TAHITI

&

FRENCH POLYNESIA GUIDE

BE A TRAVELER - NOT A TOURIST!

8%
1.50 vn

65.00
$645

Jan Prince

OPEN ROAD PUBLISHING

1st Edition

Front cover photo courtesy of Mahini Pearl Beach Resort. Back cover photos copyright©1998 by Chris Crumley, EarthWater (Virginia Beach, Virginia). Maps courtesy of Tahiti Tourist Board, except map on page 195 by James Ramage.

TABLE OF CONTENTS

7. BASIC INFORMATION   110

8. CALENDAR OF EVENTS   146

9. SPORTS & RECREATION   153

MAPS

SIDEBARS

1. INTRODUCTION

Unlike many armchair travelers and other romantics I harbored no childhood dreams to escape to Tahiti—the Isle of Illusion and Love under the swaying palms. Surely I had heard the magical name "Tahiti" when I saw the old movies about the South Seas, but they made no lasting impression on me.

But when I saw a picture of Bora Bora in a *Sports Illustrated* magazine in January 1968, I was swept away by the beauty of the island. For the next six months I read every book on Tahiti and the South Pacific that I could find in the Public Library in Houston, where I was living at the time.

When I arrived in Tahiti later that year I was prepared to accept Tahiti as she is, not as a starry-eyed tourist. I could even appreciate the wonder and beauty of a volcanic black sand beach. I knew that I would like the smell of a coconut fire and the musty odor of copra. I longed to hear the rumble of the surf crashing on the coral reef and the squawking cries of the sea birds as they fished in the lagoon. I also knew that I would enjoy the fun-loving Tahitian people, their dignity, humor and sensuous dances. I understood that it was more important to absorb the colorful sights, sounds and fragrant smells of the people and scenery around me than to see Tahiti through the lens of a camera.

My husband and I spent three weeks on Tahiti, Moorea and Bora Bora, and returned again in 1970 to do it all again. When we moved to Tahiti in 1971, I chose to discover my own Tahiti. That's what I've been doing ever since. I've experienced Tahiti as an American tourist and as an expatriate full-time resident, as a journalist, travel writer and tour guide. I've explored most of the inhabited islands in five archipelagoes, traveling by airplanes, luxury liners, inter-island cargo ships, small fishing boats and private sail boats. I've stayed in all the best hotels, at pensions and hostels, and I've lived for weeks at a time with Polynesian families in the outer islands. I learned to speak French with an American accent and enough of the Tahitian language to be understood. However, you can get by with English, gestures and smiles almost everywhere you go in these islands.

Along with all the travel information in this book are tidbits of my own experiences in Tahiti and Her Islands, which are officially known as French Polynesia. I'm confident that the travel advice in this book will help you discover your own Tahiti!

2. EXCITING TAHITI!
- OVERVIEW

Visitors to **Tahiti** often ask me which is my favorite island in French Polynesia, which island I think is the prettiest and which island I think they would most enjoy visiting.

Although I do have my favorites, each island has its own beauty, charm and specific personality. Almost everywhere you go in French Polynesia you will meet hospitable, friendly people, which helps to give meaning to the natural assets of the island. The latter question is dependent on the amount of time and interest you have to explore the islands, the people and the culture.

From the first moment I laid eyes on the lagoon of **Bora Bora** I was entranced. Each time I have returned to Bora Bora over the years I still gasp in awe at the beautiful colors of the lagoon. I find myself gazing at Otemanu and Pahia mountains from all angles around the island, and especially when I'm taking a boat trip around the lagoon.

The mountains and bays of **Moorea** are simply breathtaking, and this is the cleanest island of all, with neatly trimmed lawns and flower gardens. Here you will find the flavor of the islands by sitting beside the lagoon at sunset time and listening to Tahitian musicians playing their guitars and ukuleles and singing their favorite Polynesian songs.

The island of **Huahine** is very special to me because of the Polynesian people who live in the quiet little villages, fishing and planting vegetables and fruit in their little *fa'apu* farms in the valley. As you drive around the island you can still feel the history of Huahine when you visit the stone *marae* temples in Maeva Village.

Raiatea and **Tahaa** are ideal for sailboat chartering, and there are six yacht charter companies based in Raiatea. There are numerous *motu* islets inside the protected lagoon where you can drop anchor, watch a magnificent sunset behind Bora Bora, and listen to the roar of the surf on the reef as you fire up the barbecue on the stern of the boat, while a huge tropical moon rises above the sea.

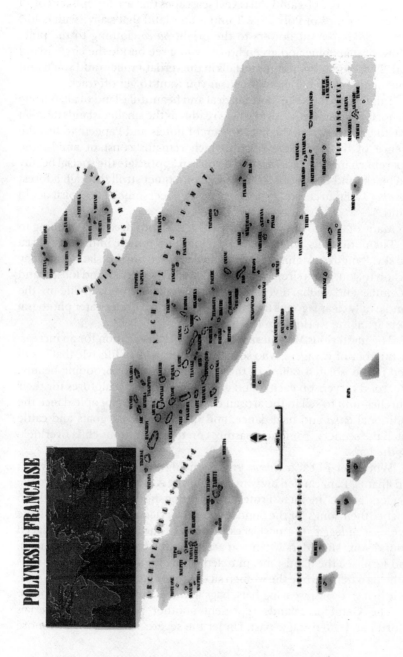

Tahiti is still the land of double rainbows for me, the regal Queen of the Pacific, and the Diadème mountain, which can best be viewed from the Fautaua bridge east of Papeete, is even shaped like a crown. A drive around the island of Tahiti will reveal seascapes that are reminiscent of all the island groups of Polynesia. Tahiti is an island that's alive with color, from the flamboyant flowers to the bright *pareo* clothing to the pink, yellow, orange, blue and green houses you'll see beside the circle island road. There are numerous waterfalls in the verdant valleys and you'll find challenging hikes in the mountains if you want to get off-track.

Tahiti is perhaps the most magical and beautiful island of all, but she will not reveal her treasures to you as readily as the smaller islands do. You have to get away from the mainstream of hotels and Papeete to feel the essence of this seductive island, which remains constant amidst the apparent changes of modern life. If you can appreciate the special beauty of a black sand beach of volcanic sand, or a quiet stroll through a forest of *mape* (Tahitian chestnut) trees, then you'll feel some of the spirit of old Tahiti.

Many of us who live on Polynesia's high islands dream of escaping to the **Tuamotu atolls**, where we can get lost between the immensity of sea and sky. Rangiroa, Manihi, Fakarava and Tikehau are the islands that may beckon to you, like a siren call, where you can live on fish and lobster and coconuts, and scuba dive among an abundance of wild life in the wonderfully clear lagoons that attract professional underwater photographers from the world's top magazines.

The mysterious **Marquesas Islands** hold a fascination for an increasing number of voyagers, who seek the authenticity of lifestyle that is still lived in the isolated valleys of these distant islands of brooding beauty. The wood carvers on each island create magnificent sculptures for their churches, and to sell in the artisan centers. The young people dance the traditional *haka* and bird dance, and the wild horses, goats and cattle watch the scenery from their pastures on the precipitous cliffs overlooking the bays.

Whenever I hear a *himene* group singing the old Polynesian hymns and chants, I am carried away in spirit to the **Austral Islands**, where the villagers gather in their Protestant meeting houses almost nightly to practice their songs for the Sunday church services. I can almost smell the *couronnes sauvages*, the necklaces of flowers and herbs that are placed around your shoulders when you arrive on the joyful island of Rurutu. And I can see the handsome, muscled young men who spend their days in the taro fields, while the women sit on *peue* mats on their terraces or in their living rooms, weaving hats, bags and mats from pandanus fronds.

The **Gambier Islands** represent another page from Polynesia's colorful and often tragic past. Under the severe staff of Father Honoré

Laval, the docile, gentle people of Mangareva were converted to Catholicism and lost their lives under the forced labor of building churches. A neo-gothic city of 116 buildings of coral and stone and a cathedral for 2,000 people is a reminder of the priest who had a driving need to build.

Here's a quick preview of what Tahiti and French Polynesia can offer you:

SOCIETY ISLANDS

The **Society Islands** are the main tourist destinations in French Polynesia. They are the islands the furthest west in French Polynesia, and the home of more than three-quarters of the population. They are divided into the **Windward Islands** or *Iles du Vent* and the **Leeward Islands** or *Iles sous le Vent*, so named because of their position in relation to the prevailing wind.

The Windward Islands include the high islands of **Tahiti** and **Moorea**, and the uninhabited volcanic crater of **Mehetia**; plus the coral atoll of **Tetiaroa**, Marlon Brando's private retreat. The mostly flat island of **Maiao** is very slowly opening its doors to the outside world. You can visit for the day aboard a VPM Dufour sailing catamaran from Moorea.

In the Leeward Islands the high islands of **Huahine**, **Raiatea**, **Tahaa**, **Bora Bora** and **Maupiti** lie 180 to 260 kilometers (112 to 161 miles) northwest of Tahiti. The atolls of **Tupai**, **Mopelia**, **Scilly** and **Bellingshausen** are the westernmost islands of the Society group. These four atolls are either uninhabited or have no tourist facilities, but you can visit by sailboat from Bora Bora. Richard Postma's *Taravana*, which operates out of the Hotel Bora Bora, is frequently chartered by movie stars and other adventurous couples to explore this hidden paradise.

The high islands of the Leeward and Windward Society group are some of the most beautiful islands in the world, offering countless photogenic scenes of saw-tooth mountain ranges, deep blue bays, green valleys and sparkling turquoise lagoons inside the fringing or barrier reefs. These are the names you've heard so much about: Tahiti, Moorea, Huahine, Raiatea, Tahaa, Bora Bora and Maupiti. On most of these islands you can explore the valleys, waterfalls and *marae* stone temples on a safari tour, or while hiking with a guide. In the opalescent lagoons you can swim, snorkel, scuba dive, water-ski, jet-ski, surf and windsurf, paddle an outrigger canoe or ride a surf bike, feed the sharks and rays, go sailing and picnic on the *motu*. And you can photograph the island, lagoon and reef while parasailing or taking a flight-seeing helicopter tour. **Tetiaroa** is easy to explore on a day tour and a haven of tranquillity for an overnight stay.

TUAMOTU ISLANDS

The **Tuamotu Archipelago** consists of two parallel island chains of 77 coral atolls and one upraised island, located between the Society and Marquesas Islands. These specks of land form one of the world's largest collections of atolls in the vastness of the blue Pacific. They are strewn across ten latitudes and stretch more than 1,500 kilometers (930 miles) from northwest to southeast and more than 500 kilometers (310 miles) from east to west. Forming the shapes of a doughnut, a bean or cigar, an egg or a slice of pie, several of these half-drowned atolls enclose lagoons that are inhabited by the black-lip *Pinctada Margaritifera* oyster, which produces the world's finest quality black pearls.

One of these atolls is **Rangiroa**, which is the second-largest atoll in the world, with a lagoon that is so large it could accommodate the entire island of Tahiti within its perimeter. You'll find international class accommodations on Rangiroa and **Manihi**, with thatched roof bungalows or rooms in pensions on **Tikehau** and **Fakarava**. There are also guest facilities with families on the atolls of **Mataiva**, **Takapoto**, **Takaroa**, **Anaa**, **Kaukura**, **Arutua** and **Nukutavake**. Several of the Tuamotu atolls are uninhabited due to a lack of water.

Lagoon excursions on Rangiroa include snorkeling through the pass, along with hundreds of fish and sharks. You can watch the dolphins, look at the fish through a glass bottom boat, visit the *motu* islets around the vast lagoon, picnic on a *motu*, fish inside the lagoon or open ocean, and parasail above the immense watery playground. Scuba diving in the Tuamotus is rated world class by the experts, especially in Rangiroa, Manihi, Fakarava, Tikehau and Mataiva. Manihi's lovely lagoon is a haven for the black lipped oyster, and you can visit a pearl farm, picnic on a *motu*, snorkel, go line or drag fishing, join a sunset cruise and learn to scuba dive. Wherever you go in the Tuamotus you will find a warm reception, laughter, music, lots of fresh air and sunshine, and an abundance of fresh fish.

MARQUESAS ISLANDS

The **Marquesas Islands** lie northwest by southeast along a 360 kilometer (223 mile) submarine chain seven to ten degrees south of the Equator. Two geographical groups are separated by 96 kilometers (60 miles) of open ocean, with a combined land area of 1,279 square kilometers (492 square miles). The southern group consists of the four high islands of **Fatu Hiva**, **Tahuata** and **Hiva Oa**, which are inhabited, plus **Mohotani** and the small uninhabited islet of **Fatu Huku**.

The northern group comprises the three high islands of **Ua Pou**, **Nuku Hiva** and **Ua Huka**, all inhabited, plus the small islets of **Motu Iti**,

Eiao and **Hatutu**, which are uninhabited. The most important island, Nuku Hiva, is about 1,500 kilometers (932 miles) northeast of Tahiti, and Hiva Oa, in the southern group, lies 1,400 kilometers (868 miles) northeast of Tahiti. The Marquesas Islands are younger than the Society Islands and do not have protective coral reefs. The wild ocean beats endlessly against the craggy, sculpted coasts, unbroken by any barriers for almost 6,400 kilometers (4,000 miles).

Accommodations are available on all the inhabited islands, either in small hotels or in family pensions. Your room and meals will be reasonably priced in the Marquesas, but the cost of land and sea transport is very expensive. Read the information on the *Aranui* in the chapters on *Planning Your Trip* and *Eco-Tourism and Travel Alternatives*. This is the best way to visit the Marquesas Islands, unless you want to stay a few days on one or more of the islands. You can also take an Air Tahiti flight to the Marquesas and board the *Aranui* there, and fly back to Tahiti if you prefer.

In the Marquesas you can visit restored archaeological sites with giant stone tikis, hike to waterfalls and high plateaus, ride horses to remote villages, scuba dive among a wealth of wild sealife, join a sailboat voyage or a dive and sail outing through the northern islands, go deep sea fishing, and watch the wood carvers at work.

AUSTRAL ISLANDS

The **Austral Islands** are the southernmost island chain in French Polynesia, lying on both sides of the Tropic of Capricorn and extending in a northwest-southeasterly direction across 1,280 kilometers (794 miles) of ocean. They are part of a vast mountain range, an extension of the same submerged chain that comprises the Cook Islands.

The Austral Islands include the high islands of **Rurutu**, **Tubuai**, **Rimatara**, **Raivavae** and **Rapa**, plus the low, uninhabited islands of **Maria** (or Hull) and the **Marotiri** (or Bass) **Rocks**. These islands lie between 538 and 1,280 kilometers (334 to 794 miles) south of Tahiti, and are separated from one another by a great distance of open ocean. These are French Polynesia's more temperate islands, where taro and potatoes, cabbages and strawberries are grown for the market in Papeete.

You can fly to Rurutu and Tubuai, and you'll need a boat to get to the other islands. Rurutu is the most lively of all the Austral Islands. You'll enjoy the communal spirit that exists here, in the taro fields, the artisan shops and in the churches. The people are enthusiastic in both work and play, and they keep their culture alive with annual tours to visit the religious and historic sites of the island.

You can visit the island by horseback or four wheel-drive vehicle, picnic on a white sand beach and hike to waterfalls and limestone grottoes with stalactites and stalagmites. Tubuai is noted for its white sand beaches, *motu* islets and fish-filled lagoon.

GAMBIER ISLANDS

At the southern end of the Tuamotu archipelago are the **Gambier Islands**, a cluster of 10 rocky islands surrounded on three sides by a barrier reef. The largest and most northerly of this group is **Mangareva**, a high island located 1,650 kilometers (1,023 miles) southeast of Tahiti. Other high islands sharing the lagoon are **Aukena**, **Akamaru** and **Taravai**, with several *motu* islets lying inside the barrier reef. The airport of **Totegegie** is built on one of the flat islets across the lagoon from Rikitea, the principal village of Mangareva. Productive black pearl farms in Mangareva provide employment and the exquisite pearls grown here are sold in Papeete and throughout the world.

You will find clean and comfortable accommodations on the island of Mangareva. In addition to visiting the churches of Father Laval, you can take boat trips to the other islands and *motu* islets that share the lagoon, visit pearl farms and enjoy a cool, pleasant climate.

TAHITI, WHERE LOVE LIVES

"Tahiti, where love lives" is the latest slogan adopted by the Tahiti Tourist office to promote Tahiti and Her Islands to the American market. This campaign is aimed at busy executives from homes where both husband and wife work and have very little time to spend together.

When you choose the Islands of Tahiti for your vacation, you will find a complete change of scenery and a rhythm of life that is slow and relaxed, very conducive to romance. Tahiti is still the Island of Love. Here we take the time to enjoy one another. Time to simply be. One of Tahiti's favorite expressions is Haere Maru, which means "take it easy." That's what you'll learn to do when you get here.

---

3. SUGGESTED ITINERARIES

CHOOSING YOUR DREAM ISLANDS

The wholesale tour operators who specialize in package programs to Tahiti and Her Islands offer vacation choices ranging from three to 15 days, which will allow you to visit from one to five islands. Some of these programs will schedule you to fly direct from the airport in Tahiti to one of the outer islands, and they sometimes include an overnight stay in Tahiti on the way back home. If you add Moorea to your itinerary, then I suggest that you fly direct from Tahiti to Moorea, providing you don't have to wait too long at the airport in Tahiti. The first flight from Tahiti to Moorea begins at 6am. If your overseas flight arrives in Tahiti in the middle of the night, as most of them do, you may want to pre-register in a hotel in Tahiti and continue your trip the next day.

The most important idea is for you to get settled into your hotel as quickly as possible, take a refreshing shower and nap, and go swimming in the lagoon when you awaken. As soon as you get out of your traveling clothes and into your swimsuit, shorts or *pareo*, you'll feel yourself starting to relax.

One of the statements I hear the most often from visitors when they arrive in Moorea is: "Oh, how I wish I had come here first." I assume this means that they wouldn't have continued their trip to the other islands had they known how much they would like Moorea.

If you are staying on the island of Tahiti you owe it to yourself to visit Moorea at least for a day. You can hop aboard an inter-island ferry or a 10-minute air shuttle flight to get to Moorea. And if you are staying on Moorea and want to go shopping and sightseeing in Tahiti, you can commute to Tahiti in the morning and return in the afternoon, the same as I do. Details for this inter-island connection are given in the *Moorea* chapter.

ONE ISLAND, ONE HOTEL

If your ideal vacation is to fly to one island, check into a hotel, unpack and settle in, then I suggest that you choose a hotel on Moorea or Bora Bora. Whether your vacation lasts for two days or two weeks, you'll find enough activity to keep you busy on land and in the lagoon. You'll be delighted with the choices of restaurants available and the entertainment provided by the various hotels on either island.

You'll have time to get to know a few of the locals and learn something about the culture of the Polynesians, if you so desire, and you can set your own pace for meals, activities and leisure time.

THE MAIN TOURIST ISLANDS

If you have 8 days/7 nights and want to see **Moorea** and **Tahiti**, I suggest you spend the first 4 nights on Moorea and the last three nights in Tahiti. When your flight arrives from Los Angeles you will be greeted at the Tahiti-Faaa International Airport and assisted to your connecting flight to Moorea. You can return to Tahiti by a 10-minute air taxi shuttle or a 30-minute catamaran trip across the Sea of Moons between the two islands. Another suggestion for an 8 day/7 night package is to fly direct from Tahiti to Bora Bora, where you'll spend four nights, then fly to Tahiti for the last three nights.

If you want to see **Bora Bora** and Moorea and do not care to spend any time in Tahiti, a 9 day/8 night package allows you to fly direct from Tahiti to Bora Bora, where you'll spend four nights before flying to Moorea for another four nights. You can fly direct from Moorea to the airport in Tahiti to connect with your international flight back to Los Angeles.

A 9 day/8 night package can also include Moorea, Bora Bora and Tahiti. You'll fly from Tahiti to Moorea, where you'll spend three nights, then fly to Bora Bora for three nights, and back to Tahiti for the last two nights.

ISLAND HOPPING

There are several island hopping possibilities available, which include a 14-day/13 night visit to the Society Islands. Upon clearing immigration and customs formalities at the Tahiti-Faaa International Airport, you will be assisted to your Air Tahiti flight to Raiatea, where you will spend two nights either on the island of Raiatea or the smaller island of Tahaa. You will fly to Bora Bora for the next three nights, continue on to Huahine for another two nights, then fly to Moorea for a four-night stay, and spend your last two nights in Tahiti. This voyage can be made by inter-island ferry or airplane.

My favorite of the island hopping itineraries is the 15 day/14 night package that takes you to Moorea for four nights, Bora Bora for three nights, Rangiroa for two nights, Manihi for three nights and Tahiti for two nights.

Air Tahiti offers six different "air passes" that will allow you to island hop among the Societies, the Tuamotus, the Marquesas and the Austral Islands. Their "Sejours dans les Iles" (Island Stays) programs include reduced rates for airfare and lodging. Details are given in Chapter 6, *Planning Your Trip*.

Should you prefer a sailing vacation, "shared yacht cruising" or "sail and dive" program, this information is given in the chapter on *Planning Your Trip* and in the individual destination chapters of *Moorea*, *Raiatea*, *Tuamotus* and *Marquesas*.

If you have already visited the Society Islands or just want to get off the track to discover another facet of Polynesia, the *Aranui* cargo/passenger ship offers 16-day round-trip voyages from Tahiti to the Marquesas Islands. The details are given in the chapters on *Planning Your Trip* and *Eco-Tourism & Travel Alternatives*.

You'll find information on the wholesale travel agencies and tour operators in the chapter on *Planning Your Trip*. Your personal travel agent will probably have their brochures that give details and prices on the wholesalers' programs for Tahiti and Her Islands.

4. A SHORT HISTORY

GENERAL HISTORY OF FRENCH POLYNESIA

THE POLYNESIAN MIGRATIONS

Archaeologists, ethnologists, anthropologists, linguists and other scholars have long debated the questions of when, why, and how the pioneer Polynesians crossed thousands of miles of open ocean to settle on these islands in the Eastern Pacific that are now called **French Polynesia**.

New archaeological evidence and improved techniques of radiocarbon dating may refine the theories, but at present most of the experts who study this subject agree that the Australoid ancestors of the Melanesian, Micronesian and Polynesian people came from Southeast Asia. They walked across the land mass that existed in the final Ice Age to reach what are now the Indonesian islands of Sumatra, Java and Borneo, and on to Australia and New Guinea, which were then joined, settling in the Southwest Pacific around 30,000 B.C.. A group of dark-skinned people called the Papuans also came from Southeast Asia, arriving in the southwestern Pacific area between 7,000 and 3,500 B.C.. Several thousands of years later, between 3,000 and 1,000 B.C., a group of lighter-skinned Austronesians from Asia forced the Papuans to moved further inland in what is now Irian Jaya and Papua New Guinea.

Some of these wanderers then set out to explore the more eastern South Pacific islands, eventually settling on every speck of land that could support life. They sailed eastward in their huge double ocean going canoes, using the sun, stars, wind, ocean currents, and the flight patterns of birds as their guides, referring to their crude stick charts to navigate to new islands. Carrying 100-500 people on board these canoes made of lashed planks with sails of pandanus matting, they brought with them their women and children, pigs and dogs, coconuts and taro, breadfruit tree seedlings and roots, shrubs and trees, as well as flowering plants,

which were to be used for food, clothing, medicines, and other househol
needs. Historians believe this eastward progress occurred over 5,00
years, and departures from a settled island were necessitated due
overpopulation, food and water shortage or because of internal fightin

The Polynesian culture is believed to have evolved in the cent
Pacific, in Tonga or Samoa, which they called Havaiki, their ances
religious center. After a pause of 1,000 years, a migratory wave from
"cradle" of Polynesia brought the new explorers even farther eastw
and some archaeologists believe that as far back as 500 B.C. the fir
these double-hulled canoes reached the Marquesas Islands. A tall
stately race of proud and cultured people settled on some of tl
islands, which they called *Te Fenua Te Enata*, or *Te Henua Te Enana*
Land of the Men."

During this time Mangaia in the Cook Islands was also settle
due to its close proximity to the Society Islands, the speculation
Tahiti and the Leeward Society Islands were also occupied
Polynesians much earlier than radio-carbon dating has indicate

In 1972 **Dr. Yosihiko H. Sinoto**, the senior anthropologist
Bernice Pauahi Bishop Museum in Honolulu, began excavatio
archaeological sites on Huahine, and unearthed a village comm
existed between 850 and 1200 A.D., which had been destroye
waves. This "Polynesian Pompeii" included remnants of
voyaging canoe that had been preserved by the mud for some

During the next migratory movement of the Polynesian
years after arriving in the Marquesas, the voyaging canoes
and west to the Tuamotu Archipelago and Mangareva,
Hawaiian Islands, and even farther eastward to discover
Easter Island, all around 850 A.D.. The great Polynesian mi
proceeded southwest, with canoes departing from the new
cultural center of Havaiki, Raiatea in the Leeward Society I
1,000 A.D. These voyagers settled in Rarotonga in the Co
in New Zealand, completing a triangle of Polynesian col
Polynesian people of French Polynesia, the Cook Is
Islanders, native Hawaiians and the Maoris of New Z
variations of the Maohi language, the native tongue of
ancestors.

In 1947 **Thor Heyerdahl**, a Norwegian ethnologis
five Viking scientists, sailed the *Kon Tiki* balsa raft a
5,000 miles (8,000 kilometers) from the shores o
Polynesia, where they crashed onto the coral reef
Tuamotus 101 days later. Heyerdahl wanted to pr
American Indians were capable of reaching the Polyn
primitive rafts, and could have been the ancestors of

Although Heyerdahl's theory was dismissed by all the experts who study the South Pacific languages and culture, fifty years after the K*on Tiki* drifted across the Pacific, he is still unrepentant in his theories about Pacific settlement. Spanish adventurer **Kitin Muñoz**, one of Heyerdahl's disciples, launched a similar project in May, 1997. Muñoz built a 70-ton reed raft in Easter Island, which he named *Mata Rangi*. He wanted to prove that the Polynesians were able to explore the ocean in all directions aboard rafts made from the *totara* reeds, which grow in Peru's Lake Titicaca, in the crater lakes of Easter Island, in Rapa and in Mangareva in French Polynesia, and in many other parts of the world. The *Mata Rangi* sank after only 18 days at sea, but Kitin Muñoz plans to launch another reed raft in Peru in 1998, and sail to Tahiti.

EUROPEAN EXPLORATION

In 1513 the Spanish explorer **Vasco Nuñez de Balboa** crossed the Isthmus of Panama and sighted the mighty Pacific Ocean. Seven years later, in 1520, **Ferdinand Magellan**, a Portuguese in the service of the Spanish, sailed to the Philippines, but the only island he sighted in Polynesia was the atoll of Puka Puka in the northeastern Tuamotu archipelago. The Spanish caravel *San Lesmes* was wrecked on the reef in Amaru in the Tuamotus around 1526, and the shipwrecked sailors supposedly married Polynesian women. In 1595 **Alvaro de Mendaña de Neira** was searching for the Solomon Islands, which he had discovered in 1567, and during this second voyage into the South Seas he discovered the southern group of the Marquesas Islands. In 1606, 80 years after the disappearance of the *San Lesmes*, **Pedro Fernández de Quiros**, who had been Mendaña's chief pilot, discovered a number of the Tuamotu Islands before continuing on to other island groups further west. This was the last of the Spanish explorations in the Pacific during that era.

In 1615-16 the Dutch explorers **Le Maire** and **Schouten** discovered several atolls in the Tuamotus, and in 1722 **Jacob Roggeveen**, another Dutch captain, sailed through the Tuamotus and passed the island of Makatea on his way to the Society Islands, where he sighted Maupiti in the Leeward Society Islands. But he failed to see Bora Bora, Raiatea or Tahaa, high islands that are visible from Maupiti.

The Dutch were then followed by the British, with **Commodore John Byron**, grandfather of the famous poet, discovering more of the Tuamotu Islands aboard the *H.M.S. Dolphin* in 1765. If any of the European explorers had found Tahiti, they left no record of their discovery.

The *Dolphin* returned to the South Seas in 1767 under the command of Captain **Samuel Wallis**, who discovered the island of Tahiti, and anchored in Matavai Bay on June 23, 1767. He was followed just 10 months later by French **Admiral Louis Antoine de Bougainville**, who also discovered Tahiti, and claimed the island for France during his visit in April, 1768. In April, 1769, Lieutenant **James Cook**, aboard the *H.M.S. Endeavour*, made his first trip to Tahiti. He returned again as Captain James Cook in 1773, 1774 and 1777. Cook visited Moorea and discovered the Leeward Islands of Raiatea, Tahaa, Huahine, Bora Bora, Tupai and Maupiti, which he named the Society Islands as they lay contiguous to each other.

In 1772 Spanish captain **Don Domingo de Boenechea** anchored his ship, the *Aguilla*, in the lagoon of Tautira on the Tahiti Iti peninsula. After claiming the island for his country and king, Boenechea sailed for Peru, but returned in 1774 to establish the first long-term European settlement on the island, with two missionaries and two military men. The Spanish rule ended in Tahiti following the death of Boenechea, when the missionaries returned to Peru.

The story of **Captain William Bligh** and the mutinous crew aboard the *H.M.S. Bounty* provided a colorful chapter in Tahiti's history, following their arrival at Point Venus in 1788.

The English Protestant missionaries from the London Missionary Society (LMS) arrived aboard the *Duff* and landed at Point Venus on March 5, 1797, to convert the Tahitians to the Gospel. **George Pritchard** of the LMS gained the confidence of **Queen Pomare IV** and convinced her that Tahiti should be under the protection of England. Although **Queen Victoria** was unwilling to declare Tahiti a protectorate of England, a power struggle between the English Protestants and the French Catholic missionaries in Tahiti almost brought England and France to the brink of war. The end result was that Queen Pomare IV and the LMS missionaries lost their battle with the French, under the guns of *La Reine Blanche*, a French warship commanded by **Admiral Dupetit-Thouars**. Tahiti became a French protectorate in 1842, and guerrilla rebellions on Tahiti and some of the other islands resisted the French invasion until 1846, when France gained control over Tahiti and Moorea.

FRENCH COLONIALISM

Tahiti and her dependencies became a full-fledged French colony on December 29, 1880, when the century-old reign of the Pomare family formally came to an end, and French nationality and rights were bestowed on all Tahitians.

The Pomare's dominions included Tahiti, Moorea, Maiao, Mehetia, the Tuamotu islands and Tubuai and Raivavae in the Austral Islands. The Marquesas Islands had already been annexed by the French in 1842. The island of Rapa became a French protectorate in 1867 and was annexed in

1881. The Gambier Islands were annexed in 1882, Raiatea and Tahaa were annexed in 1887, although the warriors in Raiatea resisted French control until the end of the century. The other Leeward Society Islands were annexed in 1888, Rurutu was annexed in 1900, and Rimatara was annexed in 1901.

In 1903 the *Etablissements Français de l'Océanie* (EFO), or French Territories of Oceania, were established, incorporating all of the French holdings in the Eastern Pacific into one colony. Copra, cotton, mother-of-pearl shell, phosphate, vanilla and fruits were exported in exchange for manufactured goods. By 1911 there were about 3,500 colonists, mostly French, living in Polynesia, plus the Chinese immigrants who had been brought to Tahiti in the 1860s to work in the cotton fields of Atimaono.

Although Tahiti was geographically far from the main theaters of the two world wars, the colony was politically involved because of its French connection. During World War I almost 1,000 Tahitian soldiers fought against the Germans in Europe, and the town of Papeete was bombarded by two German cruisers on September 22, 1914, when they sank a French navy ship in the harbor.

During World War II young men from Tahiti joined the Pacific Battalion, were shipped to Europe, and fought side by side with the forces of the Free French. Bora Bora was used as a military supply base for the American forces, with 5,000 soldiers, sailors and Seabees arriving on the small island in 1942. Besides a few cannon in the hills and some old Quonset huts, the only reminders of the American presence in Bora Bora today are some blue-eyed Tahitians with light hair and skin.

FRENCH POLYNESIA

A 1957 status changed the *Etablissements Français de l'Océanie* colony into a French overseas territory, with the official name of French Polynesia. In the early 1960s a large harbor was built in Papeete, an international airport was opened in Faaa, the French established the *Centre d'expérimentations du Pacifique* (CEP), the Pacific Experimentation Center in Tahiti, and MGM brought a big film crew to make another movie of *Mutiny on the Bounty*. All of these rapid changes brought French Polynesia into the modern age, accompanied by problems of inflation, unemployment, housing problems, pollution, emotional instability, juvenile delinquency and political discontent among an increasing number of the population.

FRENCH NUCLEAR TESTING

French Polynesia entered the nuclear age in 1963 when the French chose the Tuamotu atolls of Moruroa, 1,200 kilometers (720 miles) southeast of Tahiti, and Fangataufa, 40 kilometers (24 miles) south of Moruroa, as sites for the *Centre d'expérimentations du Pacifique* (CEP), Pacific Experimentation Center. Although the local political parties protested the invasion, President Charles de Gaulle responded by outlawing political parties.

On September 11, 1966, De Gaulle watched from an off-shore French warship as the first nuclear test was carried out, exploding in the atmosphere almost 600 meters (2,000 feet) above the turquoise lagoon of Moruroa. Between 1966-1974, the French made 41 atmospheric tests in Moruroa and Fangataufa, and between 1975-1991, some 134 underground tests were completed, by drilling a shaft deep into the coral foundation under the lagoons. President François Mitterand suspended the nuclear testing in April, 1992 and most of the 7,750 employees of the CEP returned to France or to their islands in French Polynesia. In June, 1995, France's newly elected president, Jacques Chirac, announced a new series of eight nuclear tests, to be completed by the end of May, 1996.

The shock of this announcement reverberated around the world, and on September 5, 1995, when a 20-kiloton explosion was carried out in Moruroa, the result was disastrous for France, and especially for French Polynesia's tourism and economy, which has never completely recovered. Severe rioting broke out in Papeete, with several buildings burned, the Tahiti-Faaa International Airport terminal was partially burned, and the vehicles in the parking lot were damaged and burned. On January 27, 1996, France made its sixth and final nuclear test at Fangataufa, and two days later President Chirac announced that the tests were finished forever.

Some of the 1,500 workers, technicians and scientists, who had been brought from France and Tahiti for these tests, finished their work and studies and went home, while the French Army and Legionnaires began to dismantle the two nuclear bases. That work is still underway.

INTERNAL AUTONOMY GOVERNMENT

In 1977 a statute passed by the French parliament in Paris granted administrative autonomy to French Polynesia, and domestic or internal autonomy was given in 1984, consolidated in 1990 and extended in 1996. The French Polynesian Territorial Government consists of a president elected by the territorial assembly and of ministers whom he appoints before submitting the list to the assembly's vote. The territorial assembly consists of 41 members, who are elected every five years by votes and who represent the five archipelagoes. The territory is represented in the French Parliament by two deputies and one senator, plus an advisor in the French Social and Economic Council.

A French High Commissioner represents the State in French Polynesia, and the Republic of France controls foreign affairs, territorial defense and law and order, justice, nationality and immigration, higher education and research, audiovisual communications and currency matters. The French *gendarmes* control most of the territory, and each *commune* has one or more Tahitian *mutoi* policemen, whose duties may include directing school traffic and tracking down scooters or cars that were "borrowed" on a Saturday night. His job also includes keeping peace in his own neighborhood.

Today the Tahitian flag, white with red borders at top and bottom, with an emblem representing a double outrigger sailing canoe, flies side by side with the tri-color of the French flag. The archipelagoes also have their own emblems.

POST-NUCLEAR PROGRESS PACT FOR SELF-SUFFICIENCY

A **Progress Pact** between the Territory and the French State was signed in January 1993, to compensate for the loss of financial resources due to the ending of the CEP French nuclear tests in the Tuamotu Islands. In 1994 a 10-year adjustment law and five-year development contracts were adopted, with the State providing assistance in the fields of education, training, research, health and transport infrastructures, agriculture, tourism and housing. Financial transfers from the State to the Territory will amount to 990 million francs (US $193 million) per annum until December 31, 2005.

On January 1, 1998, a Value Added Tax (VAT, TVA in French) went into effect. A one percent VAT applies to all rented accommodations, including hotel rooms, pensions and family stays, room and meal packages, all inter-island transportation by air and boat, including charter flights and chartered boat trips, and to such goods as non-alcoholic beverages, medicines, books and newspapers and magazines. A two percent VAT applies to all shops, stores and boutiques, with the exception of duty free stores, which will be exempt. A three percent VAT applies to all restaurants, snacks, bars and activity and excursion services.

The government's objective is to increase the VAT to an average of 15 percent over the first five years, and to eliminate a 10 percent tax on all imported goods during the first two years, and all local customs duties during the next three years, at a rate of one-third less per year.

HISTORIES OF THE BIGGER ISLANDS: TAHITI, MOOREA, & BORA BORA

TAHITI

Wallis Discovers King George III Island

Captain Samuel Wallis of the British Royal Navy, and his crew of 150 men, who were sailing the *H.M.S. Dolphin* during its discovery voyage, sighted the tall mountains of Tahiti Iti and Tahiti Nui five days before anchoring in Matavai Bay on June 23, 1767. The exhausted and scurvy-ridden men aboard the 32-gun frigate had left England eight months before in search of *terra Australis Incognita*, the great land mass that King George III and his geographers were convinced lay somewhere between Cape Horn and New Zealand, in balance with the northern hemisphere.

While searching for a safe anchorage the *Dolphin* was surrounded by canoes bearing more than 800 men. When the British sailors invited the natives aboard the ship, one of them climbed the mizzen chains and stood on the awning above the deck while the white men showed him trinkets. He was soon joined by a friend, and as the two men stood on the ship's deck, a billy goat butted the first fellow from behind. In terror they jumped overboard and swam ashore. They soon returned to the ship with other natives, who carried banana shoots. These curious natives inspected the goats and sheep, hogs and fowl, and then began to take everything they could lay their hands on.

Wallis' men began to trade trinkets, axes and other items in exchange for food and water, and although there were skirmishes, with some of the natives throwing stones and the white men discharging their guns, friendly relations and traffic were soon restored, although the foreigners soon learned that the natives were great pilferers.

Upon entering the beautiful harbor of Matavai Bay on June 23, the *Dolphin* struck a deep-sea rock the Tahitians called Hiro's Rock, after one of their demigods. This rock is now called Dolphin Rock on the maps.

As Wallis was too weak from scurvy to claim the new land in the name of the British King, the second lieutenant, **Tobias Furneaux**, hoisted a pennant on a long pole and went ashore on June 26, and took possession of the land Wallis called "King George's Island." The bay was named Port Royal.

Following a consultation by the Tahitian chiefs and counselors, the people formed a large torchlight procession with drums and conch trumpets to bear away the flag on its staff. The natives understood the significance of the white men planting their flag on Tahitian soil, and they sought the aid of their gods to drive the strangers away.

Imagine the surprise and joy of the men aboard the *Dolphin* the next morning when they found their ship surrounded by some five hundred canoes containing four thousand athletic paddlers and loaded with fruit, coconuts, fowl and young pigs. But the most astonishing sight to their sea-weary eyes was that of the fair young girls, standing in the middle of each canoe, nude to the waist, "who played a great many droll, wanton tricks." While the hungry sailors were enjoying the free strip-tease, the Tahitian men began to hurl fist-sized stones at the men on board the *Dolphin*. The sailors retaliated by firing the ship's cannons at the canoes, killing forty or fifty of the Tahitians and sinking a great number of the canoes. After a second attack that the men of the ship easily won, the Tahitians decided to be friendly and peaceful.

The men of the *Dolphin* spent the next five weeks trading earrings, nails and beads for foodstuffs. Then they began to engage in a "new sort of trade...it might properly be called the old trade," according to **George Robertson**, master, whose journal is the best account given. When the men had emptied their sea chests to exchange their possessions for the ladies' favors, they began to remove the iron nails and cleats from the ship. This carnal exchange began with a 20- or 30-penny nail. As demand outgrew the supply, the size of the nails increased to a 40-penny, and some of the *vahines* demanded as much as a seven- or nine-inch spike. Two-thirds of the men even pulled out the nails on which they had hung their hammocks.

The high **Chief Amo** of the powerful Teva clan of Papara was also in charge of Ha'apape (now called Mahina), the district where the *Dolphin* was anchored. Amo's wife **Purea** was chiefess of Ha'apape, and when Amo returned to Papara, Purea hospitably received Captain Wallis and his people. She personally carried Wallis ashore and had the sick men taken to a guest house, where they were massaged with coconut oil and healed with traditional Tahitian medicines until they recovered their health. In exchange for her kindness, Captain Wallis presented Purea with a looking-glass, some turkeys, a gander, a goose and a cat.

On July 27 the *Dolphin* left Tahiti, and on passing Moorea, Wallis named the island York, after the Duke of York. Wallis sailed back to England without looking further for the southern continent.

Bougainville's New Cytherea-Island of Love

Just nine months after Wallis had departed, the French explorer **Louis Antoine de Bougainville** was the second visitor from Europe to claim Tahiti for his country. Bougainville led an expedition of two ships, the *Boudeuse* and the *Etoile*, and he was also searching for the mythical *terra*

Australis Incognita. In passing through the coral atolls of the Tuamotu Islands, Bougainville named them the Dangerous Archipelago, because the outlines of the low islands were indistinct and dangerous to pass.

Bougainville's visit to Tahiti lasted from April 6-14, 1768, but he did not visit Matavai Bay, remaining instead on the eastern coast of Hitia'a, where he was anchored too close to the reef. During his visit Bougainville lost six anchors during his brief stay. He was kindly received by **Chief 'Ereti** of Hitia'a, who allowed the Frenchmen to stay in sheds on the bank of a stream while they collected water for the ships. But the chief made it clear that the visit was to be strictly limited.

One unusual incident marked this landing, when the Tahitians spotted a woman among the 314 officers and men of the two ships. Although she had sailed from France disguised as a man, the Tahitians knew immediately that she was a woman. Her secret was revealed to her shipmates when one big Tahitian man grabbed her up to run off to the hills to give her a personal welcome. Her name was **Jeanne Baret** and she had sailed as the valet of Bougainville's naturalist, **Dr. Philibert de Commerçon**. Jeanne Baret became the first white woman to visit Tahiti and to circumnavigate the world.

Bougainville, not knowing that his new island had already been "discovered" by Wallis and claimed for England, proclaimed French sovereignty over the island he called New Cytherea or the New Island of Love. He found the Tahitian love rites similar to the ancient worship of Aphrodite-Venus, whose birthplace was the Greek island of Cythera or Cytherea. Bougainville was an enlightened spirit, a mathematician, diplomat, and a sophisticated *bon vivant*. Inspired by **Jean-Jacques Rousseau's** philosophy that Europeans were overly civilized and should get back to a more natural state, Bougainville coined the phrase 'noble savage', and when he sailed away from Tahiti, Bougainville took with him a young man from Hitia'a named **Ahutoru**, a living noble savage who became the first Tahitian to discover Europe.

Cook at Point Venus

Lieutenant James Cook, who later came to be known as Captain Cook, England's most famous explorer, was the third European discoverer to visit Tahiti. Cook's ship, the *H.M.S. Endeavour*, anchored in Matavai Bay on April 13, 1769.

Cook's expedition was to take an astronomer either to the Marquesas Islands or to New Zealand for the purpose of observing the transit of the planet Venus across the sun. This event was to take place on June 3, 1769, and there would be no further opportunity to witness such a phenomenon again until 1874. Astronomers were eager to take advantage of this rare occurrence as it would enable them to ascertain the distance of the earth from the sun, the fundamental base line in all astronomical measurements. The Royal Society had sent expeditions to various parts of the world, but Cook's ship was the only one to visit the southern hemisphere.

Two months before Cook left for the South Seas, Wallis returned to England with the disappointing news that he had not found the great southern continent. When he learned of the imminent voyage Cook was to command, Wallis suggested King George III's island as the ideal spot to establish an observatory. Wallis told Cook that he and his men would find hospitable natives and an abundance of food and water on this island he discovered during his world circumnavigation just two years before.

Cook's expedition consisted of eighty-four officers and seamen and eight civilians. The civilians included **Joseph Banks**, a young botanist who later became president of the Royal Society; **Dr. Daniel Solander**, an eminent Swedish botanist and zoologist who had studied with the great Linnaeus; and astronomer **Charles Green**, who, in addition to supervising the observation of Venus, provided Cook with precise estimates of longitude, which was indispensable on such a discovery voyage.

When Cook anchored in Matavai Bay, seven weeks before the transit of Venus was expected, the *Endeavour* was given an enthusiastic welcome by the Tahitians. Crowds of natives greeted the ship with the now customary friendliness, and immediately recognized four of the officers who had visited the island with Wallis.

The high chiefess Purea did not greet Cook as the sovereign of Ha'apape, as she had received Wallis, because the Teva clan had been conquered by other chiefs, whose leader was Vairaatoa, or Tu, who later became known as **King Pomare I**.

The first thing Cook did upon arrival in what was then known to the English as King George III's Island was to build a fort to protect the astronomer and his instruments. He chose the same site that Wallis had selected, the strip of land between the beach and the river. In less than three weeks' time the fort was finished, which was 150 feet long and 80 feet wide, with five-foot high walls and two four-pounder cannons.

These precautions proved superfluous, however, for the Tahitians, especially the women, were so friendly and hospitable that the British sailors forgot their duties. Taking a lesson learned from Wallis about the nail-removing fiasco, Cook posted regulations concerning trade with the natives. He ordered that no iron be exchanged except for provisions. He also asked his men to treat the natives with "all imaginable humanity" and to use every fair means of cultivating their friendship. The natives appreciated this treatment and came to know the Englishmen affectionately by their "Tahitianized" surnames—*Tute* (Cook), *Opane* (Banks) and *Tolano* (Solander).

The major problem Cook encountered was constant pilfering. From time to time he was obliged to take one or more of the chiefs hostage against the return of missing objects. The most important item taken was the quadrant, an essential instrument for astronomical observation. Although the instrument was eventually returned, the culprit had removed it from its box and taken it apart to see what was inside, and consequently, the quadrant was useless.

On the day of the observation, there was not a cloud in the sky and the scientists were able to witness every phase of the transit from the fort at Point Venus, named in honor of the occasion. A small party took measurements from a *motu* islet inside the reef of Moorea. However, it was subsequently found that the readings were of little value because of unforeseen optical distortion caused by the irradiation of the sun.

Cook's expedition stayed in Tahiti for three months, during which time he learned much about the Tahitian way of life. He observed the native customs, manners, religion and law. He described the people's appearance (explaining their tattoos), cooking methods, foodstuffs and apparent social and political order. He also made a trip around the island in a longboat and drew a complete and accurate map of the whole coastal region of Tahiti.

By this time Cook had learned what the natives called their island and began using the name he understood it to be—Otaheite. When he asked them the name, they replied, "This is Tahiti," and in their language it sounded like Otaheite.

Several of the things Cook learned about the Tahitian way of life shocked the 41-year old seaman. "It is this," he wrote in his Journal, "that more than half of the better sort...have enter'd into a resolution of injoying free liberty in Love, without being Troubled...by its consequences. These mix and Cohabit together with the utmost freedom, and the Children who are so unfortunate as to be thus begot are smothered at the Moment of their Birth." He noted that couples lived together for years, destroying all children. His reference was to the Areoi Society that was in existence at that time, and their meetings during which "the Women in dancing...give full Liberty to their desires." He was also aghast that "both sexes express the most indecent ideas in conversation without the least emotion" and that "chastity...is but little valued. The Men will very readily offer the Young Women to Strangers, even their own daughters, and think it very strange if you refuse them; but this is merely done for the sake of gain."

However, the Tahitian people were suffering consequences of having enjoyed free liberty in love. Cook found, to his distress, that many of them, as well as his own men, were suffering from venereal disease. How they caught it is a toss-up between the men on Cook's ships or the former discoverers. The English blame the French and vice-versa.

In years to come, the ravages of venereal disease, as well as other illnesses the Europeans introduced to the islands, such as tuberculosis, small pox, measles and alcoholism, as well as the guns they brought to the natives, helped to reduce the population at an alarming rate. Cook gave the estimate of the population at over 200,000. Just 36 years later it was determined to be 8,000.

Cook and his men sailed away from Tahiti on July 13, 1769. Heading westward, he anchored in Moorea's Opunohu Bay, and took a longboat to explore Pao Pao, which he named Cook's Bay. Cook also discovered the Leeward islands of Huahine, Raiatea, Tahaa, Bora Bora, Maupiti and Tupai, located about 100 miles northwest of Tahiti. He named these six islands the Society Islands "as they lie contiguous to each other." (During the second half of the 19th century the Society Islands name was extended to comprise Tahiti and Moorea). Cook also discovered two islands in the Austral group and several of the Tuamotu atolls, before sailing on to claim New Zealand, Australia, and several other islands for his country. He returned to Matavai Bay again, as Captain Cook, on three separate occasions in 1773, 1774 and 1777, during his second and third voyages of exploration. Today there is a monument to this great discoverer at Point Venus.

"Breadfruit Bligh" & The Bounty

In the following years many ships called at Tahiti, some anchoring in Matavai Bay and others stopping at Tahiti Iti, "little Tahiti" on the Taiarapu peninsula. One of the most famous ships to drop anchor in Tahitian waters was the *H.M.S. Bounty*, commanded by Lieutenant William Bligh. The *Mutiny on the Bounty* saga is well known, as it was imaginatively told by co-authors **James Norman Hall** and **Charles Nordhoff**, two Americans who moved to Tahiti after fighting in World War I. Erroll Flynn starred in the first *Bounty* movie, which was filmed in Australia. Clark Gable and Charles Laughton played the major roles in a black and white *Mutiny on the Bounty* in 1935, which was mostly filmed in Santa Catalina, off the California coast. In 1962 MGM released another *Mutiny on the Bounty* film, starring Marlon Brando, Trevor Howard, and the Tahitian beauty, Tarita, which was filmed at Point Venus and in Bora Bora. A slightly different version entitled *The Bounty*, starring Mel Gibson and Anthony Hopkins, was filmed on Moorea in 1984. Without the bountiful *Artocarpus altilis* or breadfruit tree, one of history's greatest sea dramas might never have occurred.

Bligh first visited Tahiti with Captain Cook aboard the *Resolution*, and had taken note of the breadfruit that was the staple diet of the Tahitians.

When he returned to England, Bligh contacted his wife's uncle, who had several large plantations in Jamaica, as well as a number of ships. The English merchants in the West Indies then made a petition to King George III, requesting permission to bring small breadfruit trees from Tahiti to plant in their islands, which they intended to use as a cheap and nourishing means of feeding their slaves. Cook and others had spoken highly of this substitute for bread, which the strong and healthy Tahitians ate daily. The King agreed to their request and Bligh was appointed Captain of the voyage. He had no problem finding a crew willing to sail to Tahiti, as word had spread around Europe about the friendly and welcoming Tahitian *vahines*.

Captain Bligh began having problems with his *Bounty* crew even before the ship arrived in Tahiti's Matavai Bay on October 26, 1788. And once ashore, they had to wait five months in Tahiti before the breadfruit would be at the right stage for transplanting. The sailors happily accepted this respite from Bligh's tight discipline, and willingly adapted to the Tahitian *aita pea pea* (no problem) philosophy of life, complete with all the pleasures any sailor could ever imagine.

Bligh moved his ship from Matavai Bay to Papeete, where he had better protection from the wind. Thereafter, all the visiting ships followed suit and Papeete became the center of activity on the island of Tahiti.

While the breadfruit trees were being gathered and loaded onto the ship, Bligh became excessively severe with his men as the time drew nearer for their departure. When the *Bounty* weighed anchor on April 4, 1789, and headed toward the Leeward islands of the Society group, Bligh was faced with a moody, belligerent crew.

The punishments Bligh meted out for his men, and his insults to his officers were too harsh to endure after the idyllic life the men had enjoyed in Tahiti. Acting Lieutenant Fletcher Christian was especially disturbed, and his fury finally exploded into a dramatic mutiny, which is remembered as the most famous mutiny in history.

Bligh was hauled out of bed early on the morning of April 28, tied up and dragged on deck. He and 18 of his officers and men were put into an open launch, and the only supplies they received were a 28-gallon cask of water, 150 pounds of bread, some wine and rum, a compass, a quadrant, some canvas, and lines and sails. Then the boat was set adrift in the open ocean, a few miles from Tofua in the Tongan Islands, whose inhabitants were extremely unfriendly in those days.

Bligh's success in sailing the small open boat across 5,800 kilometers (3,600 miles) of ocean to Timor and Batavia in the Dutch Indies, is one of the most remarkable voyages in history. Only one man died during this crossing, and six others died after reaching shore.

The twenty-five men who remained aboard the *Bounty* consisted of Fletcher Christian's followers, as well as the sailors who had nothing to do with the mutiny. Christian sailed the *Bounty* to Tubuai, 568 kilometers (355 miles) due south of Tahiti in the Austral Islands, but they were unable to stay there because the natives were so hostile. The *Bounty* then returned to Tahiti and on June 6 anchored in Matavai Bay. For the next ten days the men loaded pigs, goats, a cow and a bull, cats and fowl, plus nine Tahitian men, eight women and nine children, and set sail once again for Tubuai.

Although Fletcher Christian tried to settle his group in Tubuai, they were forced to give up the idea, after a hundred natives were killed in skirmishes. They retreated to Tahiti for supplies, and when the *Bounty* left Matavai Bay for the last time, some of the British sailors remained ashore at Point Venus. Aboard the ship with Christian were eight of his fellow mutineers, six Tahitian men, twelve Tahitian women and one little girl. This small group reached the uninhabited island of Pitcairn, where they burned the *Bounty* and began a new life ashore. There was no news of Christian and his party for 18 years.

The 16 men who chose to remain in Tahiti settled down with their wives and families. Two of them had died by the time the H.M.S. *Pandora* anchored in Matavai Bay in 1791, but **Captain Edward Edwards**, who had been sent from England in search of the mutineers, arrested the remaining 14 men. The *Pandora* was shipwrecked and four of the men were drowned before they could reach England for their trial. During a court martial inquiry in England, three of the men were condemned to death and hanged, and the remaining seven were set free. **Peter Heywood** wrote the first Tahitian dictionary in prison while awaiting his trial.

Captain Bligh had also undergone a trial by the English court, which cleared his name for any guilt in the *Bounty* mutiny, and he sailed back to Tahiti, arriving in Matavai Bay on April 10, 1792, as commander of the *H.M.S. Providence* and her armed tender, the *Assistance*.

A native war was in progress when he arrived in Tahiti, but he eventually went ashore to supervise the building of storage sheds for the young breadfruit trees he had come to collect. In his journal Bligh recorded his disappointment in seeing the degeneration of the Tahitian people due to the influence of deserters from the various ships that visited Tahiti. "...little of the ancient customs of the Otaheitans remains...It is difficult to get them to speak their own language without mixing a jargon of English with it, and they are so altered that I believe in future no Europeans will ever know what their ancient customs of receiving strangers were," he wrote. He also noted that they were "...no longer clean Otaheitans, but in appearance a set of ragamuffins with whom it is necessary to observe great caution."

Bligh remained in Tahiti for three months, collecting 2,126 bread-fruit trees and 500 other plants to take back to the West Indies. The breadfruit seedlings were planted in St. Vincent and in Port Royal, Jamaica. When the trees grew and began to bear fruit, the Negro slaves refused to eat the starchy breadfruit because they didn't like the taste of the stuff.

The Arrival of the Gospel—A Different Kind of Conqueror

On March 3, 1797, the people of Tahiti felt several earthquake shocks, which were accompanied by a high sea and a terrible storm. This was the first time they had ever experienced an earthquake, and they were completely terrorized by these strange happenings. The first shock took place early in the morning, which drove the people out of their houses in confusion. At noon another shock occurred and the frightened people threw themselves prostrate upon the ground and cried out to their gods for mercy. At sunset a third shock caused many to hold night vigils, fearful that some awful calamity was at hand. On the following day, March 4th, the amazed people sighted the London missionary ship *Duff* offshore the peninsula of Tahiti Iti. They understand that this foreign ship was the cause of the commotion, and in consequence, named it *te-rapu* (The Stirrer), a name they have always retained.

By the time the *Duff* anchored in Matavai Bay on March 5, a Sunday morning, more than a hundred natives were dancing and capering on the decks of the ship, eager to make friends with the missionaries. Although the Tahitians were unarmed, Captain Wilson ordered the great guns to be hoisted out of the hold to keep the natives in awe. Instead of being intimidated by the guns, the Tahitians helped to place them into their carriages.

Aboard the ship were 18 missionaries destined for Tahiti, who settled into their new quarters on Point Venus in the former house of Captain Bligh. Most of these men were in their early 20s and only five of them were married and had their families with them. The London Missionary Society (LMS), which was composed of Episcopalians, Methodists, Presbyterians and Independents, had chosen Tahiti as their first foreign country because they felt they would not have so many difficulties in Christianiz-ing the heathen natives. The Reverend **Doctor Thomas Haweis**, the founder of the LMS, had read the accounts of Samuel Wallis, James Cook and William Bligh, who had written of their voyages to Tahiti. The shocking lack of puritanical behavior of the fun-loving Tahitians pre-sented a certain challenge to the LMS leader. He decided that a South Seas island would be a suitable place for their mission, as the climate was good, food plentiful, there were no religious prejudices, and the government seemed monarchical, but of the mildest nature.

One of the first problems the Englishmen encountered was how to deal with the beautiful and seductive Tahitian *vahines*. Several of the young missionaries were sent home soon after arriving in Tahiti because they succumbed to the alluring charms of the idolatrous women, which was an unforgivable sin according to their vows.

Among the missionaries were carpenters, bricklayers, shoemakers, tailors, weavers and a harness maker. There were only four ordained ministers in the group, who soon learned that there was more to apprehend from being caressed and exalted by the natives, than from being insulted and oppressed.

The missionaries had difficulty learning to speak the language well enough to preach the gospel in Tahitian, and the natives would scoff and ridicule them and laugh when the missionaries said that Jehovah was the only true God and their pagan rites and human sacrifices should be abolished.

Some of the Tahitians felt that the missionaries should pay them to attend the mission school, and among the students was the oldest son of **Pomare II**, the powerful chief whom the missionaries thought of as king of Tahiti. His father, Tu, who had been designated as King Pomare I by the Europeans, died in 1803.

It was not until May 18, 1819, that the missionaries baptized their first convert on the island of Tahiti, who was King Pomare II. It had taken 22 long years of hard work, persistence and tremendous faith to achieve this goal. Although they suspected that Pomare wanted to be baptized for his own personal and political gain, they had to accept him in order to get the rest of the people into the church. Following his conversion, the heathen idols and temples were destroyed in favor of the Christian religion.

Although the Tahitians seemed to accept the outward forms of Christianity, many of them still retained their old ways. The missionaries made every effort to enforce their puritan standards on the islanders, who had to cover their bodies with hot clothing. They were forbidden to sing any songs but hymns, nor were they allowed to dance, wear flowers, tattoo their bodies, or sleep together in the big houses, where they formerly enjoyed indiscriminate sex. However, the women were still as free and easy in sex matters with foreign seamen who arrived in increasing numbers aboard the whaling ships. And drunkenness among the men became common, with King Pomare II one of the worst offenders. His behavior continued to shock the puritanical missionaries, as he continued his sexual relations with both sexes. He died in 1821 at the age of 47, from a combination of alcoholism, elephantiasis and dropsy. His young son, **Pomare III**, who was being educated by the missionary **Henry Knott**, died at the age of six.

The Reign of Queen Pomare IV

Pomare II's 14-year old illegitimate daughter, Aimata, was then crowned **Queen Pomare IV**, but her accession to the crown was without pomp or ceremony. The young queen had been married at the age of ten to a chief from Tahaa named Tapoa, but she later divorced him and took a new consort named **Arifaaite**. Although her wild behavior shocked the missionaries, Queen Pomare IV eventually grew into her majestic role and she ruled Tahiti, Moorea and part of the Austral and Tuamotu groups for 50 years.

In 1827 the Protestants built their first church, made of coral stones, which was erected on the site of Marae Taputapuatea at Papetoai in Moorea, which had been a royal stone temple.

The Protestant missionaries were the only soul-savers in Tahiti for almost forty years before any competitive religions arrived on the island. In 1835 a group of Catholic missionaries landed on the island of Mangareva, 900 miles southeast of Tahiti. They eventually made their way to Tahiti, and the Protestants used all their influence to prevent the Catholics from opening a new mission.

When two Catholic priests refused to leave Tahiti, even upon written orders issued by Queen Pomare IV, **Father Honoré Laval** and **Father François Caret** were forcibly removed from the island.

The French Protectorate

When the French government learned how their Catholic priests had been treated by the Queen of Tahiti, they retaliated by sending the frigate *Venus*, under the command of **Captain Abel Du Petit-Thouars**, who arrived in 1836 to punish the Tahitian sovereign for the insult done to France in the person of the priests. The full reparation demanded that Queen Pomare write a letter of apology to the King of France, pay an indemnity of 2,000 Spanish dollars for losses suffered by the two priests, and to honor the French flag with a twenty-one gun salute. **George Pritchard**, the most prominent missionary, and two other English residents, provided the money, and the French commander provided the flag and the gunpowder for the salute. Queen Pomare wrote the required letter of apology.

Du Petit-Thouars also proposed a treaty of perpetual peace be drawn up between Tahiti and France, specifying that Frenchmen would be allowed to come and go and to trade in all the islands of the government of Tahiti, where they should be received and protected as the most favored foreigners.

As soon as he left the island, Queen Pomare and four of her principal chiefs wrote a letter to **Queen Victoria**, asking for British protection. At the persuasion of George Pritchard, the Queen of Tahiti had appealed to the Queen of England on previous occasions, asking to be made a protectorate of the British crown. Queen Victoria, who was having her own problems with France, expressed her concern for Tahiti's difficulties, but replied that it would be impossible to fulfill any defensive obligations towards the government and inhabitants of Tahiti.

Soon after receiving the letter from Queen Victoria, Queen Pomare was away from Tahiti, visiting the island of Raiatea, while George Pritchard—who had left the London Missionary Society to become the British Consul of Tahiti—was away in England. During their absence the newly appointed French consul, **Jacques Antoine Moerenhout**, a Belgian Catholic who had served for a time as the American consul in Tahiti, took advantage of this time to persuade four of Tahiti's chiefs into signing a document he had prepared, stating that Tahiti wished to be made a French protectorate.

When this petition was received by the French government, in 1842 they once again sent Du Petit-Thouars, who had been promoted to Rear Admiral, back to Tahiti aboard the flagship *La Reine Blanche*. The French had been looking for a base in the Pacific for their warships, whalers and merchant vessels, and since they had already decided to take over the Marquesas Islands, they found it convenient to establish the French protectorate in Tahiti as well.

The Tahitian chiefs admitted that they had not understood the document they had signed, but in spite of Queen Pomare's protests, the French began to take hold in Tahiti. Du Petit-Thouars used his threats and troops to force the Queen to sign a letter accepting the proposal to place the government of Queen Pomare under the protection of France's **King Louis Philippe**. Du Petit-Thouars then appointed a provisional government that included a Royal Commissioner, a military governor and a captain of the port of Papeete.

Six months later, when news of the French protectorate reached England, the Parliament accepted the French action, stipulating that the work of the Protestant missionaries should continue. Soon it came to the attention of the English that France had actually taken full possession of Tahiti in 1843, when the Tahitian flag had been replaced by the French flag, after 500 French troops had surrounded Queen Pomare's palace in Papeete, forcing the dispossessed queen to take refuge aboard an English ship in the Papeete harbor. Then George Pritchard arrived in England on July 26, 1844, aboard the H.M.S. *Vindictive* with the news that he had been arrested by the French and deported from Tahiti.

Both the French and the English governments felt humiliated by the affairs that had transpired in Tahiti, and tempers rose on both sides of the channel between the two countries. In hopes of maintaining an *entente cordiale* with Great Britain, King Louis Philippe offered to pay Pritchard

25,000 francs from his own funds. Although this offer was rejected, an accord was reached between the two governments when France apologized to England for the treatment Pritchard had suffered, and he was paid an equitable indemnity for his losses.

For three more years this affair was heatedly discussed in all circles and kept alive in the French parliament. Although France and England carefully avoided war during this time, the Tahiti problems eventually contributed to the overthrow of the government and monarchy in France in 1848, and the indemnity was never paid.

Back in Tahiti, meanwhile, the natives resisted the French presence for three years with a series of skirmishes with the military troops that had been sent over to secure the French protectorate. Queen Pomare once again sought refuge in Raiatea, where she wrote another pleading letter to Queen Victoria, beseeching her help. Queen Victoria never answered the letters, yet the Tahitian people did not want to believe that England had deserted them.

After France and England had come to terms over the George Pritchard affair, and Queen Pomare's sovereignty was restored in early 1845, she refused to return to Tahiti under French rule. She stayed in exile for two more years, and was then persuaded by a Tahitian chiefess to give up the useless struggle. After agreeing to accept the French protectorate in 1847, Queen Pomare returned to Tahiti, and remained a figurehead until she died on September 17, 1877. The Paris Evangelical Missionary Society took over from the English Protestant missionaries in 1863.

King Pomare V, the son of the queen, ruled for three years, but he lacked his mother's pride in the Tahitian heritage, preferring drinking and gambling on the visiting ships, rather than assuming any duties of his kingship. On June 29, 1880, he gave France right of sovereignty of his dependencies in exchange for an annual pension and money for his wife and two brothers. Pomare V, the last King of Tahiti, drank himself to death in 1891. The Pomare descendants are now trying to reclaim the lands they lost during the French takeover.

MOOREA

Archaeologists have found evidence of settlements on Moorea as early as 900 AD. Stone *marae* temples, somberly hidden in a grove of *mape* Tahitian chestnut trees in the Opunohu valley, are mute remains of a once powerful religion.

The first European who reported sighting this island was **Captain Samuel Wallis**, who sailed past in 1767 and named it **York Island**, after the Duke of York. When **Captain James Cook** came to Tahiti to record the transit of the planet Venus across the sun in 1769, he sent a party of scientists from Matavai Bay over to York Island, where they camped out on a small sand bank called Irioa, and set up their telescopes for the June 3rd transit. Cook's ship anchored in Opunohu Bay in 1777, during his third voyage to Tahiti, yet Pao Pao Bay became known as Cook's Bay.

Pomare I of Tahiti conquered the Marama chiefs of Moorea in 1790, and following his death in 1803, **King Pomare II** retreated to Moorea whenever necessary to avoid his warring enemies in Tahiti. Following his defeat in 1808 the king withdrew to Moorea and befriended the remaining missionaries in Papetoai village, who had also fled Tahiti when their mission station was burned at Point Venus. Pomare II helped **Henry Nott**, a missionary bricklayer, translate the Bible into Tahitian. A second mission station was opened in Afareaitu village, where **Reverend William Ellis** installed the first printing press in the South Seas. King Pomare II printed the first page in 1817, and the Gospel of Saint Luke, written in the Tahitian language was published the following year.

In 1813 the missionaries erected a place for public worship in Papetoai village, and they made their first Christian convert in 1815, when the **High Chief Patti** denounced his idolatrous gods. He later became the first Tahitian deacon, preaching in the church the missionaries built in 1827 on the site of the royal Marae Taputapuatea in Papetoai village. The octagonal shaped Ebenezer church you see there today was rebuilt in 1889 and has since been restored. A spring in the church yard is said to produce healing water, and a 2-meter- (6.5 foot-) high basaltic stone stands in the church courtyard. This kneeling stone was brought to Moorea from the big Marae Taputapuatea in Raiatea, the sacred island. The first Christian marriage was performed in the missionaries' original church, and the South Seas Academy, the first school, was opened in Afareaitu in 1821. Moorea also had the first plantations of sugar cane, cotton, coffee and rice.

King Pomare II regained his power in Tahiti in 1815 and when he returned to rule in Tahiti, he took his Christian teachings with him. In May 1819 he became the first Christian convert on the island of Tahiti, where he was baptized at Papaoa in Arue.

Queen Pomare IV also used Moorea as a place of refuge when the French raised their flag on Tahiti. When the French protectorate was established in Tahiti in 1843, Moorea also came under French rule. Today Moorea is one of the Leeward Islands of the Society Archipelago, along with Tahiti, Tetiaroa and the little island of Maiao.

BORA BORA

Historians believe that the first Maohi or Polynesian settlers on Vavau sailed their double-hulled voyaging canoes into the island's beautiful lagoon sometime during the ninth century. The name of the island was changed to Porapora in the early 1700s, during the reign of **Chief Puni**, "The Terror" of all the nearby islands. This land of brave warriors distinguished their island by conquering their neighbors on Tahaa, Raiatea, Maupiti and Tupai, and they muffled their paddles to silently approach an island at night, thus surprising their sleeping enemy. Because of these warfare tactics the island of Vavau became known by the poetic name of *Porapora i te hoe manu* (first born of the silent paddle).

In 1769 **Captain James Cook** sailed past Porapora in the *Endeavour* and claimed all the Leeward Islands for his Britannic Majesty. During his third voyage in 1777, in command of the *Resolution* and *Discovery*, Cook landed on Porapora in a ship's boat, instead of sailing the ships through the narrow passage. He recorded the event in his ship's log, writing the island's name as BolaBola. At the time of Cook's arrival Chief Puni was a half-blind old man whose forces had conquered all the islands except Huahine. Puni died around 1786.

Porapora's warriors were sent to Tahiti in 1815 to help fight the traditionalists who still practiced the cult of Oro, which involved human sacrifices. At the invitation of the islanders the first Protestant missionaries landed on Porapora in 1820 and built a church in Vaitape in 1822. The first husband of **Queen Pomare IV**, **King Tapoa II**, was from Porapora, and when France claimed a protectorate over Tahiti and its dependencies, he maintained peace on Porapora until his death in 1860. The Pomare rule ended when the Leeward Islands became a French possession in 1888.

The American Armed Forces who were stationed on Porapora in World War II called the island Bora Bora. Although there is no "B" in the Polynesian language, common usage prevails.

In February, 1942, the 1,500 Polynesians who lived on Bora Bora awoke to find five gray transport ships and several escorting warships of "Operation Bobcat" lying out in the lagoon. This joint U.S. Navy-Army task force had been sent to construct a military base for supplying fuel to Allied shipping during their long journeys across the South Pacific. The military installations on Bora Bora's main island included a small seaplane base, a submarine base, port facilities, an adequate water system, a good road and bridges around the island, Quonset huts, cannon and bunkers for the anti-aircraft guns. A beer garden for weekend relaxation was built on the white sand beach of Matira Point, and a sports facility there included a baseball diamond.

By 1943 the Seabees had constructed an airstrip on Motu Mute, on the northern side of the lagoon. Almost 5,000 troops were involved in the "friendly invasion" of Bora Bora, until June, 1946, when the base was decommissioned and turned over to the French. When they departed the

Americans left behind some 175 light-skinned, blue-eyed babies. Many of these children died due to lack of proper nutrition following the decampment of "Operation Bobcat."

Several of the men who were stationed on Bora Bora during World War II returned after the war, some to visit their *vahines* and children, and others to rekindle fond memories. The landing strip they built on Motu Mute was used for international air traffic until the Tahiti-Faaa International Airport was opened in 1961, and continued to be used for inter-island flights for many years after. The old airstrip can still be seen when you arrive by plane at the new runway on Motu Mute.

5. LAND & PEOPLE

THE LAND

Tahiti and Her Islands, officially known as **French Polynesia**, are sprinkled over 5,030 million square kilometers (almost two million square miles) of ocean in the eastern South Pacific, between the longitudes of 134º28' and 154º40 west and the latitudes of 7º50' and 27º36' south. Papeete, the capital of French Polynesia, is located on Tahiti, the largest island, and lies at 17º32' latitude south and 149º34' longitude west.

French Polynesia is east of the international date line. Tahiti is 6,200 kilometers (3,844 miles) from Los Angeles, 3,900 kilometers (2,418 miles) from Auckland, New Zealand, 4,700 kilometers (2,914 miles) from Noumea, New Caledonia, 5,700 kilometers (3,534 miles) from Sydney, 8,800 kilometers (5,456 miles) from Tokyo, 7,500 kilometers (4,650 miles) from Santiago, Chile, and 17,100 kilometers (10,602 miles) from Paris. The most northerly island in the Marquesas archipelago, Eiao, also known as Hatutu, is more than 2,000 kilometers (1,240 miles) from the Austral Island of Rapa, the most southerly island.

The word Polynesia means "many islands." The total land area of these 118 Polynesian islands and atolls adds up to only 3,500 square kilometers (1,365 square miles). The territory is geographically and politically divided into five archipelagoes: the Society Islands, Austral Islands, Marquesas Islands, Tuamotu Islands and the Gambier Islands. These island groups differ in terrain, climate and, to a lesser degree, the people. Most of the land in the archipelagoes are high islands, which are the eroded mountain tops of ancient volcanoes.

THE HIGH VOLCANIC ISLANDS

All the Polynesian islands are basically of volcanic origin. They were formed millions of years ago when volcanoes erupted from a rising column of magma in the asthenosphere called a "hot spot." The earth's crust, or lithosphere, is divided into approximately a dozen plates resting on a flexible magma known as the asthenosphere. Magma escapes from accretion zones along dorsals formed on these plates and disappears within subduction zone troughs back into the magma. The hot spots remain stationary even though the Pacific lithospheric plate moves 7 to 10 centimeters a year in a westward direction, and a periodic reactivation of these hot spots over millions of years have resulted in a linear distribution of the Polynesian islands in a southeast-northwest direction.

Five strips of islands correspond to a succession of hot-spots along the Pacific seabed. The MacDonald hot spot, southeast of Rapa, is believed to have come to life 15 or 20 millions of years ago, and is still intermittently active. Tahiti is estimated at 2.6 million years in age, whereas Bora Bora seems to have come into existence between three and four million years ago.

The volcano becomes extinct when the magma is no longer expelled through the vent. The lava on top collapses, forming a huge caldera basin, which eventually erodes and forms valleys. As the island sinks slowly into the ocean, coral begins to grow on the underwater sides of the island. These corals are millions of microscopic polyps that attach themselves to a permanent base and produce a hard outer skeleton. Generations of these rocklike formations build upon one another, creating barriers hundreds of feet deep that surround the island shores, forming a fringing reef connected to the island.

When the island disintegrates, the coral remains at the surface of the water, reaching for the light it needs to survive. A circular crust is eventually formed above the volcano, which is called a barrier reef. A channel of varying width fills with water to form a lagoon between the fringing reef and the barrier reef.

This process may take millions of years. The different stages of this evolution are illustrated by the Society archipelago. The island of Mehetia, which is near a hot spot, is a young island with no coral reef; Moorea is a high island with a coral reef; Bora Bora is nearly an atoll with a barrier reef; and Scilly is an atoll.

THE LOW CORAL ATOLLS

During **Charles Darwin's** visit to Tahiti in 1842 he climbed a mountain and discovered that the flat coral atoll is actually a high island that has sunk deeper into the ocean when the original volcano disappeared completely under the water. The old volcanic core still remains underneath the atoll, but all you see is the coral ring, which encircles the lagoon. The coral rim of the atoll indicates how big the island once was. A series of small coral islets, strung together by often-submerged coral reefs, are seldom more than a quarter of a mile wide and only a few feet above the sea. Inside this narrow strip of coral the lagoon can be the size of a salt-water pond or as big as an inland sea.

White beaches of coarse and fine coral sand create a border between the sea and the green oasis of coconut forests, flowering trees and scented bushes. The live coral gardens of the reefs and inner lagoons are filled with a fantastic variety of tropical fish, sharks, rays, turtles, crustaceans, and other marine fauna.

FLORA

From the moment you step off your plane in Tahiti you become aware that you are surrounded by flowers. The first scent is the sweet perfume of the beautiful white **Tiare Tahiti** (*Gardenia taitensis*), that a smiling *vahine* offers to welcome you to this luxuriant land of flowers.

This traditional custom of the islands existed long before there were passenger ships and airplanes. Even today when the Tahitians are traveling between the islands, they are adorned with crowns and leis of flowers. This is a sign of the traveler.

"Say it with flowers" is a way of life in Tahiti. Walk through the public market in the heart of downtown Papeete and just watch for a few minutes as the vendors sell their brilliantly colored anthuriums, birds of paradise, asters, carnations, red and pink ginger flowers, delicate orchids, vivid roses, and myriads of varied bouquets. You won't be complaining about the prices here.

Or stroll around to the side of the market late in the afternoon and see the Tahitian grandmothers and little girls creating the decorative flower crowns and leis for the evening's merrymakers. Anyone who is going out to dinner and who wants to feel festive has only to walk by the flower stands and suddenly there are flower-covered arms thrust from all directions, filling your nostrils and senses with a captivating aroma.

A drive around the island will give you an opportunity to see the many varieties of flowers flourishing in the rich soil of Tahiti. Especially in the spring and summer months (October-March) you will find a wonderful display of flowering trees and vines. The most readily identified belong to the *cassia* family: the *cassia grandis*, coral shower tree; *cassia fistula*, golden shower tree; *cassia javanica*, pink and white shower tree; and the lovely peach and cream colored *cassia hybrida*, the rainbow shower tree. One of the most exotic stars in this springtime show is the jade vine, *Strongylodon macrobotrys,* from the forests of the Philippines, whose cascading green flowers resemble sharks teeth.

The pink and purple flowers you see bordering many of the streets in the urban areas of Tahiti are cousins to the crepe myrtle you know back home. Named *lagerstroemia speciosa*, this tree is a native of India and is also called crepe myrtle in Tahiti. The *koelreuteria* or goldenrain tree, the jacaranda, with its lovely blue-violet bell-shaped flowers, the *tabebuia pentaphylla* or Tecoma tree, with its masses of lavender-pink, trumpet-shaped flowers, and the *bauhinia varigate*, known as the orchid tree, are some of the delightful sights that Tahiti's springtime brings. The Royal Poinciana, also called flamboyant or flame tree, *delonis regia*, grows to a height of 40 feet, and this most regal of all of Tahiti's springtime exhibits is in full bloom each Christmas, providing a huge canopy of red, scarlet and yellow blossoms. With their shiny green fern-like foliage, these showy trees make a brilliant contribution to the holiday season.

Take a tour to the Botanical Gardens in Papeari. Here you will find 340 acres of exotic plants, shrubs, fruits and flowers, brought from all the tropical countries by **Harrison Willard Smith**, an American who left his job as a physics professor at the Massachusetts Institute of Technology to settle in Tahiti in 1919. Smith spent the rest of his life importing plants for his gardens.

Here you will discover a forest of Tahitian *mape* chestnut trees *(Inocarpus fagifer)*, plus gardens of indigenous and imported trees and plants. These include the perfumed pua *(Fabrea berteriana)*, ylang-ylang *(Cananga odorata)*, pitate jasmine *(Jasminum rex)*, queen of the night *(Epiphyllum oxypetalum)*, ixora or jungle flame *(Ixora macrothyrsa)*, lipstick plant *(Bixa orellana)*, Indian lotus *(Nelumbium Nelumbo nucifera)*, Mickey Mouse plant *(Ochna kirkii)*, pagoda flower *(Clerodendron speciossisimum)*, dwarf poinciana *(Poinciana pulcherrima)*, shrimp plant *(Beloperone guttata)*, white bleeding heart *(Clerodendron thomsonae)*, chenille plant *(Acalpha hispida)* candle bush *(Cassia alata)* elephant ear *(Alocasia macrorrhiza)* and many more.

Called the "Grandfather of Trees" by the Tahitians, Smith distributed his seeds and cuttings to his neighbors in Papeari, encouraging them to beautify their surroundings. He even held a contest each year to see who had the prettiest garden, and Papeari was long considered to be the "flower district" of Tahiti. Thanks to the Tahitians' natural love of flowers, the entire island is a botanical garden today.

Here in the Polynesian islands, we incorporate flowers into our daily lives. Both men and women can be seen wearing a fragrant blossom behind their ears, even while performing the most humdrum tasks. Often you can hear them softly singing to themselves. Wearing flowers does make you want to sing.

HOW TO WEAR YOUR FLOWERS

"They are very fond of flowers," wrote Captain Cook, when he first visited Tahiti in 1769. "Especially of the Cape Jasmine (Gardenia taitensis, known as the Tiare Tahiti), of which they have great plenty planted near their houses; these they stick into the holes of their ears and into their hair..."

Many of the visitors to Tahiti have noticed that there is a custom of conversing through the wearing of flowers, and this language of the flowers still exists. Learn to read what they are saying when you see a big, husky man digging a ditch and wearing his Tiare Tahiti bud behind his ear; or when you see a young lady with her long hair coifed so nicely for that special evening and laced with orchids; when you see the proud Tahitian grandmothers with their woven hats and a hibiscus behind an ear.

When you wear your flower behind your right ear–it means you are single, available and looking. When you wear your flower behind your left ear–it means you are married, engaged or otherwise taken. When you wear flowers behind both ears–it means you are married but are still available. When you wear your flower backwards behind your ear–it means "follow me and you'll find out how available I am." When you wear a flower backwards behind both ears–it means anything goes. And when you see the young vahine with flowers in her hair–it means she's desperate, you'd better hurry up!

TRADITIONAL TAHITIAN FOOD PLANTS

Plants have always served as an essential part in the daily social and economic life of the Polynesians. Their ancestors, who were sailors and fishermen, had a plant-based culture, and plants provided the islanders with food, utensils, material of all kinds, ornaments and drugs.

On all the islands and atolls of French Polynesia you will find the graceful coconut palm, the "tree of life" to the Polynesians, which can be used in dozens of ways. Other trees and plants that provide traditional Tahitian foods are: breadfruit, bananas, *fei* plantains, taro, tarua, manioc, arrowroot, sweet potato and yams. Complimentary food plants include: sugarcane, pandanus, *mape* (Tahitian chestnut), ti or *auti* (*cordyline fruticosa*), *vi* Tahiti or Tahitian apple (*Spondias dulcis*), kava (*Pometia pinnata Forster*), *nono* (*Morinda citrifolia*), small ginger roots called *rea*, bamboo, the candlenut tree (*Aleurites molucanna*), the wild hibiscus called *purau* (*Hibiscus tiliaceus*), the *hotu* fruit of the *Barringtonia asiatica*, and varieties of purslane and cress, as well as several types of ferns.

THE MYSTICAL-MAGICAL INTOXICATING TI PLANT

*The ancient Tahitians had 13 varieties of the **ti plant** (Cordyline terminalis or fructicosa), which they called **auti**. The most sacred of all ti plants in old Tahiti was the Ti-'uti, which was a fine variety planted chiefly in the marae enclosures for the gods and religious uses. Beautiful varieties of ti have been introduced in recent years, but it is still the glossy green leaves that were worn by orators, warriors and enchanters that are worn today by dancers, high priests and fire-walkers.*

This small tree of the Liliaceae family is believed to possess mystical-magical qualities that will protect the house from fire, and hedges of auti surround many of the homes in the islands. The broad leaves are used as food wrappers and to line the pits where breadfruit is preserved by fermentation. The ti is also used in traditional healing for diarrhea, vomiting, abscesses or ear infections. The root can be cooked in the underground stone oven to replace the breadfruit and the taro, and the large fibrous tuber was formerly made into candy. This root is very rich in sugar, and during the reign of King Pomare II, natives from the Sandwich Islands (now Hawaii) taught the Tahitians how to build a still and produce a potent liqueur from the auti root.

Imported Food Plants

The European explorers, botanists, sailors, missionaries, traders and civil servants brought many species of economic flora to Tahiti, which flourish on most of the islands today. Among these food plants you will find varieties of: avocado, bay rum tree, Brazilian plum, cantaloupe, cashew nut, cayenne pepper, citron, coffee, custard apple, grapefruit, guava, gooseberry tree, jackfruit, Java almond, lime, lychee, mamee apple, mandarin, mango, orange, pakai, Panama cherry, papaya, passion fruit, pineapple, pistachio, pomegranate, quenette, rambutan, sea grape, soursop, Spanish plum, Surinam cherry, star apple, sugar apple, tamarind, vanilla and watermelon.

Chinese Gardens

Chinese immigrants brought their garden vegetables with them, which they plant in the high valleys of Tahiti. These colorful vegetables can best be seen at the Papeete market, where you will recognize varieties of bok choy, cabbages, carrots, cilantro, cucumbers, eggplant, ginger root, green peppers, jicama, lettuce, long beans and snap beans, parsley, pumpkins, soy bean sprouts, spinach, squashes, tomatoes, watercress, white radishes and zucchini.

Sacred Trees of Old Polynesia

The sacred trees of old Polynesia were chosen for their medicinal value, and the quality of their wood, bark, leaves or roots. Some of these trees are still used for carving into furniture, *umete* bowls, platters, small canoes, tikis and ceremonial clubs. These precious trees are the *tamanu* or *ati* (*Calophyllum inophyllum*), the *tou* (*Cordia subcordata*), rosewood or *miro* (*Thespesia populnea*), banyan or *ora* (*Ficus prolixa*), *aito* or ironwood (*Casuarina equisetifolia*), *reva* or *hotureva* (*Cerbera odollam*) and the *pua* (*Fagraea berteriana*).

LAND-BASED FAUNA

There are no snakes in Tahiti and Her Islands and there are no poisonous spiders or fearsome land animals, except for the centipede (*Scolopendra subspinipes*), which lives in dark, humid areas, under rocks and in palm frond structures. Its bite is venomous and very painful to humans. It is nocturnal by nature and its diet is made up exclusively of cockroaches, while the centipede itself is a delicacy for chickens. So don't strangle the roosters that crow outside your hotel window all night long!

Almost every home in the Polynesian islands has a few house pets in the form of the *mo'o*, a yellow lizard that lives on the ceilings, where they feed on mosquitoes and other flying insects and bananas if they're available. Sometimes these critters find their way into hotel rooms, which has been known to disrupt the tranquillity of the human occupants. These geckos are harmless, but they do seem to occasionally take delight in dropping "whitewash" on inappropriate places, such as your bed or head. The reptile population includes four gecko species and three lizard species, none of which are to be feared.

Here you will find the yellowish-red Tahitian dog, some of whom are descendants of the barkless vegetarian dogs who crossed the ocean aboard the double-hulled voyaging canoes of the pioneer Polynesians. They eat meat these days and sometimes they bark all night, in tandem with the cocks.

Along with the dog, the pig was the only domestic animal known to the Polynesian before the arrival of the Europeans. Both animals were raised for food. The pig is still baked in the underground ovens for special feasts, and dogs are still served in a "special Chinese sauce" during big celebrations. Some of the pigs have taken to the bush and wild boar hunts are organized by men on the high islands.

Captain Wallis gave a cat to the high chiefess Purea in 1767, and it found a mate somewhere, because today cats abound in all the inhabited islands and atolls.

The little Polynesian rat and its cousins, who arrived aboard ships and boats, are a threat to coconut trees without the metal bands. The *Rattus norvegicus*, a large brown rat, carries Tahitian meningitis and other contagious diseases. They also steal birds' eggs and fruit, and love to make their nests in thatched roofs.

In the Marquesas Islands you will see wild goats, sheep and cattle grazing on the precipitous cliffs overlooking the sea. Wild and tamed horses roam the plains of Ua Huka. The ancestors of these small horses were brought from Chile by Dupetit-Thouars in 1842.

A land crab called *tupa* lives in holes in the ground close to the lagoon and as far as a mile inland. When I first visited Bora Bora as a tourist I expended a lot of effort in trying to annihilate the tupas. When you cover up one of the holes they just disappear into their extensive underground network and surface from another hole. Now I know better and I feed the tupas who live beside my house. They're also edible if you pen them up and feed them coconut for ten days. Mine are getting pretty big now, but I'll just keep on feeding them.

Some would-be entrepreneur got the idea to import the African snail (*Achatina fulica*) in 1967, because he knew the French like their *escargots*. His snails were not a culinary success and what's more, they gobbled up plants in most of the gardens. Another carnivorous species, *Euglandina rosea*, was brought in to combat this greedy snail, but instead of attacking the *Achatina*, it almost wiped out the *Partula*, the tiny local snails whose shells are used by the Polynesians for making necklaces.

The mosquito and *nono* (sandfly) are two obnoxious pests that can truly ruin your vacation if you don't protect yourself from their stings. They particularly favor tourists, so be sure to bring a good insect repellent with you. I've listed a few suggestions under the Health category in the *Basic Information* chapter.

The insect population in this part of Polynesia includes the beautiful butterfly, *Danaida plexippus*, which you'll see in the daytime. The *Rhyncogonus* beetle that lives in the Marquesas Islands is found nowhere else in the world. There are about forty nocturnal species of moths, including the *Lepidopter sphingidae*, which feeds on leaves and vegetable stalks at night, and the Queensland fruit fly (*Dacus tryoni*). Over 400 different pesticides are used in massive quantities, especially on the island of Tahiti, which is a concern for the public because of the risks of pollution and toxic effects in rivers and lagoons. Fresh water shrimps and eels live in the rivers and streams.

BIRDS

Birds (*manu*) were brought into these islands by the early Polynesians and European explorers, and during the past two centuries other species have been introduced from Asia, Africa, Australasia and the Americas. Habitat changes and introduced species of birds are believed to be accountable for the extinction of certain species that formerly inhabited the Windward Society Islands. There are presently 104 known species of birds found in Tahiti and Her Islands.

Of the 27 species of sea birds nesting here, only nine reproduce in the Pacific, and Murphy's petrel (*Pterodroma ultima*) is the only species that lives in Polynesia all the time. The birds you may see include terns, boobies, noddies, frigatebirds, petrels and the graceful white tropicbirds (phaethons), identified by two long white plumes that form the tip of the tail as they soar high over the valleys from the rocky cavities where they nest. Twenty-one species of migratory sea birds have been observed as they fly from the North to the South Pacific. The white sand beaches and the bushes on the *motus* inside the reef on Tetiaroa atoll are nesting grounds for several species of sea birds, and the Tuamotu atolls have numerous bird islands. Almost a million sooty terns (*kaveka*) live on a small island offshore Ua Huka in the Marquesas Islands.

Thirteen species of land-birds coming from North America and Siberia reach these islands on a regular basis. They include two ducks and a cuckoo from New Zealand. Among the 30 species of nesting birds, almost half can be found only in French Polynesia. They include two herons, two salanganes, two warblers, one swallow, one duck, one rail, one of the limicoles, three parakeets, four wood kingfishers, four flycatchers and nine pigeons. Thirteen introduced species include the harrier, which lives in the Society Islands, and the eagle-owl in the Marquesas.

The main land bird you will see is the Indian Mynah (*Acridotheres Tristis*), which was imported to Tahiti around 1903 to eradicate a beetle that was destroying the young coconuts. The cheeky Mynah also wiped out several species of birds by robbing their nests. The turtledove (*geopelia striata*) was introduced in 1950, and the red-tailed bulbul (*Pyconotus cafer*), a native of Asia, was introduced more recently, brought in from Rarotonga in the Cook Islands. The Tahitians gave the name *vini* to several small finch-like birds, which include the chestnut-breasted mannikin (*Lonchura Castaneothorax*), common waxbill (*Estrilda Astrild*), red-browed waxbill (*Estrilda Temporalis*), crimson-backed tanager (*Ramphocelus dimidiatus*) and the gray-backed white-eye (*Zosterops Lateralis*).

The Tahiti Lorikeet (*Vini peruviana*) disappeared from Tahiti around the end of the last century, when the Swamp Harrier was introduced. This pretty little blue and white bird, also known as *lori-nonette*, is still found on some of the Tuamotu atolls, but is on the endangered species list, along with the *pihiti (Vini ultramarine-Kuhl)* of the Marquesas Islands and all the other lorikeets.

The *mo'a oviri* or wild cock is a jungle fowl of the *Gallus Gallus* family, which was introduced by the early Polynesians. The roosters are brightly colored with red, green and black feathers, and the hens are beige, brown or black. These birds can fly for several yards and they live in a free state, not really belonging to any family, but roost in trees and bushes close to a good source of food, such as my house. The roosters crow at all hours of the night, especially during the full moon, and of course, when you're trying to take a nap in the afternoon. I buy rice and bread for them and frozen chicken legs from Arkansas and Mississippi for myself. Their biggest enemies, apart from the Swamp Harrier, are little Tahitian boys, who catch the roosters and use them as fighting cocks.

OCEAN, REEF & LAGOON FAUNA

The oceanic slope is the richest part of a coral reef, and this is where you will have a better chance of finding crayfish or rock lobsters (*Panulirus penicillatus* called *oura miti*) and slipper lobsters (*Parribacus antarticus* called *tianee* in Tahitian). The near surface zones of the reef abound with surgeon-fish, parrot-fish, wrasses and red mullets. The external reef is also inhabited by various species of trigger-fish, soldier-fish, squirrel-fish, bass, perch, rock cod, angel-fish, demoiselle-fish, mullet, and gray sharks and moray eels. You may also come across a green turtle (*Chelonia mydas*) or see a rare jelly fish or an occasional sea snake in this underwater zone.

Most of the mollusks and crustacea are found on the reef flats, which are also favored by pencil sea urchins and holothurians (sea cucumbers, called *rori* in Tahitian). The trigger-fish, puffer-fish, rock cods, box-fish, rascass and butterfly cod make their permanent homes here, and parrot-fish, surgeon-fish, angel-fish and small sharks, usually the harmless black-tipped and white-tipped variety, will visit the reef flats at high tide. Submerged coral plateaus act as passages between the oceanic slopes and the lagoons, and are the homes for echinoderms, particularly sea urchins, clam shells, octopus, small sponges and anemones, annelid worms and a variety of crabs. Lizard-fish, puffer-fish and trumpet-fish are also common in this area. At high tide small schools of red mullet, jacks and parrot-fish cross the zone on their way from the ocean to the lagoons.

On the lagoon slopes, as well as in the passes and the cracks in the reef (*hoa*), which have a sandy bottom sloping gradually to the center of the lagoon, is the favorite area of sponges, sand crabs, seashells (littorinids, nerites, ceriths), oysters, pearl oysters, cowries, strombs, spider shells, cones, all types of holothuria, *Ophiuridae*, starfish, *taramea*, some species of sea urchins (*vana*), soles, sand goby (*avaava*), leopard rays and some red mullets.

The coral outcrops and pinnacles are habitats of bivalve mollusks, including the colorful velvet-mantled reef clam (*Tridacna maxima*), called *pahua* locally. Numerous small species of fishes also gather here: surgeon-fish, angel-fish, butterfly-fish, soldier-fish, harp-fish, butterfly cod, trumpet-fish, box-fish, porcupine-fish and trigger-fish.

There is almost no living coral or algae on the bottom of the lagoons, which are colonized by clam shells, pearl oysters, stony oysters and ark shells. Spider shells, a rare helmet shell or conch shell live on the softer sand bottom, but the majority of shells, including the pencil shells, miters, harp shells, olives, ceriths and several cones, remain hidden in the sand during the daytime.

The open lagoon waters are the habitat of roving fishes, including unicorn-fish (*ume*), *rotea*, *kukina*, coral trout (*tonu*), chameleon sea bass (*hoa*), lagoon sharks and stingrays. The (*lutjanus*) snappers, sweetlip, flying fish, garfish, great barracuda (*ono*), sea-pike barracuda (*tiatio*), jacks and mullets come and go between the lagoon and the ocean, and the silver scad (*ature*) also visit the lagoon for brief periods during certain seasons.

The flora of the fringing reefs is rich, and trochus are abundant in many parts of the fringing reef, but the fishes found here are usually in the juvenile stage. These may include moray eels, rock eels, rascasse, surgeon-fish, wrasses, gobies, blennies and angel-fish.

Three types of rays are found in Polynesian waters, and they are not aggressive unless threatened. The biggest danger is when a bather treads on a ray that is buried in the sand in shallow water. The most spectacular and famous member of the family is the giant manta ray (*Manta alfredi (Macleay)*, *fafa piti*), which has a wingspan up to 25 feet across and may weigh almost two tons. The spotted eagle ray (*Aetobatis nari nari Euphrasen*) is the "bird ray" (*fai manu*) to the Tahitians because of its protruding head and narrow snout. They feed on mollusks and are one of the most important predators of the valuable pearl oysters in the lagoons of the Tuamotu and Gambier Islands. Several species of rays equipped with venomous spines on their tails are found in Polynesia. The stingray (*Himantura sp.*, *fai iu*) live near coral reefs or in the brackish water of some large bays around the high islands. The pectoral fins or wings of these species, as well as those of most other rays, are tasty and considered a delicacy, sometimes appearing on the menu in seafood restaurants in Tahiti and Moorea.

Sea turtles (*honu*) were once reserved for the high chiefs and priests of Tahiti, as this marine reptile was held *tapu* (sacred and forbidden). The three species living in Polynesian waters are the leathery turtle, the green turtle and the hawksbill turtle, which are on the list of endangered species and, therefore, *tapu*. However, these turtles are still massacred for their flesh and carapaces.

The most important commercial fishes found in the ocean depths surrounding French Polynesia include several species of the tuna family, principally, the yellow fin tuna (*Neothunnus albacora macropterus, aahi*), which are fished year round. Along with the tuna, the mahi mahi dolphinfish (*Coryphaena hippurus*), is the favorite fish served in restaurants. The great barracuda (*Sphyraena barracuda, ono*), the wahoo (*Acanthocybium solandri, paere*), the deep-water swordfish (*Xyphias gladius, haura or meka*), and the salmon of the gods (*Lampris luna*), are also served in seafood restaurants. The bonito (*Katsuwonus pelamis, auhopu*) is the most commonly caught fish, and is preferred by most Tahitians to any other fish, but the taste is a bit too "fishy" for most tourists. Many other species of edible fish abound in this oceanic wonderland, which are taken home by the local fishermen for their own dinner.

Roughly one-third, or 25 species, of the species of dolphins and whales in the world are found in the waters of Tahiti and Her Islands. The spinner dolphins (*Stenella longirostris*) are the easiest to find around Tahiti and Moorea because they live the closest to shore. The humpback whales (*Megaptera novaeangliae*) can be seen and heard offshore Moorea between July and October, when they come up from Antarctica to mate and give birth. They also escape the austral winters by visiting the Australs, Gambiers and Tuamotu Islands, as well as the Leeward Society group.

According to Richard H. Johnson, an American marine biologist and local shark specialist living in Tahiti, there are an estimated 35 species of sharks in French Polynesian waters. These include: (*Alopias Vulpinus*) common thresher shark (*mao aero*), (*Carcharhinus Albimarginatus*) silvertip shark (*tapete*); (*Carcharhinus Amblyrhynchos*) gray reef shark (*raira*); (*Carcharhinus Falciformis*) silky shark (*tautukau*); (*Carcharhinus Galapagensis*) Galapagos shark; (*Carcharhinus Leucas*) bull shark; (*Carcharhinus Limbatus*) blacktip shark (*oihe*); (*Carcharhinus Longimanus*) oceanic whitetip shark (*mao parata*); (*Carcharhinus Melanopterus*) blackfin reef shark (*mauri*); (*Galeocerdo Cuvier*) tiger shark (*mao tore tore*); (*Negaprion Acutidens*) South Pacific lemon shark (*arava*); (*Triaenodon Obesus*) reef whitetip shark (*mamaru*); (*Isurus Oxyrinchus*) mako or short-finned mako shark (*mao aahi*); (*Nebrius Concolor*) Indo-Pacific nurse shark (*mao rohoi); (Rhincodon Typus*) whale shark; (*Sphyrna Lewini*) scalloped hammerhead shark (*mao tuamata*); (*Sphyrna Mokarran*) great hammerhead shark (*tamataroa*);and (*Sphyrna Sp.*) squarehead hammerhead shark (*mao afata*).

Natural Dangers

The ocean, coral reef, lagoons and coral gardens do have a few inhabitants that are not man's best friend. Sea snakes are rare in Polynesia and only one species (*Pelamis platurus*) is occasionally seen and caught along the coasts of some of the islands. This bi-colored snake has a brownish back and yellow belly and its venom is dangerous to humans. The theory is that these serpents hitch-hiked on the bottoms of ships arriving in Tahiti from islands to our west, where the snakes are prevalent.

The natural dangers you want to avoid in the lagoon are: the "crown of thorns" starfish, called *taramea* in Tahitian; the sting of the jellyfish;

burns from the Holuthurian or sea cucumber, also called sea leech, *rori* in Tahitian, and its cousin with spaghetti-like sticky tubules; burns from the sea anemone; the sting of the stone fish, called *nohu* in Tahitian; the sting of the scorpion fish and fire coral; the sting of sea urchin spines, called *vana* in Tahitian; and the highly poisonous varieties of cone shells, members of the *Conidae* family. There are 60 species of cones in Polynesia, but the most dangerous are the geographic, textile, marbled, aulicus and tulip cones. The best way to protect yourself from any of these unpleasant encounters is to wear plastic reef sandals or other appropriate shoes when walking in the lagoon or on the reef, and to watch where you put your hands and body when snorkeling or scuba diving.

The moray eel rarely attacks humans, but it will bite when it is provoked and feels threatened. Keep your hands safely out of the crevices or cavities in the coral, where the moray eel may be lurking.

Shark attacks occur most frequently in the atolls, along the exterior of the barrier reefs and in the shallow fissures between the exterior reef and the interior lagoons. Some of these attacks happen when a spear fisherman is trailing a string of fish behind him. Several scuba diving and snorkeling excursions include feeding the sharks and moray eels, who have been "tamed" by repetitious feedings.

You can avoid any potential problems by remembering to swim only in the areas where you see the locals swimming; do not swim in the ocean at night; leave your bright jewelry at your hotel when you go swimming, snorkeling or scuba diving, as it can reflect the sun and refracted light in the water, and attract the attention of moray eels and sharks; and wear protective footgear when you're swimming in the lagoons and walking on the reef.

THE PEOPLE

The 1996 census counted 219,521 residents of French Polynesia, an increase of 16.3 percent since the last census of 1988, for an average annual growth rate of 1.9 percent. The demographic distribution includes 74.1 percent of the population living in the Windward Society Islands, 12.2 percent in the Leeward Society Islands, 3.7 percent in the Marquesas Islands, 3 percent in the Austral Islands and 7 percent in the Tuamotu and Gambier Islands. The total population included 52 percent males and 48 percent females, and the greatest segment is the 0 to 19 year old group, which accounts for 42.6 percent of the overall figure.

The birth rate is 22.5 percent and the death rate is 5 percent, with both numbers representing a slight decrease since the last counting. Only 6 percent of the population is over the age of 60, which equals one senior citizen per 16 inhabitants, and one out of every three citizens in French Polynesia attends school.

Life expectancy remains 68 years for men and 72 years for women. This shorter life span in the tropics can be attributed to bad health habits: too much alcohol and tobacco and the consumption of too much sweet and fatty foods. Road accidents also take their toll, especially on the under 30 age group. The per capita ratio of deaths on the highway in Tahiti is one of the highest in the world. There are more than 47,000 cars or other four-wheel vehicles and almost 16,000 two-wheel vehicles in these islands.

The minimum wage in French Polynesia is 551,14 CFP ($5.51) per hour or 93.143 CFP ($931.43) per month, for a 39-hour work week or 169 working hours per month. Employees are covered by a French government insurance program (CPS) that includes health, workman's compensation and retirement benefits. The employer pays the majority of the premiums, as well as five weeks' vacation pay for each employee per year. The work force includes 42,000 men and 27,000 women.

The 1996 census counted 49,574 residences in French Polynesia, with an average of 4.34 people per habitation. Statistics show that 89.6 percent of the homes have a television and 82.8 percent have a refrigerator, 70.5 percent have a telephone and only 7.6 percent have air conditioning. Most people live an indoor-outdoor type existence, with windows wide open to catch the tradewinds.

The census no longer includes a breakdown by ethnic groups, which were formerly classified as Polynesians, those of Polynesian-European or Polynesian-Chinese mixed race, Europeans and Chinese, or French citizens of Chinese origin. The 1988 census reported that Polynesians and assimilated races accounted for 82.8 percent of the population, Europeans represented 11.9 percent, and the Asians comprised 4.7 percent. The Polynesians and the Chinese born in French Polynesia are French citizens.

THE POLYNESIANS

The majority of the people who live in the five island groups of French Polynesia are the **Maohi** people or Eastern Polynesians. Whether they live in the Society Islands, the Marquesas, Tuamotu-Gambiers or Austral Islands, they are commonly referred to as **Tahitians**. The Polynesians refer to one another according to their island or archipelago, such as a Marquesan, a Paumotu (native of the Tuamotu Islands), a Rurutuan or Rapan, Mangarevan, and so forth.

The Marquesas Islands were settled by two distinct racial types and some of the Marquesans have longer, narrow heads. The Marquesan women have the reputation of being the prettiest of all Polynesian women. There are striking differences in the Paumotu physical types, as well as their language and culture. Some of the men on the Tuamotu atolls are big strapping fellows, with wide flat noses, while others are more squat, with big heads, small button noses and dark brown skin. Still others have thin lips, aquiline features, slim bodies and light tan skin. The Austral Islanders resemble their neighbors in the Cook Islands, with almost blue-black hair, Spanish eyes and heavy beards. In Mangareva and the other Gambier Islands the earliest settlers appear to have been castaways from the Tuamotu archipelago, the Marquesas and Rarotonga.

Although their ancestors' idea of beauty included shutting the chiefly children inside special "fattening" houses, where they became enormous while their skin was lightened from lack of sunlight, many of today's Tahitians have adopted the western world's concept of beauty. Therefore, they are even prouder of themselves when they've bronzed their bodies for hours on the beaches, even though their skin is naturally of an amber or golden brown color.

Their hair is usually thick, black and shiny and can be curly, wavy or straight, depending on how much Chinese or Spanish blood is mingled with the Polynesian traits. They anoint their hair and soft, smooth, velvety skin with *monoi*, a wonderful emollient made from coconut oil and different flowers and herbs, which makes them smell divine and practically glow under the rays of the sun.

The Polynesians are among the tallest people in the world, broad and muscular in structure. Most of them have short, broad, well-shaped heads with high cheekbones and strong jaw lines. The average Polynesian nose is long, broad and high, with a straight profile and a depression at the root. The lips are full but not Negroid, and their teeth are perfectly shaped and very white, although today's sugary diet leaves some of them snaggle-toothed. Their long and wide almond shaped eyes reveal an ancestry that began centuries ago in Southeast Asia or Malaysia, and they are a liquid brown or hazel color. The eyes of both the men and women are very expressive, sometimes sparkling with fire, and sometimes melting with softness. Their eyes are deep-set with heavy lids and their long, thick, black eyelashes are definitely enviable.

The Tahitian male has very little body hair, although several of them wear mustaches and little goatee beards. His shoulders are often very wide and strong, and his chest is well developed and tapers down to a nice, slim waist and flat stomach. His long, well-shaped legs with the prominent thigh muscles also have nicely developed calf muscles from years of playing soccer on the beach or sports field. His big feet, which are normally flat with the toes wide apart, are good for climbing coconut trees, and he has the dexterity of an amphibious animal in the water. A Tahitian man's sports usually come before everything else. If the Saturday afternoon soccer game is canceled because the playing field is three feet under water, he quickly becomes *fiu* (bored, fed up, non-talkative, non-responsive) and nothing can appease him. Fidelity to his wife or mistress is not in his vocabulary, and several of the handsomest youths are not averse to more or less discreet bisexual relationships.

The young *vahine* usually has an erect carriage, graceful walk and perfectly proportioned body. She looks fabulous in a string bikini, *pareo*, or a Parisian gown. Some of these modern ladies are well educated, intelligent, sophisticated and liberated. They're at home in the islands and the big cities of the world, at ease among different kinds of people and circumstances.

Although some of the Polynesians remain wiry and slim all their lives, the majority have a tendency toward corpulence in their adult years. The men convey an impression of giant strength, reserve power, and unconscious poise. Some of the women are tall and majestic, with broad shoulders and other masculine features. Their movements are slow, dignified and full of pride, with an undulating movement of their bodies and long pliant fingers.

The first European visitors to Tahiti were impressed by the personal cleanliness of the people. They may take three or four cold water showers a day, and both sexes use a lime as their natural deodorant, or they will sometimes rub the sweet smelling kernel of the pandanus fruit under their armpits. A group of dancers or workers or spectators on a hot day smell only of soap, *monoi* or flowers. Being dirty or wearing dirty clothes is a matter of shame.

The Polynesians resemble or even exceed the Greeks in their intense worship of beauty, and there are many legends of bold sea rovers who made long and perilous voyages to distant lands to win a famous beauty, whose bodily charms are described in a most detailed and realistic manner. The beautiful languorous people of Tahiti are devoted to pleasure and the joy of the moment.

The first Europeans to discover Tahiti found a highly evolved aristocratic society that was divided into three distinct groups. The first was the Arii or princely caste, whose king or Arii Rahi, was considered a

POLYNESIAN ARISTOCRACY

"...Few peoples in the history of the world have had such an aristocratic social organization as the Polynesians, and the class differences were so great that one can almost call it a caste system of the Indian type." –**Love in the South Seas** by Bengt Danielsson

sacred being. The Raatira were minor chiefs and landowners, and the Manahune were the common people. The Arioi were a kind of sect or religious fraternity that originated in Bora Bora. Their rank in the society was identified by their tattoos. They excelled in dancing and good manners and lived totally promiscuous lives, killing their children at birth. They traveled like troubadours from island to island, performing erotic ballets and political skits.

The Manahune or *kaina* of today's Tahiti still forms the majority of the population. These Polynesians are the blue-collar workers, at the bottom end of the economic structure, with the least political power in French Polynesia.

THE CHINESE

Soon after the American Civil War began on April 12, 1861, the Southern states could no longer supply cotton to the textile mills in England. To fill this shortage, gentleman adventurers were sent to various parts of the world to establish cotton plantations. To Tahiti came William Stewart, a 37-year old Scotsman, who acquired 17,000 acres of fertile plains and rugged hills in Tahiti's south coast districts of Papara and Mataiea, in an area known as Atimaono. When the Tahiti Cotton and Coffee Plantation Company was formed, Stewart received permission from the Governor to import **Chinese laborers** to work in the cotton fields at Atimaono, because the Tahitians refused to become fieldhands.

The first contingent of 329 Chinese laborers arrived in Tahiti from Hong Kong on February 28, 1865. These workers were from a district around Canton and the Kwangtung Province, who spoke the Hakka dialect. Eleven months later Atimaono had a total of 1,010 Chinese workers, who lived in five villages separated according to ethnic groups. In addition to the Chinese coolies, Stewart had also recruited Cook Islanders, Gilbertese, Easter Islanders and even some Tahitians to plant cotton, coconut trees, coffee, sugar cane, fruit trees and vegetable gardens.

Rumors of Stewart's tyrannical manner of running the Atimaono plantation included tales of workers being deprived of their food, fined, beaten, imprisoned in solitary confinement and even incarcerated in fetters. In 1867 a Chinese worker named Chim Soo was reportedly executed by guillotine.

Stewart was cleared of this murder and a number of other charges against him, but his fortunes began to fail when the American Civil War was over and the Southern states were once again producing cotton. Stewart's career as cotton king was ended in 1873 and he was bankrupt when he died at the age of 53.

There was no money to send the Chinese home, so most of them took jobs to earn their return fare. About a hundred of these Chinese workers remained in Tahiti and began growing vegetables on rented land, opening small stores in Tahiti and several of the outer islands. Gradually they acquired wealth and today they are integrated in all the professions, but are primarily the merchants of French Polynesia.

Many of the Chinese intermarried with the Tahitians and were eventually allowed to become French citizens, when several families changed their names to sound more "Frenchified." Today Mr. Wong has Chinese cousins who use the name of Vongue, but most of them honor the traditions of their Chinese ancestors, including the commemoration of the death of Chim Soo, the martyred Chinese coolie of Atimaono.

THE FRENCH

French people from all walks of life began arriving in Tahiti as early as 1843, when the Protectorate was created in Tahiti, with Papeete as the government capital. French civil servants, lawyers, *notaires*, small businessmen, school teachers, medical professionals, missionaries and military men settled here, often intermarrying with the most important families of Tahiti.

Most of the French live on the island of Tahiti and her sister island of Moorea. There are small settlements of French *fonctionnaires* or retired civil servants living on Raiatea, Tahaa and Bora Bora, and in the Marquesas Islands of Hiva Oa and Nuku Hiva, with just a scattering of French on the more isolated islands.

THE EXPATRIATES

When the census was taken in 1996 there were 1,017 **expatriates** living in French Polynesia. The majority of that number consists of French Foreign Legionnaires who are stationed in the French military zone of the Tuamotu Archipelago. The next highest group includes the wives and concubines of the French military personnel stationed in Tahiti. There are some 300 Americans living in French Polynesia, primarily in the Society Islands, where they are employed in tourism and the black pearl industry, or they have retired from business.

Even though the French and other Europeans have never settled in large numbers in French Polynesia, there has been a recent influx of French moving to the Territory, and the open door policy France has granted to the citizens of the European Union is causing great concern in Tahiti. Although the local government has been assured by France that this does not mean that a Belgian or Dutchman will take the jobs that would normally be filled by Polynesians, there is still a feeling of skepticism and doubt among the local population.

THE DEMI

A *demi* is a Polynesian with mixed blood. The first half-caste or *demi* was born about nine months after the Spanish caravel *San Lesmes* was wrecked on the reef of Amaru in the Tuamotu atolls in 1526. After that came more Spaniards, followed by the Dutch and then the British sailors, who arrived in Tahiti in 1767. The French followed, and then Tahiti became a favored destination for sea-rovers, merchants, lotus-eaters, writers, painters and wastrels.

Throughout the years the pure Polynesian stock has been diminished by contact with the French, English, Americans, Germans, Russian, Swedish, Norwegians, Spanish, South Americans, Japanese, Africans—you name it. The *demi* is often very attractive and reasonably intelligent, and usually has a pretty good education, and a good job with the local government, quite frequently obtained through family connections. The *demi* can also be one of the most confused people you'll ever meet, because they live between two cultures.

On one hand they want to be sophisticated and snobbish French, and on the other hand, they are happiest when they're slurping up the *maa* Tahiti with their fingers and singing *kaina* songs in Tahitian during a boozy *bringue*. Some of them are adept at combining the two contrasting cultures. There's a saying in Tahiti that describes the dilemma of the average Tahitian-European person: "When he wakes up the morning, the *demi* doesn't know which side of the bed to get out of."

THE VERY FRIENDLY PEOPLE OF TAHITI

During a 1981 interview on the "East-West Connection" television program in Los Angeles, the hostess asked Tahiti's Minister of Tourism: "What is the racial breakdown of the majority of the people?" He replied: "We used to say in Tahiti that the whole world slept with Tahiti."

6. PLANNING YOUR TRIP

WHEN TO GO

"When is the best time to go to Tahiti?" is a question I'll answer by asking you: "What do you want to do once you get here?"

If you want to scuba dive, you'll have the best underwater visibility during the dry season. If you want to snorkel and swim in the limpid lagoons, then come between October and June, when the water temperature is at least 80º Fahrenheit. If your goal is to photograph the most marvelous sunsets, complete with a "green flash", then come in July or August, when the evening skies are more likely to be free of clouds. If you want to see Tahiti dressed in her most beautiful finery of flowering trees and ripening fruits, then come in the "springtime" months of October through December. If you want to surf the huge rollers, make your reservations for January through March.

If you intend to catch a record-setting marlin, then your guess is as good as the experts, who tell me they're now reeling in the big ones all year long, rather than just during the summer months. If you want to see the humpback whales, they come up from Antarctica between mid-July and early October, and play around the waters of Moorea. If you want to charter a yacht and sail from island to island, the balmy tradewinds blow most of the year, and are most pleasant from May to September. If your interest is outrigger canoe racing, the biggest competitions are in July, September and November. And if you want to party with the Polynesians during the biggest celebration of the year, then reserve now for a room during the Heiva Festivals that begin in late June and continue throughout most of August.

You may want to consult the *Calendar of Events* chapter before making your decision, as well as checking out the legal holidays in French Polynesia, which are listed in Chapter 7, *Basic Information*.

Another thing to keep in mind may be the school holidays, which can influence the availability of international and domestic flights, as well as accommodations in the small hotels and family operated hostels or pensions. The students in the Society Islands have a two-week vacation in mid-October, a month's holiday from mid-December to mid-January, another two weeks the first half of March, a week at the beginning of May, and a seven-week rest from early July until the last week in August. Schools in the Marquesas, Austral and Tuamotu/Gambier Islands keep the same basic holiday schedule, except for October, when they have only a three-day break during the third week, in March, when they get the entire month off, and their May break is taken during the third week of the month. If you have any questions about the exact dates, the Tahiti Tourist Board can answer them.

This means that from Christmas to the beginning of January, the end of February or beginning of March, the Easter period, the beginning of May, the longer northern-summer holiday in July-August and the beginning of October are likely to be busier.

CLIMATE & WEATHER

The climate of these islands is usually benign, sunny and pleasant, and the cool, gentle breezes of the South Pacific ocean and the northeasterly trade winds provide a natural air-conditioning system. Meteorologists consider the months of November through March as the "rainy" season, when the climate is warmer and more humid, and April through October as the "dry" season, with a cool, drier climate.

November through May are definitely warmer than the rest of the year. Most of the rain falls during the warmer season, but there are also many days of sunshine during these months, with refreshing tradewinds.

The central and northern Tuamotus have warmer temperatures and less rainfall than in the Society Islands. There are no mountains to create cooling night breezes, as the elevation of these atolls ranges from six to 20 feet above sea level. They can experience desert-like hot periods between November and April, with devastating storms and cyclones.

The Marquesas Islands are closer to the equator, and temperatures and humidity tend to be slightly higher than in Tahiti, with more rainfall in verdant Fatu Hiva and more arid conditions in Ua Huka. The Marquesas archipelago lies in the midst of a trade wind belt from the northern latitudes, bringing northeasterly winds most of the year, with seasons that are reversed to those in the Society Islands. Although there is no real rainy season, trekking through the steep valleys to visit tikis and archaeological sites in the Marquesas can be a very steamy and often muddy hike at any time of the year.

The climate in the Australs is more temperate and less rainy than in Tahiti, and the seasons are more clearly defined. These islands lie at the southern boundary of the southeast trade winds, which blow from November to March. In the cold season, from May to September, the winds are more variable and generally westerly, with temperatures of 50 to 70 degrees Fahrenheit.

French Polynesia is on the far eastern edge of the South Pacific cyclone (hurricane) belt, and has suffered serious damage from the destructive El Niño effect. The Leeward Society Island of Maupiti was 95 percent destroyed by Cyclone Osea in November, 1997. Bora Bora is still recovering from extensive damage caused by Cyclones Martin and Osea in November, and the Tuamotu atoll of Mataiva suffered major destruction caused by tropical depression Veli that hit the atoll in January, 1998. The southwest coast of Tahiti has had more than its share of floods during the 1997-98 rainy season.

Dry Season

In July, August and September the *mara'amu* tradewinds can bring blustery, howling weather and rain from the south. But the rains don't always accompany these chilling winds. I lost the roof of my house one year in July during the *mara'amu*, and I looked up to see a beautiful, bright sky filled with a moon and stars.

The dry seasons are sometimes too dry in many of the islands, when we suffer droughts and water rationing. This was especially true during July, August and September of 1997, when the fire trucks had to replenish water tanks in some of the hotels on Moorea.

Winter storms in the southern latitudes, down around the "Roaring 40s" south of the Austral Islands, can stir up some powerful waves, with 16-foot swells damaging homes and hotels throughout the Society Islands.

These inclement weather conditions should not affect your vacation plans, as the months of July through September are especially beautiful in the islands, with day after day of glorious sunshine, and cool nights good for snuggling and gazing at the Southern Cross and other tropical stars. If your hotel is located on the southern coast of any of the Society Islands, just bring along a windbreaker or sweater, and throw an extra blanket on the bed.

Wet Season

A guest activities manager in one of the resort hotels answers questions about the rainy season by stating that in these islands we have a short season of the long rains and a long season of the short rains. If I had to guess which is when, I would say that November through March would be the short season of the long rains, and the rest of the year is the long season of the short rains.

During the height of the rainy season, it can rain very heavily for days and days. During this time the trade winds stop and the temperature and humidity levels rise. When this happens the mugginess may make you feel hot, sticky and irritable if you stay indoors. The best thing to do is to take a walk in the refreshing rain or swim in the lagoon to cool off. It's true that you cannot work on your tan during this weather, but you can tour around the island and watch the double rainbows over the emerald green valley when the sun breaks through the clouds for a few minutes. This is also a great time to go shopping for your own special black pearl!

Rainfall & Sunny Days

The yearly average for **rainfall** recorded at the Tahiti-Faaa airport in 1996 was 69.44 inches (1,736 millimeters), with an average relative humidity of 77 percent. The meteorologists counted 2,688 hours of **sunshine** during the same period. The 1997 results were not yet published at publication time.

Temperatures

The weather bureau in Tahiti keeps a record of the temperatures in all the island groups of French Polynesia. They report that the yearly average temperature at the Tahiti-Faaa International Airport is a balmy 79 degrees Fahrenheit (26 degrees Celsius).

I live less than 50 feet from the edge of the lagoon on the island of Moorea, and in the living room where I am writing, the temperature at noon in mid-September was 89 degrees Fahrenheit, with a relative humidity of 88 percent. That's with 14 windows open to the tradewinds and two overhead fans turned on. While the thermometer rarely reads higher than 92 degrees Fahrenheit, the humidity often reaches 98-100 percent inside the open house during the wetter months. In July and August I shiver under three blankets when the temperature falls to 69 degrees Fahrenheit. It's a delightful change because I can exchange my habitual *pareos* for real clothes, which are too hot to wear most of the year.

In the Austral Islands, especially in Rapa, the southernmost island, which is below the tropical zone, the temperature sometimes drops to 41 degrees Fahrenheit in July and August.

WHAT TO PACK

Casual and cool are the keywords to packing for this tropical climate. Light, loose, wash and wear garments of cotton and other natural fabrics are best. Unless you are taking a cruise ship to Tahiti you can leave your formal dining clothes and coats and ties at home. Women should pack a few pairs of shorts and slacks, along with a couple of skirts and tops or comfortable dresses, plus one or two swimsuits. Men will be properly dressed in shorts and tee-shirts almost everywhere, except for dinner in a few hotels, fancy restaurants and nightclubs, where you'll have to put on long pants, an open-neck shirt and shoes. You can both buy some colorful *pareos* once you are here to complement your wardrobes. Yes, men wear them too!

Both men and women will be in style in sandals or flip-flop rubber thongs, and be sure to include protective foot gear, such as old tennis shoes, for walking on the coral reef and in the lagoons. Plastic sandals can be purchased in the islands for about $12, which can worn in the lagoon and while walking in the valleys.

A lightweight sweater or windbreaker will feel good on cool evenings, especially during the months of July-September, and anytime you are on the sea at night. Along with a hat or visor, don't forget to pack a good pair of sun glasses along with your sun block or screen. A folding umbrella or a light weight plastic rain coat that fits into a pocket or purse may also come in handy during tropical rain showers, which are refreshing rather than cold.

Some of the budget hotels and hostels or pensions do not supply face cloths, and in the backpackers lodgings you will have to bring your own soap and towel. Other useful items include an alarm clock, portable clothes line and pegs, small bags of soap powder, beach towel, pocket flashlight, sink plug, insect repellent, corkscrew, tin opener or Swiss Army knife, plastic fork and spoon, folding drinking cup and zip-lock plastic bags to contain anything spillable. Bring a small first-aid kit containing your personal medicines, aspirin, indigestion tablets, vitamins, antiseptic cream, Band-Aids or other sticking plasters. Pack your toiletries and just a few cosmetics, and you may want to bring along your binoculars.

Don't forget to bring your camera, and make sure you know how to operate it before you get here, to prevent losing that perfect shot. Be sure to include lots of film and a waterproof bag to protect your camera from salt and spray during boat excursions.

Hair-dryers are provided in the luxury hotels, and if you bring a hair-dryer, make sure it can convert to 220 voltage, or bring a small transformer. Always ask at your hotel reception before plugging in your electrical appliances. Last but not least—bring your passport, airline tickets, driver's license and all your international credit cards.

ENTRANCE REQUIREMENTS
Passports/Visas

All non-French citizens must have a valid passport to enter French Polynesia, as well as an airline ticket back to their resident country or to at least two more continuing destinations. Citizens of the United States, Canada, New Zealand, Japan, and the European Community countries may visit for a maximum of 30 days without a visa. They must have a sufficient amount of resources to cover their planned stay in the territory. This visa exemption is subject to change at short notice. A foreigner with a residence card for the US is not exempt from having a visa for visiting French Polynesia. It is advisable to contact the nearest French Consulate or an airline serving Tahiti for specific information.

Should you wish to extend your stay in French Polynesia beyond the one-month visa exemption, you can apply for another two months at the air and border police (PAF) office at the Tahiti-Faaa airport. This must be done at least one week before the exemption expires. You can also apply for the three-month visa at a French Consulate office prior to coming to Tahiti. Temporary residency visas for up to one year are more difficult to obtain, and have to be applied for at a French Consulate or Embassy before you arrive in French Polynesia.

In the US
• **Embassy of France:** *4104 Reservoir Rd., NW, Washington, DC 20007, Tel. 202/944-6195, Fax 202/944-6148*
• **French Consulates:** *934 Fifth Ave., New York, NY 10021, Tel. 212/606-3688/9, Fax 202/606-3620; 540 Bush St., San Francisco, CA 94108, Tel. 415/397-4330, Fax 415/433-8357*

Other French consulate offices are in Atlanta, Boston, Chicago, Detroit, Honolulu, Houston, Los Angeles, Miami, New Orleans and San Juan, Puerto Rico. Residents of those cities are required to apply there. If there is no French consulate in your town, please contact the French Embassy in Washington, DC, listed above.

In Canada
• **Embassy of France:** *42 Sussex Drive, Ottawa, Ontario, KIM 2C9, Tel. 613/789-1795, Fax 613/789-0279*
• **French Consulate:** *130 Bloor St. West, Suite 400, Toronto, Ontario M5S 1N5, Tel. 416/925-8041, Fax 416/925-3076*

MAKING RESERVATIONS

It is so much simpler to contact your favorite travel agent to take care of all the reservations and details in planning your trip to Tahiti and Her

Islands. Or you can arrange your entire trip by yourself, by contacting the airlines and hotels directly or going through one of the travel agencies in Tahiti. The airlines have special fares and passes, which will cost you less if you reserve two weeks to a month in advance. The airfares also vary according to whether you go in the high or peak season, the shoulder season or the basic season. Check with the airline companies to learn which season will be in effect when you want to fly. If you are traveling on a budget, ask for their lowest fares, and be sure to learn what restrictions apply.

Some of the "discounter" travel agents buy airline seats and hotel rooms at wholesale prices. Mary Anne Cook of **Discover Wholesale Travel, Inc.**, *Tel. 800/576-7770, or 714/883-1136*, specializes in the South Pacific Islands. She knows French Polynesia very well because she and her late husband, Ted Cook, created **Islands in the Sun**, a wholesale agency in California, and they sent countless numbers of tourists to Tahiti before they sold the company. Ted Cook also owned the Hotel Captain Cook in Moorea, which no longer exists.

You may also want to get a list of discounter travel agents, as well as worldwide discount air fares, from the Web site *www.etn.nl/discount.htm#disco*.

Some of the consolidators or "bucket shops" who buy and resell seats on the major international airlines include: **Air Brokers International**, *Tel. 800/883-3273*; **Council Travel**, *Tel. 800/226-8624*; and **Concorde International Travel**, *Tel. 800/207-7300*.

USING TRAVEL SPECIALISTS/AGENTS

You can contact the following offices of the Tahiti Tourist Board to request brochures, schedules and information, which they will mail to you.

• **Tahiti Tourist Board**, *300 Continental Boulevard, Suite 180, El Segundo, CA 90245; Tel 310/414-8484; Fax 310/414-8490; e-mail address: tahitilax@earthlink.net*
• **Tahiti Tourist Board**, *444 Madison Avenue, 16th floor, New York, NY 10022; Tel. 212/838-7800, ext. 253; Fax 212/838-9576*

The following companies are a few of the wholesale tour/travel operators who work directly with the professional travel agents. Should your local travel agency need additional brochures and information, they can contact a wholesale company. A few of these wholesalers will work directly with you if you contact them.

• **Islands in the Sun**, *2381 Rosecrans Ave., Suite 325, El Segundo, CA 90245, Tel. 800/828-6877, 310/536-0051, Fax 310/536-6266*

- **J&O Holidays**, *3131 Camino del Rio North, Suite 1080, San Diego, CA, 92108-5789, Tel. 800/377-1080, 619/282-3131, Fax 283-3131*
- **Jetset Tours**, *5120 West Goldleaf Circle ,Suite 310, Los Angeles, CA 90056-1268, Tel. 800/638-3273, 213/290/5800, Fax 213/294-0434*
- **Manuia Tours and Travel**, *74 Montgomery Street, San Francisco, CA 94105, Tel. 415/495-4500, Fax 415/495-2000*
- **Newmans South Pacific Vacations**, *6033 W. Century Blvd., Suite 1270, Los Angeles, CA 90045, Tel. 800/421-3326, extension 221, Fax 310/215-9705, e-mail: Kristvedt@nztp.com*
- **New Zealand Australia Reservations Office (NZARO)**, *6033 W. Century Blvd., Suite 1270, Los Angeles, CA 90045, Tel. 310-338.1538, Fax 310-215-9705, INFOFAX 800/206/3544, e-mail: nzaro@nztp.com*
- **PADI Travel Network**, *Tel. 800/729-7234*, has packages for scuba divers.
- **Tahiti Nui's Island Dreams**, *100 W. Harrison, South Tower, Suite 350, Seattle, WA 98119-4123, Tel. 800/841-4321, 206/216-2900, Fax 206/2990*
- **Tahiti Vacations**, **(Air Tahiti's wholesale tour operator)** *9841 Airport Blvd., Suite 1124, Los Angeles, CA 90045, Tel. 800/553-3477, 310/337-1040, Fax 310/337-1126, e-mail: http://www.tahiti.com/english/tahiti/vacation.html*

Travel agencies in Tahiti are mentioned in various parts of this book. Here are a few that you may want to contact from home when planning your trip, as they can give you detailed information about every aspect of traveling in French Polynesia:

- **Tekura Tahiti Travel**, *B.P. 2971, Papeete, Tahiti, Tel. 689/43.12.00, Fax (689) 42.84.60, e-mail go@tahiti-tekuratravel.com Internet: www.tahiti-tekuratravel.com.* Tekura is the most imaginative, enthusiastic travel agent in Tahiti, and she speaks excellent English. She also has a knowledgeable, qualified staff who speak good English and know how to give personalized service.
- **Tahiti Nui Travel**, *B.P. 718, Papeete, Tahiti, Tel. 689/54.02.00; Fax 689/42.74.35; Internet http://www.tahiti.com/.* This is Tahiti's largest travel agency.
- **Marama Tours**, *B.P. 6266, Faaa, Tahiti, Tel. 689/83.96.50/83.95.81/82.08.42; Fax (689) 82.16.75*, is operated by a Polynesian family. They are the local representatives for Islands in the Sun.

GETTING TO FRENCH POLYNESIA

BAGGAGE ALLOWANCES

Airline regulations for international flights entitle each first-class or business-class passenger to a baggage limit of 30 kilograms (66 pounds). Economy-class passengers are allowed 20 kilograms (44 pounds). All passengers are allowed a small handbag plus a carry-on bag that will fit under your seat, which means that it cannot exceed total measurements of 115 centimeters (45 inches).

Air Tahiti, the domestic inter-island company in Tahiti, has a baggage limit of 10 kilograms (22 pounds for each passenger). If you're connecting with an international flight within seven days, the baggage limit is 20 kilograms (44 pounds).

A baggage storage room at the Tahiti-Faaa airport terminal is open Monday to Saturday from 8am to 5pm, Sunday from 6am to 12pm, from 2 to 6 pm, and two hours prior to each international flight departure. The hotels offer free baggage storage for their guests.

BY AIR FROM NORTH AMERICA

All international flights arrive at the **Tahiti-Faaa International Airport** on the island of Tahiti. The airline companies serving Tahiti from North America usually depart from the Los Angeles International Airport, for a 7 1/2 hour direct flight to Tahiti. If you are flying to Los Angeles from another city or state, be sure to allow sufficient time between flights to make the connection. Airport check-in time is two hours before each international flight departure. When your flight lands in Los Angeles it takes a while to transfer your bags from a domestic airline terminal to the international terminal.

The following airline companies have several flights weekly between Los Angeles and Tahiti. Extra flights are added during the high seasons, which vary. The busiest seasons are generally the months of July and August and the Christmas-New Year's season.

Airlines Serving Tahiti from Los Angeles

AIR FRANCE, *Tel. 800/237-2747 in US, 800/667-2747 in Canada*, has three Paris-Los Angeles-Papeete flights a week. *The Tahiti office is on Boulevard Pomare, close to the corner of Avenue Bruat in downtown Papeete; Tel. 689/42.22.22; Fax 689/41.05.22*

AIR NEW ZEALAND, *Tel. 800/262-1234 or 310/615-1111*, has two flights a week to Tahiti. *The Tahiti office is on the ground floor of the Vaima*

6ᵈ Oakland —

Center, on the corner of rue Jeanne d'Arc and rue du General du Gaulle; Tel. 689/54.07.4754.07.40; Fax 689/42.45.44.

Air New Zealand also began a weekly charter flight service between Los Angeles and Tahiti in April, 1998, to transport the clients of Radisson Seven Seas Cruises (RSSC) who have booked a week's cruise aboard the *M/S Paul Gauguin*. The Boeing 767 aircraft leaves Los Angeles each Friday at 7pm and arrives in Papeete at 1:30am on Saturday morning. The plane leaves Papeete each Saturday at 6:30am and arrives in Los Angeles at 6pm local time. Any of the 236 seats not used by RSSC clients are available for sale to the public. In the US, contact: *Paul Goodwin or O. J. Abello at Radisson Seven Seas Cruises, 600 Corporate Drive, Suite 400, Fort Lauderdale, Florida 33334; Tel. 954/776-6123; Fax 954/772-4113; or J. C. Potier, Tel. 954/491-9434; Fax 954/491-9433. In Papeete, contact: Marie Eve Robreau, SCAT Polynésie, B.P. 596, Papeete, Tahiti; Tel. 689/45.59.13; Fax 689/45.52.56.*

AOM FRENCH AIRLINES, *Tel. 800/892-9136*, has three flights a week from Paris-Los Angeles-Papeete. This airline usually has the best fares and interesting air-hotel packages are offered by Tahiti Vacations. *The Tahiti office is located on rue des Remparts in Papeete; Tel. 689/54.25.25; Fax 689/43.62.28.*

CORSAIR AIRLINES, *Tel. 800/677-0720*, is primarily a French charter airline that flies from Paris to Oakland, then to Los Angeles and Tahiti, with one flight a week. Individuals can also buy seats, which may be a little higher than the charter fare. *The Tahiti office is located on the corner of Boulevard Pomare and rue Clappier in downtown Papeete; Tel. 689/ 42.28.28; Fax 689/42.29.09.*

AIR TAHITI NUI, *Tel. 689/46.02.02 in Tahiti; e-mail info@tahiti-airlines.pf* is Tahiti's newly formed international airline company, which is programmed to begin service between Los Angeles and Tahiti in November 1998, using Airbus A340-aircraft for three weekly flights.

By Other Air Routes

AIR CALEDONIE INTERNATIONAL, *Tel. 310/670-7302*, has a direct flight from Noumea, New Caledonia, to Tahiti once a week and a weekly flight from Noumea to Nandi, Wallis Island and Tahiti. *The Tahiti office is located at the Tahiti-Faaa International Airport, office number 6; Tel. 689/85.09.04; Fax 689/85.69.05.*

AIR FRANCE, *Tel. 800/237-2747 in US, 800/667-2747 in Canada*, has one flight a week from Tokyo. *The Tahiti office is on Boulevard Pomare, close to the corner of Avenue Bruat in downtown Papeete; Tel. 689/42.22.22; Fax 689/41.05.22.*

AIR NEW ZEALAND, *Tel. 800/262-1234 or 310/615-1111*, has one direct flight a week from Auckland, a weekly flight from Auckland, Nandi and Rarotonga, and one weekly flight from Auckland and Rarotonga. *The Tahiti office is on the ground floor of the Vaima Center, on the corner of rue Jeanne d'Arc and rue du General du Gaulle; Tel. 689/54.07.4754.07.40; Fax 689/42.45.44.*

AIR TAHITI NUI, *Tel. 689/46.02.02 in Tahiti; e-mail info@tahiti-airlines.pf* will provide two flights a week between Tahiti and Japan, starting in November 1998.

HAWAIIAN AIRLINES, *Tel. 800/367-5320 in the continental US, Alaska and Canada, and 808/838-1555 in Honolulu*, has once-a-week service between Honolulu and Tahiti. *The Tahiti office is located upstairs at the Vaima Center in Papeete; Tel. 689/42.15.00; Fax 689/45.14.51.*

LAN CHILE AIRLINES, *Tel. 800/735-5526*, has three flights per week from Santiago, Chile and Easter Island. *The Tahiti office is located upstairs at the Vaima Center in Papeete; Tel. 689/42.64.55/82.64.57; Fax 689/42.18.87.*

QANTAS AIRWAYS, *Tel. 800/227-4500*, no longer flies from Los Angeles to Tahiti, but still continues serving Tahiti with three weekly flights from Sydney and Auckland. *The Tahiti office is located upstairs at the Vaima Center in Papeete; Tel. 689/43.06.65/83.90.90; Fax 689/41.05.19.*

BY PASSENGER SHIP

Tahiti's brief cruise ship season usually begins in November and ends in April, with most of the passenger liners calling during the months of January through March. The average number of cruise ships that call in Tahiti and Her Islands is only a dozen for the entire season. These include Russian flag-carriers such as the *Delphin, Columbus and Maxim Gorky,* whose passengers are primarily from eastern Europe. The *Switzerland, Albatros, Europa, Astor* and *Saga Rose* were among the 1998 visiting ships, with more passengers from Europe, some of whom were visiting 40 countries in 129 days during their round-the-world cruise. The *Royal Viking Sun, Vistafjord, Crystal Harmony, Sky Princess* and *Seabourn Legend* usually carry mostly American passengers, with just a sprinkling of Europeans.

Ship day in Tahiti usually is limited to an early morning arrival in the harbor and a late afternoon departure, allowing enough time to make a tour of the island, perhaps to explore the coral gardens or tropical valleys and shop for post cards and souvenirs.

Several of the ships are now including the Marquesas Islands and Fakarava in the Tuamotu archipelago in their shore programs, which the passengers enjoy for their unexploited natural beauty.

World Discoverer, operated by Society Expeditions, truly takes you off the beaten track with their nature-oriented or eco-cruises through the remote islands of French Polynesia. For information call Nature Expeditions International, *Tel. 800/869/0639*, or have your travel agent contact Tahiti Vacations, *Tel. 800/553-3477 or 310/337-1040*; Islands in the Sun, *Tel. 800/828-6877 or 310/536-0051*, Jetset, *Tel. 800/4-JETSET*, or Sunmakers Travel Group, *Tel. 800/841-4321*.

Princess Cruises, *Tel. 800/421-0522 or 310/553-1770*, usually makes a few "turn-around" cruises to Tahiti. That means you cruise to Tahiti and fly home, or vice-versa, and because these one-way cruises don't require as much time at sea, perhaps you will have the time to spend a few days on one or more of Tahiti's islands. Cunard Line, *Tel. 800/221-4770*, or *212/880-7500*, operates the *Queen Elizabeth II*, which makes round-the-world cruises every few years, including Tahiti in her ports-of-call.

BY PRIVATE BOAT

The best way to visit Tahiti and Her Islands is, of course, the leisurely way. Hundreds of cruising yachts from all over the world pass through the islands each year, with some boats stopping only long enough to get provisions for the next leg of the journey, while others linger until the authorities ask them to move on.

Their contact with the villagers in remote islands is often rewarding for all concerned, with the "yachties" often getting involved in the daily lives of the friendly Polynesians. Outgoing visitors are frequently invited to join in volleyball and soccer games and fishing expeditions. The young people will take you to hunt for tiny shells that are strung into pretty necklaces, and the women will teach you how to weave hats, mats, and baskets from palm fronds. You can also eat delicious seafoods direct from the shell while standing on a Technicolor reef. In the evenings, you can sit on the pier under a starlit sky and watch the Southern Cross as you listen to the young men from the village playing melodic island tunes on their guitars and ukuleles.

There's a sailing adage that goes: "A month at sea can cure all the ills of the land." However, a month at sea with an incompatible crew can make you ill or want to kill. Sailing to Tahiti sounds so very romantic, and many people do realize their life-long dreams of anchoring inside an opalescent lagoon and tying a line around a coconut tree. It takes a month and sometimes much longer to sail from the US West Coast or Panama to the Marquesas Islands, the first landfall in French Polynesia. This long crossing is also disastrous for many relationships, so it is very important to know the dispositions of the other people on the yacht, and to be as easy-going and tolerant as you can be.

Valid passports and tourist visas are required for the captain and each crew member. The Immigration Service in French Polynesia can issue a three month visa that is good for all of French Polynesia. In addition to the required visa, each crew member must also deposit money into a special account at a local bank or at the Trésorerie Générale that is equal to the airfare from Tahiti back to their country of origin. Crew changes can only be made in harbors where there is a *gendarmerie*, and the Chief of Immigration must be advised of any crew changes.

CUSTOMS ALLOWANCES - ENTERING FRENCH POLYNESIA

In addition to your personal effects, when you come to French Polynesia you may legally bring in duty free: 200 cigarettes or 100 cigarillos or 50 cigars or 250 grams of smoking tobacco, 50 grams of perfume, .25 liter of lotion, 500 grams of coffee, 100 grams of tea and two liters of spirits. Visitors under 17 years of age are not allowed to import tobacco or spirits.

Before importing any telecommunications items, please contact the French High Commissioner's services, *Tel. 689/46.86.86, extension 630.* Prohibited items include narcotics, copyright infringements (pirated video and audio tapes), weapons and ammunition, dangerous drugs, and imitation brand names. No live animals can be imported and certification of plants is required.

CUSTOMS ALLOWANCES - RETURNING HOME

US customs allows an exemption of $400 in goods for each US resident, including one quart of liquor and 200 cigarettes.

Canadian residents may use their once-yearly $300 exemption, or their $100 quarterly exemption for goods brought home, with a limit of 1,1 liters for liquor, and 200 cigarettes.

US law allows the importation, duty-free, of original works of art. Because of concessions made to developing countries, jewelry made in Tahiti may qualify as original art, and thus be duty-free. The US customs has waivered the import duty on Tahitian black pearls or black pearl jewelry made in French Polynesia, so you will not be charged duty by the customs for these purchases. California residents will be charged a State tax on black pearls. If you purchase black pearls or jewelry, make sure to get a certificate from the place of purchase stating that the jewelry was made in the islands.

TRAVELING ON YOUR OWN

Having the time to be flexible in your travels and being open to adventure and new experiences can bring you infinite rewards in discovering wonderful places and people. If you like to travel "by the seat of your pants" you can come to Tahiti without a hotel reservation and let serendipity be your guide.

You can usually get a hotel room or a bed in a hostel or family pension without any advance notice. I have found spur-of-the-moment lodgings for friends who wanted to spend a couple of days in Bora Bora during the July Festival, which is normally overbooked at that time of year. A woman I met had just returned from Huahine, where she had intended camping out, but was invited to stay in the home of a Tahitian woman she met, who has a *roulotte* on the boat dock in Fare. A couple from Texas took a week's cruise through the Society Islands aboard the *Club Med II* sailing ship, and enjoyed themselves so much they signed on for the next trip the following week. The *Club Med II* is no longer sailing Polynesian waters, but this couple returned within the same year to visit the Marquesas Islands aboard the *Aranui*.

Tourism has not yet reached the level of saturation in these islands, and the only long lines you'll find are at the buffet tables in the hotels during a special event. You can still find a last-minute seat on an airplane, a cabin on an inter-island ship, a berth on a sailboat, or a place on any of the tours and excursions that are available on each island.

GETTING AROUND TAHITI & HER ISLANDS

BY AIR

AIR MOOREA, *Tahiti-Faaa International Airport, B.P. 6019, Papeete, Tahiti; Tel. 689/86.41.41 (Papeete); Tel. 689/56.10.34 (Moorea); Fax 689/86.42.99. The Air Moorea Terminal is in a separate building to the left of the main terminal as you exit Immigration and Customs. Just follow the marked walkway.*

Air Moorea operates an air-shuttle service between Tahiti and Moorea, with a fleet of 3 Britten Norman and 2 Twin-Otter aircraft, plus 2 Dornier 228 planes in pool with Air Tahiti. All flights to Tetiaroa are provided by Air Moorea. There are 40 scheduled flights daily between Tahiti and Moorea, with the first Tahiti-Moorea flight at 6am and the last flight at 6pm. The first Moorea-Tahiti flight is at 6:15am and the last flight is at 6:15pm. The flights operate every 30 to 60 minutes for the 10-minute hop between the two airports, and no reservations are needed. The one-way fare is 2.700 CFP ($27) if you buy your tickets locally, and 3.200 CFP ($32) if they are issued overseas.

AIR TAHITI, *Tahiti-Faaa International Airport, B.P. 314, Papeete, Tahiti; Tel. 689/86.42.42/86.40.00. The main ticket office is located up one flight of stairs at Fare Tony in downtown Papeete. Office hours are Monday to Friday 7:30am to 12pm and 1 to 4:30pm. The airport office is open daily from 6am to 5pm, and the Moana Holidays office at the Moana Nui Shopping Center in Punaauia is open all day Monday to Friday and on Saturday mornings.*

Tahiti Vacations is the Air Tahiti subsidiary in the US. Have your travel agent contact them at *Tel. 800/553-3477* or *Tel. 310/337-1040; Fax 310/337-1126.* Tour operators who specialize in Tahiti and Her Islands destination, and their retail travel agencies, will provide you with the best service. *In Los Angeles Tel. 310/414-8484, Fax 310/414-8490; in New York Tel. 212/838-7800, ext. 253; Fax 212/838-9576.*

Should you wish to deal directly with Air Tahiti you may fax your request to the reservations department in Papeete, at *Fax 689/86.40.69.* Please include names, age of children, flights/dates/time required, your contact or hotels in Tahiti and in the islands, your international inbound and outbound flights, and any information that you think may help in arranging your flight. Air Tahiti will fax your booking by return. You will be able to retrieve your ticket at the Air Tahiti ticket office at the Tahiti-Faaa International Airport when you arrive in Tahiti. This is located 50 meters (164 feet) to the right from the international arrival gate. All major credit cards are accepted.

Air Tahiti Network

Air Tahiti operates domestic scheduled flights between the islands of French Polynesia, with a network of 39 islands, covering all five archipelagoes. A modern fleet of 10 twin-turboprop aircraft comprises two Dornier 228 planes with 19-seats, four ATR 42-500 planes with 48 seats and four ATR 72-200 planes with 66 seats. All the aircraft have high wings, offering you great views of the beautiful islands if you are seated by the window.

Your travel agent can arrange an air pass for you to visit several islands, which is the most popular and least expensive means of island hopping. Tahiti is the center for the Air Tahiti flights and you will have to pass through Papeete to fly between island groups, except when you are flying from Bora Bora to Rangiroa or Manihi, and between the Tuamotus and Marquesas Islands, or between the Tuamotus and Gambier Islands.

Air Passes

Air Tahiti offers six different **air passes**, which all begin in Papeete. Take note of the restrictions applying to the number of transits allowed through Papeete before the end of the island-hopping pass. You are allowed one stopover on each island but, except for Papeete, you can transit an island so long as the flight number does not change. If you stop at the island to change flights that counts as a stopover. The tickets are valid for a maximum of 28 days and all flights (except Papeete-Moorea or Moorea-Papeete) must be booked at the beginning, although you can change your reservations for a fee of 1.000 CFP ($10). For the Papeete-Moorea sector you can use either Air Tahiti or Air Moorea. If the routing is also changed and this changes the pass classification, you will have to pay the higher fare.

Once you have taken the first flight on the pass the fare is non-refundable. Reduced fares are available for children between two and twelve years of age.

Air Passes to the Society Islands

Pass YD 215 lets you visit all six of the major islands in the Society group: Tahiti, Moorea, Huahine, Raiatea, Maupiti and Bora Bora. You are not allowed to transit in Papeete within the pass nor to fly back to Papeete before the end of the pass. This pass costs 30.500 CFP ($305) for adults and 16.200 CFP ($162) for children. Compare this cost with the point-to-point Tahiti-Bora Bora round-trip fare of 26.040 CFP ($260.40) for adults, and you will appreciate the advantage of an Air Pass.

Air Passes to the Society Islands & Tuamotus

Pass YD 213 is one of the most popular choices, especially for honeymooners and scuba divers. This pass takes you from Tahiti to Moorea, Huahine, Raiatea and Bora Bora in the Society group, and on to Rangiroa, Manihi and Tikehau in the Tuamotus. You must use the Bora Bora-Rangiroa or Bora Bora-Manihi flight, which operates three times a week from Bora Bora to the Tuamotus, but only once a week from the Tuamotus to Bora Bora. You will have more flexibility if you visit the Society Islands first. This pass costs 45.500 CFP ($455) for adults, and 23.700 CFP ($237) for children. To give you a comparison between the Air Pass and point-to-point air fares, you would pay 35.910 CFP ($359.10) if you flew from Tahiti to Manihi, and 49.140 CFP ($491.40) for a flight between Bora Bora and Manihi.

Pass YD 212 allows you to visit the same islands as the YD 213 pass, but you can transit Papeete between the Society Islands and the Tuamotus, rather than being restricted to the three eastbound flights and one westbound connection between Bora Bora and the Tuamotus. This pass costs 50.500 CFP ($505) for adults and 26.200 CFP ($262) for children.

Air Passes to the Society Islands & Australs

Pass YD 214 combines the Society Islands (Tahiti, Moorea, Huahine,

Raiatea and Bora Bora) with the Austral Islands (Rurutu and Tubuai). You are allowed to transit Papeete between the Society and Austral groups. This pass costs 50.500 CFP ($505) for adults and 26.200 CFP ($262) for children. The point-to-point round-trip fare between Tahiti and Tubuai is 51.580 CFP ($515.80), to give you an idea of the savings offered by the Air Pass.

Air Passes to the Moorea & Tuamotus
Pass YD 220 combines a visit to Moorea with Rangiroa, Manihi and Tikehau. One transit is allowed through Papeete between Moorea and the Tuamotus. This pass costs 35.000 CFP ($350) for adults and 18.400 CFP ($184) for children. You would pay 39.110 CFP ($391.10) to fly from Moorea to Tahiti and on to Manihi and back to Tahiti if you did not have the Air Pass ticket.

Air Passes to the Society Islands, Tuamotus & Marquesas
Pass YD 217 combines the Society Islands of Tahiti, Moorea, Huahine, Raiatea and Bora Bora with the Tuamotu Islands of Rangiroa and Manihi, and the Marquesas Islands of Atuona (Hiva Oa) and Nuku Hiva. You have a choice of three different route variations. You can fly from Papeete to the other Society Islands, then transit Papeete en route to the Tuamotus and the Marquesas, or vice versa. You can visit the Society Islands and fly from Bora Bora to the Tuamotus without returning to Papeete. Either before or after your visit to the Society and Tuamotu Islands you can fly to the Marquesas Islands and back, as this is a separate trip from Papeete.

The third choice combines the three groups as one continuous circuit without having to transit through Papeete. This pass costs 87.000 CFP ($870) for adults and 44.400 CFP ($444) for children. The regular fare of a round-trip flight between Papeete and Hiva Oa is 63.000 CFP ($630); therefore, you have the advantage of visiting several other islands for only $240 more.

Air Tahiti Day Tours
Air Tahiti offers day tours to Huahine, Raiatea, Bora Bora and Rangiroa, which can only be booked less than seven days prior to departure. The day tour rates range from 23.500 CFP ($235) to 29.300 CFP ($293) per person, which include the round-trip air fare from Tahiti, transfers between the airport and your hotel, picnic or lunch, and excursions. A minimum of two to four passengers is required, depending on the tour, except for the circle island tour by outrigger canoe in the lagoon of Bora Bora, which is available for even one person. Whether you travel by yourself, with a partner or a group, you may be able to join others who have booked for the same tour. If you cancel your day tour a

AN AIR TAHITI ADVENTURE

One of the most exhilarating feelings in the world for adventurers is to step off a plane onto new territory, a place you've never explored. This excitement is intensified when you land on a tropical island that you have longed to visit since you were a child. Some of us believe that the further you have to go to get there, the more rewarding your experience will be once you arrive. Remember the old song that goes: "Far away places with strange sounding names, far away over the sea, those far away places with the strange sounding names are calling, calling me." Air Tahiti can take you to 39 far-away places with such beautiful names as Huahine, Bora Bora, Tikehau, Fakarava, Kaukura, Manihi, Takapoto, Pukarua, Mangareva, Ua Huka, Nuku Hiva and Rurutu. Just pronouncing these mellifluous names can give you wanderlust.

Getting there truly is half the fun when you fly Air Tahiti. Imagine sitting in a comfortable seat inside a quiet modern aircraft and looking out the window at the incredibly blue Pacific Ocean and the magnificent islands below. Air Tahiti flies low enough so that you can see the fern-covered crenelated mountain ranges of the high islands and the sapphire and emerald lagoons inside the coral atolls. They all seem to be a mirage, a dream or a movie setting for a South Pacific film. Adding to the exotic feeling is the intoxicating perfume wafting from the flowers worn by the islanders when they travel.

It is a Polynesian custom to welcome people with floral leis when they arrive and to send them off on their journeys wearing leis and crowns of flowers, sweet smelling herbs, ferns and colored leaves. On the smaller islands almost everyone in the village goes to the airport to meet the incoming flights, and most of them bring several leis to place around the necks of their family and friends who are arriving or departing. The Rurutu airport turns into a veritable flower garden before the arrival of each Air Tahiti flight, when the flower vendors set up shop in the waiting area. The fragrance of the sauvage (wild) leis fills the air, a sweet and pungent combination of ylang ylang, sweet basil, Tiare Tahiti, avaro, and dried pineapple, threaded together with red twirls of the porohiti fruit. You'll smell the same wonderful melange of perfumes at airports in the Marquesas Islands, with the addition of sandalwood, pandanus fruit, spearmint, ginger root and other mysterious herbs. In the Tuamotu Islands you'll smell the Tiare Tahiti gardenias that adorn the floral crowns of the islanders, who may also be wearing multiple strings of brightly colored shells.

In addition to providing a means of reliable, quick and comfortable transportation, Air Tahiti is also a source of education into the Polynesian culture, which can be very entertaining.

cancellation fee will apply, and the amount charged will depend on the tour. To arrange a day tour you can call Air Tahiti in Papeete, *Tel. 689/42.70.00; Fax 689/86.40.69*; or contact your travel agent.

Island Stays

Air Tahiti's **Sejours dans les Iles** (Island Stays) program was designed to promote inter-island tourism among the residents living in French Polynesia. Although they are not advertised overseas, these packages are available to anyone as long as you buy the package locally. The packages include round-trip air fares between Tahiti and the outer island chosen, plus one or two nights at a hotel, hostel or family pension, and ground transfers. Depending on your lodging, you may also have one, two or three daily meals included, and an excursion thrown in.

Example: The Hotel Sofitel Marara in Bora Bora has a rack rate for a standard garden room of 29.000 CFP ($290) a day. Add the round-trip airfare between Tahiti and Bora Bora of 26.040 CFP ($26.040), for a total of 55.040 CFP ($550.40). With the *Sejours* program, you would pay 38.700 CFP ($387) per person for one night at the Marara, which includes your round-trip airfare, transfers, room, breakfast and one excursion. You'll need to add the 7 percent hotel tax, one percent VAT and 150 CFP per day visitor's tax to both rates.

Example: The cost of two nights' lodging at Pension Cecile on Rangiroa, with all meals included, is normally 12.000 CFP ($120) per person, and the round-trip airfare from Tahiti is 28.560 CFP ($285.60), for a total of 40.560 CFP ($405.60). With the special Air Tahiti *Sejours* program you would pay 36.000 CFP ($360), which also includes transfers. A one percent VAT should be added to the pension rates. For further information on the *Sejours* program contact Air Tahiti in Papeete at *Tel. 689/42.70.00; Fax 689/86.40.69*.

Baggage

The normal baggage allowance of 10 kilograms (22 pounds) is raised to 20 kilograms (44 pounds) on most destinations if you have arrived in Tahiti less than 7 days before the first Air Tahiti flight. If you purchase your domestic flights locally then your limit is 10 kilograms. Excess baggage fares vary according to destination. Rather than having to pay for excess baggage at each inter-island flight, you may choose the special round-trip rate available upon check-in at the Tahiti or Moorea airports.

Reconfirmations

You are not required to reconfirm your reservations with Air Tahiti, except in the following conditions. If Air Tahiti has no contact number for you then you should reconfirm a day before your scheduled flight. If you take a flight for which you have no reservation or if you should choose to travel by other means, then you should reconfirm any subsequent reservations you've already made with Air Tahiti. If you are flying to the Eastern Tuamotus or to the Marquesas Islands aboard a 19-seat Dornier 228 aircraft, you should reconfirm a week in advance.

Other Information
    Check-in time for Air Tahiti flights is one hour in advance of your flight. If you haven't checked in by 15 minutes before flight departure your reservation will be canceled. All Air Tahiti flights are non-smoking. Air Tahiti issues two new timetables every six months, one for local distribution and the other for overseas markets. The international fares are five percent higher than you would pay if you bought your ticket in French Polynesia.

CHARTER FLIGHTS
    AIR TAHITI, *Tahiti-Faaa International Airport, B.P. 314, Papeete, Tahiti; Tel. 689/86.40.11; Fax 689/86.40.69.* Aircraft available for charter within French Polynesia includes a 19-Seat Dornier 228, 48-seat ATR 42-500 and 66-seat ATR 72-200.
    AIR MOOREA, *Tahiti-Faaa International Airport, B.P. 6019, Papeete, Tahiti; Tel. 689/86.41.41 (Papeete); Tel. 689/56.10.34 (Moorea).* Air Moorea has 30-minute flight-seeing tours over Moorea, and other charter flights can be arranged.
    AIR ARCHIPELS, *Tahiti-Faaa International Airport, B.P. 6019, Faaa, Tahiti, Tel. 689/81.30.30; Fax 689/86.42.69.* Mate Galenon, who is general manager of Air Tahiti and Air Moorea, also heads this small airline, which is used for charters and emergency flight service. The fleet includes a Beechcraft Super King B200, with nine seats, and a pressurized Cessna Conquest C441, with eight passenger seats.
    WAN AIR, *Tahiti-Faaa International Airport, B.P. 6806, Faaa, Tahiti; Tel. 689/85.55.54; Fax 689/85.55.56.* This company took over the activities of Tahiti Conquest Airline (TCA) in 1996, and has a new fleet that includes a 9-seat Beechcraft 300 LW, a 19-seat Beechcraft 1900 D and a 9-seat Citation 5 Jet. Charter flights are arranged on request to visit all five archipelagoes of French Polynesia and some of the neighboring islands.

HELICOPTER SERVICE
    HELI-PACIFIC, *Tahiti-Faaa International Airport, B.P. 6109, Faaa, Tahiti; Tel. 689/85.68.00; Fax 689/85.68.08.* This company is associated with Air Moorea, and operates two AS 350 "Ecureuil" helicopters, each with 5-6 seats. Flightseeing tours and transfers from the airport to various

sites on Tahiti and Moorea are available. *See further information in destination chapter on Tahiti.*

HELI INTER POLYNESIE, *B.P. 424, Papeete, Tahiti; Tel. 81.99.00; Fax 689/81.99.99.* A 6-seat "Ecureuil" helicopter is based in Tahiti, providing sightseeing flights and charters on request to visit Tahiti and Moorea. There is also a helicopter based in Bora Bora, and two "Ecureuils" based permanently in the Marquesas Islands, where they provide transfers from the Nuku Hiva airport to Taiohae village and other nearby islands.

BY INTER-ISLAND CRUISE SHIPS, PASSENGER BOATS & FREIGHTERS

Windward Society Islands

Tahiti and Moorea are connected by fast catamarans: *Aremiti III, Tel. 689/42.88.88, Tamarii Moorea VIII-Corsaire 6000* and *Tamahine Moorea II B, Tel. 43.76.50,* which provide 30 minute crossings between Papeete and the Vaiare ferry dock in Moorea. Each boat makes several round-trips a day.

Car ferry service is provided by *Tamarii Moorea VIII-Corsaire 6000,* as well as the older *Tamarii Moorea VIII H,* the latter taking one hour to get across the channel that is called the Sea of Moons. The *Aremiti Ferry,* which is the newest and largest of the car ferries, takes about 45 minutes to traverse the channel. One-way passenger fares on these boats is 700 to 800 CFP ($7-$8). Additional information is given in *Moorea* chapter.

Leeward Society Islands

M/S PAUL GAUGUIN, *operated by Radisson Seven Seas Cruises (RSSC), which is based in Fort Lauderdale, Florida, Tel. 954/776-6123; Fax 954/772-3689. The ship is 156 meters (512 feet) long, 20,80 meters (68 feet wide), with a draft of 5,10 meters (17 feet), and it weighs 1,230 tons. The 160 outside cabins can accommodate 318 passengers, who pay from $2,509 to $5,436, depending on cabin.*

RSSC operates a charter flight service for the *Paul Gauguin* clients, using an Air New Zealand Boeing 767 plane between Los Angeles and Tahiti. See information under *Airlines* in this chapter.

This 318-passenger ship was built in France to be based year-round in Tahiti. The seven-day cruises in the Society Islands and the Tuamotu atoll of Rangiroa began on January 31, 1998. All of the 160 staterooms and suites have sweeping ocean and lagoon views and half of the staterooms have private balconies or verandas.

The largest of the **Grandes Suites** has 48 square meters (517 square feet) of living space, with a private balcony and veranda, for 29,900 French francs ($5,436). The deluxe suites are 27.400 FF ($4,981); the veranda suites are 22.700 FF ($4,127), the junior suites are 18.900 FF ($3,436), and exterior cabins in categories D, E and F are 16.500 FF ($3,000), 15.400 FF ($2,800) and 13.800 FF ($2,509), respectively. The smallest cabin is 19 square meters (205 square feet).

The rates quoted are valid through September 1998 and are based on double occupancy. Add 80 percent for single occupancy. Juniors 12 to 18 years have a reduction of 15 percent based on double occupancy if sharing a cabin with a parent. Children under 12 years are not admitted on board the ship. A 10 percent reduction is offered to newlyweds during their first year of marriage, and a 5 percent discount is accorded couples celebrating their decennial anniversaries. These rates include all meals, preselected wines with meals, non-alcoholic beverages and mineral waters, Captain's Welcome Cocktail, all nautical sports from the Marina nautical sports center except scuba diving, tips, welcome at the Tahiti-Faaa International airport and transfer to a first-class hotel (Beachcomber or Sofitel), use of hotel rooms for the morning on departure day, brunch at the hotel, transfers from the hotel to the *Paul Gauguin* in the afternoon, and transfers from the ship to the airport at the end of the cruise for international departure.

The air-conditioned cabins and suites have individual temperature control and are decorated in a contemporary motif, with exotic woods and warm colors. They each contain a queen-size bed or twin beds, white marble appointed bathroom with a real bathtub and shower, hair dryer and terry cloth robes, closed circuit television and video player, refrigerator stocked with soft drinks and mineral waters, direct dial telephone, safe, numerous shelves and spacious closets. The 252 employees include a sufficient number of cabin stewards to provide individual service 24 hours a day.

The 9-deck ship has two elegant restaurants, the **Veranda** and the **Etoile**, and an outdoor Grill, plus a 24-hour room service menu. Passengers can choose single, open seating dining at their leisure to enjoy gastronomic meals featuring Mediterranean cuisine, as well as Polynesian specialties and a barbecue evening. Menu selections are inspired by **Jean-Pierre Vigato**, a two-star Michelin chef at the Parisian restaurant **Apicius**. The **Fare Tahiti** is a museum and special information center with books, videos and other materials on the ethnic art, history, geography and culture of Tahiti and Her Islands. **La Palette** and the **Connoisseur Club** are the bars and lounges, plus there is a duty free boutique and black pearl shop, a panoramic night club and piano bar, a disco, casino, hospital and beauty salon. The **Spa** is a full spa and fitness center operated by world-famous **Carita of Paris**, including steam room, aromatherapy, thalasso-therapy, massage, facials and full beauty services. The fully-equipped **Fitness Center** features Lifecycles, Liferower, Treadmill, Stairmasters and weight machines. In addition to the swimming pool, there is a nautical sports center, **La Marina**, with a retractable water sports platform. Waterskiing, windsurfing, sailing, kayaking and snorkeling are offered, as well as a full scuba dive program for novices and experts. Nightly entertainment is presented in the main lounge. The "Gauguines" or "Gauguin's Girls" are 12 pretty Tahitian *vahines* who sing and dance and act as gracious hostesses aboard the ship.

The passengers board the *Paul Gauguin* each Saturday afternoon, with departure time at 6pm. The ship reaches Rangiroa on Sunday morning, departing on Monday in the middle of the day for the Leeward Society Islands. If the weather does not permit entry through the Tiputa pass into the lagoon of Rangiroa, an alternative stop is made in Huahine. On Tuesday the ship cruises inside the lagoon of Tahaa and docks at the Uturoa quay in Raiatea at 11am. On Wednesday it leaves Raiatea at 7am for Bora Bora, arriving at 10am. On Thursday the ship leaves Bora Bora at 5pm and arrives in Moorea at 8am on Friday morning, then leaves Moorea at 6pm on Friday, arriving in Papeete harbor at 9pm. The passengers disembark on Saturday morning.

Pre- and post-cruise packages include stays at the Tahiti Beachcomber Parkroyal and the beautiful Hotel Bora Bora at forfeit prices. In June, 1998, the *Paul Gauguin* will make an exceptional 2-week cruise to the Marquesas Islands in honor of the 150th anniversary of the birth of French painter Paul Gauguin. Some 70 direct descendants of Gauguin will pay homage to their ancestor on the island of Hiva Oa, where the artist is buried in Calvary Cemetery above the village of Atuona.

HAUMANA, *operated by Bora Bora Pearl Cruises. Reservations: South Pacific Management, B.P. 2460, 98713 Papeete, Tahiti; Tel. 689/43.43.03; Fax 689/43.17.86.*

The 147 ton mini-ship is 33 meters (110 feet) long, with 21 deluxe cabins. Three-day cruises cost 140.500 CFP ($1,405) single and 115.500 CFP ($1,155) half-double; four-day cruises are 188.500 CFP ($1,885) single and 155.000 CFP ($1,550) half-double. These rates include all meals, activities, tours and excursions. Add a 1% value added tax to the above rates, plus a port charge of 4.500 CFP ($45) per person.

Haumana means "magical spirit" in Tahitian, and that is the feeling you are intended to have when you board this new, deluxe air-conditioned four-star 21-cabin mini-ship, which was put into service in January, 1998, operating three- and four-day year-round cruises between Bora Bora, Tahaa and Raiatea. This is the first cruise ship ever based in the Leeward Islands and the first operated by local owners. The cabins are all identical, with at least two windows. They are furnished with a queen-size bed or two single beds, bathroom with shower and hair dryer, port-hole window, mini-bar, television with video cassette player, radio/music cassette/

compact disc player and telephone. The main deck offers a 45-seat panoramic restaurant. The upper deck offers a lounge for 40 and an outdoor terrace, and the reception area and boutique are located on the intermediary deck.

The three-day **Turquoise Cruise** leaves Bora Bora at 2pm every Saturday afternoon, arriving in Raiatea at 5pm, where it spends the night in the Raiatea lagoon. All day Sunday is spent in the lagoon of Raiatea and Tahaa, and the ship spends the night in the Tahaa lagoon, departing at 6:30am on Monday for Bora Bora, arriving at 8:30am. After spending the day inside the Bora Bora lagoon, the *Haumana* remains there Monday night, and the passengers disembark in Bora Bora on Tuesday from 6 to 9am.

The three-day **Jade Cruise** departs from Raiatea on Saturday between 6 and 8pm, and the ship remains inside the Raiatea lagoon Saturday night. Sunday is spent inside the lagoon between Raiatea and Tahaa, with the ship spending Sunday night in Tahaa. It leaves for Bora Bora on Monday morning at 6:30am, arriving in Bora Bora at 8:30am, and passengers have a full day in Bora Bora, including spending the night. The ship departs Bora Bora on Tuesday at 2pm and arrives in Raiatea at 5pm, with disembarkment set for 5:30pm in Raiatea.

The four-night **Sapphire Cruise** begins in Bora Bora on Tuesday, with embarkment between 12 and 2pm. Departure from Bora Bora is at 2pm on Tuesday, with arrival in Raiatea at 5pm. The ship spends the night in Raiatea and departs on Wednesday at 4pm for a 5pm arrival in Tahaa, where it spends the night. On Thursday the *Haumana* leaves Tahaa at 3pm for an arrival in Bora Bora at 5pm. The ship then spends two nights in Bora Bora, with passengers disembarking in Bora Bora from 6 to 9am on Saturday.

The 4-day **Emerald Cruise** welcomes the passengers in Raiatea on Tuesday from 6 to 8pm, and spends Tuesday night inside the Raiatea lagoon. On Wednesday the ship leaves Raiatea at 4pm and arrives in Tahaa at 5pm, spending the night inside the lagoon of Tahaa. On Thursday the ship leaves Tahaa at 3pm and arrives in Bora Bora at 5pm. Passengers get to spend Thursday night and Friday night in Bora Bora, and return to Raiatea on Saturday, disembarking in Raiatea from 5 to 7pm on Saturday evening.

The *Haumana* will not dock anywhere except to refuel. Passengers board shuttle boats to embark and disembark and to visit the islands. Complimentary activities include visits to the villages and deserted *motu* islands with white sand beaches, "Robinson Crusoe Day" on a deserted *motu*, lagoon fishing, rainy weather games, television and video, lagoon expedition cruises and kayaks. Excursions ashore that are included in the cruise rates include: the Faaroa River Cruise, and Marae Taputapuatea in

Raiatea; visits to a vanilla plantation and black pearl farm in Tahaa; and Shark and Ray Feeding, sunbathing and beachcombing on a private islet in Bora Bora.

ONO ONO, *operated by Société Anonyme SPIM. B.P. 9772 Motu Uta, Papeete, Tahiti, Tel. 689/45.35.35; Fax 689/43.83.45; e-mail: onoono@mail.pf.*

The *Ono Ono* departs from the Papeete boat dock, adjacent to the Moorea boats. The ticket office is on the quay in front of the boat. There are three round-trips each week between Tahiti and the Leeward Society Islands. This rapid launch is powered by water-jet engines, and is 48 meters (157 feet) long, 9 meters (30 feet) wide, and has a draft of 1.2 meters (4 feet). The air-conditioned boat has 450 Pullman seats, a snack-bar that serves breakfast, sandwiches, luncheon specials and full dinners, with full bar service.

The *Ono Ono* leaves Papeete each Monday and Wednesday at 9am, arriving in Huahine at 12:45pm, in Raiatea at 2pm, in Tahaa at 2:45pm and in Bora Bora at 4pm. Each Friday the boat leaves Papeete at 4:30pm, arriving in Huahine at 8:30pm, in Raiatea at 9:45pm, and in Bora Bora at 11:20pm. Each Saturday a special inter-island circuit leaves Bora Bora at 8am, arrives in Tahaa at 9am, in Raiatea at 9:45am and in Huahine at 11am. On the same day the boat leaves Huahine at 3pm, arriving in Raiatea at 4pm, in Tahaa at 4:45pm and in Bora Bora at 6pm.

The return trip to Tahiti leaves Bora Bora each Tuesday and Thursday at 7am, arrives in Tahaa at 8am, in Raiatea at 8:15am, in Huahine at 10am and gets back to Papeete at 2:15pm. Each Sunday's departure from Bora Bora is at 12pm, arriving in Tahaa at 1pm, in Raiatea at 1:45pm, in Huahine at 3pm, and returns to Papeete at 7:15pm. The *Ono Ono* arrives and departs from the Fare quay in Huahine, the Uturoa quay in Raiatea, the Tapuamu quay in Tahaa and the Fare Piti quay in Faanui on the island of Bora Bora.

One-way fares are: 4.944 CFP ($49.44) to Huahine; 5.499 CFP ($54.99) to Raiatea; 6.055 CFP ($60.55) to Tahaa; and 6.610 CFP ($66.10) to Bora Bora. Reductions are given for babies, children and passengers over 60 years. *Ono-Ono* also has packages that include lodging on Huahine, Raiatea and Bora Bora.

TAPORO VI, *operated by Compagnie Française Maritime de Tahiti. B.P. 368, Papeete, Tahiti, Tel. 689/42.63.93/43.79.72; Fax 689/42.06.17.*

This is a large freighter that takes fuel and other supplies to the Leeward Society Islands three times a week. Only 12 passengers are allowed on board and there is only one cabin. The ticket office is at the Fare-Ute quay on the far side of Papeete harbor.

The ship leaves Papeete each Monday, Wednesday and Friday at 4pm, arriving in Huahine the following day at 1:30am; in Raiatea at 4:30am, in Tahaa at 6:30am, and in Bora Bora at 10am. The return trip leaves Bora

Bora each Tuesday, Thursday and Saturday at 11:30am, arriving in Raiatea at 2pm, in Huahine at 5pm and in Papeete at 4am the following morning. One-way fares from Papeete to all islands are 1,692 CFP ($16.92) on the bridge and 20.000 CFP ($200) for a cabin with four berths.

VAEANU, *operated by Société Coopérative Ouvrière de Production Ihitai Nui. B.P. 9062, Motu Uta, Tahiti, Tel. 689/41.25.35; Fax 41.24.34.*

This freighter is 79 meters (264 feet) long and 12 meters (39 feet) wide, with a draft of 6 meters (19 feet). In 1981 this ship began its career in Polynesian waters as the *Aranui*, cruising to the Marquesas and Tuamotu Islands. It was sold and renamed in the early 1990s and now serves the Leeward Society Islands with three round-trips each week from Papeete. There are 2 triple cabins, 12 double cabins and one individual cabin on board, with bridge space for 90 passengers. There is also a dining room on board.

This passenger/cargo ship departs from the Fare-Ute quay in Papeete at 5pm on Monday, Wednesday and Friday, arriving in Huahine the following morning at 2am, in Raiatea at 5am, in Tahaa at 7:30am (Saturday only), and in Bora Bora at 9:30 or 10am. The return trip leaves Bora Bora each Tuesday at 10:30am, arriving in Tahaa at 12:30pm, in Raiatea at 2pm, in Huahine at 5pm, and in Papeete at 3am on Wednesday. Each Thursday the ship leaves Bora Bora at 12pm, arriving in Raiatea at 3pm, in Huahine at 6pm and in Papeete at 4pm. The *Vaeanu* spends each Saturday night in Bora Bora, departing at 9am on Sunday for Tahaa, arriving at 11am, arriving in Raiatea at 1pm, in Huahine at 4pm and in Papeete at 2am Monday.

The one-way fare between Papeete and all the Leeward Society Islands for bridge passengers is 1.709 CFP ($17.09) per person. Cabins cost 4.000 to 5.500 CFP ($40 to $55) per person. The Wednesday voyage from Tahiti carries fuel drums, and all passengers must sleep in cabins during this trip.

MAUPITI EXPRESS, *B.P. 158, Uturoa, Raiatea, Tel/Fax 689/67.66.69; Tahiti reservations: B.P. 4596, Papeete, Tahiti, Tel. 689/48.05.81.*

This is a newly constructed (1997) covered launch 14,50 meters (48 feet) long, that can transport 62 passengers in the open ocean and 82 passengers inside the lagoons. Two 125 horsepower Cummings engines can cruise at 20 knots. Captain Gérald Sachet operated the *Keke II* and *Keke III* service between Tahiti and Moorea during the 1970s and 1980s, with his father Pierre Sachet. Gérald also worked aboard the *Aranui* before starting his career with the *Maupiti Express*.

The boat is based in Bora Bora, providing round-trip service between Bora Bora and Maupiti each Tuesday, Thursday, Saturday and Sunday, departing Vaitape boat dock at 8:30am and arriving in Maupiti at 10am. The boat leaves Maupiti the same afternoon at 4:30pm, arriving in Bora

Bora at 6pm. Each Wednesday and Friday the *Maupiti Express* leaves Vaitape quay at 7am, for Tahaa and Raiatea. It arrives in Tahaa's Apu Bay at the Marina Iti hotel at 8am, and leaves at 8:15am for Raiatea, arriving at the Uturoa quay at 8:30am. The launch leaves Raiatea on the same afternoon at 4:30pm, arriving in Tahaa at 4:45pm, and departs from the Marina Iti pier at 5pm for Bora Bora, arriving in Vaitape at 6pm. The one-way fare is 3.000 CFP ($30), for the Bora Bora-Maupiti run or the Bora Bora-Tahaa-Raiatea service. Round-trip tickets are 6.000 CFP ($60). Reductions of 20 percent are given to people under 15 years and over 60 years.

A Day Tour of Tahaa is available for 10.000 CFP ($100) a person, which includes a guided visit to the highlights of Tahaa, including a vanilla plantation, a black pearl farm and handcrafts centers. You'll also get to taste *poisson cru* and fresh tropical fruits. Should you choose to take this tour you will be transported from Tahaa at 1:30pm, arriving in Raiatea at 2pm., and departing for Tahaa and Bora Bora during the regular scheduled service, which leaves Uturoa boat dock at 4:30pm. *Reservations can be made at Agence Blue Lagon, Tel. 66.17.28/65.67.10.*

Marquesas Islands

ARANUI, *operated by Compagnie de Transport Maritime, 2028 El Camino Real South, Suite B, San Mateo, California 94403; in US Tel. 415/574-2575; Fax 415/574-6881; e-mail cptm@aranui.com Internet://www.aranui.com The Tahiti office is located at Motu Uta, across the harbor and bridge from Papeete, Tel. 689/42.62.40/43.76.60; Fax 689/43.48.89.* See more information in chapter on *Eco-Tourism and Travel Alternatives.*

In my opinion the *Aranui* is the best way to visit French Polynesia if you have the time and interest to enjoy an authentic experience of ship-day in a small secluded valley in the Marquesas Islands. The *Aranui* is a 105 meter (343 foot) long working cargo/copra ship that accommodates 90 passengers in 36 air-conditioned cabins and on an air-conditioned covered deck.

This is not a cruise ship in the usual sense, where you put on your best finery to dine at the captain's table. You'll be more practically dressed in a cool shirt or blouse and shorts or pants that you don't mind getting wet and dirty when you get into the whaleboat for shore excursions. And don't forget your plastic sandals, protective hat, sunglasses, sunscreen and a good repellent against mosquitoes and *nono*'s (sand fleas).

The *Aranui* leaves Tahiti 15 times a year for 16-day round-trip voyages to the Marquesas Islands, with a stop at the Tuamotu atoll of Takapoto on the outbound trip, and in Rangiroa atoll on the return voyage. The *Aranui*, which means "The Great Highway" in the Tahitian language, provides a lifeline to the Marquesas Islanders, as the ship calls at each principal village and several remote valleys on all six inhabited islands. The big cargo holds contain food, fuel, cement and other building materials, trucks, fishing boats, beer, bedding and other necessities to offload in the distant Marquesas Islands. Copra, citrus fruit, fish and barrels of *noni* (*Morinda citrifolia*) are embarked to take back to Papeete.

Watching the *Aranui*'s muscular crew perform their tasks is part of the attraction and charm of this voyage. Even if hydraulics are not your favorite thing, you'll enjoy watching a pickup truck being loaded from the ship's hold onto a double platform balanced on top of two whale boats lashed together. What's even more interesting is to see how the crew gets the truck safely ashore while the waves are bouncing the whaleboats up and down.

While you're ashore visiting the sights, the Marquesan men and boys are helping the *Aranui* crew carry burlap bags of copra to the whaleboats to be shipped to the copra processing plant in Papeete. A trip aboard the *Aranui* will give you many opportunities to meet the friendly and natural Polynesians, far removed from the normal tourist scene.

The 1998 rates quoted here are based on per person double occupancy and include three meals a day and guided excursions, picnics and programmed meals on shore. Add 50 percent for single occupancy. Children 3 to 15 years sharing cabin with adults are charged $820 per person. The estimated port tax is $75 per person.

The 5 deluxe "A" class cabins are large outside cabins with a queen size bed, refrigerator and private facilities with bathtub, for $3,995 per person plus $40.70 VAT per person. There are 20 standard "A" class cabins, which are all outside, with two lower berths and private bathrooms with showers, for $3,375 per person plus $34.50 VAT per person. The 4 outside "B" class cabins with upper and lower berths, without private facilities, located in the old super-structure, and 3 "B" class inside cabins in the new superstructure, with two lower berths and no private facilities, are $2,935 per person, plus $30.10 VAT per person. Class "C" accommodations are located on the bridge deck, which is also air-conditioned and without private facilities. The dormitory style upper and lower berths are $1,980 per person, plus $20.55 VAT per person.

The ship's public facilities include air-conditioned reception, boutique, colorful dining room that seats 50, a non-smoking lounge-library, a video room and infirmary with a doctor, plus a bar, sun deck and salt water swimming pool. There is daily maid service, twice weekly laundry service and a trained host and two hostess/guides. Organized shore excursions include picnics, Marquesan feasts, horseback riding, hiking to waterfalls, stone tikis and archaeological sites, visits to wood carvers and artisan workshops, plus inland and upland tours by 4-wheel drive vehicle.

The *Aranui* itinerary given here may vary with each voyage, depending on departure date and the freight to be delivered, but the ship will call at all the villages during each trip.

Day 1 - Saturday: Boarding & Departure

A typical cruise begins with a welcome cocktail party in the ship's bar at 6pm, followed by dinner, which is usually served in two seatings. The Americans usually choose the first seating and the French dine later. The *Aranui* leaves Papeete harbor between 8 and 10:30pm and heads toward the Tuamotu Archipelago.

Day 2 - Sunday: At Sea

You can get your sea legs while exploring the ship, relax with a book on one of the sun decks, swim in the small salt water pool, read in the lounge/library and attend a lecture given by an authority on Marquesan culture or archaeology. In the evening some of the Polynesian crew play island tunes in the bar, while Yoyo prepares your favorite cocktail. Yoyo is always dressed in a *pareo* and he is an essential part of the *Aranui* experience. His favorite expression is "Aita peapea," (no problem).

Day 3 - Monday: Takapoto atoll in Tuamotu Archipelago

This atoll is 300 nautical miles northeast of Tahiti. You will go ashore in a whaleboat, wearing your life jacket. There is no pass into the lagoon and the boat has to shoot the reef to get to the dock. Have no fear, because *Aranui*'s strong and capable Polynesian crew will take care of you, assisting you ashore and even picking you up and carrying you to dry land on occasion. Your guides will lead you through the neat little village to the inner lagoon, where you will board an outrigger speed canoe to visit a black pearl farm. You will have plenty of time to look at black pearls for sale, snorkeling, enjoying a picnic on a white sand beach and a walk through a coconut plantation.

Remember to wear strong sun protection, a hat and sunglasses, and don't forget your plastic sandals and mosquito repellent. You'll be transported back to the ship at 2pm, and the *Aranui* will set a course for the mysterious Marquesas Islands.

Day 4 - Tuesday: At Sea

The guides will inform you of what you'll be doing in the Marquesas Islands, and you can attend a lecture or video film about the Marquesas, or read and sunbathe. At the reception desk you can check out reading material on the Marquesas Islands or choose a best-selling novel in the library.

Day 5 - Wednesday: Ua Pou (Hakahetau & Hakahau)

Advance your watch by 30 minutes. As dawn lightens the sky you'll see the soaring mountain spires of Ua Pou. While the crew unloads supplies and hauls sacks of copra on board, you can visit the small village of Hakahetau, with its little church, handcrafts shop and beach of flowerstones (*phonolitis*). The *Aranui* will dock in the harbor of Hakahau, the main village, where you will be guided to Paepae Teavatuu for a traditional Marquesan welcome, which includes tasting fruit and Marquesan dishes, and watching some school children perform the *haka* and bird dances. Lunch is served at Rosalie's Restaurant, where you'll taste breadfruit, octopus, roast pork, curried goat, rock lobster, *poisson cru*, taro and sweet red bananas.

You can walk off your delicious meal by visiting the Catholic church to see the carvings on the altar, which represent designs from the Bible. Late in the afternoon the *Aranui* will leave Ua Pou and head for Nuku Hiva. You can watch Theodore Oputu, the second captain, fishing from the aft bridge while a brilliant red sun dips behind the horizon, offering the bonus of a sparkling green flash just before setting. The *Aranui* Band plays music for dancing in the bar after dinner.

Day 6 - Thursday: Nuku Hiva–Taiohae to Taipivai

The *Aranui* arrives into Taiohae's spectacular bay, a giant volcanic amphitheater dominated by towering cliffs streaked with waterfalls. The ship docks at a pier near Taiohae Bay, and you can walk down the gangway and board a 4-wheel drive vehicle to the village. Protect yourself from the fierce bite of the *nono* before going ashore. A welcome ceremony includes tasting fresh guava, fried bananas and coconut candy, accompanied by a Marquesan dance show on the lawn. You'll then be driven to the cathedral (Notre Dame des Iles Marquises) to see the intricate carvings, and you'll pass the Tohua Piki Vehine (an ancient assembly place) on your way out of Taiohae village.

A caravan of pickup trucks and other 4WD's will wind up the rutted roads of the Toovii Plateau, to a height of 800 meters (2,624 feet) for panoramic views of Taiohae Bay and the *Aranui* far below. The *Aranui* dining room hostesses and Yoyo the barman spread a tempting picnic feast under the shade of a *pistache* tree, to restore your strength before you descend into Taipivai. This is the valley made famous in Herman Melville's book *Typee*, in which he tells how he and a buddy jumped a whaling ship in 1842 and lived among the hospitable cannibals of Taipivai. Hidden among the bamboo and vanilla vines are eight stone tiki gods and sacred ritual sites, a 20-minute walk into the steamy valley. The *Aranui* crew will come to fetch you at the dock and the whaleboat takes you down the Taipi river to return to the ship in the late afternoon.

Day 7 - Friday: Hiva Oa–Tahuata (Atuona–Vaitahu)

The *Aranui* docks at the pier and you can walk down the gangway and board *le truck* to go to Atuona village, the second largest town in the Marquesas Islands. This is where Paul Gauguin lived and did some of his best work, before he died in 1903, and was buried in Calvary Cemetery above the village. You'll visit Gauguin's grave and that of Belgian singer Jacques Brel, attend a welcome ceremony and Marquesan dance show performed in front of the Paul Gauguin Museum and the *Maison du Jouir* (House of Pleasure), a reproduction of his home and *atelier*. Lunch at the Hoa Nui restaurant is another Marquesan feast of *poisson cru*, duck with tamarind sauce, smoked chicken, lobster, goat, macaroni fritters, fresh water shrimp, *fafa poulet*, banana *po'e* and fresh tropical fruits.

In the afternoon the *Aranui* crosses the Bordelais channel to reach the little island of Tahuata, where you can visit the village of Vaitahu. The guides will take you to the Notre Dame de l'Enfant Jesus church, which was built by the Vatican, and is decorated with beautiful Marquesan carvings. You'll also visit a small museum inside the town hall and the arts and crafts center.

Day 8 - Saturday: Fatu Hiva (Omoa–Hanavave)

Fatu Hiva is the most lush and remote island of the Marquesas group, and the industrious residents of the village of Omoa still maintain their traditional crafts. You'll go ashore by whaleboat to a slippery pier and walk to Omoa village, where you will see women hammering mulberry, banyan or breadfruit bark on logs to make tapa cloth. Once the bark cloth is dried they decorate the *tapa* with hand painted Marquesan designs. Wood carvings, sculpted coconuts, hand-painted *pareos*, fragrant *monoi* oils and dried bananas are also made in Fatu Hiva. The *Aranui* passengers are invited to a private home, where you will see an impressive collection of ancient Marquesan woodcarvings that belonged to a former chief, Willie Grellet, which are proudly displayed today by his grandchildren.

You can join a 10-mile hike across a rugged mountain trail between Omoa and Hanavave village, with a picnic lunch, or you can return to the *Aranui* for lunch and visit Hanavave when the ship anchors in the beautiful Bay of Virgins. A secluded jungle pool awaits you at the end of the hike, where you can swim in an ideal setting for a South Pacific movie.

Day 9 - Sunday: Tahuata (Hapatoni–Hanamoenoa Beach)

When the *Aranui* anchors in front of the little village of Hapatoni, you'll be taken ashore by whaleboat and greeted at the pier by some 60 friendly, smiling Marquesan women and children. They will present you with floral crowns and take your hand to lead you to their village, where you will be served fruits and fresh juices. In addition to singing and dancing for you these happy people will show you around their village and treat you so well that you will always remember this brief visit. Hapatoni is the favorite village for many of the *Aranui* passengers.

After lunch on board the ship you can join the *Aranui* crew and other passengers for an afternoon on the white sand beach of Hanamoenoa, the prettiest beach in the Marquesas Islands. The Polynesian sailors gather around a radio to listen to a Catholic mass while quietly watching the sunset. In the evening they fish on the aft bridge.

Day 10 - Monday: Hiva Oa (Hanaiapa–Puamau)

In the morning you'll go ashore by whaleboat to visit the pretty little village of Hanaiapa, where you can buy some wooden tikis and snorkel by the boat dock. After lunch the whaleboats go ashore on the beach of Puamau, which is inhabited by the descendants of Paul Gauguin. You can travel by foot or pickup truck to visit one of the most important archaeological sites in Polynesia. At the *me'ae* Oipona, the mysterious jungle ruins of Puamau, the *Aranui* guides will point out Takaii, a stone statue 235 centimeters (7.6 feet) high, which is the biggest tiki in French Polynesia. Bring lots of film and mosquito repellent.

Day 11 - Tuesday: Ua Huka (Vaipaee–Hane–Hokatu–Haavei Bay)

Captain Taputu has to maneuver the *Aranui* into a 180 degree turn-around to safely secure the ship at the anchorage in the "Invisible Bay" of Vaipaee on the island of Ua Huka. You'll go ashore by whaleboat for a welcome ceremony of flower leis, fruit and a Marquesan dance show performed in the gardens of the *mairie* (town hall). You'll visit a small museum of Marquesan artifacts and board decorated pick-up trucks or mount a Marquesan horse for a ride across the island. A three-hour ride takes you across the mountain landscape, with breathtaking scenes of wild horses, plains, green mountains, wild goats, rocky coastlines, an offshore huge rock and the *Aranui* passing far below at just the right moment to take a photograph. You will stop to visit a botanical garden that covers 14 hectares (35 acres) and contains every kind of plant and flower you can think of that grows in this climate.

In Hane village you will visit a handcrafts center and a little museum of the sea, then dig into another gargantuan Marquesan feast at Celine Fournier's Auberge Hitikau. Lunch may include *kaveka* omelets made from the eggs of sea terns, plus goat cooked in coconut milk, *poisson cru*, pig, goat and fish cooked in an earth oven, plus rice, *fei*, *uru*, banana *po'e*, sashimi, cake, wine and coffee. If you can still walk after lunch, you may want to hike into the valley to see four stone tiki statues at a *me'ae* temple. You can also ride over to the next village of Hokatu and visit their handcrafts center, or you can stroll around the pretty village of Hane, swim from the beach or nap under a tree. After dinner the *Aranui* Band plays Tahitian songs while Yoyo pours the drinks.

Day 12 - Wednesday: Nuku Hiva (Hatiheu)
The beautiful green valley behind the little village of Hatiheu beckons you ashore, and the *Aranui* crew will take you to a slippery little dock in the whaleboat, which is a 10-minute walk to the village. The young people of the village perform a Marquesan *haka* and bird dance to welcome you, while the little school kids next door leave their class room to steal the show with their antics. You can walk for 20 minutes uphill or go by pick-up truck to the Tohua Hikokua, a huge grassy meeting area surrounded by beautiful trees and stone platforms. This restored archaeological site has both old and more recently carved tikis, and further uphill is a *me'ae* with petroglyphs. Lunch is served at Mayor Yvonne Katupa's restaurant, which has the well deserved reputation of serving some of the best food in the Marquesas Islands. A feast of breaded white tuna and lobster tails with *uru* and taro also includes roast pig and bananas from the *ahimaa* underground oven. The delicious food is accompanied by wine and music played by the same fellows who danced for you this morning.

More food and music is in store for you this evening, when the *Aranui* crew presents Polynesian Night, complete with a bountiful buffet, lots of wine, a Tahitian dance show, skits and music for dancing.

Day 13 - Thursday: Nuku Hiva–Ua Pou (Taiohae–Hakahau)
The *Aranui* will dock at the quay of Taiohae, where you have a choice of optional activities, including a helicopter flight over the island, scuba diving or horseback riding. You can also explore the village of Taiohae and visit the woodcarvers' workshops.

Around midday the ship leaves Nuku Hiva and returns to Ua Pou, where you can go ashore at Hakahau, the *Aranui*'s last stop in the Marquesas Islands. You can watch the mountains of Ua Pou fade into the distance as the sun sets and the *Aranui* heads toward the Tuamotu Islands.

Day 14 - Friday: At Sea
You'll have plenty of time to watch the ocean, sunbathe on deck, read and watch video films.

Day 15 - Saturday: Rangiroa
You'll have a wonderful opportunity to "watch the sunrise on a tropic isle," as the *Aranui* reaches the atoll of Rangiroa and enters the deep and wide Tiputa Pass to anchor inside the world's second largest lagoon. The whaleboat crew will take you to the wooden dock in front of the Kia Ora Village, your headquarters for the day. You can snorkel, take a glass-

bottom boat ride to watch the sharks and fish, or opt for scuba diving or parasailing. A picnic lunch of barbecued chicken, cold salads, fruit and wine is served on the beach adjacent to the hotel. When you return to the ship at 2pm, be sure to go to the bow to watch the *Aranui* go out the pass. Several big dolphins have a great time racing with the ship for several minutes before turning back toward the atoll.

Day 16 - Sunday: Papeete, Tahiti

The *Aranui* enters the Papeete harbor around 5:30am, and you will be served breakfast before going ashore.

Tuamotu Islands

Before planning a trip to the Tuamotu and Gambier Islands aboard any of the ships listed below, you should verify if the vessel is still in service. The treacherous reefs of the atolls are a graveyard for ships that have been wrecked on these coral shores. These distant atolls were named the Dangerous Archipelago for a good reason. The *Tamarii Tuamotu* finished its long career on the reef in Takaroa in February 1998, just before publication time. The offices of these *goëlettes* (tramp boats) are located in the port area of Motu Uta, reached by bridge across the Papeete harbor.

ST. XAVIER MARIS STELLA, *operated by Société Navigation Tuamotu, B.P. 11366, Mahina, Tahiti; Tel. 689/42.23.58; Fax 689/43.03.73. The office is in a warehouse on the inter-island goëlette pier at Motu Uta.*

This long red-hulled steel ship is a family business owned by Elias Salem, who left Lebanon in 1937 to live in Tahiti. His sons and grandsons all work on the ship, which transports fuel, cars, cement, wood and other building materials to the Tuamotus and returns to Papeete laden with copra, ice chests of fish and white sand. A maximum of 12 passengers are allowed on board. The ship smells of gasoline, rancid copra and fish, which is a nostalgic perfume for some South Seas romantics. The cabins are basically furnished and simple meals are served on board. The ship reaches Rangiroa after 20 hours at sea, then continues on to all the western Tuamotu atolls: Ahe, Manihi, Takaroa, Takapoto, Fakarava, Kauehi, Aratika, Toau, Arutua, Kaukura, Apataki, Mataiva and Tikehau. Only one day is spent in each port.

The ship leaves Papeete every 15 days and it takes 10 days to make the round-trip circuit. One way fares to any of the destinations is 5.000 CFP ($50) per person for a cabin and 2.000 CFP ($20) if you sleep on the deck. Add another 2.000 CFP ($20) per day for three meals.

AU'URA NUI III, *B.P. 9364, Motu Uta, Tahiti; Tel. 689/43.92.40, Fax 689/42.77.70.*

This is another big steel ship that serves the central and eastern Tuamotus, has cabins and offers three daily meals on board. The central

Tuamotu atolls include Anaa, Tetamanu, Faaite, Katiu, Makemo, Taenga, Nihiru, Hikueru and Marokau. The one-way fare is 6.000 CFP ($60) per person in a cabin, and 3.000 CFP ($30) on deck. The eastern Tuamotu atolls served are Hao, Amanu, Vairaatea, Nukutavake, Vahitahi, Reao, Pukarua, Takoto, Puka Puka, Fakahina, Fangatau, Napuka, Tepoto, Takume, Raroia and Anaa. The fare is 10.000 to 12.000 CFP ($100-$120) per person in a cabin, depending on the atoll, and 5.500 to 7.000 CFP ($55-$70) on deck. Add 2.200 CFP ($22) per person a day for the meals on all routes.

MANAVA III, *operated by Société Compagnie de Développement Maritime des Tuamotu, B. P. 1291, Papeete, Tahiti; Tel. 689/43.32.65; Fax 689/41.31.65. The office is at the Motu-Uta goëlette pier.*

This big steel boat offers cabins and meals and is owned by Béné Richmond, who provides service once a month to the Tuamotus and Gambier Islands. The 18-day round-trip voyages from Papeete call at Hereheretue, Nego Nego, Nukutavake, Nukutepipi, Tematangi, Tureia, Vairaatea and Vanavana in the eastern Tuamotus. The one-way fare is 12.694 CFP ($126.94) in a cabin and 7.254 CFP ($72.54) on deck. The fare from Papeete to Hao and Amanu, which is a separate voyage, is 9.284 CFP ($92.84) in a cabin and 5.305 CFP ($53.05) on deck. Add 2.500 CFP ($25) per person a day for all three meals. The 18-day monthly trip to the Gambier Islands also stops at the Tuamotu atoll of Marutea Sud (South), and in Rikitea and Tenani'a in the Gambier Islands. The cost of a cabin is 15.000 CFP ($150) and deck space is 7.500 CFP ($75). Add 2.500 CFP ($25) per person for three meals daily.

Other ships serving the Tuamotus are: *Dory and Cobia II, Tel. 689/42.30.55, Fax 689/42.06.15; Manava II, Tel. 689/43.83.84/42.25.53, Fax 689/45.31.38/42.25.53; Kura Ora II, Tel./Fax 689/45.55.45; Rairoa Nui, Tel. 689/42.91.69, Fax 689/41.04.33; Hotu Maru, Tel. 689/41.07.11, Fax 689/57.30.71; and Vai Aito, Tel. 689/43.99.96, Fax 689/43.53.04.* The eastern Tuamotus and Gambier Islands are also served by *Nuke Hau, Tel. 689/45.23.24, Fax 689/45.24.44.* None of these *goëlettes* have cabins, but you can sleep on deck, and some of them serve meals.

Austral Islands

TUHAA PAE II, *operated by Société Anonyme d'Economie Mixte de Navigation des Australes, B.P. 1890, Papeete, Tahiti, Tel. 689/42.93.67; Fax 689/42.06.09.*

This is a steel hull ship, 59 meters (196 feet) long, that carries passengers and supplies to the Austral Islands. It leaves Papeete every 15 days for Rurutu, Tubuai, Rimatara and Raivavae, and stops in Rapa once a month. The cabins are very basic, usually with four bunk beds, no portholes and no air. The showers and toilets (holes in the floor) are on a separate level from the cabins. The local passengers sleep in berths in a big open room up top, which is cooler but not private. Bring your own toilet paper, booze, towels, soap and electric fans (220 volts). The dining room serves simple but good food. There are no shore activities programmed. You can hitch a ride with some of the islanders who come to the ship to collect their merchandise from Tahiti or to load their taro and other vegetables that are being shipped to Papeete.

Fares from Tahiti to Rurutu, Rimatara and Tubuai are 6.583 CFP ($65.83) in a cabin, 5.265 CFP ($52.65) for a berth on the upper deck, and 3.761 CFP ($37.61) if you sleep on the bridge. A cabin to Raivavae is 9.487 CFP ($94.87) per person and to Rapa is 12.971 CFP ($129.71). A berth to Raivavae is 7.589 CFP ($75.89) and 10.376 CFP ($103.76) to Rapa. Bridge space to Raivavae is 5.421 ($54.21) and 7.412 CFP ($74.12) to Rapa.

BY CHARTER BOAT

If your romantic spirit is stirred at the sight of a white-sailed ship beating out to the wide sea, you can put yourself aboard your dream by chartering a sailboat in Tahiti. Comfortable modern yachts of every description are available for chartering by the day or week, with bases in Tahiti, Moorea, Raiatea, Tahaa, Bora Bora, Rangiroa, Tikihau and the Marquesas Islands of Nuku Hiva and Hiva Oa. Please check each island section for details on chartering a sailboat. Billowing sails, white against the horizon, beckon you to "come aboard" one of the sleek yachts you see gliding gracefully across the lagoon, within the protective embrace of the barrier reef that encloses Raiatea and Tahaa.

Sailing conditions are ideal in the Leeward Islands and a large variety of yachts can be chartered in Raiatea for bare-boating, day-sailing or for longer excursions with skipper and crew.

ARCHIPELS POLYNESIAN CRUISES, *B.P. 1160, Papetoai, Moorea, Tel. 689/56.36.39, Fax 689/56.35.87. US representatives are Islands in the Sun, Tel. 800/828-6877, Tahiti Vacations, Tel. 800/553-3477, and Tahiti Legends, Tel. 800/200-1213.*

Archipels is based in Opunohu Bay on the island of Moorea. Seven deep-sea Fountaine Pajot 57 sailing catamarans can be chartered to cruise the Leeward Society Islands, the Tuamotu atolls or the Marquesas Islands. Individuals can choose a "by the cabin" shared-boat cruise, paying $1,880 per person for a 7 day/6 night Society Islands cruise, $1,030 per person for a 4 day/3 night Tuamotu cruise inside the atoll of Rangiroa, or $790 per person for a 3 day/2 night cruise inside the immense lagoon. An 8-day/7 night Marquesas Island cruise is $2,050 per person. The per-passenger rates include meals and hotel services aboard in double occupancy cabins. You can also charter the entire yacht for US $2,090 per day. A yacht is kept in Raiatea for sailing the Leeward Islands and another yacht is based year-round in Nuku Hiva for cruising the Marquesas Islands. Romantic honeymoon cruises and dive cruises are also available. Please see information in the *Moorea* chapter.

DANAE CRUISES, *B.P. 251, Uturoa, Raiatea, Tel. 689/66.12.50; Fax 689/66.39.37. This nautical base is located at Uturaerae Marina.*

The *Danae III* is one of the few yachts that operates a shared-boat sailing schedule with a per person cost. The 67-foot steel ketch has four double staterooms, is fully crewed and offers complete services. One week the cruise begins in Bora Bora on Monday morning and ends in Raiatea on Saturday, anchoring in a different cove each night. The following week the cruise starts from Raiatea and ends in Bora Bora. The cost of this six-day cruise is $1,167 per person, all on-board meals and activities included. Dive Cruises are also available.

The *Danae IV* is an air-conditioned 50-foot sailing trawler with two double staterooms that is used for families, romantic honeymoon cruises or for private charters.

THE MOORINGS, *B.P. 165, Uturoa, Raiatea, Tel. 689/66.35.93/ 66.26.26; Fax 689/66.20.94. The nautical base is located at Apooiti Marina in Raiatea.*

The Moorings fleet has been operating in Raiatea since 1985 and has an average fleet of 30 boats, which include monohull sailboats from 35 to 51 feet and catamarans 42 to 47 feet long. Yachts can be chartered bareboat or with skipper and hostess/cook, and provisioning is available on request. The August 1997, edition of *Cruising World* magazine published the results of a "Bareboat charter scorecard," which voted The Moorings in Raiatea the best yacht charter base in the world. Charter rates vary from about $310 per day for a 6-passenger yacht to $670 a day for an 8-passenger catamaran.

STARDUST MARINE, *B.P. 331, Uturoa, Raiatea, Tel. 689/66.23.18; Fax 689/66.23.19.*

Stardust Marine has an office in Newport Beach, California, but their biggest market is French. The Europeans have also discovered the pleasures of cruising through the Leeward Islands, and up to eight yachts at a time are chartered by groups of Germans and Austrians. The fleet includes 17 mono-hulls ranging from 37 to 52 feet, and 3 catamarans 43 to 47 feet long, which can be chartered bareboat or with skipper and hostess/cook. Charter rates are based on low, shoulder or high season and the yacht chosen. Please see further information in *Raiatea* chapter.

STAR VOYAGE, *B.P. 119, Uturoa, Raiatea, Tel. 689/66. 40.00; Fax 689/66.11.83. The base is at the Uturoa marina.*

This French-owned company is the newest addition to the yacht charterers in Raiatea. The fleet includes Sun Odyssey mono-hulls from 32 to 42 feet long, Oceanis 381 and 461 yachts, and Privilege 37 and 42 catamarans. Weekly charter rates start at 180.000 CFP ($1,800) for a Sun Odyssey 32.1 during the low season of November through March. The high season rate, from June 27 through August 28, for the same yacht is 238,000 CFP ($2,300).

TAHITI YACHT CHARTER, *B.P. 608, Papeete, Tahiti, Tel. 689/45.04.00; Fax 689/42.76.00; e-mail: tyc@mail.pf is located on the yacht quay of Papeete and at the Apooiti Marina in Raiatea.*

The fleet includes six mono-hulls from 32 to 50 feet and six catamarans from 35 to 46 feet, which can be chartered bareboat or provisioned with skipper and hostess/cook. Charter rates range from $350 a day to $5,740 a week, depending on season and yacht. Please see information in *Tahiti* chapter.

VPM DUFOUR TAHITI, *B.P. 554, Maharepa, Moorea, Tel. 689/56.40.50, Fax 689/56.40.60, e-mail VPMyacht@mailpf*

This yacht charter company is based at the Vaiare Marina in Moorea. Another base is located in Raiatea, and they also have a yacht permanently based in Tikehau in the Tuamotu archipelago and a catamaran in Taiohae on the island of Nuku Hiva. Their fleet ranges from 35 to 98 feet, and includes some sailboats that can be chartered without a skipper. A 9 day/8 night leisure cruise aboard an 82-foot long catamaran from Tahiti to Bora Bora is about $1,450 per person, meals included. You can also choose a 10 day/9 night sporting cruise that takes you from Papeete to Bora Bora, Tahaa, Raiatea, Huahine, Moorea and back to Tahiti, or a cruise in the Tuamotus and in the Marquesas Islands. Please see information in the *Moorea* chapter.

BY CAR

In the Society Islands most of the roads that circle the islands are paved. There are a few places in Huahine, Raiatea and Tahaa where the road is not sealed but they are pretty well graded. Following heavy rains there are frequently holes in the road that can be very dangerous, especially if you are driving a scooter or bicycle. In the Marquesas Islands the 4-wheel drive vehicles (called 4x4, pronounced "cat-cat") are usually rented with driver, because the roads are abominable. You can rent a self-drive 4WD in Atuona on the island of Hiva Oa. Rangiroa has a paved road between the two passes and there's nowhere else to go by car. The Austral Islands have mostly unpaved roads, which you can drive in a normal car, except for some places in Rurutu, where a 4WD is required.

You will drive on the right side of the road in French Polynesia, just as you do in North America and continental Europe. A valid diver's license from your State or home country will be honored here. Should you buy an international driver's license, which is not at all necessary, you will still need to show your normal driver's license in order to rent a car or scooter. The minimum age is 21 years to rent a 4WD vehicle and to rent two wheel vehicles the driver must be 18 or 19 years old, depending on the island.

Speed limits are 40 kilometers per hour (24 miles per hour) in the towns and villages, 60 kilometers (37 miles per hour) on the winding roads of most of the islands and 80 to 110 kilometers (50 to 68 miles per hour) on a short stretch of freeway leading from Tahiti's west coast to downtown Papeete. Seat belts are mandatory for the driver and passenger in the front seats of vehicles, and helmets are required for anyone riding a motorcycle or scooter.

Anyone driving a two-wheel vehicle should remember to go single file. There are no bicycle paths in these islands and some of the local drivers are in a mighty big hurry to get somewhere, even with nowhere to go. After all, they take their driver's lessons from the French!

You should also be alert for drunk drivers, especially late at night, and young boys doing "wheelies" on bicycles or scooters, often with no lights at night. You also have to look out for children and dogs when you pass through the villages around the island.

Liability Insurance

Vehicle insurance includes third party liability insurance. It is possible, depending on the conditions of the driving license and age, to take a comprehensive insurance that covers collision, damage and waiver.

Automobile Rental

Europcar and **Pacificar** are the biggest names for rental cars in French Polynesia, although **Avis** and **Hertz** also have offices in the more popular tourist islands. There are also a few individuals who rent cars, scooters and bicycles. See information for each island in the *Getting Around Town* section.

By Package Tours

The travel agencies listed in this chapter can suggest package tours that include international air travel to French Polynesia, accommodations, some meals, ground transfers, inter-island travel by airplane or boat, and some tours and excursions. Should you decide on a tour package, be sure to read the fine print so that you will understand what you are paying for. You don't want to limit yourself to eating all your meals in the same hotel when there are enticing restaurants to explore on the island.

ACCOMMODATIONS

You have a choice of 3,100 classified hotel rooms in French Polynesia, with new hotels scheduled to open in 1998 and 1999, and other hotels adding more units. You will also find a selection of 700 non-classified rooms in hostels and homestays, locally referred to as pensions.

These accommodations include air-conditioned, carpeted, deluxe rooms with direct dial international telephones, individual safes, cable television and room service, similar to American hotel or motel rooms, usually in concrete buildings of two or more levels.

Mid-range rooms are available in small hotels, which may be an air-conditioned room in downtown Papeete, a self-contained, totally equipped house on Raiatea, or an attractive bungalow beside the beach in Moorea, with an overhead fan, cooking facilities and television.

The typical Polynesian style bungalows can be very elegant, especially when they are built overwater, with a glass panel or table in the floor, allowing you to have a peek at what the fish are doing in the coral gardens below. These bungalows often have thatched roofs of woven pandanus leaves and woven bamboo walls. The interior walls are sometimes covered with pandanus matting, and a chic Polynesian decor incorporates all the flamboyant colors you'll find in the tropical gardens, or it reflects the softer colors of the lagoon. Many of the newer bungalows have air-conditioning, large bathrooms with a bathtub/shower or bathtub and separate shower. They also have lighted dressing tables and living areas, plus a porch or veranda, and the overwater bungalows have steps leading into the lagoon, with a shower on the landing.

The small *fare* (FAH-rey) often has a thatched roof, overhead fan and colorful linens and curtains. Some of them are screened, and most of them have a porch or terrace. In the family operated pensions you usually have a choice of a private room or sharing a room. You can cook your own meals or eat what your hosts prepare. You may have a bathroom to yourself with a hot water shower, or share the outdoor facilities, which may have a cold water shower. On some of the more arid islands your water supply may be limited, and you may have to dip half a coconut shell into a barrel of water to take your bath. Backpackers' lodgings and campgrounds are available on several islands. Check the accommodations information for the individual islands.

INTERNATIONAL HOTEL CHAINS

The 55 unit Hotel Bora Bora is operated by the exclusive Amanresorts, North America reservations, *Tel. 800/447-7462.* **Orient Express Hotels**, *reservations 800/237-1236/800-223-6800*, operates the 80 unit Bora Bora Lagoon Resort. **Southern Pacific Hotels**, *North America reservations, Tel. 800/835-7742*, operates the 212 unit Tahiti Beachcomber Parkroyal, the 147 unit Moorea Beachcomber Parkroyal and the 51 unit Moana Beach Parkroyal. **Club Mediterranee**, *US reservations, Tel. 800/528-3100*, has 350 units at the Club Med Moorea and 150 units at the Club Med Bora Bora.

The French company **Sofitel Coralia**, *Tel. US reservations 800/221-4542*, has the 208 room Maeva Beach in Tahiti, the 110 unit Sofitel Ia Ora Moorea, the 61 unit Sofitel Heiva Huahine and the 64 unit Sofitel Marara Bora Bora. They also handle the promotion for the 45 unit Kia Ora Village and the five bungalow Kia Ora Sauvage in Rangiroa. **Le Méridien Hotels**, *North America reservations, Tel. 800/543-4300*, will open the 150 unit Le Méridien Tahiti and the 100 unit Le Méridien Bora Bora in 1998. **Outrigger Hotels**, *North America reservations, Tel. 800/688-7444*, will open the 200 unit Outrigger Hotel Tahiti during the first quarter of 1999, and the 90 unit Outrigger Bora Bora is still in the planning stage.

LOCALLY-OWNED HOTEL CHAINS

Bali Hai Hotels, *US reservations, Tel. 800/282-1401, in California, Tel. 800/282-1402*, owns the 63 unit Hotel Bali Hai and the 39 unit Club Bali Hai in Moorea, and the 33 unit Hotel Bali Hai Huahine. **Tahiti Resort Hotels (TRH)**, *reservations, Tel. 689/43.08.29*, operates the 40 room Tahiti Country Club, 40 room Moorea Beach Club, 17 unit Huahine Beach Club, the 36 room Beach Club Bora Bora and the 11 unit Rangiroa Beach Club.

The 41-unit Manihi Pearl Beach Resort, 32-unit Raiatea Pearl Beach Resort (Hawaiki Nui) and 60 unit Bora Bora Pearl Beach Resort are owned by **Financière Hôtelière Polynésienne (FHP)** and managed by **South Pacific Marketing (SPM)**, *reservations Tel. 689/42.68.55*. The Rangiroa Pearl Beach Resort will open in June 1999, with 40 units, also managed by SPM, which represents the 24 bungalow Hotel Hana Iti in Huahine, the 41 unit Te Tiare Beach Resort, which will open in Huahine in October 1998, the Keikahanui Noa Noa in Nuku Hiva, due to open with 20 units in June 1999, and the 14 unit Hanakee Noa Noa in Hiva Oa, also opening in June 1999. The existing hotels that are marketed by SPM in the Noa Noa category also include the 37 room Hotel Le Mandarin Noa Noa in Papeete, the 80 unit Moorea Village Noa Noa, the 11 bungalow Vahine Island Noa Noa in Tahaa, and the 17 room Revatua Club Noa Noa in Bora Bora.

The Bora Bora Pearl Cruises, which operates the *Haumana* passenger ship in the Leeward Society Islands, is also represented by South Pacific Marketing. **Hotel Management & Services (HMS)**, *Tel. 689/43.08.83*, will open 55 new units at Le Maitai Polynesia Bora Bora in June, 1998, incorporating the existing 10 units of Vairupe Villas to make a total of 65 units. Hotel Le Maitai Tenape will open 16 units in Raiatea during the first quarter of 1998.

7. BASIC INFORMATION

Listed here, in alphabetical order by topic, are practical information and recommendations for your trip to Tahiti and Her Islands.

BUSINESS HOURS

Several of the small restaurant/snacks and the Papeete Municipal Market, **le Marché**, open around 5am, and between 7:30-8am the post office, government offices, banks, airline offices, travel agencies and boutiques open. Many of the shops and offices still close for lunch between 12pm and 1:30 or 2pm, while others are now remaining open through the lunch period. Except for the restaurants and sidewalk cafés and bars, most of Papeete is closed down by 6pm.

The suburban shopping centers remain open until 7 or 8pm. Most businesses close at noon on Saturdays and all day Sunday and holidays. The food stores are open on Saturday afternoon and usually open on Sundays and holidays from 6 to 8am, with a few *magasins* remaining open until noon and then reopening between 5 and 7pm.

COST OF LIVING & TRAVEL

French Polynesia can be very expensive and it can also be affordable, depending on how you choose to go. I've been living in Tahiti and Moorea since 1971 and I have never ceased to be amazed at the costs. We pay the same prices as you will when we go to the restaurants and grocery stores, take a taxi or buy gas for our automobiles. Only recently have the residents begun to benefit from reductions on inter-island airfares, hotel rates and some of the excursions. Even the French visitors are surprised at the cost of living in Tahiti and Her Islands. The Japanese don't find it too expensive, but many Americans spend their entire vacation complaining about the cost of Coca-Cola, beer, water and food. Some of these tourists are so concerned with how much money they're spending that they cannot even enjoy their vacations.

Even though some of the prices here are still astronomical compared to what you'll pay in the United States, they are actually lower for many items than we paid a few years ago. I remember when a package of celery, or a head of cauliflower or broccoli cost 1.300 CFP ($13)! Now we consider ourselves lucky because we pay only 700 CFP ($7) for these precious imported items.

With the opening of the "mega" markets (Continent, Tropic Import, Cash and Carry and Casino) in Tahiti, competition brought the prices down. Larger supermarkets have also opened in the outer islands, providing a wider choice of goodies at slightly lower prices.

Hotel Rates

You won't find many real bargains for a hotel room in Tahiti and Her Islands, unless you get way off the tourist track. Have a look at the prices listed in the *Where to Stay* sections of each island chapter and you will see that a standard hotel room or bungalow in the most expensive hotels starts at 28.800 CFP ($288) double and goes up to 52.400 CFP ($540). The overwater bungalows, which are the most popular with honeymooners and other romantics, start at 24.000 CFP ($240) on Moorea and escalate to 71.000 CFP ($710) on Bora Bora. The rates for a standard double room in a medium-priced classified hotel start at 9.500 CFP ($95) in Tahiti, 6.500 CFP ($65) in Moorea, 4.500 CFP ($45) in Huahine, 5.500 CFP ($55) in Raiatea, 10.400 CFP ($104) in Bora Bora, 13.000 CFP ($130) in Rangiroa, and 7.500 CFP ($75) in Nuku Hiva.

There are no seasonal rates, but some of the hotels will reduce the Rack Rate if you walk in without a reservation during a slack period. July and August and the Christmas holidays are normally the busiest times of the year.

You will find some of the least expensive accommodations in the pensions, or family homes. These rates usually vary from 3.000 CFP ($30) a day to 10.000 CFP ($100) a day for two. Breakfast is sometimes included. A few of these facilities require a two-night minimum stay. Backpackers will pay 1.000 CFP ($10) a day for a bed in a dormitory, with reduced rates for the second day, and if you bring your tent, you can rent camping space for about 700 CFP ($7) for the first day and 500 CFP ($5) afterward. The backpacker hostels and campgrounds in Moorea often compete with one another, and lower their rates for a short period of time.

Transportation Costs

Tahiti's public transport system is provided by *le truck*, which has a brightly painted wooden cabin mounted on the rear of a flatbed truck. These colorful vehicles operate during the daylight hours, with night transportation provided from downtown Papeete to the airport and hotels on the west coast, as far as Sofitel Maeva Beach. The last run depends on what is happening in Papeete. Each *le truck* has a specific route, with the destination usually painted on the top or sides of the vehicle. The authorized stops are indicated by a blue sign with a drawing of *le truck*. Just wave to the driver to stop. Pay the driver on the right side of the cab when you get off. The minimum fare is 120 CFP ($1.20), which will get you from your hotel to downtown, and you'll have to pay 200 CFP ($2) at night. The Tahiti Manava Visitors Bureau can give you specific details on where to catch le *truck* to your destination.

Taxi fares will be one of your biggest shocks when you arrive in Tahiti. A ruling went into effect in 1990 stating that all taxis should be equipped with taxi meters, but some cabbies still have not installed the meters. Some of the drivers have stopped using the meters, claiming they are more expensive for the clients because the meter keeps running in traffic jams, which are a common occurrence when you get close to Papeete. The legal rates are supposed to be visibly displayed inside the cab and posted at the taxi stands. The flag-fall or minimum rate between 6am and 8pm is 800 CFP ($8), which is increased by 120 CFP ($1.20) for every kilometer after the first one. The minimum rate between 8pm and 6am is 1.200 CFP ($12) and 240 CFP ($2.40) per kilometer.

Between the airport and the hotels in Papeete the fare will be about 1.500 CFP ($15) during the day, and 1.000 CFP ($10) from the west coast hotels to the airport. A trip to the Gauguin Museum on Tahiti's south coast will cost 6.500 CFP ($65) one way, and a trip around the island of Tahiti is between 16.000 and 24.000 CFP ($160-$240), depending on how long you want to take. You will also be charged 100 CFP ($1) extra for each large bag of luggage transported and 50 CFP ($.50) for the smaller bags. Extra heavy bags cost more.

Rental cars are available on all the islands. You'll find the lowest fares on Tahiti, where you can rent a car for about 2.000 CFP ($20) a day, plus 35 CFP ($.35) a kilometer. An unlimited kilometer rate is 6.150 CFP ($61.50) a day, and special half-day rates are also available.

Gasoline is sold by the liter (4 liters = 1.06 gallons), and you'll pay 112 CFP (about $1.12 per liter or $4.48 per US gallon) for unleaded gas, which is used by all the rental cars. Costs are a little higher on the outer islands. Total and Mobil are sold by most service stations, and Shell has a few stations on the island of Tahiti.

ELECTRICITY

The current is 220 volts, 50 cycles in most hotels and family homes. Only the oldest hotels still use 110 volts. Most hotels provide 110-volt outlets for shavers, and hair dryers are provided in the most expensive hotels. It's best to ask the management before you plug in hair dryers, battery chargers and computers. Adapters are usually necessary for

American appliances, as the French plugs have two round prongs. You can bring your adapters with you or buy them at a general store here, and the hotels sometimes, but not always, have a transformer or converter for your electrical appliance.

FESTIVALS & HOLIDAYS

All the islands in French Polynesia celebrate New Year's Day, Missionaries Day (March 5), Good Friday, Easter, Easter Monday, May Day (May 1, which is Labor Day), Ascension Day (May 8), which is also Victory Day 1945, Pentecost (seventh Sunday after Easter), Pentecost Monday, Internal Autonomy Day (June 29), Bastille Day (July 14), Assumption (August 15), All Saints Day (November 1), Armistice Day 1918 (November 11) and Christmas Day.

All government offices, banks, airline offices, travel agencies and most private offices are closed on these days. If the holiday falls on a Thursday or Tuesday, quite often the businesses will make a bridge, giving their employees an extra day off to enjoy a long weekend.

See Chapter 8, *Calendar of Events.*

GETTING MARRIED

Tahiti, the Island of Love, has long been a favorite honeymoon destination for lovers of all ages. Getting married in Paradise has also become a popular activity for some of our visitors. In Tahiti, Moorea and Bora Bora couples from around the world are now saying "Oui" at the Mairie (Town Hall), "Hai" in the wedding chapels at the hotels, and "Eh" while standing in front of a Tahitian high priest.

Young Japanese couples choose to get married in French Polynesia to avoid the exorbitant costs of a wedding "correctly" done in Japan, which averages between $35,000-$40,000 for some 80 guests. Travel agencies and hotels in Tahiti take care of all the details, and the prospective newlyweds are already legally married according to Japanese law before they leave home. Along with their rented wedding clothes and rings, they bring a certificate of marriage, which has been completed and officially stamped at their own town hall. This paper must be translated and stamped at the French Embassy in Japan before a wedding can be performed in Tahiti.

Tying the knot in French Polynesia requires several steps and official stamps. For non-French applicants each person needs to furnish a birth certificate, must be of legal age, and must furnish a certificate of celibacy to prove that they have never been married. If they are divorced or widowed they must have the legal papers to prove that too. Birth certificates are required for any children of either party, and all these papers must be translated into French by a legal translator who has been granted an official stamp. All birth certificates must have been issued or translated in French within three months prior to application.

In addition, each spouse has to provide a pre-marriage medical certificate issued within the last two months. In order to verify if the projected marriage is not contrary to public order, the municipal authority has the right to demand a customary certificate from the foreign authorities, which can be either the ministry or consulate of your country. A certificate of residency is necessary to prove that one or both of the future spouses has an address or has established residency in one of the communes of French Polynesia for a minimum of one month's continued residency prior to the marriage date. The wedding will be performed at the Mairie in that commune.

The marriage bans will be posted for 10 days in the commune where the wedding will take place and in the last place of residence of the future spouse not residing in French Polynesia. If one of the applicants has neither address nor residence in French Polynesia, the wedding bans must be published in his/her place of residence and must be verified by a certificate of publication.

Tiki Village in Moorea specializes in creating authentic Polynesian weddings. Most lovers, however, get married back home and splurge for a fun-filled colorful wedding ceremony in the authentic tradition of old Polynesia. And it's not just newlyweds who are getting married in the Tahitian style, but also loving couples who are celebrating their anniversaries, who wish to renew their vows to one another. Polynesian weddings are also being performed at some of the international class hotels in Tahiti, Moorea, Huahine and Bora Bora.

Honeymoon Hotels

Most of the hotels with overwater bungalows have special honeymoon packages. Some of these hotels will upgrade honeymooners to overwater bungalows if there is a vacancy. Check the *Where to Stay* section of each island and contact the hotels directly for special programs for honeymooners. The sailboat charter companies also have cruising honeymoon programs.

HEALTH CONCERNS

On the island of Tahiti you will have access to a large government hospital, two private clinics and numerous medical specialists who provide good medical and dental services. In addition to the allopathic doctors, you have alternative health care in the form of homeopathic medicine, acupuncturists, Chinese herbalists, traditional Tahitian healers, massage therapy, magnetizers and thalassotherapy. Many of these specialists speak English. Moorea, Raiatea, Nuku Hiva and Tubuai have small hospitals, and all the other islands have medical centers, infirmaries or dispensaries. The more populous islands also have pharmacies and dentists. In Papeete there are optical services, where you can have minor repairs made to your eyeglasses, and should you need emergency attention for your hearing aid, that is also available.

All the islands maintain hygienic controls to combat potential epidemics of tropical diseases, such as the dengue fever, which is also known as "breakbone" fever, because of the intense pain in the head and muscles. This viral disease is carried by the *Aëdes aegypti* mosquito, which lives indoors and bites only during the daytime. In addition to a high fever, excruciating headache, pain in the joints and small of the back, and general feeling of weakness, the victims also develop an itchy body rash. Unfortunately, there is no vaccine, and you cannot take aspirin for the pains, as it may cause the stomach to bleed. The doctors can treat this disease with a *dengue cocktail*, which is an injection of Vitamin C and other vitamins, but the symptoms can last from a week to 10 days. There are several forms of *dengue*, and the most severe type can cause death in children, although this is very rare in French Polynesia.

Malaria is not present in the islands of French Polynesia, and the inhabitants generally have a high standard of health. There is an occasional outbreak of conjunctivitis, and some of the long time residents have suffered from filariasis or elephantiasis, an insect-borne disease that attacks the lymphatic system. Preventive medicine is distributed free every six months in all the islands, which keeps this disease well under control, and it is not a threat to the short-term visitor.

Pests & Pets

Mosquitoes are tropical pests, and in addition to the high cost of living and the noise of the roosters, the biggest complaints in French Polynesia are about the hungry mosquitoes, who just love fresh blood from our tourists. There's not much you can do about the inflated prices and the crowing rooster you'd love to throttle at 2-3-4-5am, but you can avoid being bitten. In the higher priced hotels, you will find an electric diffuser or mosquito destroyer that uses blue pastilles, treated with Allethrin, to ward off mosquitoes. Other lodgings usually provide mosquito coils that you can burn, or you can buy them at any food store. Keep a coil going all the time or change the anti-mosquito tablet every eight hours.

Bring a good mosquito repellent with you or go to the pharmacy once you're here and buy your defense products. I have found Dolmix Pic cream to be effective, which is sold in pharmacies. Aerogard spray or lotion is a good Australian product and can be purchased in the supermarkets. Tourists have also reported satisfactory results with *monoi* oil mixed with citronella, and this is available in most supermarkets, small *magasins* and hotel gift shops. My favorite anti-mosquito cream is Rid, which is made in Australia, but it is not sold in Tahiti. It is available in other Pacific Island groups, however. Be aware that mosquitoes will bite you day and night, and are most active when the weather is hot and sticky, which means during our rainy seasons. You have to remember to reapply your mosquito protection throughout the day or evening, especially if you are perspiring or swimming, as the water and sweat washes the product away.

On some of the islands, especially in the Marquesas, you may encounter the *nono*, which is a minuscule "no-see-um" sand fly with a nasty sting. They are most prevalent at daybreak and late in the afternoon, when they come to chew on your ankles. You might not even know you've been bitten until hours later, when the itching starts. Do not scratch it, however, as that will only aggravate the pain and cause an infected sore. Slathering yourself in oil is the best way to keep these little buggers at bay, as they just slide off your skin. Any kind of oil will do, although Avon's Skin So Soft from the States, or *monoi* oil, which is sold all over French Polynesia, will certainly smell better than cooking oil. Daily doses of 500 milligrams of vitamin B1 will help to ward off the pesky nonos.

If you do get stung by a mosquito, nono, wasp or bee, or cut yourself on coral, a good first aid treatment is to squeeze fresh lime juice on the wound to avoid infection. Cuts and scratches infect easily and take a long time to heal, so it is important to prevent any problems. Creams are also sold to take away pain from stings. Just remember to include an antibacterial cream in your traveling first aid kit, which you should definitely pack for your trip. The ingredients of such a kit will vary according to your own needs. The most important items to include would be any prescription drugs you take. Bring an extra pair of eye glasses if you use them.

Ciguatera

More than 400 species of lagoon and reef fish are potential carriers of **ciguatera**, a poisoning from eating infected fish. This phenomenon existed in some of the coral islands before the arrival of the first Europeans, and is caused by a microscopic marine organism that lives on or near the coral reef, especially reefs that have been disturbed by shipwrecks, port construction and other developments.

The larger carnivorous fish, such as the parrot fish, surgeon fish, coral bass, sea perch, snappers and jack crevallis are all potential carriers of ciguatera, as well as the big barracuda, as they tend to store the toxins found in the smaller coral fish on which they feed. The open ocean fish, such as mahi mahi, tuna, swordfish, salmon of the gods and marlin and other pelagics are safe to eat.

If you catch your own fish, it is best to get the advice of the local people before you cook it. They know which spots are more likely to be affected by ciguatera. The seafood served in the restaurants of French Polynesia is as safe as you'll find anywhere. Just avoid eating the head, gonads, liver and viscera of the fish.

Drinking Water

The Department of Health in French Polynesia reports that the tap water in Papeete has been treated with chlorine and is potable, and the water on the island of Bora Bora is drinkable. For the rest of the island of Tahiti and on all the other islands, it is advisable to drink bottled water. Eau Royale and Vaimato are two companies in Tahiti that sell bottled water, and the lab tests have given a higher rating to Vaimato for purity and cleanliness. There are also several brands of bottled water imported from France. Some of the hotels have water filter systems.

Sunshine

More vacations have been ruined from an overdose of sun than from any other factor. So many of the elderly tourists, who come ashore from their air-conditioned cruise ships, walk along the road in the heat and humidity of the noon day sun. Back home they drive round and round the parking lot, hoping to find a parking place close to the entrance to the shopping center or super market, yet when they come here, they decide to walk the equivalent of several blocks or even kilometers, with the sun blazing on their heads.

I have escorted groups of American doctors to Marlon Brando's atoll of Tetiaroa for a day tour. No matter how much they were warned about the dangers of the sun, when it was time to fly back to Tahiti in the afternoon, every doctor in the group, including the dermatologists, was red as a boiled lobster. The Tahitian name for white people is *popa'a*, which means "red lobster."

Fair-skinned people have to be especially careful in the tropics. Do your jogging, take your walk and work on your tan at the beginning of the morning or in the late afternoon, when the ultra violet rays are filtered by distant clouds low on the horizon. During your picnic on the *motu* or while riding in any open boat, make sure you apply a sufficiently strong sunscreen or sunblock (containing 25 to 50 sunburn protection factor) on all the exposed parts of your body, and wrap up like a mummy if there is no sun protector on the boat. Don't forget to rub the lotion on your feet and reapply the sunblock throughout the day, as you sweat and swim. Always wear a hat when exposed to the sun, and protect your nose and lips with zinc or a similar barrier cream.

Should you forget this advice and get yourself "cooked" while vacationing in Tahiti and Her Islands, there are several remedies to ease the pain and help the healing process. These include applying tomato juice or vinegar to the sunburned parts, as well as Calamine lotion, aloe vera gel, tamanu oil, and a range of other products, which are available at the pharmacies in your country and in Tahiti.

Diarrhea

The abundance of tropical fruits you'll find so tempting in Tahiti are also very good for you if you exercise moderation. If you go overboard on the mangoes, papayas, *pamplemousse* (sweet grapefruit), bananas, pineapple, passion fruit, custard apples, rambutan, carambolas (Chinese star apples), watermelon and other delicious fruits, you may regret it. Your system is not accustomed to so much Vitamin C, which can have a cataclysmic effect on your bowels.

The change of water, food and climate are the primary reasons for an upset digestive system. Drink bottled mineral water, eat in balanced proportions and get plenty of rest, and you will most likely avoid any disruptive problems. When you're packing for your trip to Tahiti, be sure to include a remedy for treating diarrhea. There are many products on the market from which to choose, such as Imodium and Lomotil.

Should symptoms of diarrhea manifest, it would be best to avoid the consumption of raw vegetables and chilled beverages. Eat steamed white rice and boiled eggs and yogurt, and drink lots of bottled water to restore body fluids lost through dehydration.

Sex in the South Seas

Exercise the same precautions you would apply back home. Since the arrival of the first European ships in 1767, Tahiti has earned a world-wide reputation as a sexually permissive port-of-call. Even with the strong influence of all the missionaries and church groups that have worked for over 200 years to change the sexual mores of the Polynesians, the promiscuous practices have not been completely eliminated.

Papeete is a hot-spot of very young female prostitutes and *mahu* (male transvestites), who frequent the nightclubs and bars and hang out on the corner of Boulevard Pomare and Avenue Prince Hinoi, looking for a pick-up. Safe sex in Tahiti often means that when boy meets girl for a clandestine rendezvous, they are both reasonably sure that his wives and girlfriends and her husband and/or boyfriends are not going to catch them in the act—this time. Even though there is an on-going educational program on the dangers of unprotected sexual encounters, there is still a reticence to put the knowledge into action. The Acquired Immune Deficiency Syndrome (AIDS) virus, known as SIDA in French, has already claimed several lives in Tahiti, and all the other sexually transmitted diseases are prevalent here as well.

Vaccinations

No immunizations are required for entry into French Polynesia unless you are arriving from an infected area. The U.S. State Department has a 24-hour **Travel Advisory**, *Tel. 202/647-5225; Web site http://travel.state.gov/travel_warnings.html* for up-to-date overseas health information, as well as crime and politics in foreign countries. The US Center for Disease Control in Atlanta, Georgia, gives travel advisories on an **International Traveler's Hotline**, *Tel. 404/332-4559, Fax 404/647-3000, Web site www.cdc.gov/travel/blusheet.htm.*

MAPS

Free maps of each island are available at **Tahiti Tourisme**, including a good map of downtown Papeete. The *Tahiti Beach Press* includes maps of Papeete and the islands of Tahiti, Moorea, Huahine and Bora Bora. You'll also find maps in the bookstores and newsstands. Pacific Promotion's *39 Tourist Maps of Tahiti and Her Islands* sells for about 1,000 CFP ($10) and includes the locations of all hotels and pensions. Librairie Klima *at Place Notre Dame in Papeete, Tel. 689/42.00.63*, sells oceanographic charts of the islands.

MONEY & BANKING

The **French Pacific franc**, written as **CFP** (*cour de franc Pacifique*), is the official currency of French Polynesia, and is on a parity with the French franc (5.5 CFP per FF)). The exchange rate for other currencies fluctuates daily. To determine the approximate amount of CFP you will get for one US dollar, check in your local newspaper for the number of French francs per dollar, and multiply that amount by 18.18. (Example: $1 = 5.5 French francs x 18.18 = 100 CFP).

The colorful CFP notes, which may look like play money to you, are issued in denominations of 500, 1.000, 5.000 and 10.000 francs (CFP); and coins are 1, 2, 5, 10, 20, 50 and 100 francs (CFP).

QUICK CURRENCY CONVERSION TRICK

A quick way to get an approximate dollar equivalent to the CFP is to drop the last two zeros of the price tag in Tahiti and Her Islands. For example, the cost of a pareo may be 1.000 francs or CFP, which is easy to think of as $10, and a black pearl for 150.000 francs or CFP is about $1,500.

To be more exact than the trick shown above, you should divide the cost of the item by the current exchange rate to determine the US dollar equivalent. At this writing, the exchange rate is around 108 CFP per US dollar, which means that you would actually pay $9.26 for your *pareo* and $1,389 for that beautiful black pearl. When you want to find the CFP rate in comparison to the US dollar, you multiply the amount of dollars you have to spend by the exchange rate.

Say that you have decided to buy a black pearl for no more than $1,500. You multiply $1,500 x 108, which gives you 162.000 CFP. That fabulous blue-green pendant you have fallen in love with has a price tag of 150.000 CFP, which converts to $1,389, or $111 less than your budget. Make sure you get a good discount from your sales clerk and you'll be able to buy a ring or earrings to match your pendant!

Bargaining or price haggling is not a custom in French Polynesia, but it is widely practiced in the black pearl industry. So, don't hesitate to ask for a discount when you're negotiating the purchase of a black pearl. This same technique should not be used when you're buying the $10 *pareo* or a $30 woven bag.

Ready Cash

Westpac and Socredo Banques have offices at the International Airport of Tahiti-Faaa, where you can buy CFP as soon as you arrive in Tahiti, and exchange your leftover francs for US dollars just before you leave.

Banque de Polynésie, Banque de Tahiti, Banque Socredo and Westpac have offices on the main islands. Banking hours are generally from 8am to 3:30pm, Monday through Friday, with branch offices closing two hours for lunch and remaining open until 5pm. and on Saturday morning. All the banks accept and issue travelers checks and have a currency exchange counter. Be prepared to pay the bank charge of 450-500 CFP ($4.50-$5) per transaction.

The automatic teller machine is a **TPE** (*traitement paiement electronique*), better known as a *distributeur*. All the banks listed above are now equipped with this handy service. The Banque de Tahiti has TPE machines in Tahiti, Huahine, Raiatea and Bora Bora, but not on Moorea, and you can use your American Express, Diner's Club, Mastercard and Visa cards to withdraw cash. When I asked Banque de Polynésie what international credit cards they accepted, they told me to call Socredo, which I did. Socredo's TPE machines accept Mastercard and Visa, with this service available in Tahiti, Moorea, Huahine, Raiatea and Bora Bora. Socredo also has a TPE machine at the Faaa International Airport. Westpac accepts American Express, JCB, Mastercard and Visa, with the TPE machines located in Tahiti, Moorea, Huahine, Raiatea, Tahaa, Bora Bora,

Rangiroa, Nuku Hiva and Hiva Oa in the Marques
Rurutu and Tubuai in the Austral Islands.

Currency Exchanges

An exchange office is located on the Papeete waterfront beside the passenger ship dock, just behind the Banque Socredo, and you'll find another exchange office just across the street from Club Med in Moorea. These offices are open when the banks are closed, especially on weekends, and they will supposedly give you the legal exchange rate for your dollars, pound sterling, marks, pesetas and yen.

Socredo Banque has installed an automatic currency exchange machine in the lobby of the Hotel Tahiti Beachcomber Parkroyal, and another one at the Socredo Banque Pomare, adjacent to Hotel Tiare Tahiti near the main post office on Boulevard Pomare in downtown Papeete. More of these machines are currently being installed in Tahiti, which makes it handy to exchange your American, Australian and New Zealand dollars, French francs, Italian lira, Japanese yen and German deutchmarks. The pound sterling and Swiss francs are supposed to be included in this service in the near future.

You can also exchange your dollars for CFP at your hotel, which is sometimes necessary, but you will not receive as good a rate as you'll get at the banks.

Credit Cards & Personal Checks

Visa is the most widely accepted credit card in the major tourist islands of French Polynesia, with Mastercard, American Express, JCB and Diner's Club respectively following. All the banks in Tahiti can help you with any questions regarding Visa and Mastercard. **Westpac Bank** , *Tel. 45.03.91,* and **Tahiti Tours**, *Tel. 54.02.50,* are the local representatives for American Express services; **Socredo Bank**, *Tel. 41.51.45,* handles JCB; and **Westpac**, *Tel. 46.79.79,* is the representative for Diner's Club. Some of the small hostels and pensions do not accept credit cards.

To secure a reservation in a hotel or hostel, you may send a personal check for the required deposit, but once you arrive, most businesses will not accept personal checks unless they are written on a local bank account. Some of the owners of art galleries and black pearl shops will occasionally accept a personal account on a foreign bank if you are making a big purchase.

MOVIES & VIDEO FILMS

The impact of movies showing the South Sea Islands has been so motivating that several people moved down here to live forever after seeing films such as *Tabu, Sadie Thompson* (also known as *Rain*), *Return to radise*, one or more versions of *Mutiny on the Bounty*, and the very popular *South Pacific*.

I was once the tour guide for a group of Japanese tourists, who sang "Bali Hai," "Bloody Mary," "Happy Talk" and other songs from *South Pacific* all day, as we drove around the island of Tahiti. This movie was not made in Tahiti, nor did the book or film ever indicate that Tahiti, Moorea or Bora Bora was the setting, yet many people still assume otherwise. The Bali Hai hotels on Moorea, Huahine and formerly on Raiatea were named for the movie, not the other way round. And the "Bali Hai" mountain on Moorea does not even resemble the "Bali Hai" of the movie. Still, escapist dreams are very good for tourism and for the well-being of the dreamer.

Movies to Set the Mood

Here is a list of movies that were either filmed in Tahiti, or supposedly used stories or settings from Tahiti. Perhaps you can locate a few of these in your local video rental stores. And you, too, can dream of Tahiti and Her Islands.

White Shadows in the South Seas (1927) was the first movie filmed in French Polynesia, which was shot in the Marquesas, and based on the book by Frederick O'Brien. The lovely "Polynesian" in the movie was Mexican actress Raquel Torres. *The Pagan* (1928), starred Ramon Navarro and Dorothy Janis. *Tabu* (1931) was filmed in Bora Bora, a Murnau-Flaherty production, starring Anna Chevalier as Reri. *Never the Twain Shall Meet* (1931) was a story about Tahiti, with Conchita Montenegro, that was filmed in Hawaii.

Bird of Paradise (1932), with Dolores Del Rio and Joel McCrea, was also made in Hawaii. *Mutiny on the Bounty* (1935), based on Charles Nordhoff and James Norman Hall's *Bounty Trilogy*, starred Charles Laughton as Captain Bligh, Clark Gable as Fletcher Christian and Mamo Clark as Maimiti. Most of this movie was filmed on Santa Catalina, off the California coast. This was the second *Bounty* movie; the first was an Australian production, starring Erroll Flynn. *Hurricane* (1937), John Ford's production based on Nordhoff and Hall's book of the same name, was the first of the "South Seas" films starring Dorothy Lamour and Jon Hall. *Aloma of the South Seas* (1941) was a story about Tahiti that was filmed in Puerto Rico, starring Dorothy Lamour and Jon Hall.

Son of Fury (1942), with Tyrone Power and Gene Tierny, was a Tahiti setting filmed at 20th Century Fox in Hollywood. *The Moon and Sixpence* (1941), Somerset Maugham's book about Paul Gauguin, starred George Sanders and Elena Verdugo (an Hispanic) who played the role of a Tahitian *vahine*. *South of Tahiti* (1941) starred Mexican actress Maria Montez as a Tahitian. The *Tuttles of Tahiti* (1942) was an amusing film based on *No More Gas*, a book by Nordhoff and Hall, starring Charles

Laughton and Jon Hall. *Bird of Paradise* (1951) was a remake of the film of 1932, with Debra Paget and Louis Jourdan, a story about Raiatea that was filmed in Hawaii. *Drums of Tahiti* (1953) was a made-in-Hollywood film with Dennis O'Keefe and Patricia Medina. *Cinerama South Sea Adventure* (1958) was filmed in Bora Bora, with Tahitian actress Ramine Allen-Buchin.

Enchanted Island (1958) was based on Herman Melville's book *Typee* about the Marquesas Islands. It was filmed in Mexico, with Dana Andrews and blue-eyed Jane Powell, who played a Polynesian. *Mutiny on the Bounty* (1962), MGM's successful film, was filmed in Tahiti and Bora Bora. Trevor Howard played the role of Captain Bligh and Marlon Brando was cast as the mutinous Fletcher Christian. Tarita Teriipaia, from Bora Bora, was Brando's Tahitian lady in the movie, and thus began a real-life relationship. *Tiko and the Shark* (1963) was also filmed in Bora Bora by MGM, with Hawaiian actors. *Donavan's Reef* (1963) was supposed to be Tahiti after World War II, but it was filmed on Kauai in Hawaii, with John Wayne, Lee Marvin and Dorothy Lamour.

Hurricane (1978) was the Dino de Laurentiis version of the Nordhoff and Hall book, which was also filmed on Bora Bora. Mia Farrow and Hawaiian Dayton Ka'ne played the lead roles. James Norman Hall's daughter, Nancy Hall, and her husband Nick Rutgers, were also in the film. *Beyond the Reef*, also known as *The Boy and The Shark*, was filmed on Bora Bora by de Laurentiis, immediately following the *Hurricane*, using some of the same decor. Dayton Ka'ne and Tahitian Keahi Farden were the stars. *The Bounty* (1984) was another movie version of the famous mutiny, which was filmed in Moorea with Mel Gibson as Fletcher Christian and Anthony Hopkins as a more sympathetic Captain Bligh. The *vahines* were all Tahitian. *A Love Affair* (1994) was a Warner Brothers movie filmed in Moorea, starring Warren Beatty and Annette Bening.

In addition to a government-owned audiovisual company, Tahiti has several private companies that produce video films on all the islands, from the land, sea and sky. The quality of the color is excellent and most, but not all, of these films are compatible with the American video systems. The Tahiti Tourisme office has a selection of promotional films for sale, and Tahiti Music, in front of the Notre Dame Cathedral in Papeete, has the largest choice of commercial films.

POST OFFICE & COURIER SERVICES

You can leave your American stamps at home because they won't be acceptable for mailing your postcards overseas from any of the islands in French Polynesia. I say this because I've met several Americans who do bring their stamps to Tahiti, thinking they'll be saving money on postage.

Each country has its own postal system, and in Tahiti this is an important source of revenue for the territory.

When we go on vacation most of us wait until the last few days before we mail our "Wish you were here" postcards home. As the airmail service from Tahiti to most overseas destinations takes anywhere from six to ten days to arrive, chances are the card will not get there before you do. If you post your mail from the international airport it will probably get processed faster and be put on the next departing flight.

The cost of mailing postcards to the US or Canada is 76 CFP ($.76) and it takes 94 CFP ($.94) to mail letters weighing less than 20 grams. Stamps can be purchased from all post office counters and from the hotel boutiques. A few of the newsstands and tourist shops also sell stamps, but you will have to go to the post office and stand in line if you want to make sure you've added enough postage to the envelope.

ADDRESSING A LETTER TO FRENCH POLYNESIA

When addressing a letter or package to anyone living in French Polynesia, it is necessary to include the name of the person, hotel or business, the B.P. (boîte postale) number, the zip code if known, the town or village where the post office is located, the island and the country. Example: **Jan Prince, B.P. 298, 98728 Maharepa, Moorea, French Polynesia.** *On some of the islands the PK number is used instead of a B.P., which should always be followed by the name of the village and any other specifics you may have, then the name of the island and country. Example:* **Jan Prince, Chez Wilder, PK 12.5, côté montagne, Pihaena, Moorea, French Polynesia.***

You'll notice only a few zip codes included in the addresses in this guide. This is a new addition to our postal services, and many of the businesses haven't added their zip codes to their published information. Most people don't even know what their zip code is. I haven't included the name of the country in the addresses given in this book, but each address should always include the name of the island, followed by French Polynesia.

The main post office is on Boulevard Pomare in downtown Papeete. Services include stamps for letters and parcels, express delivery service, international telephone calls, telegrams, telex, fax, phone cards and a philatelic center. This post office is open Monday to Friday 7am to 6pm, and on Saturday from 8 to 11 am for postal services, and until 6pm for telephone and fax service. The post office inside the international terminal at Faaa airport is open Monday to Friday 7am to 6pm, and on Saturday and Sunday 6 to 10 am. You can also make international phone calls from this small office. There are post offices on all the inhabited islands of French Polynesia, which are open Monday through Thursday 7am to 3pm, and on Friday 7am to 2pm.

General Delivery mail service is available at all the post offices. On the envelope you should write the person's name, c/o Poste Restante, and the name of the island, and make sure that this is followed by French Polynesia.

B.P. = *bôite postale* **or post office box**

You will note that most of the addresses listed in this book show the initials B.P., which stand for *bôite postale*, the equivalent of post office box in the US. You can write P.O. Box or B.P. and your letter to French Polynesia will be processed with no problem.

PK = *poste kilometre*, **the number of kilometers from the** *mairie* **or post office**

Should you be given an address with a PK number instead of B.P., on the island of Tahiti, this indicates how many kilometers that person lives from the *mairie* (town hall) in Papeete. On other islands, such as Moorea, the 0 kilometer can be at the post office. PK stands for *poste kilometre*, and when you're driving around Tahiti, Moorea, Huahine, Raiatea, Tahaa and Bora, you will see the kilometer markers on the mountain side of the road. Look for the red-capped white painted stone or concrete markers with the kilometer number painted in black on two sides.

The Philatelic Center of the Offices Des Postes et Télécommunications in Tahiti is located in the main post office, where you can buy sets of collector stamps, along with a stamped "first day" envelope. The themes for these beautiful stamps include the fruits, flowers, fishes and fauna of Polynesia, along with pictures of pretty *vahines*, fancy hats, outrigger sailing canoes, old *goelette* schooners and lovely seascapes. All the major post offices in the islands also carry selections of these collectors' items.

DHL Worldwide Express is located at the *Tahiti-Faaa International Airport, B.P. 6480, Faaa, Tahiti, French Polynesia, Tel. 689/83.00.24, Fax 689/83.76.27.* The office is open daily 7am to 5pm. Three-day delivery service will get your package home in a hurry, for a cost of 7.700 CFP ($77) per 500 grams.

PUBLICATIONS ABOUT TAHITI

Newspapers & Magazines

Tahiti Beach Press is a 16-page English language tabloid that is published weekly for tourists and distributed free of charge to hotels in Tahiti, Moorea, Huahine, Raiatea, Bora Bora and Rangiroa. You can also pick up a copy at Tahiti Tourisme, the airports, ferry docks, car-rental agencies, and in the restaurants and businesses who advertise in the paper. *Tahiti Today, B.P. 887, Papeete, Tahiti, French Polynesia,* is a 16-page English language quarterly tabloid that is sold to subscribers ($34 air-mail for one-year subscription to US) published by the same company, and *Tahiti Beach Press* also publishes a quarterly newspaper in French. You can also read the *Tahiti Beach Press* on the Internet at *http://www.fix.net/ percent7Ewdavis/tahiti-beach-press.html.*

La Dépêche de Tahiti and *Les Nouvelles* are Tahiti's two daily French-language newspapers. The *International Herald Tribune, USA Today, Time* and *Newsweek* are sold at Le Kiosk in front of the Vaima Center on Boulevard Pomare in Papeete, at Supersonics in Moorea's Le Petit Village, and in the boutiques of the larger hotels. *Tahiti Pacifique Magazine* is a popular monthly publication in French, with a long list of subscribers. *Air Tahiti Magazine* is published in French and English, a quarterly on-board magazine that is also available for subscription.

Books

In 1968, when I knew that I would be coming to Tahiti, Moorea and Bora for a three-week vacation, I visited the Public Library in Houston, Texas, each week for six months prior to getting on the airplane. During that period I checked out each available book on Tahiti and the South Pacific, and thoroughly did my homework before making my first visit. During my 27-year residence in Tahiti and Moorea, I have had access to the best private libraries in Tahiti, and have made my own collection of reference books and armchair favorites of old tales of the romantic South Seas. Yet, I have not even touched the tip of the iceberg in discovering the wealth of published material on Tahiti and Her Islands.

Due to the limits of space available for the subject, I will give you an abbreviated list of recommended reading and reference material, which you may still find in the public libraries, specialized book stores and secondhand shops. Free catalogs of publications may be requested from: **Bishop Museum Press**, *P.O. Box 19000-A, Honolulu, HI 96817-0916, Tel. 808/848-4135;* **University of Hawaii Press**, *2840 Kolowalu Street, Honolulu, HI 96822;* **The Book Bin**, *351 NW Jackson Street, Corvallis, OR 97330;* **Mutual Publishing**, *2055 N. King Street, Suite 201, Honolulu, HI 96819;* **Colin Hinchcliffe**, *12 Queens Staith Mews, York, Y01 1HH, England; and* **Société des Océanistes Catalogue**, *Musée de l'Homme, 75116, Paris, France.*

Reference Books

Ancient Tahiti (Bulletin 48 Bernice P. Bishop Museum, Honolulu) by Teuira Henry, is based on material recorded by her grandfather, the Reverend J. M. Orsmond, who came to Moorea as a Protestant missionary in 1817. This is my primary reference book for the plants, flowers, trees, religion, culture and legends of the Society Islands.

Ancient Tahitian Society (The University Press of Hawaii, Honolulu, 1974) is a three-dome collection by Douglas L. Oliver. These scholarly studies are an excellent reference for the history and culture of the Tahitians.

Bengt Danielsson, a Swedish anthropologist and historian, who crossed the Pacific from Peru to the Tuamotus with Thor Heyerdahl aboard the *Kon-Tiki* raft in 1947, settled in Tahiti until his death in 1997, and published a wide variety of books. They include: *The Happy Island* (London, 1952), *Work and Life on Raroia* (Stockholm, 1955), *From Raft to Raft* (London, 1960), *Forgotten Islands of the South Seas, Love in the South Seas* (Mutual, 1986), *Tahiti-Circle Island Tour Guide* (Les Editions du Pacifique, 1976), and *Moruroa Mon Amour–the French Nuclear Tests in the Pacific* (1977), by Bengt & Marie-Thérèse Danielsson.

Fatu-Hiva–Back to Nature (Penguin Books, 1976) is Thor Heyerdahl's account of the sojourn he and his wife undertook for more than a year on this lonely island in the Marquesas Archipelago, just before the outbreak of World War II.

History and Culture in the Society Islands (Honolulu, 1930), *Marquesan Legends* (Honolulu, 1930), *Polynesian Religion* (Honolulu, 1927), and *The Native Culture in the Marquesas*, Honolulu, 1923), all by Craighill Handy. *Landfalls of Paradise: The Guide to Pacific Islands* (Western Marine Enterprises, Inc., Marina del Ray, California, 1986), by Earl Hinz, who sailed the South Pacific aboard his yacht *Horizon*, along with his wife Betty. They dropped anchor in Honolulu for several years, where Earl wrote his books and magazine articles. Finally, they gave up the sea and now live in the desert near Las Vegas.

Pacific Islands Yearbook (Fiji Times, 1995) editors Norman and Ngaire Douglas, is a good reference book on all the islands, which is updated on a regular basis. *Polynesian Researches* (1829) by William Ellis, is a two-volume work by a missionary who spent nearly six years in the South Sea Islands. *Polynesia's Sacred Isle* (Dodd, Mead & Company, New York, 1976), by Edward Dodd, is part of a three-volume *Ring of Fire* set about the island of Raiatea.

Ra'ivavae–An expedition to the most fascinating and mysterious island in Polynesia (Doubleday & Company, Inc., New York, 1961). Author-anthropologist Donald Marshall describes life on Ra'ivavae, one of the Austral islands south of Tahiti.

Return to the Sea (John deGraff, Inc., New York, 1972), by William Albert Robinson, is the story of Robinson's 70-foot brigantine *Varua*, in which he sailed to Tahiti in 1945, to settle in Paea, where his house still stands. Robinson used *Varua* as a floating laboratory to travel throughout the Pacific Islands, helping to eradicate the filariasis parasite transmitted by mosquitoes that causes elephantiasis.

Robert Suggs, an American archaeologist who did seminal work for the American Museum of Natural History of New York in the Marquesas Islands during the 1950s and 1960s, has written *The Island Civilizations of Polynesia* (New American Library, Mentor Books, New York, 1960), *Hidden Worlds of Polynesia* (Harcourt, Brace and World, New York, 1963) and *Marquesan Sexual Behavior* (Harcourt, Brace and World, New York, 1966), which are interesting reading and good reference books for anyone interested in the Marquesas Islands.

Tahiti, Island of Love by Robert Langdon, is a popular account of Tahiti's history, and it's easy reading. *Tahitian Journal* (University of Minnesota Press, 1968) is a diary written by George Biddle between 1917 and 1922, along with paintings and drawings by the author. The setting is Tautira on the Tahiti-Iti peninsula, where Biddle lived among the Tahitians. *Tahitians–Mind & Experience in the Society Islands* (University of Chicago Press, 1973) by Robert I. Levy is an anthropologist's reference book for anthropologists, containing a wealth of cultural information. *The Journals of Captain James Cook* (Cambridge University, 1955, 1961, 1967), edited by J. C. Beaglehole, were published in three volumes.

Novels, Island Tales & Modern Accounts

Come Unto These Yellow Sands (Bobbs-Merrill Company, 1940) by author, artist and anthropologist Earl Schenck, combines fact with fiction in a captivating tale that takes us to various islands of the South Pacific, including Tahiti, Bora Bora and to the distant atolls of Hikueru and Vahitahi in the Tuamotus, the Dangerous Archipelago.

Manga Reva–the Forgotten Islands (Mutual Publishing Paperback Series, Tales of the Pacific, Honolulu, 1931) by Robert Lee Eskridge, tells the story of an American artist who arrived in Tahiti in 1927 aboard the SS *Makura*, became friends with Queen Marau, and set off for the remote Gambier Islands to discover the "Forgotten Islands." His book tells about Father Laval, the "mad builder priest" who ruled the Gambiers with a Jesuit rod early in the nineteenth century, and killed thousands of Polynesians who built his great Cathedral of the Jungles in Manga Reva.

Mystic Isles of the South Seas (Garden City Publishing Company, Inc., New York, 1921) by Frederick O'Brien, is based on his visit to Tahiti during one of three journeys he made to the South Seas. His story of Lovina Gooding, the colorful character who owned the Tiare Hotel in Papeete, is classic. O'Brien's *White Shadows in the South Seas* are about the Marquesas Islands, and *Atolls of the Sun* feature the Tuamotu Archipelago.

Numerous Treasure (Jacobsen Publishing Company, Inc., New York, 1930), is a Romantic Novel by Robert Keable, whose former home still stands on a bluff in Papeari, overlooking Port Phaeton and the Tahiti-Iti peninsula.

Planter's Punch (Appleton-Century-Crofts, Inc., New York, 1962) by Margaret Curtis, is an autobiographical account of an English opera singer who met and married wealthy American Carl Curtis in 1932 while sailing to the South Seas aboard the *Stella Polaris*. Curtis took his new bride home to Tahiti to live in his big white rambling house on a coconut plantation in Mahina. This house is still standing and has been known throughout the years as the Brander House, the Curtis Mansion, Martin Mansion and the White House.

Point Venus (Little, Brown and Company, 1951) by Susanne McConnaughey, is a fictional account of the English Protestant missionaries in Tahiti during the era of Queen Pomare and the French takeover.

Rainbow in Tahiti (Hammond, Hammond & Co., Ltd., London, 1951) is Caroline Guild's story of a charmed, easy life in Tahiti in the 1920s and 1930s, where she and her husband, Eastham, had an estate in Paea, near the fern grottos of Mara'a. Due to the influence of Zane Grey, who also lived in Tahiti at that time, the Guilds took up sports fishing. Carolyn landed an 823-pound black marlin in New Zealand to set a world's record.

Tahiti (Grant Richards Ltd., London) by Tihoti, the Tahitianized name of George Calderon, who visited Tahiti in 1906. He was killed in the war in Gallipoli in 1915, and the book was completed from his notes. This is truly a collector's item and is illustrated with Calderon's drawings of the people he met while wandering around the island of Tahiti.

Tales of the South Pacific (1947) and *Return to Paradise* by James A. Michener, are all-time classics by a very descriptive writer.

The Blue of Capricorn (1977) by Eugene Burdick, takes you from Polynesia, to Melanesia and Micronesia.

The Bounty Trilogy (1932) by Charles Nordhoff and James Norman Hall, comprises the three volumes of *Mutiny on the Bounty*, *Men Against the Sea* and *Pitcairn's Island*.

The Dark River (1946) by Charles Nordhoff and James Norman Hall, is set in the wild and natural *fenua 'aihere*—the Land of Forests—of the Taiarapu peninsula on Tahiti-Iti. The descriptions of this savage beauty transport us right onto the scene of this lonely land.

The Hurricane (1935) by Charles Nordhoff and James Norman Hall, is an exciting story set in the Dangerous Archipelago of the Tuamotus.

The Lure of Tahiti–An Armchair Companion (Edited by A. Grove Day and published by Mutual Publishing Company, Tales of the Pacific, Honolulu, 1986). An entertaining selection of stories by 17 authors, including Rupert Brooke, Paul Gauguin, Jack London, Pierre Loti, Charles Darwin, William S. Stone, James Norman Hall, James A. Michener and some of the early explorers.

The Moon and Sixpence (Penguin Books, 1945-1977), first published in 1919, is W. Somerset Maugham's story of Charles Strickland, a London stockbroker, who abandons family and career to become a painter in Tahiti, suggested by the life of Paul Gauguin.

To Live in Paradise (Armand Denis, 801 W. Covina Blvd., San Dinas, CA 91773, Tel. 626/909-8931). Published in 1996, this book by Renée Roosevelt Denis, a long-time resident of Tahiti and Moorea, is an autobiography that takes us from Bali to Haiti to Tahiti. Renée's book is filled with tales of adventure with her grandfather, André Roosevelt, her famous parents, her Tahitian husband and children, her years with Club Med in Moorea and her meetings with Marlon Brando on his private atoll in Tetiaroa. This book is currently available in all the bookstores in Tahiti and Moorea and in the hotel gift shops on all the major tourist islands.

Two-Thirds of a Coconut Tree (Little, Brown and Company, 1963) is the most hilarious book I've ever read about Tahiti. Author H. Allen Smith and his wife, Nelle, spent six months in Tahiti just after the international airport opened in the early 1960s. Although local residents recall Smith as being drunk the whole time he was here, his written humor was always intact. He calls names and says what he feels about everyone.

Typee: a Real Romance of the South Seas; Omoo; a Narrative of Adventures in the South Seas, a Sequel to Typee and Marquesas Islands by Herman Melville are all based on Melville's experiences in the islands.

Books Available in English in Tahiti

I am including this list so that you will know what to look for when you come here. Some of the books are available in the States. You might also contact the following bookstores in Tahiti that carry the best selection of books in English, as well as the individual publishers.

Galerie "Point Art" is the Polynesian section of the **Librarie du Vaima,** *B.P. 2399, Centre Vaima, Papeete, Tahiti, Tel. 689/45.57.44/45.57.57, Fax 689/45.53.45;* **Archipels,** *B.P. 20676, 68, rue des Remparts, Papeete, Tahiti, Tel. 689/42.47.30, Fax 689/45.10.27.* For books on art and Paul Gauguin, as well as the pamphlets listed below, contact the **Paul Gauguin Museum** at *B.P. 7029, Taravao, Tahiti, Tel. 689/57.10.58, Fax 689/ 57.42.10.* For the brochures published by **Pacific Promotion**, contact Teva Sylvain at *B.P. 625, Papeete, Tahiti 98713, Tel. 689/42.43.11, Fax 689/ 42.25.98.*

A Tahitian and English Dictionary (Haere Po No Tahiti, 1985) with introductory remarks on the Polynesian language and a short grammar of the Tahitian dialect. This was first printed in 1851 at the London Missionary Society's Press.

Atoll (Scoop - Tahiti, 1992) is an illustrated 44-page pamphlet by Jean-Louis Saquet, that illustrates the geology of the atolls, the surrounding lagoon, coral reefs and ocean shelf, and the flora and fauna that inhabit these "desert isles" of dreams.

Birds of Tahiti (Les Editions du Pacifique, 1975) with text by Jean-Claude Thibault and photographs by Claude Rives, features the land and sea birds of the Society Islands.

Black Pearls of Tahiti (Tahiti, 1987) by Jean Paul Lintilhac, is an informative, authoritative and factual book, with good photographs, providing all you want to know about the black pearls.

Bora Bora (Les Editions du Pacifique, 1974, 1980), with text by Erwin Christian and Raymond Bagnis, features the wonderful photography of Bora Bora resident, Erwin Christian.

Bora Bora, Impressions of an Island (Kea Editions, 1996), contains 95 photos by Erwin Christian.

Diving in Tahiti–a Diver's Guide to French Polynesia (Les Editions du Pacifique, 1991) by Thierry Zysman has an introduction to diving in French Polynesia, plus detailed descriptions and photographs of specific dive sites in Tahiti, Moorea, Huahine, Raiatea, Tahaa, Bora Bora, Rangiroa and Manihi.

Fishes of Polynesia (Les Editions du Pacifique, 1972, 1987), by residents Raymond Bagnis, Philippe Mazellier, Jack Bennett and Erwin Christian, is a coffee-table book with photos and descriptions of the lagoon, reef and ocean fish, and their scientific, Tahitian and English names.

Hiva Oa, Glimpses of an Oceanic Memory (Departement Archeologie, 1991) by Pierre Ottino and Marie-Noële de Bergh-Ottino, reports on their archaeological work on Hiva Oa, and their scholarly 50-page booklet is filled with historical information and maps on the Marquesas Islands.

Islands of Tahiti (Kea Editions, 1991) by Raymond Bagnis, with photos by Bora Bora resident, Erwin Christian, is a coffee-table book on all the island groups of French Polynesia.

Moorea (Millwood Press, Wellington, New Zealand, 1974), is a photographic book by James Siers.

Noa Noa by Paul Gauguin is an autobiographical account of his life in Tahiti.

Plants and Flowers of Tahiti (Les Editions du Pacifique, 1974) with text by Jean-Claude Celhay and photography by Bernard Hermann, is a colorful 143-page reference book that is very helpful for amateur botanists.

Sharks of Polynesia (Les Editions du Pacifique, 1978), with text and photography by Richard H. Johnson, an American marine biologist and shark expert, who operates Tahiti Aquatique, a nautical activities center adjacent to Hotel Sofitel Maeva Beach in Tahiti.

Tahiti Blue and Other Modern Tales of the South Pacific (Les Editions de Tahiti, Tahiti, 1990) by Alex du Prel. He is also editor of *Tahiti Pacifique Magazine*, which he publishes monthly in French from his home on Moorea.

Tahiti from the Air (Les Editions du Pacifique, 1985) by Erwin Christian and Emmanuel Vigneron, has aerial photos of French Polynesia as it was in the mid-1980s.

Tahiti, the Magic of the Black Pearl (Tahiti, 1986) by Paule Solomon is poetic, ethereal and has beautiful photographs.

Tahiti–The Other Side (Institute of Pacific Studies of the University of the South Pacific, in association with Editions Haere Po No Tahiti, 1983) is a social study made by Marc Cizeron, Marianne Hienly and several others, to reveal the people who live on the mountainside of Tahiti, far from the postcard scenery and glamour of a Polynesian Paradise.

Tahitian Island Cooking (Arapoanui Edition, 1988), with text by Jean Galopin and photography by Jean-Claude Bosmel, is a beautifully presented coffee-table book that will have your mouth watering when you read Galopin's recipes, which he prepares and serves in his Auberge du Pacifique Restaurant in Punaauia, on Tahiti's southwest coast.

Tatau–Maohi Tattoo (Tupuna Productions, 1993) by Dominique Morvan, photographs by Claude Corault and Marie-Hélène Villierme, traces the resurgence of traditional tattooing in French Polynesia. Black-and-white photos of the geometrical Polynesian tattoos.

The Dance of Tahiti (Les Editions du Pacifique, 1979), by Jane Freeman Moulin, presents the traditional dances of Tahiti from A to Z, along with photos and illustrations of the movements.

The Marquesas (Les Editions du Pacifique, 1982), with text by Greg Dening and photography by Erwin Christian, presents Te Henua Te Enata, the Land of Men.

The Tahiti Handbook (Editions Avant et Après, 1993) by Jean-Louis Saquet covers French Polynesia's geography, history, and natural history with general information on marine life, plant life, canoe design and arts and crafts.

Tuamotu (Les Editions du Pacifique, 1986), with text by Dominique Charnay and photographs by Erwin Christian, covers the history, geography, flora and fauna, and daily life in the remote atolls of the Tuamotu archipelago.

Underwater Guide to Tahiti (Les Editions du Pacifique, 1977, 1980), with text by Raymond Bagnis and photography by Erwin Christian, presents the reefs and lagoons, the living environment, distribution of living organisms and the species of inhabitants in this threatened submarine world.

Pamphlets/Booklets Sold in Tahiti
Pacific Promotion Tahiti has published a number of pamphlets on Tahiti and Her Islands, which are filled with the colorful photographs of owner Teva Sylvain, who also issues calendars and post cards. These

publications include: *Circle Island Tour Guide to Tahiti, Souvenir Guide to Bora Bora, 39 Tourist Maps of Tahiti and Her Islands, Tupai Island, Flowers of Tahiti, Orchids of Tahiti, The Fishes of Tahiti, Natural Dangers in Tahiti, Bora Bora-History and GIs in Paradise* (text by Thomas J. Larson & Alex W. du Prel), *Gauguin and the Tahitian* (text by Loana Sanford) and others.

The Société des Océanistes and Les Nouvelles Editions Latines in Paris have issued several informative pamphlets that are sold in the bookstores in Tahiti and the hotel boutiques in the islands. These include booklets on *Ancient Tahiti, Ancient Tahitian Canoes, Bora Bora, Botanical Garden of Papeari, Bougainville in Tahiti, Cartographic Handbook of French Polynesia, Childhood in Tahiti, Dancing in Tahiti, Gauguin in Tahiti, Huahine, Moorea, Painters in Tahiti, Pomare–Queen of Tahiti, Protestant Church at Tahiti, Sacred Stones & Rites of Tahiti, Short Flora of Tahiti, Stamps and Postal History of Tahiti, Tahiti From Word to Paper, Tahitian Catholic Church, Tahitians of the Past, The Fairyland of Useful Shells, Traditional Art of Tahiti, Useful Plants of Tahiti, Whaling Off Tahiti,* and others.

RADIO

Radio Television Française d'Outre-Mer (RFO), also known as Radio Tahiti, is the official station, which operates with French and Tahitian broadcasts on several AM and FM frequencies. Some of the mayors in Tahiti have their own FM radio stations, where political messages in French and Tahitian are interspersed with a musical melange of rap, rock, reggae, religion and Tahitian favorites, as well as death announcements and other local news.

Should you bring your walkman or other transistor radio with you, then you can just turn the dial from 88.6 to 106, until you find music to your liking. Don't rely on your radio for soft music for dreaming while you contemplate the clouds or classical music for a superb sunset. You'll have a hard time finding it. More than half the population here is under 20 years old, and the music is played primarily for that audience.

RETIRING IN TAHITI

A few American couples have bought retirement homes in Tahiti or Moorea. It is still possible to buy land or houses in French Polynesia, and each application is studied individually. French Polynesia is not an immigration country, and President Gaston Flosse is opposed to opening the doors even to the European Economic Community, to which French Polynesia belongs through its association with France. Contact your nearest French Consulate for the necessary papers to apply for a residence visa.

SHOPPING

All the main tourist islands have souvenir shops and arts and crafts centers, where you can find hand-painted *pareos*, locally made T-shirts, carved Marquesan bowls, ceremonial spears, drums, ukuleles, tables and tikis, plus tapa bark paintings, Tahitian dancing costumes, basketry and woven hats, shell jewelry, mother-of-pearl creations, *tifaifai* bed covers, vanilla beans, Tahitian music and video films, *monoi* oil, soaps and perfumes, and beautiful black pearls.

Tahitian Black Pearls

The emerald and turquoise lagoons of the Tuamotu and Gambier Islands of French Polynesia are a natural haven for the black-lipped oyster, the *Pinctada Margaritifera (Cumingi variety)*, which produces the world's finest black pearls. At the beginning of the 19th century the lagoons of Polynesia were filled with pearl oysters, also called *nacres*. From 1802-1940 the smoky gray mother-of-pearl shell was sought after as material for buttons. With the introduction of water-tight diving glasses the divers could go deeper and deeper to find oysters of an acceptable size, as they exhausted the ready supply. With the advent of synthetic buttons and the depletion of accessible oysters in the lagoons, the adventurous days of the famous South Seas pearl divers ended after World War II, with controlled diving seasons continuing into the 1960s.

During the highlight of the pearl diving days there was an average of one black pearl found among 15,000 oysters killed. The *Pinctada margaritifera* came very close to extinction, until researchers experimented with techniques to harvest the spawn of the *nacre* to collect the baby spats that would grow into oysters.

The first trials were made at culturing black pearls in the lagoon of Hikueru in 1962 and in Bora Bora in 1964, using the grafting technique that was invented in Japan in 1893, and refined by Mikimoto in the early 1900s. The first undersea pearl farm was established in the lagoon of Manihi in the 1970s, and the culturing of black pearls has slowly grown from an isolated experiment into an industry. In 1976 the Gemnological Institute of America (G.I.A.) gave formal recognition to the authentic character of the cultured pearls of Tahiti, and in 1989 the official designation of this gem became "Perle de Culture de Tahiti," the label decided upon by the *Confederation Internationale de la Bijouterie Joaillerie et Orféverie* (CINJO). Today there are more than 1,000 functioning pearl farms, essentially in the Tuamotu and Gambier atolls, with a few small pearl farms in the Society Islands of Huahine, Tahaa and Maupiti.

The Tahitian black pearl is French Polynesia's biggest export item and the most sought after souvenir purchase made by visitors to Tahiti and Her Islands. Just a few years ago the black pearl was virtually unknown in the United States, and today you can buy black pearl jewelry through the Home Shopper's Channel on television.

When you shop for your black pearls you can make a better choice if you know what to look for in choosing a quality pearl. The main criteria are: size, shape, surface quality, luster and color.

Black pearls range in diameter from 7 millimeters to more than 20 millimeters, but the average size is 9.5-11.5 millimeters, and anything over that is considered large. The bigger the pearl, the more it costs.

The shape or form of the pearl is judged by roundness and symmetry. They are graded as round, semi-round, semi-baroque, baroque and circle. The round pearls are rarer, therefore more expensive, but a drop or pear shaped pearl that is perfectly symmetrical can be as expensive as a round pearl.

The pearls are graded Gem, A, B, C, and D quality according to the number of flaws, pits, scratches and rays that blemish the surface. A "Gem" quality pearl is extremely rare as it is perfect, with no blemishes. About five percent of each harvest consists of "A" quality pearls, with only one or two small flaws and 90 percent of the surface remaining clean. "B" quality pearls have two to five flaws with 67 percent of the surface flawless. The majority of pearls are "C" quality, with more than five flaws and a minimum of 33 percent of the surface is clean. A "D" quality pearl has more than five flaws and looks like your dog has been chewing on it, leaving lots of tooth marks.

The most important ingredient is luster or orient, which is the radiance of the pearl, the mirror-like shine on the surface and the inner-layer quality that reflects the light.

The color of a black pearl may range from white to lunar gray, with gradations of cream, peacock green, rainbow tints, aubergine (eggplant), blue, pink and golden. Black pearls are rarely black, which may come as a surprise to you, but they are called black pearls because they come from the black-lipped oyster.

The color of the pearl depends on the color of the mantle or lip of the donor oyster used to graft into the producing oysters during the cultivating process. The grafter trims the outer mantle, the epithelium, of a donor oyster and cuts it into about 50 small pieces. Then he takes one tiny sliver of this living cell and transplants it into the gonad gland of a three-year old oyster, along with a nucleus, a small white round ball that is made from the shell of the Mississippi River mussel. The grafted oysters are then placed in wire nets and suspended from platforms under the lagoon, where they live for 18 months while the oyster is covering the nucleus with up to 16,000 micron-thin layers of mother-of-pearl, which is comprised of aragonite. The pearls that are produced from the slivers of mantle from one oyster will all be different, as there are no two pearls exactly alike. Color is also affected by the mineral salts present in the water, the degree of salinity, the plankton that the oysters feed on, and the water temperature. Although some pearl sales people will tell you that the color of a pearl does not affect the price, it actually does. Pearls with a prevalence of white or gray are priced lower and black pearls with rare hues, such as rainbow, aubergine, fly-wing green and shiny black, are more expensive.

There are numerous pearl shops in Tahiti, and if you have the stamina and the perseverance, you can check out all the most obvious boutiques and sales rooms in downtown Papeete and at the hotels. Tahiti Pearls is the biggest supplier of fine quality black pearls in the world, and they have an exquisite collection of pearls and jewelry made with pearls. At Tahiti Pearl Museum near the Protestant Temple on Boulevard Pomare in Papeete you can watch a video film and see a replica of a pearl farm, which will give you a basic education on pearls. You'll also enjoy looking at their beautiful but very pricey black pearl jewelry.

At the end of 1998, Tahiti Pearls will move to the **Vaima Center** and will open a big museum with paid entry. On rue Jean Gilbert in the Quartier du Commerce in downtown Papeete, behind Tahiti Sports, you have several choices of black pearl shops. Pai Moana Pearls has their own pearl farm in Manihi, managed by American marine biologist, Doctor Rick Steger, who is the partner of Peter Ringland, a Canadian expatriate, who also has two shops on Moorea. They have a nice selection of unset pearls, and I personally like the goldwork of their jeweler, Jacques, who can create your jewelry for you overnight. Facing Pai Moana Pearls is Pacific Black Pearls, which offers a good quality-price ratio and a large selection of loose and set pearls.

My recommendation for choosing your pearl is to find a sales person you like and a pearl that "winks" at you. I sold pearls on a part-time basis in Moorea for five years, and I learned that certain pearls naturally attract the attention of the person who should be wearing them. They have their own magic, you know. In the outer islands, such as Moorea and Bora Bora, some of the pearl shops are owned by people who have their own pearl farms and jewelers, or they own the shop, so there's no middle man to pay. Therefore, they can sell the pearls at a lower price than in Papeete. Plus you have the advantage of being able to walk outside the boutique and look at the pearls in the natural light, which truly brings out the beauty of this living jewel, especially in the early morning, at sunset time and on cloudy days. The same tactic won't work on a bright sunny day at noon.

People often ask if a pearl costs less when you buy it from a pearl farm, such as on Manihi and Rangiroa. The answer is yes, but the best pearls are usually shipped to Tahiti to be set into jewelry, or sold at auction to the big name buyers from overseas. In Tahiti and Moorea you will find black pearl pendants mounted in 18-carat gold starting around $100.

You will probably be warned against buying black pearls from street vendors. This notice is to protect you against the possibility of receiving stolen goods and buying inferior merchandise. Get a receipt and a certificate of origin and authenticity for each pearl you buy. And keep in mind there is no import duty on black pearls when you pass through US Customs on your way home.

STAYING OUT OF TROUBLE

When you're packing your bags for a trip to Tahiti please do not include any drugs that are illegal in your country. They are also illegal here and the French Immigration and Customs authorities do not consider the importation of any stupifiants as a light matter. "Dope dogs" are trained to sniff out anything suspicious in your luggage when it's unloaded from the plane. Heavy fines and jail sentences are a sure way to ruin a good vacation. Should you decide to risk it anyway, then please use discretion and do not give or sell any illegal drugs to a local person. This is a very small place and news travels amazingly fast via the "Coconut Radio".

When I first came from Houston, Texas, to Tahiti as a tourist in 1968 I remember that I was so afraid of theft that I took my handbag with me when I took a ride across the beautiful Bora Bora lagoon aboard an outrigger sailing canoe. Inside the bag were my passport, return plane tickets, travelers checks, money, driver's license and other important papers. After I moved to Tahiti I learned to relax more and to leave the watch and handbag in my hotel room when I went out in a boat. Many times there were no doors to lock and no windows to close.

Due to the increasing hotel room thefts, most of the rooms are now more protected. Experience has taught me to lock the valuable papers inside the safe provided in some of the hotels, or at least to lock the door to the hotel room or bungalow, and to close the windows. I've also had to learn to take the same precautions at home, although I do still sleep with the unscreened windows open.

For Police, dial 17.

The shops, boutiques and especially the *roulottes* (mobile diners) in Papeete are complaining of increased thefts, and you should watch out for purse-snatchers in the city, which also includes pre-teenage girls. The delinquency problems are not so pronounced that you have to be afraid to take your eyes off your suitcase at the airport. Please don't let fear ruin your vacation, when you should be relaxed and carefree, but just be cautious.

If you want to discover Papeete-by-night, stay in the main stream of lighted streets, sidewalk cafés and bars, where lots of people are on the

streets. Avoid drunk Tahitians and you'll enjoy yourself more. A municipal police station is close to Papeete's municipal market, adjacent to the
Loto (lottery) building on rue Edouard Ahnne. You can also dial 17 at any
telephone booth without having to deposit coins, and you will be
connected to the *gendarmerie*, the French national police station.

Women Traveling Alone

If you're a woman traveling alone or with a girlfriend, then you should
be aware that things are not the same as they were in the "good old days"
of the 1970s, when I could roam around Papeete all by myself and pop into
any nightclub to dance the night away in complete safety. I will no longer
walk by myself in downtown Papeete after dark, although rape, robbery
and aggressions are certainly not confined to the shadows of night.

Another word to the wise for women alone: do not sunbathe in the
nude or even topless on secluded beaches. Some of the Tahitian males see
this as an open invitation, and they will pursue you, even if it takes all day.
This warning needs to be heeded in the remote islands as well as in the
more popular tourist islands.

I do not want to frighten you away, but a form of rape called *motoro*
existed in these islands long before the Europeans arrived, and this
traditional "courtship" is still practiced. The *tane haere po* (guys who creep
around in the dark) are always on the lookout for sexual adventures, and
they still crawl through windows to achieve their goals. I've had some
problems with this myself, both at home and whenever I travel to the outer
islands. Thankfully, my unexpected visitors have not been physically
abusive, and I still travel by myself, but with caution. Some of the more
adventurous females I've known have actually booked a flight to a specific
island and hotel or pension when they've learned that the boys will crawl
through their windows at night!

Tahitian men are very charming and are always ready for romance,
or at least sexual encounters. Should you succumb to the erotic mist that
covers these tropical isles, then be sure that you provide your own
protection against sexually transmitted diseases, which exist in Tahiti and
Her Islands just as they do back home. Do not rely on your partner for
anything except a brief moment of pleasure, which is not even guaranteed.

A woman visiting the islands by herself is often open to all kinds of
experiences, which may include being invited to stay in the home of a
Tahitian family. Should this happen to you, then chances are you'll create
a lifelong friendship and wonderful memories. Just use your female
intuition in making your decision.

TAXES

Value Added Tax (VAT)

The 8 percent government tax that was formerly added to the cost of a room in the classified hotels and cabins of cruise ships based in French Polynesia was reduced to 7 percent during 1997, in anticipation of the Value Added Tax (VAT) that became effective January 1, 1998.

For the first year, from January 1 through December 31, 1998, this VAT, (TVA in French) will add 1 percent to all rented accommodations, including hotel rooms, pensions and family stays, as well as "room and meal" packages. The 1 percent VAT also applies to all inter-island transportation by air and boat, including charter flights and chartered boat trips. The 1 percent VAT also applies to such goods as non-alcoholic beverages, medicines, books and newspapers and magazines.

A 2 percent VAT applies to all shops, stores and boutiques, with the exception of duty free stores, which will be exempt. The 3 percent VAT applies to all restaurants, snacks, bars and activity and excursion services.

Some of the local businesses have chosen to absorb the VAT to avoid an increase in prices. As an example, Air Tahiti's air fares on January 1, 1998, remained the same as those of December 31, 1997, with the domestic airline carrier absorbing the 1 percent VAT instead of passing it on to passengers. Neither do visitors pay a VAT on telecommunications operations such as telephone calls and fax messages. International airlines and visiting foreign flag cruise ships will be exempt from this indirect tax levied by the government on the value added to goods on services.

The government's objective is to increase the VAT to an average of 15 percent over the first five years. At the same time, the government has an objective of eliminating a 10 percent tax on all imported goods during the first two years and eliminating all local customs duties during the next three years, at a rate of one-third less per year.

The rates quoted in this guide do not include the VAT. The cost of local transportation, activities and excursions may increase during 1998 to compensate for the VAT; therefore, the rates quoted in this book are subject to change at any time.

Bora Bora Tourist Tax

All visitors staying on Bora Bora began paying a tourist tax on January 1, 1998, regardless of what type of accommodation they buy. The tax amounts to 150 CFP ($1.50) per person, per day, for all stays in classified hotels, pensions, hostels or campgrounds, and includes passengers aboard all cruise ships. All children ages 2-12 accompanied by a parent are exempt from the new tax.

TELEPHONES & TELECOMMUNICATIONS

Dial 19 to reach a long-distance operator in Tahiti from any of the islands of French Polynesia. They all speak good English and are very efficient and courteous. Dial 3612 for information on telephone numbers within French Polynesia, and 3600 for overseas information. The telephone numbers for government offices, hotels and other private businesses, as well as all home phone numbers, contain only six digits.

Public pay phones are easily identifiable booths of metal and glass, with black letters on a yellow background. There are several phone booths in the most populous islands, and you will probably even find a public phone in the most remote village of the Marquesas Islands, the Gambiers, or Rapa in the Austral Islands.

There are a few pay phones that still take coins, but most of them require a *télécarte*, a phone card that you can buy at any post office and in many shops and newsstands. These plastic cards are often decorated with some of the same scenes as the postage stamps, and are collectors' items as well. They are sold for 1,000 CFP, 2,000 CFP and 5,000 CFP ($10, $20 and $50), and include 30, 60 and 150 units, respectively. A signal on the phone states how many units remain on your card as you talk with your party.

Calling Tahiti

When dialing direct to Tahiti and Her Islands, dial the proper International Access Code + 689 (Country Code) + the local number. The International Access Code if calling from the US is 011. Therefore, if you were calling me at the *Tahiti Beach Press*, you would dial 011+689+42.68.50.

The same codes apply when sending faxes. When transmitting telex messages from the US, the code 702 or 711 + FP must precede the telex number.

Calling Home from Tahiti

To call overseas from anywhere in Tahiti and Her Islands, dial 00, then the country code (1 for the US and Canada), followed by the area code and phone number. You can dial direct from your hotel room or by going to the nearest post office or phone booth. In the post offices you give the postal clerk the number you are calling and he will direct you to one of the booths when your call is placed.

To call Hawaii, the US mainland or Canada from Tahiti between 6am to midnight costs 135 CFP ($1.35) per minute. Between midnight and 6am you will pay 100 CFP per minute.

At the post office you can pay directly for the call, place a collect call or charge the call to your AT&T, MCI or similar long-distance calling card if you live in the US or Canada. If you live in Hawaii and have a Hawaiian

Telephone Company GTE card, that is also acceptable. Canadians with a Teleglobe Canada card can also use it in Tahiti.

Calling Within Tahiti and Her Islands

When calling from a public phone, local calls on Tahiti cost 50 CFP ($.50) for the first five minutes. Calls from Tahiti to Moorea cost 50 CFP per minute, and calls to the other islands cost a minimum of 100 CFP ($1) a minute. Just dial the six-digit telephone number, as there are no area codes within the territory.

Many individuals and several businesses on the island of Tahiti now carry their mobile Vini phones almost wherever they go, just like in the States. These numbers have a prefix of 77, and a Vini network is currently being installed on Moorea.

Should you be tempted to dial one of the numbers with a 36 prefix, be prepared to pay 96 CFP ($.96) for the first one and a half minutes, and 64 CFP ($.64) per each additional minute. This type of service is used primarily by encounter agencies, escort services and tarot card readers, and for weather reports.

Calling from Hotels

Whether you dial direct from your hotel room or go through the hotel switchboard, the surcharge can often double the cost of your international call.

TELEVISION

People living on the island of Tahiti and some of the Moorea residents have access to two free channels televised by Radio Television Française d'Outre-Mer, **RFO Tahiti**, the French government-owned station. RFO's Channel 1 also reaches most of the remote island groups of French Polynesia, with direct broadcasts replacing the recorded programs that used to arrive in the outer islands a week or two after the event.

Channel 1 begins each morning at 6am and continues throughout the day until sign-off time around 11:30pm or midnight. In addition to the local and international news in Tahitian and French, this station presents American soap operas, game and talk shows, Disneyland cartoons, classical dance performances, local events, sports matches live from France, educational programs, far too many cops and robbers series, and movies, all in French except for an occasional made-in-Hollywood circa 1950s black and white movie in English. A plus for us is that all the commercials, which are not very many, are shown just before and immediately following the evening news. Then we are left in peace to watch the program without dozens of interruptions throughout the evening.

Channel 2 comes on the air at 9am and signs off around midnight. The programs seem to be geared toward more educational programs, rather than strictly senseless entertainment. But the movies at night can be truly off-the-wall.

In addition to RFO, Tahiti residents and some homes and hotels on Moorea now have the option of subscribing to Canal + (Plus) and Telefenua, two cable television services. Canal + features live sports broadcasts from France and America, plus some movies in both languages. Telefenua has the CNN, ESPN and HBO channels, and is the closest we'll get to receiving American broadcasts until we hook up to another satellite, which is also in the works.

Has television changed the lives of the Polynesians? My answer is an unqualified yes! The old adage that "ignorance is bliss" was still in effect when I first came here, and I have seen the changes as the people have evolved or degenerated with their newly acquired knowledge, which is due in a very large part to the television programs they've absorbed, like a dry sponge sucks in water. I know several people who have no television in their homes, nor do they want one. But they're usually not Tahitian.

TIME

The island of Tahiti, as well as all the rest of the Society Islands, the Tuamotu-Gambier archipelago and the Austral Islands, is 10 hours behind Greenwich mean time. These islands are in the same time zone as Hawaii, and are two hours behind US Pacific Standard time and five hours behind US Eastern Standard time. You'll add one hour difference in time between Tahiti and the US when daylight saving time is in effect in the US. This means that between the first Sunday in April and the last Sunday in October, when it is noon in Tahiti, it is 6pm in New York and 3pm in Los Angeles; and between the last Sunday in October and the first Sunday in April, when it is noon in Tahiti, it is 5pm in New York and 2pm in Los Angeles.

The Marquesas Islands, which form the most eastern archipelago in the territory, are a half-hour ahead of the rest of French Polynesia. Therefore, when it is noon in Tahiti, it is 12:30pm in the Marquesas.

French Polynesia is east of the international date line, with the same date as the US. These islands are one day behind Tonga, Fiji, New Zealand and Australia. Tahiti is 20 hours behind Australian Eastern Standard time.

TIPPING

The brochures published by the Tahiti Tourist office state that tipping is not expected in Tahiti and Her Islands. In tour guides and brochures you will read that tipping is considered contrary to the Polynesian custom of hospitality, or that a Tahitian will be offended if you try to tip them.

It is still true that tipping is not the custom here, nor will you be expected to tip, even if someone does render a service beyond the call of duty. No one here has their hand out in anticipation of a tip. However, if you do want to tip someone, you will make them happy and you'll feel good about it yourself, because you are probably accustomed to tipping back home.

The *Tahiti Beach Press* prints a notice in each weekly publication, encouraging tourists to write a letter of thanks (*mauruuru* means "thank you" in Tahitian) to the newspaper if someone has been especially nice or has gone out of their way to help the visitor. This letter nominates that helpful person for the Mauruuru Award, which is presented by the Tahiti Tourisme office each September during World Tourism days. The winners can be people who work in the tourist industry, as well as any other resident, and they are awarded a round-trip airline ticket to California, Australia or France.

Tipping at Hotels & Restaurants

At the bottom of the menu in some restaurants you'll occasionally see a notice that tips are appreciated. There may also be a "Tips Accepted" sign posted in some obvious place inside the restaurant. At the Linareva floating restaurant in Moorea a huge bottle containing dollars and francs sits on a table near the entrance to the converted ferry boat. I asked one of the waitresses what happens to the money when the jug is full, and she said that all the employees get to spend a weekend on Tetiaroa, or they divvy up the tips among all the staff. Other restaurants use the tips for their Christmas party.

The bellmen or *bagagistes* in the hotels also appreciate the tips they receive, even though the hotel management discourages this practice. I've asked many of these young men how they feel about receiving tips, and some of them said that they just indicate to the hotel guest to put the money in their shirt pockets, and that way they can truthfully say they didn't have their hand out.

Tipping Guides

I worked as a free-lance tour guide in Tahiti for 17 years, in addition to my newspaper job, and I can assure you that all of the tour guides and drivers happily welcome tips. Some of the European guides have also told me that they make it clear to the tourists that they want tips. This is exactly the attitude that the Tahiti Tourist office is trying to prevent, and Tahitian guides and drivers do not use this aggressive approach.

Tipping Taxi Drivers
Chances are you won't feel much inclined to tip taxi drivers when you discover how expensive the fares are. But it's still up to your discretion whether to tip. The president of the taxi drivers' union in Tahiti said that only one percent of people tip them, and these tippers are Americans.

WEIGHTS & MEASURES

French Polynesia is on the metric system, but for your convenience, I have converted kilometers to miles, meters to feet, kilos to pounds, liters to gallons, and Celsius to Fahrenheit, where appropriate. To facilitate your own conversions, here are the equations:

1 meter = 3.28 feet	1 foot = 0.30 meters
1 meter = 1.09 yards	1 yard = 0.91 meters
1 square meter = 10.7639 square feet	1 square foot = 0.09 square meter
1 square meter = 1,1960 square yards	1 square yard = .08 square meter
1 hectare = 2.4710 acres	1 acre = .04 hectares
1 kilometer = .62 miles	1 mile = 1.61 kilometers
1 liter = 1.06 quarts	1 quart = 0.95 liters
4 liters = 1.06 gallons	1 gallon = 3.79 liters
1 kilogram = 2.20 pounds	1 pound = 0.45 kilograms

Temperature Guide

0º Celsius = 32º Fahrenheit	=	Freezing point of water
10º Celsius = 50º Fahrenheit	=	Winter in the Austral Islands
20º Celsius = 68º Fahrenheit	=	Comfortable for you, chilly for some of Tahiti's residents
30º Celsius = 86º Fahrenheit	=	Quite warm-almost hot
37º Celsius = 98.6 Fahrenheit	=	Normal body temperature
40º Celsius = 104º Fahrenheit	=	Heat wave conditions
100º Celsius = 212º Fahrenheit	=	Boiling point of water

WHERE TO FIND MORE INFORMATION ABOUT TAHITI & FRENCH POLYNESIA

• **Tahiti Tourisme**, *300 Continental Boulevard, Suite 180, El Segundo, CA 90245; Tel 310/414-8484; Fax 310/414-8490; e-mail address: tahitilax@earthlink.net.* Contact this office to request brochures, schedules and information that you want to be mailed to you.
• **Tahiti Tourisme**, *444 Madison Avenue, 16th floor, New York, NY 10022; Tel. 212/838-7800, ext. 253; Fax 212/838-9576.* This office is also equipped to mail out requested brochures and information upon request.

- **Tahiti Tourisme**, *B.P. 65, Papeete, Tahiti, French Polynesia; Tel. 689/ 50.57.00, Fax 689/43.66.19; e-mail address: tahiti-tourisme@mail.pf Internet site: www.tahiti-tourisme.com* This is the main office for overseas promotion, which is located *in the building adjacent to Tahiti Manava Visitors Bureau.* A tour guide to the small hotels and pensions, plus video films, posters, T-shirts, caps and sun visors, can be purchased in the promotional materials department.
- **Tahiti Manava Visitors Bureau**, *B.P. 1710, Papeete, Tahiti, French Polynesia, Tel. 689/50.57.00, Fax 689/45.16.78.* This office, formerly known as GIE Tahiti Animation, *is on the harbor side of the Papeete waterfront in Fare Manihini.* Here you will find brochures and informational sheets on lodgings, activities, tours and excursions, ferries, boats and air services to the outer islands, maps and anything else related to tourism. English-speaking Tahitian hostesses are on duty from 7:30am through 5pm Monday through Friday, and from 8am until noon on Saturday.
- **Territorial Service of Tourism**, *B.P. 4227, Papeete, Tahiti, French Polynesia, Tel. 689/50.57.00, Fax 689/48.12.75.* Please contact this office if you have any complaints or helpful comments. *They are located in the same complex as Tahiti Manava Visitors Bureau and Tahiti Tourisme.*
- Other Internet sites include the **World Travel Net-World Country Guide**: *http://www.world-travel-net.co.uk/country/tah_cin.htm* and **TahitiWeb**, which is the Internet guide to Tahiti's web sites: *http:// www.tahitiweb.com/*
- **Chamber of Commerce**, **Industry and Trade in French Polynesia**, *rue du Dr. Cassiau, Papeete, Tahiti, French Polynesia, Tel. 689/54.07.11, Fax 689/54.07.01.* Use this contact for questions regarding any business or trade in Tahiti.
- **Polynesian Cultural Center (OTAC)**, *B.P. 1709, Papeete, Tahiti, French Polynesia, Tel .689/42.88.50, Fax 689/42.85.69.* OTAC is in charge of the annual Heiva I Tahiti Festival each July, and selected cultural events throughout the year. There is a library on the premises.
- **Société des Etudes Océaniennes**, **Mr. Robert Koenig**, *c/o Territorial Records, Tipaerui, B.P. 110, Papeete, Tahiti, French Polynesia, Tel. 689/ 41.96.03, Fax 689/58.23.33.* Researchers may obtain permission to use the library and archives.
- **Friends of Tahiti**, *55 Lehigh Aisle, Irvine, CA 92612, Tel. 714/856-2695, Fax 818/887-5897, e-mail hcc@tahiti.com* A quarterly magazine, available by subscription, keeps you informed on what's happening with the Tahitians in California and the Californians in Tahiti. You can also visit FoT at its new web site on the Internet: *www.tahiti.com/ english/magazine/fot.htm.*

8. CALENDAR OF EVENTS

JANUARY

New Year's Day. It's serious party time on all the islands of French Polynesia, when many people return to their natal islands to celebrate for almost a month. There are *bringues* (parties) almost every night, with crowds of Tahitians singing to the tune of the ukuleles, guitars, "gut bucket" bass, and spoons rattled in the big Hinano beer bottles that are quickly emptied of their original contents. A tradition in Tahiti is to drive around the island on New Year's Day, stopping to visit family and friends and swimming in the rivers and lagoons along the way. The Tahiti Manava Visitor's Bureau organizes a circle island tour for visitors. You will ride in a flower decorated *le truck*, complete with a band of musicians playing the guitar and ukulele and singing Tahitian songs. You stop at several of the most beautiful natural sites to visit waterfalls, public gardens, public parks and beaches, with a traditional Tahitian lunch served at noon, followed by a dance show.

Chinese New Year. Tahiti's Chinese community will welcome in the Year of the Tiger on January 28, 1998, and the Year of the Cat on February 16, 1999. Celebrations include parades, the Dance of the Lion and Dragon, and open house at the Chinese temple in the Mamao suburb of Papeete, with traditional dances, martial arts demonstrations, food tasting, calligraphy, paintings, fortune telling and fireworks.

FEBRUARY

The Moorea International Blue Marathon. A 42,195 kilometer scenic marathon is held on the island of Moorea each February, an increasingly popular event that attracts competitors from all over the world. A 21 kilometer Mini-Marathon and a 6 kilometer Fun Run are also held in conjunction with the international event. The Association of International Marathons and Road Races will hold a World Congress in Tahiti February 17-18, 1999.

Cultural Exhibitions. A six-week exhibit of Polynesian Cultural Traditions starts each year at the beginning of February, with arts and crafts shows and demonstrations at Place Vaiete on the Papeete waterfront. Traditional medicine, massage, tattooing, basket weaving, wood carving, lei making and other handcrafts are featured. This annual exhibit corresponds with the arrival of several passenger cruise ships, which dock at the quay adjacent to the exhibits.

MARCH

Missionaries Day. March 5 is a public holiday to commemorate the arrival of the first English Protestant Missionaries on March 5, 1797. Reenactment ceremonies are held at Tahiti's Point Venus, in the stadiums and churches, and also in Moorea's Protestant churches and stadium in Afareaitu.

National Women's Day. The women's associations from throughout French Polynesia meet in Papeete on March 8 to discuss the Women's Condition. These meetings are punctuated by songs, dances and skits.

APRIL

International Triathlon in Moorea. This competition is unique because of the picturesque landscape in which the three disciplines take place: a 1.5 kilometer swimming competition, a 40-kilometer bicycle race, and a 10-kilometer run. Almost the whole population of Moorea participates in this event, either as competitors or supporters, in a typical Polynesian celebration of singing and dancing.

MAY

Annual World Qualifying Surfing Series in Tahiti. Several of the top professional surfers in the world will face the impressive rollers offshore Teahupoo on Tahiti-Iti during the Gotcha Tahiti Pro Surfing challenging match. The Black Pearl Vahine Pro surfing competition is held for female contestants at the same time and same place.

Annual Miss Tahiti and Miss Heiva Contest. Beauty queens from all the island groups will compete for the coveted title of Miss Tahiti . Miss Heiva I Tahiti will reign during the Heiva Festival in July and the Mini-Heiva celebrations in August.

Oxbow World Master Championship is an international competition for professional surfers, held at Taapuna beach.

Traditional Maohi Sports Festival in Tahiti. This demonstration of traditional Polynesian sports includes fruit-carriers' races, javelin throwing, coconut tree climbing, husking coconuts, stone lifting competitions and lots of *maa Tahiti*, food cooked in an underground oven.

Week of the Outer Islands at the Papeete Market in Tahiti. All the distant archipelagoes of French Polynesia are featured in a week-long exhibit of arts and crafts, music, songs and dances performed by artisans from the Australs, Tuamotu-Gambiers, Marquesas and Leeward Society Islands. This colorful event takes place in mid-May.

Heiva Upa Rau. These are the Polynesian music awards, which are held annually in mid-May, when the best singers and musicians receive prizes from Tahiti's Cultural Center and the local recording studios.

JUNE

World Environment Day. This event on June 5th includes a special environmental awareness program throughout French Polynesia, involving school children, youth and church groups and visitors. Guided tours are organized to visit the beautiful valleys, such as Fautaua, Papenoo and Lake Vaihiria, and a trek to the top of Aorai, 2,066 meters (6,776 feet) altitude, Tahiti's second highest mountain.

Visit to Tourist Sites Around Tahiti. This two-day event takes place in early June, giving you a chance to visit Tahiti's most spectacular sites along with Tahitian musicians and traditional dance groups, who entertain you while posing in a living tableau for you photographers. You'll discover the east coast on the first day, stopping at Point Venus and the Three Cascades of Faarumai in Tiarei. The second day takes you to Tahiti's west coast sites of Vaipahi gardens and waterfall in Mataiea, the Fern Grotto of Mara'a in Paea, and the Marae Arahurahu.

International Tahiti Black Pearl Festival. Local and international jewelers exhibit their most beautiful creations using the *poe rava*, the Tahitian black pearl, in mid-June. Black pearl auctions are accompanied by fashion shows of jewelry and clothes at the Papeete *mairie* (city hall), and a gala evening of dining and dancing in one of the major hotels.

Heiva I Tahiti. The Tahiti Festival is the biggest event of the year. There are daily activities, but the main events are scheduled for Thursday-Sunday each week. In addition to the traditional sports events listed above, Tahiti's competitions also include stone-lifting, outrigger sailing canoe races, horse races and bicycle races. Outrigger canoe races are held inside the lagoon and in the open ocean. The month-long program includes a fire walking ceremony, sound and light shows, reenactment ceremonies at the Marae of Arahurahu and in the Papenoo Valley, professional and amateur song and dance competitions, a race of restaurant and bar waiters, and all night balls. Carnival type rides and fairground booths called *baraques* are set up in two locations, where the kids of all ages can munch popcorn and cotton candy and jump on the ferris wheel, merry-go-round and other thrilling rides.

Arts and Crafts Festival. This is a main event during the July activities in Tahiti, with daily exhibits of handcrafts from all the island groups. Daily demonstrations of traditional arts and crafts are accompanied by live concerts, song and dance competitions, Polynesian meals, varied games and a month of fun.

Annual Tahiti International Pro/Am Golf Open. This popular event is held each year during the Heiva I Tahiti Festival, attracting golfers from many parts of the world, who compete for the $40,000 cash prizes at the Olivier Breaud International Golf Course in Atimaono, on Tahiti's south coast of Papara.

Anniversary of Internal Autonomy Day with a Hiva Vaevae Parade in Papeete. This is the biggest folkloric parade of the year, held along Boulevard Pomare in downtown Papeete to celebrate the anniversary of a French parliamentary statute that was adopted in 1984, giving French Polynesia increased self-governing powers. In addition to Miss Tahiti and Miss Heiva I Tahiti, you will see all the dance groups, youth groups, church groups, sports groups and special interest groups parading on foot, roller blades, bicycles, motorcycles, horses, in pirogues, cars and trucks and aboard decorated floats.

JULY

Heiva Festivals on all the Islands. The schedules vary, but these festivals usually begin during the month of July. Each island has traditional sports competitions, including fruit carriers' races, javelin-throwing, copra chopping contests and outrigger canoe races, arts and crafts stands and games for children. The singing and dancing contests are the highlight of each festival, which usually lasts from four to six weeks. The most popular outer island festivals take place on Bora Bora, Raiatea and Tahaa.

Highlights of the Tahiti Festival include the song and dance competitions and a special evening of Laureates. There are outrigger canoe races inside the lagoon and in the open ocean, and the 84-kilometer (52-mile) Tahiti-Moorea-Tahiti race. A fire-walking ceremony occurs at Mahana Park in Punaauia, and the colorful re-enactment ceremonies at Arahurahu Marae in Paea will be held each Saturday during the month of July.

Horue International. Surfing competitors from overseas will test their skills against Tahiti's best surfers on the waves in Papara. This event is organized by the Popoti Surf Club.

French Bastille Day Holiday Parade. France's National Holiday of July 14th is celebrated throughout French Polynesia with parades, parties and all night balls. Large hotels also organize special evenings for this event. A military parade is staged on Boulevard Pomare along the Papeete waterfront, followed by a champagne party at the residence of the French High Commissioner. Horse races are usually scheduled for that afternoon.

Annual Te Aito Individual Marathon Outrigger Canoe Race. Almost 300 individual outrigger canoe racers compete in this 20-kilometer course in Tahiti's Matavai Bay, which is held at the end of July. The Aito (Polynesian warriors) winners of this race qualify to compete in the Super Aito competitions.

AUGUST

Mini Heiva Festivals. The Hotel Tahiti Beachcomber Parkroyal invites the winners of the Tahiti Festival song and dance competitions to perform during a nine-evening Mini Heiva Festival under the stars. Gastronomic feasts are served on the hotel's *motu*, followed by first class entertainment. The Hotel Moana Beach Parkroyal Bora Bora hosts a three-night Mini Heiva Festival and feast on their beach, featuring the best song and dance groups in Bora Bora, and the Hotel Moorea Beachcomber Parkroyal presents the best dance groups during their four-night Mini Heiva Festival, complete with sumptuous buffet dinners on the beach.

Tahiti Agricultural Fair. This big event, which is held after the Heiva Festival is over, presents the fruits, vegetables, flowers and livestock from Tahiti, Moorea and some of the other islands. Exhibit booths offer food tastings and information to the tune of live music. Fruit carriers' races and other traditional competitions are held, and the best fruits and vegetables are chosen. A *Vahine Faapu* (Miss Farm Girl) is chosen.

SEPTEMBER

Moorea-Tahiti Super Aito Individual Outrigger Canoe Channel Race. Along with the local paddlers who qualify for this most important individual pirogue competition, a few foreign paddlers are invited to race from Moorea's Temae Beach to Point Venus in Tahiti. The winner receives $4,000 in cash. This annual competition is also called the Budweiser Channel Race.

Taapuna Surf Masters is an international event that will take place in September at Taapuna beach.

Annual Tahiti Flower Show. Floralies is the biggest floral exhibit of the year, organized by the Harrison Smith Association at Place Tarahoi in

Papeete. This festival of tropical colors and scents, which always coincides with World Tourism Day on September 27, is dedicated to Tahiti's "Grandfather of the Trees," Harrison W. Smith, who created the Botanical Gardens in Papeari on Tahiti's south coast.

World Tourism Week. Tahiti, Moorea and Bora Bora all participate in this annual celebration in honor of our visitors. World Tourism Day is September 27, and that entire week is filled with traditional singing and dancing shows, arts and crafts exhibits, and Polynesian bands playing music in the streets while hostesses distribute flowers to tourists. The airports, hotels, tourist offices, *les trucks*, banks and other offices are decorated with flowers for the occasion.

OCTOBER

Te Avaava Nui Longboard Classic is an international competition organized by the Tahiti Surf Club held in Papenoo.

Annual Aito Man (Iron Man) International Triathlon on Moorea. This competition features 3.8 kilometers of swimming, 180 kilometers of bicycling, and 42.195 kilometers of running.

Pacific Raid. This is a five-stage, three-island cross country competition with participants choosing between mountain biking or running on Tahiti, Moorea and Huahine.

7th International Heineken Cup Kayak/Surf-ski. Contestants paddle 60 kilometers (37 miles) from Vairao on the west coast of Tahiti Iti to Punaauia on the northwest coast.

Carnival in Tahiti. Hihglights are a Carnival Queen and King, decorated floats and a parade of the giant sized heads and figures. Activities include a masked ball at Place Vaiete in Papeete.

NOVEMBER

All Saints Day. The graves in the cemeteries and in the yards of private homes are weeded and cleaned in preparation for this annual event. Flower stands are set up all around the island of Tahiti on this public holiday, and families decorate the graves with dozens of fresh and plastic flowers. That night the cemeteries are lighted with candles as the families sing hymns and recite prayers for their departed loved ones.

Annual Hawaiki Nui Outrigger Canoe Race. This is a three-day marathon competition between the Leeward Islands of Huahine, Raiatea, Tahaa and Bora Bora, with hundreds of paddlers. This is the ultimate pirogue competition, with foreign canoe clubs participating.

Annual Va'a Hine outrigger canoe race is a women's competition held during the Hawaiki Nui race.

Stone Fishing Ceremony (Moorea and Bora Bora). This traditional fishing technique, which involves beating the water with stones tied on a rope, is a colorful, festive occasion that you don't want to miss. The two-day events take place during the last two weeks of November.

DECEMBER

Tiare Tahiti Days. Tahiti's national flower, the fragrant white Tiare Tahiti (*gardenia tahitensis*), is honored during this three-day annual event during the first week of December. On the major tourist islands of Tahiti, Moorea and Bora Bora, the airports, hotels, some restaurants, tourist offices, post offices and banks are decorated with garlands of Tiare Tahiti blossoms, and Tiare Tahiti flowers are presented to tourists on the streets.

Tahiti Surf Club Open will be held in Papenoo.

Pineapple Festival in Moorea. Moorea is the pineapple island and pays tribute to this sweet, delicious fruit each year in mid-December.

Marquesas Islands Festival Days. A three-day sales exhibit of Marquesan arts and crafts is held each year just before Christmas at the Territorial Assembly Hall in Papeete. Carved wooden bowls, tikis, ceremonial spears and ukuleles are the most sought after items, along with tapa bark paintings, sandalwood jewelry and smoky dried bananas. Marquesan dancers entertain you with their traditional performances and you can sample foods that are unique to the Marquesas Islands.

Christmas in Tahiti. Santa Claus or "Papa Noel" arrives in Tahiti by outrigger canoe, jet-ski, helicopter or horse, accompanied by Polynesian musicians as he distributes candies to the children in Papeete. The major hotels in the tourist islands and several restaurants present special menus and entertainment on Christmas Eve and Christmas Day, which also include roast turkey with chestnut dressing. And the perfect French wine to accompany the meal, of course!

9. SPORTS & RECREATION

BOAT RENTALS & RIDES

In Tahiti you can rent a four-person fishing boat with a six-horse-power engine for 2.500 CFP (about $25) per hour or 10.000 CFP ($100) for eight hours, or a 140-horsepower boat for 6.000 CFP ($60) an hour, up to 24.000 CFP ($240) for eight hours, plus fuel. In Rangiroa a boat with pilot will cost you 7.500 CFP ($75) per hour or 50.000 CFP ($500) per day. Glass bottom boat rides start at 1.800 CFP ($18) for an hour's excursion, and you can go on a sunset cruise for 2.000 to 3.000 CFP ($20 to $30).

CANOE RACES

The **Moorea-Tahiti Super Aito Individual Outrigger Canoe Channel Race** is an international pirogue competition that is held each September. This annual competition, which is also called the Budweiser Channel Race, is the most important individual pirogue competition of the year, when local and foreign paddlers race from Moorea's Temae Beach to Point Venus in Tahiti.

The **International Heineken Cup for Kayaks** takes place in October. Contestants from several countries will race 60 kilometers (37 miles) from Vairao on the west coast of Tahiti Iti to Punaauia on the northwest coast of Tahiti Nui.

The **Annual Hawaiki Nui Outrigger Canoe Race**, each November, is the biggest and most exciting pirogue race of the year. More than 60 teams and 1,000 men from local and international canoe clubs compete in this three-day sports event, paddling from Huahine to Raiatea, Raiatea to Tahaa and Tahaa to Bora Bora. The **Annual Va'a Hine outrigger canoe race** is a women's competition held during the Hawaiki Nui race, when women's teams paddle from Raiatea to Tahaa.

FISHING

Game fishing in Tahitian waters reaches its peak months during March and April, with fishing competitions held from the end of September to April. Sports fishing is available all year, however, with good results. The game fish usually found around these islands are: blue marlin, Pacific sailfish, big eye tuna, mahi mahi (dorado), wahoo, yellow fin tuna, ocean bonito and tiger shark.

Off-shore game fish found outside the reef also include jack crevally, blue crevally, rainbow runner, dog tooth tuna and barracuda. Sports fishing boats charge 45.000 to 60.000 CFP ($450-$600) for a four-hour fishing expedition, with full-day outings available on request.

GOLF

The 18-hole **Olivier Breaud International Golf Course** of Atimaono is located 25 miles from Papeete in the southwest coast communes of Papara and Mataiea. The annual **Tahiti International Pro/Am Golf Open** is held each June or July, attracting players from several countries, who compete for the $40,000 cash prizes.

HIKING

Trekking to the interior valleys and climbing mountains should be done with a qualified guide. Most of the high islands have interesting trails and local guides to show you the way.

HORSEBACK RIDING

There are riding stables on Tahiti, Moorea, Huahine, Raiatea, Bora Bora, Nuku Hiva and Ua Huka. Most of the horses are from the Marquesas Islands, originally of Chilean stock. A few Equestrian Clubs also have thoroughbreds from New Zealand. A one-hour ride costs 1.000 CFP ($10) on Nuku Hiva, 2.000 CFP ($20) on Moorea, 2.800 CFP ($28) on Huahine and 4.000 CFP ($40) on Bora Bora.

MARATHONS, TRIATHLONS & RAIDS

Almost every weekend in Tahiti or Moorea there is a marathon, triathlon or bicycle race held. One of the most popular international competitions is the **Moorea Blue Marathon**, a 42.195 kilometer (26.16 mile) race that is held on the island of Moorea each February. A Half-Marathon and 6 kilometer (3.7 mile) Polymat Fun Run/Walk are also included. Following the Moorea Blue Marathon, a Bora Bora Beach Run is held, with competitors racing along the white sand beach of Point Matira. The next Moorea Blue Marathon is set for February 20, 1999, and the Association of International Marathons and Road Races will hold a World Congress in Tahiti on February 17-18, 1999, prior to the Moorea Blue Marathon.

The **Moorea International Triathlon** is held in April, and includes a 1.5 kilometer (.93 mile) swimming competition, a 40-kilometer (24.8 mile) bicycle race and a 10-kilometer (6.2 mile) run.

The **Annual Aito Man (Iron Man) International Triathlon** on Moorea is held in October. This competition includes 3.8 kilometers (2.4 miles) of swimming, 180 kilometers of bicycling (111.6 miles) and 42.195 kilometers (26.16 miles) of running.

A **Pacific Raid** is a five-stage, three-island cross country competition with participants choosing between mountain biking or running on Tahiti, Moorea and Huahine. This event is held in October.

For further information on these international competitions, contact: *Barbara Lansun of Pacific Events Marketing at Tahiti Manava Visitors Bureau in Tahiti, Tel. 689/50.57.38; Fax 689/45.16.78; e-mail: blansun@tahititourisme.pf.*

SCUBA DIVING

The clear, tropical waters of Tahiti and Her Islands are ideal for year-round diving, providing a diversity of magnificent dive sites in the lagoons, passes and outer coral reefs. Because French Polynesia covers such a vast area, with varying degrees of latitude and longitude, the underwater scenery is different from archipelago to archipelago, from island to island.

All scuba divers must have a certificate from a doctor indicating that you are in good health, plus a certificate indicating the depth specifications allowed. A medical exam can be taken in Tahiti for the necessary papers, and examinations are available to obtain diving diplomas.

Around the island of Tahiti you will find some of the best scuba diving conditions for the beginner or the veteran diver who needs a reorientation. Due to the location of dive centers on the west coast of the island, in the lee of the prevailing easterly winds, you will find minimal currents and calm surface conditions. There is good visibility, with colorful small reef fish, friendly moray eels, eagle rays, small white-tip sharks and nurse sharks. Dive attractions also include a sunken inter-island schooner and a seaplane, and a vertical cliff on the outer reef that descends to infinity from a plateau 4.5 meters (15 feet) deep.

Moorea's special diving features are the feeding of moray eels, barracuda and large lemon sharks, plus a friendly encounter with leopard rays and large Napoleon fish. A sunken ship is clearly seen in the translucent waters of Papetoai.

Bora Bora is famous for its multihued lagoon, but also for the abundance of large-species marine life that inhabit this environment, especially the graceful manta rays that are sometimes found in groups of 10 swimming inside the lagoon and in the pass.

In the lagoon surrounding Huahine Nui and Huahine Iti you can feed sharks and see large schools of barracudas, big red snappers, tuna, turtles, rays and Napoleons.

The lagoon that is shared by Raiatea and Tahaa attracts large schools of pelagic fish, leopard rays and a few manta rays. Divers can watch or join in the feeding of the large blue-green Napoleon fish, pet moray eels, and observe white-tip, black-tip and gray sharks.

In the Tuamotu atolls you will find world-class diving in luminescent waters with very good visibility inside the lagoons and passes. Rangiroa is one of the top diving destinations in the world. This is the largest atoll in the Southern Hemisphere and the second largest in the world, after Kwajalein in the Marshall Islands. Rangiroa's two most famous diving spots are the Avatoru and Tiputa passes through the coral reef. Schools of sharks, squadrons of eagle rays, jacks, tuna, barracuda, manta rays, turtles and dolphins swim through these passes when the very strong currents from the ocean flow into the lagoon or rush back out to sea.

Manihi is famous for the black pearl farms inside its crystal clear lagoon. Excellent diving conditions are favorable for beginners and experienced divers. The sites include a beautiful variety of coral gardens, big Napoleon fish, black-tip reef sharks, gray sharks, eagle and manta rays, schools of snappers and big tuna fish. One favorite site is a breathtaking wall that drops 3 to 1,350 meters (10 to 4,500 feet). When the famous French diver Jacques Cousteau explored the lagoon in Tikehau he said that it contained more fish than any of the other lagoons in this part of the Pacific. The inhabitants ship parrot fish from the Tikehau lagoon to Tahiti by airplane and fishing ships. Fakarava is the second largest atoll in the Tuamotu archipelago, where scuba diving is the most spectacular in the Garuae Pass, which is one kilometer (.62 miles) wide and 16 meters (52 feet) deep. Experienced divers will be treated to a panorama of underwater life that includes manta rays, dolphins, barracudas, tiger sharks, hammerhead sharks and whale sharks. A virtually unexplored scuba diver's paradise awaits discovery on the atoll of Makemo, which will probably be the next dive site developed.

The northern group of the Marquesas Islands offers underwater caves with large fauna, recommended for adventurous, experienced divers only. Some of the world's most famous underwater photographers come here to dive and photograph the dozens of manta rays, leopard rays, stingrays, friendly hammerhead sharks and pigmy killer whales that inhabit the open waters surrounding the islands.

In the southern latitudes of the Austral Islands the humpback whales are a big attraction for scuba divers just offshore the island of Rurutu. These mammals, which are 14 to 18 meters (46 to 59 feet) in length, are seen during the months of July through October, when they come up from Antarctica to mate and give birth, while escaping the austral winters. Several humpbacks also visit Moorea, Tahiti and the Tuamotu atolls.

There are more than 30 scuba diving clubs in French Polynesia, located on the islands of Tahiti, Moorea, Huahine, Raiatea and Bora Bora in the Society Islands, the atolls of Rangiroa, Tikehau, Manihi, Fakarava and Hao in the Tuamotu archipelago, on Nuka Hiva in the Marquesas Islands, and on Rurutu and Tubuai in the Austral Islands. Please check each destination chapter for information on the most popular diving clubs used by tourists.

For certified divers a one-tank dive costs 5.000 to 5.500 CFP ($50-$55), and each dive shop has forfeit prices for several dives. Scuba diving lessons are also available from qualified international instructors, who teach the French system of CMAS and the American system of PADI. Dive packages are also available.

SCUBA DIVING TERMS

For the uninitiated in the vernacular of scuba diving, **PADI** *is the* **Professional Association of Diving Instructors.** *An OWDI is an overwater diving instructor. The PADI system of training divers is used in North America. The techniques differ from those of the French system of* **CMAS** *(Conféderation Mondiale des Activités Subaquatiques), which is the World Underwater Federation. The diving monitors and instructors in Tahiti and Her Islands are qualified to teach both PADI and CMAS.*

The **FFESSM** *is the* **Fèderation Française des Activités Subaquatiques,** *or French Underwater Federation. A level of B.E. training in the FFESSM equals a CMAS one star rating; the first echelon or level equals a two-star rating in CMAS; and autonomous diver equals a three-star rating in CMAS. In France a monitor (moniteur) is more qualified than an instructor. A moniteur d'Etat is the equivalent of a State instructor, with levels of BEES 1, 2 or 3. BEES 3 is the highest level you can reach, except for a moniteur federal, who is not supposed to accept money for giving lessons. All the instructors and monitors in Tahiti can still be paid for their services.*

Dive Cruises

More information is given on the sailing charter yachts in the chapter on *Planning Your Trip.*

Archipels Croisières has an exclusive 8 day/7 night Dive Aboard Cruise in the Marquesas Islands for $2,450 per person. Dive Aboard Cruises in the Tuamotus are "by the boat only" for $2,450 a day.

Danae Cruises has weekend dive cruises in the Leeward Islands, and 6 day/5 night dive cruises that will take you to Raiatea, Tahaa, Bora Bora and Tupai. The longer cruise costs $1,600 per diver if there are only two people, and $1,450 per person for four divers. All meals and diving equipment are included.

VPM Dufour Yachting offers 8 day/7 night Dive Cruises in the Tuamotu archipelago aboard an 82-foot catamaran. On Monday you fly from Papeete to Fakarava by Air Tahiti and board the *Nemo*. You will dive the passes of Fakarava, Kauehi and Toau during the week and fly back from Fakarava to Tahiti the following Monday.

SURFING

International competitions

The **Horue International Surfing** competition is held at Tahiti's Papara beach in July. The **Taapuna Surf Masters** is held at Taapuna beach in September. The **Te Avaava Nui Longboard Classic** takes place in Papenoo in October. The first **Tahiti Surf Club Open** will be held December 5 and 6, 1998, and December 12 and 13 in Papenoo.

International Professional competitions

The **Annual World Qualifying Surfing Series** takes place in May. The **Gotcha Tahiti Pro Surfing** and the **Black Pearl Vahine Pro** are held in May, followed by the **Oxbow World Master Championship**. Some of the world's top professional surfers will match skills offshore Teahupoo on the Tahiti Iti peninsula.

TENNIS

Tahiti's climate is ideal for playing tennis at any time of the year, by scheduling a match in the early morning or at sunset time, to avoid the hottest hours of a tropical day. Tennis courts are located at all the major hotels in Tahiti, Moorea, Huahine, Bora Bora and Rangiroa.

10. TAKING THE KIDS

The 1996 Census in French Polynesia counted 219,521 people living in five island groups. Of this number 42.6 percent of the inhabitants are under the age of 20 years. On the other end of the scale, only 6.2 percent of the population are over 60 years old.

Tahiti and Her Islands are a haven for the young! So bring your kids and let them enjoy the attention they'll receive from the friendly Polynesians, who adore babies and little children. If they're still young enough to be picked up easily, that will be even more fun for the child and the Tahitians, who love to kiss and hug little people, little puppies and anything that is still a baby. When they get older and bigger, that's another story for the animals and local kids, but the Tahitians will still treat visiting children with genuine warmth and patience.

International airline companies and Air Tahiti give preferential seating to families traveling with children. Kids generally pay only half the adult fare on international airline routings. Air Tahiti gives a 50 percent discount to children between two and eleven years, and the fare for babies under two years is 10 percent of the adult fare. Most of the hotels, hostels, guest houses and pensions will let the kids stay for free if sharing a room with their parents, or they only charge for an extra bed.

Your travel agent can make all the reservations for you, securing spacious bulkhead seats on airlines and determining which flights are least crowded. They can also seek out the best deals on lodging and meals.

When traveling with children of any age, make sure their vaccinations are up to date and bring their health records and any special medications they made need. In the event of an emergency, there are medical facilities on all the islands. Mamao hospital in Tahiti has a modern pediatric department. Make sure that your repatriation insurance also covers your child.

Rascals in Paradise, *650 Fifth St., San Francisco, CA 94107, Tel. 800/ 872-7225* or *415/978-9800* organizes South Pacific tours for families with kids, including visits with local families.

TRAVELING WITH BABIES

Hopefully, you'll be at least two people to bring a baby on a long airplane flight to Tahiti. Bring a suitcase filled with baby supplies, including a sufficient supply of disposable diapers, food, light clothes that cover the whole body, a sun hat, favorite toys, Q-Tips, baby wipes, a first aid kit with sunblock, mosquito repellent, baby aspirin, thermometer and a treatment for diarrhea. The supermarkets and small *magasin* stores carry fresh or powdered whole milk, bottled mineral water, dry cereals that must be cooked, canned fruits and jars of baby food, but you'll pay much more for these items in Tahiti than you will back home.

Bring a stroller with sunshade or cloth carrier for your baby, or a car seat-sleeper combination. Only a few of the hotels can provide cribs and high chairs for babies.

TODDLERS & LITTLE TIKES

Along with the shorts, T-shirts, sweater, waterproof shoes and sun hat you pack for your small children, you should also include some of their favorite snacks, books and toys. If they're big enough to snorkel, pack their own snorkel gear, plus a bucket and shovel and inflatable beach ball. In their first-aid kit be sure to include some preventive drops for swimmer's ear. Cleanse and treat any minor cuts or abrasions immediately to prevent staph infection. Make sure they're protected from the hot tropical sun and mosquitoes and that they drink a sufficient amount of water throughout the day.

JUNIORS & ADOLESCENTS

The warm climate, natural setting, aquatic games and lack of poisonous creatures make Tahiti and Her Islands a paradise for children of all ages. Many of the hotels have swimming pools and beach activities, such as outrigger paddle canoes, pedal boats, surf bikes and windsurf boards. Swimming or playing in the reef-protected lagoon waters is also relatively safe, as long as you keep an eye on the little ones, because there are no lifeguards. Children enjoy lagoon excursions, picnics on the *motu*, feeding the fish, rays and sharks, sailing and other water activities. Some of the scuba diving centers will accept divers as young as eight years. You can rent bikes on most of the islands.

MacDonald's is located in downtown Papeete, and Kentucky Fried Chicken will open a second outlet in Tahiti during 1998. On several of the islands you'll find hamburgers, sandwiches, pizzas, tacos, pancakes and crêpes. All the food stores carry some American snacks and good ice cream. Some of the hotels have children's menus and discount buffets and Tahitian feasts for children under 12 years. The more luxurious hotels have room service, which can be convenient for families, and several of the moderate range hotels and pensions provide kitchen facilities.

BABY-SITTERS

Hotels that welcome children generally have no problem arranging baby-sitters. Of course, it's better to have a sitter who speaks English. If you're in Moorea and need a baby sitter, you can contact Elizabeth Roometua *at the Sofitel Ia Ora, Tel. 56.12.90,* or at home *Tel. 56.36.05.* She is an American mother of three children, and she's willing to help you find a baby sitter. In Huahine you can contact Dorothy Levy *at the Snack Vakalele at the airport, Tel. 68.85.69.* Dorothy has two children of her own and is an Earth Mother to everyone else.

In Bora Bora, contact Robin Teraitepo *at Chez Ben's in Matira* at their restaurant that is located *on the mountain side between the Hotel Bora Bora and Matira Point. Tel. 67.74.54.* Robin is from California and she and her husband Ben serve American style food, including good pizzas, pastas, tacos and sandwiches.

11. ECOTOURISM & TRAVEL ALTERNATIVES

The Ecotourism Society of America defines an **ecotour** as: Purposeful travel to natural areas to understand the culture and natural history of the environment, taking care not to alter the integrity of the ecosystem, while producing economic opportunities that make conservation of the natural resources beneficial to local people.

Ecotours can vary from bird watching safaris to botanical investigations to tours that focus on local dance styles, or language, or archaeological interests. What they have in common is that they use local guides, seek to educate the client about the natural and cultural world and the environmental issues surrounding it, and actively promote the conservation of each tour site.

The development of ecotourism is a direct response to public interest in the environment, which has risen dramatically in the last 30 years. The market for ecotourism has taken a well known fact—that beautiful pristine environments and unspoiled cultures are good for tourism—and turned it into a defining edict: that ecotourists want to learn about these places and cultures, and that they want to have something to do with conserving them.

French Polynesia is an ideal region for ecotourism as it offers many unspoiled areas of terrestrial and marine flora and fauna to explore, and the Maohi culture is still largely intact. Even though there are environmental problems (some directly related to high-end tourism), even on the more populated islands of Tahiti and Moorea there are still places where an interested person or group can spend a quiet day in a natural setting. There are other islands, such as Huahine, Raiatea and Tahaa, which are better preserved, and many islands in the Tuamotu and Marquesas archipelagoes are still relatively wild. Almost all of the islands are accessible by air.

IAORA TAHITI ECOTOURS (ITE), *B.P. 6845, Faaa, Tahiti; Tel. 689/56.46.75; Voice Mail/Fax 689/42.73.10; e-mail: murphy@mail.pf.*

ITE is the first ecotour company based in French Polynesia, which owners Philipe Siu and Francis (Frank) Murphy plan to be fully operational by mid-1998. Philipe Siu is an oceanographer and fisheries biologist and has worked in French Polynesia as a government research scientist and environmental specialist for the past 28 years. He is a founding member of Iaora Te Natura, Fédération des Associations de Protection de l'Environnement, and Te Manu (ornithological society). Frank Murphy is a geographer and biologist and was most recently the director of the University of California Berkeley Biological Field Station in Moorea. He has extensive experience organizing and conducting natural history tours and university field courses in California, Mexico and French Polynesia. He has lived in Moorea for six years, has traveled widely in French Polynesia, and has taught university students about the natural history of these islands.

The main goal for Iaora Tahiti Ecotours is to design, promote and conduct the most comprehensive and highest quality ecotours in Polynesia. ITE will use the existing tourist infrastructure of hotels, pensions and transportation for all tours, and will train carefully chosen young Tahitians who have an interest in the natural history of their islands. These guides will conduct tours on Moorea, Bora Bora and Rangiroa, and eventually to other islands. Each of the tours will have an average of 10 clients, and the trained guide will remain with the clients throughout the tours, looking after their needs and introducing them to the natural history of each site. In addition to their knowledge of the nature and culture of these islands, the tour guides will also be trained in the latest lifesaving techniques and emergency evacuation procedures.

They will also be people with common sense and a sense of humor, so that you can have fun as you acquire new knowledge and appreciation of the natural and cultural world of Polynesia. ITE will also utilize special resource people who are knowledgeable about particular subjects or particular sites. Included under the broad heading of "natural history" are: geology, geomorphology, oceanography, ecology, conservation, biology, human history and culture, and a variety of environmental issues. The teaching will be done as short lectures in the field and longer organized discussions at other times, using local experts for guest lectures according to the special interests of the group.

The prices quoted for the following tours include double occupancy lodging, three meals a day, all group transport and planned excursions. Single occupancy rooms are available for added fee. Cost does not include non-group activities, personal food and drink, nor international airfare.

Society Islands Odyssey

Society Islands Odyssey is a 7-day tour for 10-12 people to discover the general natural history of Tahiti, Raiatea and Bora Bora. The trip will begin on the legendary island of Tahiti, where you will stay for two days, touring the shore and valleys and visiting all the best historical and natural sites and exhibits. Then you will fly to the sacred island of Raiatea, which was the epicenter of Polynesian religion. On your first day there you will visit the most important temple in all of Polynesia and stop on the way back for a refreshing swim in a tropical river. The following day will be spent exploring the immense lagoon and visiting the adjacent island of Tahaa.

On the next day you will fly to Bora Bora, where you will disappear from the normal tourist scene to visit a tropical garden of fruits and flowers enjoyed only by the clients of Iaora Tahiti Ecotours. On the second day in Bora Bora you will explore the world-famous lagoon and its small coral islets that ring the island. On the last day you will take a morning flight back to Tahiti and you will be taken on a special historical tour of the town of Papeete and then be given time to shop for books or souvenirs, or just to relax and people-watch in a sidewalk cafe. The estimated cost is $1,895.

General Itinerary:

Day 1: Arrival on Tahiti; orientation; relax, trip to Museum
Day 2: Excursion around Tahiti; Botanical Garden, Gauguin Museum, Point Venus
Day 3: Fly to Raiatea, visit Marae Taputapuatea
Day 4: Lagoon tour to Tahaa
Day 5: Travel to Bora Bora; land tour
Day 6: Lagoon trip in Bora Bora
Day 7: Travel to Tahiti; special historical tour of Papeete

Across the Sea of the Moon

This is a 10-day tour for 10-14 people to learn about the natural and cultural history of Tahiti, Moorea and Tetiaroa. The Sea of the Moon lies between the enchanted South Sea isles of Tahiti and Moorea, and the beautiful atoll of Tetiaroa is just over the horizon. The trip will begin on the legendary island of Tahiti where you will stay for three days, hiking in lush tropical valleys, exploring rugged shorelines, and visiting all of the best historical and natural sites and exhibits.

Next you will fly to the atoll of Tetiaroa for two days and two nights, with time to explore the lagoon and many of the small islets that ring the atoll. You will see nesting seabirds and swim in quiet lagoon waters teeming with fish. Then you will travel to Moorea for a three-day visit, where you will tour the island and investigate the shore, lagoon and valleys. You will visit ancient temple sites and present day villages and towns. The final day will be devoted to the preparation and celebration of a traditional Tahitian feast, complete with song and dance. The estimated cost is $2,295.

General Itinerary:

Day 1: Arrival and orientation; relax at hotel, afternoon trip to Museum

Day 2: Excursion around Tahiti; Botanical Garden, Gauguin Museum, Point Venus

Day 3: Hike to a waterfall in one of Tahiti's valleys

Day 4: Fly to Tetiaroa; spend day on lagoon; stay at Marlon Brando's resort

Day 5: Spend day exploring on Tetiaroa; stay at Brando's resort

Day 6: Travel to Moorea; afternoon trip to sacred temple sites; Hotel Bali Hai

Day 7: Excursion around Moorea; Hotel Bali Hai

Day 8: Boat trip on lagoon and to motu; Hotel Bali Hai

Day 9: Free day on Moorea; optional hikes and beach trips; Hotel Bali Hai

Day 10: Prepare and partake in traditional feast and celebration; Hotel Bali Hai

Islands Through Time

This is a 14-day tour for 6-8 people to learn about the general natural history of Tahiti, Moorea and Rangiroa. This trip combines exploration on two exquisite volcanic islands with a cruise aboard a luxury yacht to the deserted coral islands of the second largest atoll in the world. The theme for this trip follows Charles Darwin's theory of reef and oceanic island evolution and will include a wide variety of natural history and cultural topics. The trip begins with a stay on the legendary island of Tahiti, the youngest of all the islands in the archipelago, where you will explore the coastal valleys and take a helicopter ride over the spectacular ridges and through the heart of the volcano.

On the island of Moorea you will investigate ancient temple sites and snorkel in the crystalline lagoons. Then you will fly to Rangiroa at the northern end of the Tuamotu Archipelago. This is an atoll island, where the original volcano has subsided and the remaining reef and reef islands encircle a huge azure lagoon. You will spend a week here sailing the lagoon, snorkeling among a myriad of tropical fish, and strolling along deserted shores. The last day will be spent in Papeete, with time for shopping and sightseeing in the capital city of French Polynesia. On the land portion of this trip you will stay in some of the best hotels in the region, and on the water you will cruise aboard a top-of-the-line 60 foot sailboat. The estimated cost is $4,625.

General Itinerary:
Day 1: Arrival and orientation at hotel
Day 2: Drive around Tahiti
Day 3: Helicopter tour of Tahiti; move to Moorea
Day 4: Tour of Moorea; visit to marae; snorkeling
Day 5: Boat tour of Moorea; visit to motu; snorkeling
Day 6: Travel to Rangiroa; board boat
Day 7-11: Sail the lagoon; explore motu; snorkel; fish; relax
Day 12: Return to Tahiti
Day 13: Free day on Tahiti (shopping, museums, etc.)
Day 14: Departure

DR. MICHAEL POOLE, *CRIOBE, B.P. 1013, Papetoai, Moorea; Tel./ Fax 689/56.14.70; e-mail criobe@mail.ps.*

Michael Poole is an American marine biologist who has lived in Moorea for more than 10 years, studying the 25 local occurring species of dolphins and whales, some of whom live year-round in the waters surrounding Moorea and Tahiti. For his Ph.D. in marine biology, Michael studied at the University of California at Santa Cruz, with Doctor Kenneth Norris, the world's foremost authority on dolphins and whales. Michael chose to come to Moorea for his research work, where the University of California at Berkeley has a biological research station, the Gump Center, located beside Cook's Bay. He is currently associated with the Centre de Recherches Insulaires et Observatoire de l'Environnement (CRIOBE) in Opunohu Bay on Moorea. Michael is also a research associate with the Institute of Marine Sciences at the University of California Santa Cruz. To carry out his research projects, which take him to several other islands in French Polynesia, he depends on grants from foundations, businesses, philanthropists and individuals. He also offers internship programs to interested individuals who wish to participate in the research as "hands-on" field assistants.

Michael has identified over 200 spinner dolphins (*Stenella longirostris*), of which 150 live around Moorea, and humpback whales (*Megaptera novaeangliae*) come up from Antarctica to mate and give birth between July and October. These giant mammals can be seen offshore Moorea, and Michael has a whale-watching and reporting network set up throughout the islands of French Polynesia.

In addition to his internship programs, Michael leads 3-4 hour educational tours twice a week, working with Moorea Boat Tours to give tourists an opportunity to observe the dolphins and whales in their natural environment. The enthusiasm he feels for the mammals he studies is very contagious. Michael is a man who truly loves his work, a teacher who enjoys sharing his knowledge with people.

TEFAARAHI ADVENTURE TOURS, *B.P. 290, Maharepa, Moorea; Tel. 689/56.41.24, Fax 689/56.31.91.*

Derek Grell was the manager of the Hotel Bali Hai Moorea in 1988 when he bought land in a high valley in Maharepa. This volcanic amphitheater had been used as a coffee, cacao and vanilla plantation. While clearing his land in 1994, Derek discovered several petroglyphs carved in the basaltic boulders around the plantation. Archaeologists from Tahiti's Centre Polynésien des Sciences Humaine at the Museum of Tahiti and Her Islands (CPSH) have determined that Derek's land contains the largest collection of petroglyphs that has been discovered south of the Marquesas Islands. At least 50 rocks are chiseled with figures depicting humans, turtles, fish, birds and enigmatic symbols. In these ancient rocks you can see a high priest, a boat or space ship, fat people, stick people, one-armed people and even a compass face or sun dial.

Derek's mountain safari excursion will take you by 4-wheel drive vehicle to visit his property and petroglyphs. He operates 3-hour educational tours for 3.500 CFP ($35), which also include a little hiking from the road to his petroglyphs and plantations. He also leads excursions to Moorea's waterfalls, *marae* temples and highlights around the island. Half- or full-day customized tours are also available.

ARANUI, *Compagnie de Transport Maritime, 2028 El Camino Real South, Suite B, San Mateo, California 94403; in US Tel. 415/574-2575; Fax 415/574-6881; e-mail cptm@aranui.com Internet://www.aranui.com*

The *Aranui* is a 104-meter (343 feet) long working copra-cargo-passenger ship based in Tahiti, offering 16-day round-trip voyages to the Marquesas Islands, with stops in the Tuamotu atolls enroute. There are accommodations for 90 passengers in comfortable, attractive air-conditioned cabins and dormitories, and the ship's dining room, reception, library-lounge, boutique, infirmary, video room, and bar are all air-conditioned.

If you want to get off the beaten path of tourism and discover the authentic lifestyles of the Polynesian people, the *Aranui* offers the best opportunity for this experience. The passengers who choose the *Aranui* are normally well-educated, travel-wise people who have an idea of where they're going, and usually they have already done some background reading on the Marquesas before boarding the ship. An onboard library and video films will help to further your knowledge during the trip. Multilingual guest speakers lecture on Marquesan history, culture, archaeology, art, flora and fauna.

Shore excursions to Marquesan archaeological sites include *me'ae* stone temples, *tohua* assembly places, *paepae* house platforms, stone tikis and petroglyphs. Your guides will take you to the Catholic churches to see the magnificent wooden sculptures carved by Marquesan artisans, and to the handcrafts centers to purchase *umete* bowls, platters, tikis, war clubs, saddles and ukuleles carved from beautiful local woods. You will also find tapa bark cloth, made and painted entirely by hand, carved coconut shells, fragrant *monoi* oils, sandalwood leis and smoky-flavored dried bananas.

Guided trips take you to visit small museums, a botanical garden, vanilla and coconut plantations and noted gravesites, including those of the French painter Paul Gauguin and Belgian singer Jacques Brel in Hiva Oa. You can hike through a tropical rain forest in Fatu Hiva, ride a horse across the island of Ua Huka, picnic on a mountain in Nuku Hiva, see the flower stones (*phonolitis*) in Ua Pou, and enjoy traditional Marquesan *kai kai* feasts that include fresh lobster and curried goat cooked in coconut milk. Optional activities include a helicopter ride above the island of Nuku Hiva or scuba diving with the orcas, manta rays and sharks offshore Nuku Hiva. You can also scuba dive and snorkel in the magnificent lagoon of Rangiroa on the voyage back to Tahiti.

Rates for the 16-day voyage, including accommodations, all meals and guided excursions, range between $1,980 and $3,995 per person. See detailed information in the *Planning Your Trip* chapter.

DR. ROBERT C. SUGGS, *2507 Culpepper Road, Alexandria, Virginia 22308; Tel. 703/780-2242; Fax 703/780-4630.*

Doctor Suggs works with a specialized travel agency to organize elite anthropological/archaeological tours. He received his doctorate from Columbia University in 1959, and was a Research Assistant at the American Museum of Natural History for four years. From 1959 until he retired he was engaged in other scientific research. His first book, *The Island Civilizations of Polynesia*, was published in 1960 and translated into eight languages. *Hidden Worlds of Polynesia*, published in 1962, was a chronicle of a year Doctor Suggs and his wife Rachel spent in Nuku Hiva in 1957 and 1958. He also authored *Lords of the Blue Pacific*, a book for juveniles, *Marquesan Sexual Behavior*, and *The Archaeology of Nuku Hiva, Marquesas Islands, French Polynesia*, a monograph for the American Museum of Natural History, Volume 49.

After many years' absence, Doctor Suggs returned to Tahiti and the Marquesas Islands in 1993, and since then he has become involved in various archaeological scientific and educational projects that continue to bring him back to French Polynesia. In addition to lecturing aboard the *Aranui*, Doctor Suggs has also cruised as guest speaker aboard the *World Discoverer* and the *Royal Viking Sun*, on behalf of the Smithsonian Institute.

WORLD DISCOVERER is a German-built ship that is 285 feet long, 50 feet wide and has a draft of 15 feet, which is operated by **Society Expeditions** for adventure and eco-cruises to remote islands. The 140-passenger ship has 71 cabins on seven decks, each with an outside view, lower beds, private bathroom and temperature control. The Observation Lounge gives you a 180 degree view of the islands, lagoons and sea. The Marco Polo Dining Room serves Continental cuisine prepared by European chefs, and the spacious public areas also include the Discoverer and Lido Lounges and Bars, a lecture hall and cinema, a limited fitness center with sauna, a beauty salon and gift shop, a medical center with physician, a library and a sun deck with pool. A team of naturalists will travel with you to introduce you to the flora and fauna of land and lagoon, using a fleet of Zodiacs to go ashore where there are no docking facilities.

The 1998 cruise schedule includes six visits to French Polynesia, where you will embark or disembark in Papeete. These cruises will take you to Tahiti, Moorea, Huahine, Raiatea, Bora Bora, Mopelia, Rangiroa and Mataiva, as well as to other islands and atolls in the Pacific. You can get information and rates on these eco-cruises by contacting your travel agent. See further information in the *Planning Your Trip* chapter.

12. FOOD & DRINK

I've listened to big beefy American men comparing prices as they stood in a hotel swimming pool beside Moorea's Cook's Bay, totally ignoring the incredible beauty of the mountains and lagoon, as they talked about how they managed to cut costs on their trip to Moorea. One of them bragged that he had collected free packages of coffee, tea, sugar, cream, mustard, ketchup, mayonnaise, crackers and other condiments from the fast food outlets in his town, and had brought them along.

Others described all the snacks, soft drinks and alcohol they had packed into a cooler for the trip. None of these people were eating in the hotel or nearby restaurants. They spent their week surviving on processed snack foods they brought with them, plus the crusty French *baguette* bread, luncheon meats, cheese and crackers bought at the nearest food store. Although the hotel has a no-food-in-the-room policy, it is usually ignored, and some of the guests are unwilling to spend 200 CFP ($2) for a cup of coffee in the hotel restaurant.

If you decide to travel on a very tight budget, please try not to let the high prices occupy so much of your attention that you cannot even enjoy these magnificent islands. You may want to have a look in the larger supermarkets in Tahiti, where there are delicatessen counters with a varied selection of prepared foods. The smaller *magasins* in Tahiti and the outer islands sell tasty take-away meals of rice with chicken, meat or fish, and containers of *poisson cru* for about 500 CFP ($5). The mobile diners, *les roulottes*, are now found in all the Society Islands, where you can have a good meal for under $10. There are also small, inexpensive restaurant/ snacks, which are listed under *Where to Eat* for each island.

You can buy a soft drink for 100 CFP ($1) at some of the coin-operated vending machines and from a few of the *roulottes* and snack bars, and this same canned drink will cost you as much as 450 CFP ($4.50) in a hotel bar. Tahiti's favorite locally brewed beer is Hinano, which sells for about 125 CFP ($1.25) for a small can or bottle in grocery stores, and for up to 450 CFP ($4.50) in some restaurants and bars. Most restaurants serve *vin ordinaire* (table wine) by the carafe, and an acceptable quality of Bordeaux can be purchased at the grocery stores for around 1.200 CFP ($12).

For most of us, one of the greatest pleasures of traveling to a foreign country is to sample the local cuisine. If your budget allows a few meals in a restaurant while you're visiting Tahiti, Moorea, Bora Bora or any of the other islands in French Polynesia, then chances are you will have a superb meal.

LA NOUVELLE CUISINE TAHITIENNE

The hotels and restaurants in Tahiti have earned a reputation among gourmet visitors for serving choice cuisine. The chefs have united the flavors of Europe and the Orient, spiked with a fresh tropical island accent. Whether he came from France, Switzerland, Italy, South America or Asia, each newcomer brought his little sprig of thyme, his chili pepper, soybean or ginger, perhaps to ward off the effects of home sickness in a foreign land.

Culinary choices feature French *haute cuisine*, seven-course Imperial dinners from the provinces of China, Vietnamese *nems*, Italian pasta, Algerian *couscous*, Spanish *paella*, spicy West Indian specialties and Alsatian *choucroute*. These imaginative and creative chefs have also introduced a *nouvelle cuisine Tahitienne* that is a combination of the traditional recipes of their own home countries and the fresh bounty of the Polynesian waters and fruit orchards. Dishes may include fresh local snapper infused with vanilla sauce, a lagoon *bouillabaisse*, reef clams in garlic butter, sautéed crab with ginger, *varo* with champagne and cream, roast duck with papaya or chicken drumsticks with *fafa* and taro.

To accompany these memorable meals are fine French wines and champagnes, locally brewed beer, or a selection of imported beers. Most of the bars bill themselves as a "Bar Americaine" and serve mixed cocktails. Freshly squeezed orange, grapefruit or pineapple juices are sometimes available, or you will be served fruit juices from the cartons of the Moorea Fruit Juice Factory and Distillery. Perrier and a wide variety of carbonated waters are stocked, as well as the most popular soda pops, sometimes including carbonated diet drinks. Bottled waters from Tahiti and France are also served.

SNACK BARS, FAST FOODS, SALONS DE THÈ, & PATISSERIES

You'll find an abundance of small restaurants in Tahiti and Her Islands that are advertised as Snacks or Restaurant/Snacks. Most of these places are clean and serve daily specials of local style home cooking. The food is usually delicious and inexpensive. The choices often include *poisson cru* with coconut milk, beef or lamb stew, an assortment of curry dishes, fresh lagoon fish, chicken and vegetables, prawns in garlic sauce, pork and taro, chow mien, or *maa tinito haricots rouge*, which is a Chinese dish of red beans, macaroni, pork or chicken, Chinese vermicelli noodles and a few more good things.

Fast foods have definitely arrived on the scene in Tahiti, with international and local style hamburger stands popping up all over the island. MacDonald's has a prime site in downtown Papeete and Kentucky Fried Chicken has an outlet in Punaauia, with a second location soon to open in downtown Papeete. Now you hardly have to pause at all in your shopping to have a bite to eat. You can walk up to a sidewalk food stand and order a *casse-croûte*, a ham and cheese *croissant*, a small pizza or a *Panini* sandwich. Or you can beat the heat of the Papeete streets while enjoying some of the world's best ice cream.

Salons de thè serve a variety of teas and *infusions*, as well as *espressos* and vanilla flavored coffee from Pacific plantations. *Patisseries* provide people watching in air-conditioned comfort while nibbling on your choice of flaky pastries.

LES ROULOTTES

Les roulottes are mobile diners (roach coaches) that set up shop each evening along the cruise ship dock on the Papeete waterfront and serve hot meals until the wee hours of the morning. These colorful food vans provide good, fast food at reasonable prices, as well as a bar stool, where you can sit and watch the waterfront scene of Papeete-by-night.

You can order barbecue steaks, chicken and shish-kabob, served with French fries, *poisson cru*, or *salade russe*, which is potato salad with beets. Specialty diners serve pizza cooked in a wood-burning stove, *couscous*, fish and chips, Tahitian food, barbecue veal and freshly wokked hot delicacies from the provinces of China. Your dinner can be a veritable moveable feast, with a tempting choice of *crêpe*s for dessert. No alcohol is served here, but the bars and nightclubs are just across the street.

TAHITIAN FEASTS

Several hotels and individually-owned restaurants in Tahiti and the other tourist islands feature regular Tahitian feasts. The *tamaara'a* (tah-mah-AH-rah-ah) is Tahiti's equivalent to the luau served in Hawaii, only much more authentic. This feast features *maa Tahiti* (MAH-ah), foods that are cooked for several hours in an underground *ahima'a* (ah-HEE-mah-ah) oven. These usually include roast pig, *taro* root, *tarua* root, breadfruit, yams, bananas, *fei* (fey-ee) plantains, *fafa* (taro leaves cooked with chicken and coconut milk that tastes like spinach), and accompanied by coconut sauces. Dessert is a gooey pudding called *po'e*, (PO-eh), which is made with bananas, papaya, pumpkin or other fruits and flavored with coconut milk.

The national dish of Tahiti is *ei'a ota* (ee-ah OH-ta), which the French call *poisson cru*. It's made with small cubes of fresh tuna or bonito fish that have been marinated in lime juice and mixed with chopped tomatoes, grated carrots, thinly sliced onions and cucumbers and coconut milk. It's delicious and even better with a French *baguette*. If you have an adventurous palate then you'll want to try *fafaru*, slices of fish marinated in a stinky sauce that most Tahitians just adore. The traditional manner of eating *maa Tahiti* is with your fingers, although forks are normally supplied. Most hotel restaurants also serve a buffet of Continental foods along with the Tahitian dishes. In hotels the *tamaara'a* is normally accompanied by Tahitian music and an hour-long folkloric dance show. The colorfully costumed entertainers perform the traditional dances of Tahiti and the musicians play exciting music on their drums, guitars and ukuleles. The dancers may even invite you to dance the *tamure*.

VEGETARIAN MEALS

Tahiti is not a paradise for dieters or vegetarians. Most of the restaurants serve rich entrees made with real butter, knowing that few people go out to diet. It is difficult to get a piece of grilled fish or steak without having a generous serving of parsley butter on the top. Lagoon fish and prawns are usually served with the heads intact, so if you're squeamish about having your dinner looking at you, order a fish filet or something else. Vegetarians usually have a choice of rice, potatoes, green beans and salads, plus fresh fruits, French cheeses and tempting desserts. A few restaurants do have vegetarian plates. These are indicated in the Where to Eat section of each island.

13. TAHITI'S BEST PLACES TO STAY

HOTEL BORA BORA

Point Raititi in Bora Bora. Tel. (689) 60.44.60, Fax (689) 60.44.66; Reservations Tel. (689) 60.44.11, Fax (689) 60.44.22, US & Canada Bookings toll free at (800) 421-1490, (800) 447-7462, Year round Rack Rates from $395 per double bungalow per night (EP). Meal Plan with Breakfast & Dinner is $68 per person, Meal Plan with Breakfast, Lunch & Dinner is $72 per person. Special Honeymoon Packages Available.

The Hotel Bora Bora is my favorite hotel anywhere in the world. This 37-year old establishment is to the hotel industry what the QE 2 is to the cruise ship business: it has stately, royal class and the comfort of a privileged country club. The Hotel Bora Bora is as solid to me as the Otemanu mountain that rises from the heart of the island behind the hotel.

Since it's opening in June, 1961 the Hotel Bora Bora has frequently been rated in guide books as one of the world's top resort hotels. The Hotel Bora Bora has been a member of the prestigious Amanresorts since 1988. The *Condé Nast Traveler* Gold List for 1998 gives the Hotel Bora Bora the fourth highest rating for location and atmosphere and the fifth highest rating for rooms and service among the 18 hotels chosen in the Australia and Pacific Nations area. The 55-room hotel received the seventh overall highest average rating in this area, which includes accommodations in Australia, Fiji, French Polynesia and New Zealand.

This luxurious resort has attracted some of the world's most discriminating travelers and it is a favored destination for stars of the cinema, television and stage, plus several leaders in politics and business. Many of these personalities return again and again, where they can still find the magical charm that entranced them during their first visit. Often these repeat visitors celebrate their special wedding anniversaries in the same bungalow where they spent their first honeymoon. Some of them have given the name of the bungalow to their babies, who were conceived while the parents were spending their honeymoon at the Hotel Bora Bora. And several of these children come to this hotel years later for their own honeymoons.

The gracious staff of the Hotel Bora Bora always accommodate the guests, yet keep their distance. This friendly and professional approach has helped to earn a favorable reputation for the hotel.

Seventeen acres of luxuriant tropical flowers and exotic foliage border three lovely beaches of fine white sand. Sea birds nest in the fronds of the towering coconut palms and the surf tenderly laps the shore. The vast sparkling lagoon of Bora Bora is a tableau of at least seven shades of blue and green. The coral gardens are one of the hotel's best attributes. The hotel management encourages the guests to feed the fish in the lagoon, and there are hundreds of tropical fish of every hue, including the graceful manta rays, who perform their ballet nightly next to the boat dock and below the deep overwater bungalows.

Amidst this exclusive setting on the peninsula of Point Raititi, the Hotel Bora Bora offers 55 individual guest bungalows. Your choice of accommodations includes four deluxe bungalows on the beach, with an elevated sundeck built on columns with steps leading to the edge of the waterline. These bungalows have a bedroom facing the sea and a separate lounge overlooking the sundeck. Fourteen superior bungalows are located on the beachfront, offering a spacious bedroom, bathroom and sitting area leading to a small patio facing the sea. Each bungalow has a hammock nearby, where you can enjoy the beach and sea breeze. Five garden bungalows are of the same design as the superior bungalows.

Six premium overwater bungalows are situated on a coral reef in a deeper section of the lagoon, surrounded by marine life. Each of the luxurious units features a spacious bedroom with a king-size four-poster bed, a bathroom with a venetian blind indoor panel and a sundeck terrace with a pandanus shade over the top level and a shower at the water level next to the steps set into the lagoon. Nine overwater bungalows are of the same design as the premium overwater units, but they are set over shallow water in the lagoon, nearer to the boat dock and the main walkway.

A new category of accommodation at the Hotel Bora Bora offers *fares* or villas, which provide guests with a living room, bedroom with king-size four-poster bed, sitting room, a bathroom and a large sundeck. Three premium *fares* (Numbers 21, 27 and 29) are situated in prime beach locations on the Matira side of the resort. Eight pool *fares* are surrounded by a rock garden wall for added privacy, enclosing a small swimming pool and outdoor sun pavilion for two. Six *fares* are situated within the beachfront area or in the gardens, and some feature an outdoor Jacuzzi tub on the sundeck.

All the spacious bungalows are built in the Polynesian style with hand-tied thatched pandanus roofs, ceiling fans and natural woods. The decor is neutral with plenty of natural light, drawing the vivid colors of the lagoon and gardens into every room. All accommodations have free standing bathtubs and separate showers, hair-dryers, private bars, coffee and tea facilities, radio/cassette players, personal safes and dual 110/220 voltage. Telephones are optional.

The main building of the Hotel Bora Bora is located on a bluff overlooking Point Raititi. From the Matira Terrace Restaurant you can watch the hotel's outrigger sailing canoes skimming across the lagoon while you enjoy a bountiful breakfast buffet. The French *chef de cuisine* ensures that the menu upholds the reputation of the hotel, and each dinner is a gourmet's treat. The Pofai Beach Bar is ideal for light lunches while you're relaxing on the beach.

High-tide Tea is served on the beach late in the afternoon, flavored with fresh vanilla beans from the island of Tahaa, and accompanied by banana or coconut cookies. My favorite place to watch the sunset behind the island of Maupiti is from the Matira Terrace Bar, where colorful cocktails are accompanied by Polynesian musicians playing some of the romantic songs of the island.

The reception area, guest relations and activities desks, and the Shop Bora Bora boutique are located in the main building. The Pofai Shoppe, next to the hotel's two complimentary tennis courts, basketball court and volleyball court, is a general store that sells souvenirs, post cards, local jewelry, film, cheeses, caviar, cold drinks and champagne.

Fare Raititi game room is set up for billiards and table tennis. You'll find a selection of local and international newspapers in the lounge here, as well as a paperback book exchange, video and television with international broadcasts. Other free of charge activities include snorkeling, outrigger paddle and sailing canoes, garden tours, flower crown and lei making lessons, *pareo* tying, *tamure* lessons, *poisson cru* demonstrations, and a twice-daily shuttle bus service to Vaitape village.

Paid activities include circle island tours, horseback riding, jeep safaris, helicopter excursions, glass bottom boat rides, barrier reef trips, snorkeling safaris and shark feeding, ray ballet and coral gardens, speedboat rentals, airport express, blue lagoon cruises, saltwater fly fishing, offshore fishing, scuba diving, jet ski tours, and sunset champagne trips on the resort's 46-foot sailing catamaran.

Honeymooners are welcomed at the Hotel Bora Bora as very special guests. The *Honeymoon* package includes a bed of flowers in your room, champagne and a tropical fruit platter, a candlelight dinner with wine served on your terrace, and a private sunset sail aboard an outrigger sailing canoe. A *Beyond the Ordinary* program includes a three-night private sailing charter aboard the 50-foot sailing catamaran *Taravana*. Should you desire to exchange vows or reaffirm them, the hotel will arrange a *Polynesian Ceremony* or a *Marriage of Hearts Ceremony*. When you return to the Hotel Bora Bora with your children, be assured that baby-sitting service is available.

KIA ORA SAUVAGE RANGIROA

Motu Avea is a private islet 25 miles or one hour by boat from Kia Ora Village in Rangiroa, Tel. (689) 96.03.84/96.02.22, Fax (689) 96.04.93/96.02.20, US & Canada Bookings toll free (800) 221-4542, Fax (914) 472-0451, Year round Rack Rates $240 per double beach bungalow per night (EP), Meal Plan with Breakfast, Lunch & Dinner is $70 per person, Round-trip Boat Transfers between Kia Ora Village and motu $75 per person.

Do you harbor secret dreams of escaping to a desert isle, far, far away, and living the simple life—a modern version of Robinson Crusoe's experience? Are you looking for a little haven of peace, where you can fish for your dinner, breathe pure sweet air, sunbathe *au naturel*, listen to the thunder of the surf on the reef, and gaze at the Southern Cross or an enormous full moon?

Kia Ora Sauvage is lost from the big world and all its problems. You have to go a little further these days to find a paradise of peace and tranquillity. First you have to fly to Tahiti, then to Rangiroa, then take an hour's boat ride across the lagoon to get there. But it's definitely worth the trip. Tahiti Vacations' clients have voted this little hotel their favorite holiday destination. What they like best about the Kia Ora Sauvage is the Polynesian tradition, which is scrupulously guarded.

Five little thatched roof bungalows are located on the white sand beach of a 4-hectare (9.88-acre) islet named Motu Avae Rahi, which means "isle of the big moon." I've stayed here twice during the full moon, and during my last trip in April, 1997, all the guests stood on the beach under the enormous bowl of the sky and gazed at the huge full moon, the Hale-Bopp comet, the Southern Cross and the other wonders of the celestial universe, while Ugo, the manager, gave his guests a lesson in astronomy.

Ugo's father, Robin Angely, was one of the three founders of the Kia Ora Village. When the Kia Ora Sauvage was opened in 1991, Ugo and his wife Celine were put in charge of the hotel, which was created to give people a Robinson Crusoe type experience. Ugo likes to make a play on words by joking that he is Robin's son. He and Celine do a super job of running the place and keeping their guests happy. They are assisted by another couple, and Napoleon, Ugo's dog, is the mascot of the island and a favorite pet of all the guests.

Each of the attractive and comfortable bungalows accommodates two or three people. The bedspreads on the king-size bed and single bed are a tapa cloth design in brown and beige, with matching curtains and cushion covers for the queen's chair and the dressing table stool. A step-down bathroom has a coral floor, a tiled shower with cold water, and a huge clam shell lavabo. You can sit on your terrace and read or watch the small lagoon sharks swimming close to the white sand beach as they arrive for their twice-daily feeding when Ugo and Taufa, his all-purpose handy man, clean the fish for lunch and dinner.

In keeping with the *sauvage* or wild, natural theme, the hotel has no electricity. Taufa sets two lighted petrol lamps on your steps each evening, and you should also bring a small flashlight.

Ugo makes twice-daily radio contact with the Kia Ora Village, to learn of new arrivals and to order food supplies and more ice for the rum punches and other drinks he'll prepare for you at the bar. He blows a *pu* (triton) shell to summons you to meals, which are served family style inside the restaurant or under the shade of Tiare Kahaia trees on the beach. Fresh lagoon fish and shellfish from the coral reef are daily fare, which are supplemented by Celine's creative salads, chicken and meat dishes. Her French toast is a favorite breakfast choice.

You can work off the calories by paddling an outrigger canoe or windsurfing to a nearby *motu*. You can also go spear fishing with Ugo or accompany him to the fringing reef to collect *maoa* sea snails and *pahua* clams for dinner. You'll walk through incredible walls of crystallized coral that rise six feet above the sea. These miniature cathedrals are called *feo*, which Ugo says are over four million years old. He'll also invite you to come along to explore *motu* islets that are even more wild than Kia Ora Sauvage. You are free to do whatever you want, or nothing at all. That's the whole idea of playing "cast-away."

MANIHI PEARL BEACH RESORT

On Manihi atoll in the Tuamotu archipelago, just an hour and 15 minutes by direct flight from Tahiti. Tel. (689)96.42.73, Fax (689) 96.42.72. US bookings (607) 273-5012, Fax (607) 273-5302, E-mail: sales@tahiti-nui.com Internet: http://www.tahiti-nui.com Year round Rack Rates from $260 per double beach bungalow per night (EP). Honeymoon Packages are available. Meal plan with Breakfast & Dinner is $59.50 per person, Meal plan with Breakfast, Lunch and Dinner is $82.50 per person.

Manihi is a world removed from time and care, a tiny green oasis floating in the desert of the sea, with a name as exotic as the trade winds and coconut trees, and a lagoon as pretty as a mother-of-pearl shell. Manihi Pearl Beach Resort is the only hotel on the atoll and it is one of the most beautiful and pleasant resort hotels you'll find anywhere.

Renaud Coquille is the general manager of Manihi Pearl Beach Resort, the first of a chain of deluxe four-star Pearl Beach Resorts to be built in French Polynesia. The 22 beach bungalows and 19 deluxe overwater bungalows are located on the site of the former Kaina Village, a small hotel that opened in 1977 and was operated until the end of 1995 by Mareva and Guy Coquille, Renaud's parents. Renaud attended hotel schools in Tahiti and France and visited his parents in Manihi only during his school vacations. When he became manager of the Manihi Pearl Beach Resort in 1996, Renaud brought his Spanish wife, Veronica, and their young two daughters to live full time on the premises. Veronica runs the boutique and makes sure the rooms are perfect for your arrival.

I think that the overwater bungalows in this hotel are the prettiest of all the deluxe accommodations in French Polynesia. The roof is thatched palm leaves and the wooden walls are covered with matting of pandanus fibers. The soft blonde-beige hard wood furniture matches the golden tones of the split bamboo trim, and geometric Polynesian tattoo designs are carved into the wood between the wall and ceiling, around the full length mirror and around the exterior base of the bungalow. The king size bed and day bed have neutral beige covers with accent cushions the color of the turquoise and emerald lagoon, which is visible from almost every angle.

The glass top coffee table that allows you to view the fish below your bungalow has become almost *de rigeur* in overwater bungalows, but the Manihi Pearl Beach Resort gives you additional fish watching possibilities with windows on two sides of a writing desk, where you'll also find a telephone and small lamp. Glass tables on each side of the bed and glass panels in the bathroom keep you in touch with what's happening in the lagoon at all times. A light can be turned on at night to attract the fish and you can even watch a family of blue, green, turquoise and red parrot fish nibbling their dinner while you're brushing your teeth after your own meal!

The lagoon is always in view if you choose to open the shutters between the bathroom and bedroom. A triple sliding glass door leads to the terrace, with heavy blackout curtains for privacy and light beige sheers for diffused lighting. The railing of the terrace is made of decorative *miki miki* branches, fragrant bushes that grow on the coral shores of the atolls. Two *chaises longues* welcome sunbathers and lagoon gazers, and a curved stairway leads you down into the warm waters of liquid crystal.

In addition to the fabulous bungalows at Manihi Pearl Beach Resort, I also like the big salt water swimming pool between the white sand beach and the lagoon. The restaurant serves French cuisine and some local dishes, and you can get a sandwich at the bar between lunch and dinner if you want a lighter meal. Activities are centered around the lagoon, with emphasis on scuba diving. Frenchman Gilles Petre runs the Manihi Blue

Nui dive center on the premises, and his American wife, Wendy, takes care of his reservations.

Because the Manihi Pearl Beach Resort is a small hotel, it is easy to get to know the employees and other guests. The feeling here is that of a small village, not at all a Club Med ambiance. Renaud Coquille sets a friendly pace in his own quiet, gentle way, and he has a team of employees who follow suit.

HOTEL MOANA BEACH PARKROYAL

Beside the lagoon at Point Matira on Bora Bora. Tel. (689) 60.49.00, Fax (689) 60.49.99. US Bookings toll free at (800) 835-7742, e-mail prkroyal@mail.pf Year round Rack Rates from $498 per double beach bungalow per night (EP). Honeymoon packages are available. Meal Plan with Breakfast & Dinner is $68 per person, Meal Plan with Breakfast, Lunch & Dinner is $98 per person. Special Honeymoon Packages Available.

Built over the turquoise and jade green Bora Bora lagoon are 41 thatched roof bungalows, and just steps from the water are 10 bungalows on the fine white sand beach. Nearby are the buildings housing the hotel's reception, restaurant and bar, boutique and activities lounge.

Each spacious bungalow looks like a setting out of a South Seas movie. They are a very attractive combination of hardwood, woven pandanus fronds and golden bamboo, and the decor is light, airy, colorful and very tropical. There is a large master bedroom, a sitting room and sundeck. From the covering on the king size bed to the paintings on the walls, the colors and designs of the decor are elegantly and tastefully Polynesian.

Hibiscus blossoms and frangipani flowers are everywhere—in the bathtub, on the separate toilet, next to the tea and coffee maker, among the complimentary soaps, shampoos and bath gel, on the lighted dressing table with its hair-dryer, on the television, and the bedside table, which also has a radio panel and control for the overhead fan. Brightly colored flowers are scattered across the big comfortable bed, on top of the well-stocked mini-bar and refrigerator, on the writing table and even on the glass coffee table, through which you can watch the flora and fauna of the lagoon beneath your overwater bungalow. Vanilla vines twine around the bamboo ceiling and a picture window frames the postcard views of Otemanu mountain, the island of Tahaa and the sparkling clear lagoon.

These lavishly decorated junior-suites were designed for lovers. Simply display your bamboo "do not disturb" sign outside the door and create a world of your own. The bedside telephone can be used for direct dialing international calls, or for ordering delicious meals from room service. Upon request a memorable breakfast will be delivered to your overwater bungalow. The flower-ornamented tray arrives at your steps aboard an outrigger canoe, and a *pareo*-clad *vahine* or *tane* presents your meal with a smile and "Ia Ora Na" greeting. Twice-daily maid service keeps the room always clean and filled with flowers and lots of fluffy towels. Blackout curtains provide complete privacy and two lounge chairs on the deck are ideal for hand-in-hand star-gazing. Step down from your deck into the warm embrace of the clear lagoon for the feel of paradise.

Should you lovers decide to visit the rest of the hotel, you will discover that the hotel has a lovely white sand beach, and a cool oasis of greenery to welcome you when you arrive by car. You need only walk across the road from the entrance to watch a spectacular sunset from the western side of Matira Beach. The Vini Vini Bar has special cocktails and a musical trio, who play their guitars and ukuleles between 6-7 each evening, and during dinner in the Noa Noa Restaurant, while you dine on a gourmet meal of French specialties and *la nouvelle cuisine Tahitienne*, an imaginative alliance of local seafoods and fruits prepared with a French flair. Entertainment includes a *pareo* show, demonstrations of Tahitian cooking, crab races or a slide show presenting the Tahitian black pearls that are sold in the hotel boutique or how to grow and use vanilla.

Franck De Lestapis, the young bachelor manager of the Moana Beachcomber Parkroyal Bora Bora, will happily orchestrate a Polynesian wedding ceremony for you on the beach at sunset, should you so desire. You can choose a full-on traditional Polynesian wedding ceremony for 185.000 CFP ($1,850) or a mini version for 85.000 CFP ($850). You can also get married in the Faanui Protestant Church and sail away into the sunset for an hour on the Bora Bora lagoon, with your wedding cake and champagne, for 185.000 CFP ($1,850).

Romantic dinners for two and romantic picnics can be arranged at your request. One of the most popular events for lovers is the 3-hour Moonlight Dinner Cruise aboard a double-decker outrigger canoe, for 7.200 CFP ($72) per person. The cruise begins just in time to watch the golden moon rising over the island. You dine on a delicious bouillabaisse, breathe in the soft tropical sea breeze, and listen to the surf crashing on the barrier reef and the on-board musicians singing "Bora Bora." Raise your glass in a toast to one another, Bora Bora and romance.

The Beach Boys at the sports *fare* will give you pointers on how to use the snorkeling equipment, windsurf boards or glass-bottom outrigger paddle canoes for two. The activities director will explain the hotel's full range of land and water sports, which include shark- and ray-feeding safaris, and a visit to a lagoonarium. You can take a catamaran cruise, sailing picnic cruise, sunset cruise, glass-bottom boat ride, go water-skiing, scuba diving, deep-sea or lagoon fishing, parasail above the lagoon, picnic on a *motu* islet, ride horses, explore the mountains by jeep safari, ride around the island on a guided bus tour or in a private limousine. You can also rent a car or bike around the island and discover Bora Bora's charms on your own. Or you can just remain in your private overwater bungalow, order from room service and be romantic.

TAHITI BEACHCOMBER PARKROYAL

Beside the lagoon at Point Tata'a on the border of Faaa and Punaauia, facing the island of Moorea. Tel. (689) 86.51.10, Fax (689) 86.51.30, US & Canada Bookings at (800) 835-7742, e-mail prkroyal@mail.pf Year Round Rack Rates from $293 per double room per night (EP), Meal Plan with Breakfast & Dinner is $68 per person, Meal Plan with Breakfast, Lunch & Dinner is $98 per person. Special Honeymoon Packages Available.

This is Tahiti's "can-do" hotel. The professional staff is very efficient and the management makes sure that your stay will be more than satisfactory. This is a favorite hotel for honeymooners, business people, incentive groups and individual travelers.

Southern Pacific Hotels inaugurated the hotel in 1974, which operated as a Travelodge for several years before changing names and owners. The Tahiti Beachcomber is now a member of the prestigious Parkroyal collection of 4 1/2 to 5 star hotels. The 180 air-conditioned rooms and suites in the three-story buildings have been renovated and refurbished several times and are very attractively decorated, with a choice of king- and queen-size beds or twin beds, plus a sitting area. Many of the rooms have a private balcony or terrace overlooking the island of Moorea.

The hotel's overwater bungalows are built in the Polynesian style, with thatched roofs, natural woods and private sun decks with steps leading into the lagoon. There are 17 deluxe overwater bungalows grouped around a private island, reached by a bridge from the main property. The hotel's newest addition are 15 beautifully appointed junior suites built over the lagoon at the legendary Point Tata'a, which you can reach by golf cart or a leisurely stroll through the hotel gardens. All the overwater units are air-conditioned and also have an overhead fan and screened windows and sliding glass doors. If your budget can cover the cost, the overwater junior suites offer the most intimacy. Imagine yourself reclining on a deck chair at night, drinking fine French champagne and gazing at the Southern stars from the privacy of your overwater balcony.

All rooms and bungalows have separate bathrooms with bathtubs and courtesy Parkroyal soaps, *monoi* and bath gels. Each room has a stocked mini-bar, coffee and tea making facilities, hair-dryer, color television with cable, radio, direct dial telephone, twice-a-day maid service, and same-day laundry and dry-cleaning service. Three free laundromats are provided for your convenience. Room service is available from 7am to 10pm, and guests staying in the overwater bungalows can be served breakfast by outrigger canoe. These guests also receive a complimentary basket of fruit upon arrival.

In the reception area of the main building is a lobby with comfortable sofas and easy chairs, where you can watch the Tahitian "mamas" display their crafts work several times a week. There are desks for guest activities, rental cars, excursions, and day trips to outer islands. Also on this level you'll find a beauty parlor, duty free gift shop and newsstand, a Tahiti Pearls boutique, a currency exchange, and function rooms that are used for conferences, seminars and art shows. One of the hotel's three bars is in the corner of the lobby. You can take the elevator or the stairway to the ground level, where you will find the spacious Tiki Bar and open-air Tiare Restaurant, which has all-day dining. The air-conditioned Hibiscus Restaurant is on the second floor and is used for special occasions. Le Lotus Restaurant and Bar has the most romantic setting of any restaurant on the island, with a lovely view of Moorea. See more information on these two restaurants under the *Where to Eat* section of the chapter on Tahiti.

The 35 acres of landscaped tropical gardens surrounding the hotel include two flood-lit tennis courts, a golf park with a driving range, pitch and putt, and a jogging trail. In addition to two large fresh water swimming pools, an outdoor Jacuzzi and four white sand beaches, you'll find a nautical center, where you can book glass bottom boat rides, snorkeling excursions, sailing picnics, a day-sail to Moorea, or a popular sunset cruise. Water sports include Hobie Cats, windsurfing, water-skiing, pedal-boats, surf-bikes, snorkeling, scuba diving, and speedboat trips to sunbathe on the hotel's private pontoons within the reef protected lagoon.

Each guest is given an Activities Rainbow of daily happenings at the Tahiti Beachcomber Parkroyal. These include a folkloric marketplace, demonstrations of Tahitian cuisine, fashion and dance, slide shows, Happy Hour with musical entertainment in the Tiki Bar several nights a week, and a visit to the Papeete market early on Sunday mornings. A Barbecue Dinner and Tahitian dance show is held in Te Tiare Restaurant each Wednesday night. A *Soirée Merveilleuse* Seafood Buffet is held on the beach each Friday night, with a team of dancers and musicians performing a torch lit show on and around the hotel's private beach and lagoon. A Candlelight Dinner Show each Saturday evening includes Tahitian dancing, and each Sunday's feature is a Tahitian breakfast buffet, a Buffet Brunch with a dance show, and a Tahitian Feast in the evening, also with a Tahitian dance show.

This hotel receives my highest recommendation for your place to stay on the island of Tahiti.

HOTEL BALI HAI HUAHINE

B.P. 341, Fare, Huahine, Tel. (689) 68.84.77, Fax (689) 68.82.77. US Bookings toll free at (800) 282-1401. Year Round Rack Rates from $115 per double poolside bungalow (EP). Meal Plan with Breakfast & Dinner is $45 per person, Meal Plan with Breakfast Lunch & Dinner is $69 per person.

The saga of the Bali Hai "Boys" from Moorea added a new chapter in 1973, when American expatriates Hugh Kelley, Muk McCallum and Jay Carlisle opened the 10-bungalow Bali Hai Huahine. Most of the employees spoke only Tahitian and had never seen a tourist. When the hotel began to entertain the guests with a Tahitian dance show on Saturday evenings, the young men from the island flocked to the hotel to look at the lady tourists. The hotel manager gave them lessons in social etiquette vis-à-vis American or European women.

Tour operators discovered that the tourists were enchanted with Huahine, where they found the true Polynesia they had hoped to find when they made their reservations back home.

Over the years the Hotel Bali Hai Huahine added more attractive bungalows, combining the natural products of the island into a blend of bamboo, pandanus, wood and stone. Today there are 15 garden bungalows, 10 rooms overlooking the swimming pool with a waterfall, 11 bungalows built at the edge of a palm-shaded lake filled with water lilies, and 7 bungalows built along a soft white sand beach that overlooks a lagoon that offers excellent swimming in the clearest shades of turquoise and blue. Down the beach toward Fare, which is just a five-minute walk from the hotel, cruising yachts tie a line around a coconut tree and come to the Bali Hai bar to relax with a cold beer, Bloody Mary or Maitai.

The restaurant serves meals to suit the tastes of their clientele, who come from the States, Italy, Spain, France and New Zealand. The menu boasts of the "real" Salade Niçoise, which even includes the anchovies. Nina took my order for a filet of mahi mahi in lemon butter sauce for 1.400 CFP ($14), which was melt-in-your-mouth deliciously fresh. Nina has worked at the Hotel Bali Hai since it opened. She is in charge of the dining room and bar, where she has learned English, Spanish and Italian, in addition to her French and Tahitian. Her husband Kaukura is from the Cook Islands, and he worked his way up through the Bali Hai chain to become manager of the hotel in Huahine.

You can learn a bit of Huahine's history and folklore without even leaving the hotel grounds. In the reception area is a display window containing adzes, fishhooks, whale tooth pendants, tapa beaters and wooden bowls that were found on the hotel grounds during various phases of construction. They date back to Circa 850, when a settlement of people inhabited the site adjacent to where the hotel is located today. The handcrafts "mamas" demonstrate how to make marinated fish, how to weave the fibers of the island's trees into pretty hats, bags, fans and other useful items. And the girls who tend bar will teach you how to dance the *tamure*, which you can put into practice during the Friday night buffet and Tahitian dance show. The young men of the island still flock to the hotel to look at the tourist ladies on Friday nights. Not that much has changed in Huahine. It still maintains its very basic charm.

HOTEL BALI HAI MOOREA

B.P. 26, Maharepa, Moorea Tel. (689) 56.13.59, Fax (689) 56.13.27. US Bookings toll free at (800) 282-1401, in California toll free at (800) 282-1402. Year round Rack Rates from $115 per double room per night (EP). Meal Plan with Breakfast & Dinner is $45 per person, Meal Plan with Breakfast, Lunch & Dinner is $69 per person.

The Bali Hai birds that nest in the palm fronds greet you as you walk from the hotel parking to the main building. These squawking sea terns are the sound of the tropics, making a sawing cry as they fly among the coconut trees that tower over the Hotel Bali Hai's four-acre garden.

Moorea is shaped like a heart and is an island for lovers of all ages. The Hotel Bali Hai has a special treat for its honeymooners, who receive preferential rooming. Should the hotel be less than full, newlyweds will be upgraded. That room will be lovingly decorated with myriads of brightly colored tropical blossoms. And the bride and groom will find a giant heart of flowers on their bed.

This American-owned hotel, located at the entrance to Cook's Bay, has 63 Polynesian style units. The 9 overwater bungalows have a see-through trap door in the floor, where you can watch the underwater marine life. You can sunbathe on your private balcony and step down into the lagoon for a swim with the inquisitive fish. There are 4 bungalows half over the water, 4 beach bungalows, 6 bungalows with an ocean view, a 2-bedroom suite, 26 bungalows in the gardens and beside the pool, and 12 lanai rooms. Each unit has a king- or queen-size bed and single bed, a sitting area with overhead fan, a large bathroom with hot water shower, and a mini-refrigerator. The bungalows have tea and coffee making facilities.

The reception, boutique, activities desk, restaurant and bar are covered by an immense thatched roof, with an outdoor dining terrace on the beach. Gnarled old *tamanu* and South Seas almond trees provide handy perches for the birds and photograph souvenirs for the tourists. A swimming pool on the road side of the property has a waterfall at one end and a swim-up bar on the other side. Guests can play tennis, paddle an outrigger canoe or surf bike, take a Liki Tiki snorkeling excursion or a sunset cruise, or sign up for a picnic on the *motu* with Hiro Kelley at "What to Do on Moorea Tours."

You can watch a Tahitian dance show each Wednesday evening on Barbecue Night at the Bali Hai Canoe Grill and Restaurant. You can join a handcrafts show and listen to Tahitian *Ute* singing of olden times on Saturday evening. And you can watch a free camera show and dance performance on Sunday afternoon following a traditional Tahitian feast prepared in the underground oven. There's also video in the bar, demonstrations of how to weave a palm frond basket, create a flower *hei* or crown, learn to tie a *pareo*, and *tupa* crab races if you want to place a bet.

MOOREA VILLAGE NOA NOA

Beside the lagoon in Haapiti, Tel. (689) 56.10.02, Fax (689) 56.22.11, Year Round Rack Rates from $80 per double garden bungalow per night (EP), Meal Plan with Breakfast & Dinner is $39 per person, Meal Plan with Breakfast, Lunch & Dinner is $54 per person.

This is one of the best hotel bargains you'll find in French Polynesia, plus you will have the bonus of staying in a hotel that has a lot of other great things going for you. When Didier Revel, the manager, began working here in 1976 there were only 10 units. Now he has to look after 80 bungalows, all attractively designed in the traditional or modern Polynesian style. The 10 most recently completed units were finished in August, 1997 and were given Marquesan names. Half of the spacious bungalows have thatched pandanus roofs and the other five have red-wood roofs. They all have woven bamboo walls, screened windows and sliding glass doors with screens, plus a spacious private veranda with carved *tiki* posts. Inside the bungalows you'll find a bedroom with a double bed, *armoire* hanging closet and a full-length mirror. Two single beds are in the living room, which is one big room that also comprises the dining room and kitchen. All the necessary equipment and supplies you'll need to prepare meals have been added: a refrigerator, 4-burner stove, sink, toaster, coffee maker, dishes, pots and pans. An overhead fan and television will also make your stay more pleasant, and you'll be happy to find American style plugs in each new bungalow. But don't forget that the electricity is 220 volts. The bathroom has a shower with hot water.

Four of the older bungalows have kitchens and they all have the charm of the old South Seas, with golden bamboo walls, pandanus roofs and verandas. A very special bungalow has been built on a *motu* that was built 20 years ago, within easy swimming distance from the white sand beach that stretches in front of the hotel grounds. This hideaway for lovers rents for 10.000 CFP ($100) a night, and has a double bed, water, electricity, refrigerator and all the privacy and romance you could wish for.

The restaurant and bar overlook the beach and lagoon, with a long dining terrace on stilts in the sand. Between the reception and activities area and the boutique is a good size swimming pool, also facing the sea. A tennis court is across the street and a volley ball net is on the beach. You'll never have to complain about having nothing to do at the Moorea Village, because something's almost always going on. Free activities include snorkeling equipment, tennis rackets, outrigger paddle canoes, an excursion to the *motu* by outrigger speed canoe and canoe races.

You can rent bicycles and paddle boats, have a barbecue on the *motu*, and cruise the lagoon under the full moon. An extensive list of land and lagoon excursions is posted in the reception area. A Tahitian orchestra plays *kaina* music three nights a week, and Happy Hour is held daily except Saturday from 5:30 to 7pm, with half-priced beer and cocktails.

Each Saturday evening the pace steps up for the barbecue buffet, with *pareu*, coconut and *tamure* demonstrations, followed by fire dancing around the pool. Then it's your turn to dance the Tahitian waltz. Sunday is Tahitian *tamaara'a* day, when the *ahima'a* underground oven is opened to reveal the roast suckling pig, breadfruit, taro and other Tahitian foods. This is the most authentic and delicious Tahitian feast you'll find on Moorea, and the servings are very generous. You eat with your fingers and you'll still be licking them when the Tahitian dance show begins after lunch.

14. TAHITI

Queen of the Pacific

Polynesian mythology tells of a lovely *vahine* named Terehe, who defied the gods of great Havai'i on the island of Raiatea by swimming in the river during a period of sacred restriction. The angry gods caused the young maiden to be overcome by a feeling of numbness and she sank to the bottom of the river and was swallowed by a giant eel. Terehe's spirit then possessed the eel, who thrashed about, tearing away the earth between Raiatea and Tahaa. The eel's body was magically transformed into a fish, which swam away from Havai'i toward the East. Tu-rahu-nui, artisan of Ta'aroa, the supreme god, guided the fish in its course, and the warrior Tafai used a powerful ax to cut the sinews of the fish, to stabilize the new land. Thus were formed lofty mountain ranges, winding gulfs, an isthmus, bluffs and caves. The insouciant soul of Terehe lives today in this transplanted land called **Tahiti**.

Tahiti Nui Mare'are'a, Great Tahiti of the Golden Haze, the Polynesians sang. This is Tahiti of many shaded waters; various are the songs of the birds. Great Tahiti, the mounting place of the sun. The Tahitian people of old had to boast, because the people of Raiatea, the sacred island of Havai'i, regarded Tahiti as a plebeian island with no gods.

When the Europeans discovered Tahiti, beginning with the arrival of English Captain Samuel Wallis in 1767, followed by Frenchman de Bougainville, Captain James Cook, Captain Bligh and the famous *Bounty* crew, they too shouted the praises of this seductive island, where dreams are lived. Explorers, artists, writers and poets, sea-weary sailors and beachcombers of all makes spread the word. The myth of Tahiti as an earthly paradise was born.

Throughout the years Tahiti has become known as the Land of the Double Rainbows, the Romantic Isle, Beloved Island, Isle of Illusion, Island of Love, the Amorous Isle and the World's Most Glamorous Tropic Isle. Tahiti, the living Spirit of Terehe, is hailed as the most famous island in the South Seas—Queen of the Pacific.

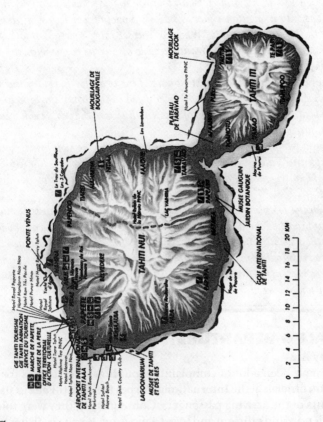

TAHITI

CIE TAHITI TOURISME
CIE TAHITI ANIMATION
SERVICE DU TOURISME

MARCHE DE LA PERE
OFFICE NATIONAL
D'ACTION CULTURELLE

AEROPORT INTERNATIONAL
DE TAHITI FAAA

LAGOONARIUM

MUSEE DE TAHITI
ET DES ILES

Hotel Royal Papeete
Hotel Mandarin Nao Nao
Hotel Kon Tiki Pacific
Hotel Prince Hinoi
Hotel Royal
Papeava
Hotel Tiare Tahiti
Hotel Matavai Tiare PHNC
Hotel Tahiti Nao Nao

Hotel Maeva Tahiti
Hotel Tahiti Beachcomber
Parkroyal

Hotel Sofitel
Maeva Beach

Hotel Tahiti Country Club

POINTE VENUS

MAHINA

ARUE

PIRAE

PAPEETE

FAAA

PUNAAUIA

PAEA

TAHITI NUI

PAPENOO

MOOREA

Le Trou du Souffleur
Les 3 Cascades

MOUILLAGE DE
BOUGAINVILLE

TIAREI

HITIAA

Les Lavatubes

FAAONE

Hotel Relais de la Maroto PHNC

Lac Vaihiria

MUSEE GAUGUIN
JARDIN BOTANIQUE

GOLF INTERNATIONAL
DE TAHITI

Vallée de la
de Papara

PAPARA

MATAIEA

PAPEARI

PLATEAU
DE TARAVAO

TARAVAO

PUEU

AFAAHITI

Hotel Te Anuanua PHNC

TAUTIRA

TAHITI ITI

TEAHUPOO

VAIRAO

Maison de Pomare

MOUILLAGE
DE COOK

0 2 4 6 8 10 12 14 16 18 20 KM

A TAHITIAN PROPHECY

The ancient Tahitian seer named Pau'e prophesied: "There are coming children of the glorious princess, by a canoe without an outrigger, who are covered from head to foot." **King Pomare I,** *hearing him say so, inquired how a canoe without an outrigger could hold its balance and not upset; so to illustrate his subject, Pau'e took an 'umete (wooden trough) and set it afloat with a few stones placed in it in a pool of water close by; then turning to the King he said: "What will upset that 'umete without an outrigger. It is balanced by its breadth, and so also is the canoe without an outrigger that is coming."*

Pau'e also said: "There will come a new king to whom this government will be given, and new manners will be adopted in this land; the tapa and the cloth-beating mallet will go out of use in Tahiti, and the people will wear different, foreign clothes."

Three days afterwards Pau'e died, and a little later the Dolphin arrived with Captain Wallis, when the people exclaimed: "There is the canoe without the outrigger of Pau'e, and there are the children of the glorious princess!"

When the Dolphin coasted the Taiarapu peninsula of Tahiti Iti, the natives approached the ship, headed by a man who held up a banana shoot, which to them was an effigy of their own persons, and after a welcome speech, he dropped it into the sea, signifying that their intentions were friendly and that the sea was sacred to all, for the Tahitians regarded it as a great moving marae or temple. –Extract from "Ancient Tahiti" by Teuira Henry.

ARRIVALS & DEPARTURES

Arriving By Air

There have been a lot of complaints about how long it takes for the Immigration officials at the **International Airport of Tahiti-Faaa** to stamp the passports of the arriving passengers. Consequently, they were told to be more friendly and efficient and to get a move on. If you are flying from a cold country to Tahiti, then make sure you can take off heavy garments once you arrive here, especially if you are continuing on to Moorea, Bora Bora or any of the other outer islands. You'll probably arrive in the cooler hours of the dawn, but once the sun rises you'll be sweltering in sweaters, woolens and polyesters. So layer your traveling clothes.

If you are on a package tour you will be met inside the baggage room or immediately outside the Customs area. The tour operators hold signs listing the names of their arriving guests. Westpac Bank has a currency exchange booth in the baggage area, and another branch in the main terminal, and Banque Socredo has an ATM machine in the terminal. If you need to make a phone call, book a room or continuing flight, rent a car, pick up a map, post a letter, go to the restroom, eat or drink, or shop for a gift, you can do it all inside the modern airport terminal.

The airport is located at PK 5.5 (3.4 miles), west of downtown Papeete. A taxi ride between 8pm and 6am will cost you 2.500 CFP ($25) to go downtown, and 1.500 CFP ($15) to go to the Tahiti Beachcomber Parkroyal, Tahiti Country Club, Sofitel Maeva Beach and any hostels and guest houses that are on the west coast in the vicinity of the airport. The taxi driver will also charge you 100 CFP($1) for each large bag, 50 CFP ($.50) for small bags and more for extra heavy bags. If you arrive in the daytime and want to save money, you can walk out to the main road and catch *le truck*. When you leave the airport you'll turn right on the main road (Route 1) to go to the west coast hotels, and turn left to go downtown and to the east coast. You have a choice of the old coastal route or the freeway, (Route 5), which is called the RDO. You'll see the freeway entry almost in front of the airport.

If you are flying to Moorea you can push your baggage cart to the Moorea terminal, which is to the left of the main terminal. Just follow the signs. The first flight to Moorea is at 6am. If you are flying to any of the other outer islands the Air Tahiti counter is at the extreme right of the main terminal when you come out of the Customs area. A baggage storage room in this area is open Monday to Saturday from 8am to 5pm, Sunday from 6am to 12pm, from 2 to 6 pm, and two hours prior to each international flight departure. The hotels have a baggage storage room, which is free for their guests.

Arriving By Boat

If you arrive in Tahiti on board a passenger cruise ship you will disembark at the **Quai d'Honneur**, the visitor's dock in downtown Papeete. A currency exchange machine and Banque Socredo are located on the quay and the Tahiti Manava Visitor's Bureau is under the shade trees to the right, also adjacent to the quay. Tour buses, taxis, guides and tourism representatives meet each ship's arrival, and a Tahitian dance show is often performed for the visitors.

Before arriving in the port of Papeete by yacht you must notify the port authorities on channel 12 of your arrival. You can anchor at the quay or beside the beach, and you will need to complete an arrival declaration at the harbor master's office, which is beside the Quai d'Honneur, across the road from the Tahiti Manava Visitor's Bureau. The harbor master's office is open Monday to Thursday from 7 to 11:30am and from 1 to 4pm, and on Friday to 3pm. The offices of the air and border police and customs are in the same building. The office hours for the air and border police are Monday to Friday from 7:30am to 11am and from 1:30 to 3:30pm. The customs office is open Monday to Friday from 7:30 to 11:30am and from 2:30 to 5pm. Anchorages are also available at the Yacht Club in Arue and the Marina Taina in Punaauia. Yachts are no longer allowed to anchor at Maeva Beach. Each crew member is required to have a return air ticket or pay a repatriation bond to your home country.

For Americans and Canadians this cost is 89.000 CFP ($890), and for residents of Hawaii and other Pacific regions, the cost is 79.000 CFP ($790) per person. See more information in Chapter 6, *Planning Your Trip*.

Departing By Air
You should reconfirm your international flight no later than 72 hours before your departure date. Check-in time for departing international flights is 1 1/2 hours prior to departure. There is no airport departure tax. You can exchange your francs for dollars at the Banque Socredo or Westpac offices inside the terminal. Once you pass Immigration and go into the international departure lounge, you will find several duty free shops, which sell cigarettes, liquors, Tahitian music and video films, French perfumes and Tahitian black pearl jewelry.

Departing By Boat
The cruise ship company or travel agency that arranges your cruise will give you details of what you will do when you arrive in Tahiti to board a passenger ship. Groups are met at the airport and transferred to a hotel until time to board the ship, when they will be transferred by boat to the Quai d'Honneur in Papeete, where the ship is moored.

If you are departing by private yacht you must advise the air and border police in Papeete of your final departure, and the police will issue a release from the bond that you were required to post upon arrival. This document must be presented to the police on the last island you visit before leaving French Polynesia, and your bond will be refunded.

ORIENTATION

Tahiti is located in the Windward Islands of the Society archipelago of French Polynesia. This is the largest of the 118 islands and atolls, with a population of more than 150,000 people living in 12 *communes* on Tahiti Nui (big Tahiti) and Tahiti Iti (little Tahiti), also known as the Taiarapu peninsula.

Tahiti Nui and **Tahiti Iti** are shaped as a turtle, a lady's hand mirror or a reclining figure 8. Geologists say that these two majestic green islands emerged from the sea in separate volcanic births millions of years apart. Comprising a total of 1,042 square km. (402 square miles) of land, Tahiti

Nui and Tahiti Iti are joined by the narrow isthmus of **Taravao**, 60 kilometers (37 miles) from the noise of **Papeete** by the south coast and 54 kilometers (34 miles) by the north coast.

The circle island tour around the coastal road of Tahiti Nui is 114 kilometers (71 miles). Away from the metropolitan area close to Papeete the paved roads are two lanes, with very few straight stretches, and there are no street lights and very few guard rails at the edge of the seaside cliffs. The northeast coast is less developed, with numerous waterfalls and deep verdant valleys, modest homes and beautiful flower gardens beside the road. Here you will find the golden-brown sands of the volcanic beaches and cool streams ferrying tiny boats of flower blossoms to the sea. A fringing reef borders the shoreline in a few places, but most of the coast is battered by the waves of the frequently turbulent open ocean.

The southwest coast is much more congested, with houses and traffic, and high fences around the luxurious homes that often conceal ocean views to the motorists. A few white sand beaches border the shoreline and the shimmering turquoise lagoon is protected by a coral reef. Beyond the reef, across the Sea of Moons, is the island of Moorea.

Tahiti Iti has 18 kilometers (11 miles) of paved road on the eastern and western coasts and a 7 kilometer (4 mile) interior road that leads past dairy farms and citrus groves to a panoramic view of the Plateau of Taravao. Beyond the road's end of the peninsula's southern tip lies the *fenua 'aihere*, the magnificent bush land, and the steep sea cliffs known as Te Pari. You can explore this coast by boat or hike across the rivers and volcanic bluffs.

PAPEETE

The busy, bustling town of **Papeete**, on Tahiti's north coast, is the capital of French Polynesia. This is the administrative center for the 219,521 people who live in the five archipelagoes that comprise this French Overseas Territory.

Papeete (Pah-pay-eh-tay) is a Tahitian word, which "means a basket of waters." The town is spread along the waterfront on Tahiti's north coast, 5 kilometers (3 miles) east of the airport, facing the island of Moorea across the Sea of Moons. Papeete harbor is an international port, as well as home base for inter-island passenger launches, copra freighters, fishing boats and ferries and a small fleet of French naval ships. Among the winding streets of Papeete and its environs you will find the territorial medical center and hospital, two private clinics, a cosmedical center, pharmacies, French and Tahitian government offices, tribunal courts, *gendarmerie*, municipal police, port authorities and post office with international communications. Services also include the tourist bureau, banks, airline offices, shipping and travel agencies, television and radio stations, newspapers in French and English, hotel and technical schools, Lycée and university, cathedrals and temples, sports centers and stadiums, health clubs and gyms, a cultural center, museums, art galleries, movie theaters, shopping centers, boutiques, crafts centers and a public market.

A lot of negative publicity has circulated about Papeete, which is hot and dirty. The sidewalks are uneven and even dangerous, so that you must watch where you are walking, or you may sprain an ankle in a hole in the sidewalk. The crime rate for purse snatching and other petty thefts has increased over the past several years, and prostitutes of all sexes (including Polynesia's third sex, the *mahu*) is rampant. The traffic is bottleneck at all hours during the day, with the diesel engines of trucks and cars emitting stinky, smoky fumes in the air. The tradewinds do help to clear the air quickly, unless you are riding behind one of these vehicles. Even the residents get a headache when we go to town. Trash pick-up varies, and people still litter the streets and sidewalks while they're walking around near the market or waiting for *le truck* just across the street from the Tahiti Manava Visitors Bureau.

On the up side of the coin, the mayor of Papeete and the local government are making some efforts to improve the situation. A municipal police station was recently opened near the public *marché*, and more security personnel are now patrolling the streets. You will see the occasional street person sitting on the sidewalk near the entrance to a shop, but it is still rare in Tahiti for anyone to ask passersby for money.

The yacht quay facing the waterfront street of Boulevard Pomare was rebuilt in 1996, with an attractive boardwalk. Planters of colorful bougainvillea, benches, street lamps and discreetly hidden garbage cans are welcome changes for the international yachts that tie up to the wharf. In 1997 another section of the waterfront was converted, when the sidewalk adjacent to the bonito boat dock was paved in the same Bomanite design as the yacht quay. This area, which is adjacent to the tourist office, is now called Temarii a Teai Square, after a popular ship captain of Tahiti's yesteryear. Here you will find informational panels about Papeete, with handy telephone numbers of tourist interest. Frequent arts and crafts exhibits take place here, and it is a popular meeting place for strollers who want to sit in the sun or shade, smell the briny air and feel the breezes as they watch the activity along the waterfront from a quieter distance.

The improvement program will soon include a nice sidewalk along the waterfront, extending all the way to the Olympic swimming pool adjacent to Tahiti's Cultural Center. A landfill project already underway at the edge of the lagoon will provide 2 hectares (4.9 acres) as the site for

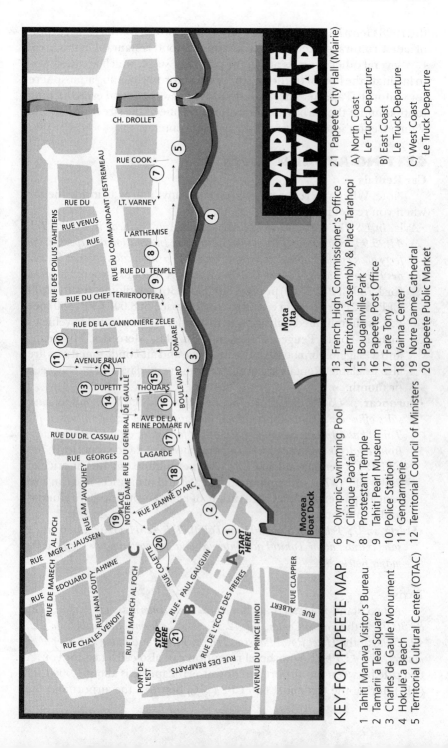

PAPEETE CITY MAP

CH. DROLLET

RUE COOK

LT. VARNEY

L'ARTHEMISE

RUE DU TEMPLE

RUE DU CHEF TERIIEROOTERA

RUE DE LA CANNONIERE ZELEE

RUE DU

RUE VENUS

RUE

RUE DES POILUS TAHITIENS

RUE DU COMMANDANT DESTREMEAU

POMARE

AVENUE BRUAT

DUPETIT

THOUARS

BOULEVARD

AVE DE LA REINE POMARE IV

RUE DU DR. CASSIAU

RUE GEORGES

LAGARDE

RUE DU GENERAL DE GAULLE

PLACE NOTRE DAME

RUE JEANNE D'ARC

RUE AM JAVOUHEY

RUE AL FOCH

RUE MARECH MGR. T. JAUSSEN

RUE DE MARECH AHNE

RUE EDOUARD

RUE NAN SOUTY AHNNE

RUE CHALES VENOIT

RUE DE MARECH AL FOCH

RUE COLETTE

RUE PAUL GAUGUIN

RUE DE L'ECOLE DES FRERES

RUE DES REMPARTS

AVENUE DU PRINCE HINOI

PONT DE L'EST

RUE ALBERT

RUE CLAPPIER

START HERE

STOP HERE

A

B

C

Moorea Boat Dock

Mota Uta

KEY FOR PAPEETE MAP

1 Tahiti Manava Visitor's Bureau
2 Tamarii a Teai Square
3 Charles de Gaulle Monument
4 Hokule'a Beach
5 Territorial Cultural Center (OTAC)
6 Olympic Swimming Pool
7 Clinique Paofai
8 Prostestant Temple
9 Tahiti Pearl Museum
10 Police Station
11 Gendarmerie
12 Territorial Council of Ministers
13 French High Commissioner's Office
14 Territorial Assembly & Place Tarahopi
15 Bougainville Park
16 Papeete Post Office
17 Fare Tony
18 Vaima Center
19 Notre Dame Cathedral
20 Papeete Public Market
21 Papeete City Hall (Mairie)

A) North Coast
   Le Truck Departure
B) East Coast
   Le Truck Departure
C) West Coast
   Le Truck Departure

the 1998 Heiva I Tahiti Festival in July. Plans also call for the construction of a new cultural center and a panoramic seafood restaurant in this area.

Several other projects are in the planning stage, which are designed to facilitate the flow of traffic and to create a more welcoming atmosphere for visitors to Papeete. They include adding new roads and even building tunnels under the harbor, and transforming one of the streets beside the Vaima Center into an open-air pedestrian center.

GETTING AROUND TOWN
Car Rentals

Note: When you rent a car, do not leave anything at all inside the car when you're not in it.

• **Avis**, *in US Tel. 800/230-4898, is known as Avis-Pacificar in Tahiti, Tel. 41.93.93, with a sales office at the Tahiti-Faaa International Airport, at the ferry dock on the Papeete waterfront, and with a main sales office at 56, rue des Remparts at the Pont de l'Est in Papeete.* A 5-door Citroen AX rents for 1.780 CFP ($17.80) per day, 36 CFP ($.36) per kilometer and 1.200 CFP ($12) for insurance, or for a forfeit price of 8.000 CFP ($80) per day, with unlimited mileage and insurance. Other available vehicles include Fords, Peugeots, Renaults, Suzukis, Mercedes, Hyundais, and a Piaggio Mini-bus. Automatic drive and air-conditioned cars are also available. Rentals are available for several days and by the week or month.

• **Europcar**, *in US Tel. 800/227-7368, in Tahiti, Tel. 45.24.24, has its main sales office on Avenue Prince Hinoi in Papeete, and branch offices at the Tahiti-Faaa International Airport, at the ferry dock on the Papeete waterfront, at all the major hotels and in Taravao.* A Fiat Panda rents for 1.700 CFP ($17) per day and 36 CFP ($.36) per minute or a forfeit price of 7.600 CFP ($76), with unlimited mileage and insurance. You can also rent a 2-passenger Fun Car, a variety of Fiats, automatic drive Hondas and a mini-bus.

• **Hertz**, *in US Tel. 800/654-3001, in Tahiti, Tel. 42.04.71/82.55.86, has a sales counter at the Tahiti-Faaa International Airport and sales desks at the major hotels.*

Taxis

A taxi stand is located at the *Tahiti-Faaa International Airport, Tel. 83.30.07,* at the *Vaima Center, Tel. 42.33.60,* at *Le Jasmin Sidewalk Cafe, Tel. 42.35.98,* at the *Hotel Royal Papeete, Tel. 42.11.83,* and *at the Papeete public market, Tel. 43.19.62.* Your hotel reception can also call a taxi for you. A taxi ride between the airport and downtown Papeete is about 1.500 CFP ($15) during the day and 1.000 CFP ($10) between the airport and the west coast hotels as far as Sofitel Maeva Beach. See hotel rate structures in the *Basic Information* chapter.

Limousine Service

Tiare Limousine, *Tel. 43.15.97*, has an 8-seat Lincoln Town stretch limousine, complete with air-conditioning, free bar, leather seats, sun roof, video, and an English-speaking chauffeur-guide. The hourly rates are 15.000 CFP ($150); a Tahitian Black Pearl shopping tour is 4.500 CFP ($45) one-way only; and the limousine can be rented for special occasions such as weddings, complete with champagne.

Tour & Transport Companies

When you book your visit to Tahiti through a travel agent, your ground transportation is normally part of the package. If you are traveling on your own, you can save money by contacting one of the following tour and transport companies to drive you between your hotel and the airport or ferry dock. **Marama Tours Tahiti**, *Tel. 83.96.50 or 83.95.81*; **Paradise Tours**, *Tel. 44.40.40 or 42.49.36 on weekends*; and **Tahiti Nui Travel**, *Tel. 54.02.00*.

Le Truck

Tahiti's public transport system is provided by *le truck*, which has a brightly painted wooden cabin mounted on the rear of a flatbed truck. These colorful vehicles operate during the daylight hours, with night transportation provided from downtown Papeete to the airport and hotels on the west coast, as far as Sofitel Maeva Beach. The last run depends on what is happening in Papeete. Each *le truck* has a specific route, with the destination usually painted on the top or sides of the vehicle.

The authorized stops are indicated by a blue sign with a drawing of *le truck*. Just wave to the driver to stop. Pay the driver on the right side of the cab when you get off. The minimum fare is 120 CFP ($1.20), which will get you from your hotel to downtown, and you'll have to pay 200 CFP ($2) at night. The Tahiti Manava Visitors Bureau can give you specific details on where to catch *le truck* to your destination.

WHERE TO STAY

DOWNTOWN PAPEETE

Moderate

HOTEL LE MANDARIN NOA NOA, *B.P. 302, Papeete, Tahiti. Tel. 689/42.16.33; Fax 689/42.16.32. EP Rates: standard room 12.500 CFP ($125) single; 14.000 CFP ($140) double; mini-suite 14.000 CFP ($140) single; 16.000 CFP ($160) double. Third person 2.000 ($20) CFP. Meal plan* *with breakfast and dinner is 3.800 CFP ($38) per person; meal plan with breakfast, lunch and dinner is 5.700 CFP ($57) per person. Add 7% hotel tax to room rates and 1% value added tax to room rates and meal plan. All major credit cards.*

On Rue Colette in downtown Papeete, two blocks inland from the waterfront and across the street from the Mairie of Papeete. 32 air-conditioned rooms and five suites on five floors, with elevator. Each room has a queen size bed or twin beds, private bathroom with shower, refrigerator or mini-bar, tea and coffee facilities, television, video and telephone. There are two Chinese restaurants and bars and a coffee shop in the hotel and around the corner. This is a clean and comfortable hotel, conveniently located for downtown activities.

MATAVAI HOTEL RESORT AND SPORTS CENTRE, *B.P. 32, Papeete, Tahiti. Tel. 689/42.67.67; Fax 689/42.36.90. EP Rates: standard room 12.000 CFP ($120) single; 16.000 CFP ($160) double; 20.000 CFP ($200) triple; 24.000 CFP ($240) quadruple. Bridal suite with Jacuzzi 25.000 CFP ($250). Add 7% hotel tax to room rates and 1% value added tax to room rates and meal plan. Round-trip transfers provided. All major credit cards.*

This 138-room hotel was operated as a Holiday Inn until 20 years ago. It is located about a kilometer (.6 miles) from the center of Papeete in Tipaerui several blocks inland, and 4.5 kilometers (3 miles) from the airport, where there is a direct phone for free transportation to the hotel. Each room has individually controlled air conditioning, two large double beds, direct dialing telephone system, color television with video program, tub/shower, and balcony or terrace. You will enjoy bringing your family here, and there is no charge for children under 12 who share the room with their parents, unless an extra bed is required. Neither is there any charge for baby cribs.

The hotel has two restaurants, two bars, room service, guest laundry room, elevators, ice machines, a travel agency in the lobby, and a gift shop. The physically challenged guest will find wheelchair access throughout the hotel. The children will be delighted with the two big swimming pools. One of these pools has a slide, and the other pool, which is 22 meters (72 feet) long, also has a kiddy's pool and adjacent play area for children. An open air giant size chessboard and 18-hole mini-golf course will keep the family occupied for hours. Plus you will find a fitness gym, tennis court, badminton court, two squash courts, table tennis, billiards and darts. All the outdoor play areas are floodlit.

HOTEL TIARE TAHITI, *B.P. 2359, Papeete, Tahiti. Tel. 689/43.68.48; Fax 689/43.68.47. 417. Blvd. Pomare, on waterfront adjacent to Papeete Post Office. EP Rates: Standard room 12.000 CFP ($120) single/double; ocean view 13.500 CFP ($135) single/double; panoramic view 15.500 CFP ($155) single/ double; panoramic suite #502, 18.000 CFP ($180). Third person 2.000 CFP*

($20). Add 7% hotel tax to room rates and 1% value added tax to room rates and meal plan. All major credit cards.

Tahiti's newest downtown hotel, adjacent to the Papeete Post Office on the waterfront of Boulevard Pomare, opened in December, 1996, with 44 rooms in a five-story building with elevator. The front rooms have private balconies overlooking the yacht quay, harbor and Moorea. Each room has air-conditioning, telephone, television, and tea/coffee facilities.

HOTEL PRINCE HINOI, *B.P. 4545, Papeete, Tahiti. Tel. 689/42.32.77; Fax 689/42.33.66. EP Rates: 9.500 CFP ($95) single/double; 11.200 CFP ($112) triple; additional person 1.700 CFP ($17). Meal plan with breakfast and dinner is 3.250 CFP ($32.50) per person; meal plan with breakfast, lunch and dinner is 5.450 CFP ($54.50) per person. Add 7% hotel tax to room rates and 1% value added tax to room rates and meal plan. All major credit cards.*

A six-story concrete building on the corner of Boulevard Pomare and Avenue Prince Hinoi in the heart of Papeete's night club and disco district. The 72 air-conditioned rooms are very basic, with telephone and television. There is an elevator, restaurant and small bar, plus a private gambling club, which you can easily join.

HOTEL ROYAL PAPEETE, *B.P. 919, Papeete, Tahiti. Tel. 689/42.01.29; Fax 689/43.79.09. EP Rates: Standard room 9.000 CFP ($90) single; 10.700 CFP ($107) double; 12.200 CFP ($122) triple; deluxe room 10.500 CFP ($105) single; 12.000 CFP ($120) double; 13.500 CFP ($135) triple. Meal plan with breakfast and dinner is 3.800 CFP ($38) per person; meal plan with breakfast, lunch and dinner is 6.300 CFP ($63) per person. Add 7% hotel tax to room rates and 1% value added tax to room rates and meal plan. Mastercard, Visa.*

An old colonial style hotel on Boulevard Pomare opposite the boat docks for ferries to Moorea and Leeward Society Islands. Some of the 71 air-conditioned rooms on three floors can be very noisy, so be sure to request a room on the quieter side, which can be reached by elevator or a wide stairway. There are telephones but no television in the rooms. This is where most of the expatriate residents of Tahiti's outer islands stay when we need to be in Papeete overnight. The staff here is friendly and the bar and restaurant are very popular with local clientele. You also have a choice of two nightclubs and a casino for entertainment.

HOTEL KON TIKI PACIFIC, *B.P. 111, Papeete, Tahiti. Tel. 689/43.72.82; Fax 689/42.11.66. EP Rates: single 8.500 CFP ($85); double 9.900 CFP ($99); twin-bed room 10.300 CFP ($103). Third person 2.000 CFP ($20). Add 7% hotel tax to room rates and 1% value added tax to room rates and meal plan. All major credit cards.*

This is a popular hotel with the French military men as it is located at the lower end of Boulevard Pomare, opposite a naval base in the Papeete harbor. More than half of the 36 air-conditioned rooms have balconies facing the waterfront, which can be noisy, especially at night when the nearby bars and nightclubs are in full swing. There's no restaurant but the hotel has a casino.

Inexpensive

SHOGUN, *B.P. 2880, Papeete, Tahiti; Tel. 689/43.13.93; Fax 689/ 43.27.28. On rue du Commandant Destremeau between Avenue Bruat and rue de la Canonniere Zelee. EP Rates single/double: room road side 5.000-6.000 CFP ($50-$60); room yard side 6.500 CFP ($65). Third person 1.000 CFP ($10). Bed in dormitory 2.000 CFP ($20). Add 1% value added tax to room rates. American Express, Visa.*

The report on this small hotel is a big NO! Unsuspecting tourists check in and want to leave the same day. It has been removed from the recommended list of lodgings published by the Tahiti Tourist office. The location is not in the most desirable part of town, and the owner has a rather unsavory reputation. Otherwise, it is convenient to the inter-island ships, and you can catch *le truck* to the airport at the front door. There are seven simply furnished air-conditioned rooms with private bathrooms and hot water, and a six-bed dormitory with shared bath facilities.

MAHINA TEA, *B.P. 17, Papeete, Tahiti; Tel. 689/42.00.97. A 10-minute walk from downtown area, in Sainte-Amélie valley behind the gendarmerie on Avenue Bruat. EP Rates room single/double: 4.000 CFP ($40); single for three days 3.400 CFP ($34); double for three days 3.700 CFP ($37); single per month 60.000 CFP ($600); double per month 65.000 CFP ($650); studio single/double per month 80.000 CFP ($800). Add 1% value added tax to room rates. No credit cards.*

This aging family-operated hotel is still a bargain for budget travelers who don't mind the faded façade and well-worn furnishings in the two-story, aquamarine-colored concrete structure. The 15 rooms with private bathrooms are located upstairs, as are the six studios with kitchens and bathrooms. Hot water is available in the evenings. The rooms are clean and linens are provided, and some of the rooms have balconies. The reception area on the ground level also doubles as a communal television room, which is decorated with photographs of the Ceran-Jerusalemy family and guests. A few of the clients have lived here for years and others are students from the outer islands. There have been several complaints about the noise of the roosters, but this is also a problem in many of the more expensive hotels throughout the islands.

TAHITI BUDGET LODGE, *B.P. 237, Papeete, Tahiti. Tel. 689/ 42.66.82; Fax 689/43.06.79. In Mission quartier next to College Lamenais on rue Frère Alain at the end of rue Edouard Ahnne. From Boulevard Pomare near Papeete Public Market go inland five blocks on rue du 22 Septembre, cross rue du*

Marechal Foch, and continue down rue Edouard Ahnne. EP Rates: communal room up to three people 1.900 CFP ($19) person; private room with communal bathroom 3.900 CFP ($39); private room and private bathroom 4.800 CFP ($48) single/double. Add 1% value added tax to room rates. Visa.

This hostel has been removed from the recommended lodgings published by the Tahiti Tourist office due to hygienic problems. When the situation is corrected it will be added to the list again. This place is popular with backpackers, in-transit visitors going to or coming from the outer islands, and newly arrived French people who work in Papeete. The eleven rooms in a motel-like building include private and communal facilities, including a dormitory. It has a snack-bar area, kitchen facilities, a guest laundry and an open garden space. The windows are not screened and the front of the hostel can be noisy, so try to get a room in the back, away from the communal kitchen and lounge.

CHEZ MYRNA, *B.P. 790, Papeete, Tahiti. Tel. 689/42.64.11. In Tipaerui valley, a five minute walk inland from rue du Commandant Destremeau, a few hundred meters from Hotel Matavai. Minimum two nights, breakfast included; dinner on request. EP Rates: Day 3.500 CFP ($35) single, 4.500 CFP ($45) double; week 23.000 CFP ($230) single, 29.000 CFP ($290) double; per month 70.000 CFP ($700) single, 90.000 CFP ($900) double; per month without meals 55.000 CFP ($550) single, 70.000 CFP ($700) double. Additional bed 1.000 CFP ($10) day. Add 1% value added tax to room rates and meal plan. No credit cards.*

Myrna and her husband Walter Dahmmeyer have a clean concrete two-bedroom house with a double bed in each room. There's hot water in the shared bathroom and house linens are furnished. Myrna is a good cook and she'll serve your meals on the terrace. You can also walk to nearby restaurants, snack bars and *magasins.*

TEAMO HOSTEL, *B.P. 2407, Papeete, Tahiti. Tel. 689/42.00.35/ 42.47.26; Fax 689/43.56.95. In Mission quartier at 8, rue du Pont Neuf, Fariimata, around the corner from Tahiti Budget Lodge. EP Rates: Room single 1.200-1.500-3.500 CFP ($12-$15-$35). Additional bed 1.000 CFP ($10). Two rooms in apartment 8.000 CFP ($80). Round-trip transfers provided from airport with paid reservation. House linens for rent. Add 1% value added tax to room rates. Mastercard, Visa.*

This six-room house was removed from the recommended listings compiled by the Tahiti Tourist office due to unsatisfactory sanitation and lack of sufficient toilet facilities for the number of guests accommodated. There are still complaints about the cramped quarters and noise. There are three dormitory rooms, one with four single beds and two with six single beds; three rooms, each containing a double and a single bed or one double and two single beds. The shared bathrooms have hot water and you can prepare your meals in the communal kitchen. There is also a two-room apartment, with a double bed and two single beds in each room, plus an equipped kitchen and private bathroom with hot water. In addition to a television room and lending library, there is also a covered terrace, where backpackers from various corners of the world gather to discuss their adventures.

NORTHEAST COAST: PIRAE TO MAHINA
Expensive
HOTEL ROYAL MATAVAI BAY, (ex-Hyatt Regency Tahiti) on Tahara'a Hill in Arue, overlooking Matavai and Point Venus, closed in mid-January 1998, for an extensive building and renovation project, which will take a minimum of 18 months to complete. Plans are to add 57 rooms to the existing 190 units, which will be located in a fifth "upside-down" building on the edge of the Tahara'a bluff.

Moderate
HOTEL ROYAL TAHITIEN, *B.P. 5001, Pirae, Tahiti. Tel. 689/ 42.81.13; Fax 689/41.05.35. On the beach in Pirae, on Tahiti's north shore, 4 kilometers (2.5 miles) east of Papeete. EP Rates: Standard room 14.500 CFP ($145) single; 16.000 CFP ($160) double. Third person 3.000 CFP ($30). Meal plan with breakfast and dinner is 5.000 CFP ($50) per person; meal plan with breakfast, lunch and dinner is 7.000 CFP ($70) per person. Add 7% hotel tax to room rates and 1% value added tax to room rates and meal plan. All major credit cards.*

The 40 air-conditioned rooms are located in two-story motel-type contemporary structures beside a spacious garden with a small river meandering toward the sea. The rooms have telephone, refrigerator and tea/coffee facilities, bathtubs and a private balcony or terrace overlooking the tropical gardens. This land was once owned by Tahiti's royal family. You can swim in the lagoon beside a black sand beach and sunbathe on the open terrace overlooking the sea. Very good meals are served in the thatched roof Tahitian style dining room or under the shade of almond trees on the terrace. This is a popular place with local diners, and the Happy Hour crowd who come to the spacious bar on Friday evenings to dance to tunes played by Tahiti's favorite musicians.

Inexpensive
VAIMANA FARE, *PK 10.5, Mahina, Tahiti. Tel. 689/48.07.17; Fax 689/43.87.27. In Mahina Commune, behind the Mahina High School, beside the Toaru river, with access to a black sand beach. EP Rates: bungalow single/ double 6.500 CFP ($65) per day; 6.000 CFP ($60) after one week. Additional bed 2.000 CFP ($20) day. Monthly rental 85.000 CFP ($850). Add 1% value added tax to room rates. No credit cards.*

This is a large, quiet family property with majestic pistachio and monkeypod trees and numerous fruit trees, including mango, *pamplemousse*, oranges, citrons and star apples. You will be welcome to whatever fruit is in season. A family atmosphere reigns here, with a welcoming Polynesian spirit. There are five bungalows on the premises and two are available for short-term rentals. In one bungalow there is a double bed, a mezzanine with four beds, plus a kitchen and bathroom with hot water. The other bungalow contains a double bed and sofa bed, kitchen, bathroom with hot water and washing machine. House linens are furnished.

You can walk to Point Venus in 15 minutes and the closest beach is popular with wind surfers, whose destination is Motu Martin. You can also visit the *motu* in Grand's 20-foot boat, and he will take you fishing or to Moorea if you desire, but you must have insurance coverage for these outings. The Grands will also drive you to the Tahiti-Iti peninsula for an extra charge. There are supermarkets nearby and you can catch *le truck* to town.

AIRPORT AREA: FAAA-PUNAAUIA
Expensive

HOTEL LE MERIDIEN TAHITI, *B.P. 380595, Punaauia 98718, Tahiti. Tel. 689/47.07.07; Fax 689/47.07.08; in US 800/543-4300. Beside the lagoon in Punaauia, 15 kilometers (9.3 miles) from downtown Papeete and 9 kilometers (6 miles) west of the international airport. 150 units. EP Rates single/ double: garden view room 30.000 CFP ($300); lagoon view room 33.000 CFP ($330); junior suite 44.000 CFP ($440), overwater bungalow 46.000 CFP ($460); deluxe suite 66.000 CFP ($660); presidential suite 99.000 CFP ($990); roll-away bed 7.000 CFP ($70). Meal plan with breakfast and dinner is 7.000 CFP ($70) per person; meal plan with breakfast, lunch and dinner is 10.800 CFP ($108) per person; American buffet breakfast 2.000 CFP ($20); Lunch-set menu at Le Fare Te Moana beach restaurant 3.800 CFP ($38); buffet dinner at La Plantation restaurant 7.000 CFP ($70). Add 7% hotel tax to room rates and 1% value added tax to room rates and meal plan. All major credit cards.*

Le Méridien Tahiti is scheduled to open on May 15, 1998, on 4.5 hectares (11.12 acres) of land close to the Museum of Tahiti and Her Islands and just 20 minutes from the Atimaono International Golf Course. Facilities include 12 air-conditioned overwater bungalows with thatched roofs and 138 air-conditioned guest rooms and suites in four-story concrete buildings. The overwater bungalows are 60 square meters (646 square feet) in size and feature a spacious living area opening onto an outdoor deck providing direct access to the crystal clear waters of the lagoon. The suites include 5 junior suites, 2 deluxe suites and one presidential suite. Each guest room has an ocean view. Each room and bungalow includes international direct dial telephones, mini-bar, coffee and tea facilities, room service, and all the other amenities found in international class resort hotels.

In addition to a business center, boutique, travel agency and car rental desk in the main building, there will be five conference and banquet rooms accommodating from 20 to 500 people. A buffet restaurant will serve an eclectic mix of local and European cuisine; a beachside restaurant will have a casually elegant Polynesian ambiance, and there will be a beach bar and main hotel bar. The 2,000 square meter (215,278 square feet) sand bottom swimming pool, prolonged by a river, is claimed as the largest in the world. Watersports, tennis and pétanque (French bowls) are some of the activities offered, as well as a white sand beach facing the sunset and the island of Moorea.

HOTEL TAHITI BEACHCOMBER PARKROYAL, *B.P. 6014, Faaa 98702, Tahiti. Tel. 689/86.51.10; Fax 689/86.51.30; Telex 702/276FP; in US 800/835-7742. e-mail prkroyal@mail.pf Beside the lagoon at the border of Faaa and Punaauia, 7 kilometers (4.3 miles) west of Papeete and 2 kilometers (1.2 miles west) of the airport. EP Rates: garden side room 29.300 CFP ($293) single or double; lagoon side room 32.400 CFP ($324) single or double; bungalow on the motu 37.600 CFP ($376) single or double; overwater bungalow 45.300 CFP ($453) single or double; third person add 6.000 CFP ($60); suite 64.800 CFP ($648). Meal plan with breakfast and dinner is 6.800 CFP ($68) per person; meal plan with breakfast, lunch and dinner is 9.800 CFP ($98) per person. Add 7% hotel tax to room rates and 1% value added tax to room rates and meal plan. All major credit cards.*

The grounds cover 14 hectares (35 acres) of lush tropical gardens. The 212 units include 180 rooms in main building, 17 overwater bungalows and 15 junior suite overwater bungalows. All rooms have airconditioning, direct dial telephone, radio-television, and private terraces, and are equipped with hairdryers, mini bar, refrigerator, tea and coffee making facilities. Services include activities desk, travel desk and car rental desk, duty free boutique, beauty salon, black pearl shop, three restaurants and bars, room service, guest laundry, nautical activities center, tennis courts, golf park with driving range, pitch & putt, two swimming pools and a helipad. See more information in chapter on *Best Places to Stay.*

HOTEL SOFITEL MAEVA BEACH, *B.P. 60008, 98702 Faaa, Tahiti. Tel. 689/42.80.42; Fax 689/43.84.70; Reservations 689/41.04.04; Fax 689/ 41.05.05; Telex 702/214FP; in US 800/221-4542. Beside the lagoon in Punaauia, 7.5 kilometers (4.6 miles) west of Papeete and 2.5 kilometers (1.5 miles) west of the airport. EP Rates: garden side room 20.000 CFP ($200) single or double; lagoon side room 23.000 CFP ($230) single or double; panoramic room 25.000 CFP ($250) single or double; suite 40.000 CFP ($400) single or*

*double; third person add 4.500 CFP ($45). Meal plan with breakfast and dinner
is 5.600 CFP ($56) per person; meal plan with breakfast, lunch and dinner is
8.100 CFP ($81) per person. A supplement charge of 1.500 CFP ($15) per person
is added during the high season, January 1-15, July 15-31, August 20-31, and in
December. Add 7% hotel tax to room rates and 1% value added tax to room rates
and meal plan. All major credit cards.*

This hotel opened in 1969, offering a fabulous view of the island of
Moorea across the Sea of Moons. It was entirely refurbished in 1994, and
includes 224 air-conditioned rooms in a pyramid shaped building. These
consist of 208 standard rooms, 14 rooms with a scenic view and two suites.
Each room has a terrace or balcony, bathtub, direct-dial phone, color
television, tea and coffee facilities and hair-dryers. Room service is
available. In the lobby are desks for car rentals, tours and activities, plus
a gift shop. Seminars and banquets can be held in the Paevai Room, which
seats 250 people theater style; in the 70-seat Gauguin Room; and in the
Diademe Room, which has 15 seats.

In addition to a swimming pool, there are two lighted tennis courts,
a golf driving range and nautical activities center. The Sakura is a Japanese
teppanyaki restaurant and the Bougainville is an open-air restaurant for
200 people. Tahitian dance shows are presented here on Friday and
Saturday evenings, and each Sunday afternoon another dance show is
performed following the Tahitian *tamaara'a* feast, which has become a
popular tradition at the Maeva Beach. You can get snacks or drinks at the
Moorea Bar beside the swimming pool, and listen to a musical trio each
Friday and Saturday evening at the bar La Terrasse. The Maeva Beach is
operated by the Sofitel Coralia French hotel chain, which also has hotels
in Moorea, Huahine and Bora Bora.

Moderate
OUTRIGGER HOTEL TAHITI, *reservations in US and Canada Tel.
800/688-7444, e-mail reservations@outrigger.com. Internet www.outrigger.com.
200 units beside the lagoon in Auae, 1.6 kilometers (1 mile) from downtown and
3.5 kilometers (2.2 miles) from the airport. EP Rates: between 12.000 CFP and
15.000 CFP ($120-150). Add 7% hotel tax to room rates and 1% value added
tax to room rates and meal plan. All major credit cards.*

The 70 unit Hotel Tahiti was closed in March, 1997, to be demolished
and reconstructed as the Outrigger Hotel Tahiti, which is due to open
during the first quarter of 1999. The site has been enlarged by landfill,
providing 2.5 hectares (6.2 acres) of lagoon front property. The new hotel
will have 200 rooms, including bungalows in the gardens and beside the
lagoon. Most of the rooms will be located in a three-story building, with
views of the island of Moorea or Papeete harbor. The air-conditioned
rooms will have two double beds or a king size bed, and some of the rooms

will have an exterior terrace, a larger bathroom and a solarium. A restaurant and bar, reception area and lobby will be built, and there will be a swimming pool facing the lagoon. There is no beach here, but there will be a pier. The Outrigger Hotel Tahiti will carry the Outrigger's three-paddle rating, which means that it will be a superior hotel with first class services and a convenient location.

TAHITI COUNTRY CLUB, *reservations: Tahiti Resort Hotels, B.P. 13019, Papeete, Tahiti, Tel. 689/43.08.29; Fax 689/41.09.28; Telex 702/428FP. On the mountainside in Punaauia, 7 kilometers (4.3 miles) from Papeete and 2 kilometers (1.2 miles) from the airport. EP Rates: room 14.000 CFP ($140) single, double or triple. Meal plan with breakfast and dinner is 4.000 CFP ($40) per person; meal plan with breakfast, lunch and dinner is 5.600 CFP ($56) per person. Round-trip transfers 2.000 CFP ($20) per person, including assistance and baggage handling and fresh flower lei greeting for international arrival. Add 7% hotel tax to room rates and 1% value added tax to room rates and meal plan. All major credit cards.*

This hotel is located between the Tahiti Beachcomber Parkroyal and the Sofitel Maeva Beach, and you can catch *le truck* at the foot of the hill to go to Papeete or the airport. The 40 air-conditioned rooms in two-story buildings have telephones, television, bathtubs, and some are equipped with mini-refrigerators. There is a restaurant with indoor outdoor dining, plus snack bar beside the swimming pool. There is an activities desk in the lobby and you also have free access to the tennis courts. This is a handy in-transit hotel on your way to or returning from the outer islands. An additional 66 rooms are currently under construction, which will give the hotel two more buildings, with 36 rooms expected to be completed by June, 1998, and the remaining 30 rooms due for completion in December, 1998.

MOANA SURF TOURS, *B.P. 6734, Faaa, Tahiti, Tel./Fax 689/43.70.70. PK 8.3 in Punaauia Commune on mountain side. A dormitory with 5 beds, sharing a kitchen and bathroom with hot water. Linens included. The rate of 10.000 CFP ($100) per day includes bed in dormitory, breakfast and dinner, round-trip transfers to the airport and best surfing spots. Add 1% value added tax to room rates and meal plan. No credit cards.*

Moana David is one of Tahiti's professional surfers and he competes in international surfing events around the world. If you want to learn all the secrets of surfing in Tahiti, he is your best contact.

Inexpensive

HEITIARE INN, *B.P. 6830, Faaa, Tahiti. Tel. 689/83.33.52/82.77.53. PK 4.3 in Faaa Commune, on seaside next to airport. Round-trip transfers provided. EP Rates: non air-conditioned room 4.000 CFP ($40) single, 4.500 CFP ($45) double; air-conditioned room with bathroom 6.000 CFP ($60) single,*

*6.500 CFP ($65) double. Add 1.000 CFP ($10) per person for breakfast. Add 1%
value added tax to room rates. No credit cards.*

This six-room hostel is just two minutes from the airport, across the
road from a French military base. There is a double bed in each of four
rooms and a single bed in two rooms, with five of the rooms air-
conditioned. Several of the rooms have private bathrooms and the others
share a bathroom, all with hot water. The kitchen is communal and there
is a swimming pool nearby. This is a spacious and clean hostel, with a large
outdoor tiled terrace. You can catch *le truck* on the road in front. There
are restaurants, snack bars and supermarkets within an easy walk.

CHEZ FIFI, *Cité de l'Air, Route Mea Ma, Faaa, Tahiti. Tel. 689/
82.63.30. PK 5.5 mountainside, in Faaa Commune, close to airport. Round-trip
transfers provided. Meals on request. Breakfast included. EP Rates: room 3.500
CFP ($35) single, 6.000 CFP ($60) double. Add 1% value added tax to room
rates and meal plan. No credit cards.*

Formerly known as Chez Sorensen, this three-bedroom concrete
house is across the road from the airport, a walk of just 180 meters (200
yards). You'll have a double bed and private bathroom with hot water, and
share the kitchen. The living room is a large open deck. This is a good
choice as a transit hostel.

CHEZ LOLA, *B.P. 6102, Faaa, Tahiti. Tel. 689/81.91.75. PK 4.5
mountainside in the Sainte-Hilaire neighborhood in Faaa Commune, one
kilometer inland from airport. Round-trip transfers provided at all hours. Meals
on request. Breakfast included. EP Rates: room 3.500 CFP ($35) single, 5.000
CFP ($50) double. Add 1% value added tax to room rates and meal plan. No
credit cards.*

Lola rents out two bedrooms in her family home, which is a modern
concrete house above the airport. There's hot water in the bathroom,
which you'll share with the other guests. House linens are provided. You'll
also have use of the living room, dining room, television and terrace. Not
only does Lola meet you at the airport upon arrival, but she will drive you
to the main road to catch *le truck* to Papeete, and come to fetch you at the
airport after you've finished your sightseeing and shopping. You'll enjoy
her generous meals.

CHEZ VA'A, *B.P. 828, Papeete, Tahiti. Tel. 689/42.94.32. PK 8,
mountain side in Nina Peata neighborhood in the Punaauia Commune. Round-
trip transfers provided. Breakfast included. EP Rates: room 3.500 CFP ($35)
single, 5.000 CFP ($50) double. Add 1 % value added tax to room rates and meal
plan. No credit cards.*

This guest room is far from the main road, but you will enjoy the
relaxed atmosphere, swimming pool and the hospitality of your hostess.
There is a double bed in the bedroom, and you will share the bathroom
with bathtub and hot water. House linens provided.

TAHITI AIRPORT LODGE, *B.P. 2580, Papeete, Tahiti. Tel. 689/ 82.23.68; Fax 689/82.25.00. PK 5,5 Cité de l'Air in Faaa Commune, overlooking and next to airport. Round-trip transfers provided. Breakfast included. Dinner on request. EP Rates: room 3.000-4.000-6.000 CFP ($30-$40-$60); bed in dormitory 2.000 CFP ($20). Add 1% value added tax to room rates and meal plan. No credit cards.*

This two-story colonial style house, with a panoramic view of the lagoon and the island of Moorea, is just a three-minute ride from the airport and five minutes from downtown. It has three attractively decorated bedrooms on the ground floor; one room has a double bed, private bathroom with bathtub and hot water, a fan and television. The other two rooms have a double bed and single bed, a fan and shared bath facilities with hot water. The living room and kitchen are communal. Upstairs is a seven-bed dormitory and three communal bathrooms with hot water, a fan, living room and terrace.

Owners Charles and Marguerite will take you around the island, to visit the archaeological sites, to the beach, or on a picnic. The Tahiti Manava Visitor's Bureau has received good reports from tourists who have stayed here. It is run by an elderly couple who lock the gate at night, but will wait up for all the guests to arrive safely back at the pension before going to bed.

SOUTHWEST COAST: PUNAAUIA TO MATAIEA
Moderate

RELAIS DE LA MAROTO, *B.P. 20687, Papeete, Tahiti. Tel. 689/ 57.90.29; Fax 689/57.90.30. Turn left at the sign at PK 46.5 in Mataiea Commune, 28.8 miles from Papeete. Drive up the winding, unpaved mountain road, past Lake Vaihiria 473 meters (1,551 feet) and keep climbing. EP Rates: 8.800 CFP ($88) standard room single/double; 17.500 CFP ($175) suite single; 35.000 CFP ($350) suite double. Meals on request. Meal plan with breakfast, lunch and dinner includes round-trip transfers and excursion. Round-trip transfers by 4x4 car 14.500 CFP ($145) per person with lunch included; round-trip transfers by helicopter 17.000 CFP ($170) per person. Add 1% value added tax to room rates and meal plan and 3% value added tax to excursions. All major credit cards.*

If your preferences include quiet mountain retreats in a cool, peaceful setting of tree ferns, waterfalls, archaeological sites and wild beauty in every imaginable shade of green, then you'll be happy at Maroto Inn. This is Tahiti's only mountain lodging, located in the center of the island in the historic Papenoo Valley, at the convergence of Vaituoru and Vainavenave rivers. This valley was formerly inhabited by thousands of Maohi people. Several of the basaltic house platforms, petroglyphs, meeting sites and *marae* temples of stone have been restored, and you can hike from the hotel to explore the interior of the island, where you'll find tunnels, grottos, caves and lava tubes.

The hotel buildings were originally used to house construction crews who are building several hydroelectric dams in the Papenoo Valley, and they are not deluxe. Only 10 standard rooms and two suites are being used for guests, although the motel-type solid concrete structures contain 38 rooms. The standard rooms have four bunks, a bathroom with hot water and a terrace overlooking the mountain peaks and lush valley. The two suites can each sleep three people. Another large building houses the reception area, private living room, convention room, dining room and bar, kitchen, game room and boutique.

The restaurant serves a fixed menu of French cuisine and offers a good choice of wines. I have eaten only one meal here, during a day tour, which was steak, green beans and potatoes, for 2.000 CFP ($20). A can of Hinano beer was 400 CFP ($4). Although I can appreciate the effort of getting supplies up the mountain, I thought the food was way overpriced and not good. Hopefully, a new chef has made improvements since my visit. If you are on a tight budget and will be spending just one night here, then you may want to buy your food at the snack beside the turnoff from the main road. It is very good and inexpensive.

Please do not try to drive up this tortuous mountain road unless you have a strong four-wheel drive vehicle, and do not attempt it even then if it's raining, which is very frequently. The drive down the other side of the Papenoo Valley takes you through several rivers, which can become very dangerous during the sudden deluges, causing the level of the river to rise very quickly. Several tourists have been trapped overnight in this valley because their vehicles were not powerful enough to ford the rivers. The hotel provides transportation and you can also get there by helicopter, or you can hike. Several tour companies have daily excursions across the interior of the island and they stop for lunch at Relais de la Maroto.

LE BELLEVUE, *B.P. 13451, Punaauia, Tahiti. Tel./Fax 689/58.47.04. PK 16, mountainside, in Punaauia Commune, 9.9 miles from Papeete. EP Rates: single/double 15.000 CFP ($150) for minimum two nights; third person 7.500 CFP ($75) for two nights; room per week 21.000 CFP ($210) single/double; third person 6.000 CFP ($60); monthly rental 63.000 CFP ($630) single/double. Add 1% value added tax to room rates. No credit cards.*

Jacques and Jeanine Richard have a one-room studio, with a beautiful view of the mountains and Moorea, which has one double bed with a private bathroom and hot water, an equipped kitchen and house linens.

HITI MOANA VILLA, *B.P. 10865, Paea, Tahiti. Tel. 689/57.93.93; Fax 57.94.44. PK 32, 19.8 miles from Papeete beside the lagoon in Papara Commune, 10 minutes from golf course and surfing beach. Round-trip transfers from airport 2.000 CFP ($20) per person. EP Rates: bungalow 8.000 CFP ($80)* *single/double; 10.000 CFP ($100) three-four people for two-night minimum. Additional bed 1.000 CFP ($10). Reduced rates for longer stays. Add 1% value added tax to room rates and 3% value added tax to excursions and car rentals. No credit cards.*

Each of the four modern concrete bungalows beside the Papara lagoon has a bedroom with double bed, a living room with two sofa beds, overhead fan, television, an equipped kitchen, private bathroom with hot water and a narrow terrace overlooking the lagoon. House linens are provided. In addition to a swimming pool, you'll also have the advantage of a private pontoon. Paddle canoes, an aluminum boat and bicycles are available for additional fees, and you can also rent a car at reduced rates, or ask Steve Brotherson to take you on a land or lagoon excursion. Restaurant Nuutere is across the street and supermarkets and snack bars are close by.

LES BOUGAINVILLEES MOTOR INN, *B.P. 63, Papeete, Tahiti. Tel. 689/53.28.02; Fax 689/43.77.11. PK 22.1, seaside, in Paea Commune, 13.7 miles from Papeete, with private access to beach and 20 minutes from golf course. EP Rates: suite 3.500 CFP ($35) single/double; add 1.000 CFP ($10) per day for extra person. Minimum stay three nights. Reduced rates for longer stays. Add 1% value added tax to room rates and meal plan. No credit cards.*

Three brightly decorated air-conditioned apartments are located in a two-story colonial style building, with private terraces overlooking a pretty tropical garden and swimming pool. Each apartment has a bedroom with a king-size bed, a spacious living room with two sofa beds, a modern bathroom with tub/shower and hot water, a completely equipped kitchen, and a private laundry with washing machine and ironing board. House linens and all cooking and dining facilities included, as well as free cable television. In addition to the swimming pool, you'll have private access to a white sand beach and sun deck, with beautiful panoramic views of the lagoon, Moorea and the tropical sunsets.

Inexpensive
PAPARA VILLAGE, *B.P. 12379, Papara, Tahiti. Tel. 689/57.45.74; Fax 689/57.79.00. PK 38.1 on mountainside across road from surfing area, less than a mile from the golf course and 23.6 miles from Papeete. EP Rates: 5.000 CFP ($50) single; 7.500 CFP ($75) double; third person 2.500 CFP ($25); family bungalow up to four people 15.000 CFP ($150). Meals served on request. Add 1% value added tax to room rates and meal plan. No credit cards.*

This colonial style pension is located at the foot of the green mountains of Papara, overlooking the lagoon and the peninsula of Tahiti-Iti. On the same property Thomas Chave has built a traditional Tahitian village, complete with an authentic *marae* stone temple. Here you'll find Tahitian style hospitality along with comfortable and attractive accommodations. Two standard bungalows each contain a double bed and single bed, private bathroom facilities with hot water, refrigerator, tea/coffee facilities, fan and television. A double bungalow has two bedrooms, each with a double bed and two single beds, shared bathroom with hot water. Facilities and amenities also include a living room with fan, television and terrace, dining room, equipped kitchen, washing machine, house linens and a swimming pool.

TE MITI, *B.P. 130088, Punaauia, Tahiti. Tel./Fax 689/58.48.61. PK 18.5, mountainside, 11.4 miles from Papeete in Lotissement Papehue, in Paea Commune, 100 meters (328 feet) after the Paea sign, across road from Mahana Park public beach. Round-trip transfers 2.000 CFP ($20) per person. EP Rates: standard room single/double 5.500 CFP ($55); large room 6.000 CFP ($60); small room 4.500 CFP ($45); bed in dormitory or additional bed 1.500 CFP ($15). Reduced rates after one week. Monthly rentals available. Breakfast included. Add 1% value added tax to room rates and meal plan. Mastercard, Visa.*

A "Bed and Breakfast" sign on the mountain side of the circle island road points the way to this hostel, which is located on a quarter-acre of land with lots of fruit trees. This hostel is a good choice for surfers and sunbathers, as it is just 200 meters (218 yards) from Tahiti's prettiest white sand beach. Two clean, modern houses provide five large bedrooms, with overhead fans and plenty of storage space, and a four-bed dormitory, mosquito nets and house linens. There is a living room, communal bathroom with hot water, and spacious patio. A refrigerator is provided for guests but there are no cooking facilities. Bicycles, snorkeling equipment and outrigger paddle canoes are available for rent. This is a highly rated hostel according to the tourist feedback at the Tahiti Manava Visitor's Bureau. Frédéric and his wife are a young, dynamic couple who treat their guests very well.

CHEZ ARMELLE, *B.P. 380640, Tamanu, Tahiti. Tel. 689/58.42.43; Fax 689/58.42.81. PK 15.5 on seaside in Punaauia Commune, 9.6 miles from downtown. Look for the Chez Armelle sign on the road shortly after the Mobil Station and Plage de Toaroto sign. Take the small access road to the right past the first home and head toward the beach. Round-trip transfers 1.000 CFP ($10) for two people. EP Rates: room 4.500 CFP ($45) single; 6.000 CFP ($60) double. Additional bed 1.000 CFP ($10). Breakfast included. Add 1% value added tax to room rates and meal plan. All major credit cards.*

This pension/snack is located beside a white sand beach, close to the Museum of Tahiti and Her Islands and Taapuna, one of Tahiti's most popular surfing spots. Each of the eight rooms in the house has a double bed, overhead fan and a private bathroom with hot water. House linens are furnished. You'll share the living room and shaded beach-side patio with the other guests. Her snack is open daily. You can rent bicycles, snorkeling equipment and surfboards, and Armelle will arrange island tours and excursions for you. The feedback from tourists who have stayed here is mixed. Some like it, some say it's dirty, and some say that Armelle didn't seem to be in a very good mood during their stay.

TAHITI ITI PENINSULA - TARAVAO
Inexpensive

CHEZ JEANNINE, *B.P. 7310, Taravao, Tahiti. Tel. 689/57.07.49/ 57.29.82; Fax 689/57.07.49. PK 4.4 on the Taravao Plateau. Round-trip transfers 1.000 CFP ($10) per person. EP Rates: bungalow single/double 6.000 CFP ($60) day, 30.000 CFP ($300) week, 80.000 CFP ($800) month; room single/double 4.000 CFP ($40) day, 20.000 CFP ($200) week, 50.000 CFP ($500) month. Add 1% value added tax to room rates and 3% value added tax for snacks and restaurants not involving meal plan. Mastercard, Visa.*

Jeannine is a vivacious Vietnamese lady who will cook you delectable dishes from her home country and French cuisine in her L'Eurasienne restaurant next to the pension. She has expanded her facilities to include four bungalows and five guest rooms. The bungalows each contain a double bedroom on a mezzanine and private bathrooms with hot water and house linens included. Each of the five rooms has a double bed and private bathroom with hot water, along with house linens. There is also a washing machine and swimming pool on the premises, but no kitchen facilities.

TE ANUANUA, *PK 10, Pueu, Tahiti. Tel./Fax 689/57.12.54. Beside lagoon in Pueu Commune on Tahiti-Iti Peninsula, 42 miles from Papeete. EP Rates including breakfast single/double/triple: yard-side bungalow 5.500 CFP ($55); garden bungalow 6.500 CFP ($65); beach-front bungalow 7.500 CFP ($75). Meals on request. Add 1% value added tax to room rates and meal plan and 3% value added tax for snacks and restaurants not involving meal plan. Mastercard, Visa.*

Te Anuanua means "the rainbow" in Tahitian, and you will probably see a few double rainbows in this lush tropical setting beside the lagoon, with a view of the mountains of Tahiti-Nui. This small hotel operated for years as an excellent local style restaurant, and a few rooms were eventually added. The hotel has seen better days. Four double bungalows provide eight rooms, with a double bed, private bathroom with hot water, overhead fan, house linens and terrace in each unit. There is room for a third mattress on the floor or on the terrace, which is enclosed by a colonial style lacy white wooden railing. House linens are provided, but they are not of the finest quality. When I stayed here with two girlfriends in October, 1996, we asked for blankets, as the pouring rain made us quite chilly. The covers came in all sizes and shapes and some had holes in them, but they were clean and served the purpose.

A small white sand beach and swimming pool beside the lagoon are more recent additions, and swimming off the dock is delightful. Snorkeling equipment is provided. My shell-collecting friends were ecstatic with their unusual "finds" in the lagoon, which they thankfully left intact. The atmosphere is definitely Polynesian and Hilda Lehartel and her staff from the Pueu village are very accommodating and gracious. The food served in the spacious dining room or on the covered terraces is highly recommended, especially the Tahitian buffet that is served each Sunday noon. The discotheque gets going every Friday night, with a live Tahitian band and all night dancing, so if you're in need of tranquillity, this is not the time to be here.

FARE NANA'O, *B.P. 7193, Taravao, Tahiti. Tel. 689/57.18.14; Fax 689/57.76.10. In Faaone Commune at PK 52 beside lagoon, just two kilometers (1.2 miles) from Taravao, 32.2 miles from Papeete by the east coast and 38.4 miles by the west coast. Round-trip transfers 6.000 CFP ($60) for two people. EP Rates single/double: fare or bungalow 5.000-5.500-6.500-7.500 CFP ($50-$55-$65-$75). Third person 1.000 CFP ($10). Special rates for long stays. Breakfast and dinner on request. Add 1% value added tax to room rates and meal plan. No credit cards.*

If your fantasy of life on a tropical island includes living in a tree house or a thatched roof *fare* in the lagoon, then you'll be happy to discover Fare Nana'o. Six bungalows on piles are creatively designed and built from natural materials, in and among the trees and along the beach, where you have a marvelous view of the sea and the peninsula of Tahiti-Iti.

All the *fares* offer a quiet, relaxed atmosphere, and you'll certainly feel in harmony with Nature here. The rooms are large and airy and very unusual. Fare Aito is built in a tree, with a double bed; Fare Hiti is a bedroom by the sea with a large double bed; Fare Heremiti is also on the sea, with a drawing room below and two double beds upstairs; Fare Tanetua and Fare Avae both have a double bed and a sleeping couch, plus a full kitchen with refrigerator and stove. The outhouse for these *fares* has a white coral floor, green plants and modern toilet facilities. Fare Motu Iti has a double bed, fully equipped kitchen and private bathroom with hot shower. House linens furnished. You'll find supermarkets, restaurants and snack bars in the nearby village of Taravao. For an extra fee Monique will drive you around to see the sights and arrange for boat excursions, picnics and hiking around the peninsula. If your taste runs to the offbeat, Fare Nana'o is especially recommended.

MEHERIO ITI, *B.P. 3695, Papeete, Tahiti. Tel. 689/57.74.31. PK 11.9 in Vairao village on Tahiti-Iti peninsula, 44.5 miles from Papeete. Round-trip transfers 2.000 CFP ($20) per person. EP Rates: garden bungalow, single/double 6.000 CFP ($60); beach bungalow single/double 7.000 CFP ($70); additional* *person 700 CFP ($7) per day. Add 1% value added tax to room rates. No credit cards.*

This is the only lodging on the west coast of Tahiti-Iti, and it offers three bungalows, with private equipped kitchens, private bathroom with hot water, a living room, terrace, and house linens. You can buy food at the snack bars and *magasins* nearby.

LE BON JOUIR, *B.P. 9171, 98713 Motu Uta, Tahiti. Tel. 689/ 57.02.15; Tel/Fax 689 43.69.70. Beside the lagoon on the south coast of Tahiti Iti in an area called Te Pari, beyond the end of the road. Round-trip boat transfers 2.000 CFP ($20) per person. Private parking for cars 500 CFP ($5) per day. EP Rates: bungalow single/double 4.000 CFP ($40); bungalow for one to three people 8.000 CFP ($80); bungalow for one to six people 12.000 CFP ($120); studio for five people 10.000 CFP ($100); dormitory for 10 people 2.000 CFP ($20). Meal plan with breakfast and dinner 3.500 CFP ($35); child under 12 years 500 CFP ($5). House linens furnished. Add 1% value added tax to room rates and meal plan and 3% value added tax to excursions. No credit cards.*

There are three bungalows, three dormitories and a studio on this property between the mountains and the lagoon at the end of the peninsula of Tahiti Iti. Access can only be made by boat in this untamed bushland. This is an ideal place for individuals or groups who want to get off the beaten track. The three bungalows have private kitchens and bathrooms with hot water. The studio has a private bathroom and you can share the kitchen with the people who sleep in the dormitories. Activities include hiking into the interior of Te Pari and exploring the lagoon and nearby *motu* islet. The mornings here are especially magnificent, as you can see the sun rising from behind the horizon of the sea.

WHERE TO EAT
WEST OF PAPEETE TO PUNAAUIA
Expensive

COCO'S, *PK 13.5, (seaside) Punaauia. Tel. 58.21.08. American Express, Mastercard and Visa. Open daily for lunch and dinner.*

This is where you want to go to celebrate that special occasion. I have received letters from people who've eaten here at my suggestion, and they gave Coco's a four-star rating. You begin your evening with a glass of champagne on the lawn beside the lagoon, watching the last rays of the sunset fade into mauve and purple behind the peaks of Moorea. You are in a tropical setting of casual elegance, with orchids and ferns, a gentle surf kissing the shore and romance in the air. Your dining table may be inside the open dining room or in the gardens. The frequently changing menu offers *la nouvelle cuisine Française*, which is attractively presented, gracefully served and very pleasing to the palate. An American style bar is separate from the dining room and serves all your favorite beverages.

AUBERGE DU PACIFIQUE, *PK 11.2, (seaside) Punaauia. Tel. 43.98.30. American Express, Mastercard and Visa. Open for lunch and dinner Monday-Saturday. Closed Sunday.*

Most of my gourmet friends in Tahiti agree with me that this is the best restaurant on the island for a gastronomic dining experience. The frequently changing menu always offers exotic choices, which may include wild game of rabbit, venison or pheasant, and other specialties from the various regions of France. Pressed duck is the *pièce de resistance*, or you can order roast duck with papaya, mahi-mahi soufflé, sautéed crab with ginger, grilled meats and an incredible selection of other delectable delights. Apple or mango fritters in coconut milk are a favorite dessert, and the homemade sorbets are made of lime, mango, pineapple and soursop.

Owner Jean Galopin was a cook at Maxim's and Tour d'Argent in Paris, and he has been setting new taste trends in Tahiti since 1974, harmoniously blending the abundance of nature and the eternal traditions of *haute cuisine*. He was named a Maître Cuisinier or Master Chef of France in 1987, and has published a beautifully illustrated book entitled *Tahitian Island Cooking*.

Auberge du Pacifique is located beside the lagoon, with a lovely view of Moorea. You can dine in an air-conditioned salon or in the main dining room, which has an indoor-outdoor setting under the stars. Be sure to visit the air-conditioned wine cellar, which is stocked with an excellent selection of the best *crus* of France.

LE LOTUS, *PK 7, Faaa. Tel 86.51.10. All cards.*

This overwater restaurant is part of the Hotel Tahiti Beachcomber Parkroyal, adjacent to a sand bottom swimming pool with an outdoor Jacuzzi and swim-up bar. This is where you will find the best salad bar on the island, available at lunch for 2.000 CFP ($20). The price changes when you select your grilled meats or seafood of the day and create a starter course at the generous salad bar. Open daily from 12noon-2:30pm.

You can also return to Le Lotus at tea-time, from 3-6:30pm, to sample pastries, ice cream, sherbets and pancakes while you gaze at the beautiful island of Moorea across the lagoon. Or you may prefer to sip a tropical cocktail as the sun sets behind the mountains of Moorea and the outrigger canoe paddlers glide past in the opalescent lagoon. You'll think you're in a movie setting.

Gourmet dinners are served from 7-9:30pm Tuesday through Saturday. You may choose to dine à la carte or select your own menu of appetizer, main course and dessert. These are grouped into *fine bouche* for 4.950 CFP ($49.50), *gourmet* for 6.100 CFP ($61) and *dégustation* for 6.950 CFP ($69.50). Cold appetizers may be asparagus salad with truffles vinaigrette or chartreuse of red tuna marinated and served with cream of seaweed and lemon. Hot appetizers include tournedos of salmon with herbal cake, and boneless quail served with strawberry vinegar. Your main course may be lobster cake, served with frogs' legs, scallops and *calamari salpicon*, guinea fowl roasted with broad beans and red beans, served with goose liver foie gras, or medallions of beef filet with forest mushrooms, flambéed at your table. A truffle of chocolate and coffee mousse may tempt your sweet tooth, and the *tart tatin* with apples and calvados sauce is very satisfying. Wesley Smith, an expatriate from Chicago, plays soft music on the piano each evening while you dine. He knows all your old favorites. This is one of Tahiti's most beautiful and romantic restaurants.

TIARE RESTAURANT, *PK 7, Faaa. Tel 86.51.10. All cards.*

This is the main restaurant at the Tahiti Beachcomber Parkroyal, offering all day dining, starting with a Parisian breakfast at 5am, and followed by a full breakfast buffet, light meals or *table d'hôte* menu for lunch, and dinner from 6:30-10pm, featuring French and Polynesian cuisine. An a la carte grill dinner and Tahitian dance show are presented each Wednesday night. The most popular event of the week is the *Soiree Merveilleuse*, the Marvelous Evening, for 5.990 CFP ($59.90), that is held on the beach on Friday night. Following a seafood buffet that includes oysters on the half shell and small rock lobster tails, entertainment is provided by one of the professional dance groups of Tahiti. This show often includes fire dancing under the stars on the white sand beach.

A Tahitian brunch buffet for 2.860 CFP ($28.60) is served in the restaurant every Sunday morning, and a Tahitian feast is held each Sunday evening in the coconut grove beside the beach. You will want to photograph the opening of the *ahimaa*, the underground oven, when the roast pig, taro, breadfruit, bananas and other food is removed. The cost of 5.100 CFP ($51) also includes a Tahitian dance show that follows the feast. This hotel does the best job of feeding and entertaining hundreds of people. Following the Tahiti Festival or Heiva I Tahiti held each July, the Beachcomber presents the Mini-Heiva, a nine-evening program of sumptuous buffets and performances by the winning song and dance groups. And throughout the year, in addition to the three special evenings each week, the hotel will organize other festive events, and if you happen to be in Tahiti then, you don't want to miss it.

CAPTAIN BLIGH, *PK 11.4 (seaside), Punaauia. Tel. 43.62.90. American Express, Mastercard and Visa. Open for lunch and dinner. Closed Sunday night and Monday.*

Just seven miles from Papeete, on Tahiti's "Gold Coast" overlooking Moorea, this overwater restaurant may be the largest in the South Seas. Roger and Juliette Gowan, who also own the Gauguin Museum Restaurant in Papeari, know how to feed lots of people, and this restaurant can accommodate at least 300 diners. The cuisine is international, with emphasis on fish and seafood, and a deluxe buffet is served each Sunday noon, including Tahitian specialties. A lobster dinner and Polynesian dance show is presented each Friday and Saturday evening, for 2.800 CFP ($28). Marguerite Lai and her "O Tahiti E" dancers perform. This group won the grand prize for the best dance group during the 1997 Heiva I Tahiti Festival.

A pier beside the restaurant leads to the Lagoonarium, where you can play peek-a-boo with the fish, turtles and sharks you see through the windows of underwater tanks. When you dine in the restaurant you get free admission to the Lagoonarium. Dick Johnson at Tahiti Aquatique, adjacent to Sofitel Maeva Beach, has a boat excursion to the Lagoonarium, which can also include lunch in the restaurant.

Moderate

CASABLANCA, *Marina Taina, PK 9 (seaside), Punaauia. Tel. 43.91.35. Mastercard, Visa. Open daily for lunch and dinner.*

Formerly known as La Boudeuse, this is a popular restaurant with French residents of Tahiti who like a nautical scene while dining. If you enjoy traditional French cuisine, you'll be sure to like the food and the view of Moorea just beyond the boats, lagoon and reef. *Couscous* is served every Wednesday for lunch and each Thursday evening. You will appreciate the light lunch selections, such as tuna tartare with potatoes or other vegetables, for 1.500 CFP ($15). Saturday night includes Jazz on the Grass.

LE GRAND LAC, *PK 4.2, (seaside) Faaa. Tel. 85.05.53. American Express, Mastercard and Visa. Open for lunch and dinner. Closed Sunday.*

The cuisine of Singapore and Hong Kong are served in this popular air-conditioned restaurant, and take-away meals are also available. The food doesn't need enhancing, but perhaps you'll be interested in learning that Hinano Teanotoga, the daughter of Joe, the owner, was crowned Miss Tahiti 1997, and won the title of third runner-up in the Miss France 1997 competition.

SNACK CARO, *PK 10.2 (mountain side), Punaauia. Tel. 43.87.43. No credit cards. Open for lunch and dinner. Closed Sunday.*

Nothing fancy about this place, where you can eat on a shaded terrace or in the dining room. The attraction at Caro's is the mouth-watering Chinese food, which is served cafeteria style. You will be happily pleased.

Inexpensive

PACIFIC BURGER, *PK 15, Tamanu, (seaside) Punaauia. Tel. 42.40.84. No credit cards. Open 9am-3pm and 5:30-9pm Monday-Thursday, and from 9am-9pm on Friday through Sunday.*

This is a very popular spot for families because of the small swimming pool and playground in front, and also because the food is very good and not expensive. You can munch on cheeseburgers, chiliburgers, hot dogs, salads and *poisson cru*, or you can order *paella* and *couscous*, and each Sunday there is *veau a la brôche*, veal on a spit. The people who work here are young and friendly and most of them speak English.

KENTUCKY FRIED CHICKEN, *Taina Beach, PK 9, Punaauia. Tel. 48.16.66. Mastercard, Visa. Open 10am-10pm during the week and until midnight on weekends.*

This KFC franchise was introduced to Tahiti in July, 1996, with the opening of one outlet adjacent to Marina Taina. You can eat your chicken on the terrace, inside the restaurant or drive through and go, just like at home. A small playground and beach attracts the children.

DOWNTOWN PAPEETE
Expensive
LA CORBEILLE D'EAU, *Blvd. Pomare, Paofai. Tel. 43.77.14. American Express, Mastercard and Visa. Open for lunch and dinner, except for Saturday noon and all day Sunday. Reserve.*

You won't find the daily luncheon specials listed on a sidewalk chalkboard at this small, elegant restaurant. The name is the French version of Papeete, which means "water basket" and it's located in the block just west of the Protestant Temple across from the waterfront. If you're walking from downtown it is worth the few extra steps to experience the gastronomic French cuisine that is served in a very intimate air-conditioned setting. The appetizers range from 1.600-2.400 CFP ($16-$24), and the main courses include just four choices each of meat and fish.

You may decide on the *emincé de dos de saumon fumé crème d'aneth et oeufs de saumon* for 2.900 CFP ($29), or a *duo de chevreuil et magret de pigeon aux deux sauces* for 3.400 CFP ($34). A cheese platter or *Sancerrois (crottin de chavignol cuit dans la crème)* for 1.700 CFP ($17) naturally cleanses the palate, then you may choose from the *chariot de desserts* for 1.300 CFP ($13). You may not understand what you're reading on the menu, but the *maître d'hotel* will graciously explain it all to you, as well as suggesting the appropriate wines for your meal. There's a selection of the month, which was a 1988 Côte de Nuits Village (Drouhin) for 6.500 CFP ($65) a bottle, the last time I was here. La Corbeille D'Eau was voted 1996 restaurant of the year by Tahiti's Junior Chamber of Commerce.

L'O A LA BOUCHE, *Passage Cardella. Tel. 45.29.76. American Express, Mastercard and Visa. Open for lunch and dinner. Closed Saturday noon and Sunday. Reserve.*

Bruno and Jean-Charles have one of the best rated restaurants in Tahiti, right in the heart of Papeete. The name indicates that you'll be salivating when you order their original specialties of *la nouvelle cuisine Française*. You may want to order the *perroquet caramélisé au miel*, a sumptuous dish of parrot fish in caramel honey. Or perhaps your taste buds will tempt you to try the *tresse d'agneau au gingembre confit*, lamb cooked in crystallized ginger. The Coquille St. Jacques with shrimp is another good choice, and the smoked duck salad will please the palate. Creative vegetarian dishes can also be prepared. In this air-conditioned restaurant with a decor of understated elegance, you'll enjoy every bite of anything you order.

LA PETITE AUBERGE, *rue des Remparts at the Pont de l'Est. Tel. 42.86.13. All major credit cards. Open for breakfast, lunch and dinner. Closed Saturday. Reserve.*

A small, intimate air-conditioned restaurant decorated as a French country inn, complete with checkered table linens and fireplace. This is a favorite gathering place for cognizant gourmets of fine French cuisine from the provinces of Normandy and Brittany. Menu choices include *paella, couscous,* seafoods, game and casseroles, often served in an ambiance of a Parisian cabaret to the accompaniment of an accordion, Spanish guitar or other impromptu entertainment provided by the regular clientele. A fine selection of French wines.

LE RETRO SAINT GERMAIN, *Entry is on street level of Vaima Center on rue LaGarde behind Le Retro sidewalk cafe, which faces Blvd. Pomare. Tel. 42.86.83. All major credit cards. Open daily for lunch and dinner.*

Do not confuse this restaurant with the sidewalk cafe in front, although they both belong to the same establishment. You'll take a trip back to "Gay Paree" of the 1930s when you enter this plush air-conditioned restaurant with the red velvet upholstery and Tiffany lamps. Here you can be a true gourmet while dining on terrine of mahi mahi with a saffron sauce for 1.300 CFP ($13), raw salmon with cream and chives for 1.800 CFP ($18), foie gras for 2.700 CFP ($27), rack of lamb with a *coulis* of mango for 1.900 CFP ($19), or a grilled T-bone steak with a green pepper sauce for 2.700 CFP ($27). You can order a glass of wine for 430 CFP ($4.30), or a bottle of white or red wine from an extensive selection, priced from 1.510-9.910 CFP ($15.10-$99.10). The champagnes are also tempting. Kako, the owner, imports entertainment from other countries for special occasions, which have included samba dancers from Brazil.

LE CAFE DES NEGOTIANTS, *10 rue Jean-Gilbert, Quartier du Commerce. Tel. 48.08.48. Mastercard, Visa. Open for lunch and dinner. Closed Saturday noon and all day Sunday.*

You will find this small air-conditioned French bistrot from the waterfront street of Boulevard Pomare by following the side street behind Tahiti Sports. Some of the regular clients are black pearl negotiants, who have their jewelry shops and offices on this street. The salads are very creative and you may prefer a smaller portion for 995 CFP ($9.95) or a big salad for 1.900 CFP ($19). An *omelette aux cèpes* is 1.250 CFP ($12.50) and escargots are 1.850 ($18.50) a dozen. Your main course may be *Colombo d'agneau Creole* for 1.650 ($16.50), *coq au vin* for 1.880 CFP ($18.80), filet of mahi mahi with papaya sauce for 2.350 ($23.50), or *tournedos rossini au fois gras* for 2.950 CFP ($29.50). There is an extensive menu of fine French wines, which can be sold by the glass or bottle. And should you decide on champagne, you may also want to order the foie gras for 3.500 CFP ($35).

MOANA ITI, *Blvd. Pomare. Tel. 42.65.24. American Express, Mastercard and Visa. Open for lunch and dinner. Closed Sunday.*

For the past 20 years Jean-Jacques has been serving fine French cuisine in his air-conditioned restaurant across from the waterfront, in the block just west of Avenue Bruat. His specialties include rabbit simmered in white wine, for 1.700 CFP ($17), and *tournedos* (tenderloin of beef) with *cèpes*, for 2.300 CFP ($23). His fresh seafood dishes, according to season, may be raw oysters, marinated mussels or grilled salmon, imported from France. He also carries a good selection of Alexis Lichine wines.

MORRISON'S LE GARDEN, *on fourth level of the Vaima Center. Tel. 42.78.61. Mastercard, Visa. Open for lunch and dinner. Closed Saturday noon and Sunday.*

Take the private, outside elevator between L'Oasis and Air New Zealand to reach this rooftop restaurant with indoor/outdoor dining on the huge wooden terrace surrounding a swimming pool. Workers from the travel agencies and airline offices in Papeete meet here for lunch to gossip while feasting on the *plat du jour* for 1.400 CFP ($14), salads priced from 1.400-1.800 CFP ($14-$18) and carpaccio of tuna or beef for 1.500 CFP ($15). If you choose to come for dinner you may want to try the parrot fish in vanilla sauce for 1.700 CFP ($17), rack of lamb with sweet garlic for 1.800 CFP ($18), filet mignon with peppercorn and caramel sauce for 2.400 CFP ($24), or a basket of shrimp sautéed in curry sauce for 2.500 CFP ($25). The restaurant gets its name from Jim Morrison of The Doors rock band, and during special weekends this is a gathering place where you may hear rock or jazz music performed by visiting American groups.

Moderate

LE MANAVA, *Corner of Ave. Bruat and Ave. Commandant Destremeau. Tel. 42.02.91. American Express, Mastercard and Visa. Open for lunch and dinner. Closed Saturday noon and all day Sunday.*

Specialties from the Pèrigord region of France are featured in this air-conditioned restaurant, which is located near the government buildings downtown. The luncheon crowd includes politicians, judges and business people, who may order the plat du jour, which can be *boeuf bourguignon* for 1.500 CFP ($15), with a *salade de choux* for 800 CFP ($8), or something fancier and more costly. You can also stop for a cup of coffee or glass of wine and sit at the bar inside or in the gazebo restaurant outside.

JACK LOBSTER, *Vaima Center, Lower Plaza. Tel. 42.50.58. Visa. Open for lunch and dinner. Closed Saturday noon and Sunday.*

If you're feeling a little homesick or you are not too adventurous in your eating preferences, then you'll feel better once you walk into this restaurant, which is decorated in the old country style of America, complete with red and white checkered tablecloths. The menu choices will have your mouth watering even before you taste your cheeseburger for 1.100 CFP ($11), chili con carne, 1.200 CFP ($12), chicken enchiladas or beef fajitas. If you're really hungry you may want to order the T-bone steak for 2.200 CFP ($22), or the special ranchero platter with Corona and tequila, for 2.500 CFP ($25). A gigantic seafood platter is served each Wednesday and Saturday for 5.000 CFP ($50). Use the stairway behind the newspaper stand on Boulevard Pomare side of the Vaima Center.

ROYAL KIKIRIRI, *rue Colette, between rue Paul Gauguin and rue des Ecoles. Tel. 43.58.64. Visa. Open Monday and Tuesday 6:30am-2pm, and Wednesday-Saturday 6:30am-2pm and 7:30-9:30pm. Closed Sunday.*

When this restaurant first opened my friends at the Tahiti Tourist office were raving about it. I waited for a few years to give it a try and then wondered why I didn't go sooner. This is an undiscovered gem of a restaurant for people who enjoy French or Chinese cuisine. What I really like is the selection of fish, which can be mahi mahi, moon fish, grouper, parrot fish, red snapper or various lagoon fish, steamed whole with ginger and green onions, salted lemon or black beans. You can order a tasty tofu dish with minced pork and chicken, tenderloin of beef, shrimp curry or fresh crab. Desserts may include juicy oranges from the Marquesas or sweet lychees from Taravao. The small, simply decorated air-conditioned dining room is on the second floor above a typical Tahitian bar, where the sound of the guitar and ukulele can be heard in the evening, along with a few off-key exuberant voices.

LA ROMANA, *3, rue du Commandant Destremeau. Tel. 41.33.64. American Express, Mastercard and Visa. Open for lunch and dinner. Closed all day Saturday and Sunday noon. Reserve.*

This is a very busy restaurant near the complex of government offices. Here you can dine in total pleasure on French, Italian or Tahitian cuisine, with an excellent menu and very efficient, friendly service. The bar serves a large selection of mixed and tropical drinks. The menu includes fried shrimp with tartar sauce for 1.800 CFP ($18), breaded veal cutlets for 1.850 CFP ($18.50), and shrimp flambéed with champagne for 1.950 CFP ($19.50). The thin crust pizzas are of superior quality and the vegetarian pizza, for 950 CFP ($9.50), is visually a work of art and tastes simply divine. The *poisson cru*, for 1.100 CFP ($11), is also very good. Live music on Friday evenings.

LE MANDARIN, *26, rue des Ecoles. Tel. 42.16.33. All major credit cards. Open daily for lunch and dinner.*

If you're in downtown Papeete and are in the mood for excellent Chinese food, this air-conditioned restaurant just around the corner from the Hotel Mandarin will be a very good choice. The upstairs dining room, which is decorated in an elaborate Chinese Mandarin motif, serves authentic Cantonese specialties, using local seafoods and fresh produce. The menu changes weekly, featuring unusual dishes such as a soup made from chicken and *bêche de mer* (sea cucumber), *cigale de mer* (slipper lobster) and steamed limande (flounder). The talented chef will also prepare you an unforgettable dinner of Peking duck or *ta pen lou* (Chinese seafood fondue) if you give him a day's advance notice. The wine cellar contains a varied selection of the best of Bordeaux.

DRAGON D'OR, *rue Colette. Tel. 42.96.12. All major credit cards. Open for lunch and dinner. Closed Monday.*

This is the tried and true Chinese restaurant of Tahiti, in the heart of Papeete across the street from the Papeete Mairie (Town Hall). Robert Wong, who also owns the Hotel Royal Papeete, opened this restaurant in 1964, and his family still serves mouthwatering specialties from Canton.

This was the first Chinese restaurant I visited when I moved to Tahiti in 1971, and I'll never forget my lesson on how to eat *nems*, the Vietnamese egg rolls that are so popular in Tahiti. You wrap your *nem* in a leaf of lettuce, add fresh mint and dip it into a special Chinese sauce. Then enjoy a taste treat that will have you asking for more. I later added *chop soy special* to my repertoire of culinary favorites when I'm lunching alone here. On top of the crispy noodles the chef piles a sumptuous concoction of meat, chicken, shrimp, broccoli, snow peas, celery, mushrooms and other Chinese vegetables.

Most people eat family style when two or more dine in Chinese restaurants. This way you'll have a larger variety of foods, which should definitely include the Chinese style *poisson cru* that is a specialty of the "Golden Dragon". The decor in this comfortable, air-conditioned restaurant never changes. The walls are decorated with murals of China, complete with twinkling lights. You can sit at the bar while waiting for your table if you forget to reserve.

LA SAIGONNAISE, *Ave. Prince Hinoi. Tel. 42.05.35. Visa. Open for lunch and dinner. Closed Sunday.*

To reach Papeete's only Vietnamese restaurant if you're walking from downtown Papeete, follow Avenue Prince Hinoi from the waterfront to the first traffic light, and continue straight ahead, walking on the left side of the street until you see the restaurant in the next block. You can relax in the small, air-conditioned dining room while choosing your meal from a varied menu. In addition to the soups and salads, which are light and pleasing to the palate, you'll want to try some of Jeannot's house specialties of fish, chicken and pork dishes.

L'APIZZERIA, *Blvd. Pomare. Tel. 42.98.30. Mastercard, Visa. Open for lunch and dinner. Closed Sunday.*

Here is a garden restaurant serving Italian specialties on the waterfront since 1968. Located 228 yards west of the Papeete Post Office, this is a very popular restaurant with the luncheon crowd. In addition to a choice of 15 succulent pizzas cooked in a wood-burning oven, you may also want to try the lasagna, veal sautéed in Marsala wine, or a simply delicious barbecued steak. The salads are well prepared and the *poisson cru* is freshly prepared on order. The only drawback here is the roar of the traffic, which passes just beside the shaded terrace. If you want to talk and be heard, then take a table inside.

LOU PESCADOU, *rue Anne-Marie Javouhey. Tel. 43.74.26. No credit cards. Open for lunch and dinner. Closed all day Sunday and on Monday evening.*

This very lively Italian restaurant is the kind of place where you can whoop and shout. This is Tahiti's most popular pizza parlor, and you can also order Italian or French Provençale specialties. Mario, the owner-chef, sets the ambiance with good cheer, good smells and good food. Even the decor is boisterous and happy, with murals of waterfront scenes from the Mediterranean coast, Chianti wine bottles tied to the support posts, with checkered tablecloths and bottles of spicy olive oil on the tables. There is a well-stocked bar and the place is air-conditioned. The waitresses are mostly big Tahitian "mamas" who have been with Mario for many years, and they all wear ample sized tee-shirts sporting Mario's face with a grizzled beard. These friendly and hard-working girls have been known to dance on the tabletops with Julio Iglesias and other visiting celebrities. You'll find Mario's place behind the Cathedral of Notre Dame, on the same street as the Clinique Cardella.

BIG BURGER, *rue du General de Gaulle. Tel. 43.01.98. American Express, Mastercard, Visa. Open for breakfast, lunch and dinner. Closed Sunday.*

This indoor-outdoor restaurant is on the corner of Fare Tony, across the street from the Vaima Center. This was perhaps the first of the "fast-food" restaurants, but the tendency here is to linger over a meal or a beer *pression* rather than eating on the run. Hamburgers are on the menu, but there's a lot more besides. You can order a pizza for 800 CFP ($8), stuffed roasted veal or escalope of turkey for 1.300 ($13), shrimp in whisky for 1.400 ($14), and a filet of tenderloin for 1.700 CFP ($17). They also have a very good selection of fresh salads. Their *salade Niçoise* (Mediterranean salad) is consistently the best and most generous in town. Add a few slices of crusty French bread and a glass of red wine and you've got a very satisfying lunch for about 1.000 CFP ($10).

LE RETRO, *Street level of Vaima Center, Blvd. Pomare. Tel. 42.86.83. All major credit cards. Open daily with non-stop service until 11pm.*

This is an all-purpose restaurant for breakfast, lunch and dinner, a snack, *salon de thé* and bar, with an ice cream parlor and fast food counter. Here you can order a hamburger for 550 CFP ($5.50), a club sandwich for 750 CFP ($7.50), grilled mahi mahi for 1.700 CFP ($17) or filet mignon steak for 1.800 CFP ($18). You can get a pizza or crêpes to go, or try a hot Italian Panini sandwich for 360-550 CFP ($3.60-$5.50). American friends living in Moorea claim they get the best ice cream in the world here, with a choice of 38 flavors, including apricot, kiwi, cantaloupe, peach, pear, mango, passion fruit, or something more familiar, such as chocolate praline. The service isn't the world's fastest, however, and you'll have a good chance to practice your discipline of patience while waiting for someone to take your order if you're sitting at one of the sidewalk tables. But if you're not in a hurry, this is a great place to people watch, as it is on the waterfront street across from the boat docks.

LE PARC BOUGAINVILLE, *Adjacent to Papeete Post Office. Tel. 53.25.50. Visa. Open daily 5am-11pm.*

You may have heard of Acajou's, which was the most popular restaurant in Tahiti for many years. Chef Acajou has moved just a little further down the street, in the park beside the post office, where he now serves his faithful followers in a refreshing setting beside Queen Pomare's cool spring. This is the ideal spot to pause in your busy day of shopping and sightseeing. The extensive menu includes freshly squeezed fruit juice for 450 CFP ($4.50), hamburgers for 370 CFP ($3.70) and omelets from 550-780 CFP ($5.50-$7.80). Acajou's daily specials may include Chinese style chicken and vegetables for 790 CFP ($7.90), steak Teriyaki for 1,290 CFP ($12.90), a mahi mahi filet for 1.450 CFP ($14.50) or a filet mignon for 1.750 CFP ($17.50). You can get a beer or wine here, but no other alcoholic beverages are served.

PATISSERIE HILAIRE, *street level of Vaima Center, rue du General de Gaulle, Tel. 42.68.22. No credit cards. Closed on Sunday.*

This is Papeete's largest and most popular *patisserie*, and the glass walls on two levels provide a great view of people walking by on the sidewalk. In addition to the homemade ice cream and sorbets, pastries, salads and sandwiches, the chocolates and other candies are also a specialty of the house.

Inexpensive

L'OASIS, *Street level of Vaima Center, on corner of rue Jeanne d'Arc and Ave. General de Gaulle. Tel. 45.45.01. No credit cards. Open 6am-6pm. Closed Sunday.*

You can buy a sandwich or *casse-croûte* from the kiosk counter and eat as you go, or you can sit on the covered dining terrace and watch the daily drama of people passing, while sipping a cold *pression*. You can serve yourself from the salad bar and dine on the daily specials of French food in the air-conditioned restaurant.

LA MARQUISIENNE, *rue Colette. Tel. 42.83.52. No credit cards. Open Monday-Friday 5am-5pm, on Saturday until 3pm and on Sunday until 9am.*

The smell of the coffee will lure you into this air-conditioned pastry shop, but you won't regret following your nose, because you'll discover a wonderful selection of French pastries, quiches, slices of pizza and sandwiches that will make you glad you came. And the coffee is as good as it smells.

LE MARCHE, *the Papeete Public Market, rue Edouard Ahnne, one block inland from Blvd. Pomare. Tel. 42.25.37. Diners, Mastercard, Visa. Open 5:30am-4:30pm. Closed Sunday.*

On the ground floor of the public market is a take-out counter where you can get a selection of very good Chinese pastry, sandwiches, *casse-croûtes* and fries. Coffee and soft drinks are also available here, but you have to eat and drink standing up.

Go up the escalator to the second floor of the public market and you will find the cheapest coffee, tea or chocolate in town, at 150 CFP a cup. You can order two eggs with ham for 450 CFP ($4.50) or a steak for 700 CFP ($7). Freshly squeezed pineapple or orange juice is 400 CFP ($4). A hamburger costs 550 CFP ($5.50) and a *poisson cru* with coconut milk is 950 CFP ($9.50). Lunch service is cafeteria style, with daily specials. *Couscous* is served each Thursday for 1.100 CFP ($11) and Friday is *maa Tahiti* day, for 1.800 CFP ($18). A live Tahitian band keeps you entertained while you eat, playing music from 11am-1:30pm. (You are not allowed to take food from the first floor to eat upstairs).

POLYSELF, *8 rue Paul Gauguin. Tel. 43.75.32. No credit cards. Closed Sunday.*

This is a clean, air-conditioned restaurant where you can choose a breakfast of papaya and yogurt, a chicken *chao pao*, or a fried *merou*, a small grouper fish from the lagoon that is served, complete with head and tail, in a special Chinese sauce. The action really gets going at lunch time, when the bank and office workers pass through the cafeteria line, choosing *poisson cru*, salads and daily specials of fish, chicken, meat and vegetables, cooked in a combined local style of Chinese, French and Tahitian.

SNACK ROGER, *Place Notre Dame. Tel. 42.80.38. No credit cards. Closed Sunday.*

This is a quiet restaurant at mid-morning, where you can linger over a coffee and croissant. But watch out for the hungry herd who arrive at lunch time, to devour Roger's daily specials. His *poisson cru* is famous among local diners.

SNACK GABY, *rue Edouard Ahnne, across from Papeete Public Market. No credit cards. Open for lunch only. Closed Sunday.*

This is where I go when I want to eat well, but quickly and inexpensively. **Gaby**, who is Chinese, lived in California and speaks very good English. His restaurant is very clean and you can choose the daily specials, mostly Chinese dishes such as chicken and lemon sauce, chow mien, beef and vegetables or *maa tinito haricots rouges*, from a cafeteria style display of prepared foods. It will cost you about 800 CFP ($8). His clients are mostly Tahitians, who eat an early lunch. The food is sold out by 1:00pm.

SNACK RAUREA, *rue Georges LaGarde. Tel. 43.69.11. No credit cards. Closed Sunday.*

This little snack is located *on a side street behind the Pharmacie du Vaima, which is on Avenue General de Gaulle across from Fare Tony and Big Burger.* It's worth taking the trouble to find it, but you should get there before 11:30am if you want lunch. This is a choice restaurant for the employees of nearby banks, travel agencies and other offices, who want to eat well, quickly and cheaply. The daily specials are marked on a chalk board on the wall. You can order a whole or half portion of *poisson cru* with coconut milk, which is served with rice if you wish. Other choices frequently include *maa tinito haricots rouges*, ragout of beef, chicken with mushrooms and beef and vegetables. No alcoholic beverages are served. The food here is very good, the decor is simple and the people who work here do not speak much English, but you'll still be glad you came. You can eat a very satisfying lunch for less than 1.000 CFP ($10).

SNACK SAN FRANCISCO, *rue Paul Gauguin. Tel. 42.68.37. No credit cards. Open for breakfast and lunch. Closed Sunday.*

I've always liked this little snack shop, operated by a Chinese family, which serves excellent *poisson cru* for breakfast and throughout the normal business day in Papeete. More conventional breakfast choices include yogurt, fruit, fruit salad and *café-pain-beurre* (coffee, bread and butter). This is where I normally go for a good *café au lait* and *chao pao poulet*, otherwise known as a Chinese dough ball filled with chicken. I've never seen tourists in here, but I think you will appreciate the cleanliness, food and the ice cream.

MACDONALD'S TAHITI, *rue General de Gaulle, Tel. 53.37.37. No credit cards. Open daily 6am-11pm.*

It took them a long time to do it, but MacDonald's finally found their way to Tahiti in late 1996. Other fast food places have suffered from loss of business, as school kids, government officials and visiting South Pacific dignitaries stand in line to order their Big Macs and sausage biscuits. You won't find the bargains here that you are used to back home, but the residents of Tahiti are happy to take advantage of the special promotions when "le triple cheese" goes on sale for 350 CFP ($3.50).

KENTUCKY FRIED CHICKEN announced in February 1998 that it will build an outlet on rue General de Gaulle in downtown Papeete, in a location formerly occupied by Chic Boutique. This is just a block from MacDonalds.

LE MOTU, *street level of Vaima Center, on the corner of rue General de Gaulle and rue Georges LaGarde. No credit cards.*

This kiosk *on the back side of the Vaima block* serves a good selection of takeout sandwiches, cheese *croissants* and crusty *casse-croûtes*, as well as soft drinks and ice cream.

EAST OF PAPEETE TO MAHINA
Expensive
LE LION D'OR, *rue Afareii, Pirae. Tel. 42.66.50. All major credit cards. Open for lunch and dinner. Reserve. Closed Sunday.*

This is an excellent seafood restaurant just five minutes from Papeete via Avenue Prince Hinoi to Pirae, on the right side of the road adjacent to the Banque de Tahiti and a pharmacy. The air-conditioned restaurant is upstairs, with a lovely decor of pink and white linens and fresh flowers on the tables. Seafood choices include grilled lobster, mahi-mahi stuffed with shrimp, escargots and their special seafood platter. Perhaps you will prefer frog legs, tournedos Rossini, Roquefort steak or *steak tartare au cognac*, followed by a selection of eight salads and something sinfully delicious from the dessert menu.

The last time I ate lunch here, Elisabeth, the owner, had a drawing among her guests to win a lovely black pearl from her own pearl farm in the Tuamotu atolls. No, I wasn't holding the lucky number, but I felt like a winner anyway, because I had truly enjoyed my *sole meunière aux amandes*, accompanied by a bottle of Blanc de Blancs wine.

LE BELVEDERE, *Fare Rau Ape Valley, Pirae. Tel. 42.73.44. American Express, Mastercard, Visa. Open daily for lunch and dinner.*

You will feel on top of the world in this rustic and cheerful setting, 600 meters (1,800 feet) above the sea, overlooking Point Venus and Moorea. Marlon Brando's atoll of Tetiaroa is visible, some 42 kilometers (26 miles) to the north. The mountains of Huahine, an island 150 kilometers (93.2 miles) from Tahiti, can be seen on a clear evening at sunset, with the help of a telescope on the terrace.

Le Belvedere's bright yellow *le truck* provides unforgettable transportation from your hotel, and you will feel and smell the change of air as *le truck* winds up the one lane road with some 70 hairpin curves, climbing through the Fare Rau Ape Valley. Wild mountain ferns mingle their fragrance with the scent of the tall eucalyptus trees that grow in a wild profusion of verdure, along with giant mangoes, cashew trees, *causaurina* pines, acacias and wild hibiscus *purau* trees. By the time you get to the restaurant you will probably have begun to make friends among the other passengers, who are also laughing a little nervously while eyeing the precipitous drop-off on one or both sides of the road. You can come for lunch and a swim in the pool. You can take the first dinner service that gets you to the restaurant in time to photograph a panoramic sunset. Or you can come later for a romantic dinner under the stars. Whatever the time of day, you will be rewarded with breathtaking seascapes. You can also get to Le Belvedere by helicopter, enjoying a bird's eye view of the scenery en route.

The restaurant is a combination of a wooden Swiss chalet and Polynesian decor. There are four dining areas, but you will probably want to sit on the terrace for the best view, if the air isn't too chilly. That expression is not normally used to describe any other place in these tropical islands. Maurice Brichet, the French owner-chef of Le Belvedere since the late 1960s, claims that during the "winter" months of June, July and August, he has had to close the windows of the restaurant and light a fire in the fireplace, just like in a real Swiss chalet!

The *fondue bourguignonne* (beef fondue) is a specialty, with tender slices of New Zealand beef that you cook to your own taste. This is accompanied by a salad bar, hot French fries, tasty sauces and carafes of white or red wine, with ice cream and coffee served afterward. The cheese fondue and seafood fondue are also great favorites for couples or large groups, who have a great time trying to recapture a piece of meat or shrimp that fell into the cooking pot. Other favorite selections include French onion soup, mahi-mahi, *couscous* and pepper steak. The ride back down the mountain is always a happy one, and you'll probably join the rest of the revelers in singing "Roll Me Over in the Clover" and other bawdy songs. The tourist menu, which includes transportation, a choice of beef or cheese fondue, fish or steak, is 4.500 CFP ($45) per person. The seafood fondue is 1.600 CFP ($16) more. Reserve for your transportation. Pick-up at the hotels on the west coast begin at 11:30am for lunch, 4:30pm for sunset and dinner, and 7pm for the last service.

Moderate
LE CHEVAL D'OR, *Fariipiti, Taunoa. Tel. 42.98.89. American Express, Mastercard, Visa. Open for lunch and dinner. Closed Sunday noon.*

Whenever I eat here I always order the *riz Cantonnais Cheval D'or*, which is fried rice with bits of shrimp and fish, the house specialty of the "Golden Horse". Some of my other choices are the roast suckling pig in coconut sauce, eggplant stuffed with fish paste, and shrimp cooked in a spicy sauce and served on a sizzling platter. This air-conditioned restaurant is almost always packed with Chinese, French, Tahitian and American residents, which gives me the impression that it's a popular restaurant with everyone who knows how to find it. You'll need transportation and a map to get here from downtown. The simplest way is to turn right at the traffic light off Boulevard Pomare, just past Hotel Royal Papeete, and follow Avenue du Chef Vairaatoa about 12 blocks until you come to Cours de l'Union Sacrée. Turn left and head toward the sea, where you'll find the restaurant in front of you where the inland road ends.

DAHLIA, *PK 4,2, Arue. Tel. 42.59.87. American Express, Diners, Visa. Reserve for lunch or dinner. Closed Sunday.*

I am among those aficionados who think that this is the best Chinese restaurant in Tahiti. Some of my Chinese friends prefer other restaurants, but I believe you will be very happy with anything you order here. You can choose shrimp, chicken, beef and tofu sizzling platters, which are very popular. The chicken and cashews, beef and broccoli, crystal shrimp and pork with taro are also good. The air-conditioned restaurant is located on the seaside, across the road from the French military base in Arue, and it is packed every day at lunch with French soldiers, Chinese families and the rest of us. You won't be seated after 1pm, as most Chinese restaurants close early after the luncheon crowd has gone.

Inexpensive
SNACK MAMA ELISA, *Point Venus, Mahina. Tel. 48.30.26. No credit cards. Open daily until late afternoon.*

The black sand beach at Point Venus helped to put Tahiti on the world map because it was the landing site of Captains Samuel Wallis, James Cook, William Bligh and the English Protestant missionaries. In addition to the tour groups who come here daily, the local people use Point Venus as a playground for soccer games, outrigger canoe races and swimming in the surf. Mama Elisa's snack has developed over the years from an ice cream and soft drink stand into a good restaurant with daily specials and salads, priced under 1.000 CFP. I like to go there to sit under the majestic *causaurina* pines and rubber trees and eat a salad of shrimp and pineapple.

AROUND THE ISLAND
Expensive
NUUTERE, *PK 32.5, Papara (mountain side). Tel. 57.41.15. Visa. Open for lunch and dinner. Closed Tuesday.*

This is indeed a restaurant of gastronomic French cuisine served in a pleasant Tahitian setting of thatched roof, tropical gardens, wicker furniture, white table cloths and freshly cut flowers on the table. This French-Tahitian combination is also reflected in the food, which combines the lobster, sea shrimp and river shrimp from the Tahiti-Iti peninsula with savory sauces. A theme dinner is served each Friday evening, which can include *paella, couscous, bouillabaisse, tripes à la Catalane*, rabbit stewed in white wine sauce, *coq au vin* and other imaginative dishes. The wines are from the best vineyards in France. I've never gotten away from here without paying less than 10.000 CFP ($100) per person, but that's because we ordered Chateauneuf de Pape in the twisted bottles, T-bone steaks flown in from New York and fresh strawberries in chocolate sauce for dessert. But I'm still licking my lips when I think about the meals I've enjoyed in this restaurant.

AUBERGE DU PARI, *PK 17.8, Teahupoo, Tahiti-Iti. Tel. 57.13.44. Mastercard, Visa. Open daily for lunch and nightly on reservation.*

Chez Dany, as this gourmet restaurant is called, is almost at the end of the road on the west coast of the Tahiti-Iti peninsula, on the seaside in Teahupoo village. This is an ideal spot to linger over a long lunch of shrimp, crab, lobster and fine French cuisine, while sharing a bottle of wine and gazing at one another and the distant white line of the coral reef across the blue lagoon. You won't be rushed to leave. Dany understands the mesmerizing effect of the ocean breeze, the sun dancing in sparkling bubbles on the lagoon and the tropical splendor of the surrounding gardens. She and her staff do their part to satisfy the palate with the best quality of food carefully prepared and served on a shaded terrace or in the dining room, also open to the marvelous view.

BOB TARDIEU, *PK 51.8, Faaone. Tel. 57.14.14. American Express, Mastercard, Visa. Open daily for lunch. Dinner is served Wednesday-Saturday.*

Bob serves an excellent choice of Mediterranean French dishes and seafood on his seaside dining terrace in Faaone, which overlooks the east coast of the Tahiti-Iti peninsula. This is a good restaurant for a luncheon stop while driving around the island, and you can linger over a long, very satisfying lunch or *digestif*. You will appreciate the special ambiance of Bob's restaurant if you speak a little French, or have visited any of the villages in the south of France or in Corsica, where the men spend all day playing *boules* (French bowls), while drinking carafes of red wine and smoking their Gitanes. Bob comes from that background, and his excellent cuisine and bawdy sense of humor strongly reflect his origins.

For several years I lived in Taravao, just two kilometers from Bob's place. The first time I went to Bob's I was very impressed by his fish soup, which was made from three kinds of fish, rock lobster and *cigale de mer*, a slipper lobster that is found in the Polynesian lagoons. A week later I asked Bob to prepare the same soup to take home for a dinner party. He invited me into the kitchen, where two cats were enjoying a fish meal on the table, and he gave me the entire pot of soup, a container of *rouille*, a bowl of grated cheese and a package of croutons to go with the meal. I hesitated to take his dishes, protesting that he didn't even know me. "You'll bring them back tomorrow," he assured me with a smile. Bob's became a frequent luncheon stop whenever I had visitors from overseas. The last time I was there, with Australian friends, Bob went fishing in the lagoon in front of the restaurant while our lunch of fresh heart of palm salad, giant shrimp cocktails and enormous platter of broiled lobster was being prepared in the kitchen. When he returned to the dining terrace, his pet goat accompanied him and proceeded to tap dance on the table with her forepaws. The Australians are still talking about that a year later and can't wait to go back again.

GAUGUIN MUSEUM RESTAURANT, *PK 50.5, Papeari. Tel. 57.13.80. American Express, Mastercard, Visa. Open daily for lunch only.*

You'll enjoy this luncheon stop whether you are touring the island by rental car, by taxi or in a 50-passenger bus with guide. This popular restaurant is built over the lagoon in Papeari, 50.5 kilometers (31 miles) west of Papeete and just 364 meters (400 yards) west of the Paul Gauguin Museum and Harrison Smith Botanical gardens. Chances are you'll be able to admire a double rainbow over Tahiti-Iti while dining on grilled mahi mahi, shrimp curry and Continental cuisine, complete with home-made coconut or lime pie. Or you may prefer the buffet of salads and Tahitian food, with fresh fruits and coconut for dessert. The maitai rum drinks are a house specialty, and after a few of these, you'll be happier if you're not driving. Englishman Roger Gowan and his Chinese wife Juliette have been serving tourists for more than 20 years and their staff are people from Papeari, some of whom have worked in the kitchen right from the beginning. Roger and Juliette are also owners of Captain Bligh restaurant in Punaauia.

Moderate

TE HONO, *PK 60, Taravao. Tel. 57.21.84. Mastercard, Visa. Open daily.*

This two-story restaurant whose name means "the turtle" has a panoramic view of the green hills of the isthmus that connects Tahiti-Nui with Tahiti-Iti. It is situated in the heart of Taravao, beside the turn-off to the east coast of Tahiti-Iti, and is operated by Marcel and Denis Vanquin, two Chinese brothers who formerly operated the *magasin* Taiarapu, which gave way to the big Casino supermarket next door. Open since August, 1997, a chef from Hong Kong prepares Chinese and French cuisine, served from 10am-2pm, and 5-9pm; on Sundays and holidays, the restaurant is open from 5am-3pm. Fast-food service and take out meals are available on the street level, or you can dine leisurely in the air-conditioned restaurant upstairs.

TE ANUANUA, *PK 10, Pueu, Tahiti-Iti. Tel. 57.12.54. American Express, Mastercard, Visa. Open daily for breakfast, lunch and dinner.*

Here you can spend the day or several, as Te Anuanua (the rainbow) is also a small hotel beside the lagoon on the east coast of the Tahiti-Iti peninsula, 42 miles from Papeete. You can dine beside the lagoon on a spacious covered terrace in a relaxed atmosphere and a lovely, tranquil setting. You can also swim just off the pier in clear, clean water. Hilda Lehartel, the manager, selects the freshest seafoods and best cuts of meat from New Zealand for her clients. The cuisine is French and Tahitian, with an array of fresh fruits from the abundant orchards of Tahiti-Iti. A very popular Tahitian buffet is served each Sunday at noon.

L'EURASIENNE, *PK 4, Taravao Plateau. Tel. 57.07.49. Mastercard, Visa. Open for lunch and dinner and all day on weekends.*

Jeannine will prepare you a tasty meal of Vietnamese specialties and or have her French chef cook you a gastronomic meal. Jeannine's English is almost non-existent, but you will certainly enjoy the Vietnamese crêpes, spring rolls, Tonkinese soup or stuffed chicken wings in a spicy sauce that she cooks for you. Jeannine also makes her own liqueur and will serve you a shot on request, but don't bother asking what's in the bottle because it's an old Vietnamese secret, and she's not about to explain why there's a serpent coiled around the bottom of the jug.

Inexpensive
CHEZ MYRIAM, *PK 60, Taravao. Tel. 57.71.01. American Express, Mastercard, Visa. Open Monday-Saturday 7am-10pm.*

This friendly air-conditioned restaurant and open terrace snack bar is on the mountain side at the crossroads of Tahiti-Nui and Tahiti-Iti. Myriam is a Chinese-Tahitian lady who speaks English and likes to meet people, and she serves traditional French cuisine and quality Chinese food.

SNACK JARDIN BOTANIQUE, *PK 51.5, Papeari. Tel. 57.17.59. No credit cards. Open daily for breakfast and lunch.*

After you've visited the Paul Gauguin Museum and strolled through the Harrison Smith Botanical gardens, you'll be able to quench your thirst or enjoy a full meal at the snack bar beside the parking lot. You can sit beside the lagoon or dine indoors, with a choice of hamburgers, salads, excellent *poisson cru* or daily specials of fish, chicken or steak. Soft drinks, milkshakes and beer are also available.

SEEING THE SIGHTS
Papeete Highlights
It's fun to walk around Papeete if you do it in the cool of the morning. Everyone gets going early around here, so you won't have any problems with closed shops if you begin your stroll around 7:30am. Your first stop should be at the **Tahiti Manava Visitor's Bureau** on the waterfront side of Boulevard Pomare, at the corner of rue Paul Gauguin. This building is also called Fare Manihini, which is the Tahitian word for "Visitor's

House." The pretty and helpful hostesses speak good English and will give you a map of the city and answer any questions you may have. You can also follow the map shown here, taken from the *Tahiti Beach Press*.

Just outside the Visitor's Bureau on the right is the **Captain Tamarii a Teai Square**, named in honor of a former Tahitian merchant marine officer. This is an attractive place with benches and shade trees, where you can relax and enjoy watching the sailboats and bonito boats after your stroll. Have a look at the informational panels, which include a list of handy phone numbers and maps, plus information on the birds and fish that are found around Tahiti.

All set to go? Walk along the recently renovated **yacht quay** and check out the sailboats from many countries around the world whose owners are living their dreams of cruising the South Pacific. You'll also see the maxi-catamarans and dive boats that are loading passengers for a day sail to Tetiaroa, Marlon Brando's atoll. Across the Papeete harbor you'll see container ships and inter-island cargo vessels docked at **Motu Uta**, and chances are you'll also see one or more of the fast catamarans and ferries that connect Papeete with Moorea. This is the busiest of all the French-owned harbors in the world, due to the passenger traffic between Tahiti and Moorea. When you reach a parking lot you'll see the **Charles de Gaulle Monument**. This is a tribute to the Polynesian soldiers who were part of the Pacific Battalion, and fought with General de Gaulle's Free French forces during World War II. There are benches here for resting.

Continue on along the waterfront to **Hokule'a Beach**, where you'll see a monument in the form of twin canoe hulls imbedded in stone. This is in honor of the *Hokule'a*, a replica of an ancient Polynesian voyaging canoe, which was built in Hawaii and sponsored by the Hawaiian Voyaging Society to retrace the sailing routes of the Polynesian pioneers who settled the tiny specks of land that make up the Polynesian triangle. The *Hokule'a* made its first voyage to Tahiti in 1976, navigating by the winds, stars and sea currents, and arrived in Tahiti to an overwhelming welcome by thousands of Tahitians. The beach here is polluted and swimming is not allowed. You'll see numbers of outrigger canoes on supports and upside down on the grass in this area. You'll also see some of Tahiti's canoe teams practicing for the next big race, which is a national passion.

Your destination on this side of the street is the new site for the **Heiva Festival** activities, that is currently under construction. The work is supposed to be finished in time for the Tahiti Festival in July 1998, and the song and dance competitions will be held here if it gets done in time. The **Office Territoriale d'Action Culturelle, (OTAC),** is Tahiti's cultural center, library and theater/concert hall. This is also being renovated. Here you'll find a snack bar and public toilets. (Bring your own paper wherever you go in these islands). The **Olympic swimming pool** is just beyond OTAC.

Now you'll head back toward the center of town. First, you have to get across the street, which can be quite tricky and even dangerous in Papeete, even though there are pedestrian zones and traffic lights. Once you've negotiated crossing the four lanes of Boulevard Pomare, you'll see the **Clinique Paofai**, then the **Protestant Temple**, which is part of the Evangelical Society of French Polynesia. The missionaries from the London Missionary Society brought the Gospel to Tahiti in 1797 and the Protestant religion is predominant in the Society Islands today.

The **Tahiti Pearl Museum** is just past the church, where you'll see some exquisite black pearl jewelry in the window display cases. They'll show you a video film of how the pearl is grown, if you want to take the time now. Otherwise, continue on down Boulevard Pomare to Avenue Bruat and turn right at the traffic light. (This museum will close at the end of 1998 and will move to the Vaima Center). Walk a block and cross the street with the green light on rue du Commandant Destremeau, which changes to rue du General de Gaulle at this corner. Walk a block or two up Avenue Bruat and see the government buildings. Here you'll find the French court or tribunal, the Police station, the *gendarmerie*, and the new offices of the President of the French Polynesian Territorial Government and the building for the Territorial Council of Ministers. Go back to rue du General de Gaulle and continue back toward the center of town, passing more government buildings.

On your right is **Place Tarahoi**, where Queen Pomare IV lived in an elaborate mansion before the French took control in 1842, and used Tarahoi as their headquarters. The French High Commissioner has his office and home in the building on the right, and the **Territorial Assembly** meets in the modern building to the left. In the Assembly Hall there are frequent exhibits of handcrafts made by artisans from the various island groups of French Polynesia. In front of the building is a monument to **Pouvanaa a Oopa** (1895-1977), a man from the island of Huahine who was a decorated hero fighting for France during World War I. He became an even bigger hero to the Tahitian people when he was sentenced to prison in France while seeking independence for his own country. After spending 15 years behind bars during the 1960s and 1970s Pouvanaa returned to Tahiti, but was sent back to France again, this time as Tahiti's representative in the French Senate.

Cross rue du General de Gaulle again in the crosswalk between Place Tarahoi and the rear of the **Papeete Post Office**. Double back toward the West for a few yards until you see the green oasis of **Bougainville Park** on your right, adjacent to the post office. A gurgling stream meanders through the tree-shaded gardens. This was Queen Pomare's favorite bathing pool when she lived at Place Tarahoi, and it was from this little river that Papeete received its name: *Pape* (pah-pey) means water in the Tahitian language; and *ete* (eh-tey) means basket; therefore, Papeete means water basket. Before the houses were equipped with water pipes, the people used to come to this spring, with their gourds wrapped in woven leaves, and take the *pape* home in their *ete*.

If you need a rest **Le Parc Bougainville** is an outdoor restaurant that provides a good place to take a break. You can get bottled waters, freshly squeezed fruit juices and a cold beer here. You can also get a key to the toilets from the waiter.

Louis Antoine de Bougainville never laid eyes on this site, because he spent all of his brief visit to Tahiti on the east coast of Hitiaa. However, he was the first French discoverer, so the park bears his name. His statue stands between the **two cannons** that are adjacent to the sidewalk on the Boulevard Pomare side of the park. The one nearest the post office was taken from the *Seeadler*, a World War I German raider that belonged to the luckless Count Felix von Luckner. His ship ran aground on Mopelia atoll, in the Leeward Society Islands, in 1917, after having captured 14 British, French and American ships in the South Pacific. The other gun comes from the *Zélée*, a small French navy vessel that was sunk in Papeete harbor in 1914 when the German raiders *Scharnhorst* and *Gneisenau* bombarded Papeete.

After you've walked around the cannons continue on toward the center of Papeete on Boulevard Pomare. Turn right on rue Jeanne d'Arc beside the **Vaima Center** and you'll see the **Cathédrale de l'Immaculée Conception**, which is usually called the **Cathedral of Notre Dame**. This cathedral was built in 1875 and has been restored twice since. If the door is unlocked go inside, where it is quiet and cool, and look at the paintings of the Crucifixion.

Cross over to the left side of the street at the Pharmacie de la Cathedrale, which is on the corner opposite Place Notre Dame. Walk past Tahiti Voyages travel agency and Tahiti Music and turn left at the end of the block. The sidewalk here is usually quite crowded with Tahitians who are shopping or hanging out, talking with friends. Walk past the police station and you'll see the public market, the **Marché Municipale**, which is the heart and bread basket of Papeete. The Tahitian "mamas" and even young men sell orchids, anthuriums, ginger flowers, roses, and other flowers of every imaginable hue. Past the flower vendors inside *le Marché* you'll see traditional Tahitian fruits and tubers on the left of the aisle and vegetables sold by the Chinese are on the right.

The fish and meat markets are off to the right and upstairs you'll find all kinds of locally made products, including some nice *tifaifai* bed covers or wall hangings and lots of seashells. Outside *le Marché* are hundreds of colorful *pareos*. The cotton ones were made in Tahiti and the uni-colored ones with fringe are imported.

When you leave *le Marché*, go out the door closest to the counters selling woven hats, bags and grass skirts. Walk straight ahead on rue Colette for one block until you come to rue Paul Gauguin. Turn right at the corner and you'll see the **Mairie of Papeete** on the left. This impressive building is the town hall, called *Hôtel de Ville* in French and *Fare Oire* in Tahitian. This building is a replica of Queen Pomare's royal palace that once stood at Place Tarahoi. The elaborate new building with crystal chandeliers and pink marble imported from Italy, was inaugurated in 1990. Former French President **François Mitterand** was the guest of honor for the dedication ceremonies. Walk up the steps into the building and take the elevator to the third floor. There are frequent art exhibits on display in the room to the left as you get off the elevator. Don't hesitate to walk around the building and admire the decor, and be sure to see the stone carvings in the gardens all around the outside of the building. They were made by sculptors living in Tahiti, the Marquesas and Easter Island.

If this two hour walk is too long for you, it can be shortened by crossing Boulevard Pomare at Avenue Bruat, after you have visited the waterfront and the Charles de Gaulle Monument. You can head inland on Avenue Bruat to see the government buildings and continue the above itinerary from there. You will eliminate the extra walk to the Cultural Center and Protestant Temple.

The **Papeete Harbor Boat Discovery**, *Tel. 43.66.05*, is a guided boat tour of the Papeete port and the Punaauia lagoon for a maximum of six passengers. Look for the boat *Poti Tere I*, at the Boulevard Pomare yacht quay on the Papeete waterfront.

Around the Island

Most tour drivers follow the northeast coast through Papeete's neighboring *communes* of Pirae, Arue and Mahina. The first stop is at the **Tahara'a Lookout Point** *at PK (poste kilometre) 8.1 in Arue*. When **Captain James Cook** sailed the *Endeavour* into Tahiti's Matavai Bay in 1769, he sighted a single tree (*Erythrina indica*) with bright red-orange flowers growing on the promontory above the bay. He used the tree as a navigational landmark and named this reference point "One Tree Hill." Although the gnarled old tree has disappeared, this lookout provides a spectacular panoramic view of the island of Moorea, the Sea of Moons, the coral reef and lagoon, and Tahiti's majestic fern-softened mountains.

The next stop will be at **Point Venus** *at PK 10 in Mahina*. This historic site beside Matavai Bay is where English **Captain Samuel Wallis** of the *H.M.S. Dolphin* came ashore in 1767, to become the first European to discover Tahiti. When Captain Cook led an expedition of scientists to

Tahiti to observe the transit of the planet Venus across the sun on June 3, 1769, he named the site Point Venus. **Captain William Bligh** and the *Bounty* crew came here in 1788 to collect breadfruit plants, and representatives of the **London Missionary Society** waded ashore in 1797, in search of souls to save.

In addition to the monuments in honor of Captain Cook and the missionaries, you'll see a lighthouse, snack bar, arts and crafts stands, toilet facilities, tropical gardens and a black sand beach, usually decorated with topless sunbathers, mostly French women. Raise your gaze from the bare twin peaks on the beach and look up at the double summit of Tahiti's highest mountain, Mt. Orohena, reaching 2,241 meters (7,353 feet) high into a crown of clouds. Point Venus is a lovely spot to photograph the bathing beauties as well as the tropical sunset, with a magnificent view of the nearby island of Moorea.

Continuing along the east coast you'll see the surfers riding the waves offshore Papenoo, the **Blow Hole of Arahoho** and the **Three Cascades of Fa'arumai** *in Tiarei at PK 22.* The Vaimahuta waterfall is easily reached in five minutes by walking across the bridge over the Vaipuu river and following a well defined path under a cool canopy of wild chestnut (*mape*) trees and *Barringtonia asiatica (hutu)* trees. Countless waterfalls cascade in misty plumes and broken curtains down the mountainside to tumble into a crisp, refreshing pool. This is a good swimming hole, but don't forget your mosquito repellent.

Back on the circle island road you will pass country villages, modern concrete homes and modest little *fare* huts brightly painted in yellow, pink and blue. Flowers and hedges of every shape and hue border the road and breadfruit, mangoes, papaya and banana trees fill the luxuriant gardens. Birdhouse-shaped boxes stand by the road in front of each home, ready to receive the daily delivery of fresh French *baguettes* that are baked by the Chinese and eaten by the Tahitians as their staple food.

At PK 37.6 in Hitiaa your guide may point out a plaque beside the bridge. The French explorer, **Louis Antoine de Bougainville**, made a deed of annexation in April, 1768, when his ships *Boudeuse* and *Etoile* dropped anchor just inside two islets offshore the village. Bougainville proclaimed French sovereignty over the island, which he named New Cytherea. He placed the deed in a bottle and buried it in the ground between the river and the beach. Bougainville's ships lost six anchors during his 10-day visit.

At PK 60 you'll be in the village of **Taravao**, the isthmus that connects Tahiti Nui with Tahiti Iti, the Taiarapu peninsula. If you're saving your discovery of Tahiti Iti for another delightful day, then continue on to **Papeari**, where you'll find the **Harrison W. Smith Botanical Gardens** *at PK 51.2, adjacent to the* **Paul Gauguin Museum**. Protect yourself from mosquitoes and stroll through the 137 hectares (340 acres) of tropical gardens, streams and water lily ponds. You will see hundreds of trees, shrubs, plants and flowers gathered from tropical regions throughout the world by Smith, who was an American physics teacher who escaped to the South Seas in 1919 and created his own Garden of Eden in Tahiti.

The most impressive part of this park is a natural forest of Tahitian *mape* trees, with their convoluted roots above the ground. This grove provides a cool and pleasant walk, with a small stream meandering through the shaded garden. A main attraction in the gardens are two huge land turtles, which were brought to Tahiti in the 1930's from the Galapagos Islands. These pets placidly pose for photographs and will stop eating to raise their long wrinkled necks and stare at the cameras. Beyond the snack bar is **Motu Ovini**, where Smith's house is still standing, just a few feet from the lagoon.

This site offers excellent swimming in an outstanding natural setting, with underground springs blending with the salt water of the lagoon, providing a buoyancy that will keep you floating for hours. You'll find fresh water showers, toilets and changing rooms on the premises. An entrance fee of 400 CFP ($4) for people over 12 years entitles you to visit the botanical gardens, picnic on the *motu* or swim all day in the most refreshing water in the world. Open daily 9am to 5pm.

Sharing the same parking lot with the Botanical Gardens is the **Paul Gauguin Museum**, which is open daily 9am to 5pm. This is a memorial to the late French artist, with a few original works located in the Salle Henri Bing. Reproductions of Gauguin's paintings and carvings are exhibited in three buildings beside the sea. In the second building you can see where the originals of the works of art are located today. Three ancient stone *tiki* from the island of Raivavae stand in the gardens surrounding the museum. Admission is 600 CFP ($6) for adults and 300 CFP ($3) for people between 12 and 18 years old.

Most tour buses stop for lunch in the vicinity of Taravao or Papeari, where you have a good selection of restaurants and snack bars. The most popular luncheon choice is the **Gauguin Museum Restaurant** *at PK 50.5 in Papeari*. This very spacious restaurant and bar is built over the lagoon, just 400 yards west of the Paul Gauguin Museum and Harrison Smith Botanical gardens. (See description in Tahiti-Where to Dine section).

The latter half of your tour will take you to the **Vaipahi Gardens and Cascade**, *at PK 49 in Mataiea*. Take a pleasant stroll through these public gardens and discover a sparkling waterfall at the end of a short path. Huge tree ferns and giant leaves of elephant ear plants provide a natural setting for the cascade, which is a popular photographic choice for travel brochures on Tahiti. The gardens are filled with luxuriant vegetation, including *rambutan* fruit, fragrant *pua* flowers, ground orchids and the exotic jade vine. Crotons and hibiscus add to the flamboyance in these gardens of dancing color.

LAND OF THE DOUBLE RAINBOW

When you stop at the Vaipahi Gardens and Cascade in Mataiea, look out over the lagoon and perhaps you'll catch sight of a double rainbow, arching over the peninsula of Tahiti Iti. This is where I fell in love with Tahiti during my first visit to the island in 1968. There's magic in the air here, a haunting beauty that touches the soul.

If you're making the island tour on your own, then stop at the **Vaima River**, *PK 48.5 in Mataiea*, very close to the public gardens. This is one of Tahiti's favorite watering holes, complete with underground springs that bubble up like a cold Jacuzzi. Leave your car in the parking lot and wade waist-deep through the clear, refreshing river. Wild hibiscus (*purau*) trees lend their shade and purple water hyacinths add their color to the scene. This is a welcome treat on a hot sunny day.

On the southwest coast you'll pass the **Atimaono Golf Course** *at PK 40.2*, where international championship tournaments are played each July. A little further on you'll see the black sand beach of **Papara**, where world-class surfers compete. *At PK 36 in the heart of Papara*, you will find the **Seashell Museum**, with its display of more than 5,000 different types of shells, half of which are specific to the Polynesian Islands. Fish, corals and other treasures from the Polynesian lagoons are displayed in an aquarium. The **Musée du Coquillage** is open daily 8am to 5pm, with an admission of 300 CFP ($3) for adults and 200 CFP ($2) for children. The **Tiare Rau Artisan Center**, *adjacent to the Seashell Museum*, has an interesting exhibit of local arts and crafts.

Several of the tour guides will stop at the **Ava Tea Distillery and Tasting Room** *at PK 26.8 in Paea*. You may be interested in learning how the liqueurs and *eau de vie* are made from coconuts, ginger root, *pamplemousse* grapefruit, mangoes and other tropical fruits. You are welcome to taste all the flavors, and if you imbibe too much and drowse on the bus, then you can take the **West Coast Tour** another day to see what you missed.

The side road leading into the valley to the **Marae of Arahurahu** *is at PK 22.5 in Paea*. Follow the road to the parking area and walk a few steps to the two restored open-air stone temples, which were used in pre-Christian days for religious ceremonies, meetings, cultural rites, sacrifices and burials. Should you coincide your visit with the **Heiva I Tahiti Festival** in July, then you can attend a colorful reenactment ceremony. The themes include the crowning of a king and royal weddings, with a cast of dozens of beautifully costumed Tahitian dancers, musicians, warriors and *tahua* priests. An entrance fee of around 1.800 CFP ($18) for adults and 800 CFP ($8) for children applies only during these special programs.

The **Fern Grottos of Mara'a** *at PK 28.5 in Paea*, are joined by a flower-bordered walkway. The **Paroa cave** is the largest of three natural grottos, where overhead springs drip through wild ferns and moss, forming a pool where children play. **Queen Pomare** used to bathe here and **Paul Gauguin** wrote of swimming inside this cave. Drops of water from the overhead ferns reflect rainbow hues in the rays of the afternoon sun.

When touring by car you'll enjoy stopping at **Mahana Park**, *at PK 18.2, at the border of Paea and Punaauia*. This public park has a white sand beach facing the island of Moorea, with a tranquil lagoon for swimming. There are public toilets and showers and you can rent a pedal-boat, surf bike or kayak. You can picnic at one of the tables or dine in **La Mangue Verte** restaurant on the premises.

On the west coast of the island you'll see a sign *on the sea side at PK 15.7 in Punaauia,* directing you to the **Museum of Tahiti and Her Islands (Musée des Iles)** *at Fisherman's Point (Pointe des Pêcheurs).* The modern museum presents the natural environment, Polynesian migrations, history, culture and ethnology in four exhibit halls. On display are stone and wooden tiki, hand-hewn canoes, intricate sculptures, tapa bark, seashells and other traditional Polynesian objects and tools. In the reception area you may locate the book you've been wanting to read about Tahiti's colorful past, but be prepared to pay breathtaking prices for these old treasures. The admission price is 500 CFP ($5) for adults, no charge for students, and the museum is open from 9:30am to 5:30pm, except Mondays, when they are closed all day. Walk out to the beach and watch the surfers before you continue your tour. Breathe deeply and smell the fresh salty air.

In the communes of Paea and Punaauia, you will catch glimpses of Tahiti's lovely beachfront properties, often containing old Polynesian style homes built of pandanus and woven bamboo. The millionaires' modern villas are up in the mountains, overlooking the island of Moorea. Here suburbia Tahiti blends the past with today. The thatched roof *fare*, colonial mansions and concrete homes are neighbors with schools, shopping malls, used car lots and video shops. Supermarkets sell foods for all tastes and boutiques sell surfboards and beachwear from California and Hawaii.

From 1897 to 1901, the artist **Paul Gauguin** lived in a comfortable villa at *PK 12.6 in Punaauia*, before he left for the Marquesas Islands in search of a wild and savage beauty. Your guide will point out the **2+2=4 school** that was built adjacent to Gauguin's former property.

One last stop before heading back to your hotel is sometimes made at the **Lagoonarium**, *at PK 11.4 in Punaauia*. Four big fish parks are built into the lagoon, filled with thousands of fish, sharks, moray eels and turtles. The walls of the Lagoonarium are beautifully covered in coral, shells and sea urchin spines, and glass cases contain magnificent collections of seashells, mother-of-pearl shells, black pearls and other treasures from the sea. If you arrive at noon you can watch the daily shark feeding show, and if you dine in the **Captain Bligh Restaurant**, *adjacent to the Lagoonarium*, you will have free entry. Otherwise the admission fee is 500 CFP ($5) for adults and 300 CFP ($3) for children 3 to 12 years old. The Lagoonarium is open daily 9am to 5pm.

Island Guided Tours

You can book your sightseeing tours through the travel desk at your hotel in Tahiti and see the island with a knowledgeable guide aboard an air-conditioned bus, mini-van, Mercedes luxury car or stretch limousine.

A **Half Day Circle Island Tour** costs 3.500-4.000 CFP ($35-$40), with daily tours available between 8:30am and 12:30pm, or between 1:30 and 5:30pm. Unless specified, these tour rates do not include lunch or entrance fees to the museums and other sights. A **Full Day Circle Island Tour** starts at 4.000 CFP ($40) with a pickup at your hotel at 9:30am, returning around 3:30pm, The **West Coast Tour**, which is sometimes sold as the **Gauguin Tour**, is a four-hour excursion in the morning or afternoon, and sells for 3.500 CFP ($35).

The **East Coast Tour**, also known as the **Explorer Tour**, is a half-day excursion to discover Tahiti's less inhabited side of the island. This tour is 3.000 CFP ($30). A **Polynesian Orientation Tour** is a half day tour combining a visit to the City of Papeete with a drive through Tahiti's West Coast to the Museum of Tahiti and Her Islands. The cost of 3.500 CFP ($35) also includes admission to the museum.

A knowledgeable guide who speaks good English is essential for your introduction to the sights and stories of Tahiti. For 17 years I worked as a tour guide in Tahiti, in addition to my journalistic endeavors, and I will recommend the best guides so that you'll be able to make an agreeable choice when you book a tour.

Bernie's Circle Island Tour, sold by Paradise Tours, *Tel. 44.40.40 or 42.49.36* on weekends, will surely please even the most reticent of visitors. Bernie Kamalamalama, who is part Hawaiian, advertises that his tour is worth his weight in pleasant memories for you, and that's really saying a lot. Bernie would make his Polynesian ancestors very proud, as they believed that bigger is better. In addition to being one of the sweetest and most helpful people you'll meet anywhere, Bernie is also a very good guide.

Marama Tours Tahiti, *Tel. 83.96.50 or 83.95.81*, has a number of guides who do a good job of telling Tahiti's tales. Teva Cowan was taught by his dad Emile, who taught me to be a guide way back when. Emile and his wife Mata, both Polynesians, are owners of the company. Angèle Teriitanoa is also an entertaining guide who works for them.

William Leeteg of **Adventure Eagle Tours**, *Tel. 77.20.03*, is the son of Edgar Leeteg, the famous black velvet painter who lived in Moorea until he died following a motorcycle accident in 1953. William has a great sense of humor and will maybe even sing for you as he drives you in his air-conditioned 9-seat minivan to visit the island.

You can also buy a copy of Bengt Danielsson's *Circle Island Tour Guide* and rent a car for a do-it-yourself excursion. If you have the time and the inclination, I suggest that you take a guided tour around Tahiti Nui (big Tahiti) and on another day rent a car and drive around the island, stopping where you choose and exploring both coasts of Tahiti Iti (little Tahiti), as well as driving up the **Plateau of Taravao**, where you will see horses and cattle grazing in rolling green pastures bordered by eucalyptus trees and orange groves.

Mountain & Waterfall Tours

Excursions by four-wheel drive vehicle (4x4) are designed for you to get off the beaten track and up into the mountains and valleys of Tahiti. The "Queen of the Pacific" will disclose a few of her mysteries and magic as you are driven in air-conditioned or open-air Land Rovers or Jeeps through the tropical forests of giant ferns, centuries old Tahitian *mape* chestnut trees, wild mango and guava trees, and more waterfalls than you can count.

Patrice Bordes and his team of drivers at **Tahiti Safari Expedition**, *Tel. 42.14.15*, are recommended by *Géo Magazine* for their efficiency and expertise. Patrice was the pioneer of the inner island tours in 1990, and he advertises that "your parents and grandparents can accompany you without tiring." These excursions, however, are not for the frail, as the unpaved roads can be quite bumpy, and most uncomfortable if you are sitting on the bench in the back. These lush green valleys get a lot of rain and you will also get wet unless the side flaps are closed, creating a hothouse effect for the passengers, who can no longer see the misty beauty of the rainforest.

A **Half Day Mountain Tour** can be made in the morning or afternoon for 3.500 CFP ($35). This excursion takes you to a height of 5,000 feet up **Mount Marau** via the **Tamanu Canyon**. A **Half Day East Coast Tour** also includes the **Blowhole of Arahoho** and the **Fa'arumai Cascades of Tiarei**, and costs 5.000 CFP ($50).

A **Full Day Across the Island Tour** for 7.000 CFP ($70), lunch not included, will take you from the **Papenoo Valley** in the north to **Mataiea** in the south, crossing the main crater of Tahiti. You will see restored stone temples called *marae* and ancient **petroglyphs** carved in black basaltic boulders. You can visit a hydroelectric dam, swim in natural pools, shower under the sparkling waterfalls, traverse Tahiti's unique tunnel and photograph **Lake Vaihiria**. At an altitude of 465 meters (1,550 feet) above the sea, this is Tahiti's only fresh water lake. You can pack your lunch or dine on a fixed menu of French cuisine at the **Relais de la Marotto**, a hotel and restaurant in the mountains that was originally built to house the workers who built the dams.

It is not advisable to attempt to make this tour in a rental car, nor in a lightweight 4x4 vehicle. It can even be dangerous as the sudden rains very quickly swell the rivers into raging torrents. On many occasions tourists have been trapped overnight in these mountains because they couldn't get across the rivers. It rained constantly on the day I made this trip and three huge bulldozers lined up in a row to prevent our Land Rover from floating downstream with the force of the current. We did lose contact with the ground, but only momentarily. We forded the rivers four times, which I found exciting. But when I told this to one of the former Safari drivers he said that they used to cross the rivers at least 20 times. Still, this is an interesting tour and the scenery is outstanding.

The **Safari Maroto Tour** is also operated by Teva Wilkes of **Nave Nave Adventure Tours**, *Tel. 43.43.30*; Jean Pierre Cogulet of **Tahiti Safari Excursions**, *Tel. 58.26.12*; **Kiwi Safari Tours**, *Tel. 41.31.82*; **Marama Tours Tahiti**, *Tel. 83.96.50 or 83.95.81*; **Paradise Tours**, *Tel. 44.40.40 or 42.49.36 on weekends*; and **Tahiti Nui Travel**, *Tel. 54.02.00*.

Helicopter Tours

A helicopter tour offers the best of Tahiti's scenic sights, giving you a close-up look at the tallest mountains, dipping into the lush green valleys to hover like a hummingbird in front of a sparkling waterfall, and soaring over the lagoon, reef and sea. Go early in the morning before the clouds veil the view.

Heli-Pacific, *Tel. 85.68.00*, has two AS 350 "Ecureuil" helicopters, each with 5-6 seats, ready to let you soar above Tahiti in sound-proof comfort. A 20-minute flightseeing tour called "Discover Tahiti" costs 15.000 CFP ($150). The "Tahiti Experience" is a 35-minute tour for 25.000 CFP ($250) that takes you over the Papenoo Valley with its magnificent waterfalls, to the crater of a dormant volcano, then on to view Lake Vaihiria from the heights, the Golf Course of Atimaono, Punaruu Valley and the Diademe, Tahiti's mountain that is shaped like a crown. A 45-minute "Tahiti Island Tour" for 32.000 CFP ($320) will let you soar over Papeete, Point Venus and Matavai Bay, the Papenoo Valley, the highest peaks of the eastern coast and the beautiful Tahiti Iti peninsula. Transfers are made from the Tahiti-Faaa International Airport to the Golf Course of Atimaono or to the Maroto Valley, where you can dine at the Relais de la Maroto.

Heli-Inter Polynesie, *Tel. 81.99.00*, has a 6-seat "Ecureuil" helicopter available for tourist flights, transfers to Moorea and specific charters on request.

NIGHTLIFE & ENTERTAINMENT

Reputed as the South Seas heart of hedonism, Papeete by night is prowl-about time. The shops are closed and nightclubs swing. Sounds of disco, zouk, biguine, reggae, calypso, rock, waltz and jazz compete with the pulsating rhythm of the *tamure*, Tahiti's tantalizing national dance.

Some of Tahiti's larger hotels feature folkloric dance shows and Tahitian orchestras for dancing, and there are frequent all-night balls presented by the various sports clubs and friendship organizations on the island. These events always include live music and entertainment and the Tahitians never tire of seeing their professional or amateur dance groups performing the *ori Tahiti*. After the show the beautifully dressed Tahitians, Chinese and French diners fill the dance floor, where they glide so gracefully to the upbeat tunes of the fox trot and Tahitian waltz. When the tempo suddenly erupts into the sensual *toere* drum beat of the hip-swiveling, rubber-legging *tamure*, the floor is suddenly packed with Tahitians, who involve their whole being—body, mind and soul—into vigorously performing their national dance.

Most of the bars, nightclubs and casinos are located in the heart of Papeete, along the waterfront street of Boulevard Pomare and rarely no more than one block inland. The nightclubs and casinos require proper attire. This means that the women cannot wear shorts and the men should wear a shirt, rather than a tank top, plus shoes, rather than rubber thongs or going barefoot. The nightclubs usually charge an entry fee for men, which includes one drink, and unescorted ladies get in free, sometimes with the bonus of a complimentary first drink.

Local Style

LA CAVE *inside the Hotel Royal Papeete on Boulevard Pomare, Tel. 42.01.29,* is a large nightclub where you will find the flavor of Tahiti's good old days. A live band plays Tahitian waltzes and the hip-swiveling, rubber-legging *tamure* music every Friday and Saturday night from 9:30pm to 3am. This is the most popular nightclub in Tahiti for people of all ages.

LE KIKIRIRI, *on rue Colette between Avenue Prince Hinoi and the Mairie of Papeete (town hall), Tel. 43.58.64,* is a true Tahitian bar. This is one of the liveliest places in town when the musicians tune up for an evening of *kaina* music, playing the songs of the islands on their guitars and ukuleles, strumming the chords of a gut bucket bass or rattling two spoons together in a beer bottle. The revelers enthusiastically sing and dance as they get happy on Hinano beer or Johnny Walker whisky. Open Thursday, Saturday and Sunday from 4pm to 3am and all day Friday. The Tahitian orchestra plays from 9pm to 3am and the place rocks.

LE MAYANA dance club, the ex-Rolls Club, *is in the Vaima Center on rue General de Gaulle, above the movie theater. Tel. 43.41.42.* This air-conditioned disco offers local atmosphere and music, which means anything from the Tahitian two-step to the latest dances to come out of Paris and Martinique. Open on Friday from 3:30pm to 3am, on Saturday from 9pm to 3am and on Sunday evenings from 8pm to midnight.

LE TAMURÉ HUT *is part of the Hotel Royal Papeete, with a separate entrance on Boulevard Pomare. Tel. 42.01.29.* A Tahitian orchestra plays music for dancing Tahitian style every Friday and Saturday night from 9pm to 4am. The bar is open on Fridays starting at 2pm, with a musical trio playing between 4pm and 8pm and Happy Hour cocktails between 5-6pm.

Discos & Jazz

LE 106 is one of the oldest private dance clubs in Papeete, *located at the other end of town on Boulevard Pomare, adjacent to the Moana Iti restaurant. Tel. 42.72.92.* There's no entry charge, but you must take care of your "look" to be permitted. Simply ring the bell at the front door downstairs and then join Papeete's "in crowd" and dance to taped music for all tastes. Open nightly.

LE MANHATTAN DISCOTHÈQUE, the ex-Calypso, *is in the Hotel Kon Tiki on Boulevard Pomare*, and is open daily from 10pm to 3am., featuring "toere rock" by local musicians.

MORRISON'S CAFÉ, *is in the Vaima Center, with a private elevator located on rue General de Gaulle, adjacent to the Air New Zealand office. Tel. 42.78.61.* This is an indoor/outdoor restaurant and café built around an outdoor swimming pool. Sounds of sweet jazz sing out over the rooftops of Papeete, played by American musicians who are frequently imported to liven up the scene. This café is named after Jim Morrison (of The Doors), and the musical ambiance is a combination of American rock music, jazz and modern Tahitian rock bands.

LE PARADISE NIGHT *on Boulevard Pomare, across from the French naval station*, is the most popular spot for a European ambiance, but it can also resonate to an Afro-Caribbean rhythm. This is a complex of Le Night restaurant, Le Paradise nightclub and Le Chaplin's brasserie, cocktail and video lounge. This complex is open daily from 10am to 3am. Each Wednesday night is *karaoke* night, starting at 8pm, and Thursdays are Polynesian nights, with a candlelight dinner and music for dancing. *Reserve at Tel. 42.73.05* for the evening hours. No entry fee required.

LE PIANO BAR, *on rue des Ecoles*, is very crowded and smoke-filled, but if you want to see a female impersonator strip show Tahitian style, this is the place to go. The transvestite *mahu* dancers, Polynesia's "third sex," are friendly and may even ask you to dance in front of the mirrors with them, regardless of your sex. If you can stand the smoke, this can be a fun place.

LET THE MUSIC PLAY

The Tahitian custom of inviting someone to dance is rather subtle. You are sitting at the bar or a table, alone or with friends. A young man begins to stare at you, trying to get your attention, or perhaps returning your own flirtatious glance. When he catches your eye, he just lifts his eyebrows and nods his head toward the dance floor. You can ignore him, shake your head negatively, or raise your own eyebrows in a positive reply and meet him on the dance floor. Tahitian men assume that if a woman isn't dancing with anyone, she is available for him as a dance partner, even if she is sitting with a man.

Dancing with a Tahitian **tane** *involves little or no conversation. Normally there is no desire for introductions before or during the first few dances. People are there to dance, and grab a feel, perhaps, but not to talk. Each trip to the floor lasts for the duration of two songs, played to similar tempos. This gives you a good opportunity to get to know one another, with little or no conversation transpiring between you. But there is definitely a communication going on.*

If you continue to dance with the same man, for the first hour or so of the evening he is very polite and dances beautifully, as he holds you at a respectful distance. He smells divine, wearing the best perfume of his sister, wife or live-in vahine, the mother of some of his children. After he has drunk a few bottles of Hinano beer he becomes more relaxed and informal. Also much more intimate. He squeezes you close and his hands become freer in their wanderings around your body. He might ask you to leave with him after the dance, as he nuzzles your neck and presses his body close to yours. The next hour after that is when you have to start holding him up, if you are still on the scene by that time.

Friendly Bars

The bar inside the **HOTEL ROYAL PAPEETE** is a friendly and comfortable meeting place for American expatriates, residents of the outer islands and older locals. Jackie, the bartender, has been serving drinks here for 20 years. The bar is air-conditioned and has a few stools and tables.

Tahiti's "hot spots" include several sidewalk bars, where you can people watch. **LE RETRO** *is in the Vaima Center on Boulevard Pomare,* and is a respectable place to have a drink, a cup of coffee or a meal. Down at the other end of Boulevard Pomare, on or near rue des Ecoles and Avenue Prince Hinoi, are a variety of bars, where you will see a continuous parade of young prostitutes, both male and female, as they make their nightly rounds looking for business. You'll also see the French legionnaires, French soldiers, and young French sailors off the ships, who are looking for some action.

Casinos

Should you feel in the mood to tempt Lady Luck, you'll find casinos in the hotels **Prince Hinoi**, **Royal Papeete** and **Kon Tiki Pacific**, *all on Boulevard Pomare.* There are many more casinos in or near town, but these are the easiest to locate. If you are staying in one of these hotels you can ask for a free admission card. Otherwise, you'll have to buy a membership card for 1.000 CFP ($10), which entitles you to free drinks and the game tables, where you have a choice of blackjack, roulette, mahjong and poker. There are no slot machines in Tahiti.

SPORTS & RECREATION

Biking

Rando Cycles *at PK 20,200, just before the Centre Auto in Paea, Tel. 41.22.08,* rents mountain bikes. Tahiti's inner valleys are relatively safe for bikers, but only the foolhardy would attempt to ride a bike on the circle island road. You can also take your all-terrain bike to the outer islands.

Bowling

The **Bowling Club of Tahiti** is located at *PK 5,6 in Arue, Tel. 42.93.26.* You can rent shoes and all necessary equipment and there is a restaurant and bar on the premises. The club is open Tuesday through Saturday from 5pm to 1am and on Sunday from 7 to 10pm, and is closed on Mondays.

Golf

If golf is your game you can tee off at the **Olivier Breaud International Golf Course of Atimaono**, *at PK 40,2 in Papara, Tel. 57.43.41 or*

57.40.52. Located between the mountains and the sea 25 miles from Papeete on Tahiti's southwest coast, you'll find an 18-hole course 6,774 yards, par 72 for men and par 73 for women. The greens are planted with hybrid Bermuda grass from Hawaii. Two artificial lakes and wide, hilly fairways surrounded by fruit trees add to the beauty and pleasure of this course, which attracts professional and amateur golfers from overseas, who compete in the annual Tahiti International Pro/Am Open, held each July. A modern Club House has locker rooms and showers for men and women, a bar and a restaurant serving French and local foods. There is a swimming pool, spa pool and a driving range, plus a pro shop for sales and rentals. The course is open Monday to Friday from 8m to 4pm and on weekends from 8am to 5pm. and the greens fee is 4.650 CFP ($46.50). Clubs rent for 2.200 CFP ($22), the golf cart is 600 CFP ($6), and an electric car is 3.800 CFP ($38).

Hui Popo Tours, *Tel. 57.40.32*, arranges round-trip mini-bus transfers for players or visitors, departing from the resort hotels. If you are staying in the Hotels Tahiti Beachcomber Parkroyal, Sofitel Maeva Beach or Meridien, the cost is 3.500 CFP ($35) per person and 6.000 CFP ($60) per couple. The transfer fee is more from the hotels in Papeete and the Hotel Royal Tahitien.

Hiking

Feel like taking a hike? Tahiti's mountains and valleys and rugged Te Pari coast offer an interesting choice of treks. Even though you may be tempted to set out on your own to discover the lava tubes, burial caves and hidden grottos, my advice is to go with a guide and the proper equipment. The weather can be variable in the heights, and sudden downpours can suddenly swell the rivers, making them impassable for several days.

Vincent Dubousquet of **Polynesian Adventure**, *Tel. 43.25.95*, is a professional guide who specializes in 14 different hikes on Tahiti and Moorea. Eric LeNoble of **Tahiti Evasion**, *Tel. 41.35.07*, knows all the best places on Tahiti and Moorea, for mountain and valley walks. Pierre Wrobel of **Te Fetia O Te Mau Mato**, *Tel. 43.04.64/81.09.19*, will help you discover the natural park of Te Faaiti in the Papenoo Valley or the Plateau of Taravao. Mata Rangimakea of **Presqu'ile Loisirs**, *Tel. 57.00.57*, will guide you on the easiest and the most difficult hikes on the Tahiti Iti peninsula, including Te Pari. Zena Angelin of **Le Circuit Vert**, *Tel. 57.22.67*, has specialized in trekking Te Pari coast for many years. Guillaume of **Tiare Mato**, *Tel. 43.92.76*, will take you to the Pass of the Diadème or on a 5-day walk on an atoll in the Tuamotu archipelago.

The **Tahiti Manava Visitors Bureau** on the Papeete waterfront has a list of the qualified tour guides on all the islands.

The **Fautaua Valley** is one of the easiest walks, which most people accomplish in four to seven hours. The waterfall here was the romantic setting included in *The Marriage of Loti*, a novel written by a French sailor named Louis Marie Julien Viaud, who came to Tahiti in the 1880s. A minimum of two people are required for this outing, which will cost 7.000 CFP ($70) per person, and 5.000 CFP ($50) if there are three or more people. The rates include road transfers and a snack.

You should be in good physical condition and not subject to vertigo to climb **Mount Aorai**, which at 2,066 meters (6,776 feet), is the second highest peak on Tahiti. This trek can be done in eight hours for some hikers and in two days for others. The cost, including transfers and snack, is 7.000 CFP ($70) per person, with a minimum of two.

Beyond the road's end on the peninsula of Tahiti Iti lies the **fenua 'aihere**, the magnificent bush land and the formidable sea cliffs known as **Te Pari**. Only the most physically fit bodies and adventurous souls attempt this challenging trek around the untamed coast. The monumental Te Pari cliffs, with their ravines strung in plumes of falling water, descend straight into the ocean. Slippery barriers of basaltic rock guard this isolated coast, and fuming rollers splash with unrestrained force against the solid wall.

During the day you will visit old *marae* temples, burial caves, grottos and rocks carved with petroglyphs. In the evening you can fish, catch lobsters on the reef and search for fresh shrimp in the rivers. Two-day hikes can start from the village of Teahupoo on the west coast or from Tautira on the east coast. A minimum of four people is required, for a cost of 11.000 CFP ($110) each, which includes road and boat transfers and meals.

Other hikes on Tahiti take you to the **Tipaerui Valley** behind Papeete, **Te Faaiti Valley** in Papenoo, the **Tamanu Plateau** in Punaauia, the **Tuauru Valley** in Mahina, to the **lava tubes** of Hitiaa, and the most challenging of all, to the beautiful crown mountain called **Le Diadème**.

Horseback Riding

Most of the horses in Tahiti are from the Marquesas Islands, descendants of Chilean stock. The equestrian clubs now have thoroughbreds from New Zealand as well. You can ride by the sea or in the mountains with a guide, who will take along a picnic lunch upon request. The **Club Equestre de Tahiti**, *at the Pirae Hippodrome race track, Tel. 42.70.41*, and **L'Eperon de Pirae**, *Tel. 42.79.87, in a nearby stable*, have both races of steeds for your riding pleasure.

Tropical Ranch *at Te Tiare Center in Punaauia, Tel. 45.34.34*, will guide you up the mountains overlooking Moorea. **Le Centaure Ranch** *at PK 53.1 in Papeari, Tel. 57.70.77*, offers an entirely different view of Tahiti, with trails winding through the valleys overlooking Tahiti's southern coast.

Squash

The **Hotel Matavai**, *Tel. 42.57.68*, has two lighted squash courts, used on a first-come, first-served basis.

Tennis

Tahiti's climate is ideal for playing tennis year-round, by scheduling a match in the early morning or at sunset time, to avoid the hottest hours of a tropical day. Tennis courts are located at the following hotels: **Tahiti Beachcomber Parkroyal, Sofitel Maeva Beach, Tahiti Country Club and Hotel Matavai**.

Sports clubs and private tennis clubs also have their own courts, where you can play for a nominal fee and meet some of the local resident players. These include the **Tennis Club of Fautaua**, *just to the west of downtown Papeete, Tel. 42.00.59*; **Fei Pi Tennis Club** at *PK 3.2 in Arue, Tel. 42.53.87*; and the **Excelsior Tennis Club** *in the Mission Quarter of Papeete, Tel. 43.91.46*.

Deep Sea Fishing

Zane Grey put Tahiti on the world map of outstanding deep-sea fishing spots in the 1930s, when the American novelist had his own fishing camp in Vairao on the Tahiti Iti peninsula. Game fishing has become a year-round sport in Tahiti, and your chances are very good of reeling in a big blue marlin, sailfish, swordfish, yellow fin tuna, mahi mahi, wahoo, ocean bonito or tiger shark. You may also catch jack crevally, blue crevally, rainbow runner, dog tooth tuna and barracuda just outside the reef.

You have a choice of several professional fishing boats throughout the islands, whose crew compete in local tournaments in preparation for the **Tahiti International Billfish Tournament**, which is held every two years.

Tahiti Sporting & Adventure, *Tel. 689/41.02.25/41.02.27; Fax 689/45.27.58*, is a government nonprofit company located at the Marina Taina in Punaauia. They will book one of 12 fishing boats represented by the organization, with a choice ranging from a 29-foot Blackfin to a 61-foot Davis, complete with air-conditioning. Half-day charters start at 40.000 CFP ($400) for a half-day excursion and 65.000 CFP ($650) for a full-day fishing trip.

American expatriate Captain Chris Lilley, who lives in Moorea, *Tel. 56.15.08; Fax 41.32.97*, has been fishing Tahitian waters for more than 15 years, and he can take you to the favorite hideouts of the really big ones. Even if the prize catches have gone visiting elsewhere that day, you will still

have a great time with Chris. Enthusiasm, dedication and angling exper-
tise are the keys to his successful charters. His 31-foot Bertram Sportfisher,
Tea Nui, is professionally equipped with all Penn International reels.
Chris charges 50.000 CFP ($500) for a half-day excursion, or 13.000 CFP
($130) per person on a share basis.

Nautical Centers & Clubs
   Tahiti Aquatique, *Tel. 41.08.54 (direct line)/42.80.42, ext. 0951, is
located beside the pier at the Hotel Sofitel Maeva Beach*, and is open daily
8:30am to 5pm. Owner Richard "Dick" Johnson, an American marine
biologist who made Tahiti his home 25 years ago, has a motto that "we
offer just about anything you might want to do on or below the sea." He
does offer more than 20 activities. You can sunbathe from a floating
pontoon, go snorkeling, scuba diving, water-skiing, rent a motor boat, go
deep sea fishing and sailing. You can rent a pedal boat, a kayak, a windsurf
board, Sunfish sailboat, underwater camera, video equipment and scuba
diving gear.
   Maeva is a royal Tahitian double canoe with a glass-bottom floor, that
is used for lagoon excursions. Rates are 2.000 CFP ($20) for a Snorkeling
Safari, Glass Bottom Boat ride, Sunset Cruise or a guided visit to the
Lagoonarium, one of the world's largest underwater observatories in a
natural setting. Here you will see the sharks and fish being fed at noon.
You also have the option of dining at the Captain Bligh overwater
restaurant for lunch or dinner. You'll surely want to join a Shark
Encounter excursion, donning mask and snorkel to watch the underwater
feeding as 10 or more black tip sharks come to eat the fish your guide
hands out. This outing is made in the late afternoon, around 4:30pm, lasts
for 1 1/2 hours and costs 2.000 CFP ($20). A 2-hour Dolphin Cruise is
made aboard the deluxe catamaran *Enjoy* and costs 5.000 CFP ($50). The
Maeva is also available for a 2-hour Sunset, Harbor and Cocktail Cruise
and dinners for 20 people.
   The **Tahiti Beachcomber Parkroyal Watersports Activities Center**,
Tel. 86.51.10, ext. 5168, is open daily from 8:30am to 5pm. Even if you are
not staying at the hotel, you can take part in the activities by making
reservations. A Fish Feeding, Snorkeling Safari starts at 10am, for 2.000
CFP ($20), the Moray Eels are fed at 11:30am (no charge), and the Glass
Bottom Boat excursion starts at 2pm, for 2.000 CFP ($20). You can rent
snorkeling equipment, get a boat ride to a private floating pontoon, go
fishing on the reef, hop aboard a boat for a lagoon cruise, water-ski, scuba
dive, paddle a kayak, rent a pedal boat, windsurf board or speed boat and
sign up for a Sunset Sailing Cruise.

Sailing Charters

Tahiti Yacht Charter, *B.P. 608, Papeete, Tahiti, Tel. 689/45.04.00; Fax 689/42.76.00; e-mail: tyc@mail.pf has an office at the yacht quay on the Papeete waterfront.*

Nicole Poureau will help you to charter a monohull or a catamaran, with or without skipper and hostess/cook. You have a choice of six Oceanis or Feeling boats ranging from 32 feet to 50 feet, or one of six catamarans, which may be a Tobago 35, Venezia 42, Kennex 445 or Bahia 46. Provisions can be added on request and the dinghy, windsurf and diving equipment are included. You can board the yacht in Papeete or the outer island of your choice, as conveyance service is available.

Charter rates between September and June start at 35.000 CFP ($350) per day or 245.000 CFP ($2,450) per week for an Oceanis 350, and go up to 82.000 CFP ($820) per day or 574.000 CFP ($5,740) per week for a Kennex 445. The rates are 3.000 CFP ($30) to 9.000 CFP ($90) more per day in July and August. The daily rate for a skipper-guide, which is mandatory for the First and Kennex yachts, is 12.000 CFP ($120) per day. You will have to pay 10.000 CFP ($100) per day for a hostess, who will also take care of the cooking and all galley duties. A spinnaker sail is 20.000 CFP ($200) extra per week. Should you request conveyance services, you will be charged 32.000-70.000 CFP ($320-$700), depending on the distance between islands. A deposit of 180.000 CFP ($1,800) is required before you board the yacht. Tahiti Yacht Charter also has a base on the island of Raiatea.

Day Sailing Excursions

You'll find day sailing easy to arrange once you're here, simply by booking with your hotel activities desk or walking along the quay at the Papeete waterfront, across from the post office, and talking with the captain of the boat you choose to fulfill your dream.

Aqua Polynésie, *Tel. 85.00.00,* is a 46-foot deep-sea catamaran that is based at *the yacht quay on Boulevard Pomare in Papeete.* Patrice Poiry operates half day cruises for 40.000 CFP ($400), full-day cruises for 100.000 CFP ($1,000) and sunset cruises for 25.000 CFP ($250). Sunset/dinner cruises are also available. The boat can be chartered for one or two week cruises in the Society Islands, the Tuamotus and Marquesas Islands.

Enjoy is a 12-meter (40-foot) Fontaine Pajot sailing catamaran based at the Tahiti Beachcomber Parkroyal, *Tel. 86.51.10.* This luxury yacht can be chartered one day in advance for your private excursion of 5 hours for 50.000 CFP ($500). Day sailing cruises to Moorea for a maximum of 10 passengers, leaving at 8:30am and returning at 5pm., costs 80.000 CFP ($800) per charter. You can also sail for an hour for 14.000 CFP ($140).

Jet France, *B.P. 1089, Papetoai, Moorea, Tel. 56.15.62*, is a 22.5 meter (75 foot) maxi sailing catamaran owned by Jean-Jacques Besson, that is based at the yacht quay in Papeete. Day cruise charters to Marlon Brando's atoll of Tetiaroa leave Papeete at 7am and return between 6-8pm., for 9.500 CFP ($95) per person, including a picnic and visit to Bird Island.

Va'a Rahi, owned by VPM Dufour Yachting Nouvelles Frontière, *Tel. 41.34.03*, is the newest and largest addition to the fleet of maxi-catamarans based at the yacht quay in Papeete, since its arrival in October, 1997. It's name means "big boat" in Tahitian, and that it is, with a length of 30 meters (98 feet), a width of 12 meters (40 feet), a mast that is 33 meters (108 feet) high, 500 square meters (5,382 square feet) of sails and two 200 horsepower engines. Captain Pierre Nougarolles welcomes up to 71 passengers aboard for daily outings to Tetiaroa. You'll leave the Papeete dock at 7am and return around 6:30pm, with the better part of the day spent on shore at Tetiaroa. A fare of 12.000 CFP ($120) buys you the joy of sailing aboard this magnificent yacht, with lunch served under a shelter on the beach or in the Hotel Tetiaroa dining room. You'll have ample time to swim, snorkel, snooze in the shade of a coconut palm and visit Bird Island.

Scuba Diving

The protected lagoons, passes and outer coral reefs offer ideal conditions for scuba diving year-round and you'll discover an abundance of dive clubs on the island of Tahiti. The diving instructors are highly qualified and speak English.

Richard (Dick) Johnson is an American marine biologist and international instructor for PADI and CMAS, who owns **Tahiti Aquatique** and **Paradise Dive Travel** at the **Sofitel Maeva Beach**; *direct line Tel./Fax 41.08.54*, or you can contact him through the hotel at *Tel. 42.80.42, ext. 0951*. Dick or one of his assistants will take you to discover several beautiful locations, which may include: "**The Aquarium**," a calm, clear, fish feeding site; "**The Wrecks**," a ship and aircraft on the same dive; and "**The Tahiti Wall & Shark Cave**," an outer reef drop-off with canyons, crevices and shark cave. The small sharks are fed by hand. Dick specializes in shark behavior and has published a *Sharks of Polynesia* book, which you will find in the hotel boutiques and bookstores. The scuba diving rate for experienced divers is 5.000 CFP ($50), and you can rent your equipment. Tahiti Aquatique offers a dive coupon program, which entitles you to two dives for 9.000 CFP ($90), equipment included. Dick will also give you an introductory lesson for 8.000 CFP ($80), or exams for your FFESSM, CMAS and PADI certificates.

You can also go scuba diving with **Polynesie Nautisme Charter**, *located at the Tahiti Beachcomber Parkroyal, Tel. 45.08.68/86.51.10, ext. 5168*. The rates are the same as Dick Johnson charges.

Tahiti Charter Island, *on the Papeete quay*, is managed by Frenchman Alain Vattant, *Tel. 45.07.75/77.02.33*. This is Papeete's unique dive operation, which uses a 12-meter (40-foot) Bayliner air-conditioned cabin cruiser named *Zackitty* to take 20 divers to the best dive sites, mostly outside the lagoon next to the coral barrier reef. The *Zakitty* has two-hour dive excursions, departing three times on Tuesdays and twice each Wednesday, Thursday and Friday. The rates for exploratory dives are 3.500 CFP ($35); night dives cost 4.000 CFP ($40) and 5.000 ($50) with your meal included. A package of 10 dives is 27.000 CFP ($270). A diving trip to Moorea, departing Papeete at 8am and returning at 5pm, is 12.000 CFP ($120) each, including two dives, breakfast and lunch. A day trip to Tetiaroa, departing at 7am and returning at 6pm, includes two dives, breakfast and lunch for 16.000 CFP ($160) each. A two-day dive-cruise to Moorea or Tetiaroa is 50.000 CFP ($500) per person, 40.000 CFP ($400) per person for a group of four divers, and 35.000 CFP ($350) each if you have six divers on board. These rates cover all meals and four dives, including one night dive. Introductory dives can be included during the weekend excursions to Moorea and Tetiaroa.

Some of the other dive centers on Tahiti are: **Tahiti Plongee**, *between Tahiti Beachcomber and Maeva Beach hotels in Punaauia, Tel. 41.00.62*; **Yacht Club of Tahiti Diving Center**, *PK 4 in Arue, Tel. 42.23.55*; **Les Copains D'Abord Diving Center** *at the Marina Aquatica at PK 27 in Paea, Tel. 43.10.65*; **Dolphin Sub** *at the Nauti-sport Marina in Fare Ute, Tel. 45.21.98*; **Eleuthera** *at Marina Taina in Punaauia, Tel. 42.49.29*; and **Ta'i Tua**, *at the Marina Puunui on the west coast of the Tahiti Iti peninsula, Tel. 57.77.93*.

Surfing

The Tahitians claim that surfing was invented by their Maohi ancestors, and the chiefs of Tahiti used to compete with one another on long wooden boards. Surfers come to Tahiti from all around the world to surf the edges of the passes, and international surfing champions have found challenging waves offshore Teahupoo at the end of the Tahiti Iti peninsula. Between October and March strong swells from the north bring sizable waves, and from April to September the Antarctic winds from the south produce powerful waves that are great for riding the tube.

Prime surf spots include the break at the mouth of the **Papenoo river** *at PK 17 on Tahiti's northeast coast*. Southwest of Papeete the **Taapuna pass** *at PK 15, close to Fisherman's Point in Punaauia*, is a favorite reef break spot for local surfers. Further along the coast you'll find the **Taharuu black**

sand beach at *PK 36 in Papara*, where the waves are good enough for the popular **Horue open**, an international competition held each July. The **Black Pearl Horue Pro Surfing** championships, which are held in April or May, attract big name surfers and the international press to the beautiful untamed coastline of **Te Pari**, *at the southern tip of Tahiti Iti*. The passes of **Hava'e**, **Te Ava Ino** and **Tapueraha** are good for riding the waves to the left, and **Te Ava Piti** pass sends you to the right.

You can check on the surfing conditions in Tahiti and Moorea by dialing "**Allo Surf**," *Tel. 36.70.06*. This service keeps you informed on the latest conditions of wind, weather and the big surfing swells. Moana David of **Moana Surf Tours**, *B.P. 6734, Faaa, Tahiti, Tel./Fax 689/43.70.70*, provides lodging, breakfast and dinner, round-trip transfers by *le truck*, and daily surfing for a minimum of two and a maximum of five surfers. The all-inclusive price is 10.000 CFP ($100) a day. Moana is a pro surfer who competes in international events in several countries

Spectator Sports

Soccer is Tahiti's favorite sport, and enthusiastic crowds gather at the **Fautaua Stadium** near Papeete on week nights and during weekends to cheer their team to victory.

Outrigger canoe racing is the top traditional sport. At almost any time of the year you will see the muscled young men practicing for the next big *pirogue* race. The racing season begins around May, and the best teams of male and female paddlers compete in the Heiva Festival races in July, which are held inside the lagoon and in the open ocean. More races are held in August and September to select the teams who will compete in the **Hawaiki Nui Pirogue Race** that is held each November. During this three-day event, the paddlers race from Huahine to Raiatea, then to Tahaa and on to Bora Bora.

Surfing competitions are becoming more frequent and some of them are attracting the world-class surfers, who have discovered the formerly secret surfing spots of the locals. Tahitian-style **horse racing** is held on special occasions at the **Pirae Hippodrome**, where jockeys used to ride bareback, wearing only a brightly colored *pareo* and a crown of flowers. Safety regulations now require saddles and helmets. You can place your bets, but the payoffs are very small.

Cockfighting is another Sunday afternoon event. Although it is officially illegal, everyone seems to know where the fights will take place on a certain day. Ask at your hotel for specific details.

Almost every weekend in Tahiti or Moorea you will find a marathon or triathlon or bicycle racing event going on. Other competitions are held for Hobie Cats, wind surfers and jet-skiers, as well as tennis, golf, *petanque* or bocci-ball, volleyball, basketball, boxing, archery, rugby and track.

SHOPPING

Tahiti is not a shopper's paradise, but some of the merchandise is different from what you're used to seeing back home. Made-in-Tahiti items can be good souvenir purchases, but be aware that some of the wooden masks, clothing and pearly shells that are sold in boutiques and curio shops were imported from Indonesia, or the Philippines. The *pareu* or *pareo*, which is called a sarong or lava lava in other countries, is Tahiti's national garment. It is made from a piece of cotton fabric approximately two yards long and one yard wide and tie-dyed, air-brushed or hand painted. You will find these in shops along the Papeete waterfront, at sidewalk stands, in arts and crafts centers all around the island, in hotel boutiques, and displayed at the colorful kiosks set up permanently outside and upstairs at **le Marché**, the municipal market in the heart of Papeete. Fabrics to make your own *pareos* or brightly patterned shirts and dresses are sold by the meter at **Tahiti Art**, the **Venus** fabric stores and other Chinese-owned shops in the vicinity of the public market.

Polynesian style bikinis, beach wear and ball gowns are fabricated by local factories and *couturières* in attractive hand-blocked materials. You'll find the choicest selections in the hotel boutiques, and in dozens of shops in Papeete, including **Tahiti Art**, **Marie Ah You**, **Celina** and **Tiare Shop** on Boulevard Pomare, **Anémone** on rue Marechal Foch, **Shop Gauguin Curios** on rue Gauguin, **Tamara Curios** in Fare Tony Center, **Vaima Shirts**, **Bikini Boutique** and several other shops in the Vaima Center. **Tahiti Shirts**, on Boulevard Pomare, carries several lines of quality shirts that are designed by young artists in Tahiti.

Matamua, *on Boulevard Pomare*, sells wall hangings, tapestries, lampshades, candles, jewelry boxes, paintings and engravings, all with Polynesian designs. You can also watch the craftsman as he engraves the sculpted patterns onto the fabrics.

Pacific Curios *on Avenue Prince Hinoi* carries a good selection of carved Marquesan bowls, ceremonial spears, drums, ukuleles, tables and tikis, plus many other gift items. You can also find Polynesian wood carvings at **Manuia Curios** beside the Cathedral, and in **Mareva Curios** in Fare Tony on the waterfront.

Shop upstairs at **le Marché** for Tahitian dancing costumes, basketry and woven hats, plus shell jewelry, mother-of-pearl creations, *tifaifai* bed covers or wall hangings, embroidered cushion covers and wood carvings.

Handcrafts stands or artisan centers are located in almost every village around the island, and the major hotels have arts and crafts demonstrations several times a week. You can buy very pleasing souvenir gifts directly from the person who created them.

Monoi oil is an especially nice and inexpensive purchase, and is made from coconut oil and the essence of flowers. The most popular fragrance is that of the Tiare Tahiti, the white gardenia. Other floral choices of *monoi* are made with Pitate, Ylang Ylang, Tipanie (Frangipani or Plumeria), and you can also buy vanilla, coconut and sandalwood scented *monoi* products. *Monoi* oil can be used as a moisturizing lotion, a perfume, suntan lotion, mosquito repellent, hair dressing and a massage lotion. This can be purchased, along with *monoi* soaps, shampoos, bath gels and balms, in pharmacies, super markets, hotel boutiques and in many shops in Papeete and all around the island.

Tahitian vanilla beans make an unusual souvenir item, and are found in **le Marché** and in souvenir shops and grocery stores. Candies, cookies, *confitures* and coconut toddy, all Tahiti products, are good for gifts. And don't forget the Tahitian musical choices, in cassettes, compact disks and on video films of the islands.

French perfumes are sold at prices lower than in Paris or New York, plus there are French fashions, crystal ware and French *patés* and cheeses. Duty Free Shops are found in Papeete and at the International Airport of Tahiti-Faaa.

Tahiti's biggest export item is the black pearl, which is also the most sought-after souvenir item. Exquisite jewelry, fashioned of black pearls, 18-karat gold and diamonds, can be purchased in Tahiti, as well as unset pearls of all sizes, shapes, quality and prices. Shops selling these jewels of the sea are found on practically every block in downtown Papeete, in addition to all the hotel boutiques.

DAY TRIPS & EXCURSIONS

Day Trip to Moorea

Moorea is only 17 kilometers (11 miles) across the channel from Tahiti, and the rugged profile of her mountains beckon you to cross the **Sea of Moons**, so named by the ancient Polynesians, and come on over to have some fun. This is where the residents of Tahiti go when they need to "escape" for a day or weekend. If your plans don't include a stay on Moorea, then a day tour is certainly on the "must do" list.

You can book your excursion with any of the travel agencies listed below, who will make all the arrangements so that you can be totally carefree. Following are some of the standard tours:

A **Moorea Island Tour** includes all transfers in Tahiti and Moorea, the round-trip by high speed catamaran, a full circle island tour of Moorea, plus a drive up the mountain to the **Belvedere** lookout point. Other highlight stops include **Cook's Bay**, the **Papetoai Church** and the **Tiki Village Cultural Center**. This excursion leaves your hotel in Tahiti at 8:30am and you'll return at 5:30pm. The travel agencies in downtown Papeete can give you a better rate than the more convenient travel desks in the hotels. The hotel agencies sell the Moorea Day Tour by boat anywhere between 9.000 CFP and 14.000 CFP ($90 to $140), depending on whether or not you want lunch included. You will pay a supplementary fee if you wish to go by boat and return by Air Moorea or fly both ways.

The **Moorea Land and Lagoon Tour** for 12.500 CFP ($125), also leaves your hotel at 8:30am, returning at 5:30pm. The cost includes all transfers, the high speed catamaran, and a bus tour from the boat dock in Moorea through **Cook's Bay** to the **Belvedere** lookout point. In **Opunohu Bay** you'll board a **covered catamaran** for a tour of the beautiful lagoon, with time for swimming and snorkeling. A picnic lunch on a private *motu* islet is included. Should you wish to fly back to Tahiti the airfare is extra.

You can also visit Moorea quite easily on your own. The least expensive way will cost you a minimum of 2.240 CFP ($22.40) for land and sea transportation. You can catch l*e truck* from your hotel to downtown Papeete, get off on Boulevard Pomare by the Banque de Polynesia, cross the street to Fare Manihini, the Tahiti Manava Visitors Bureau, and walk along the wharf a couple of blocks until you come to the dock for the Moorea ferries. You'll see the ticket offices for *Aremiti III* (*Tel. 42.88.88*) and *Tamarii Moorea VIII* Corsair 6000 Fast Ferry *(Tel. 43.76.50)*. One-way fares are 700 to 800 CFP ($7 to $8), depending on how competitive the two operating companies feel at the time.

The schedules for both catamarans are almost similar, with *Tamarii Moorea's* Corsair 6000 fast catamaran usually leaving about five minutes before the *Aremiti III* departure. Most tourists like to take the luxurious, air-conditioned and comfortable *Aremiti III*, because it is easier to get on board, whereas the other boats have steep stairways. The service from Papeete to Moorea starts at 6:25am Monday through Friday, and at 7:15am and 7:30am on Saturday and Sunday, respectively. Visitors usually like to take the boat that leaves Papeete at 9:05am on Monday through Friday, and at 9:15am on weekends. You will arrive in Moorea just 30 minutes later, which gives you time for a full day of discovering this lovely island.

You can reserve a guided tour of Moorea through your travel desk, or you can choose one of the mini-buses that you'll see waiting at the **Vaiare** boat dock in Moorea. You can also rent a car or a scooter in the main terminal. Both **Avis** and **Europcar** have sales counters here, and the hostesses at the **Moorea Visitors Center** booth will give you details on the island and all the activities.

Should you decide on the least expensive way, then just walk across the parking lot to the main terminal. In front of this building you will see several big buses, and at least two of them will be loading passengers. The bus nearest the *Aremiti III* usually serves the **North Coast** of Moorea, passing by the hotels Sofitel Ia Ora Moorea, Hotel Bali Hai, Maeva Cook's

Bay Resort, Club Bali Hai, Moorea Lagoon (closed for reconstruction), Moorea Beachcomber Parkroyal, Moorea Beach Club, Les Tipaniers, Club Med, Hibiscus and Moorea Village. The second bus goes around the **South Coast** of Moorea, passing by Hotel Linareva, the Tiki Village, Moorea Village, and Hotel Hibiscus, stopping at Le Petit Village, which is within easy walking distance of Club Med and the hotels in that vicinity. Be sure to ask the bus driver which direction he's headed, and you pay him 200 CFP ($2) before boarding the bus. There's just one standard fare.

The **best beach** on the island is adjacent to the **Sofitel Ia Ora**, which is the nearest hotel to the ferry dock. If your desire is to swim in crystal clear water and just hang out around the beach and swimming pool, then this is your answer. Elizabeth and Maco, an American woman and her Tahitian husband, are in charge of the activities. Have a talk with them and decide how you can best spend your day. You can paddle an outrigger canoe or pedal boat, windsurf, ride a surf bike, glass bottom boat, or take a boat trip to the *motu*. You can also join a tour bus to explore the highlights of Moorea.

If you want to see the coastal sights of Moorea, then take one of the buses to **Haapiti**, and get off at the end of the line, which is at the **Moorea Visitors Center** in Le Petit Village. From there you can walk across the street to the island's **second best white sand beach**. You can also choose one of the hotels in the vicinity as your home for the day. They all have public showers and toilets and you'll find several restaurants, snack bars, boutiques and **black pearl shops** within easy walking distance of Le Petit Village.

The **Tiki Theatre Village** is another good choice for your self-made day tour or an excursion arranged by your travel agent. The beach here is not as pretty as some others on the island, and the lagoon is very shallow and warm close to the shore. But you will certainly find all the entertainment you want. Here in this typical **Polynesian village**, you'll see Tahitians weaving palm fronds, dying *pareos*, making floral crowns, sculpting wood or stone, tattooing and creating jewelry from black pearls. You can paddle a canoe or go fishing on the reef with the boys from the Tiki Village. You can eat lunch in the **Papayer Restaurant** and watch a mini-show of **Polynesian dances** performed in the white sand. Just remember that you have to take the south bound bus to get there, and don't forget that Tiki Village is closed on Mondays.

If you visit Moorea on a Sunday, you may want to go to the **Hotel Bali Hai**, where a traditional Tahitian feast is prepared in the underground oven. Be sure to take pictures when the oven is opened at 12:30pm. A buffet of Tahitian food and international dishes includes beverages, for 3.500 CFP ($35), and a one-hour camera and dance show is performed on the terrace. If you get here early enough you can join a morning tour.

There is a small man-made white sand beach and the snorkeling is good at the edge of the reef. You can also swim in the fresh water swimming pool.

The buses depart from **Le Petit Village** one hour before each arrival and departure of the ferries. Therefore, if you are taking the last boat from Moorea to Tahiti, which leaves at 4:40pm Monday through Thursday, 4:20pm on Friday, 4:45pm on Saturday, and at 5:45pm on Sunday, just stand beside the road an hour before departure time and wave for the driver to stop.

When you get back to Papeete you'll have to walk back to the *le truck* stop, where you'll find a *le truck* that will take you to the hotels on the west coast, but there will be fewer of them running on weekends.

Day Trip to Bora Bora

Booking your Day Tour to Bora Bora with the travel agent at your hotel tour desk is the easiest way to have all the details taken care of for you. Your departure time depends on the day you want to go, as the **Air Tahiti** flight schedule varies. You will be picked up at your hotel around 6am, approximately one hour before your scheduled flight. The flight time to Bora Bora is 45 minutes in a very comfortable ATR72 aircraft. The airport is located on **Motu Mute**, an islet that lies within the barrier reef, separated from the main island by the multihued lagoon. The Bora Bora shuttle boat to **Vaitape village** leaves the airport 20 minutes after your arrival, and you can admire the changing blues and greens of the lagoon during the 25-minute crossing. Transfers from the boat dock in Vaitape to the hotels are made by mini-van or *le truck*.

If you book a Day Tour with the **Moana Beach Parkroyal** you will be met at the Vaitape boat dock and transferred to the hotel, where you will be shown to a changing room to put on your swimsuit. At 9:15am you will board a motorized outrigger canoe for a lagoon tour around the island. Stops will be made for you to walk on the living coral reef, dip into the water to watch a thrilling shark feeding show, swim with the stingrays, and to wade ashore on a palm-shaded *motu* to taste a coconut and fresh fruit. Around 12:45pm the boat will bring you back to the hotel, where you can shower and change before having lunch in the Noa Noa Restaurant or on the Vini Vini Terrace beside the beach. A tourist menu includes a starter course, main course and dessert. Drinks are not included.

You will have ample time to swim and snorkel in the blue-silk lagoon. In mid-afternoon, depending on your return flight, you will be transferred back to the airport on Motu Mute, 1 3/4 hours before your flight departure. Should you prefer to visit the Lagoonarium or explore the island on a Safari Tour, that can also be arranged. The individual cost of this day tour is 13.200 CFP ($132), and 11.400 CFP ($114) each for two or more people. Air fare is not included. A Day Room can be rented for a supplementary price of 9.000 CFP ($90).

If you want to spend a day on a *motu* the **Bora Bora Lagoonarium** will send a boat to the airport dock to pick you up. If you are only two passengers then you will take the regular shuttle boat to Vaitape boat dock and be transferred by bus to the Bora Bora Lagoonarium office, and then be transferred by boat to the islet. When you choose this excursion you will tour the island by outrigger speed canoe, watch the shark feeding, snorkel inside the natural aquarium and eat lunch on the *motu*. You will not see Bora Bora by land.

You can create your own Day Tour to Bora Bora, but you will need to get a current copy of the Air Tahiti schedules. The **Tahiti Tourist** offices in Los Angeles or New York can mail this to you on request. The normal round-trip airfare from Tahiti to Bora Bora is 24.800 CFP ($248). Some of the travel agencies in Tahiti do not recommend a Bora Bora Day Tour because of the travel time and cost involved. They will try to sell you an overnight trip instead, which I also recommend.

Day Trip to Tetiaroa

Marlon Brando's private atoll of Tetiaroa is ideal for a day trip to a tropical islet surrounded by white beaches of powdery sand and a sparkling lagoon of warm turquoise water. This beautiful and peaceful atoll is just 42 kilometers (26 miles) north of Tahiti, less than 20 minutes by chartered airplane.

If you buy a **Tetiaroa Day Tour** at your hotel tour desk you will pay 24.500 CFP ($245), which includes all transfers, round-trip airfare, lunch, an excursion by boat to Bird Island, and free time to snorkel, swim, fish or paddle an outrigger canoe inside the protected lagoon. You will be picked up at your hotel at 7:30am to go to the airport, and you will return at 4:30pm.

You can book your own day tour at the **Hotel Tetiaroa** office, *Tel. 82.63.02*, which will cost you 18.000 CFP to 20.000 CFP ($180 to $200), depending on the time of year and whether or not promotions are in effect. Catch *le truck* in front of your hotel and get off on the main road in front of the airport. Then walk to the **Air Moorea terminal**, *which is in a separate building to the right of the International terminal of Tahiti-Faaa*. The **Tetiaroa office** in Tahiti shares the terminal in Tahiti with **Air Moorea**. The flights leave from 8-8:30am and leave Tetiaroa around 3:30 to 4pm. A barbecue on the beach is held each Wednesday and Saturday, with tropical punch and wine included.

If you go on Sunday then you'll be treated to Polynesian food inside the screened dining room, also with punch. Lunch and the trip to **Bird Island** are included in your fare. The only difference between a do-it-yourself day tour and the excursion sold at the travel desks is the ground transportation in Tahiti.

You can also go to Tetiaroa for the day aboard a sailboat or motor yacht. These boats anchor outside the reef on the south side of the atoll. A thatched roof shelter has been built on the beach for picnics ashore, and a trip to Bird Island is always included in these excursions. Please see a partial list of the boats in the chapter on Tetiaroa. The Tahiti Manava Visitors Bureau in Papeete can give you a current list when you arrive. Or you can walk along the Papeete waterfront and check out the boats yourself.

Aremiti Excursions, *at the Ferry Boat Dock in Papeete, Tel. 42.88.88,* have a day tour to Tetiaroa for 14.000 CFP ($140) per person, which includes a round-trip aboard the air-conditioned motor launch *Aremiti*, a guided tour to Bird Island, lunch on a private beach with drink included, and time for snorkeling inside the lagoon or at the wall of the reef. The boat leaves Papeete at 7am and returns at 5:30pm.

Jet France and *Va'a Rahi* also have day charters to Tetiaroa. See information above under *Sports & Recreation (Day Sailing Excursions).*

Day Tours to Other Islands

Huahine is 35 minutes by air from Tahiti, **Raiatea** is a 40-minute flight, and **Rangiroa** is just 55 minutes by Air Tahiti. All these islands have direct flights from Tahiti and a convenient flight schedule, which will allow you a full day of discovery on each island. The travel agencies can arrange all the details, including a hotel base for lunch, sightseeing tours, snorkeling equipment and changing facilities.

Here are the main travel agencies that can arrange your Day Tours to suit your requests.

Tekura Tahiti Travel, *B.P. 2971, Papeete, Tahiti. Tel. 689/43.12.00, Fax (689) 42.84.60, e-mail go@tahiti-tekuratravel.com Her web site is WWW.tahiti-tekuratravel.com.* Tekura has an office on the third level of the Vaima Center in Papeete. She is the most imaginative, enthusiastic travel agent in Tahiti, and she speaks excellent English. She also has a knowledgeable, qualified staff who speak good English and know how to give personalized service.

Tahiti Nui Travel, *B.P. 718, Papeete, Tahiti. Tel. 689/54.02.00, Fax 689/42.74.35.* This is the largest travel agency, with travel desks in most of the hotels. You can also visit their main office in the Vaima Center in Papeete.

Marama Tours Tahiti, *B.P. 6266, Faaa, Tahiti. Tel. 689/83.96.50/ 83.95.81/82.08.42 (after hours) and mobile phone 77.80.11, Fax (689) 82.16.75.* They have a counter at the Tahiti-Faaa International Airport, and a travel desk at Sofitel Maeva Beach.

Paradise Tours, *B.P. 2430, Papeete, Tahiti, Tel. 689/42.49.36/ 44.40.40 (toll free), Fax (689)42.48.62,* has counters in many of the hotels. And **Tahiti Tours**, *B.P. 627, Papeete, Tahiti, Tel. (689) 42.78.70, Fax (689) 42.50.50,* is an affiliate of Tahiti Nui Travel, with an office on rue Jeanne d'Arc in Papeete, the street between Boulevard Pomare and the Notre Dame Cathedral in the center of town.

PRACTICAL INFORMATION
Churches

Many religions and denominations are represented in French Polynesia. Some 47 percent of the population are Protestants, 37 percent are Catholics, and the other 16 percent are either Mormon, Seventh Day Adventists, Sanito, Jehovah's Witnesses, Buddhists, Jewish, Bahai, Assembly of God or with no religion.

Following are the main numbers for the religious offices on the island of Tahiti: **Protestant Evangelical Church**, *Tel. 42.00.29/42.0093*; **Catholic Church**, *Tel. 42.02.51*; **Christian Center of the Good News Church**, *Tel. 82.05.72*; **Israelite Synagogue**, *Tel. 41.03.92*; **Alleluia Church**, *Tel. 42.83.57*; **Jehovah's Witnesses**, *Tel. 54.70.00*; **Mormons**, *Tel. 50.55.05*; **Neo-Apostolic**, *Tel. 57.32.78*; **Sanito**, *Tel. 42.03.26*; **Church of the New Testament**, *Tel. 43.84.71*; **Seventh Day Adventists**, *Tel. 42.03.78*; **Tibetan Gelugpa Buddhism**, *Tel. 57.49.32.*

CHURCH SERVICES

*Church services on Sunday morning will offer you an insight into the Tahitian culture away from the hotel scene. You'll enjoy the singing, which is best in the Protestant Churches, called **Eglise Evangelique**. The missionaries taught the Tahitians to sing the old time hymns in the early 1800s, and over the years the people have transformed the old religious songs into their own versions called himene. The singing is a capella, with the men sitting behind the women and the kids running around everywhere. Hats are worn to church but not flowers. Be prepared to sit on the side up front, where you can look at the parishioners and they can smile back at you. They are used to visitors and will warmly welcome you.*

Clubs & Associations

Alcoholics Anonymous, *Tel. 43.21.63*; **Chamber of Commerce, Industry and Trade in French Polynesia**, *Tel. 54.07.00*; **Kiwanis Club**, *Tel. 82.47.66*; **Lion's Club**, *Tel. 42.05.97*; **Polynesian Cultural Center (OTAC)**, *Tel. 42.88.50*; **Red Cross**, *Tel. 42.02.76*; **Rotary Club**, *Tel. 50.52.70*;

Société des Etudes Oceaniennes, *Tel. 41.96.03*; **Soroptimist**, *Tel. 83.61.60*; **Women's Council of French Polynesia**, *Tel. 57.11.94*.

Currency Exchange

Banque de Polynésie, *Tel. 46.66.84, Boulevard Pomare*, open Monday to Thursday 7:45am to 3:30pm, Friday 7:45am to 4pm, Saturday 8am to 12pm; **Banque de Tahiti**, *Tel. 41.70.00, rue Cardella*, open Monday to Friday 7:45am to 3:30pm; **Banque Socredo**, *Tel. 41.51.23, rue Dumont d'Urville,* open Monday to Thursday 7:15am to 3:30pm, Friday 7:15am to 2:30pm; and **Westpac Banque**, *Tel. 46.79.79, Place de la Cathédrale,* Monday to Friday 7:45am to 3:30pm. A branch office of Banque de Tahiti is located on the second level of the Vaima Center, open Monday from 2 to 5pm, Tuesday to Friday 8 to 11:30am and 2 to 5pm. See information on Ready Cash and Currency Exchanges in *Basic Information* chapter.

Hairdressers & Barbers

The larger hotels have a beauty shop, with English-speaking *coiffeurs*. There are numerous beauty salons in Papeete, and usually all you have to do is stop in and ask if they can take you. I usually have good luck on short notice at **Veronique Coiffure**, *Tel. 45.13.30, on the right side of rue du Marechal Foch just before the Pont de l'Est.* She's not inexpensive, but she's good. **Absalon**, *Tel. 42.86.45* for women and *Tel. 42.86.56* for men, is another popular hair stylist, also on the right side of rue du Marechal Foch, coming from the Cathedral in the center of town.

Hospitals & Doctors

You can find English-speaking doctors, dentists, nurses and other medical personnel in Tahiti, but they are not common. The Mamao Hospital and the two private clinics are open 24 hours. There is also a hospital in Taravao. See Health Concerns in *Basic Information* chapter for further details.

Mamao Hospital, *Tel. 42.01.01/46.62.62*, is the government operated medical center on *Avenue Georges Clemenceau in Mamao, a suburb just east of Papeete.* **Clinique Cardella**, *Tel. 46.04.25*, and **Clinique Paofai**, *Tel. 46.18.18*, are two privately owned clinics in Papeete. **S.O.S. Medecins**, *Tel. 42.34.56* is an emergency unit of doctors and other medical personnel, who will come to the hotel to attend to your needs.

Optique Vaima, *Tel. 42.77.54, in the Vaima Center,* and **Pacific Optic**, *Tel. 42.70.78, in the Quartier du Commerce, one block inland from Boulevard Pomare,* will repair your glasses while you wait.

Surdité de Polynésie, *Tel. 43.33.04, in the Quartier du Commerce, close to the Tracqui store,* will solve your hearing aid problems while you're in Tahiti.

Laundry Service

All the larger hotels provide laundry service, and can arrange to have your dry cleaning done. **Lavex Sa M'Plaix**, *Tel. 41.26.65*, is the name of an automatic laundry *on Boulevard Pomare in downtown Papeete, close to Broadway Tobacco shop between Avenue Prince Hinoi and rue Clappier.* They're open Monday to Saturday 6am to 8pm and on Sunday from 6am to 12pm. A 7 kilogram (15 pound) basket of laundry costs 700 CFP ($7) to wash, 800 CFP ($8) to dry and 4.000 CFP ($40) to iron.

Pharmacies

There are half a dozen pharmacies in the Papeete area, and several around the island. One of the easiest to find in Papeete is the **Pharmacie du Vaima**, *Tel. 42.97.73, on rue de Général de Gaulle at rue Georges La Garde, behind the Vaima Center close to MacDonald's Hamburgers.* The pharmacist is Nguyen Ngoc-Tran, who speaks English. The pharmacies rotate night and weekend/holiday duty, so it is best to check with your hotel to find out which one is available should you need medical supplies after hours. The medicines sold in French Polynesia are French brands.

Restrooms

There are public toilets on the Papeete waterfront across the road from the Tahiti Manava Visitor's Bureau, adjacent to Banque Socredo and the Port Captain's office. You'll also find public toilets in the building that houses the Tamarii Moorea freight bureau, at the ferry dock on the Papeete waterfront. Bring your own paper just in case, and do not be surprised if they are not clean. You will definitely prefer using the restrooms in the hotels and restaurants downtown.

Around the island, you'll find public restrooms at the main tourist stops, such as Point Venus, the Blowhole of Arahoho and the Three Cascades of Tiarei, the Paul Gauguin Museum, the Vaipahi Gardens and Waterfall, and at the Fern Grottoes of Mara'a.

15. MOOREA

Scientists say that **Moorea** (Mo-oh-RAY-ah) is shaped like an isosceles triangle, and romantics believe the island is in the form of a heart. I think it looks like a swimming turtle. Geologists say that Moorea is twice as old as Tahiti and once contained a volcano that reached 3,300 meters (11,000 feet) into the sky. Polynesian legend tells us that Moorea was created when a magical fish swam from the lagoon of Raiatea and Tahaa to become the island of Tahiti; and the second dorsal fin of this enormous fish grew into land that was called "Aimeo i te rara varu" for the eight mountain ridges that separate the island. The traditional shortened name of this island was Aimeho, Aimeo or Eimeo. Following a vision by one of the Polynesian high priests, the name was later changed to Moorea, which means "yellow lizard."

Moorea offers you the tropical South Seas island that you expect to find when you fly to Tahiti, just 17 kilometers (11 miles) across the Sea of Moons. Some people say it's worth the airfare to Tahiti just to see Moorea. Others say that Moorea was created so that people on Tahiti would have something to stare at across the sea.

Moorea's magnificent beauty covers an area of 136 square kilometers (53 square miles), which is the south rim of a crater that was formed following cataclysmic explosions eons ago. The lofty cathedral-shaped peaks and jade velvet spires that you will see reflected in the lapis lazuli waters of **Cook's Bay** and **Opunohu** (belly-of-the-stonefish) **Bay** are the basaltic remains of the crater's interior wall.

The volcanic peaks of the mountain range resemble a fairy castle or a serrated shark's jaw, dominated by **Tohive'a** (hot spade) at 1,207 meters (3,983 feet), **Mou'a Roa** (long mountain), with an altitude of 880 meters (2,904 feet), resembles a shark's tooth. This is the most photographed of the spectacular wonders, and it is often pointed out to visitors as "Bali Ha'i." **Mou'a Puta** (split rock), the 830 meter- (2,739 foot-) high mountain with a hole in its top, is a tempting challenge for hikers. The hole is said to have been made by the spear of Pai, a favorite son of the gods of old

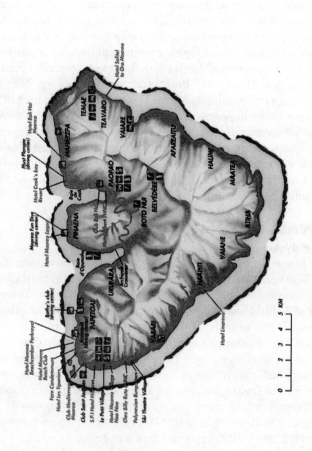

MOOREA

Polynesia, who was warned that Hiro, god of thieves, wanted to steal the sacred **Rotui** mountain and take it home to Raiatea. The warrior Pai threw a spear from Tahiti that pierced the top of Mou'a Puta and the noise woke up all the roosters on Moorea, who crowed so loudly that the thieves were forced to flee. But Hiro did manage to take a piece of Rotui's crest and this stolen land can be seen on top of a mountain in Raiatea, covered with the *toa* (ironwood) trees similar to those that grow on **Mou'a Rotui**.

Moorea's crystalline lagoons, filled with gardens of fanciful coral and exotic sea creatures, are said to have been a gift from Ruahatu, king of the ocean. The azure waters of the fjord-like bays were specially created by this benevolent god. Tane, the Polynesian god of beauty, bordered the lagoons with white sand beaches and planted an abundance of fragrant white Tiare Tahiti blossoms among the majestic coconut palms.

The September 1997 edition of *Condé Nast Traveler* reported that Moorea was voted Number 1 in the "island environment" category by readers who participated in the magazine's 10th annual Top 100 Readers' Choice Awards. Among the Top 20 islands the readers placed Moorea in sixth position, just behind Bora Bora.

ARRIVALS & DEPARTURES

Arriving By Air

Air Moorea, *Tel. 86.41.41 in Tahiti*, provides seven-minute air taxi service between Tahiti and Moorea with at least 19 flights daily. The Air Moorea terminal is within easy walking distance from the **International Airport of Tahiti-Faaa** and the domestic terminal. You can push the free luggage carts from one terminal to another. There are restrooms and a snack and bar counter in the small Air Moorea terminal in Tahiti. The nine- and eighteen-passenger planes depart from the Faaa airport in Tahiti every half hour from 6 to 9am and from 4 to 6pm. In between these peak hours the flights are once an hour, departing from Tahiti on the hour. No reservations are required unless you want to specify a certain flight time. The one-way fare is 2.700 CFP ($27) if you buy your ticket locally and 3.200 CFP ($32) if you buy it overseas.

You can also charter an airplane to Moorea with **Air Moorea** or **Air Tahiti**, *Tel. 86.41.41*, **Air Archipels**, *Tel. 81.30.30*, **Air Oceania Tahiti**, *Tel. 82.0.47*, and **Wan Air**, *Tel. 85.55.54*. Helicopter flights can be organized with **Heli-Pacific**, *Tel. 85.68.00*, and **Heli Inter Polynesie**, *Tel. 81.99.00*.

The modern **Temae Airport** terminal in Moorea has restrooms, a restaurant-bar, car rental agencies, tour and excursion companies, and an informational stand operated by the tourist bureau. Taxi service is usually available for all arriving flights, and there is a taxi phone at the main entrance. There is no bus or *le truck* service provided to the airport. If you are not carrying heavy bags and wish to walk about four blocks to the main road to catch *le truck*, you want to be sure that you schedule your arrival with that of the ferries from Tahiti, when the public transportation service will be operating. You can stand beside the Total Station and wave down the first bus that passes, which will be going toward Cook's Bay.

Arriving By Boat

The **Moorea Boat Dock** in Papeete, *a couple of blocks east of the Tahiti Tourist Office on the waterfront*, is where you will find the *Aremiti III, Tel. 42.88.88*, a luxurious air-conditioned catamaran with 450 seats and a bar, which was put into service in 1995 to transport you to Moorea in 30 minutes. Fast catamaran service is also provided by the *Tamarii Moorea VIII, Tel. 43.76.50*, which was put into service in 1996, with space for 42 cars and a few hundred passengers. The owners like to boast that this ferry crosses the channel between Tahiti and Moorea in 12 minutes due to the speed of its Corsair 6000 engine, but it actually takes 30 minutes from dock to dock. Should you have any difficulty climbing stairs or prefer not to be blasted by television noise (in French) during your trip to Moorea, then I advise you to take the *Aremiti III*. The crew on this line are extremely helpful. One-way fares are 800 CFP ($8), but the competitive lines frequently drop the fares to get the business. Each line also has a larger car ferry, with one-hour crossings between the two islands.

Both of the fast catamarans provide five to six round-trip crossings daily Monday through Saturday, and four to five trips on Sundays. The *Aremiti III* leaves Papeete each Monday at 5, 6:25, 7:25 and 9:05am, 12:15, 4:10 and 5:30pm. On Tuesday through Friday the 5am boat is eliminated, and on Friday afternoon the boat leaves Papeete at 3:15 instead of 4:10pm. The Saturday departures from Papeete to Moorea are at 7:15 and 9:15 am, 12:15, 2, and 4pm. On Sundays the boat leaves Papeete at 7:30 and 9:15am, and at 3:30 and 5pm. You will find public telephones, car rental agencies, taxi service, a tourist bureau information counter, toilets and snack bars at the **Vaiare Ferry** terminal.

Public transportation is provided by buses or *le truck*, with vehicles waiting in front of the terminal upon the arrival of the catamarans from Tahiti. Give the driver the name of your destination and verify that you're getting onto the right bus, as one goes on the north coast to **Cook's Bay** and onward to the **Club Med** area, and the other bus heads in the opposite direction, towards **Afareaitu** and on to **Haapiti** and the **Club Med** area, by way of the south coast. You pay the driver 200 CFP ($2) before boarding, and pull the cord, ring the bell or holler "stop" when you want to get off.

Departing By Air

Air Moorea, *Tel. 56.10.34*, has flights to Tahiti every half hour from the Temae Airport in Moorea between 6:15 and 9:15am and from 3:15 and 6:15pm. Hourly flights leave Moorea between 9:15am and 3:15pm. On Sundays and long weekends the last flight to Tahiti departs at 6:45pm. Reservations are advised for the early morning flights. You can also take a 30-minute "flight-seeing" excursion with Air Moorea.

Air Tahiti, *Tel. 86.42.42/86.41.84* on weekends n Tahiti or *Tel. 56.10.34* in Moorea, stops in Moorea daily enroute to Huahine, Raiatea and Bora Bora, and again on the return trip to Tahiti. This is very convenient if you are flying between Moorea and the Leeward Society Islands. Onward fares to Huahine are 11.550 CFP ($115.50) and 16.800 CFP ($168) to Bora Bora. From Moorea to Papeete the fare is 3.200 CFP ($32) on this flight.

Departing By Boat

The *Aremiti III, Tel. 56.31.10*, leaves Moorea for Papeete Monday through Friday at 5:55, 7 and 8am. An 11am departure is made on Monday, Tuesday and Thursday, and at 11:45am on Wednesdays and 11:15am on Fridays, to coincide with the school program. The afternoon boats leave Moorea at 3 and 4:40pm Monday through Thursday, and at 2 and 3:50pm on Friday. On Saturday the boat leaves at 6:05, 8 and 9:45am, and at 1, 3, and 4:45pm. The Sunday schedule is at 8:15am, 3, 4:15 and 5:45pm. Ticket counters are located at the Vaiare ferry dock in Moorea. The *Tamarii Moorea* ticket window is in the main terminal and the *Aremiti* sales office is at the far end of the parking lot.

ORIENTATION

A paved road hugs the coast for 60 kilometers (37 miles) around Moorea, where you'll see thatched roof *fares* with bamboo walls, little shacks with tin roofs and lovely villas with stone walls. Most of the 11,682 inhabitants live on the mountain side of the road, with a sprinkling of homes along the white sand beaches. Gardens of fruit and flowers border the road and during the summer months (November-March) you will see the flamboyant red and yellow Royal Poinciana trees in bloom. You can happily take pictures on this beautiful island without having electric lines mar the photograph. All the cables are underground.

Moorea doesn't have a town or central shopping area. The administrative center is in the village of **Afareaitu**, which most visitors never see except from a tour bus. Located on the eastern coast facing Tahiti, this sleepy little settlement contains the principal *mairie* (town hall), local government offices and hospital. Most of the churches, schools, supermarkets, small *magasin* stores, banks, boutiques and restaurants are located in the communes of **Maharepa**, **Pao Pao**, **Papetoai** and **Haapiti**. With just a few exceptions the hotels, hostels, family pensions and campgrounds are found beside **Cook's Bay** or beside a white sand beach in **Haapiti**.

Moorea's clear lagoon invites you to come on in for a swim, or you can snorkel, scuba dive, water-ski and jet-ski. You can view the fish and coral through a glass bottom boat, take an Aqua Walk on the sandy bottom of the lagoon gardens, or go diving in a yellow submarine. You can zoom across the lagoon in a motorboat, pirogue or lagoon jet, and you can let the tradewinds propel you on a windsurf board. There are sailing excursions, beach barbecues, shelling expeditions and fishing trips. You can take a dolphin cruise, sunset cruise or moonlight cruise. Professional lessons are available for all water sports, as well as for tennis at various hotel courts, and for horseback riding by the sea.

You can take your aerial photos during a helicopter ride or airplane tour of Moorea. You can discover the island by rental car, scooter, bicycle or on foot. Guided tours will show you Moorea's most breathtaking scenery, around the coastal road, in the interior valleys, up the mountains and to the waterfalls of Afareaitu. You can visit a fruit juice factory and distillery, and sample a tall cool drink at a lively Happy Hour. At the hotels and at Tiki Theatre Village you can photograph traditional dance shows, learn to tie a *pareo*, grate a coconut and dance Tahitian style.

Moorea's excellent restaurants and snack bars have menu selections for all tastes and prices for all budgets. The highlight of your culinary explorations in Moorea should include a *tamaara'a*, an authentic Tahitian feast.

GETTING AROUND

Car, Scooter & Bicycle Rentals

• **Albert Rent-a-Car**, *facing Hotel Bali Hai, Tel. 56.30.58, Club Bali Hai, Tel. 56.19.28, and Club Med, Tel. 56.33,75,* rents a Fiat Panda for 5.000 CFP ($50) for 4 hours, 6.000 CFP ($60) for 8 hours, 6.500 CFP ($65) for 24 hours and 12.000 CFP ($120) for 2 days. A Ford and an open-sided Mini-Moke start at 5.500 CFP ($55) for 4 hours, and a Jeep starts at 5.000 CFP ($50) for 4 hours. Scooters rent for 3.000 CFP ($30) for 4 hours, 4.000 CFP ($40) for 8 hours, 4.500 CFP ($45) for 24 hours and 8.000 CFP ($80) for 2 days. Insurance and free mileage are included in all rentals.

• **Avis-Pacificar**, *Tel. 56.12.58, has a sales office at the Moorea Airport and the Vaiare Ferry Dock.* A 5-door Citroen AX rents for 5.000 CFP ($50) for 5 hours, 6.600 CFP ($66) for 8 hours and 7.400 CFP ($74) for 24 hours. A Peugeot 106 or a Mini- Moke costs 200 CFP ($2) more per hour. These rates include unlimited mileage and insurance, or you can rent a car without mileage and insurance included. Rentals are available for several days and by the week or month.

• **Europcar**, *Tel. 56.34.00, has sales offices at the Moorea Airport, Vaiare Ferry Dock, Hotel Moorea Beachcomber Parkroyal, Hotel Sofitel Ia Ora, opposite Maeva Cook's Bay Resort, and the main office is opposite Club Med.* A Fiat Panda rents for 5.000 CFP ($50) for 4 hours, 6.000 CFP ($60) for 8 hours, 7.000 CFP ($70) for 24 hours, and 13.000 CFP ($130) for a weekend. An air-conditioned Mazda 323 or Jeep Korando diesel starts at 10.000 CFP ($100) for 4 hours. A Fun Car is a cross between a car and a scooter and rents for 4.500 CFP ($45) for 4 hours. Scooter rates start at 4.000 CFP ($40) for 4 hours. These rates include unlimited mileage and insurance. You can also rent a car without mileage and insurance included. Bicycles and mountain bikes cost 1.200 CFP ($12) for 4 hours, 1.500 CFP ($15) for 8 hours, 2.000 CFP ($24) for 24 hours and 3.000 CFP ($30) for a weekend.

• **Rando-Cycles**, *Tel. 56.35.02*, rents mountain bikes for 1.500 CFP ($15) a day, or 8 hours. *Their office is facing Vaiare Ferry Dock*, and they will deliver a bike to your hotel on request.

Several of the hotels rent bicycles to their guests. Check with your hotel activities desk for details.

Taxis

You'll find a taxi stand at the airport, *Tel. 56.10.18*, from 6 am to 6:30pm. Some of the drivers don't use their taxi meters, so be sure to negotiate the fare before you get in. Let me warn you that they're expensive. The fare between the airport and ferry dock is 1.000 CFP ($10) for a distance of 2.4 miles (3.9 kilometers). It will cost you 1.150 CFP ($11.50) from the airport to Hotel Bali Hai, 1.300 CFP ($13) to the Cook's Bay Resort Hotel, 1.500 CFP ($15) to the Club Bali Hai in Pao Pao, 3.300 CFP ($33) to Moorea Beachcomber Parkroyal, 3.500 CFP ($35) to Club Med and 3.600 CFP ($36) to the Moorea Village.

Tour & Transport Companies

Some of the Tour and Transport Companies handle round-trip transfers between the airport and ferry dock and your hotel. They will also provide taxi service if you want to dine out in the evening or arrange a special shopping tour. The average fares for the taxi from the ferry dock or the airport are: 800 CFP ($8) to Hotel Sofitel Ia Ora Moorea or to Hotel Bali Hai; 1.000 CFP ($10) to Cook's Bay Hotel or Club Bali Hai; 1.500 CFP ($15) to Hotel Moorea Lagoon; and 2.000 CFP ($20) for all locations between Hotel Moorea Beachcomber Parkroyal and Hotel Moorea

Village. (See the *Land Excursions* listings for Transport Companies that provide this service).

Buses & Le Truck

Public transportation is provided by various kinds of buses and a couple of the traditional wooden bodied *les trucks*. Some of these vehicles are hand-me-downs from the big transport companies in Tahiti. The Bluebird buses and yellow school buses were brought in from California, and are in pretty good shape, but the advertising space inside the bus is void of the publicity you will find anywhere in the States. All these vehicles operate schedules that coincide with the arrivals and departures of the ferries from Tahiti, and with the school programs.

The **bus terminals** *are located beside the Tourism Committee's Visitors Bureau at Le Petit Village opposite Club Med in Haapiti, and at the Vaiare Ferry dock.* The buses leave Le Petit Village Monday through Thursday at 4:45am, 5:45am, 6:45am, 9:45am, 1:45pm and 3:45pm. On Friday a supplementary *le truck* leaves Le Petit Village at 12:45pm. The Saturday schedule is 4:45am, 6:45am, 8:45am, 9:45am, 11:30am, 1:45pm and 3:45pm. The Sunday schedule is 4:45am, 6:45am, 1:45pm, 2:45pm and 4:45pm. From Le Petit Village terminal the buses and *le truck* head in both directions around the island to get to the Vaiare Ferry dock. You just stand beside the road and wave to the driver to stop, and you pay 200 CFP ($2) when you get off.

You can use this service for other purposes in addition to your arrival and departure transfers, and you can even go around the island for 400 CFP ($4), as long as you coordinate your plans with the bus schedules, which operate between 6am and 6pm.

WHERE TO STAY
COOK'S BAY AREA: TEMAE TO PIHAENA
Expensive

HOTEL SOFITEL IA ORA MOOREA, *B.P. 28, 98728 Maharepa, Moorea, Tel. 689/56.12.90, 689/41.04.04 in Papeete, Fax 689/41.05.05. In US Tel. 914/472-0370 or 800/763-4835, Fax 914/472-0451, Internet: http://www.sofitel.com Beside the lagoon at PK 2 in Temae, on northeast coast facing Tahiti, 2 kilometers (1.2 miles) from the airport and 2 kilometers from the ferry dock. 110 bungalows. EP Rates single/double: 23.200 CFP ($232) garden bungalow; 27.800 CFP ($278) beach bungalow; 34.650 CFP ($346.50) deluxe beach bungalow; 44.000 CFP ($440) overwater bungalow. Third adult 4.500 CFP ($45). No charge for children under 12 sharing room. Add 5.600 CFP ($56) per person for breakfast and dinner, and 8.100 CFP ($81) per person for 3 meals daily. Add a supplement of 1.500 CFP ($15) per day for the high seasons of January 1-15, July 15 to August 31, and December 20-31. Add 7% government* *room tax and 1% value added tax to room rates and meal plan. All major credit cards.*

The 110 comfortably appointed Polynesian style cottages are spread over the lagoon and throughout 35 acres of gardens. Your accommodation choice includes 47 garden bungalows, 33 beach bungalows, 10 deluxe beach bungalows and 20 overwater bungalows. All rooms have a bathroom with shower, a minibar, individual safe and direct dial phone. The garden and beach bungalows have overhead fans and the 10 deluxe beach bungalows and 20 overwater bungalows, which opened in December, 1996, each have air-conditioning, hair dryer, color television and tea and coffee facilities. All the bungalows have thatched roofs and are decorated in a tasteful Tahitian style, using bamboo, woven pandanus mats and *tifaifai* appliqué bed covers. The windows and doors are screened and each bungalow has a terrace overlooking Moorea's best white sand beach and clearest lagoon, where swimming and snorkeling is ideal year round.

La Perouse is a Tahitian-style open air restaurant, where dinners are served, featuring Tahitian and international cuisine. The Molokai restaurant is on the beach, adjacent to a spacious bar, where you can enjoy breakfast and lunch in an informal setting, while gazing at the lagoon and the island of Tahiti across the Sea of Moons. You'll find a conference and banqueting room, a wedding chapel and black pearl shop on the premises and a boutique and gift shop adjacent to the reception area. An activities desk and car rental desk are also located in the lobby. Baby sitting services are available on request for approximately 1.000 CFP ($10) per hour.

Among the spacious grounds are a nautical activities center, two tennis courts, a volleyball court and an overflowing swimming pool beside the white sandy beach. Complimentary sports and leisure activities include windsurfing, French bowls, volleyball, Polynesian outrigger paddle canoes, snorkeling equipment, parlor games, a coconut show, slide show and *pareo* show. A Polynesian show with fire dancing is presented each Tuesday, Thursday and Saturday evening, following special buffets.

Moderate
HOTEL BALI HAI, *B.P. 26, Maharepa, Moorea Tel. 689/56.13.59, Fax 689/56.13.27, reservations 689/56.13.52, in California 800/282-1402, in rest of US 800/282-1401, Fax US 714/427-6119, e-mail balihai@pacbell.com Beside lagoon at PK 5, between Moorea airport and Cook's Bay, 5 kilometers (3 miles) from the airport and 9 kilometers (5.5 miles) from the ferry dock. 63 rooms and bungalows. EP Rates single/double: 11.500 CFP ($115) standard room; 14.000 CFP ($140) pool-side bungalow; 16.000 CFP ($160) garden-side bungalow; 17.000 CFP ($170) lagoon view bungalow; 19.500 CFP ($195) beach-front bungalow; 25.000 CFP ($250) lagoon-side bungalow; 28.000 CFP ($280) garden suite; 42.000 CFP ($420) deep overwater bungalow. Third adult*

4.000 CFP ($40). Add 4.500 CFP ($45) per person for breakfast and dinner, and 6.900 CFP ($69) per person for 3 meals daily. Add 7% government room tax and 1% value added tax to room rates and meal plan. All major credit cards.

This American-owned hotel is located at the entrance to Cook's Bay with 63 Polynesian style units. There are 9 overwater bungalows, 4 bungalows half over the water, 5 beachfront bungalows, 6 bungalows with an ocean view, a 2-bedroom garden suite, 9 garden bungalows, 16 poolside bungalows and 12 lanai rooms. Each overwater bungalow unit has a king size bed and single bed and all the other bungalows contain a queen size bed and single bed. All units have a sitting area with overhead fan, a large bathroom with hot water shower, and a mini-refrigerator. The bungalows have tea and coffee making facilities. The reception, boutique, activities desk, restaurant and bar are covered by an immense thatched roof, with an outdoor dining terrace on the beach.

A swimming pool on the road side of the property has a waterfall at one end and a swim-up bar on the other side. Guests can play tennis, paddle an outrigger canoe or surf bike, take a *Liki Tiki* snorkeling excursion or a sunset cruise, or sign up for a picnic on the *motu* with Hiro Kelley at "What to Do on Moorea Tours." Weekly entertainment includes Happy Hours, special barbecue nights, a Tahitian feast each Sunday noon, Tahitian dance shows, arts and crafts demonstrations and tupa crab races. John Hogan, the resident manager, is the fourth "Bali Hai Boy." He's been greeting guests at the hotel since the 1960s.

See more information in the *Best Places to Stay* chapter and the sidebar on the next page.

CLUB BALI HAI, *B.P. 26, Maharepa, Moorea Tel. 689/56.13.68, in California 800/282-1402, in rest of US 800/282-1401, Fax 689/56.19.22, Telex 331FP. Beside the lagoon at PK 8 in Cook's Bay, near Pao Pao, 8 kilometers (5 miles) from the airport and 12 kilometers (7.5 miles) from the ferry dock. 39 rooms and bungalows. EP Rates single/double: 9.000 CFP ($90) mountainside room; 12.000 CFP ($120) bay view room; 18.000 CFP ($180) beach-front bungalow; 24.000 CFP ($240) overwater bungalow with kitchen. Third adult 3.000 CFP ($30). Add 4.500 CFP ($45) per person for breakfast and dinner. Add 7% government room tax and 1% value added tax to room rates and meal plan. All major credit cards.*

Club Bali Hai overlooks the panoramic beauty of Cook's Bay and the surrounding mountains of cathedral peaks and spires. The 39 units include 21 overwater bungalows and 18 rooms in a two-story colonial style building. The thatched roof bungalows are Polynesian in decor, with a bedroom, separate kitchen/dining area and terraces facing the spectacular scenery. The bathrooms have hot water showers. These bungalows are usually occupied by the Vacation Time Share guests, who return year after

HOTEL BALI HAI NOSTALGIA & UTE SINGING

For many return visitors and expatriate American residents of French Polynesia, going to the Hotel Bali Hai is a long-established habit. I stayed here for a week in 1968 and again in 1970 when I was a tourist, and have stayed here countless times when I became a resident of Tahiti. Now that I live on Moorea I still keep going there for lunch, Happy Hour or special barbecue nights. The best Tahitian folkloric show on the island is the Ute (oo-tey) singing presented at the Hotel Bali Hai each Saturday at 6:15pm, when Tahitians from Papetoai village sing the old Polynesian himene (Tahitian hymns) on the terrace outside the **Boom Boom Bar**. As you listen to the harmonious voices and watch the last fading glow of sunset across the lagoon, you can feel the nostalgia for the South Seas, the Polynesians and the good old Bali Hai.

The "Bali Hai Boys" earned a reputation for hospitality, enthusiasm and charm soon after they opened the hotel's first eight bungalows in 1962. **Hugh Kelley, Jay Carlisle** and **Don "Muk" McCallum** were young men from California, who chose to give up the rat race of their former jobs and create their own Garden of Eden, complete with lots of golden-brown Eves.

No tourists ever received more personal attention from the owners of a hotel than we clients who stayed at the Hotel Bali Hai during the growing years. At that time personal attention was about all they had to give the guests, and the Bali Hai Boys were fabulous hosts, full of fun, friendliness and high energy. When a group of reporters from Life Magazine came to the hotel the three "Boys" seduced them with the charms of Moorea and the Hotel Bali Hai, where American tourists could find an authentic culture in a natural environment, while enjoying at least a minimum of creature comforts. When the Hotel Bali Hai made the cover of Life Magazine their success was assured. Throughout the years journalists from national magazines, big city newspapers and travel books gave them good write-ups, and satisfied tourists also helped to spread the word.

The Bali Hai empire developed with the addition of more bungalows, then by opening Bali Hai Hotels on the islands of Huahine and Raiatea, and taking over the old Aimeo Hotel at Cook's Bay on Moorea, which is now the Club Bali Hai. The Raiatea property has since been sold, leaving three hotels for the "Boys" to manage. Hugh Kelley, the head of the team, celebrated his 70th birthday in November, 1997, surrounded by his 10 Polynesian children and some of their kids. Muk went back to California several years ago. Kelley and Jay are still playing their roles as the "Bali Hai Boys" and you might even see them at Happy Hour or the Ute show.

year. The rooms are basically furnished, but be sure to request a bay-side room as the road-side is very noisy most of the day.

There is a restaurant and snack bar, two bars, a boutique, tennis court, fresh water swimming pool with a waterfall and a small white sand beach. *Liki Tiki* snorkeling excursions and sunset cruises are made aboard a covered double canoe. Happy Hour at Club Bali Hai each Tuesday and Friday evenings is an "event" not to be missed. A Tahitian band plays guitars and ukuleles and the tourists, yachties, expatriate American residents and locals all have a great time meeting one another around the big friendly bar beside the bay. The staff, headed by Rose Tetuamahuta, the pretty and efficient manager, are all Tahitians who have worked for the "Bali Hai Boys" for years. Rental cars, scooters and bikes can be rented across the street.

MAEVA COOK'S BAY HOTEL (Cook's Bay Resort Hotel), *B.P. 30, Maharepa, Moorea. Tel. 689/56.10.50, Fax 689/56.29.18. Beside lagoon at PK 7 on east side of Cook's Bay, 7 kilometers (4.3 miles) from the airport and 11 kilometers (7 miles) from the ferry dock. 94 rooms and bungalows. EP Rates single/double: 6.500 CFP ($65) standard room; 8.500 CFP ($85) air conditioned room; 8.500 CFP ($85) garden bungalow; 9.500 CFP ($95) lagoon bungalow. Third adult 2.500 CFP ($25). Family room 10.000 CFP ($100). Add 3.800 CFP ($38) per person for breakfast and dinner. Round-trip transfers from ferry dock or airport, 1.200 CFP ($12) per person. Add 7% government room tax and 1% value added tax to room rates and meal plan. All major credit cards.*

During the past five years the Cook's Bay Resort Hotel has been a favorite choice for budget-minded American visitors, as the price is right and the ambiance is mostly American with a flavor of Polynesia. In February, 1998 the hotel was sold to Béatrice and François Michel, a young French couple from Normandy. Changes are already being made, starting with the name of the hotel. The new owners plan to give the buildings and grounds some much needed maintenance work, in order to bring it up to the standard of a good moderate-priced establishment.

The main building has 70 rooms in a two-story neo-colonial style structure, and there are 24 individual Tahitian style bungalows. All accommodations have overhead fans, refrigerators, hot water kettles and a view of the ocean. This hotel is located at the entrance to Cook's Bay and the view from the lagoon-side bar and Le Jardin restaurant or the overwater restaurant and bar at Fisherman's Wharf is truly breathtaking. The snorkeling adjacent to the pier is some of the best you'll find in Moorea.

The big swimming pool in the gardens is the center of social life, where you'll meet other guests and perhaps form friendships as you sunbathe by the pool, swim a few laps or swap stories over a sandwich and cold beer from the pool bar. Hotel activities include snorkeling equipment and outrigger paddle canoes at no charge. Tahitian dance shows are performed each Tuesday evening following a barbecue dinner, on Thursday evenings after a Tahitian feast, and on Saturday night, along with a Tahitian cookout. The M.U.S.T. Scuba Diving center is just next door and the long pier adjacent to the hotel is a handy place to board a boat to go on a lagoon excursion, picnic tour or sunset cruise. Bicycles can be rented at the Cook's Bay Boutique across the street, where you'll also find the Cook's Bay Pizza.

HOTEL MOOREA LAGOON *has been sold to the Louis Wane Group of Tahiti, who will close the hotel at the end of April, 1998, and will reopen at the end of 1999 as an Outrigger Hotel. Reservations: in US and Canada Tel. 800/ 688-7444, e-mail reservations@outrigger.com. Internet www.outrigger.com*

This sale was announced just 10 days prior to closing. The hotel site is beside the lagoon at PK 13.9 between Cook's Bay and Opunohu Bay, 14 kilometers (8.7 miles) from the airport and 18 kilometers (11 miles) from the ferry dock. The hotel is located in 12 acres of tropical gardens and coconut trees, along a small white sand beach. Only a few of the 45 Polynesian style bungalows will be kept, and a series of overwater bungalows will be built. A restaurant and bar will be built beside the beach, the swimming pool will be moved, and the tennis court will be moved to the mountain side of the road. This hotel is not close to a shopping area or to any other restaurants.

Inexpensive

MOTEL ALBERT, *Pao Pao, Moorea. Tel. 689/56.12.76. Mountainside at PK 8 in Pao Pao, across from Club Bali Hai, 8 kilometers (5 miles) from the airport and 12 kilometers (8 miles) from the ferry dock. EP Rates: room with double bed for one or two people, 4.000 CFP ($40) for one night, 3.000 CFP ($30) for two or more nights, 70.000 CFP ($700) per month; two-room bungalow for one to five people, 7.000 CFP ($70) for one night, 6.000 CFP ($60) for two or more nights, 80.000 CFP ($800) per month; two double bedrooms, 100.000 CFP ($1,000) per month. Extra bed add 1.000 CFP ($10) per day for short stays. Add 1% value added tax to room rates. No credit cards.*

This is a good choice if you are traveling on a tight budget and want to be in the Cook's Bay area, where you can see the famous mountains surrounding the bay. You'll also be within easy walking distance of supermarkets, restaurants and snacks. The 18 units are on a hillside slope decorated with fruit trees and pretty flower gardens. There are 10 two-room bungalows and 8 apartments with kitchens. All units have private bathrooms with hot water, and covered terraces. House linens are furnished.

CHEZ DINA, *PK 12.5, Pihaena, Moorea. Tel. 689/56.10.39. At PK 12.5 in Pihaena, on mountainside between Cook's Bay and Opunohu Bay, 12.5* *kilometers (7.8 miles) from the airport and 16.5 kilometers (10 miles) from the ferry dock. EP Rates: 4.500 CFP ($45), one to three people per day; 5.000 CFP ($50) one to five people per day. Transfers from ferry dock or airport to pension 500 CFP ($5) per person. Add 1% value added tax to room rates. No credit cards.*

Dina's three bungalows are across the street from a small white sand beach and the lagoon. You have a choice of two small or one family-size thatched roof *fares*, each with a kitchenette, terrace and linens furnished, except for towels. Paddle canoes and bicycles are provided for guests. Dina's clientele are usually French or Europeans who speak French. The premises can be quite noisy.

VILLAGE FAIMANO, *Papetoai, Moorea. Tel. 689/56.10.20, Fax 689/56.36.47. Beside lagoon at PK 13.9, close to the Hotel Moorea Lagoon, 14 kilometers (8.7 miles) from the airport and 18 kilometers (11 miles) from the ferry dock. EP Rates: garden bungalow 7.500 CFP ($75) single/double, 8.500 CFP ($85) triple; beach bungalow 9.000 CFP ($90) three-four people; family bungalow 11.500 CFP ($115) four-six people per day. Minimum stay two nights. Reduced Rates for longer stays. Meals served on request. Deposit required. Round-trip transfers 2.000 CFP ($20) per person. Add 1% value added tax to room rates. All major credit cards.*

The location here is very pretty, with a white sand beach and clear lagoon that offers easy swimming. This is a very popular weekend destination for Tahiti residents, and the ambiance is often local style. Your choice of 7 Tahitian style bungalows includes two family size *fares*, each with two rooms with a double bed in each, a mezzanine with a double bed, two single beds in the living room, plus a kitchen and private bathroom with hot water. Or you can rent one of the four smaller *fares*, each with a bedroom and double bed, single beds in the living room, kitchen and private bathroom with hot water. Snorkeling equipment and outrigger paddle canoes are available and you can sunbathe on a floating dock within a few laps from the shore.

FARE NANI, *B.P. 117, Papeete, Tahiti. Tel. 689/56.19.99 or 689/82.79.37. Beside lagoon at PK 13.9, adjacent to Hotel Moorea Lagoon, 14 kilometers (8.7 miles) from the airport and 18 kilometers (11 miles) from the ferry dock. EP Rates: 6.000 CFP ($60) garden bungalow; 7.000 CFP ($70) beach bungalow for two adults and two children under 12 years. Extra mattress add 1.000 CFP ($10) per day. Add 1% value added tax to room rates. No credit cards.*

This pension has the same white sand beach and ocean view as the Hotel Moorea Lagoon and Village Faimano. Three *fares* each have a double bed and a single bed, a private kitchen and bathroom with cold water, plus house linens. Paddle canoes are available for exploring the lagoon.

CHEZ FRANCINE, *B. P. 659, Maharepa, Moorea. Tel. 689/56.13.24. Beside lagoon at PK 14.5 close to Hotel Moorea Lagoon, 14.5 kilometers (9 miles)* *from the airport and 19.5 kilometers (12 miles) from the ferry dock. EP Rates: 6.000 CFP ($60) room single or double per day, 35.000 CFP ($350) per week; 7.500 CFP ($75) room with kitchen single or double per day, 45.000 CFP ($450) per week; 12.000 CFP ($120) house per day, 72.000 CFP ($720) per week. Add 1% value added tax to room rates and meal plan. No credit cards.*

You can choose one of two rooms, with or without a kitchenette, or rent the house. Each room has a private bathroom with hot water. Linens are furnished and paddle canoes are available.

WEST COAST: PAPETOAI TO HAAPITI
Expensive
HOTEL MOOREA BEACHCOMBER PARKROYAL, *B.P. 1019, 98729 Papetoai, Moorea. Tel. 689/55.19.19, Fax 689/55.19.55, in US 800/ 835-7742, e-mail: prkroyal@mail.pf. Beside the lagoon at PK 24 between Papetoai and Haapiti, 24 kilometers (14.8 miles) from the airport and 28 kilometers (17.3 miles) from the ferry dock. 146 rooms and bungalows. EP Rates: air-conditioned room 28.800 CFP ($288); garden bungalow 30.900 CFP ($309); beach-front bungalow 35.000 CFP ($350); overwater bungalow 39.100 CFP ($391). Add 6.000 CFP ($60) for third adult. Add 6.800 CFP ($68) per person for breakfast and dinner, and 9.800 CFP ($98) per person for 3 meals daily. Add 7% government room tax and 1% value added tax to room rates and meal plan. All major credit cards.*

This luxurious hotel is a member of the prestigious Parkroyal collection of 4 1/2 to 5-star hotels managed by the Southern Pacific Hotel Corporation. It covers 3.9 hectares (9.8 acres) of land on a mini-peninsula on the northwestern side of Moorea, between Opunohu Bay and the tourist hotels and shops in the Club Med area of Haapiti. The 10-year old hotel has 49 air-conditioned rooms and 1 suite located in colonial style two-story concrete buildings, each with a balcony or lanai overlooking the lagoon. The 26 garden bungalows, 20 beach bungalows and 50 overwater bungalows are all built in the traditional Polynesian design, with thatched roofs. These are all junior suites, with a separate sitting area, overhead fans and a sundeck with outside shower. Standard amenities in all rooms and bungalows include a king size bed or twin beds, direct dial telephones, color television with video programs, mini-bar/refrigerator, complimentary tea and coffee making facilities, hair dryer, 240/110 volt electrical outlets and complimentary grooming items. The air-conditioned rooms have a combined shower/bathtub and a bidet, and the bungalows have separate bath and shower.

An enormous thatched roof building houses the reception, Fare Nui restaurant for 250 diners, Fare Hana poolside restaurant for 150, Motu Iti bar with seating for 70 people, a conference room for 150 theater-style seats, a guest relations activities desk, tour desk, car and scooter rental desk, gift shop and black pearl shop. Guest services include room service, laundry and valet service, iron and ironing board, currency exchange, safety deposit boxes, and mail and postal service.

The hotel's facilities include a fresh water swimming pool, two tennis courts, white sand beaches, and a complete aquatic sports center with outrigger paddle canoes, glass-bottom boat, Aqua 6 underwater boat, sailing and fishing boats, picnics on the motu and sunset cruises. Bathy's Club has a dive center here. The Dolphin Quest park is a big attraction for people who want to play with the dolphins in an enclosed environment. Helicopter rides are available with a landing pad on the hotel grounds. In addition to a daily program of activities presented at the hotel, you will also have an interesting choice of excursions to discover the romantic beauty of Moorea's seashore and interior valleys.

A *Soirée Merveilleuse* held each Saturday evening is a gastronomic buffet, featuring a variety of fresh seafoods, usually served on the beach under the stars and tropical moon. A Tahitian dance group performs on a stage set between two graceful coconut trees.

Moderate

MOOREA BEACH CLUB, *B.P. 1017, Papetoai, Moorea. Tel. 689/ 56.15.48. Reservations: Tahiti Resort Hotels, B.P. 13019 Punaauia, Tahiti, Tel. 689/43.08.29, Fax 689/41.09.28, Telex 702/428FP. Beside lagoon at PK 25 between Papetoai and Haapiti, 25 kilometers (15.5 miles) from the airport and 29 kilometers (18 miles) from the ferry dock. 40 rooms. EP Rates: air-conditioned room 12.000 CFP ($120) single, double, triple. Add 4.000 CFP ($40) per person for breakfast and dinner, and 5.600 CFP ($56) per person for 3 meals daily. Add 1.800 CFP ($18) per person for transfers from ferry dock or airport. Add 7% government room tax and 1% value added tax to room rates and meal plan. All major credit cards.*

The Moorea Beach Club is adjacent to Les Tipaniers and shares the same pretty white sand beach, dreamy lagoon and possibility of a wide variety of water activities. This hotel has 40 rooms in two-story motel type buildings. The ground level rooms are air-conditioned and have terraces, and the upstairs units have overhead fans and balconies. All the rooms have queen size or twin beds, a sitting area, mini refrigerators and combined bathtub and shower, with 110 volt and 220 volt electricity. They used to have telephones and color television, which have now been removed from the rather spartan furnishings. In addition to the main restaurant and bar, a snack bar serves light lunches beside the tiled swimming pool. Complimentary activities include two tennis courts, volley ball, *petanque* (French bowls), snorkel equipment, outrigger paddle canoes, windsurf boards, floating dock, *pareo* show and coconut show. Each Wednesday evening is Polynesian Night, with a *tamure* show, traditional Tahitian foods and a Tahitian folkloric dance show. Each Saturday evening is theme night, featuring foods and music from the Caribbean, Asia or Spain. In the main building you'll find a small boutique and travel desk. The hotel has seen better days and a renovation project is supposedly on the planning board.

MOOREA FARE CONDOMINIUMS, *B.P. 1052, Papetoai, Moorea Tel. 689/56.26.69, Fax 689/56.26.22. Beside the lagoon at PK 25 adjacent to Moorea Beach Club, 25 kilometers (15.5 miles) from the airport and 29 kilometers (18 miles) from the ferry dock. 43 bungalows. EP Rates: 15.500 CFP ($155) garden bungalow with kitchen double/triple, 18.000 CFP ($180) for five or six people; 18.400 CFP ($184) beach bungalow, double/triple, 20.400 CFP ($204) for five or six people. Add 7% government room tax and 1% value added tax to room rates and meal plan. Mastercard, Visa.*

If you bring your family and want a place on a white sand beach where you can cook your meals, the 43 bungalows all have kitchens and sleeping space for several people. Families from Tahiti often spend the weekends here, as the kids can swim in the Moorea Beach Club pool and in the lagoon and there are plenty of water activities available in the vicinity. The bungalows have overhead fans, hot water showers and private terraces.

HOTEL LES TIPANIERS, *B.P. 1002, Papetoai, Moorea. Tel. 689/ 56.12.67, Fax 689/56.29.25, in US 800/521-7242, Fax 213/256-0647. Beside the lagoon at PK 25 in Haapiti, between Moorea Beach Club and Club Med, 25 kilometers (15.5 miles) from the airport and 29 kilometers (18 miles) from the ferry dock. 22 bungalows. EP Rates: standard room 8.500 CFP ($85) single, 10.200 CFP ($102) double; garden bungalow with kitchen 12.000 CFP ($120); seaside bungalow with kitchen 13.500 CFP ($135) single or double; Add 1.900 CFP ($19) per extra person. Add 3.600 CFP ($36) per person for breakfast and dinner. Add 7% government room tax and 1% value added tax to room rates and meal plan. All major credit cards.*

"Les Tipaniers" means frangipani or plumeria, the trees of white, pink, orange and yellow flowers you will see and smell throughout the gardens of this very Polynesian style hotel. The 22 thatched roof bungalows are rather close together and the best choice is one of the beach bungalows, where you can sit on your terrace and admire the white sandy beach and aquamarine lagoon. Across this watery playground are three *motu* islets, which you can reach by outrigger paddle canoe. The small bungalows, all with balconies, have screens on the windows but not on the sliding glass doors, and 13 bungalows have fully equipped kitchenettes. The beachside restaurant-bar is open for breakfast, lunch and sunset cocktails, and the main restaurant is open for dinner. Free activities include canoes, snorkeling gear, volley-ball, ping-pong, French bowls and bicycles. The Tip'Nautic activities center will arrange your outings on the lagoon and you can go for a dive with Scubapiti, which is also on the premises. You can easily walk to several restaurants, shops, boutiques and black pearl shops from your hotel.

LES TIPANIERS ITI, *an annex to the main hotel, is located beside the lagoon at PK 20 in Papetoai, 5 kilometers (3 miles) from Hotel Les Tipaniers, 20 kilometers (12.4 miles) from the airport and 24 kilometers (14.8 miles) from the ferry dock. 12 beach bungalows with kitchens can accommodate up to six people. EP Rates: 7.500 CFP ($75). Meal plan available. Add 7% government room tax and 1% value added tax to room rates and meal plan. All major credit cards.*

"Little Tipaniers" has five thatched-roof bungalows with kitchenettes and beds for four people. A sun deck type wharf overlooks the entrance to magnificent Opunohu Bay, and for 500 CFP ($5) you can catch a shuttle boat here to go to the beach at the main hotel or to the *motu* islets. A complimentary land shuttle service will take you to Les Tipaniers in the morning, returning after lunch, and you can go back to the main restaurant in the evening for dinner.

CLUB MEDITERRANEE MOOREA, *B.P. 575, Papeete, Tahiti. Tel. 689/55.00.00, Fax 689/55.00.10, in Papeete Tel. 689/42.96.99, Fax 689/ 42.16.83, in US 800/528-3100. Beside the lagoon at PK 26 in Haapiti on northwest coast, 26 kilometers (16 miles) from the airport and 30 kilometers (18.6 miles) from the ferry dock. 350 rooms. AP Rates: 14.000 CFP ($140) single; 28.000 CFP ($280) double, all meals and most activities included. Add 7% government room tax and 1% value added tax to room rates and meal plan. All major credit cards.*

Each of the 350 bungalows at Club Med can sleep two people, for a total capacity of 700 GM's (*gentils membres*). You'll find the ideal setting of white sand beach, clear warm lagoon and three *motu* islets nearby to enjoy a social, fun-filled vacation with a wide range of organized activities. Club Med has a huge dining hall and a smaller, more intimate restaurant, plus 2 bars, a boutique, black pearl shop, library, bank, activities desk, travel desk and disco. The package price covers lodging, all meals, the use of five tennis courts, water-skiing, scuba diving, snorkeling, glass-bottom boat, outrigger paddle canoes, windsurfing, yoga classes, body sculpting, water aerobics, boat trips to the *motu*, picnics on a private *motu*, nightly entertainment and frequent Tahitian dance shows. An extensive program of optional activities includes a day trip to Tetiaroa by plane or boat and a day trip to Bora Bora.

HOTEL HIBISCUS, *B.P. 1009, Papetoai, Moorea. Tel. 689/56.12.20, Fax 689/56.20.69. Beside the lagoon at PK 27 in Haapiti, next door to Club Med, 27 kilometers (16.7 miles) from the airport and 31 kilometers (19.2 miles) from the ferry dock. 30 bungalows. EP Rates: garden bungalow 11.000 CFP ($110) single, double or triple; beach bungalow 13.000 CFP ($130) single, double or triple. Add 1.000 CFP ($10) for additional bed. Add 3.900 CFP ($39)* *per person, for breakfast and dinner, and 6.900 CFP ($69) per person for 3 meals daily. A Continental breakfast is 780 CFP ($7.80). Add 7% government room tax and 1% value added tax to room rates and meal plan. All major credit cards.*

The 30 thatched roof bungalows are compact but comfortable, and with the aid of brightly colored tie-dyed sheets and curtains the rooms are quite cheery. Each bungalow contains a double bed and a single bed, with space to add another single bed. They have tiled bathrooms with hot water showers, a separate toilet compartment, double sinks, a kitchen corner with a mini-refrigerator and three-burner hot plate, plus cooking and eating utensils, wardrobe closet, ceiling fan, and a covered terrace with table and chairs, where you can enjoy your meals in privacy. Should you feel like eating out, you can try the French, Italian and Tahitian home style food at the Sunset Restaurant and Pizzeria, built over the white sand beach in front of Hotel Hibiscus. In addition to a fresh water swimming pool in the spacious gardens, you can paddle an outrigger canoe to the three *motu* islets across the lagoon, rent a pedal boat for 500 CFP ($5) per hour, or pay 5.000 CFP ($50) for a two-hour rental of a Moana Loca Boat, a motor boat for four passengers that doesn't require a permit. The white sand beach in front of the hotel is the center of all kinds of nautical activities. Sylvette and Jean-Claude Perelli, the managers of Hotel Hibiscus, are very helpful and friendly, and will make sure that your visit is a happy event.

FARE VAIMOANA, *B.P. 1181, Papetoai, Moorea. Tel./Fax 689/56.17.14. Beside the lagoon at PK 27 in Haapiti, west of Club Med, 27 kilometers (16.7 miles) from the airport and 31 kilometers (19.2 miles) from the ferry dock. 11 bungalows. EP Rates: garden bungalow 9.000 CFP ($90) single or double, beach bungalow 12.000 CFP ($120) single or double. Add 2.000 CFP ($20) for additional adult. Add 3.300 CFP ($33) per person for breakfast and dinner, and 5.000 CFP ($50) per person for 3 meals daily. Add 7% government room tax and 1% value added tax to room rates and meal plan. All major credit cards.*

This small hotel is built along a pretty white sand beach, close to other hotels, restaurants, boutiques and black pearl shops. The white concrete bungalows are topped with pandanus roofs, attractively decorated with bamboo furniture and precious woods and seashells. Each bungalow can sleep up to four people and has a private terrace facing the lagoon. They are equipped with an overhead fan, private bathroom with hot water shower, telephone and individual safe. The thatched roof restaurant is open to the sea, with a Polynesian flavor, tastefully decorated with flowers and ferns and Marquesan tikis. You can watch television or play games in the salon or watch the sunset from the central patio. The rooms are not screened and the ambiance here is very French.

HOTEL MOOREA VILLAGE NOA NOA, *B.P. 1008, Papetoai, Moorea. Tel. 689/56.10.02, Fax 689/56.22.11. Beside the lagoon at PK 27 in Haapiti,* *west of Club Med, 27 kilometers (16.7 miles)) from the airport and 31 kilometers (19.2 miles) from the ferry dock by the north coast. 80 bungalows. EP Rates: 8.000 CFP ($80) garden bungalow, single, 9.000 CFP ($90) double, 11.500 CFP ($115) for three or four people; 10.500 CFP ($105) beach bungalow single, 12.500 CFP ($125) double, 13.500 CFP ($135) for three or four people; 15.000 CFP ($150) garden bungalow with kitchen; 15.000 CFP ($150) double for beach-front bungalow with kitchen, 17.000 CFP ($170) for three-four people, and 19.000 CFP ($190) for five-six people. Add 3.900 CFP ($39) per person for breakfast and dinner, and 5.400 CFP ($54) per person for 3 meals daily. Add 7% government room tax and 1% value added tax to room rates and meal plan. All major credit cards.*

This hotel is popular with Australians and New Zealanders, who appreciate the value for money aspect as well as the location, service and wide range of activities available. The 80 Polynesian style bungalows, all with verandas, are located in the garden or along a white sand beach and 14 are equipped with kitchens. The windows and doors are screened, there is an overhead fan in the bedroom, hot water showers, televisions, and beds for three or four people. There is a reputable restaurant and bar, boutique, activities desk, fresh water swimming pool, 2 tennis courts and free use of outrigger paddle canoes and snorkeling equipment. A Saturday night barbecue and Sunday noon Tahitian feast are followed by Tahitian dance shows, and a Tahitian trio plays island tunes for Happy Hour three nights a week. Unusual tours and excursions are listed in the reception area at the activities desk. See more information in *Best Place to Stay* chapter.

HOTEL LINAREVA, *B.P. 1, Haapiti, Moorea. Tel./Fax 689/56.15.35. Beside the lagoon at PK 34 in Haapiti, 21 kilometers (13 miles) from the ferry dock and 25 kilometers (15.5 miles) from the airport around the south coast. 5 bungalows. EP Rates: garden room with kitchen 7.200 CFP ($72) single, 8.200 CFP ($82) double; beach-front room with kitchen 9.500 CFP ($95) single, 10.500 CFP double ($105); beach-front bungalow with kitchen 11.200 CFP ($112) single, 12.200 CFP ($122) double; suite with kitchen 15.600 CFP ($156) for up to four people. Add 1.700 CFP ($17) for additional adult. Add 7% government room tax and 1% value added tax to room rates and meal plan. All major credit cards.*

Eric Lussiez and Florian Pilloud, who own the very popular floating restaurant Linareva-Le Bateau, also have five bungalows in the gardens overlooking a white sand beach and Moorea's sunset sea. The Polynesian style bungalows are equipped with kitchens, private bathrooms with shower and bathtub, overhead fans and television. Bicycles, snorkeling gear and outrigger canoes are available for guests and there's a sunbathing deck beside the restaurant and bar. Although this hotel is far from most activity, you can join the fun at Stephanie's Oasis, a bar and hangout for tourists next door.

POLYNESIAN BUNGALOWS, *B. P. 1234, Papetoai, Moorea. Tel. 689/ 56.30.20/56.30.77, Fax 689/56.32.15. Beside the lagoon at PK 30 in Haapiti adjacent to Tiki Village, 26 kilometers (16 miles) from the ferry dock and 30 kilometers (18.6 miles) from the airport around the south side of the island. 10 bungalows. EP Rates: garden bungalow 8.000 CFP ($80) single or double. Add 1.000 CFP ($10) for third adult. Add 7% government room tax and 1% value added tax to room rates. All major credit cards.*

These are not Moorea's most ideal bungalows unless you want to be next door to the Tiki Theater Village. These concrete units with thatched roofs, owned by Maria and Guy Dupont, have a double bed in the sleeping-living-kitchen area, and a mezzanine reached by a ladder, where you'll find more beds, with a total accommodation capacity of five people. You'll find a refrigerator and tea/coffee facilities in the kitchen corner. The private bathrooms have hot water showers and hairdryers. An overhead fan will help to keep you a little cooler and a terrace provides a nice place to sit and admire the swaying palms towering above the gardens of croton and hibiscus.

The beach is only 80 meters (262 feet) distant, where you can watch the Tiki Village activities as you wade in the tepid lagoon or watch a spectacular sunset to the sound of *pu* shells, blown by the muscular tattooed men who perform several times a week during the special Tahitian Evenings at Tiki Theater Village.

Inexpensive

FARE MATOTEA, *B.P. 1111, Papetoai, Moorea. Tel. 689/56.14.36. Beside the lagoon at PK 29 in Haapiti, 25 kilometers (15.5 miles) from the ferry dock and 29 kilometers (18 miles) from the airport, by way of the south coast. EP Rates: 8.500 CFP ($85) bungalow up to four people per day; 10.500 CFP ($105) up to six people per day. Deposit required. Add 1% value added tax to room rates. No credit cards.*

Eight houses are placed rather far apart on a very spacious grassy property by the sea. Five of the *fares* contain one room with a double bed and two sofa beds, and the other three each have two rooms with a double bed and private kitchen, with a communal bathroom and hot water. Linens furnished. You'll need a car or scooter to get around.

FARE MANUIA, *Haapiti, Moorea. Tel. 689/56.26.17. Beside the lagoon at PK 30 in Haapiti, 26 kilometers (16 miles) from the ferry dock and 30 kilometers (18.6 miles) from the airport, by way of the south coast. EP Rates: garden bungalow 8.000 CFP ($80) up to four people per day, 10.000 CFP ($100) up to six people per day; beach bungalow 12.000 CFP ($120) up to six* *people per day. Add 1.000 CFP ($10) per day for extra mattress. Two night minimum. Add 1% value added tax to room rates. No credit cards.*

The five fairly new *fares* include two with a bedroom with a double bed and two single beds, kitchen and bathroom with hot water, plus three units with a double bedroom and two double mattresses on the mezzanine, kitchen and private bathroom with hot water. House linens are furnished and outrigger paddle canoes are available for your use. This pension is far from the stores and restaurants, so you'll be better equipped by renting wheels. Jeanne speaks pretty good English.

MOOREA FARE AUTI URA, *Tiahura, Haapiti, Moorea. Tel. 689/ 56.14.47; Fax 689/56.30.22. On mountainside at PK 27, across road from Moorea Camping and 500 meters from Club Med, 27 kilometers (16.7 miles) from the airport and 31 kilometers (19.2 miles) from the ferry dock. EP Rates: 6.000 CFP ($60) per day single or double. Add 2.000 CFP ($20) per day for third adult. Two night minimum. Add 1% value added tax to room rates. Mastercard, Visa.*

You'll have access to a white sandy beach by walking across the road and through the Moorea Camping grounds. Five bungalows in the garden each have one room, a mezzanine, private kitchen and bathroom with hot water and a terrace. Linens furnished. These bungalows are well situated close to hotels, shops and boutiques, and the long white sand beach provides all kinds of activities and entertainment.

CHEZ BILLY RUTA, *Haapiti, Moorea. Tel. 689/56.12.54. Beside the lagoon at PK 28 in Haapiti, 28 kilometers (17.4 miles) from the airport and 32 kilometers (19.8 miles) from the ferry dock. EP Rates: room 3.000 CFP ($30) person; bungalow 4.000 CFP ($40) person per day; bungalow with kitchenette 5.000 CFP ($50) person per day. Add 500 CFP ($5) daily for extra mattress. Add 1% value added tax to room rates. No credit cards.*

The best thing going here is the white sand beach and lagoon just in front of the small bungalows. The bungalows are okay for young surfers and others who are traveling on a low budget. Five bungalows have a kitchenette and private bathroom with cold water, and seven bungalows have two single beds and a private bathrooms with cold water and no kitchenette. You'll also find 10 rooms with a double bed, a communal kitchen and bathroom with cold water. House linens are furnished for bungalows and rooms. There's a huge dance hall next door to the bungalows, which gets really noisy on Saturday nights.

MOOREA CAMPING, *Tiahura, Haapiti, Moorea. Tel. 689/56.14.47; Fax 689/56.30.22. Beside lagoon at PK 27 in Haapiti, 500 meters from Club Med, 27 kilometers (16.7 miles) from the airport and 31 kilometers (19.2 miles) from the ferry dock. EP Rates: seaside "fare" 4.000 CFP ($40) single or double per day; mezzanine "fare" 5.000 CFP ($50) up to four people; bed in dormitory 1.000 CFP ($10) person per day, 800 CFP ($8) person for each additional day; room 3.000 CFP ($30) single or double, 2.000 CFP ($20) for each additional* *day; camping 800 CFP ($8) person per day, 700 CFP ($7) person for each additional day. Add 1% value added tax to room rates. No credit cards.*

This is a good gathering place for backpackers and campers and adventurers from all parts of the globe. You'll find simple but clean accommodations, a pretty white sand beach and lots of organized activities available for your choice. There are five *fares* with a double bed on the ground floor, plus another double bed on the mezzanine, and a private bathroom with hot water and refrigerator. Seven rooms have double or single beds, and a 6-room dormitory *fare* has four beds in each room. A communal kitchen and dining room are built beside the beach, and the communal bathrooms have cold water. House linens furnished. Camp ground available.

CHEZ NELSON AND JOSIANE–BACKPACKERS' BEACH CLUB, *Tiahura, Haapiti, Moorea. Tel. 689/56.15.18. Beside the lagoon at PK 27 in Haapiti, 27.5 kilometers (17 miles) from the airport and 31.5 kilometers (19.5 miles) from the ferry dock. EP Rates: 3.000 CFP ($30) single or double first day, 2.500 CFP ($25) for each additional day; family "fare" 6.000 CFP ($60) single or double; beach cabin 2.500 CFP ($25) single or double, 2.200 CFP ($22) for each additional day; bed in dormitory 1.200 CFP ($12), 1.000 CFP ($10) for each additional day; camping 700 CFP ($7) person and 500 CFP ($5) per person for each additional day. Add 1% value added tax to room rates. No credit cards.*

In addition to a campground by the sea, this backpacker's hostel offers three family size *fares*, each with a double bed, private kitchen and bathroom with hot water. You'll also have a choice of four smaller *fares* with kitchens, sharing the bathroom and hot water showers, plus five beach cabins with two single beds, sharing the kitchen and bathroom with hot water. In addition, two dormitories each have five rooms with two single beds. These guests also share a communal kitchen and bathroom with cold water. House linens furnished. This is a popular campground and backpacker's hangout, and Josiane has all the information on activities available on land or sea. Her temper gets a little short sometimes, as she possesses what the French call *caractère*.

AFAREAITU
Inexpensive

CHEZ PAULINE, *PK 9, on mountainside in center of Afareaitu village, 5 kilometers (3 miles) from the ferry dock and 9 kilometers (5.6 miles) from the airport. Tel. 56.11.26. EP Rates with breakfast included: room with single bed 4.000 CFP ($40); room with two beds 5.000 CFP ($50); room with five beds. 10.000 CFP ($100). All meals served on request. Add 1% value added tax to room rates and meal plan. No credit cards.*

This is Moorea's oldest hotel, with five big rooms located in an old colonial style wooden house with a deep veranda. One room has four single beds and the other four rooms each have a double bed and a single bed, plus there are five single beds on the veranda. The mattresses are recent and the place is clean and very colorful. All guests share the old fashioned bathroom.

The surrounding gardens are filled with fruit trees, exotic flowers and vines and lots of ferns. Pauline Teariki, who operated this pension until she died at 83 years of age, earned a great reputation for her delicious food. Her recipes are still followed, and you'll certainly have a few memorable meals served in the dining *fare*, which has a sand floor and thatch roof. If you are looking for a scene right out of the pages written by Somerset Maugham, then you'll find it at Chez Pauline. The only problem with that idea is that you may be the only characters in this scenario, as guests are few and far between these days.

WHERE TO EAT
COOK'S BAY: MAHAREPA TO PAO PAO
Expensive

TE HONU ITI, *PK 8, beside Cook's Bay, Pao Pao, Tel. 56.19.84. Mastercard, Visa. Open daily 11:30am-3pm and 6-9:30pm.*

To the ancient Polynesians the turtle, *honu*, was a sacred animal, reserved only for the privilege of their highest chiefs and priests. Restaurant Te Honu Iti (the little turtle) is today's privileged place for gourmets in search of Moorea's finest French cuisine. You may even say it's worth the airfare to Tahiti just to gaze at the romantic scenery of Cook's Bay, bordered by pineapple fields and fairy castle mountains. You will have the best view while dining on the overwater terrace of this simply decorated but well placed restaurant.

Roger Igual, owner and master chef of Te Honu Iti, won the *Concours National de la Poêle d'Or* in 1974. This is France's most prestigious diploma for chefs. That same year Roger brought his cooking skills to Tahiti, and settled in Moorea in 1991.

The menu at Te Honu Iti includes a varied selection of seafoods: salmon of the gods, shark and *meka* (swordfish) from the ocean depths, *cigales* (slipper lobsters), mussels, shrimp and calamaris. Roger's famous French dishes of *coq au vin, civet de porcelet* and *Tournedos Rossini* can be followed by a locally made sorbet of corosol, mango or papaya. His most popular desserts are the rich *profiteroles* or papaya baked in coconut cream. A special tourist menu gives you a choice of meat or fish, a green salad, dessert and a glass of wine or beer, for 2.400 CFP ($24). The luncheon menu includes hamburgers, fresh tuna burgers, fresh fruit salads and mango milkshakes. Roger's faithful staff includes his Chinese wife and two sons. Free transportation is provided from Hotels Moorea Lagoon, Bali Hai, Cook's Bay Resort and Club Bali Hai.

LE COCOTIER, *PK 4.7, mountainside, Maharepa. Tel. 56.12.10. American Express, Diners, Visa. Open 11:30am-2:30pm 7:30-9:30pm. Closed Sunday.*

The management of this small restaurant has changed frequently over the years, but it has always served a good quality of French cuisine and seafood. A chalkboard beside the road tells you whether the *plat du jour* is *choucroute, couscous, poulet champignons* or *saumon des dieux*. Some of the regular clientele are French doctors and school teachers, who get together once a month to sample the culinary skills of the amateur chefs in the group. Pascal, the manager and chef, invites you to be chef of the day and bring your friends along to enjoy your special recipe.

LE PECHEUR, *PK 6, mountain side, Cook's Bay, Maharepa. Tel. 56.36.12. American Express, Mastercard, Visa. Open 11am-2:30pm and 5:30-9:30pm. Closed Sunday all day and Monday at lunch.*

Here you will find good seafood in a Tahitian setting. While having lunch inside the thatched roof restaurant you have a clear view of the shining turquoise waters of Cook's Bay across the road. And at night the tiki torches will light your way into this welcoming restaurant, complete with fishnets and bamboo fish traps. Syd Pollock, the owner, has been in the hotel and restaurant business in Moorea for almost 30 years. He owned the Maui Beach hotel and nightclub in Haapiti when I first met him in 1971, and he later built the Coconut House in Maharepa. Both hotels are gone now, and Syd devotes his energies and talents to his two restaurants, Le Pêcheur, which he took over for the second time in mid-1997, and Alfredo's, his Italian restaurant in Pao Pao.

The chalkboard in front of the restaurant lists the seafood specials, which may include fresh crabs and lobster, salmon of the gods (moon fish), *thazar* (wahoo), and shrimp from the farm in Opunohu Bay. Lasagna and *osso bucco* and a few other pasta dishes have been added to the menu just in case you don't want to eat seafood.

Moderate
ALFREDO'S, *PK 8.5, mountain side, Cook's Bay, Pao Pao Tel. 56.17.71. American Express, Mastercard, Visa. Open 11am-2:30pm and 5:30-9:30pm. Closed Monday noon.*

This is my favorite restaurant in Moorea. I go here often for the food, music, ambiance and fun. Syd Pollock, who also owns Le Pêcheur, gives you a choice of Italian or French cuisine, and whatever you order will be good most of the time. The scampi and garlic shrimp, for 1.800 CFP ($18), are especially recommended, although I usually choose the scallop of veal with Milano sauce, which is a tomato-garlic combination, served with spaghetti, for 1.800 CFP ($18). You can also order from a choice of 10 pizzas, for 1.150 CFP ($11.50). The decor fits the menu, with green and red table cloths, just like in Italy, and white patio furniture for a light-hearted setting. Whether you dine inside the restaurant or on the covered terrace, you'll be able to hear the music Syd chooses from his collection of jazz, soft Brazilian sambas and old favorites sung by Louis Armstrong or Frank Sinatra. Manager Christian Boucheron and his team provide very friendly service, which does slow down when the place fills up. Free transportation is provided from the hotels in the Cook's Bay area, and this restaurant is almost always crowded with American tourists in the evening, creating a very lively atmosphere.

LE MAHOGANY, *PK 5, mountainside, Maharepa. Tel. 56.39.73. Mastercard, Visa. Open 11am-2:30pm and 6-9:30pm. Closed Wednesday.*

Blondine is the attractive Tahitian lady who owns this large wooden restaurant, which is located beside the Horue gym, Moorea's only health club. When coming from the ferry dock or airport this will be the first restaurant you see. A street-side chalkboard lists the daily specials, which may be rabbit in white wine sauce, *blanquette de veau, sole meunière* or *ragout*, beef stew. In addition to the French cuisine, Blondine serves Chinese and Tahitian dishes at moderate prices, and you can also get a sandwich and freshly squeezed pineapple juice. The ambiance is definitely local style. A few times I've been here in the evening when Blondine and all her clients were dancing.

CAPRICE DES ILES, *PK 7.4, mountain side, Cook's Bay, Maharepa. Tel. 56.44.24. Mastercard, Visa. Open 11:30am-2pm and 6-9:30pm. Closed Wednesday.*

Sylvette and Patrick Giraud-Porquez are a young French couple with a determination to make their restaurant a success. They took over the rambling thatched roof location that was formerly known as Fare Manava, a Chinese restaurant that closed several years ago. After making the necessary repairs to the building, they opened the Caprice des Iles in April, 1996, providing a new gathering place for residents and visitors to the island. Lunch specials are printed on the chalkboard outside, which may be chicken and lemon sauce, fried chicken, leg of lamb or grilled mahi mahi. Some of the chef's dinner creations include *bavarois de saumon fumé, profiterole de langoustes*, and fresh Moorea shrimp in passion fruit vinegar. Traditional dishes are beef filet with morilles, sweet and sour pork with pineapple, and duck filet. The Chinese food they serve is also good. Live musical entertainment adds to the ambiance on Friday or Saturday evenings.

CHEZ JEAN-PIERRE, *PK 9, beside the quay in Cook's Bay, Pao Pao. Tel. 56.18.51. Mastercard, Visa. Open 11:15am-2:30pm and 6:15-9:30pm. Closed Wednesday.*

This is the only restaurant on this side of the island that features Chinese food. Jean-Pierre Tetuanui, who is Tahitian with a Chinese wife, serves succulent suckling pig roasted to a crisp, accompanied by a bowl of coconut milk. The fried shrimp is good and I like the *aubergine farcie*, the stuffed eggplant. Some of the local connoisseurs of Chinese cuisine don't give this place a high rating, but I've never been disappointed with my choices. Free transportation is provided if your hotel is in the Cook's Bay vicinity.

FISHERMAN'S WHARF, *PK 7, Cook's Bay, Maharepa. Tel. 56.10.50. All credit cards. Open 6:30-9pm. Closed Sunday and Monday.*

This spacious overwater restaurant has a fantastic view of Cook's Bay and the peaked mountains that fringe the mirror-like waters of the bay and lagoon. It is part of the Maeva Cook's Bay Resort Hotel complex, separated from the main hotel by a parking lot and a few bungalows. This is primarily a seafood restaurant, where you can get an order of fish and chips, but the menu also includes chicken and meat dishes. The quality of the food depends on who's in the kitchen. The service can be very slow.

LA CASE, *PK 5.5, seaside on Cook's Bay, Maharepa. Tel. 56.42.95. American Express, Mastercard, Visa. Open 9am-2:30pm and 5-9:30pm. Closed Wednesday.*

In May, 1997, Eric and Claudie Berset opened the only Swiss restaurant in French Polynesia, taking over the place that had formerly served cuisine from the Antilles. Eric, who is the chef, is from Gruyère in the mountains of Switzerland, and his menu features several cheese dishes. You may want to try the pork steak with a *gratin* of gruyère, the *ravioli* of escargots on a bed of leeks, or the *tagliatelles* with ham and cream.

Inexpensive

PATISSERIE LE SYLESIE, *PK 5, Maharepa, in shopping center on mountain side, along with Socredo Banque and the post office. Tel. 56.15.88. Mastercard, Visa. Open daily 6:30am-6pm.*

Here is the ideal place to sit and write your post cards while enjoying something good to eat and drink. You can exchange your dollars at the bank, buy post cards at Kina newsstand, write them at Le Sylesie and mail them at the post office, all in the same small center. In addition to a tempting selection of ham and cheese croissants, quiches and pizzas, you may want to try a *pain bagnat* filled with chicken or ham, for 480 CFP ($4.80). A hamburger or fishburger is 380 CFP ($3.80) and a hot-dog with fries is 600 CFP ($6). The *poisson cru* here is only 500 CFP ($5), and is very good. After 11am they serve steak and fries, with rice or salad for 880 CFP ($8.80), shrimp curry for 1.000 CFP ($10) and mahi mahi for 1.280 ($12.80). In addition to the fresh fruit juices, you can also order beer and cider. You will also have a good choice of ice creams and you don't want to miss the *parfait au mimosa* for dessert.

L'ANANAS BLEU, *PK 8, across the road from Club Bali Hai in Pao Pao. Tel. 56.12.06. American Express, Mastercard, Visa. Open 7am-3pm. Closed Monday.*

This is the place you'll want to go for a very affordable breakfast, snack or lunch. Ham or bacon and eggs are 400 CFP ($4), waffles, pancakes, and crêpes are 300-500 CFP ($3-$5) and a fruit plate is 500 CFP ($5). This was the old Snack Crêperie and that name is still on the front, along with a Top Burger Drive-In sign.

This is my favorite luncheon stop and I recommend the hamburgers with fries for 600 CFP ($6) and the *poisson cru* for 800 CFP ($8). The chalkboard beside the road often announces grilled lagoon fish (served whole with head and eyes intact), chicken curry, roast chicken or beef stew, each for less than 1.000 CFP ($10). Grilled lobster is 2.800 CFP ($28). Soft drinks are 200 CFP ($2), iced tea is 300 CFP ($3), and you can order a milkshake for 350 CFP ($3.50). No alcohol is served.

The "Blue Pineapple" is operated by Matahi Hunter, with the assistance of his parents, Vero and Charley Hunter, who ran the Hotel Aimeo (now Club Bali Hai) for many years, along with Christa Winkelstroeter, Vero's sister. Matahi learned to cook at the hotel school in Tahiti, and now uses his talents to satisfy his clients, who are local residents as well as tourists.

JULES ET CLAUDINE, *PK 9, beside the quay and fish market in Cook's Bay, Pao Pao. No credit cards. Closed Sunday.*

This is a stationary *roulotte* where you can order your *casse-croûte, poisson cru, steak-frites, chow mien* or other quickly prepared foods, and sit at the tables in the courtyard of Te Fare Hotu Rau, the Fish Cooperative. Or you can take it with you. The servings are generous and you can eat for under 1.000 CFP ($10). The quality of the food varies.

SNACK ROTUI, *PK 9.5, beside Cook's Bay, just after Are's Supermarket and Supersonics. Tel. 56.18.16. No credit cards. Closed Monday.*

You can sit on a stool at the sheltered counter, eat at one of the tables in back or pick up a sandwich and soft drink, a *poisson cru, chow mien,* or other prepared Chinese dishes served with rice for 500 CFP ($5). Don't resist having a piece of yummy chocolate cake at this popular fast food snack. The tuna *casse-croûtes* for 120 CFP ($1.20) are also good here, and you'll have a good view of the sailboats anchored in Cook's Bay.

WEST COAST: HAAPITI
Expensive

LINAREVA-LE BATEAU, *PK 34, Haapiti. Tel. 56.15.35. All credit cards. Open daily 11am-9pm.*

When the *Tamarii Moorea* finished its long career ferrying passengers and freight between Tahiti and Moorea, it metamorphosed as a floating restaurant, safely anchored in the lagoon in front of Hotel Linareva. Eric Lussiez and Florian Pilloud lovingly restored the old boat, outfitting the dining room and bar with large windows, polished wood, shining brass and nautical antiques.

Whether you are touring Moorea with a guided tour or rental vehicle, you'll want to stop here for lunch and return again for dinner. This is not only Moorea's most unusual restaurant, with a panoramic view of the reef and mountains, but the cuisine is also highly praised by Moorea's most discerning gourmands. I think it's the best restaurant on the island because of the varied selection of appetizers and fish dishes offered. The menus are printed in French and English on two chalkboards, with appetizers on one board and the main courses on the other.

The first course choices range from 850 CFP ($8.50) for vegetable soup to 2.900 CFP ($29) for *foie gras*. They include a Greek salad with feta cheese, an endive salad with Roquefort cheese, fried calamaries and *crabe au gratin*. The main course dishes are priced at 1.750 CFP ($17.50) to 2.450 CFP ($24.50), offering mahi mahi in ginger sauce, parrot fish in vanilla sauce, barracuda in a pink peppercorn sauce, jack fish, salmon of the gods, reef lobster or shark in a parsley garlic sauce. There are also several shrimp and meat dishes. The bar serves a wide range of exotic cocktails and the wine list is extensive.

An afternoon snack service has been added to the dining repertoire, with a modified version of the menu available between 2-6pm daily except Sunday. During these hours you may order a hot-dog for 400 CFP ($4), a hamburger with fries for 980 CFP ($9.80), soups, salads, omelets, and a delicious pasta with salmon ravioli and basil cream sauce, for 1.250 CFP ($12.50).

Transportation is available from hotels as far away as the Moorea Beachcomber Parkroyal, for 400 CFP ($4) per person. Reserve before 6pm for this service.

L'AVENTURE, *PK 27, seaside, Haapiti. Tel. 56.23.36. American Express, Mastercard, Visa. Open 12-2pm and 7-9pm. Closed Monday night and Tuesday.*

Classical French cuisine is prepared by Chef Bernard Frerot, and Carole Stiehr oversees the dining service in this intimate restaurant. If you like rich sauces, then you'll love Bernard's cooking. For lighter fare, there's always *poisson cru*.

LE PAPAYER, *PK 30, at Tiki Village in Haapiti. Tel. 56.18.97/ 56.10.86. American Express, Mastercard, Visa. Open daily 12-3pm and 6-10pm nightly except Monday.*

This is a good luncheon choice while you are visiting the traditional Tahitian style Tiki Village. The thatched roof open-air restaurant overlooks the lagoon and coral reef, providing a romantic setting as well as good food. If you feel like becoming a Tahitian Chief and wining and dining your Princess in tropical splendor, then reserve the Royal Floating Fare, a private houseboat, where your lunch will be served by canoe and set upon a glass bottom table on the terrace. You can enjoy your meal and admire the beautiful multicolored fish while taking in the spectacular surroundings.

A big buffet of Tahitian food and international dishes is served in Le Papayer restaurant each Tuesday, Wednesday, Friday and Saturday evening, when the Tiki Theater Village dancers and musicians present a spectacular Polynesian show. Please see further information in the *Nightlife & Entertainment* section of this chapter.

Moderate

LES TIPANIERS, *PK 25, seaside, Haapiti. Tel. 56.12.67. All credit cards. Beach Bar Restaurant open daily 7-9:30am and 12-2 p.m. Main restaurant open daily for dinner 7-9pm.*

This is one of the most delightful places to spend the day, swimming in the lagoon, participating in a variety of water sports, or reading in the shade beside a white sand beach. Breakfast and lunch are served in the beachside restaurant. You can order burgers, salads and pizza, or one of the daily specials. Fine Italian cuisine is served for dinner in the thatch-roof restaurant in the gardens, featuring fresh homemade pastas, spaghetti, lasagna and fettucine. French dishes include fish soup, lamb sirloin with goat cheese and mahi mahi with vanilla sauce.

PIZZERIA SUNSET, *PK 27, on the beach at Hotel Hibiscus, Haapiti. Tel. 56.26.00. All credit cards. Open daily 7am-10pm.*

Here you can eat pizzas, grilled meats and homemade pastas all day long, or sip a cold beer while sitting at a picnic table on the open deck overlooking the white sand beach, the lagoon and the *motu* islets in front of Club Med.

LAGOON CAFE, *PK 26 in Le Petit Village, Haapiti. Tel. 56.39.41. American Express, Mastercard, Visa. Open 11am-2:30pm and 5:30-11pm. Closed Sunday.*

This open terrace restaurant was formerly the Chinese Café, but the name and cuisine were changed in 1996, when owners Maire and Jean-Pierre began receiving fresh fish from the lagoon of Kaukura in the Tuamotu archipelago. These shipments of parrot fish, sea bass, blue jack, grouper and red snapper arrive by plane three times a week, along with crustaceans in season. Jean-Pierre, who is a veritable French *saucier*, uses this wealth of seafood to create a delicious *soupe de poissons "avé"*, complete with garlicky *rouille* and croutons. A sumptuous seafood platter is prepared each Saturday night for 3.800 CFP ($38). Special entertainment is often provided by jazz and blues musicians or Tahitian dance groups.

LA PLANTATION, *PK 26, on mountain side just past Le Petit Village in Haapiti. Tel. 56.45.10. American Express, Mastercard, Visa. Open every night 6-11 p.m. and for lunch on weekends only, from 11:30am-2pm.*

This large open-air restaurant, with seating for 60 inside and almost as many on the partially shaded terrace by the street, has been known by various names during several brief reincarnations. Monique and Charles Boursier are a young couple from Narbonne, France, who reopened this restaurant as La Plantation in February, 1997. They hired a French chef who is well known locally, and began serving European and Chinese cuisine.

I have enjoyed most of the dishes I've eaten here. The *tournedos* of mahi mahi with sesame seed sauce is delectable, and the *civet* of shrimp plantation is also good. The Chinese dishes I've eaten are nothing to rave about. I've found the chicken with lemon sauce too crispy and fatty, and the fried rice simply rice that is fried, with no vegetables added. Luncheon specials are printed on the sidewalk chalkboard. Wines from Bordeaux and Bourgogne are featured.

A nice touch is the *tiare* Tahiti flower the hostess puts behind your ear when you enter the restaurant. You will also be served a small appetizer of mousse of mahi mahi while you wait for your dinner. This restaurant was formerly a cabaret, and the stage and piano remain, providing the right ambiance for the Friday night jazz sessions that begin at 8:30pm and continue on into the night.

Inexpensive

LE MOTU, *PK 26, Haapiti, in St. Jacques Center, right across street from Club Med. Tel. 56.16.70. Mastercard, Visa. Open 9:30am-9pm. Closed Sunday night and all day Monday.*

This is a good choice for salads, quiches, pizzas and other light snacks, or for full meals. Here you have an unusual selection of sandwiches that are served on half a loaf of the crusty French *baguette*. My favorite is the ground beef sandwich, which is grilled hamburger meat, with lettuce, tomatoes, onions and mayonnaise spread on a *baguette*. It is much bigger and better than the hamburgers on buns and costs only 400 CFP ($4). The Italian ice cream is a specialty, and you can choose your soft drink or juice from the refrigerator. The bar is well stocked and there are several imported beers in the cooler.

DANIEL'S PIZZA, *PK 34,1 seaside, close to Linareva in Haapiti, Tel. 56.39.95. No credit cards. Open 11am-9pm. Closed Thursday.*

This is where you'll find the best pizza on the island. Daniel has built a wood-fired pizza oven in his garage and you can sit on a stool and eat at the wooden counter or take it with you. No alcohol is served. Look for his sign beside the road on the seaside just before you get to Hotel Linareva.

TAHITIAN FEASTS

CHEZ SERGE, beside road on mountainside at PK 22 in Papetoai Village, Tel. 56.13.17. Mastercard and Visa. Serge prepares maa Tahiti in the underground oven every Wednesday night and Sunday noon. This is the place where local residents go to eat in the thatched roof restaurant with a sand floor, or to take food home. He charges 2.500 CFP ($25) per person for the full range of typical Tahitian dishes. Serge is a Frenchman with a Tahitian wife, and he grows all his own fruits, vegetables and pigs for the underground oven. His snack style restaurant and bar is open seven days a week for lunch and dinner, specializing in fresh fish, shrimp, lobster and Tahitian food.

HOTEL BALI HAI, PK 5, Maharepa, Tel. 56.13.59. All major credit cards. A Tahitian tamaara'a takes place every Sunday at noon, with a welcome punch, floral crowns and the opening of the ahima'a underground oven. In addition to the traditional Tahitian foods you have a salad bar and a selection of foods you will recognize. A group of Tahitians from one of the villages presents a one-hour dance show and folkloric camera show on the terrace. The cost is 4.000 CFP ($40) per person or 3.500 CFP ($35) if you reserve a day in advance.

MAEVA COOK'S BAY HOTEL, PK 7, Maharepa, Tel. 56.10.50. All major credit cards. A Tahitian tamaara'a is held on the beach beside the pool house each Thursday evening, followed by a Tahitian dance show. Wine is included in the price of 3.800 CFP ($38) per person.

HOTEL MOOREA VILLAGE, PK 27, Haapiti, Tel. 56.10.02. American Express, Mastercard, Visa. Sunday is Tahitian tamaara'a day, when the ahima'a underground oven is opened at 12:45pm to reveal the roast suckling pig, breadfruit, taro and other Tahitian foods. This is the most authentic and delicious Tahitian feast you'll find in a hotel on Moorea that includes a Tahitian dance show, and the servings of roast suckling pig, poisson cru and Tahitian vegetables are very generous. You can even have fafaru if you feel adventurous. You eat with your fingers and you'll still be licking them when the Tahitian dance show begins after lunch. The cost of 3.800 CFP ($38) per person includes wine.

HOTEL SOFITEL IA ORA MOOREA, PK 2, Temae, Tel. 56.12.90. All major credit cards. The Tahitian underground oven is opened at 6:30pm each Saturday evening and a tamaara'a buffet is served in La Perouse Restaurant, followed by a Polynesian dance show at 7:45pm, which may also include fire dancing. The cost of 4.900 CFP ($49) per person is for the food and show only.

TIKI THEATER VILLAGE, PK 30, Haapiti, Tel. 56.18.97/56.10.86. American Express, Mastercard, Visa. A big buffet of Tahitian food cooked in the underground oven is served in Le Papayer Restaurant each Tuesday, Wednesday, Friday and Saturday evening, when the Tiki Theater Village dancers and musicians present a spectacular Polynesian show, complete with fire dancing. Total price for welcome punch, dinner with house wine, visit to the Tiki Village and the dance show is 6.500 CFP ($65). Please see further information in Nightlife & Entertainment section of this chapter.

AFAREAITU-MAATEA
Moderate
   CHEZ PAULINE, *PK 9, on mountain side in center of Afareaitu village. Tel. 56.11.26. No credit cards. Open 7am-7pm. Closed Sunday.*
   Pauline Teariki was a pioneer of tourism in Moorea, and operated her pension and adjacent restaurant until she died in October, 1996, when she was 83 years old. Her family is continuing the long tradition of serving delicious local style food. Here you don't order what you want; you get what's been prepared, which can be fresh local shrimp, crab or lobster, chicken or meat dishes, served with an interesting variety of locally grown vegetables.
   Pauline's daughter-in-law, Anna Bouvier, has everything prepared according to Pauline's tried and true recipes, including a powerful rum punch with fresh vanilla. Be sure to see Pauline's small museum collection of wood and stone *tiki*s, which she found in the mountains and valleys of Moorea. Please reserve.

SEEING THE SIGHTS

   Look for the **PK** (*poste kilometre*) markers on the mountain side of the road, which are placed one kilometer (.62 miles) apart. The signs are in concrete in the shape of Moorea, which resembles a heart. PK 0 is located at the old post office in **Temae**, close to the airport road. If you're coming from the airport and turn right onto the circle island road, you'll soon see the PK 1 marker opposite Lake Temae, which is actually a swamp. The distance markers continue on around the northwest coast to the village of **Haapiti** to PK 35, and then there's a gap in the numbering system. Here you'll want to photograph the **Mou'a Roa** and **Tohivea mountains** that rise in the distance behind the soccer field. On the seaside is a Protestant Church. The next marker you'll see will be PK 24, where another lovely landscape of the mountains is visible from the courtyard of the Catholic church, **Eglise de la Saint Famille**. The PK numbers then descend from PK 24 to PK 4, where you'll find the Ferry dock at **Vaiare Bay**, and then on down to PK 0, where you'll see the old Temae post office again. The new post office is in the commercial center of **Maharepa** at PK 5.
   At the end of Opunohu Bay at PK 18 you can leave the circle island road and turn left onto a partially paved inland road that passes through the **Opunohu Valley**. Here you will see horses, cows, sheep and goats grazing in verdant green pastures under the shadow of Moorea's sacred **Rotui mountain**. There is an agricultural school in this valley and the students look after the livestock. Beside this road, in a forest of *mape* Tahitian chestnut trees, are restored *marae* temples of stone and ancient archery platforms, where the Maohi chiefs and priests used to worship

and play. **Le Belvedere** is a popular destination at the top of a steep and winding road, and from the **Lookout Point**, at the end of a torturous road, you have the visual pleasure of **Cook's Bay** and **Opunohu Bay** far below, which are separated by Mt. Rotui. You continue on along the *route des ananas* (the pineapple road), where you'll see the mountain slopes of Pao Pao valley covered with pineapple plantations. Forests of mahogany, teak, acacia and mangoes shade the rutted red dirt road, which leads you back to the circle island road at PK 9 in the village of **Pao Pao**.

Land Tours

The **Moorea Highlights Tours** take you by minivan or large bus to Opunohu Bay, Cook's Bay, the Maraes in the Opunohu Valley and the Belvedere Lookout point. This tour usually lasts at least two hours and sells for 1.500 CFP ($15) a person. The **Circle Island Tour** takes you on a four-hour voyage around the coastal road, with stops at the Belvedere Lookout and pineapple plantations, a visit to the **Moorea Fruit Juice Factory & Distillery**, the *maraes*, Opunohu Bay and Cook's Bay. This tour sells for 2.000 CFP ($20) per person.

A full-day **Circle Island Tour** costs the same, because the difference in time is spent eating lunch, which is not included in the rates listed. The **Safari Tours** are usually half-day tours, varying according to the guide, which sell for 4.500 CFP ($45) if you book through a hotel, and 3.500 CFP ($35) if you reserve directly with the guides. A **Shopping Tour** around the Cook's Bay area costs about 1.500 CFP ($15) round-trip for hotels in that area. Should you want to shop in the **Club Med** area, the cost is 2.000 CFP ($20) one-way from the Cook's Bay area.

Note: Several tourists have complained that they were ripped off by some of the people who sell the land tours. While being transported from the Ferry dock to their hotels, they have been subjected to some high pressure salesmanship, and wound up buying the circle island tour and the safari tour. Later they discovered that the safari tours also take them around the island, and they can see the same sights that they had already seen the day before on the circle island tour, plus the addition of discovering the high mountains and waterfalls of Moorea. When they understood the difference, they canceled their circle island tours and took the safari tours.

Here are some of the companies and guides who will be happy to show you Moorea:

Albert Transports, *Tel. 56.13.53/56.19.28*. Rico Haring manages this family business, providing a combined circle island tour and interior island tour with shopping. Highlights include Opunohu Bay and Cook's Bay with a stop at the Belvedere lookout, the Moorea Fruit Juice Factory and Tiki Village. This daily tour starts at 9am and costs 2.000 CFP ($20).

A 3-hour **Photo Jeep Safari** takes you to the waterfalls and the scenic sights daily at 9am and 1:30pm, for 3.500 CFP ($35). Albert's guides are usually his sons, who grew up in the tour business. They don't let the facts stand in the way of a good story and they may even entertain you with tales of their many wives and girlfriends, following in the footsteps of their dear old dad. Private taxi service is also available.

Benjamin Transports, *Tel. 56.11.69/56.26.50*. Half-day excursions include stops at the Belvedere lookout and pineapple plantations, a visit to the Moorea Fruit Juice Factory & Distillery, the Opunohu *maraes*, Opunohu Bay and Cook's Bay. Full-day excursions will take you in a private air-conditioned car with stops at the Protestant temple in Papetoai, the Belvedere, the *marae* and Opunohu Bay. Shopping tours and private taxi service are also available. Some of the guides speak very little English.

Billy Transports, *Tel. 56.12.54*. Half-day excursions with stops at the main sites, including Opunohu and Cook's Bays, the *marae* in Opunohu, and Le Petit Village for shopping. Another half-day excursion takes you to the Belvedere lookout, to photograph pineapple plantations, visit the *marae* in Opunohu and the two bays.

Hei Maire Tours and 4x4 Safari, *Tel. 56.26.50*. This is a new company that will show you the Belvedere Lookout Point, the plantations, Fruit Juice Distillery, the *marae*, the waterfall and some long-eared prehistoric eels that live in a small river.

Julienne's Safari Tour, *Tel. 56.48.87*. Half-day tours leave the Moorea Village at 8am and 2pm daily, taking you around the island, up into the valley and stopping at many extra places you'd not normally visit on a tour. In addition to all the other stops mentioned in this section, Julienne also takes you to the fish market of Pao Pao, the airport, the ferry boat dock to see the fruit vendors, to the public beach of Toatea, to a vanilla farm, the hospital and town hall of Afareaitu, the waterfall, the Tiki Village, and even to the pharmacy. The tourists are happy with her tour, which is 4.000 CFP ($40) per person, fruit and drinks included.

Moorea Transports, *Tel. 56.12.86*. Full-day guided excursion with stops at the main interest sites, including the *marae* in Opunohu valley and the Belvedere lookout. You'll stop for lunch at **Linareva's** floating restaurant. This 6-hour tour is 2.000 CFP ($20).

A half-day mountain **Safari Tour** for 3.500 CFP ($35) takes you to the Belvedere lookout, the Moorea Fruit Juice Factory & Distillery and to the waterfalls in Afareaitu. These guides speak good English. Transfer service is also available.

Torea Nui Transport & Safari, *Tel. 56.12.48*. A 3-hour tour takes you to the Belvedere panoramic lookout, the *marae* temples in Opunohu valley, the pineapple and vanilla plantations and to the Moorea Fruit Juice

Factory & Distillery, where you can taste different liqueurs made with the fruits of Moorea.

A 4 1/2 hour **Safari Tour** will show you the interior of the island, with the *maraes*, pineapple and vanilla plantations, Belvedere, rivers, and the water falls of Afareaitu, plus a stop at the Moorea Fruit Juice Factory & Distillery to do a little taste testing. Transfer service and private taxi also available.

EDNA PAUTU, HEINUI TOURS

*Edna Pautu is a tour guide in Moorea who won the **Mauruuru Award** contest in 1997, an annual competition organized by **Tahiti Beach Press** and **Tahiti Manava Visitors Bureau**. Edna received the most nominations through letters written by people who had toured with her or visitors she had rescued as they walked beside the road in the tropical sun. When she appeared at the awards ceremony to receive her certificate and round-trip airline ticket to Paris, Edna had her leg in a cast, healing from a bad fall she took during a tour. While she was demonstrating how a pineapple grows on the slopes of the mountain overlooking Pao Pao Valley, one of the tourists in her group followed Edna down the mountain and lost her balance. Edna's strong body broke the fall of the tourist but she also broke her leg, which has resulted in several months' healing and rehabilitation.*

*At press time we learned that Edna will soon start her own Transport and Safari company, which will be called **Heinui Tours**, Tel. 56.24.90. By the time you visit Moorea Edna will be driving her own mini-van and guiding tourists around the island again. If you book your tour with Edna you'll be well pleased with your excursion, because she truly goes all out to help the tourists.*

Mountain Safari Excursions

Aimeo Safari Tours, *Tel. 56.14.11*. Heitapu Hunter has received rave reviews from many people who have taken his half-day tours to visit the Pao Pao and Opunohu valleys, which include a stop at Belvedere lookout, the Moorea Fruit Juice Factory & Distillery, Mou'a Puta mountain and the *marae* temples. Heitapu also takes you off-track to visit his private family domain in the Pao Pao valley.

Inner Island Safari Tours, *Tel. 56.20.09*. Alex and Ghislaine Roo A Haamataerii operate half-day inner island photo tours in air-conditioned and open jeeps through the tropical valleys, up to the highest panoramic viewpoint in Moorea's majestic mountains. You'll stop at the *marae* temples in Opunohu valley, discover grapefruit, vanilla and pineapple plantations, and learn all about the history, culture and daily lives of the people of Moorea. A waterfall tour is accessible only to 4-wheel drive vehicles and requires a 15-minute hike uphill. Be sure to bring your camera. These are very well informed guides, whose English is good. Transfer and taxi service also available.

Painapo 4x4, *Tel. 56.42.43/60.60.06*. Ronald Sage was the first person to start the Moorea Safari Tours by Landrover several years ago and his tours are still packed, mostly with people staying at Club Med. This excursion takes you through Moorea's verdant Opunohu valley, past vanilla and coffee plantations, pineapple fields, and through gardens of lush tropical fruits. The highlight of the tour is a visit to a private domain, operated by the government's Economie Rurale as an agricultural school. Past lush meadows and orange groves, the road winds upward through the undergrowth of ferns and bamboo, climbing to the foot of the Mou'a Roa mountain, where you have an unequaled view of Moorea's beauty of land and sea, with the two bays of Opunohu and Cook far below. You'll also stop at a *marae*, the Moorea Fruit Juice Factory & Distillery and visit the waterfalls in Afareaitu. **Moorea Rally Discovery** and **Papeete Adventure** are other excursions Ronald Sage has created. These rallies may include shopping, touring and treasure hunts.

Tefaarahi Adventure Tours, *Tel. 56.41.24*. Derek Grell is an American expatriate who married a lovely Chinese-Tahitian *vahine* and settled on Moorea. His mountain safari takes you to visit his private property in the mountains of Maharepa, where 1,000-year old petroglyphs depicting Polynesian gods are carved into the boulders. This is an unusual educational and ecotourism adventure. This 3-hour excursion for 3.500 CFP ($35) includes hiking to the petroglyphs.

Derek will also take you on a 4-hour excursion, where you will discover Moorea from the mountains to the sea, visit the bays, viewpoints and waterfall, plus the Tefaarahi plantation and petroglyphs. This tour is 4.500 CFP ($45). An 8-hour complete island tour for 5.500 CFP ($55) includes all the above stops, plus a visit to the *marae* temples, Moorea Fruit Juice Factory & Distillery, a lunch stop (lunch not included), and time for a refreshing swim.

Special Activities & Sightseeing Stops

Douglas Pearson, *Tel. 56.36.15*, is an Englishman who has lived in these islands for many years. He leads original, unusual and very informative walks and bicycle trips to discover nature and life on a small island. You can also join Douglas' Star Gazing Discoveries of the Southern night sky in all its aspects—astronomy, mythology and constellations galore. An evening of Menu Stories includes many menus of legends and island stories. If you're still a Polly Wog Douglas will baptize you into the realm of King Neptune or Ruahatu, the Polynesian god of the sea. You'll have to provide the transportation as his only wheels are on a bicycle.

Visit a private botanical garden at the **Kellum Stop**, *PK 17.8 on the beach side in Opunohu Bay*, and let Mari Mari Kellum, *Tel. 56.18.52*, tell you about her parents who were given the Opunohu Valley as a wedding gift in the 1920s. Mari Mari still lives in their old colonial style house, surrounded by majestic trees and a large variety of plants and flowers. The gardens are closed Sunday through Tuesday. The best time to visit is in the morning on Wednesday through Saturday. Admission 300 CFP ($3).

The **Opunohu Agricultural School** has a **Fare Boutique**, *Tel. 56.11.34*, on the right as you drive up the mountain to visit Le Belvedere. It's open daily from 10am to 2pm, selling fresh fruit juice, vanilla beans, dried bananas, coffee beans, homemade jams and hand-painted *pareos*, all made by the students, who will show you the school farm.

Tahitian Weddings are performed at the **Tiki Theater Village** for lovers who get married back home and want to splurge for a fun-filled colorful wedding ceremony in the authentic tradition of old Polynesia. It's not just newlyweds who are getting married in the Tahitian style, but also loving couples who are celebrating their anniversaries or who want to renew their vows. The ceremony takes place on a *marae* stone altar with a true Tahitian priest officiating. Olivier Briac and his Tiki Village artisans will transform you into a Tahitian prince and princess for your wedding ceremony for a marriage made in Paradise. Contact Olivier Briac *at B.P. 1016, Haapiti, Moorea, Tel. 689/56.18.97, Fax 689/56.10.86.*

Tattoos can be designed by masters of the art for those of you who wish to wear a permanent souvenir of your trip to Moorea. Roonui is one of the best and his little Tattoo *fare* is easy to find, in front of Club Med adjacent to the Boutique Souvenir, Tel. 56.37.53/56.16.87. You can also get tattooed at Tiki Village. The cost of a Maohi tattoo depends on the design, and you'll pay at least 5.000 CFP ($50) for the simple drawing.

Tropical Aquarium Center, *PK 7.1 in Maharepa, Tel. 56.24.00*, has several tanks filled with brightly colored fish from the lagoon, as well as the dreaded stonefish (*nohu*). Behind the aquarium and black pearl shop you can visit an experimental black pearl farm, where oysters are grown in big tanks. You can learn about the process of grafting the oyster and how the pearls develop.

There are sea turtles in a pen, as well as birds and coral that owner Teva Yrondi has dyed in bright colors. Teva's idea of creativity also includes cutting the black pearls into half and sculpting them into facets like diamonds and other stones. Open 9am-12pm and 2:30-5:30pm except Monday. Free entry.

NIGHTLIFE & ENTERTAINMENT

A karaoke bar attracts tourists and local residents at the **Hotel Sofitel Ia Ora**, *Tel. 56.12.90*, each Tuesday and Thursday night, between 8:45pm and 10:30pm. No cover charge, but you are expected to buy a drink, of course.

CHEZ BILLY, *PK 28 in Haapiti, just past Moorea Village, Tel. 56.12.54*, is a big dance hall built over the white sand beach. This is where you go on Friday and Saturday nights if you want to let your hair down and dance Tahitian style. Just watch out for the flying beer bottles when the Tahitian *tanes* get a little more than drunk. Shoes, long pants and T-shirts or shirts are required for men and there is a cover charge of 1.000 CFP ($10), which includes a drink.

CLUB MED, *Tel. 55.00.00*, has nightly entertainment after dinner, when the G.O.'s (*gentils organizateurs*) get on stage to perform cabaret acts, way-south-of Broadway plays, can-can dances, skits and comedies. Even if you're not staying at the Club you can join the fun for a fee. At 7 p.m. you can eat dinner in the main dining room, watch the theater show and dance the night away in the disco, for 5.500 CFP ($55). Your wine and beer are included with your meal in the dining room, but if you want to drink in the bar you have to buy some plastic beads before you can order a drink. Starting at 9:30pm on weekends you can watch the G.O. show and stay for the disco, for 2.500 CFP ($25). A special lunch-plus-activities fee of 5.500 CFP allows you to spend half a day at Club Med, from 10am to 4pm, enjoying water-skiing, tennis, beach volley ball, outrigger canoes and boat trips to the *motu*. Be sure to call and confirm the rates and activities before you show up at the guard house gate.

STEPHANIE'S OASIS, *PK 34,2, beside the lagoon next to Linareva in Haapiti*, is a boutique by day and a bar by night. Marc and Stéphanie Quattrini closed their café in January 1998, and have opened a place for tourists to hang out at night. If you're looking for something to do that won't cost a lot of money and will give you a chance to meet other people, just call Stephanie at *Tel. 56.41.19*. Their services include round-trip transfers from the hotels. You can play a game of darts, checkers or chess, and drink pitchers of sangria or beer at the picnic tables on the lawn. The bar is open from 5:30pm to 9:30pm.

TIKI THEATER VILLAGE, *PK 30 in Haapiti*, is a cultural and folkloric center, which you can visit by day or in the evening. Multilingual guides lead you through the village of thatched roof *fares* where you will see demonstrations of how to carve tikis from stone, how to sculpt wooden bowls, weave a hat, make a floral crown and tie-dye a *pareo*. You can get a traditional Tahitian or Marquesan tattoo and learn how the ancient Tahitians built their homes and meeting houses. You can swim in the lagoon, paddle an outrigger canoe, go fishing with the Tiki Village dancers or sunbathe on the beach. You can enjoy lunch in **Le Papayer** restaurant and watch a mini-dance show, or reserve the **Royal Floating Fare** for your romantic lunch for two. Tiki Village opens daily at 10am except on Mondays. You can attend the **Maohi Lagoon Show** each Tuesday, Thursday and Sunday, with a visit to a **black pearl farm** and a demonstration of how the oyster is grafted. You will be picked up at your hotel by outrigger canoe or by bus at 9:45am and transferred back to your hotel after lunch and the dance show. The entry fee at Tiki Village is 2.000 CFP ($20) without food and 5.000 CFP ($50) with lunch.

Each Tuesday, Wednesday, Friday and Saturday evening the 70 dancers and musicians at the Tiki Theater Village present a Polynesian extravaganza. You will arrive by outrigger canoe and be welcomed on the beach around 6:15pm with a fruit drink or rum punch. Then you will be immersed in the culture and tradition of Polynesia, with demonstrations of arts and crafts and dancing techniques. After the opening of the *ahima'a* underground oven a bountiful buffet is set out, featuring Tahitian specialties, Continental cuisine, barbecued fish, chicken and meats, along with a salad bar and dessert table.

While you are enjoying your meal you'll be treated to a very lively demonstration of how to wear the *pareo*. After dinner the big show gets underway at 8:45pm in the open air theater with a white sand floor. This spectacular dance show includes several fire dancers, all muscular men with beautiful tattoos. Everyone here works very hard and puts all their energy and enthusiasm into entertaining you. I highly recommend this **Great Polynesian Revue**, the food and the visit through the village. The entry fee for dinner and the show is 6.500 CFP ($65). Reserve at your hotel or *Tel. 56.18.97/56.10.86.*

Several of the hotels have barbecues, special theme evenings, and especially Tahitian feasts, followed by Tahitian dance shows. The *Tahiti Beach Press*, an English-language free newspaper that is distributed to all the hotels each Thursday, has a Special Events page that will inform you where the action is on any night of the week.

SPORTS & RECREATION
Hiking
Tropic Escape takes you into the green sanctuary of Moorea's valleys and mountains. Costa Rimy, *Tel. 56.42.49*, teaches hiking, first aid and security, plus he is an amateur archaeologist. For 4.000 CFP ($40) per person he will guide you on a half-day trek to cross the mountain path from Vaiare to Pao Pao, which he classes as a very easy walk. For the same price you can climb up to the Three Coconuts, which is a four to five hour medium-challenge hike.

A full-day walk of seven to eight hours is 6.000 CFP ($60), and you must be in good physical condition and not subject to vertigo to attempt the climb to Mou'a Rotui, the sacred mountain, or to Mou'a Puta, the mountain with a hole in the top. The prices charged include land transport, food and walking equipment such as backpacks and raincoats.

Vincent Dubousquet of **Polynesian Adventure**, *Tel. 43.25.95*, leads hikes in Tahiti and Moorea. You can also contact Eric, *Tel. 41.35.07* or Guillaume, *Tel. 43.92.76* of **Tiare Mato** in Tahiti. These two guides take hikers up Mt. Rotui and Mou'a Puta.

Horseback Riding

Rupe Rupe Ranch *is on the mountainside at PK 2 in Teavaro, between the Hotel Sofitel Ia Ora and the Vaiare Ferry dock*. Christian Dauzou, *Tel. 56.26.52*, organizes exhilarating rides along the white sand beach, into the Teavaro valley, and even sunset promenades. The horses are from the Marquesas Islands and come equipped with saddles. A 1 1/2 hour excursion costs 3.000 CFP ($30), with daily departures at 8:30am and 2:30pm.

Pegasus Ranch, *Tel. 56.34.11, is on the mountainside at PK 2.2 in Maharepa*. For 2.000 CFP ($20) you can take a guided ride across a coconut grove, along the beach and to the Temae *motu*, which is not an offshore islet but is connected to the main island. This place is noted for mosquitoes and *nonos*, so be sure to use your repellent. Daily rides are at 8:30am, 10:30am and 2:30pm.

Tiahura Ranch *is at PK 27 in Haapiti, on the mountainside close to the Moorea Village*. Terai Maihi and Carole Bayet, *Tel. 56.28.55*, can accommodate a maximum of 8 riders for guided excursions into the valley, daily between 9am-11am. Between 4pm and 6pm the Marquesan horses will also transport you to a panoramic viewpoint to watch the sun dip behind the horizon. Each outing costs 3.000 CFP ($30).

Helicopter Tours

Heli-Pacific, *Tel. 85.68.00*, has two AS 350 "Ecureuil" helicopters, each with 5-6 seats, ready to let you soar above Moorea in sound-proof comfort. A "Moorea Highlights" 20-minute tour costs 15.500 CFP ($155). A "Moorea Discovery" tour is a 35-minute excursion that is available daily, taking you over the mountains, valleys, bays, lagoon and coral reef. Special flights are available for aerial photography and for transfers between the Tahiti-Faaa airport and Moorea. The Club Med and Hotel Moorea Beachcomber Parkroyal have helipads.

Heli-Inter Polynesie, *Tel. 81.99.00*, has a 6-seat "Ecureuil" helicopter available for tourist flights, transfers to Moorea and specific charters on request.

Day Sailing

Manu is a 10.8 meter (36-foot) sailing catamaran owned by Bernard Calvet, which operates out of the *Moorea Beachcomber Parkroyal Nautical Center, Tel. 55.19.19, ext. 1138*, offering half-day sailing excursions to visit Cook's Bay and Opunohu Bay. This light craft needs only the slightest breath of wind to send you gliding briskly across the lagoon. A 3-hour sail costs 5.000 CFP ($50), departing daily at 9:30am and 1:30pm. A sunset cruise aboard *Manu* leaves the dock at 5pm and returns at 6:30pm. Drinks are included in the price of 2.500 CFP ($25). *Manu* is also available for private charters for a maximum of six people. A half-day charter is 30.000 CFP ($300) and a full day sail is 50.000 CFP ($500).

Day Tour to Tetiaroa by Boat

Pacific Charter, *Tel. 56.45.98/56.44.38*, operates a *Tahiti Cat* power boat that takes only 1 1/2 hours to get to Marlon Brando's atoll of Tetiaroa from Moorea. The boat leaves at 7am and returns at 5pm, with an American breakfast served on arrival, a picnic on the beach and a visit to Bird Island. Captain Jean-Michel Raffin has to anchor the boat outside the reef and you'll walk across the coral to get to the inner lagoon. The cost is 17.000 CFP ($170) per person. Be sure to bring your plastic shoes for walking on the reef, snorkeling gear, a hat, sun glasses and sun protection cream.

Deep Sea Fishing

Captain Chris Lilley has a 31-foot Bertram Sportfisher named *Tea Nui* that is professionally equipped with a flybridge, Penn International reels and all that you need to realize your dream of catching marlin, tuna, wahoo or mahi mahi offshore Moorea. Chris, who is an American, has 15 years' experience in local waters. His half-day fishing excursion is 50.000 CFP ($500), or you can arrange shares and pay only 13.000 CFP ($130) per person. You can reach Chris at *Tel. 689/56.15.08 or Fax 689/41.32.97*.

Lagoon Excursions, Snorkeling & Picnics on the Motu

"A Coconut Cookout With Maco" takes places every Tuesday and Friday, leaving the Sofitel Ia Ora at 9am and returning at 3:30pm. You board the *Spirit of Moorea*, a 36-foot outrigger canoe. Maco, your Polynesian guide, will share his paradise with you as you travel through Moorea's crystal clear blue lagoon to a private "coconut *motu*."

While you swim and snorkel in the coral gardens or relax on the white sand beach, Maco will prepare your lunch of chicken and fish grilled on a barbecue. Salads, fresh tropical fruits, beer, wine and juice are included in the price of 4.500 CFP ($45). Maco will even show you how to open your own coconut and how to wear the *pareo*. You'll enjoy his humor. For

DOLPHIN & WHALE WATCHING

Doctor Michael Poole is an American marine-biologist who lives in Moorea and has devoted his life's work to the study of dolphins and whales. He is a very good teacher who loves sharing his knowledge with other people. The enthusiasm he feels for the mammals he studies in their natural environment is very contagious. Michael leads 3-hour Dolphin and Whale Watch expeditions every Thursday and Sunday morning, working with Captain Heifara Dutertre of Moorea Boat Tours, Tel/Fax 56.28.44. Heifara begins collecting a maximum of 20 passengers at their hotel docks between 7:30 and 8:30am, and Michael boards the 8.7 meter (29-foot) Fiberglas boat Enoha at the Hotel Bali Hai pier. Then the search begins, as you head out the pass into the open ocean. The wild spinner dolphins (Stenella longirostris) are the easiest to find and the most fun to watch because of their acrobatic aerial leaps. Michael will tell you that 150 of these mammals live around Moorea all the time.

When the sea is calm and the mammals seem approachable, you can even swim with the dolphins and pilot whales. The giant humpback whales can be seen and heard offshore Moorea between July and October, when they come up from Antarctica to mate and give birth. These are the most exciting mammals to watch as they frolic close to the shore and splash in the vicinity of the surprised surfers, who ride the waves beside the passes.

reservations and pick-up call the Hotel Sofitel Ia Ora at *Tel. 56.12.90*, or Maco and Elizabeth *at Tel. 56.36.06.*

Mahana Tours, operated by Moise and Fellie Ruta, *Tel. 56.20.44/ 55.19.19, ext. 1138, operates out of the Hotel Moorea Beachcomber Parkroyal.* Their Glass Bottom Boat ride is 1.800 CFP ($18) for a one-hour excursion across the lagoon. A full-day excursion by double-decker boat includes a picnic on the *motu*, for 5.000 CFP ($50), departing each Tuesday, Wednesday and Thursday at 11:30am and returning at 3:30pm. They also have jet-ski and wave runner rentals.

Moana Lagoon Excursions also have barbecue picnics on the *motu*, with time for snorkeling and shelling and viewing Cook's Bay and Opunohu Bay from the water. This daily tour lasts five to six hours and costs 4.000 CFP ($40). A **Moana Lagoon Safari** lasts from 9:30am to 1:30pm and takes you to the same places without a picnic and costs 3.000 CFP ($30). These excursions are operated by the **Albert Tours** family, *Tel. 56.13.53/56.19.28* for reservations.

Moorea Boat Tours is owned by Heifara Dutertre, *Tel/Fax 56.28.44.* His 8.7 meter (29-foot) Fiberglas boat *Enoha* has a 140 horsepower engine,

Tues
Wood - Scuba
Thurs
Fri'

Pearl

MOOREA 309

a protective canvas top and will seat 20 people. He offers a full-day circle island tour inside Moorea's lagoon, complete with local music, fish feeding, snorkeling and shelling, a picnic on the *motu*, and demonstrations of how to open and use a coconut, how to wear the *pareo* and how to prepare *poisson cru*. This tour costs 6.500 CFP ($65) for people over 12 years of age, and operates each Wednesday and Friday, from 9:30am to 3:30pm.

Every Sunday and Thursday morning a 3-hour **Dolphin and Whale Watch** excursion (see sidebar above), guided by Doctor Michael Poole, takes you outside the reef to search for the dolphins and whales that inhabit local waters. This tour costs 4.500 CFP ($45) for adults, 3.000 CFP ($30) for children 5 to 12 years, and 1.500 CFP ($15) for kids 3 to 5 years old. Supplementary excursions are sometimes made on Tuesday afternoons. A 4-hour circle island tour without picnic is 3.500 CFP ($35), and a boat trip to the *motu* with a picnic lunch is 3.500 CFP ($35) per person, departing at 11:30am and returning at 3:30pm. Captain Dutertre also rents his boat with skipper for private tours. A 3 1/2 hour excursion is 30.000 CFP ($300) and a 7-hour tour is 50.000 CFP ($500).

Moorea Transport, *Tel. 56.12.86*, has half-day outrigger speed canoe excursions to the *motu* each Tuesday, Thursday and Saturday, at 9am. This excursion includes feeding the sharks and fish and snorkeling for 2.000 CFP ($20). The original *motu* picnic party is a 5-hour excursion each Monday, Wednesday and Friday, with hotel pick-up starting at 9am. A barbecue picnic lunch is included for 4.500 CFP ($45).

What To Do On Moorea Tours, *based at the Hotel Bali Hai, Tel. 56.13.59*, will take you on a **Liki Tiki Motu Picnic Tour** to one of the *motu* islets facing Club Med. You can be assured of a memorable day of swimming, snorkeling and sightseeing. During a 3-hour stop on the *motu* you'll picnic on grilled chicken or mahi mahi, with salads, fruits and a free bar of beer, soft drinks, wine and rum punch. The price of 4.000 CFP ($40) per person includes a coconut show. If you purchase your picnic tour 24 hours in advance you can save 300 CFP ($3). This tour operates on Tuesday or Friday, with a free pick-up from your hotel at 9am., returning five to six hours later.

You can board the 50-passenger *Liki Tiki* catamaran with a thatched roof shelter for a one-hour **Snorkeling Excursion** starting at 2:30pm daily except Tuesday. This memorable experience costs 700 CFP ($7).

An **Outrigger Lagoon Excursion Around Moorea** departs from the Hotel Bali Hai dock at 9:30am each Monday, Wednesday and Saturday, taking you to visit Cook's Bay and Opunohu Bay, with a snorkeling stop and a visit to a *motu*, where you'll be served complimentary fresh fruit, soft drinks and tropical juices. This tour is 3.500 CFP ($35) or 3.000 CFP ($30), if you sign up 24 hours in advance.

Hiro Kelley, who owns **What to Do on Moorea Tours**, will also take you on a **Glass Bottom Boat Shelling & Fish Feeding Snorkeling Tour** at 2pm daily except Sunday. Inside the clear waters of the Temae lagoon near the Hotel Sofitel Ia Ora you can pet a tame barracuda and see fish of every imaginable color. Hiro will teach you how to find live shells, but they must remain in their natural habitat for future expeditioners to appreciate and for ecological stability of the fragile life of the reefs. This 1 1/2 hour tour costs 2.500 CFP ($25) with round-trip transportation, or 1.700 CFP ($17) if you provide your own transport. You can also join a **Sunset Cruise** at 4pm or go on a **Moonlight Cruise** when the tropical moon is the most romantic.

Nautical Activities Centers

Moorea Beachcomber Parkroyal Nautical Activities Center, *Tel. 55.19.19, ext. 1138.* You'll find a variety of interesting activities here, which are available to hotel guests and anyone else who wants to explore the lagoon. In addition to snorkeling, windsurfing, scuba diving, day sailing, parasailing, fishing, lagoon tours, and pedal boat rentals, you can also get a round-trip boat transfer to a *motu* for 700 CFP ($7), water-ski for 2.000 CFP ($20) for a 15-minute tour, join a fish-feeding expedition in the lagoon for 1.500 CFP ($15), take a sunset cruise for 2.000 CFP ($20), view the coral gardens through a glass bottom boat for 1.800 CFP ($18) or from an *Aquascope* half submarine for 2.500 CFP ($25).

Sofitel Ia Ora Moorea Nautical Activities Center, *Tel. 56.12.90, ext. 4134.* You can rent a pedal boat for 700 CFP ($7) per hour, go water-skiing for 1.500 CFP ($15), ride a glass bottom boat or join a snorkeling excursion for 1.700 CFP ($17) and tour the island by boat with a picnic on the *motu* for 4.500 CFP ($45). Surf bikes and windsurf boards are also available for rent.

Tip'nautic is a nautical base located at *Hotel Les Tipaniers, Tel. 56.12.67*, open daily except Monday. You can rent a kayak for 1.000 CFP ($10) for 2 hours, after paying a deposit of 10.000 CFP ($10). You can catch a boat to the *motu* for 700 CFP ($7), water-ski for 15 minutes for 1.500 CFP ($15), join a **Shark Discovery** excursion for 1.500 CFP ($15), or **Discover the Two Bays** of Opunohu and Cook's by boat for 3.000 CFP ($30). Manager Jean Marcel has an 8-passenger motor boat for these excursions and he is a qualified sports teacher.

Sailing – Charter Yachts

Archipels Polynesian Cruises, *B.P. 1160, Papetoai, Moorea, Tel. 689/56.36.39, Fax 689/56.35.87. US representatives are Islands in the Sun, Tel. 800/828-6877, Tahiti Vacations, Tel. 800/553-3477, and Tahiti Legends, Tel. 800/200-1213.* The main office for **Archipels Croisieres Polynesiennes**

is on the mountainside at PK 16 in Opunohu Bay. General Manager François Profit will help you plan your own sailing holiday aboard one of the seven Archipels 57 sailing catamarans, whether you want to visit the Leeward Society Islands, the Tuamotu atolls or the Marquesas Islands.

Each catamaran has a Fiberglass hull, is 17.5 meters (57 feet) long and 8.20 meters (28 feet) wide, with a draft of 1.20 meters (4 feet) and 160 square meters (190 square yards) of sail area. The 4 air-conditioned guest cabins, each with its own private bathroom, can sleep a total of 8 passengers. There's a spacious living area, galley, 2-crew cabin and large cockpit protected by a permanent sun-roof. Technical equipment includes 2 engines, a generator, fresh water maker, large refrigeration space, ice maker, dishwasher and washing machine. An inflatable dinghy with a motor, windsurfing board, snorkeling and fishing equipment, ocean kayak, cassette deck and compact disk player, television and video are some of the leisure equipment available, and each yacht has radio transceivers, navigational equipment, automatic pilot and radar. Diving equipment is provided for the yacht based in the Marquesas Islands, and a Diving in the Marquesas Cruise is an Archipels' exclusive, working in conjunction with the Marquesas Diving Center.

Archipels Croisieres charters primarily to individuals or "by the cabin" in a shared-boat cruise, or you can charter the entire yacht for US $2,090 per day. This rate includes fuel for the boat and dinghy, all meals and hotel services aboard and airport/yacht transfers. The per-passenger rates also include meals and hotel services aboard, double occupancy cabins, airport/yacht transfers and all the excursions and events specified in the program you choose. An 8-day/7 night Marquesas Island cruise is $2,050 per person; a 7 day/6 night Society Islands cruise is $1,880 per person; a 4 day/3 night Tuamotu cruise inside the atoll of Rangiroa is $1,030 per person, or $790 per person for a 3 day/2 night cruise inside the Rangiroa lagoon. Dive Aboard Cruises "by the boat only" cost $2,450 a day in the Tuamotus or the Marquesas Islands.

VPM Dufour Tahiti, *B.P. 554, Maharepa, Moorea, Tel. 689/56.40.50, Fax 689/56.40.60, e-mail VPMyacht@mailpf.* The main base for this yacht charter company, run by Jacqueline and Christian Gallé, is located at the Vaiare Marina. The fleet includes 8 monohull sailboats ranging from 35 feet to 62 feet, 6 Nautitech 435 or 475 catamarans, a Lagoon 57 catamaran and two 82-foot Nemo maxi-catamarans for 16 passengers. The biggest boat in the VPM Dufour fleet is *Va'a Rahi*, a 98-foot maxi-cat for 71 passengers that is based at the yacht harbor in Papeete, used for day-sailing tours to Tetiaroa. This company has a yacht charter base in Raiatea and keeps a boat permanently based in Tikehau in the Tuamotus and a catamaran in Taiohae in the Marquesas Islands.

Bareboat and skippered charters and special sports cruises are possible for itineraries that will take you to visit the Society Islands, the Tuamotus and the Marquesas Islands. These include sail-dive cruises, where you fly to Fakarava from Tahiti and board the 82-foot long *Nemo* catamaran for a week-long dive cruise in the Tuamotus, then flying back to Tahiti. This 8 day/7 night charter with all meals included costs 9,675 French francs (about US $1,750) during the high season of July through October, sharing a double cabin. The low season rate between November and March is 8,650 French francs (about US $1,570). Airfares are not included.

Scuba Diving

Each dive center in Moorea is headed by a qualified English-speaking instructor. All diving equipment is available, and dive packages with special lodging can be arranged. Bring a health certificate from your doctor with you, plus a certificate stating the depth specifications you are qualified to dive. The protected lagoons, passes and outer coral reefs offer ideal conditions for scuba diving year-round.

Bathy's Club Moorea, *B.P. 1247, Papetoai, Moorea, Tel. 689/56.31.44, Fax 689/56.38.10, e-mail: bathys@mail.pf.* This PADI five-star center is located at the Moorea Beachcomber Parkroyal. Four PADI instructors speak English, French and Spanish, and are very experienced in underwater guided tours inside the lagoon, on the coral shelf and in the open ocean around Moorea. The dive gear is new, safe and comfortable and two boats are available to ensure safety and congeniality. Full service features air fill, professional video service, dive shop, certification, and lessons for beginners or certified divers. A specialty of Bathy's Club is meeting the sharks and stingrays that live inside the lagoon. Open daily from 8am to 6pm, with four dives per day.

Moorea Fun Dive, *B.P. 737, Maharepa, Moorea, Tel. 689/56.40.74/ 56.40./38, Fax 689/56.40.74, e-mail: fundive@mail.pf.* This dive shop was located at the Hotel Moorea Lagoon before the hotel was sold and closed at the end of April, 1998, for rebuilding as an Outrigger Hotel. At publication time the owners were looking for a new site in the same area, which they will surely find before you arrive. They offer introductory and exploration dives for 4.500 CFP ($45), including equipment and transfers. Night dives are 5.500 CFP ($55), and a forfeit price of 5 dives costs 4.200 CFP ($42) per dive. The dive school is headed by FFESSM, CMAS and PADI instructors.

M.U.S.T. (Moorea Underwater Scuba Diving Tahiti), *B.P. 336, Pao Pao, Moorea, Tel. 689/56.17.32/56.15.83, Fax 689/56.15.83.* This popular dive shop is located beside the pier at the Maeva Cook's Bay Resort, open daily except Monday. Exploration dives are made at 9am and 2pm, with a choice of 20 different spots. Philippe Molle is a CMAS three star international monitor and ex-PADI Open Water Instructor. He or his two well qualified dive instructors will accompany you as you hand feed the black tip sharks, giant moray eels and Napoleon fish, and they will take you to the wreck of an old sailing warship. Your diving experience will be recorded on video tape, which you can watch at 5pm at the club.

One dive is 5.000 CFP ($50) and five dives cost 22.500 CFP ($225). Night dives are 1.500 CFP ($15) more. You will pay 6.500 CFP ($65) for one lesson and 22.000 CFP ($220) for four lessons. All rates include the instructor, boat, one tank and weight belt. You can rent all the necessary equipment at the M.U.S.T. dive shop.

Scubapiti Moorea, *Hotel Les Tipaniers, B.P. 58-H, Haapiti, Moorea, Tel. 689/56.20.38/56.12.67, Fax 689/56.29.25.* PADI and CMAS instructors are available to take you for an exploration dive for 4.500 CFP ($45) or give you lessons for 5.500 CFP ($55). The boat transport for a maximum of 10 kilometers (6.2 miles) is included and equipment rental is extra. While you are exploring the underwater world of clown fish, groupers and sharks, two camera men will follow you to video tape your dive, which you can then see on an instant replay system. This tape is available for purchase as a souvenir of your vacation memories.

MOOREA'S BEST DIVE SITES

Moorea's dive sites offer special treats of feeding the large lemon sharks and a rendezvous with the friendly giant-sized Napoleon fish. Divers also see black and white-tip sharks, gray sharks and moray eels.

The water is clear with insignificant currents, assuring easy dives that attract scuba divers from all over the world. One of the most popular sites is "Le Tiki", where you'll be able to feed the wild sharks, including lemon sharks more than 2.4 meters (8 feet) long. The Toatai Pass through the barrier reef offers drift diving among nurse sharks, leopard rays and schools of jackfish. A site known as "Napoleon Plateau" offers Napoleon fish that weigh up to 80 pounds, as well as sharks. Inside the lagoon is a site called "The Wreck", which is an artificial haven for fish, with the ship's hull spread over 82 feet, complete with anchors, chains and a gangway. Other sites include the "Ray Corridor", "The Canyon", "The Blue Island", the "Shark Dining Room", the "Bali Hai Wall", "Temae", "Atiha", the "Avamotu Pass" and the "Taotaha Pass", all offering a concentration of eels, barracudas, coral fish, rays or sharks.

Shark-Feeding

Patrice Pater of **Te Aho Nui Activities** leads shark-feeding excursions daily between 9:30am and 12pm. For 2.000 CFP ($20) per person he will take you through the pass near the Moorea Beachcomber Parkroyal, where you will go to Opunohu Bay to a site called "Le Tiki". You can feed the sharks and fish and on the way back to the hotel you can swim with the stingrays. Patrice picks up his clients at the hotels in the Haapiti area. You can reserve with the activities desk of one of these hotels even if you are not staying there.

What To Do On Moorea Tours also has shark and fish-feeding tours each Thursday and Saturday morning. During this 4-hour excursion you can meet the friendly sharks and fish Hiro Kelley grew up with inside the lagoon near the Sofitel Ia Ora. You can even swim with the sharks if you have the courage. This tour normally costs 2.500 CFP ($25), but Hiro will give you a special price of 2.000 CFP ($20) if you sign up a day in advance. Reserve at *Tel. 56.13.59*.

Moorea Transport, *Tel. 56.12.86*, has a 2-hour Shark and Fish Feeding Tour for 2.500 CFP ($25) each Tuesday, Thursday and Saturday, with hotel pick-ups starting at 9am.

More Water Fun

Aquascope is a half submarine that puts you under the surface of the water, where you can view the coral gardens and colorful fish without getting wet. You'll find this excursion *at the Moorea Beachcomber Parkroyal Nautical Center, Tel. 55.19.19, ext. 1138*. The cost is 2.500 CFP ($25) and you can take a ride every day between 9am and 3pm.

Aqua-Walk is a novel way to say hello to the fish in the lagoon in Moorea. Jean-Michel Raffin of **Pacific Charter**, *Tel. 56.45.98/56.44.38*, takes you on board his traditional double pirogue and heads toward the lagoon between two *motu* islets facing Club Med. Then you put on a diving helmet that looks like those used in Jules Verne's *20,000 Leagues Under the Sea* movie, which weighs 40 kilograms (88 pounds). You don't feel the weight when you are under the water, however, and you can actually walk around on the bottom of the lagoon just as you would walk on any land. An air hose connected to a compressor on board the canoe allows you to descend to a depth of 3 meters (10 feet). Your Aqua-Walk lasts about 25 minutes and costs 3.500 CFP ($30). You can reserve through your hotel and he'll pick you up at the Moorea Beachcomber Parkroyal, Moorea Beach Club or Hotel Hibiscus.

Polynesian Parasailing is a way to let you float over Moorea's lagoon without getting your feet wet. This activity is available two or three times daily except Thursday at *the Moorea Beachcomber Parkroyal Nautical Activities Center, Tel. 55.19.19, ext. 1138*. For 5.000 CFP ($50) you have a 10-

minute ride aloft, up to 180 meters (600 feet) above the lagoon, where all you can hear is the wind.

Vaimana is the name of a **yellow submarine** that will transport you to the realm of Ruahatu, King of the Ocean, the home of more than 200 species of fantastically colored fish and magnificent coral gardens. **I.T.S. Moorea**, *Tel. 56.17.56*, headed by Axel Mesnard and Vanessa Bicay, *is based at the Moorea Beachcomber Parkroyal*. There are four tours starting at 8:30am each morning except Monday. Following a briefing you will be transported by boat across the lagoon to board the submarine, which can accommodate three passengers and the pilot. For the next 45 minutes you dive to depths varying from 20-60 meters (66-197 feet), visiting the "Rose Garden" with its enormous coral heads in the form and color of a rose; or you will go to another one of the popular scuba diving sites in Moorea, where you may see Napoleon fish and rays. When the *Vaimana* surfaces at the end of the dive you will return to the hotel dock by boat. The cost of this excursion is 14.500 CFP ($145) per person per dive, or 40.000 CFP ($400) for three people who go together. Children under 12 pay 10.000 CFP ($100), and children under 7 years are not accepted.

Voyage To The World Of Mu is a new excursion that takes you aboard the *Enoha-Iti* covered boat to Opunohu Bay, where you can snorkel among the fish and rays. You'll discover Ruahatu, the Polynesian King Neptune, and some 14 huge stone tikis created by Tihoti, a resident artist-sculptor of Moorea. Then you will go ashore to walk through the centuries old trees and lovely flowers in the **Kellum Gardens**. The price of 3.500 CFP ($35) includes free pick-up at your hotel at 9am or 1pm, snorkeling equipment and fresh fruit and juices, plus the 3-hour boat excursion and snorkeling adventure and the Kellum Gardens. *Tel. 56.18.83*.

SHOPPING

When you take a guided circle island tour of Moorea the bus will most likely stop at a boutique and a black pearl shop, which are probably owned by the guide's family or friends. If you rent a car or scooter or bike around the island you'll have a better chance of finding out which shops suit you best. The **Golden Nugget** in Maharepa is an art gallery and black pearl shop. Owner A. J. Kerebel is a goldsmith and a painter and you'll quickly detect that he is a fan of the American Southwest. The **White House** or *Maison Blanche* in Maharepa, close to the Hotel Bali Hai, is a popular tourist stop. The carved wooden masks and bamboo "rain sticks" filled with rattling seeds are imported, as well as a lot of other souvenir items, but some of the *pareos*, T-shirts and bikinis were made in Tahiti or Moorea.

Island Fashions in Maharepa has *pareos* from Moorea, bikinis from Hawaii and California, as well as Hawaiian style shirts made in California, which are popular with local men and tourists. Ron Hall, the owner of

Island Fashions, is an American who has lived in Moorea since the 1970s. He is a super salesman and he'll give you a great lesson in black pearls and show you his collection of black pearls and black pearl jewelry. Aad van der Heyde, who owns the **Van der Heyde Art Gallery** next door to Ron, has his own oil paintings displayed all around his enclosed garden. Inside his shop you'll find authentic primitive art from throughout the South Pacific, more of Aad's paintings, coral and wood sculptures from the French Polynesian Islands, and displays of black pearl jewelry from Aad's black pearl farm in Ahe in the Tuamotu archipelago.

Honu Iti Boutique in Cook's Bay has Tahitian clothing and souvenirs, as well as *pareos* and trinkets imported from Indonesia. They also have some pretty black pearl jewelry. **Galerie Baie de Cook**, across from Club Bali Hai in Pao Pao, is a museum of ancient Polynesian canoes and artifacts and an art gallery featuring the paintings, sculptures and carvings of artists who live on Moorea.

In the Club Med area of Haapiti you'll find a number of boutiques that carry *pareos*, T-shirts, swimsuits and gift items. **Le Petit Village** is a small shopping center with a supermarket, black pearl shops, boutiques and a magazine stand. **Pai Moana Pearls** is between the Club Med and Le Petit Village. Ask Roger Abernathy, the manager from Missouri, to give you the nitty-gritty on how the black pearl is formed. The **Black Pearl Gem Company (BPGC)**, also facing Club Med, has a good selection of unset pearls and a jeweler on the premises. The prices are right and the service is friendly and helpful. **Galerie Api** is at PK 26 in Haapiti, beside the lagoon close to Club Med. Owner Patrice Bredel exhibits paintings by resident artists, quality prints, old engravings and primitive art.

PRACTICAL INFORMATION

Banks

Socredo Banque, *Tel. 56.13.06, is in the same shopping center as the Maharepa Post Office*, and you'll find an ATM ready cash window here. Open Monday through Friday 8am-12pm and 1:30-4:30pm. *Across the road in the Centre Noha is the* **Banque de Polynesie**, *Tel. 56.14.59.* Open 7:45am-12pm and 1:15-3:45pm. *Less than a block down the road towards Pao Pao* you'll find the **Banque de Tahiti**, *Tel. 56.13.29, on the lagoon side.* Open 8am-12pm and 1:30-4:30pm. The **Westpac Banque**, *Tel. 56.12.02, is located in Le Petit Village in the Club Med area of Haapiti.* Open 9am-12pm and 1:30-4:30pm. All the banks are closed on weekends and holidays. The banks charge a commission of 515 CFP ($5.15) for each transaction, and 561 CFP ($5.61) commission for Visa and Mastercard cash advances

You'll also find a **Change Bureau**, *Tel. 56.43.78, in the Club Saint-Jacques center across the street from the Club Med entrance gate.* This office is open Tuesday through Sunday and the hours fluctuate according to the number of tourists in the area.

Books, Newspapers & Magazines

- **Kina Maharepa**, *Tel. 56.22.44, is in the same commercial center as the Post Office and Socredo Banque.*
- **Supersonics**, *Tel. 56.14.96, is in Le Petit Village in the Club Med area of Haapiti.*

Churches

If your hotel is in the Cook's Bay area, the Protestant church at *PK 5 in Maharepa* is a good choice. The Protestant church Ebenezer at *PK 22 in Papetoai Village* is octagonal and was built on the site that was once the royal Marae Taputapuatea, where heathen gods were worshipped. The first church in the South Seas was built here in 1827 and rebuilt in 1889. It has since been restored a few times. Another Protestant church is located at *PK 35 in Haapiti*, and the beautiful Catholic church, Eglise de la Saint Famille Haapiti, is at *PK 24 on the mountain side.*

Dentist

Dr. Jean-Marc Thurillet, *Tel. 56.32.44, has an office in the Centre Noha, opposite the post office in Maharepa.* He has modern equipment and good dental knowledge and techniques. He is Vietnamese-French and his English is not fluent, but he can communicate.

Doctor

Dr. Christian Jonville, *Tel. 56.32.32, has an office in the Centre Noha, opposite the post office in Maharepa.* He and his partner, Dr. Senegal, both speak English. The office hours are 7am to 12pm and 2 to 6pm Monday through Friday, 7am to 12pm on Saturday, and 8 to 10am on Sunday. Dr. Hervé Paulus, *Tel. 56.10.09, has an office in Le Petit Village, opposite Club Med.* He specializes in sports injuries.

Drugstores

Pharmacie Tran, *Tel. 56.10.51, is at PK 6.5 in Maharepa.* The hours are 7:30am to 12pm and 2 to 5:30pm Monday through Friday, 7:30am to 12pm on Saturday and 8 to 10am on Sundays and holidays. Dr. Tran is Vietnamese and speaks good English. In case of emergency, knock on the door. The **Pharmacie of Haapiti**, *Tel. 56.31.05/56.41.16, is located on the mountainside at PK 30.5.*

Hospital

The 20-bed government **Hospital of Afareaitu**, *Tel. 56.24.24/56.23.23, is at PK 9 in Afareaitu Village.* Seriously ill or injured patients are evacuated by helicopter or airplane to Mamao Hospital in Tahiti.

Laundry/Dry Cleaning

Le Petit Village opposite Club Med has a Laundromat. They wash and dry your clothes for you.

Police

The French *gendarmerie, Tel. 56.13.44, is at PK 7 in Maharepa.* Open daily 7am to 12pm and 2 to 6pm.

Post Office & Telecommunications Office

The **Maharepa Post Office**, *Tel. 56.10.12, is located in the shopping center at PK 5.5.* Hours are 7:30am-12pm and 1:30-4pm Monday through Thursday, and on Fridays it closes at 3pm. It's also open on Saturdays 7:30-9:30am. All telecommunications and postal services are available here. In the village of Papetoai a **mobile Post Office** is open Monday through Friday from 8am-12pm and from 1:30-3:30pm, and from 8-10am on Saturdays. Most hotel boutiques also carry a few postage stamps.

Tourist Information

The **Moorea Tourist Information Center**, *Tel. 56.29.09, has an office at Le Petit Village shopping center opposite Club Med.* Hours are Monday to Saturday from 8am to 5pm. There is also a counter *at the Vaiare Ferry dock*, which is open in the mornings Monday through Saturday, and you can pick up brochures at the airport counter all day.

16. TETIAROA

Tetiaroa is an atoll located just 42 kilometers (26 miles) north of Tahiti, enclosed by a reef that is 55 kilometers (34 miles) in circumference. Inside this protective ring of coral are 12 small *motu* islets scattered around a magnificent lagoon, whose sparkling clear water shades from aquamarine to turquoise to royal blue. This is your ideal desert isle, complete with coconut palms swaying in the tropical breeze, a salty tang in the air, abundant sunshine, miles of empty white sand beaches and a natural aquarium of tropical fish and coral gardens.

When the first Europeans arrived in Tahiti in 1767, Tetiaroa was owned by the high chief **Tu** (who later became known as **King Pomare I**) and his family, who escaped to Tetiaroa to rest and relax. The wives and children of Tahiti's royal family also used Tetiaroa as a beauty spa, where they spent months sequestered from the sun to lighten their skin, and stuffing themselves with fattening foods. In those days, the Polynesian ideal of beauty was to be plump and white.

In 1904 Tetiaroa was ceded to a dentist living in Papeete named Dr. Walter Williams, purportedly in exchange for dental work performed on members of the Pomare family. Williams served as the British consul in Tahiti between 1923 and 1935, and his daughter eventually sold the abandoned atoll to American actor **Marlon Brando** in 1965.

Brando came to Tahiti in 1962 to star in one of the movie versions of *Mutiny on the Bounty*, with many of the scenes being filmed at Point Venus and Matavai Bay, where the *Bounty* actually anchored when Bligh and his crew landed in Tahiti in 1788. Brando played the role of the mutinous Fletcher Christian, and **Tarita Terepaia**, a lovely girl from Bora Bora, played his leading lady in the movie and became Brando's *vahine* in real life.

Tetiaroa was then transformed into the private domain of Brando, Tarita and their two children, Tehotu and Cheyenne, where he could occasionally get away from the stressful life of being a movie star. There is only one small pass through the barrier reef into the lagoon of Tetiaroa, and Brando had a small airstrip built on one of the islets, Motu Onetahi.

Brando's simple bungalows were built primarily from the trunks and fronds of the coconut tree, with coral and sand floors. Tetiaroa Village was eventually opened to the public as a small hotel resort with a reception, restaurant, bar and boutique, also made from coconut palms. Some of the bungalows were blown away during cyclones (hurricanes) in 1983, and the hotel was closed while repairs were made. Tarita still manages the hotel, and it is once again a popular playground and rustic resort.

Tetiaroa is your ideal place if you seek peace and tranquillity. Here you can fulfill your escapist dreams for a day, an overnight visit or a week. The only sounds you hear are the wind blowing through the *causaurina* trees, the cries of sea birds, the thud of a coconut falling, and the thunderous roar of the ocean as the turquoise waves break into seafoam on the coral reef surrounding the atoll.

ARRIVALS & DEPARTURES

Arriving By Air

The Tetiaroa office in Tahiti shares the terminal in Tahiti with **Air Moorea**, and charters small planes from Air Moorea for the 20-minute flight to Tetiaroa. The morning flights leave the Faaa airport in Tahiti at 8am. and the afternoon flights depart at 3:30pm. If you are staying in Moorea and want to visit Tetiaroa, you can fly from Moorea to the air terminal in Papeete and hop on the plane there. When there are several passengers from Moorea making the trip, the plane will pick you up in Moorea just after 8am and bring you back by 4:30pm.

Arriving by Boat

Although the atoll of Tetiaroa belongs to Marlon Brando, the interior lagoon belongs to territorial waters. You can join a day-tour or overnight trip departing from the Papeete waterfront and visit Tetiaroa by sailboat or motor yacht. Or you can leave by boat from Moorea. All the boats take you to one of the *motu* islets on the other side of the coral atoll, far removed from the hotel grounds. They anchor outside the reef, as there is not a large enough pass for the boats to enter the lagoon through the coral gardens. You are then taken ashore by dinghy, landing within walking distance of Bird Island. A picnic lunch is usually served on the beach. See more information on boats in *Tahiti* and *Moorea* chapters.

Va'a Rahi, *Tel. 41.34.03*, has daily sailing excursions to Tetiaroa for 12.000 CFP ($120) aboard a maxi-cat that is 30 meters (98 feet) long. The boat leaves the Papeete dock at 7am and returns around 6:30pm. Lunch is served on the beach or in the Hotel Tetiaroa dining room.

Jet France, *Tel. 56.15.62*, leaves Papeete daily at 7am and returns between 6-8pm. The cost to sail aboard the 22.5 meter (75-foot) maxi-cat is 9.500 CFP ($95) per person, including a picnic on Tetiaroa.

TETIAROA

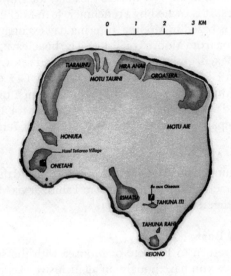

Piraeus II, *Polynesie Yacht Charter, B.P. 20589, Papeete, Tahiti, Tel. 45.17.14/53.43.83*, is a 22.5 meter (75-foot) motor yacht that will take you from Moorea or Papeete to Tetiaroa in just 1 hour and 15 minutes in air-conditioned comfort. Each Tuesday and Thursday the boat leaves from the pier adjacent to **Moana Cook's Bay** in Moorea at 8am, returning at 5:30pm. Every Wednesday, Friday, Saturday and Sunday you can depart at 8am from the boat dock in front of the Papeete post office, and return at 5:30pm. The cost of 14.500 CFP ($145) per person includes breakfast. Snacks and drinks are extra.

Tahiti Cat, *Pacific Charter, Tel. 45.04.00/56.45.98/56.44.38.* This aluminum catamaran is 11.7 meters (39 feet) long, with two 435 horse-power engines. It is owned by Frenchmen Jean-Michel Raffin and Paul Courset, and is based in Moorea, offering day excursions for 18 passengers to Tetiaroa from Moorea or Tahiti. The boat leaves from the dock of the Moorea Beachcomber Parkroyal at 7am and returns at 5:30pm. The crossing takes 1 1/2 hours and the cost of 17.000 CFP ($170) per person includes an American breakfast and a picnic lunch on the beach, with beer, wine and juice. A special Saturday excursion for 14.500 CFP ($145) per person departs from the Papeete boat dock at 7am.

Departing By Air

The morning flight leaves Tetiaroa at 8:30am and the afternoon flight leaves at 4pm, returning to the airport in Tahiti, or via Moorea if there are enough passengers to warrant a stop.

Departing By Boat

You will return to Papeete or Moorea with the same captain who brought you, as you have bought an all-inclusive excursion.

ORIENTATION

You can easily walk around the small islet on Tetiaroa where the airport and hotel are located. As Tetiaroa is a privately-owned atoll, the only people living here are the employees of the hotel and their families, who all live on the main islet of Onetahi.

WHERE TO STAY

HOTEL TETIAROA, *B.P. 2418, 98713 Papeete, Tahiti, French Polynesia, Tel. 689/82.63.02/82.63.03, Fax 689/85.00.51. 9 bungalows and 6 small houses. All rates include round-trip airfare from Tahiti, AP meal plan and excursion to Bird Island. 1 day/1 night 31.000 CFP ($310) single/56.000 CFP ($560) double/72.000 CFP ($720) triple: 2 days/1 night 35.000 CFP ($350) single/64.000 CFP ($640) double/84.000 CFP ($840) triple: 2 days/2 nights*

40.000 CFP ($400) single/74.000 CFP ($740) double/102.000 CFP ($1,020) triple. Add 7% government room tax and 1% value added tax to room rates and meal plan.

The 9 well-worn bungalows are very simply built of coconut logs and thatch. There are also 6 small wooden *fares* or houses beside the beach, which are in much better condition than the bungalows. Both types of lodgings include electricity and private bathrooms with hot water. Mosquito nets cover the beds as the windows and doors are unscreened. The hotel also has a small boutique and a television/video set, and there is a thatched roof beach bar beside the lagoon.

WHERE TO EAT

Every Wednesday and Saturday the hotel serves a barbecue picnic lunch on the white sand beach. All other meals are served in the thatched roof screened restaurant. The cuisine is a combination of French and Tahitian. The Sunday lunch is *maa Tahiti*, which includes roast pig and traditional Tahitian foods cooked in an underground oven.

SEEING THE SIGHTS

You will be welcomed with a fruit punch drink at the reception *fare* beside the airstrip and escorted to your changing rooms or hotel bungalows. After you have put on your swimsuits you are taken on a boat ride across the calm lagoon to visit Tahuna Iti, the *motu* that is better known as **Bird Island**. Tetiaroa is a sanctuary for thousands of sea birds, who lay their eggs on the white powdery sands of the beaches. Here you can easily observe crested terns, brown noddy birds, red- and blue-footed booby birds, white-bellied gannets, petrels, the beautiful white fairy terns with black eyes, and the occasional red-breasted frigate birds, whose fledglings of fluffy white feathers are larger than their mothers. A surprise treat for some visitors is to watch a baby bird opening his shell and taking its first glimpse of the world outside.

The ruins of a *marae* temple built of coral stone can be seen adjacent to the airstrip, and the remains of an old village and *marae* are located on Motu Rimatuu, adjacent to Motu Tahuna Iti.

SPORTS & RECREATION

You can swim, snorkel, fish and dive in the lagoon, which in some places is 30 meters (100 feet) deep. Snorkeling equipment and outrigger paddle canoes can be rented at the hotel. Bring your own fishing and diving gear. Each afternoon is free for snorkeling, swimming, walking around the small islet or simply snoozing in the sun.

PRACTICAL INFORMATION

The tropical sun is very strong and bright on Tetiaroa, and only a minimum of shade is provided by the trees. You can get sunburned here even on cloudy days, so, along with your swimsuit, be sure to bring a wide brimmed hat or visor, sunglasses, a beach cover-up, T-shirt or *pareo*, suntan lotion and plastic sandals or other protective shoes for walking on coral beaches. And don't forget your mosquito repellent.

17. HUAHINE

Huahine (WHO-ah-HEE-nay) is a magical island. I discovered the special qualities of Huahine in 1977, when I was shipwrecked on the reef in Parea, on the south end of Huahine Iti, during a dark and stormy night, while sailing with American friends aboard their luxury yacht. The story has a happy ending, because the yacht was saved and we were adopted into a Tahitian family in Parea. I stayed there for six weeks just because the people were so nice.

On that first morning in Parea, from the cockpit of the yacht that was embedded on the coral reef, I watched the early dawn turning the whole world pink from the mountains to the village to the sea. There is a certain light and color of the air on this island that I haven't found anywhere else. The senses are heightened so that the colors of nature seem more vivid, the air more calm, yet at the same time charged with a feeling of anticipation. I realized that I was listening more intently for—perhaps the primeval call of the jungle.

Twenty years later I still have the same feeling for Huahine. The people are happy and relaxed and they have maintained their traditional lifestyle of fishing and farming. Family and friends are more important than television and Internet. And there's a definite aura of sexual energy in the air. The mountains of Huahine form the shape of a beautiful Tahitian woman when seen from the sea in the moonlight.

Huahine is 175 kilometers (110 miles) northwest of Tahiti, the nearest of the Leeward Society Islands to the capital of Papeete. The two islands that comprise **Huahine-Nui** and **Huahine-Iti** (big and little Huahine) are connected by a bridge and have a combined surface area of 73 square kilometers (28 square miles). Legend claims that the two islands were once united and the isthmus was formed when Hiro, a great warrior and god of thieves in Polynesian mythology, sliced his canoe through the island, dividing it and producing two beautiful bays on each side of the isthmus. Folklore tells us that Hiro used the Leeward Islands as his favorite hangout, and on Huahine you can see Hiro's paddle and parts of his anatomy in the stone formations of the cliffs overlooking the channel.

A common barrier reef surrounds the two islands, with several passes providing openings from the sea to the deep harbors. Off-shore *motu* lie inside the reef, where watermelons and cantaloupe are grown in the white coral sand. These islets are surrounded by white sand beaches, ideal for a picnic outing with snorkeling in the living coral gardens.

The road winds 32 kilometers (20 miles) around the two islands, passing through the little villages of Fare, Maeva, Faie and Fitii on Huahine Nui, and Haapu, Parea, Mahuti, Tefarerii and Maroe on Huahine Iti. The modest homes of the 5,411 inhabitants are built beside the lagoon in the small villages. Another road, called *la route transversale*, crosses part of the island of Huahine Nui, and is best explored by Land Rover or Jeep or any four-wheel drive vehicle, which are called 4x4 (cat-cat) in French. This rutted and often muddy road is close-hemmed by giant ferns and vines that look as though Tarzan might be seen swinging around these parts.

Skirting the shoreline and climbing a little higher into the fern-covered mountains, you will see spectacular views of natural bays and seascapes, with the white foam of the indigo ocean leaping into spray on the coral reef, giving birth to sapphire and emerald lagoons. One multihued bay near the village of Haapu is pointed out on tours as "Gauguin's palette." All around both islands are plantations of vanilla, coffee and taro, and groves of breadfruit, mango, banana and papaya. Trees of *purau* and kapok grow among tangled masses of untamed wilderness. Swiftly flowing streams make their way from their mountain origins, winding through the *mape* forests to form delightful pools for fresh water shrimp.

Mou'a Tapu is the sacred mountain overlooking the prehistoric village of Maeva, which is built beside Lake Fauna Nui. The mountain forms a pyramid, and the people of Maeva say there is a power spot on its summit, which is 429 meters (1,407 feet) high. A tiki of white coral and a Tiare Taina (gardenia) bush are found here. You can reach this spot by going up the road where the television antenna is located on the southern side of the mountain.

According to ethnohistory, Maeva was the ancient capital of Huahine, and all its ruling families lived there and worshipped in their individual *marae* temples of stone. The great Marae Manunu on the coral islet on the opposite side of Maeva Village was the community temple for Huahine Nui, and Marae Anini at Point Tiva in Parea was the community *marae* for Huahine Iti.

HUAHINE

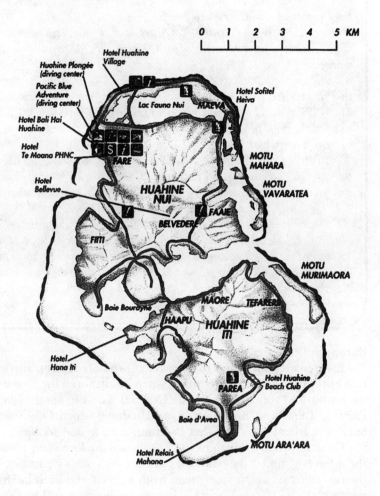

HUAHINE'S ARCHAEOLOGICAL SITES

The royal village of **Maeva** *was the traditional headquarters of Huahine, the capital of a complex and highly centralized system of government. This was the only place in all the Polynesian triangle where the royal families lived side by side. The people of Maeva say that the sacred mountain of Mou'a Tapu protected them. Each of the eight district chiefs of Huahine held court at Maeva and ruled in his province through envoys. Each royal household had a marae stone temple in Maeva as well as in his provincial seat. When the children of each household approached maturity, they, too, each had a temple erected. Consequently, there are some 200 maraes in Maeva.*

Doctor Yosihiko H. Sinoto, Senior Anthropologist of the Bernice P. Bishop Museum in Honolulu, restored several of the marae temples in Maeva Village and on nearby Matairea Hill in 1967 and 1968. He also restored the stone fish weirs in Lake Fauna Nui, which were used by the ancient fishermen of Maeva.

In 1972 Doctor Sinoto began excavation of two archaeological sites on the grounds of the Hotel Bali Hai in Huahine. Over a period of years he and his assistants unearthed a village community that existed between 850 and 1200 A.D., which had been destroyed by tidal waves.

Doctor Sinoto has restored some 200 sites, including 35 marae temples, plus council platforms and housing sites on Matairea Hill in Maeva Village. At the Fare Pote'e, an oval-shaped traditional meeting house built over Lake Fauna Nui, is a museum that tells the story of the royal village. Here you can pick up a map of Matairea Hill and follow a cultural and scenic hiking trail to visit the restored sites.

European Discovery

Lieutenant James Cook (who was later promoted to Captain) was the first European to discover Huahine, when he anchored the *Endeavour* in the harbor of Farenui-Atea on July 15, 1769. You can see the islands of Raiatea, Tahaa and Bora Bora from Huahine, which Cook named a Society of Islands, 'because they lay contiguous to one another'.

Cook returned to Huahine in 1773 aboard the *Resolution*, along with the *Adventure*, under the command of Captain Tobias Furneaux. When the two ships set sail, a young man from Raiatea who lived in Huahine went with them. His name was Mai but the Englishmen call him Omai. He became the first Tahitian to discover England, where he was presented to King George III on July 17, 1774. Cook brought Omai back to Huahine in 1777 during his third and final voyage to the South Seas.

After Cook's departure there were few Europeans who visited Huahine, until 1808-09, when a party of Protestant missionaries from the London Missionary Society made it their headquarters for nearly a year. When Christianity was adopted in Tahiti in 1818 the missionaries returned to Huahine and opened a station. A first-hand account of this story is told by the Reverend William Ellis in *Polynesian Researches*.

Huahine's warrior-queen Teha'apapa defended her island against the aggressions made by the men of Bora Bora, and she won a great naval battle against the forces of Tahiti's Queen Pomare, who tried to gain control of Huahine. In 1846 Teha'apapa won a land battle against French troops at Maeva, and 24 Frenchmen are buried in Maeva Village, surrounded by seven broken cannon. Huahine defended its independence until 1888, when the regent Marama accepted the French protectorate. In 1898 Huahine became a French colony, but it was not until 1946 that the people of Huahine became French citizens, 58 years after the residents of Tahiti.

ARRIVALS & DEPARTURES

Arriving By Air

Air Tahiti has three to six flights daily between Tahiti and Huahine. The 35-minute non-stop flight is 9.240 CFP ($92.40) one-way for adults tax included. There is one flight daily with a stop in Moorea, which costs 11.550 CFP ($115.50) one-way. **Air Tahiti reservations**: *Tahiti, Tel. 86.42.42/86.41.84; Moorea, Tel. 56.10.34; Huahine, Tel. 68.82.65.*

If you have hotel reservations then you will be met at the airport and driven to your hotel. There are also taxis at the airport, as well as **Avis-Pacificar**, **Europcar** and **Hertz** counters. **Sofitel Heiva** has a direct line from the airport and there are two public phones, one for coins and one for phonecards. Brochures of hotels, pensions and activities are available in a wall rack on the left of the arrival gate. The **Vakalele** snack bar and **JoJo's** boutique are located in the airport terminal.

Arriving By Boat

Ono-Ono, *Tel. 45.35.35; Fax 43.83.45; e-mail: onoono@mail.pf*, departs from the Papeete boat dock, *adjacent to the Moorea boats*, each Monday and Wednesday at 9am, arriving in Huahine at 12:45pm. Each Friday it leaves Papeete at 4:30pm, arriving in Huahine at 8:30pm. Each Saturday a special inter-island circuit arrives in Huahine from Bora Bora, Tahaa and Raiatea at 11am. *The ticket office is located on the boat dock in Papeete.* One-way fare between Papeete and Huahine is 4.944 CFP ($49.44). Be at the dock one hour prior to departure.

Taporo VI, *Tel. 42.63.93/43.79.72; Fax 42.06.17*, departs from *the Fare-Ute quay on the far side of the Papeete harbor*, each Monday, Wednesday and Friday, at 4pm, arriving in Huahine the following day at 1:30am. One-way fare to Huahine is 1,692 CFP ($16.92) on the bridge and 20.000 CFP ($200) for a cabin with four berths.

Vaeanu, *Tel. 41.25.35; Fax 41.24.34,* departs from the *Fare-Ute quay in Papeete* at 5pm on Monday, Wednesday and Friday, arriving in Huahine the following morning at 2am. One-way fare for bridge passengers is 1.709 CFP ($17.09) and cabins cost 4.000 to 5.500 CFP ($40 to $55) per person. All the inter-island transport boats dock at the quay in Fare, the main village of Huahine, and it would be advisable to arrange with your hotel or pension to have someone meet you when you arrive in the middle of the night.

Departing By Air

You can fly from Huahine to Raiatea or Bora Bora or return to Moorea or Tahiti by **Air Tahiti**, *Tel. 68.82.65 in Huahine.* Tickets can be purchased at the airport. If you already have reservations and a ticket, reconfirmations should be made one day in advance, and most hotels will take care of this for you. Check-in time at the airport is one hour before scheduled departure.

Departing By Boat

You can continue on to Raiatea, Tahaa and Bora Bora by boat from Huahine, or you can return to Papeete. But let me warn you that the return trip can be very uncomfortable when the sea is rough, which is quite often. Complaints about seasickness aboard the *Ono Ono* are most frequent. So, if you're not a hardy sailor, perhaps you'll want to consider flying back to Tahiti.

The **Ono Ono,** *Tel./Fax 68.85.85,* leaves Huahine for Raiatea, Tahaa and Bora Bora each Monday and Wednesday at 1pm, and for Raiatea and Bora Bora each Friday at 8:45pm. The Huahine-Papeete passages leave the boat dock in Fare each Tuesday and Thursday at 10:15am, arriving in Tahiti at 2:15pm. The Saturday inter-island circuit leaves Huahine for Raiatea-Tahaa-Bora Bora at 3pm. On Sundays the departure time from Huahine is at 3:15pm, arriving in Papeete at 7:15pm.

The **Taporo VI** leaves Huahine at 5:30pm each Tuesday, Thursday and Saturday, arriving in Papeete at 4am the following morning. Buy your tickets on board.

The **Vaeanu** leaves Huahine at 6pm each Tuesday, arriving in Papeete at 3am on Wednesday; departures on Thursday are at 7pm, arriving in Papeete at 4am on Friday; and the Sunday departures leave Huahine at 5pm, arriving in Papeete each Monday at 2am. Buy your ticket on board the ship.

ORIENTATION

To get from the airport in Huahine to the hotels you will turn right to reach the road that circles the island of Huahine-Nui. When you come to this road you will turn right to go to the Hotel Bali Hai Huahine, the main village of **Fare** (pronounced Fah-rey) and the Hotel Bellevue. Turn left if you want to go to **Maeva Village** and the Sofitel Heiva. You can drive in either direction to reach Huahine-Iti and the hotels Hana Iti, Relais Mahana and Huahine Beach Club. If you arrive by boat you will disembark on the dock at Fare, right in the center of Huahine's "downtown" area. Fare looks like a sleepy little village, shaded by acacia and South Seas almond trees, but traffic jams are already a daily occurrence, while people search for a parking place close to the Champion Supermarket, which opened in 1997.

This store is on the waterfront street opposite the quay, along with the Banque de Tahiti, pharmacy, snack bars and small restaurants, pensions, car, scooter and bicycle rentals, service station, scuba diving center, plus other food stores, general merchandise and clothing stores, boutiques, a photo shop and jewelry shop. The post office, *gendarmerie*, private doctors and a 15-bed dispensary are within easy walking distance.

GETTING AROUND
Car, Scooter & Bicycle Rentals

Rental cars, scooters and bicycles are available at the airport and the Fare boat dock, in all the larger hotels and at most of the pensions.

Avis Fare Nui, *Tel. 68.73.34*, has a sales counter at the airport and inside the Super Farenui store in Fare. A 5-door Ford Fiesta rents for 5.200 CFP ($52) for 4 hours, 6.300 CFP ($63) for 8 hours and 7.300 CFP ($73) for 24 hours. A 2-place Mega Ranch costs 5.800 CFP ($58) for four hours, 6.800 CFP ($68) for 8 hours and 7.900 CFP ($79) for 24 hours. Scooter rentals start at 4.500 CFP ($45) for 4 hours and 5.000 CFP ($50) for 8 hours. These rates include unlimited mileage and insurance. Gas is extra.

Hertz, *Tel. 68.72.00*, has car rental offices *at the airport and on the quay in Fare.*

Europcar, *Tel. 68.82.59*, has sales offices beside the entrance to the Hotel Bali Hai, on the quay in Fare, and sales desks at all the hotels. A Fiat Panda rents for 4.500 CFP ($45) for 3 hours, 5.000 CFP ($50) for 4 hours, 6.000 CFP ($60) for 8 hours, 7.000 CFP ($70) for 24 hours, and 13.000 CFP ($130) for a weekend. A Fun Car is a cross between a car and a scooter and rents for 4.000 CFP ($40) for 3 hours and 4.500 CFP ($45) for 8 hours. Scooter rates start at 3.500 CFP ($35) for 3 hours. These rates include unlimited mileage and third party insurance. Gas is extra.

Tropic 2000, *Tel. 68.70.84*, is located in the same building as the **Photo Shop**, adjacent to the Pharmacy in Fare. Car rental rates vary from 5.000 CFP ($50) for 4 hours to 7.500 CFP ($75) for 24 hours.

Bicycles

Avis Fare Nui, *Tel. 68.73.34*, rents bicycles for 1.200 CFP ($12) for 4 hours and 1.500 CFP ($15) for 8 hours. Longer rentals possible.

Europcar, *Tel. 68.82.59*, rents mountain bikes for 1.100 CFP ($11) for 3 hours and 1.600 CFP ($16) for 8 hours. Bicycles can be rented for 1.000 CFP ($10) for 3 hours and 1.500 CFP ($15) for 8 hours. Longer rentals possible.

Huahine Lagoon, *Tel. 68.70.00*, has beach bikes with a basket or mountain bikes for rent.

JoJo Locations, *Tel. 68.89.16*, also rents bicycles *on the quay in Fare*.

Taxis

Taxi service is provided by **Enite Excursions**, *Tel. 68.82.37*; **Lovina Excursions** *Tel. 68.88.06*; **Maeva Nui Taxi Service** *Tel. 68.81.76*; **Alan Parker**, and a couple of other taxis that wait at the airport and boat dock.

Le Truck

The local transportation service, *le truck*, operates between the boat dock in Fare and the outlying villages around Huahine Nui and Huahine Iti, coordinating their runs with the arrivals and departures of the inter-island ferries and school hours. The name of the destination is painted on the wooden sides of each *le truck*. Although the fares are affordable for all budgets, hopping aboard a *le truck* is not recommended if you don't know your way around Huahine, and especially if you don't speak any French or Tahitian. But if you are adventurous, this is a fun way to discover the island and its inhabitants.

WHERE TO STAY

Expensive

HANA ITI, *B.P. 185, Fare, Huahine, Tel. 689/68.85.05, Fax 689/68.88.53; reservations, South Pacific Marketing, B.P. 718, Papeete, Tahiti, Tel. 689/43.90.04, Fax 689/41.39.23, New York reservations office, Tel. 800/225-4255/212, 696-4566, Fax 212/689-1598. Near the village of Haapu on Huahine Iti, overlooking the Bay of Bourayne, 12 kilometers (7.5 miles) from the airport. 24 bungalows. EP Rates: 54.000 CFP ($540) single/double deluxe bungalow; 64.000 CFP ($640) single/double special bungalow; third adult 5.000 CFP ($50) per night. Add 7.800 CFP ($78) per person for breakfast and dinner; add 10.800 CFP ($108) per person for 3 meals daily. Round-trip* *transfers from airport 2.400 CFP ($24). Add 7% government room tax and 1% value added tax to room rates and meal plan. All major credit cards.*

This very exotic hotel is a dream realized by American owner Tom Kurth, who bought 26.05 hectares (64.3 acres) of land from Julio Iglesias, the Spanish singer. Tom and his sons created a virtual Garden of Eden, with over 500 different kinds of plants added to the untamed beauty of the virgin forest of tropical trees that covers the hillside and slopes down to the beach.

Hana Iti, which means small bay, opened in 1991. Each of the 24 one-of-a-kind luxury villas or *fares* is secluded, with privacy guaranteed. Some are reminiscent of tree houses, tucked into the arms of banyan trees. Other villas are embedded in volcanic rock with tiny cascades of water trickling through their showers, and feature sundecks perched on the edge of cliffs. Others are built on stilts, some as high as 6 meters (20 feet) off the ground, which creates a sense of being suspended in the jungle. All the thatched-roof villas offer views of the lagoon and Raiatea across the ocean, and provide 360 degree views of the magnificent valleys and mountain peaks of Huahine Iti.

Each *fare* is at least 90 square meters (1,000 square feet) in size, divided into separate living areas on three or more levels for lounging, sleeping and bathing, connected by spiral stairs or a walk around a living tree. They were painstakingly built of precious wood from Fiji, volcanic stone and seashells. All have verandas and an outdoor Jacuzzi. Each unit is decorated with hand-painted tapa bark from Tonga and Fiji, imported Balinese batiks, bamboo couches and screens of Filipino capiz shells. A mosquito net forms a canopy over the king size beds. The toilet is transformed into a throne when you sit in the Queen Pomare chair, and the wash basins are giant clam shells with cowry shell faucets.

You'll find a complimentary refrigerator-bar and overhead fans. There are no phones or air-conditioning in these back-to-Eden *fares*, which sometimes resemble an upscale Freddy Flintstone abode or an eclectic Balinese hangout for a modern-day Tarzan. The *fares* now have a weathered look, which Tom Kurth calls "Mother Nature's art work." You have to be part mountain goat to negotiate some of the stone stairways, and the daytime humidity in this gorgeous jungle is overwhelming. Still, it's a fabulous setting for agile lovers who want to play chase. No children under 12 are allowed.

To get to the reception or beachfront dining/bar facilities from your lofty summit dwelling, you order a four-wheel shuttle van by intercom. Room service is available only for Continental breakfasts. The open-air dining *fare* on the beach has a roof design like the Thai concept of reaching for the sky. Every table overlooks the lily pond, with a front row view during the Tahitian dance shows. A thatched roof bar beside the white sand beach has swinging chairs and Tom's creative arrangements of driftwood, coral and huge triton shells decorate the tables.

The fresh water swimming pool and Jacuzzi are surrounded by tropical foliage and fed by a waterfall cascading 120 feet down the mountainside. You can also swim to a floating sun dock in the lagoon, paddle an outrigger canoe, windsurf, sail a Hobie cat, or snorkel. These are all free activities. The tennis courts are no longer usable, and the hotel shows other signs that it is suffering severe financial difficulties.

SOFITEL HEIVA, *B.P. 38, Fare, 98731 Huahine, Tel. 689/68.86.86, Fax 689/68.85.25, reservations Tahitires, Tel. 689/41.04.04, Fax 689/41.05.05. In US Tel. 914/472-0370 or 800/763-4835, Fax 914/472-0451, Internet: http://www.sofitel.com Located 8 kilometers (5 miles) from the airport at the end of the motu in Maeva Village. 61 rooms and bungalows. EP Rates 22.500 CFP $225) single/double garden room; 32.000 CFP ($320) single/double garden bungalow; 48.000 CFP ($480) single/double beach bungalow; 60.000 CFP ($600) single/double overwater bungalow; third adult 4.500 CFP ($45). Add a supplement of 1.500 CFP ($15) per day for the high seasons of January 1-15, July 15 to August 31, and December 20-31. Add 5.600 CFP ($56) per person for breakfast and dinner; add 8.100 CFP ($81) person for 3 meals daily. Round-trip transfers from the airport by mini-van cost 1.600 CFP ($16) per person, and round-trip transfers by air-conditioned limousine are 3.920 CFP ($39.20) per person. Add 7% government room tax and 1% value added tax to room rates and meal plan. All major credit cards.*

The Sofitel Heiva opened in 1989 and is built on nearly two hectares (5 acres) of tropical gardens, complete with stone *marae* temples, on the tip of the Maeva peninsula between two white sandy beaches and a coconut plantation. The 61 Polynesian style thatched-roof bungalows include 6 suites over the water, one suite on the beach, 11 beach bungalows, 19 lagoon side bungalows and 24 individual garden rooms with a private terrace.

All the rooms are equipped with overhead fans, mini-bar, direct-dial phone, tea and coffee facilities, a bathroom with hot water shower, 220 volt electricity, and hair dryers on request. The overwater suites have a semi-circular living room and a large bedroom, with one king size bed or two twin beds. There is a dressing table with stool and a full length mirror and spacious closets. The big bathrooms have two lavabos, shower or bathtub and a private toilet, lots of fluffy towels and a collection of Sofitel's own brand of soap, shampoo, lotion and suntan oil. The decoration is all Polynesian, with bamboo, wicker and rattan furniture, woven pandanus mats and wall coverings, Tahitian quilted bedspreads and framed *tapa* bark cloth wall hangings. A window through the floor reveals families of multihued fish nibbling on live coral in the lagoon below the bungalow. There are reclining chairs on the covered terrace, and steps leading down into the warm shallow water, where Lake Maeva merges with the lagoon.

An immense thatched roof covers the Omai Restaurant, Manuia Bar, reception area and library. Public facilities include a boutique, black pearl shop, tour desk and car rental desk. The island style motif is expanded by draped tapa hangings and Polynesian paintings. Outside is a fresh water swimming pool with waterfall, the sports *fare* and pier.

Nautical activities range from an outrigger canoe tour to visit the sacred eels in Faie village for 2.300 CFP ($23) to a full-day deep sea fishing expedition for 85.200 CFP ($852). Land activities include archaeological tours, horseback riding, and a personalized tour of Huahine by air-conditioned limousine for 24.000 CFP ($240). The hotel has a daily program of free entertainment, such as *tamure* lessons, Huahine slide shows, learning how to make coconut candies and discovering the plants in the hotel gardens. Happy Hour is held nightly from 9 to 10pm, with an additional Happy Hour on Wednesday and Thursday from 5 to 6pm. A Polynesian dance show is performed on Thursday evening following a buffet, and on Saturday nights following the Polynesian feast.

TE TIARE BEACH RESORT, *B.P. 36, Fare, Huahine, Tel. 689/ 68.80.12. Reservations: South Pacific Marketing, B.P. 718, Papeete, Tahiti. Tel. 689/43.90.04; Fax 689/41.39.23. Located on the coast of Fitii, 20 minutes by boat from the main village of Fare. 41 bungalows. EP Rates: garden bungalow 26.000 CFP ($260) single/double; beach bungalow 42.000 CFP ($420) single/ double; overwater bungalow 42.000 CFP ($420) single/double; third adult add 4.000 CFP ($40). Add 6.200 CFP ($62) per person for breakfast and dinner; add 8.500 CFP ($85) per person for all three meals; Continental breakfast add 1.450 CFP ($14.50); full American breakfast add 1.950 CFP ($19.50); outrigger canoe breakfast add 2.900 CFP ($29) per person; romantic breakfast on the beach add 2.600 CFP ($26) per person; private honeymoon champagne dinner under the stars add 7.800 CFP ($78) per person. One-way transfer add 900 CFP ($9). Add 7% government room tax and 1% value added tax to room rates and meal plan All major credit cards.*

This hotel is scheduled to open in October, 1998, with 19 garden bungalows, 6 beach bungalows and 16 overwater bungalows, located beside the Fitii lagoon. The site covers 11.40 hectares (28.17 acres) of tropical plants and flowers, including 3.5 hectares (8.65 acres) of flat ground. The deluxe bungalows have air-conditioning and fans, a mini-bar and refrigerator, coffee and tea facilities, a bathroom with hot water shower, hair dryers, safes, television, international direct dial telephones and a sundeck. The overwater bungalows also have Jacuzzi bathtubs.

The main building has an overwater restaurant and bar. There will be a boutique, swimming pool, tennis court and nautical activities center, offering snorkeling equipment, outrigger canoes, kayaks, lagoon fishing, deep-sea fishing, sunset cruises, scuba diving, outrigger canoe tours, glass bottom boat excursions, water skiing, jet skiing and windsurf boards. Jeep safaris and other land excursions will be operated from the boat dock in Fare village, as there is no road leading to the hotel.

Moderate

HUAHINE BEACH CLUB, *B.P. 39, Fare, Huahine, Tel. 689/68.81.46, Fax 689/68.85.86; reservations Tahiti Resort Hotels, B.P. 13019, Punaauia, Tahiti, Tel. 689/43.08.29, Fax 689/41.09.28. Located 20 kilometers (12 miles) from the airport on the southern coast of Huahine Iti in Parea Village. 17 bungalows. EP Rates: 18.000 CFP ($180) single/double/triple garden bungalow; 20.000 CFP ($200) single/double/triple beachside bungalow; 22.000 CFP ($220) single/double/triple bungalow on beach. Add 4.000 CFP ($40) per person for breakfast and dinner; add 5.600 CFP ($56) per person for 3 meals daily. Round-trip transfers from airport 1.800 CFP ($18) person. Add 7% government room tax and 1% value added tax to room rates and meal plan. All major credit cards.*

The Huahine Beach Club opened as a Tahiti Resort Hotel in 1989 and is considered the flagship hotel of this chain. The 9 beach bungalows and 8 garden bungalows across the road have all been rebuilt following a fire in 1993. These thatched roof traditional Polynesian style bungalows have 54 square meters (600 square feet) of living space, with a king size bed and sitting area under the ceiling fan, a mini-refrigerator, sunken bathroom with hot water shower and garden, and a private terrace. The decor is South Seas cool, with rattan furniture, woven mats on the walls and tastefully selected bedspreads, curtains and cushions.

The main building houses the reception, dining room, boutique and activities desk, and the bar is in a separate thatched roof building. The hotel offers complimentary use of the fresh water swimming pool, snorkeling equipment, outrigger paddle canoes, windsurf board, *petanque* (bocci-ball) and volley ball. Free entertainment also includes a coconut show, *pareo* tying demonstrations and live Tahitian music in the evenings. A Tahitian *tamaara'a* feast is held once a month or when the hotel is full.

The long white sand beach in front of the hotel is bordered by centuries old *tamanu* trees, and the historic Marae Anini stone temple is sheltered under the trees close to the pass. Motu Araara is across the lagoon from the hotel beach, providing a tempting destination for a picnic and swim in the liquid turquoise beauty of a deep swimming hole called *la piscine*. Bring your mosquito repellent. Boat and land tours will take you to visit Huahine Iti, and you can rent a car, scooter or bicycle for your own exploring.

You can also walk around the village of Parea and meet the inhabitants, watch the young men of the village playing soccer, see the children coming home from school, and attending church services and listening to the beautiful singing. This is an opportunity to experience the authentic life on a small Polynesian island. Parea became my special place in 1977 when the yacht I was sailing aboard was shipwrecked on the reef beside the pass. I lived six weeks with the *mutoi*, the local policeman and his family. My favorite friend in Parea was a 14-year old boy named Tino, who is now the cook at Huahine Beach Club.

An additional 24 rooms are to be added to this hotel, with 12 rooms scheduled for completion by June, 1998, and another 12 to be finished in December, 1998, which will give the hotel a total capacity of 41 rooms.

HOTEL BALI HAI HUAHINE, *B.P. 341, Fare, Huahine, Tel. 689/68.84.77, Fax 689/68.82.77; reservations B.P. 26, Maharepa, Moorea, Tel. 689/56.13.59, Fax 689/56.19.22; in US Tel. 800/282-1401. Located four kilometers (2.5 miles) from the airport and one kilometer (.6 mile) from Fare Village. 33 bungalows and 10 rooms. EP Rates: 11.500 CFP ($115) single/double poolside bungalow; 13.500 CFP ($135) single/double garden bungalow; 15.500 CFP ($155) single/double lakeside bungalow; 19.800 CFP($198) single/double bungalow on beach; third adult 3.000 CFP ($30). Add 4.500 CFP ($45) per person for breakfast and dinner; add 6.900 CFP ($69) per person for 3 meals daily. Round-trip transfers from airport 1.200 CFP ($12) person. Add 7% government room tax and 1% value added tax to room rates and meal plan. All major credit cards.*

This was the first international class hotel in Huahine, and it still remains one of the favorite destinations for guests who want a true Polynesian experience in a beautiful location. The manager and staff are all Polynesian, mostly from Huahine. The thatched roof bungalows include 7 beach bungalows, 15 garden bungalows, 11 lake-side bungalows and 10 rooms beside the swimming pool. The bungalows are screened and have a queen-size bed and one or two twin beds, overhead fans, mini-refrigerators, sunken bathrooms with hot water shower and hair dryer. The current is 110 volts and each room is limited to 900 watts. The restaurant and bar are beside the soft white sand beach facing the pass of Fare, a favorite surfing spot. A special buffet is served on Friday evenings, followed by a traditional Tahitian dance show. In addition to the fresh water pool with underwater bar stools, there is a tennis court, and guests can paddle an outrigger canoe to explore the beautiful turquoise lagoon. Near the reception desk in the lobby is an activities and car rental desk and the boutique carries sundries and souvenirs.

This is my favorite hotel in Huahine. It is simple, relaxing, and located in an exquisite setting, just a five minute walk to Fare village. One of my favorite activities here is to awaken with the dawn so that I can photograph the lake and its bridges during a very brief magical moment, when the luminescence of the sky is reflected in the still water, shaded by the palm trees and lakeside bungalows. And just before sunset time, I love to swim in the warm lagoon in front of the hotel. See chapter on *Best Places to Stay*.

RELAIS MAHANA, *B.P. 30, Fare, Huahine, Tel. 689/68.81.54, Fax 689/68.85.08. Located at Avea Bay on Huahine's best white sand beach, (25 kilometers) 15.5 miles from the airport, on the southwest side of Huahine Iti, just outside Parea Village. 22 garden and beach bungalows. EP Rates: 16.000 CFP ($160) single/double garden bungalow; 18.000 CFP ($180) single/double beach bungalow; additional person 3.000 CFP ($30) per night. Add 3.700 CFP ($37) per person for breakfast and dinner. Round-trip transfers from airport 2.000 CFP ($20) per adult and 1.400 CFP ($14) for children 3-11 years. Add 7% government room tax and 1% value added tax to room rates and meal plan. All major credit cards. Note: The hotel will be closed from November 15 to December 15, 1998.*

This small hotel was built in 1985 and remodeled in 1992. It is owned and operated by the Paiman family, French people from New Caledonia, who keep the grounds and the 22 shingle-roofed bungalows clean and in good condition. I have been allowed to see the rooms and I have eaten lunch here, but I have never chosen to stay at this hotel because I don't get a feeling of warmth and reception from the management. They run their hotel with strict military-like precision. If that doesn't bother you, then you will have the advantage of enjoying Huahine's prettiest snorkeling grounds and white sand beach.

There are 12 bungalows for one or two people, including 7 beach and 5 garden units, and 10 bungalows will sleep three or four people in 4 beach and 6 garden units. One of the double beach bungalows is equipped to receive disabled people with wheelchairs. The bungalows are equipped with large double beds, a ceiling fan in the bedroom, a mini-refrigerator, a bathroom with hot water showers and a terrace with a table and armchairs. The one-bedroom bungalows also have a desk.

There is a restaurant and bar, with another mini-bar/ snack on the beachfront, a reception desk, boutique and a living room. Guests pay to use a mini-launderette. Free activities include pedal boats, canoes, kayaks, bicycles, snorkeling equipment, ping-pong, books, tennis, swimming pool, *petanque* (French bowls), and video movies are shown on rainy days. The hotel's paid activities include water-skiing for 2.000 CFP ($20), glass bottom boat excursion for 2.200 CFP ($22), snorkeling excursion, 2.000 CFP ($20) per hour, and a tour around Huahine Iti by boat for 3.000 CFP ($30) per person. The hotel can also arrange deep-sea fishing, scuba diving, horseback riding, and minibus and safari tours. You can rent a car or scooter from Europcar across the street.

HUAHINE VILLAGE, *B.P. 295, Fare, Huahine. Tel. 689/68.87.00; Fax 689/68.86.99. Located beside the lagoon four kilometers (2.5 miles) from the airport and 3 kilometers (1.9 miles) from Fare village. 28 bungalows. EP Rates:*

garden bungalow 8.000 CFP ($80) single/double; beach bungalow 10.000 CFP ($100) single/double. Add 3.000 CFP ($30) for additional person. Add 4.000 CFP ($40) per person for breakfast and dinner; add 5.800 CFP ($58) per person for 3 meals daily. Round-trip transfers 600 CFP ($6). Add 7% government room tax and 1% value added tax to room rates and meal plan. Visa.

This beachfront hotel is located between the airport and Fare village, with 6 beach bungalows and 22 garden bungalows, all with thatched roofs and simply furnished in *pareo* fabrics. Each room has an overhead fan, a mini-refrigerator, coffee and tea facilities, and private bathroom with hot water shower. There is a fresh water swimming pool, an activities desk and car rental desk in the lobby, a restaurant, bar and boutique.

PENSION MAUARII, *98731, Parea, Huahine, Tel./Fax. 689/68.86.49. Beside a white sand beach in Parea, 17 kilometers (10.6 miles) from the ferry dock and 19 kilometers (11.8 miles) from the airport. 3 bungalows, 1 fare and a dormitory. EP Rates: room 6.500 CFP ($65) single, 7.500 CFP ($75) double; mezzanine 9.000 CFP ($90) double; "fare" 35.000 CFP ($350); bungalow 9.000 CFP ($90) single, 10.000 CFP ($100) double, 15.000 CFP ($150) quadruple; bed in dormitory 2.400 CFP ($24); additional person 1.000 CFP ($10). Add 3.000 CFP ($30) per person for breakfast and dinner; add 5.000 CFP ($50) per person for 3 meals daily. Weekly and monthly rates available on request. Transfers from airport 1.800 CFP ($18). Add 1% value added tax to room rates and meal plan. No credit cards.*

This pension is located on Huahine Iti beside a beautiful white sand beach just outside Parea village. The main building is a deluxe Polynesian style *fare pote'e* or traditional meeting house, with an overwater terrace. The two rooms contain a king size bed, and guests share the bathroom with hot water shower and large living room with a lending library. The three bungalows are beside the lagoon or with a garden view, each with a king size bed and a double bed, a bathroom with cold water and a terrace. The dormitory on the mezzanine has 10 mattresses, and guests share a communal bathroom with cold water. The restaurant serves a Continental breakfast for 1.000 CFP ($10) and the menu includes excellent food prepared by Willie Flohr, who specializes in fish and seafood, and he can also create some tasty Chinese dishes. Marcelle and Willie, who were born in Huahine, are both fluent in English.

Inexpensive

HOTEL BELLEVUE, *B.P. 21, Fare, Huahine, Tel. 689/68.82.76/ 68.81.70, Fax 689/68.85.35. Located on the mountainside overlooking Maroe Bay, 7 kilometers (4 miles) from Fare village. 8 rooms and 12 garden bungalows. EP Rates: 3.500 CFP ($35) single, 4.500 CFP ($45) double, 5.000 CFP ($50) triple standard room; 6.000 CFP ($60) single, 7.000 CFP ($70) double, 8.000 CFP ($80) triple, and 9.000 CFP ($90) quadruple for bungalow. Add 3.200*

CFP ($32) per person for breakfast and dinner; add 5.700 CFP ($57) per person for 3 meals daily. Round-trip transfers from airport 1.000 CFP ($10). Add 7% government room tax and 1% value added tax to room rates and meal plan. Mastercard, Visa.

This small hotel is owned by Eliane and François Lefoc, a Chinese couple from Huahine who have earned a reputation for their delicious seafood from the lagoons of Huahine. They operated a restaurant and bar on these premises for three years before they built the bungalows in 1983. Most visitors to Huahine see the Hotel Bellevue when they are riding around the island in a tour bus. It is perched on the top of a knoll overlooking the tranquil scenery of Maroe Bay and the hills beyond. This is one of those places that is discovered by travelers who have the time to get to know an island, its people and its delightful secrets.

Each of the 12 colonial style bungalows contains a double bed, a single bed, a bathroom with hot water provided by solar heating, and individual terraces overlooking the fresh water swimming pool and the view of Maroe Bay. The rooms are upstairs over the family living quarters and are rented only when necessary.

Eliane and François do not speak much English, but they say a lot with their eyes and gestures. She very willingly drives the guests to the village and to visit the island. You can also walk down to the road and catch *le truck* into Fare. The gardens here would please any botanist, and the lobster, soft-shell crabs, *varo* (sea centipede) and fresh fish that are served will transform your visit to Huahine into a holiday for *gourmands*.

CHEZ GUYNETTE CLUB-BED, *B. P. 87, 98731 Fare, Huahine, Tel. 689/68.83.75. In the center of Fare village, opposite the ferry dock and 3 kilometers (1.9 miles) from the airport. 7 rooms and an 8 berth dormitory. EP Rates: room 3.300 CFP ($33) single, 3.900 CFP ($39) double, 4.500 CFP ($45) triple); bed in dormitory 1.400 CFP ($14). Minimum stay 2 nights or pay supplement of 300 CFP ($3). The room rates include a 1% value added tax. Mastercard, Visa.*

If you arrive in Huahine by inter-island ferry boat you can walk across the road from the boat dock and you'll be at Chez Guynette, which is now operated by my friend Marty Temahahe, an American expatriate who bought the pension in April, 1998. The hostel has 7 rooms, each with a double bed and a cot and a private bathroom with cold water. There is also an 8-bed dormitory, sharing an outside communal bathroom with cold water, and a big, clean and homey kitchen. The windows are all screened and each room has an electric fan. Sheets are furnished, but you should bring your own towels and soap. In the reception area Marty has all the information posted on the activities available on Huahine, and Moe, her Tahitian husband, runs the snack bar. You'll enjoy eating the meals and snacks prepared in the local style, as well as American specialties, even if you're not sleeping in the pension. You'll be right in the middle of village life on a tropical island here, with the benefit of walking across the road to a white sand beach for a wonderful swim in the warm lagoon.

Guest Houses & Camp Sites

Guest houses in Huahine include: **Poetaina**, *Tel. 68.89.49*, with a 3-story concrete house in Fare; **Chez Henriette**, *Tel. 68.83.71*, with 6 *fares* in Haamene Bay; **Pension Meri**, *Tel. 68.82.44*, with 2 houses in Fare; **Chez Lovina**, *Tel. 68.88.06*, with 3 bungalows, 6 *fares* and a campground in Fare; **Fare Tehani**, *Tel. 68.71.00*, with 2 family size *fares* in Fare; and **Chez Ella**, *Tel. 68.73.07*, with 2 houses and a cottage in Fare.

In the Maroe Bay area there are houses and villas to rent. These include **Residence Loisirs Maroe**, *Tel. 42.96.09*, with a 4-bedroom villa; **Maisons Standing**, *Tel. 82.49.65*, with 4 houses; **Villa Bougainville** and **Villa Oiseau de Paradis**, *Tel. 68.81.59*, with 2 houses; and **Villa Pitate**, *Tel. 68.85.63*, with a family style bungalow. **Motel Vanille**, *Tel. 68.71.77*, near Fare village, has six bungalows and a swimming pool and serves family style meals.

Backpackers and campers will find inexpensive accommodations at **Camping Snack Vanaa**, *Tel. 68.89.51*, on Motu Maeva, which has 13 small *fares* and a campground; and at **Ariiura Camping**, *Tel. 68.85.20*, in Parea on Huahine Iti, which has 12 small *fares* and a campground.

WHERE TO EAT

The hotel restaurants usually have very good food, but if you want to see what's happening in Fare village, the following restaurants and snack bars serve pretty good food for reasonable prices. You'll also find a few *roulottes* (mobile diners) and small snack bars on the quay of Fare, which are open when the inter-island boats arrive from Papeete or Bora Bora during the wee hours of the morning.

TIARE TIPANIER RESTAURANT, *Tel. 68.80.52, is adjacent to the Mairie of Fare (town hall).*

Huahine residents consider this the best restaurant in town. Part of it is operated as a snack, serving hamburgers, pizzas and omelets, and the other part is a French restaurant. Steaks are 1.250 CFP ($12.50), a variety of fish dishes each cost 1.400 CFP ($14), an *escalope cordon bleue forestière* is 900 CFP ($9), and you can take your pick of live lobster in a tank, for 1.800 CFP ($18). Open for lunch and dinner except Sunday. Mastercard and Visa accepted.

ORIO BAR AND RESTAURANT, *Tel. 68.83.03, built overwater at the quay in Fare village.*

A simple restaurant where you can watch the bonito boats coming in as you sip a sunset cocktail on the terrace. Owner Jacqueline Itchner is a

Huahine lady who serves some good breaded shrimp for 1.400 CFP ($14), mahi mahi or salmon-of-the-gods with pepper or Roquefort sauce for 1.600 CFP ($16), and lobster in spicy coconut sauce, starting at 1.500 CFP ($15), according to the size of the lobster. Open 11am to 2:30pm and 6:30 to 9:30pm. Closed Friday night and Saturday noon. Mastercard and Visa accepted.

TE MARARA, *Tel. 68.74.33, is at the edge of the beach at the beginning of Fare village when you come from the airport.*

Owner Vahinetua Fontaine serves a Continental breakfast from 7 to 9am, and French cuisine and seafood for lunch and dinner. Open daily. Happy Hour on Friday evening. All cards.

TE VAIPUNA, *Tel. 68.70.45, is opposite the Fare quay.*

This small air-conditioned restaurant serves mainly Chinese dishes, with a few French and local selections. Open 6 to 9:30am, 11am to 2:30pm and 6 to 9:30pm. Mastercard and Visa accepted.

LA PAPAYE VERTE (**The Green Papaya**), *Tel. 68.73.13, in Fare village opposite the quay.*

This is a snackbar with a few umbrella-covered tables and a coral floor. You can eat breakfast, lunch and snacks here from 8am to 6pm. An omelette with ham, cheese and mushrooms costs 300 CFP ($3), *poisson cru* is 700 CFP ($7), fish and chips are 400 CFP ($4), and fresh fruit juices, which include a choice of *pamplemousse* (grapefruit), pineapple, papaya, watermelon or lime, cost 500 CFP ($5). No credit cards.

CHEZ GUYNETTE, *Tel. 68.83.75, facing the waterfront of Fare village.*

Chez Guynette is often open when all other restaurants and snack bars are closed in Fare. Light meals are served and you may even find a sub-sandwich prepared by American owner Marty Temahahe, or a delicious *poisson cru* created by her Tahitian husband, Moe, who wears the chef's hat.

VAKALELE, *at the Huahine Airport.*

Dorothy Levy's snackbar, open for all Air Tahiti arrivals and departures. Meeting Dorothy is worth the trip to Huahine. She also runs the Fare Pote'e museum in Maeva village. Dorothy will create a special smoothie or fruit juice and sandwich for you while she fills you in on the history and culture of the island.

SEEING THE SIGHTS

Ariiura Paradise is a back-to-Eden garden of revival and conservation of Polynesian herbal medicine. Cecile Tehihira and Hubert Bremond have planted more than 200 varieties of herbs, flowers, ferns, fruits and trees in their hillside garden *beside Maroe Bay*. Over 150 of these plants are used by the islanders for *raa'u Tahiti*, traditional medicine. Native healers visit the gardens twice a month to collect medicinal plants and to treat people who have health problems. Some of the organized tours stop here.

Fare Pote'e is a museum and handcrafts center, built over the water at Lake Fauna Nui in Maeva Village. This is a replica of a traditional meeting house of classic Polynesian oval shape, with a high curved roof of pandanus thatch, bamboo walls, and a floor of halved coconut trees, overlaid with woven slats of bamboo. The exhibits include a variety of useful tools that were used by the Polynesians before the arrival of the Europeans. Kites, canoes, tops and other traditional games are also displayed, as well as musical instruments and a copy of the wooden headrest used by Omai, the first Tahitian to discover England.

Arts and crafts made by the residents of Huahine are for sale, and you can get a map of the hiking trails on nearby Matairea Hill, where you can see the restored *marae* temples of stone, the house and council platforms and other work in progress. The Fare Pote'e is managed by Dorothy Levy, who is half-American. She has a great, outgoing personality and is a wealth of information on Huahine's history and culture. The museum is open Monday to Friday 9am to 3pm, and on Saturday from 9am to 12pm. Free admission.

Local Motion Farm, *Tel. 68.86.58, is located in Vaiorea Bay at Port Bourayne close to Fitii Village.* Look for the sign at the junction just past Hotel Bellevue. Gilles Tehau Parzy has created a botanical garden in 3 hectares (7 acres) of tropical fruit trees, flowers and exotic plants. A special **Botanical Tour** has been designed for rainy days, but you can also enjoy this activity when the sun shines. After watching a video film of the island you will be served appetizers and fresh fruit drinks made from fruits grown on the farm. Rubber boots and raincoats are provided if necessary, for your wanderings through the gardens, where you can photograph three of Huahine's bays from the panoramic viewpoints. Then you'll sit down to a gastronomic meal of tonic exotic salads, seafood or shellfish, a gourmet dessert and vanilla-flavored coffee or tropical herbal teas. This experience costs 2.950 CFP ($29.50) per person, all inclusive, and is available on Monday, Wednesday, Thursday and Friday, from 10am to 2pm.

Each Tuesday and Saturday a **Lagoon Safari** aboard a giant-size covered twin-hull canoe takes you on a snorkeling excursion, with a picnic of fresh grilled fish and other foods cooked on a white sand beach. The cost is 6.800 CFP ($68) per person, including two fruit juices and water. Each Wednesday and Friday you can join a **Magical Sunset Cruise** from 5 to 6:30pm, with fruit juice cocktails and Tahitian dancing included for the 3.500 CFP ($35) per person. Free transfers to board the canoe in Fitii are provided.

Land Tours

Felix Tours, *Tel. 68.82.26*, offers half-day Circle Island Tours by mini-van. The morning tour starts at 9am and ends at 12:30pm and the afternoon tour is from 1:30 to 5:30pm., for 3.500 CFP ($35) per person. You will visit all of the interesting sites on both islands, including some of the most important prehistoric archaeological remains in all of Polynesia. The stops include: Marae Manunu on Motu Maeva, the largest stone temple on Huahine; the ancient stone fish traps in Lake Maeva, which are still in use; the prehistoric archaeological center of Maeva Village; the blue-eyed sacred eels of Faie Village; the Mato Ere Ere panoramic view of Huahine Nui and Huahine Iti at Maroe Bay; a viewpoint of the beautiful Mahuti Bay on Huahine Iti; the picturesque white sand beach at Ave'a Bay on Huahine Iti; and a visit to Fare, the capital and commercial center of Huahine.

Huahine Land Safari 4x4 is a four-wheel drive excursion led by Sylvie and Jacques Espieussas, *Tel. 68.89.21*, that takes you off the track into the hidden valleys and sites of Huahine. The half-day tours are available daily at 9am and 2:30pm., for a cost of 4.000 CFP ($40). You'll even visit the plantation of Gilles Parzy, where you can sample dried bananas, and fruit confitures flavored with vanilla. This is an interesting botanical experience for lovers of nature and green open spaces.

Lovina Excursions, Tel. *68.88.06*, **Enite Excursions**, *Tel. 68.82.37*, and Edna Flohr at **Maeva Nui Taxi Service**, *Tel. 68.81.76*, also provide Circle Island Tours and Archaeological Tours.

Helicopter Excursion

Heli-Pacific, *Tel. 85.68.00*, and **Heli-Inter Polynésie**, *Tel. 68.86.86*, provide helicopter service in Huahine. From the helipad at the Sofitel Heiva Huahine you'll embark on a 7-minute flight over Motu Topatii and south to Tefareii Village, reaching heights up to 660 meters (2,200 feet) above Huahine, for 5.800 CFP ($58). A 20-minute sunset flight includes champagne, for 16.000 CFP ($160) per person.

A Picnic Excursion includes a 7-minute helicopter flight, then you'll transfer to a four-wheel drive vehicle to reach a secluded site, for 12.000 CFP ($120) per person. You can also fly over Huahine Nui and Huahine Iti by helicopter for 30.000 CFP ($300) or be transferred from the airport to the Sofitel Heiva Huahine by helicopter for 2.600 CFP ($26) one way. Reserve at your hotel.

SPORTS & RECREATION

Horseback Riding

La Petite Ferme (the little farm), *Tel. 68.82.98, is located on the ocean side of the road between Fare Village and the airport.* Pascale or Yvan will take you riding on trained Marquesan horses along the beach and on the shores of Lake Maeva, for 2.800 CFP ($28) for one hour and 3.500 CFP ($35) for two hours. An all-day trail ride with picnic is 8.500 CFP ($85) and a 2-day overnight trail and camping expedition with meals is 13.500 CFP ($135). Open daily 8am to 6pm. Please reserve at least a day in advance. Boarding house facilities are also available.

Boat Rental

Huahine Lagoon, *Tel. 68.70.00*. Jean-Luc Eychenne rents a boat with motor that doesn't require a permit. All safety equipment is included. The rates are 3.000 CFP ($30) for two hours, 5.000 CFP ($50) for four hours and 8.000 CFP ($80) for eight hours. Masks, fins and snorkel are included, as well as ice-box and map of the lagoon. Gas is extra.

Deep Sea Fishing

Moana Tropicale Excursions, *Tel. 68.87.05*, is owned by Robertino Lee, a professional fisherman who operates the *Terei'a Nui II*, a 35-foot deep-sea fishing vessel *based at the quay in Fare*, that takes guests along on half-day or full-day outings in the lagoon or in the open ocean. Yellow-fin tuna, mahi mahi, marlin and other pelagics live outside the barrier reef that surrounds the islands.

The Sofitel Heiva Huahine offers half-day deep-sea fishing excursions for 55.200 CFP ($552) and full-day outings for 85.200 CFP ($852).

Lagoon Excursions & Picnics on the Beach or Motu

Huahine Boat Cruising is owned by Teva Colombani, *Tel. 68.72.72*, a young Polynesian man who will take you on a Safari Day Tour from 10am to 4pm, with drinks and lunch, on a Sunset Cruise from 5-7pm with drinks, or on a Full Moon Cruise, starting at 8pm, with dinner and drinks. Special tours are arranged on request. Teva's boat *Amatahiapo II* is an 8 meter (27-foot) Fiberglass catamaran with a 175 horsepower Mercury engine and a sun roof.

Jet-Ski Excursions

Mark, *Tel. 68.83.15*, provides full day jet-skiing excursions with picnic for 15.960 CFP ($159.60). **Jojo's**, next door to Chez Guynette, rents surf-skis for 500 CFP ($5) for two hours.

Outrigger Canoe Excursions

Matairea Tours is owned by Tina and Parka, a Tahitian couple who love their island and its lagoon. Their outrigger speed canoe for the snorkeling and picnic excursion *leaves the Fare quay* at 10am Tuesday through Saturday, returning at 5pm. The cost is 5.000 CFP ($50) including drinks. They will take you to the world of tropical fish, friendly stingrays and coral gardens. Your picnic lunch is served on the pretty white sand beach of Ave'a Bay on Huahine Iti, where you'll enjoy snorkeling in Huahine's most beautiful coral gardens. They will even teach you over 25 different Tahitian words for the coconut. *Tel. 68.83.79/ 68.86.21 after 8pm or you can call Tina at her office in the daytime at Tel. 68.70.16.*

Vaipua Cruises Safari, *Tel. 68.86.42*, is managed by Colette Teaurai. Her son Abinade will meet you at the quay in Fare at 9:30am and take you on an excursion around the lagoon in his outrigger speed canoe, which holds 20 passengers. You can swim with the rays, snorkel and hunt for shells in the best spots. Your barbecue lunch of chicken or fresh fish with local vegetables and fruits will be prepared on the white sand beach of Motu Topatii in Tefareii. Soft drinks and beer are included for the price of 5.000 CFP ($50) for anyone over 12 years old, and 2.500 CFP ($25) for 4-11 years. They will teach you how to weave protective sun hats and other items from the coconut fronds. The tour ends at the Fare boat dock at 4pm.

Vaipua Cruises II is a new outrigger speed canoe that is available for 4-hour excursions and photo/video tours for 3.500 CFP ($35), without picnic.

Lovina Excursions, *Tel. 68.88.06*, will also arrange picnics on the *motu* or boat transfers to the *motu* islets.

Sailing Charter Yachts

There is no yacht charterer based in Huahine. You can rent a sailboat from one of the charter companies based in Tahiti, Moorea or Raiatea and sail to Huahine, or you can arrange for a yacht to be delivered to Huahine in time for your arrival. See chapter on *Planning Your Trip.*

Scuba Diving

Pacific Blue Adventure, *Tel. 68.87.21, is located on the quay in the main village of Fare.* Didier Forget is an international PADI and CMAS diving instructor who leads lagoon and ocean dives for beginners and certified divers. He has an outing at 9am and 2pm daily, taking divers to the best sites inside the lagoon or in the open ocean, adapting to the diving level of the participants. The cost is 5.000 CFP ($50) for one dive, 18.000 CFP ($180) for four dives, and night dives are 1.500 CFP ($15) more. All equipment is included as well as transfers from your hotel.

Surfing

American surfers discovered the passes of Huahine more than 20 years ago, and a couple of them are still here, now sharing their favorite surf spots with their children. The local surfers jealously guard the passes with the best breaks, and a few foreign surfers have been given black eyes when they intrude. The big attraction in Huahine is the consistency and perfect shape of the waves rather than their size. Three of the best breaks are in the Fare area, and another good site is at the Araara pass in Parea on the southern tip of Huahine Iti. Try to find a local surfer to accompany you to the passes, which may eliminate any problems from the other surfers.

SHOPPING

In addition to the boutiques and black pearl shops in the resort hotels, you can also find original creations and some imported items in the boutiques in Fare and around the island. **Jojo's Boutique** at the airport carries film, books, T-shirts and *pareos*. **Jojo's Photo Studio** on the main street in Fare also has film, video cassettes, hand-painted *pareos*, post cards and locally made clothing. The **Huahine Lagoon** in Fare is an art gallery and boutique. **La Palme d'Or** on Fare's main street has black pearls and other jewelry.

The **Tima'i Te Nui Taue** has the most original clothing and souvenir items, including pottery made by Peter Owen, an American resident of Huahine. **Chez Atiho** is a little *fare* adjacent to the Marae Manunu on Motu Maeva, where you can buy mother-of-pearl and shell jewelry. At the **Fare Pote'e** in Maeva Village you can buy *tifaifai* quilts or wall hangings, wood sculptures, woven hats and bags and *monoi* mosquito repellent made from coconut oil and citrons.

PRACTICAL INFORMATION
Banks

Huahine has three banks, which are all located in the main village of Fare. **Banque de Tahiti**, *Tel. 68.82.46*, has an ATM window. Open Monday through Friday 7:45-11:45am and 1:30-4:30pm. **Banque Socredo**, *Tel. 68.82.71*, also has an ATM window. **Banque Westpac**, *Tel. 68.82.31*.

Doctor

There are three private doctors in Fare who speak good English, and the 15-bed government infirmary, *Tel. 68.82.48, is also in Fare.*

Drugstore

The **Pharmacy of Huahine**, *Tel. 68.80.90*, is on the main street of Fare opposite the boat dock. Open Monday to Saturday from 7:30 to 11:30am and 2:30 to 5:30pm. The pharmacist speaks English.

Police
The French gendarmerie is beside the lagoon in Fare, *Tel. 68.82.61.*

Post Office and Telecommunications Office
The **Post Office**, *Tel. 68.82.70,* is in Fare, on the bypass road opposite the Hotel Bali Hai entrance. All telecommunications and postal services are available here. Hours are Monday to Thursday from 7am to 3pm, Friday from 7am to 2pm.

Tourist Bureau
A tourist information bureau is located on the quay in Fare. Hours are 8am to 12pm Monday through Friday. You'll also find brochures of hotels, pensions and activities at the airport on the wall to the left of the arrival gate.

18. RAIATEA

A panorama of green carpeted mountains, azure shoals and indigo bays greets your eyes as your Air Tahiti flight descends at **Raiatea** (Rye-ah-TEY-ah). The Temehani plateau rises to heights of 792 meters (2,598 feet) in the north, and Mount Tefatoaiati touches the clouds at 1,017 meters (3,336 feet) in the south. Small coral islets seem to float at the edge of the bays, rising from the submarine foundation that surrounds Raiatea and the smaller island of Tahaa. Eight passes provide entry into the vast lagoon.

Raiatea does not have the glamour of its neighboring island of Bora Bora. There are no white sand beaches except around the *motu* islets, and the tourists facilities do not include world-famous luxury resorts. Neither does it have the dramatic skyline of Moorea nor the majesty of the mountains of Tahiti. Raiatea's big attraction lies in the ideal conditions it offers for year-round sailing, scuba diving and fishing. There are five major yacht charter bases on the island, three scuba diving centers and several game fishing boats.

Raiatea is 220 kilometers (136 miles) to the west-north-west of Tahiti. It is the largest of the Leeward Society Islands, which also include the high islands of Tahaa, Huahine, Bora Bora and Maupiti, plus the coral atolls of Tupai, Mopelia, Scilly and Bellinghausen. It has a surface area of 170 square kilometers (105 square miles) and is shaped rather like a triangle. When I look at a map of Tahaa and Raiatea together and see the barrier reef that protects the two islands, I think that it looks like a *penu*, the phallic-shaped stone pestle used by the Polynesians to prepare their traditional medicines of plants and herbs. Tahaa is the head of the *penu* and Raiatea is the base.

Havai'i, The Sacred Island

Raiatea means "clear sky" and is still referred to as the **Sacred Island of Havai'i**, the ancestral home of the **Maohi** people. The Polynesian Creation Chant tells how Havai'i was created by the god Ta'aroa, as the birthplace of land, the birthplace of gods, the birthplace of kings and the birthplace of man. And it was to Havai'i, deep within the sacred Temehani mountain, that the souls of the dead must return.

According to Polynesian mythology, fragments of the sacred island broke off to create other lands, swimming like a fish to become the Windward Islands of Tahiti, Moorea, Maiao, Mehetia and Tetiaroa. Havai'i was also the cradle of royalty and religion in Eastern Polynesia, as well as the center of the Maohi culture, history and heraldry.

Ta'aroa, the creator god, was considered too aloof for the dynamic religion that soon developed among the ancient Polynesians. He was eventually retired to the background, along with the god **Tane**, while **Oro**, the son of Ta'aroa, came to be revered as the god of war, harvest, music and the founder of the famous Arioi society of troubadours and comedians. Long before Oro was born at Opoa the national *marae* of Havai'i or Havaiki was called Tinirauhinimatatepapa o Feoro, which means "Fruitful myriads who engraved the rocks of Feoro."

When Oro became very powerful and was acknowledged as the supreme every day god of the earth and sky, the name Feoro was changed to Vaiotaha, meaning "Water of the man o' war bird," because this bird was Oro's shadow and the water meant human blood. To his *marae* were taken most of the heads of decapitated warriors, which were cleaned and stacked in shining white rows on the black stones of the temple. The name was later changed to **Taputapuatea**, which means "Sacrifices from abroad," and it became an international *marae*, where chiefs were brought for investiture. All other *marae* temples were founded by bringing a sacred stone from Taputapuatea or one of its descendant *maraes*.

The sacred pass of **Te Ava Moa** at Opoa in Raiatea offered frequent scenes of grandeur as great double canoes from many islands sailed into the lagoon, streaming long pennants from Hawaii, Tonga and New Zealand. The deep-toned sound of drums and the conch shell trumpets announced the arrival of delegations from island kingdoms throughout the Polynesian triangle, who were members of a friendly alliance.

At Opoa, the **Tamatoa** dynasty was reputed to go back 30 generations to **Hiro**, who was Raiatea's first king. Tradition says that Hiro and his associates built a great canoe and sailed away to Rarotonga and New Zealand, leaving two of his sons behind. One succeeded him as King of Raiatea and the other was the King of Bora Bora. During the meetings of the friendly alliance at Opoa, King Tamatoa was entitled to wear a red feather belt or *maro*, a sign of the highest honor, as he welcomed the visiting delegations. Each group of pilgrims brought human sacrifices to offer to the blood-thirsty Oro, and awesome ceremonies were held in the open air temple of Marae Taputapuatea for the festivity of the gods, to render respect and sacrifices to Oro on his home soil.

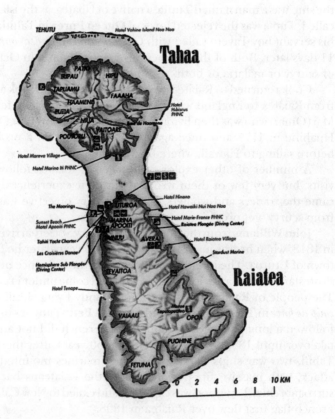

TEHUTU

Hotel Vahine Island Noa Noa

Tahaa

PAIPAI
TAPUAMU
TIPAU
HIPU
HAAMENE
FAAAHA
RUTA
NIUA
PAITOARE
POUTORU

Hotel Hibiscus PHNC
Baie de Haamene

Hotel Mareva Village

Hotel Marina Iti PHNC

Hotel Hinano
Hotel Hawaiki Nui Noa Noa
UTUROA
The Moorings
MARINA
APOOITI
Hotel Marie-France PHNC
Raiatea Plongée (Diving Center)
Sunset Beach
Motel Apooiti PHNC
Tahiti Yacht Charter
Les Croisières Danae
Hemisphere Sub Plongée
(Diving Center)
NUNUU
TUMARAA
AVERA
Hotel Raiatea Village
Stardust Marine

Hotel Tenape
TEVAITOA
VAIAAU
Motel
Tepua-pua-tea
OPOA

Raiatea

PUOHINE

FETUNA

0 2 4 6 8 10 KM

These pagan rites ended with the arrival of the missionaries. Oro and the lesser gods were banished and Marae Taputapuatea is now silent, except for an occasional reenactment ceremony, which does not involve human sacrifices!

European Discovery

Captain James Cook was the first European to discover Raiatea, when he anchored the *Endeavour* in the lagoon at Opoa in July, 1769. On board the ship was a man named **Tupia**, a native of Uliatea, as the island was then called. Tupia was the rejected lover of **Queen Purea** in Tahiti, and he and his servant boy Tayeto sailed with Cook when the *Endeavour* left Uliatea 11 days later. Both of the Polynesians died in Batavia in October, 1770, of scurvy or malaria or both.

Cook returned to Raiatea in September, 1773, and took a young man from Raiatea to England with him. This was a 22-year old fellow named Mai (**Omai**) who was then living in Huahine. Cook brought Omai back to Huahine in 1777 and once again visited Raiatea on a prolonged visit before sailing to Hawaii, where he was killed.

A number of other explorers touched at Raiatea following Cook's visits, but very few of them wrote about their experiences. After them came the traders and whalers, whose primary objective was to recover from scurvy, get provisions and find a woman.

John Williams from the London Missionary Society arrived in Raiatea in 1818, when he was just 21 years old. A few years later he founded the town of Uturoa. The island remained under the influence of the English Protestant missionaries long after Tahiti had come under French control. The people of Raiatea are still predominantly Evangelical. Following a *coup de force* in Tahiti by French **Admiral Du Petit-Thouars** in 1842, there followed a long period of instability. The French did not attempt a real takeover until 1888. In 1897, more than 50 years after the conquest of Tahiti, two war ships filled with French marines mounted a full-scale attack, with massive fire-power, driving the Raiateans back, until surrogate chief Teraupoo was captured and exiled to New Caledonia. The French flag first flew over Raiatea in 1898.

Raiatea Today

The Raiatea airport is at the northern tip of the island and the town of Uturoa is southeast of the airport. A road, mostly paved, encircles the island for about 150 kilometers (93 miles), following the contours of the deeply indented coastline, with occasional forays into the exuberant vegetation of the valleys. Raiatea's 10,000 inhabitants live beside the road in Uturoa and in the villages and hamlets of Avera, Faaroa, Opoa, Puohine, Fetuna, Vaiaau, Tevaitoa and Apooiti.

Driving in a southeasterly direction from Uturoa you will see the **Raiatea Pearl Beach Resort (Hotel Hawaiki Nui)** on your left, and pass impressive new homes and lovely flower gardens on both sides of the road. By the time you reach Avera you are in the country. At PK 6 you will see the **Raiatea Village**, just before a curve to the right that takes you down the deeply indented road that winds quietly around the edge of the **Faaroa Bay**. Your senses are heightened as you breathe in the perfumes of fresh mountain ferns, wild mangoes, kava, kapok and ripening bread-fruit.

This deeply indented bay merges with the **Apoomau River**, which is navigable by small ships and boats for a distance of four kilometers (2.5 miles) into the interior. At the mouth of the river is a spring containing effervescent water. I've been told by a woman from Raiatea that people come from Hawaii and New Zealand to drink this water, which is guarded by the spirit of the spring. Photos that are taken here always show an extra person, or part of a face, which is supposedly that of the spirit. But this image fades in time.

A road from Faaroa Bay takes you into the interior of the island for 8 kilometers (5 miles), connecting with Fetuna at the southern tip of the island. Winding through the fertile valleys and wide flatland, you will pass plantations of pineapple, tapioca, papaya and vanilla, and farms with horses, cows, pigs and chickens. Far below the lacy fronds of acacia trees bordering the road you can see the wild, untamed southern coast of Raiatea. If you continue along the coastal route instead of cutting across the valley, you will come to **Marae Taputapuatea** at PK 32, 19.2 miles from Uturoa center, just beyond the village of Opoa. This is Raiatea's most famous landmark. The huge slabs of coral flagstone and basaltic rock slumber under the shade of coconut palms, a shrine to Polynesia's rich and varied Maohi culture.

Between Puohine and Fetuna a new road has been built along an embankment, forming ponds where oysters and mussels are cultivated. The *motu* beside Nao Nao pass into Faatemu Bay is a popular picnic site for visiting cruise ships. The US Navy built a landing strip nearby when they occupied the island of Bora Bora during World War II.

Along the west coast you will see mountain streams meandering to the sea and gaily colored cocks following their harem of clucking hens. The fishermen still use stones to enclose their fish ponds, instead of wire netting. You can see them mending their nets on the beach, while their children play in the shallows of the lagoon. There are no stores in these remote settlements, except for the mobile *magasins* operated by the Chinese vendors, who make their daily rounds with fresh *baguettes*, frozen chickens and Piggy Snax.

TIARE APETAHI-RAIATEA'S
ENDANGERED FLOWER

In the heights of the sacred Temehani mountain grows the **Tiare Apetahi**, *refreshed by the cool, dense clouds and mountain showers. When touched by the first rays of the rising sun, this rare white flower bursts open with a slight exploding sound.*

The five-petalled Tiare Apetahi is the symbol of Raiatea, and it is believed that this particular variety of the Campanaulacées family grows nowhere else in the world.

Legend says that the delicate petals represent the five fingers of a lovely Tahitian girl who fell in love with the son of a king and died of a broken heart because she could not hope to marry him.

In order to protect the rapidly disappearing Tiare Apetahi, which the flower vendors in Raiatea were selling at the airport, the local government has declared it an endangered species. Offenders may be fined up to one million French Pacific francs (about $10,000) if caught. Repeat offenders can be given a maximum fine of six months imprisonment and nine million French Pacific francs (about $100,000).

The lagoon narrows between Vaihuti and Vaiaau Bays, with several palm-shaded *motu* islets seeming to float on air above the lagoon. Sharp peaks delineate the central mountain chain and in Vaiaau valley are remnants of fortifications that were built by the warriors of Faterehau, the great chiefess of Raiatea, who opposed the takeover by the French in 1897.

Behind Tevaitoa village the magnificent **Temehani Plateau** rises in formidable walls of basalt. The historic peaks shimmer in shades of blue and gray, and countless waterfalls cascade in misty plumes to splash far below into crisp pools fringed with tropical fern trees and shrubbery. **Marae Tainuu** is on the shoreline in the middle of the village. The Protestant church here is the oldest on the island, and partially covers the flagstones of the *marae*. Petroglyphs engraved in the basaltic stones include a Polynesian sun dial and 10 turtles, depicting a sort of Polynesian treasure hunt that the Maohi warriors had to perform to achieve valor and esteem.

Copra drying in the sun, pigs grunting in the mud, and quiet oyster farms beside the road are left behind as you arrive at Apooiti Bay and see the sleek charter yachts moored at **Apooiti Marina**. Soon you round the north end of the island, pass in front of the airport and end your tour back in Uturoa.

Although there is an increase in the flow of traffic here in the town center, life is still unhurried and the calm, friendly feeling of a small island lingers still. It is this wonderful magic of Polynesia that tempts you to return again to Raiatea.

ARRIVALS & DEPARTURES

Arriving By Air

Air Tahiti has one to four direct flights daily between Tahiti and Raiatea and one or two flights with stops in Huahine. The 40-minute non-stop flight is 10.605 CFP ($106.05) one-way for adults, tax included. **Air Tahiti reservations**: *Tahiti, Tel. 86.42.42/86.41.84; Huahine, Tel. 68.82.65.*

If you have reservations with a hotel, pension or yacht charter company, then you will be met at the airport and driven to your hotel. Avis and Europcar have sales counters at the airport and there are also taxis that meet the arrival of each flight. An information desk is operated by the Visitors Bureau at the airport.

Arriving By Boat

All the inter-island transport boats dock at the quay in Uturoa, the main town of Raiatea, and it would be advisable to arrange with your hotel or pension to have someone meet you when you arrive in the middle of the night. The car rental agencies will also meet you at the Uturoa quay. A Visitors Bureau is adjacent to the quay.

Ono-Ono, *Tel. 45.35.35; Fax 43.83.45; e-mail: onoono@mail.pf* departs from the *Papeete boat dock, adjacent to the Moorea boats,* each Monday and Wednesday at 9am, arriving in Raiatea at 2pm. Each Friday it leaves Papeete at 4:30pm, arriving in Raiatea at 9:45pm. *The ticket office is located on the boat dock.* One-way fare from Papeete to Raiatea is 5.499 CFP ($54.99). Be at the dock one hour prior to departure. A special weekend inter-island circuit arrives in Raiatea from Bora Bora and Tahaa each Saturday at 9:45am, and from Huahine at 4pm the same day.

Taporo VI, *Tel. 42.63.93/43.79.72; Fax 42.06.17,* departs from *the Fare-Ute quay on the far side of the Papeete harbor,* each Monday, Wednesday and Friday, at 4pm, stopping in Huahine and arriving in Raiatea the following day at 4:30am. One-way fare to Raiatea is 1,692 CFP ($16.92) on the bridge and 20.000 CFP ($200) for a cabin with four berths.

Vaeanu, *Tel. 41.25.35; Fax 41.24.34,* departs from the *Fare-Ute quay in Papeete* at 5pm on Monday, Wednesday and Friday, stopping in Huahine and arriving in Raiatea the following morning at 5am. One-way fare for bridge passengers is 1.709 CFP ($17.09) and cabins cost 4.000 to 5.500 CFP ($40 to $55) per person.

Maupiti Express, *Tel. 67.66.69,* arrives in Uturoa from Bora Bora and Tahaa each Wednesday and Friday at 8:30am. The one-way fare is 3.000

CFP ($30). Passengers under 15 years and over 60 years have a 20 percent reduction. *Reservations office in Tahiti, Tel. 48.05.81.*

Departing By Air

You can fly from Raiatea to Bora Bora, Maupiti and Huahine, or return to Tahiti by **Air Tahiti**, *Tel. 66.32.50/66.30.51 in Raiatea.* Tickets can be purchased at the airport. If you already have reservations and a ticket, reconfirmations should be made one day in advance, and most hotels will take care of this for you. Check-in time at the airport is one hour before scheduled departure.

Departing By Boat

You can continue on to Tahaa and Bora Bora by boat from Raiatea, or you can return to Papeete with a stop in Huahine.

Ono Ono, *Tel. 66.24.25*, leaves Raiatea for Tahaa and Bora Bora each Monday and Wednesday at 2:15pm, and for Bora Bora each Friday at 10pm. The Raiatea-Huahine-Papeete passages leave the boat dock in Uturoa each Tuesday and Thursday at 9am, arriving in Tahiti at 2:15pm. A special inter-island circuit operates each weekend, leaving Raiatea for Huahine at 10am each Saturday, and departing for Tahaa and Bora Bora at 4:15pm Saturday afternoon. On Sundays the departure time for Huahine and Tahiti is at 2pm, arriving in Papeete at 7:15pm.

Taporo VI, *Tel. 66.32.29*, leaves Raiatea at 5:30am each Tuesday, Thursday and Saturday, for Tahaa and Bora Bora. At 3pm on the same days the ship departs for Huahine and Tahiti, arriving in Papeete at 4am the following morning. Buy your ticket on board.

Vaeanu, *Tel. 41.25.35*, leaves Raiatea at 6:30am each Tuesday for Bora Bora, and at 3pm each Tuesday the ship leaves Raiatea for Huahine and Papeete, arriving in Papeete at 3am on Wednesday. Each Thursday the ship leaves Raiatea for Bora Bora at 7am and departs for Huahine and Tahiti on Thursday afternoon at 4pm, arriving in Papeete at 4am on Friday. On Saturday the *Vaeanu* leaves Raiatea at 6:30am for Tahaa and Bora Bora, and returns to Tahiti each Sunday, leaving Raiatea at 2pm, arriving in Papeete each Monday at 2am. Buy your ticket on board the ship.

Maupiti Express, *Tel. 67.66.69*, departs from the Uturoa quay each Wednesday and Friday at 4:30pm, for Tahaa and Bora Bora. The one-way fare is 3.000 CFP ($30). Passengers under 15 years and over 60 years have a 20 percent reduction. *Reservations office in Tahiti, Tel. 48.05.81.*

ORIENTATION

The town center of **Uturoa** (oo-too-RO-ah), which means "long jaw," is two kilometers (1.2 miles) south of the airport. This is the second largest town in French Polynesia. Here you will find the administrative seat for the Leeward Islands. Buildings reminiscent of former colonial days stand adjacent to modern government buildings, post office, banks, boutiques, general stores, supermarkets and small restaurants. There is a hospital, *gendarmerie*, courthouse, a Catholic school, a Lycée, technical schools and boarding facilities for students from throughout the Leeward Islands. A community nautical center and marina are on the edge of town, and the public market, port facilities and shipping warehouses in the center of Uturoa provide the focal point of a relaxed pace of business life.

Mount Tapioi rises 294 meters (964 feet) behind Uturoa, with a television relay at the summit. You can hike up or drive 3.5 kilometers (2.2 miles) to the top in a 4WD, where you'll enjoy the panoramic view of Tahaa and Huahine, Bora Bora and Maupiti.

Big projects are now underway to modernize Uturoa's public facilities. A quay for tourist ships is being built, which will almost double the existing pier to 280 meters (918 feet). This is to accommodate the *Paul Gauguin*, which began service in January 1998, and for two *Renaissance* ships, which will begin cruises in French Polynesia within the next year. A new port captain's office, warehouses, cold storage for fish, public restrooms and arts and crafts center will be built, and a public garden will be created along the waterfront. The public tennis courts will be renovated and other sports facilities added. The Chinese businessmen in Uturoa are being encouraged to update or rebuild their old wooden stores that added a certain charm to the Uturoa of yesteryear, an image that will soon disappear.

GETTING AROUND
Car, Scooter & Bicycle Rentals
Avis-Pacificar, *Tel. 66.34.06/66.34.35/66.15.59*. The sales office at the airport is open for each flight and a car will be delivered to the Uturoa boat dock on request. A Citroen AX rents for 4.600 CFP ($46) for 5 hours, 6.000 CFP ($60) for 10 hours and 6.900 CFP ($69) for 24 hours. These rates include unlimited mileage and insurance. Longer rentals available.

Europcar, *Tel. 66.34.06. Sales offices are located at the airport, in the Raihere Agency in Uturoa and at the Raiatea Pearl Beach Resort.* A Fiat Panda rents for 5.000 CFP ($50) for 4 hours, 6.000 CFP ($60) for 8 hours, 7.000 CFP ($70) for 24 hours, and 13.000 CFP ($130) for a weekend. A Fun Car is a cross between a car and a scooter and rents for 4.500 CFP ($45) for 4 hours and 5.000 CFP ($50) for 8 hours. Scooter rates start at 4.000 CFP ($40) for 4 hours. These rates include unlimited mileage and third party insurance. Gas is extra. Europcar also offers a special Raiatea package for 9.000 CFP ($90), which includes a Fiat Panda and a bungalow, or 12.000 CFP ($120) for a Fiat Panda and a boat.

Hertz, *Tel. 66.15.59/66.16.17,* **Garage Motu Tapu**, Tel. 66.33.09, and **Opeha Locations**, Tel. 66.31.62, also have car rentals.

Bicycles

Europcar, *Tel. 66.34.06,* rents bicycles and beach bikes for 1.200 CFP ($12) for 4 hours and 1.500 CFP ($15) for 8 hours. Longer rentals possible.

Taxis

Taxis are usually available at the Uturoa airport for each flight arrival, and a taxi stand is located near the public market in the center of Uturoa. *Tel. 66.20.60.* You can also contact René Guilloux, *Tel. 66.31.40;* Marona Teanini, *Tel. 66.34.62;* or Apia Tehope, *Tel. 66.36.41.* There are seven taxis in Raiatea, and the drivers pride themselves on their good reputation. Germain Guilloux, president of the taxi union in Raiatea, said that they have not had a big problem with taxi drivers in 20 years.

Le Truck

A *le truck* service operates between the public market in Uturoa and each village, coordinating their schedules with the arrivals of the ferries and school hours. They charge a minimal fee to transport passengers to their destination in Raiatea.

WHERE TO STAY

Expensive

RAIATEA PEARL BEACH RESORT (Hotel Hawaiki Nui,) *B.P. 43, Uturoa, Raiatea. Tel. 689/66.20.23; Fax 689/66.20.20. Reservations: South Pacific Marketing, B.P. 718, Papeete, Tahiti. Tel. 689/43.90.04; Fax 689/ 41.39.23. Beside the lagoon, two kilometers (1.2 miles) south of town. Round-trip transfers from the airport or ferry dock: 1.400 CFP ($14) per person. EP Rates: garden room 13.000 CFP ($130) single/double; garden bungalow 17.000 CFP ($170) single/double; lagoon bungalow 21.000 CFP ($210) single/double; overwater bungalow 29.000 CFP ($290) single/double. Add 2.500 CFP ($25) for extra person. Continental breakfast is 950 CFP ($9.50); meal plan with breakfast and dinner is 6.000 CFP ($60) per person; meal plan with breakfast, lunch and dinner is 7.500 CFP ($75) per person. Add 7% hotel tax to room rates and 1% value added tax to room rates and meal plan. All major credit cards.*

The Raiatea Pearl Beach Resort (Hawaiki Nui) is the most luxurious hotel on Raiatea. The 32-room hotel opened as the Hawaiki Nui in December, 1994, on the site formerly occupied by the Hotel Bali Hai Raiatea, which was part of the hotel chain operated by the "Bali Hai Boys" of Moorea, until it burned down in 1992. Raiatea Pearl Beach Resort is locally owned and it is managed by Frenchman Robert Cazenave, who is also president of the Tourism Committee in Raiatea.

The hotel is situated on the fringe of the lagoon in Tepua Bay, with rooms and bungalows built in the Polynesian style with thatched roofs and bamboo furniture. The 12 garden rooms, 8 garden bungalows, 3 lagoon bungalows and 9 overwater bungalows are all screened and equipped with a king size bed and a single bed, overhead fan, refrigerator/mini-bar, television, video and stereo system, telephone, safety deposit box, hair dryer and coffee/tea making facilities. The garden bungalows offer a lounge area, while the overwater bungalows have a veranda overlooking the lagoon and steps leading down into the warm blue waters. A glass floor in the overwater bungalows lets you watch the fish at night as they feed in the coral gardens below.

The Raiatea Pearl Beach Resort has an indoor-outdoor bar and its restaurant has earned a good reputation for fine French cuisine and seafood specialties. There is no beach here, but there is a long pier for sunbathing, a fresh water swimming pool overlooking the lagoon and tennis courts across the road. A boutique is beside the hotel entrance and an activities desk in the reception area will arrange tours and excursions to help you discover the mountains, valleys, rivers, *motu* and lagoons of Raiatea and its sister island of Tahaa.

Moderate

HOTEL LE MAITAI TENAPE, *Tel./Fax 689/66.14.50; reservations Hotel Management & Services, B.P. 13037, Punaauia, Tahiti, Tel. 689/ 43.08.83/Fax 689/43.08.93. Beside the lagoon in Tumaraa, 4 kilometers (2.5 miles) from the airport and 7 kilometers (4.3 miles) from the ferry dock. EP rates: 12.000 CFP ($120) single/double; add 2.500 CFP ($25) for additional person; air-conditioned suite 24.000 CFP ($240) for maximum 4 people. Add 7% hotel tax to room rates and 1% value added tax to room rates and meal plan. All major credit cards.*

This 2-story colonial style hotel is scheduled to open during the first quarter of 1998, with 15 rooms and an air-conditioned suite. The hotel is situated on two hectares (4.9 acres) of land on the northwest coast of Raiatea, with 120 meters (394 feet) of beach facing the islands of Bora Bora and Maupiti, and the spectacular sunsets. Each room will contain a king-size bed or twin beds, television, direct dial telephone, air-conditioning, mini-bar, individual safe, a separate bathroom with a hot water shower, and a covered terrace.

Public facilities include a restaurant and bar, swimming pool, front desk, lounge, activities desk and boutique. A wide range of services and activities, including a Scubapro/SEA scuba diving base on the property, will be available for guests. Le Maitai Tenape belongs to the same locally owned chain as Le Maitai Polynesia in Bora Bora. Other Maitai hotels will be built in Rangiroa and Moorea.

HOTEL ATIAPITI, *B.P. 884, Uturoa, Raiatea. Tel./Fax 689/66.16.65. Beside the lagoon in Opoa, near Marae Taputapuatea, 30 kilometers (18.6 miles) from the ferry dock and 32 kilometers (19.8 miles) from the airport. Round-trip transfers 2.000 CFP ($20) per person. EP Rates: beach bungalow 8.500 CFP ($85) single/double; garden bungalow-suite 12.000 CFP ($120) single/double; third adult add 1.000 CFP ($10). Meal plan with breakfast and dinner is 3.500 CFP ($35), meal plan with breakfast, lunch and dinner is 6.000 CFP ($60) per person. Add 7% hotel tax to room rates. Add 1% value added tax to room rates and meal plan. Mastercard, Visa.*

Formerly operated as Hotel Te Moana Iti, this is the only accommodation available anywhere near the famous Marae Taputapuatea. Six modern concrete bungalows are well spaced in a hectare (2.5 acres) of land beside a white sand beach. The grounds are planted with fruit trees and flowers—orchids, Tiare Tahiti, gardenias and hibiscus. Each of the six bungalows has a bedroom with a king size bed, living room with tamanu wood furniture, mini-bar, television and terrace overlooking the sea and the distant island of Huahine. Marie-Claude admits that she is a very good cook, and her seafood specialties include crab, lobster and fresh shrimp from the rivers of Raiatea. Activities include scuba diving from the pontoon, a picnic on the bird's *motu*, walking on the reef, swimming in the river, horseback riding, hiking to waterfalls and safari tours.

CHEZ MARIE-FRANCE, *B.P. 272, Uturoa, Raiatea. Tel. 689/66.37.10; Fax 689/66.26.25. e-mail diveta@mail.pf. Beside the lagoon in Tepua Bay, 2.5 kilometers (1.5 miles) south of Uturoa center. Round-trip transfers are extra. EP Rates: bungalow 7.000 CFP ($70) single, 8.000 CFP ($80) double, 9.000 ($90) CFP triple, and 10.000 CFP ($100) quadruple. Add 1.000 CFP ($10) per person for one night only. Room 4.000 CFP ($40) single/double; add 500 CFP ($5) per person for one night only; bed in dormitory 1.200 CFP ($12); add 300 CFP ($3) for one night only. Meal plan with breakfast and dinner is 3.500 CFP ($35) per person, meal plan with breakfast, lunch and dinner is 5.200 CFP ($52) per person. Add 1% value added tax to room rates and meal plan. Deposit required for reservation. All major credit cards.*

There are a lot of activities squeezed into this property between the road and the bay. A large house has four big rooms, each with telephone, television, overhead fans and private bathroom with hot water. House linens are furnished. There is also a large bunkhouse style *fare* of woven bamboo with six rooms containing double or single beds and overhead fans. There is a communal kitchenette and bathrooms with hot water. Bed linens are furnished and towels are available on request. A restaurant serves snacks, take-out meals and full course lunches and dinners. The bar is open during lunch and dinner. Marie-France's husband, Patrice Philip, operates the Raiatea Plongée Scuba Diving Center, Raiatea Safari Tours and a Yacht Services marina from here, and there is a swimming pool just outside the bedrooms.

SUNSET BEACH MOTEL, *B.P. 397, Uturoa, Raiatea. Tel. 689/ 66.33.47; Fax 689/66.33.08. Beside the lagoon in Apooiti, 5 kilometers (3 miles) from the ferry dock and 2 kilometers (1.2 miles) from the airport. Round-trip transfers are provided. EP Rates: bungalow 6.500 CFP ($65) single, 7.500 CFP ($75) double, 8.500 CFP ($85) triple and 9.500 CFP ($95) quadruple. Add 1.000 CFP ($10) for fifth adult. Add 1.000 CFP per bungalow for one night only. Camping 1.000 CFP person per day. Reduced rates for longer stays. Add 1% value added tax to room rates. Deposit of 6.500 CFP ($65) required for reservations. Mastercard, Visa.*

If you are looking for a quiet, comfortable place to spend several days or weeks, you'll find this small hotel very suitable for your desires, as it offers one of the best values in the islands. The 21 American style wooden bungalows are placed far apart on a 10 hectare (24.7 acre) property that is still a working coconut plantation. The bungalows are all on the waterfront with a fabulous view of Tahaa and Bora Bora. Each bungalow has screened windows and sliding glass doors, and contains a bedroom with a double bed, a living room with three single beds and television, a picnic table, a completely equipped kitchen, private bathroom with solar hot water, house linens, portable fan, covered terrace and carport. A narrow strip of white sand beach fronts the property, and you can sunbathe on the long private pier or feed the fish at the end of the dock. Outrigger paddle canoes are provided, and for 2.500 CFP ($25) you can rent a boat for five people to go to the *motu*. Free transfers are provided for shopping expeditions in town. An activities book with photos and descriptions of land and lagoon excursions is provided for each bungalow, and if you want to take an excursion they will pick you up at Sunset Beach.

Separated from the bungalows by a large garden is a campground for up to 25 tents, with a large equipped kitchen and big covered dining terrace. Campers share the communal cold water bath facilities, with access to a pay phone, laundry, luggage room and library on the premises.

Sunset Beach is managed by 27-year-old Moana Boubee, whose grandfather bought this property 40 years ago. After finishing a three-year hotel school course in Tahiti, Moana took over from his mother, Eliane, who is a school teacher in Raiatea. His enthusiasm and friendliness are welcome assets, and he speaks good English. He has seven employees to help run the estate, which includes plantations of papaya, pineapple, vanilla and copra. A breakfast of fresh fruit grown on his farm will be delivered to your bungalow on request.

HOTEL RAIATEA VILLAGE, *B.P. 282, Uturoa, Raiatea. Tel. 689/ 66.31.62; Fax 689/66.10.65. Beside the lagoon in Avera, 10 kilometers (6.2 miles) southeast of the town center. Round-trip transfers 1.000 CFP ($10) per person. EP rates: waterfront bungalow 5.000 CFP ($50) single; 6.000 CFP ($60) double; 7.000 CFP ($70) triple; 8.000 CFP ($80) quadruple. Add 7% hotel tax and 1% value added tax to room rates. Deposit required for reservation. Mastercard, Visa.*

There are 10 Polynesian style wooden bungalows with thatched roofs; 5 are on the lagoon front beside a man-made white sand beach, and the other 5 are in the gardens behind. Each attractively furnished *fare* has a bedroom with a double bed, a spacious living room with two single beds, an individual bathroom with hot water, a dining area and kitchenette, and a covered terrace overlooking the lagoon. House linens and daily maid service are provided. You can rent a car for 6.500 CFP ($65) for eight hours, or a bicycle for 800 CFP ($8) a day. You can also catch *le truck* on the road just in front of the reception. The restaurant is presently being rebuilt.

PENSION YOLANDE, *B.P. 298, Uturoa, Raiatea. Tel. 689/66.35.28. Beside the lagoon in Avera, 10 kilometers (6.2 miles) southeast of town. Round-trip transfers 3.000 CFP ($30) per car. Rates: room 5.000 CFP ($50) single/ double; 6.000 CFP ($60) triple. Meal plan with breakfast and dinner is 3.500 CFP ($35) per person; meal plan for with breakfast and dinner for child 5-11 years is 1.750 CFP ($17.50). Complete pension with all three meals is available. Add 1% value added tax to room rates and meal plan. Deposit required for reservation. No credit cards.*

This pension has a large thatch roof bungalow by the sea, built in the traditional Polynesian style, with four rooms, each with one double bed and one single bed. There is a kitchenette and private bathroom with hot water in each room; house linens are furnished. A family style restaurant serves tasty local dishes. Outrigger paddle canoes are provided.

KAOHI NUI RANCH, *B.P. 568, Uturoa, Raiatea. Tel./Fax 689/ 66.25.46. On mountainside in Avera, 6 kilometers (3.7 miles) southeast of town. Round-trip transfers are provided. Breakfast on request. EP Rates: room 5.000 CFP ($50) single/double; bed in dormitory 1.500 CFP ($15). Add 1% value added tax to room rates and meal plan. Deposit required for reservation. No credit cards.*

The grounds resemble a Western movie setting, with a corral, bank (reception area) and saloon. Lodging is in a one-bedroom house with a double bed and single bed, fan, private bathroom with hot water, and private terrace. A large four-bedroom house is used as a dormitory, with two single beds in each room and shared bathroom with hot water. House linens and anti-mosquito products are furnished. The kitchen and open air living room are communal. Bicycle rentals and horseback rides.

Inexpensive
   HOTEL HINANO, *B.P. 196, Uturoa, Raiatea. Tel. 689/66.13.13; Fax 689/66.14.14. On the main street in the center of Uturoa, a two-minute walk from the ferry dock. Round-trip transfers from the airport on request. EP Rates: standard room 4.500 CFP ($45) single; 5.500 CFP ($55) double; standard room with air-conditioning 5.500 CFP ($55) single; 6.500 CFP ($65) double. Third person 1.000 CFP ($10). Add 7% hotel tax and 1% value added tax to room rates. All major credit cards.*

   This is the only hotel in the downtown area of Uturoa. The hotel is located upstairs over a bank on the town side and a restaurant is on the side facing the boat dock. Augustin Moulon bought this old hotel in 1994 and has totally upgraded the 10 rooms, each with a private bathroom and hot water showers. Four of the rooms are air-conditioned and six have overhead fans. An inner patio is reminiscent of Mexico, with a tiled floor and huge potted plants. It no longer looks like a flophouse, as it did for many years.

   PENSION MANAVA, *B.P. 559, Uturoa, Raiatea. Tel. 689/66.28.26; Fax 689/66.16.66. On mountainside in Avera, 6 kilometers (3.7 miles) southeast of town. Round-trip transfers are provided. Breakfast on request 500 CFP ($5) for a simple breakfast, 800 CFP ($8) for Continental. Other meals are available. EP Rates: room with kitchen and communal bathroom 3.500 CFP ($35) person; bungalow with kitchen and private bathroom 4.500 ($45) CFP person; bungalow with kitchenette and private bathroom 5.500 CFP ($55) person. Add 1% value added tax to room rates and meal plan. Deposit required for reservation. No credit cards.*

   Four clean and attractive bungalows and a large house are located in a pretty setting of trees, grass and flowers. Two bungalows have individual kitchens and toilets with solar hot water. Two bungalows have individual toilets with hot water and share a kitchen. In the large *fare* are two bedrooms with shared kitchen and a bathroom with hot water. Each bungalow has screened windows and a covered terrace. Linens are furnished.

   BED-BREAKFAST RAIATEA BELLEVUE, *B.P. 98, Uturoa, Raiatea. Tel. 689/66.15.15; Fax 689/66.14.15. On the mountainside behind the Lycée of Uturoa, two kilometers (1.2 miles) from the airport and one kilometer from the ferry dock. Round-trip transfers 1.500 CFP ($15). Breakfast on request. EP Rates: double room 2.950 CFP ($29.50) person. Add 1% value added tax to room rates and meal plan. No credit cards.*

   Just a 15-minute walk from the center of Uturoa. Six rooms, each with one double bed, fan and television, refrigerator, private bathroom with hot water and terrace. House linens are furnished and you can enjoy the swimming pool.

PETER'S PLACE, *Avera Taputapuatea, Raiatea. Tel. 689/66.20.01. On the mountainside in Avera, 6.1 kilometers (3.8 miles) southeast of town. Arrival transfer is provided; departure transfer is 500 CFP ($5). EP Rates: Room 1.200 CFP ($12); 1.400 CFP ($14) for one night only. Camping is 700 CFP ($7) per camper. Deposit required for reservation. Add 1% value added tax to room rates. No credit cards.*

On the mountainside, 50 meters (164 feet) from the lagoon at Vairahi. One large plywood *fare* with eight rooms containing a double or single bed, a bamboo and thatch open-air communal kitchen and dining room, and shared bathroom facilities with hot water. House linens are furnished. The campground is large enough for 15 tents and has lots of shade trees.

WHERE TO EAT

Moderate

LE CLUB HOUSE, *Tel. 66.11.66, at the Apooiti Yacht Harbor. Open daily for breakfast, lunch and dinner. All major credit cards.*

This is the largest restaurant on the island, with seats for 200 diners. The thatched-roof building has a bamboo motif, with indoor-outdoor dining facing the sailing yachts moored at the marina. The menu includes French cuisine and local dishes such as chicken curry, mahi mahi and grilled lobster. This is a good place to have a sunset drink and gaze at the picture postcard scene before you.

QUAI DES PECHEURS, *(Fisherman's Wharf), Tel. 66.36.83, is on the waterfront at the Uturoa boat dock. Open daily for breakfast, lunch and dinner, specializing in poisson cru and other fish dishes. Visa.*

This is not fancy dining, as you eat on the terrace adjacent to the boat dock, but it is probably the favorite hangout for visitors off the ships and ferry boats who want to drink a cold beer and eat a pizza. It is also popular with locals, especially on weekends, when you will probably need reservations. Seafood and Chinese dishes are featured. At 10pm each Friday and Saturday the restaurant becomes the Disco Quaidep, where you are fanned by the tradewinds as you dance. If you approach through the ramshackle fence on the dock side, you may be repelled by the overwhelming smell of urine, following a night of disco. If you enter from the town side you may be more tempted to order something to eat.

LE MOANA, *Tel. 66.27.49, is upstairs in the Léogite Building, opposite the public market on the main street of Uturoa. Open for lunch and dinner. Closed Sunday noon and all day Monday. Reservations are advised on weekend evenings as this is a popular place with locals. Visa.*

Owner Alphonse Léogite speaks excellent English and serves good Chinese food, which includes such unusual dishes as sea cucumber with ginger and seafood with shredded taro. Main courses cost 900 to 1.800 CFP ($9 to $18). American Express, Mastercard and Visa. Each Friday and Saturday after the dinner service is finished, the restaurant is transformed into the Club Zenith Discothèque at 10pm.

LE JADE GARDEN, *Tel. 66.34.40, is on the mountain side of Uturoa's main street in the downtown shopping area. Open Wednesday through Saturday from 11am to 1pm and 6:30 to 9pm. Closed Sunday, Monday and Tuesday. Mastercard and Visa.*

I've always enjoyed my meals here, which feature Cantonese dishes for 1.000 to 1.600 CFP ($10 to $16) for the main course choices. There are two air-conditioned dining rooms, and the one upstairs is nicer.

Inexpensive

CHEZ MICHELE, *Tel. 66.14.66, occupies the ground floor of the Hotel Hinano, facing the boat dock. Open for breakfast, lunch and dinner. Closed Saturday night and Sunday. No credit cards.*

Chinese, European and Tahitian dishes are served in a small in-door restaurant. The quality of the food is good and includes steak, chicken and fish specialties, prepared in the local style, which are priced around 1.000 CFP ($10) a plate.

MOEMOEA, *Tel. 66.39.84, is between the Uturoa quay and the main street in the center of town. You'll recognize it from its blue awning. Open for breakfast and lunch, and closed Saturday afternoon and all day Sunday. No credit cards.*

This is a local style outdoor cafe, where you can order the *plât du jour*, which is usually a combination of Chinese, Tahitian and French dishes for about 1.000 CFP ($10). You can also get a great hamburger here, and watch the boats loading for their trip back to Tahaa.

LE GOURMET PATISSERIE, *Tel. 66.21.51, is in the Westpac Bank building on the main street in Uturoa. Open Monday to Saturday 6am to 6pm, and from 7 to 10 pm on Friday and Saturday evenings. Mastercard, Visa.*

This is where you'll find your breakfast pastries, starting at 150 CFP ($1.50) and burgers and salads for lunch, from 300 CFP ($3). Daily specials are also served Monday through Friday 11am to 1pm. Pizza and spaghetti are featured on Friday and Saturday evenings, from 700 to 1.200 CFP ($7 to $12).

SNACK RESTAURANT TEANAU, *on lagoon side at PK 25 at Vaiaau Bay on the west coast. Tel. 66.17.28.* Local dishes are prepared and there's a boutique next door.

SNACK BAR TEMEHANI, *Tel. 66.15.59, is located at the airport,* providing drinks and sandwiches, and a special luncheon plate.

SEEING THE SIGHTS

Marae Taputapuatea is Raiatea's most famous landmark. Seven *marae* temples of stone face the Te-Ava-Moa pass at Opoa. This international *marae* has been in existence since 1600 A.D. and was the most important *marae* in eastern Polynesia during the pre-Christian era. Raiatea was then known as Havai'i, the Sacred Island.

Marae Tainuu is located beside the sea in the little fishing village of Tevaitoa on the northwest coast of Raiatea. Petroglyphs engraved in the basaltic stones include a Polynesian sun dial and 10 turtles, depicting a sort of Polynesian treasure hunt that the Maohi warriors had to perform to achieve valor and esteem.

Almost Paradise Tours, *Tel. 66.23.64*, is owned by American Bill Kolans, who will take you in his minibus on a 3-hour tour to visit Marae Taputapuatea and five other *marae* temples. Bill's tours are highly praised by English-speaking visitors, who learn about the migration, anthropology and navigation of the ancient Polynesians. He gives detailed explanations of the rocks, gods, religious ceremonies and human sacrifices performed at this international *marae*. Cost is 3.000 CFP ($30) per person.

Jeep Safari Raiatea, *Tel. 66.15.73*, is operated by Mirella and Petero Mou Kam Tse, who can take a maximum of 8 passengers in their 4x4 Land Rover. Daily departures are at 9m and 2pm, for 4-hour tours through the mountain valleys, with stops at vanilla plantations, Marae Taputapuatea and at a black pearl farm. Petero drives and Bernadette Sarccione is the very knowledgeable guide who speaks fluent English. Bernadette will remind you of Bloody Mary from the movie *South Pacific*. She will explain the botanical treasures of the hidden valleys and tropical plantations and tell you all about the cultivation of the black pearl oyster. This tour costs 3.500 CFP ($35), including refreshments.

Raiatea 4x4, *Tel. 66.24.16*, is operated daily at 8am and 1:30pm by Maria and Gérard Duvos. This 4-hour mountain safari is made in an open four-wheel drive vehicle, taking you to visit the hills and deep valleys, with time for a swim in a river. Stops are made at a vanilla plantation and at Marae Taputapuatea.

Raiatea Safari Tours, *Tel. 66.37.10*, is owned by Patrice Philip of Chez Marie-France and Raiatea Scuba Diving. A photo safari tour shows you the secret sites of Raiatea during a 4-hour excursion, for 4.000 CFP ($40).

NIGHTLIFE & ENTERTAINMENT

CLUB ZENITH DISCOTHÈQUE, *Tel. 66.27.49, is upstairs in the Léogite Building in "downtown" Uturoa, which also operates as Le Moana Restaurant during meal times.*

The disco opens at 10pm each Friday, Saturday and Sunday. The cover charge is 1.000 CFP ($10) and drinks are 500 CFP ($5).

DISCO QUAIDEP, *Tel. 66.36.83, is at le Quai des Pêcheurs restaurant beside the boat dock in Uturoa.*

The disco opens at 10pm each Friday and Saturday, with a cover charge of 500 CFP ($5) for women and 1.000 CFP ($10) for men, including the first drink.

SPORTS & RECREATION

Horseback Riding

Kaohi Nui Equestrian Tourism Center, *Tel. 66.25.46*, is on the mountainside at PK 6 in Avera. Sylvianne and Patrick Marinthe lead 2-hour rides for 3.500 CFP ($35) and half-day rides for 4.500 CFP ($45), using saddled Marquesan horses of Chilean stock. A picnic can be arranged for a ride into the valley, stopping to swim at the waterfalls. Lodging is also available.

Glass Bottom Boat Excursions

Carlo Zanotta, *Tel. 66.10.24*, operates glass bottom boat excursions, departing five times daily from the *Raiatea Pearl Beach Resort pier* starting at 8:30am. The one-hour excursion costs 1.000 CFP ($10) for adults and 500 CFP ($5) for children 5 to 15 years old.

Motor Boat Rental

Raiatea Location, *Tel. 66.34.06*, operated by Patrick Bardou, has small boats for rent. These include a 12-foot Fiberglass unsinkable boat with a 6-horse power engine that requires no permit or a 15-horse power engine that does require a license. Wave runners can also be rented, with a picnic included on request.

Deep Sea Fishing

Game fishing is especially rewarding in the Leeward Society Islands, where prize catches of marlin, yellow fin tuna, mahi mahi and wahoo are frequent events. The Raiatea Haura Club holds local competitions several times a year, and the private charterers report good fishing year-round.

Sakario, *Tel. 66.35.54*, is a 28-foot Bertram Flybridge cruiser owned by Captain Joseph Chaussoy. Half-day charters last for five hours and include drinks, for 35.000 CFP ($350). Full-day charters include drinks and a picnic lunch, for 60.000 CFP ($600). Sakario is the current holder of the International Game Fishing Association Women's World Record of Pacific Blue Marlin. The prize-winning fish was caught on 130-pound line and weighed 385 kilograms (848 pounds).

Te Manu Ata, *Tel. 66.32.14*, is a 28-foot Bertram owned by Captain Jean-Luc Liaut, who also provides half-day fishing expeditions for 3.500

CFP ($350) and full-day outings for 60.000 CFP ($600). **Tahiti Sport Fishing**, *Tel. 66.32.69*, also has fishing charters.

Lagoon Excursions

Faaroa River is a cool, green haven bordered by wild hibiscus *purau* trees and modern homes. One of the most popular excursions is to explore this historic river by outrigger speed canoe. Around the year 1350 hundreds of brave Maohi families left Raiatea from this river, navigating their voyaging sailing canoes by the wind, stars and ocean currents to settle in Hawaii, the Cook Islands, the Samoas and finally in New Zealand. Their Polynesian descendants are called Maori in New Zealand and Tahitians in French Polynesia.

A **Day Tour to Tahaa Island** takes you on a 30-minute boat ride across the protected lagoon that is shared by Raiatea and Tahaa. On the main island you will visit a picturesque little village and a vanilla farm. Then you will explore the lagoon by boat, visiting a black pearl farm and stopping on a *motu* islet to swim and snorkel in the clear lagoon waters.

Trips to the Motu provide an ideal destination by canoe or speedboat, where you will find white sand beaches, privacy, and time for daydreaming and swimming in the lagoon. Should you wish to make a day of it, your hotel will pack a picnic lunch for you.

Manava Excursions, *Tel. 66.28.26*, provides excursions by outrigger speed canoe, offering half-day trips to the **Faaroa river** and **Marae Taputapuatea**, for 2.500 CFP ($25) per person; a picnic on **Motu Nao Nao** on the south coast, for 3.500 CFP ($35) each; a day trip to **Tahaa** to visit a black pearl farm, fish park, vanilla plantation and stop for a swim at a *motu*, for 2.750 CFP ($27.50) per person. An all-day tour of Tahaa and the *motu* islets, with a picnic of grilled fish and fresh fruits, costs 3.750 CFP ($37.50). Andrew, your guide, will also take you to a nearby *motu* and return at your convenience, for 1.000 CFP ($10) per person.

Raiatea Safari Tours, *Tel. 66.37.10*, charges 3.000 CFP ($30) per person for a boat trip to visit the Faaroa River, with a snorkeling stop on the reef and *motu*. A half-day boat trip to Tahaa is 3.500 CFP ($35), and a full-day trip around Tahaa is 5.500 CFP ($55). Fishing inside the lagoon is 2.000 CFP ($20) for line fishing and 4.000 CFP ($40) for troll fishing. Owner Patrice Philip also performs a **Snorkeling and Underwater "Tubalade" Show**. Scuba gear is provided and you can float on the surface in shallow water and watch the Scuba Tour instructors feed thousands of colorful tropical fish in a natural aquarium. These include Napoleon fish weighing up to 100 kilograms (220 pounds), giant trigger fish, moray eels, puffer fish, sharks and perhaps even Jules or Juliette, the pet barracuda. This snorkeling and underwater show costs 2.800 CFP ($28) per person, and departs from the pier at Chez Marie-France.

Tahaa Pearl Tour, *65.67.80*, is operated by Bruno Fabre, who can take from two to 10 people in his covered outrigger speed canoe for half- or full-day excursions. He departs daily from the Uturoa quay in Raiatea, and takes you to Tahaa to visit a vanilla plantation. You will eat lunch with a local family and then visit the pearl farm, where you will be given a demonstration of how the black lip oyster is cultivated to produce black pearls. Stops are also made at the fish parks inside the lagoon. The all-day tour is from 9am to 4pm and costs 6.000 CFP ($60) for adults and 4.500 CFP ($45) for children, lunch included.

Tahaa Transport Services, *Tel. 66.17.28, Blue Lagon Agency in Raiatea or Tel. 65.67.10 in Tahaa.* Yves Guilbert has a 9-place *Navette des Iles* mini-truck for guided excursions of Tahaa, visiting the vanilla farms, fruit farms and pearl farms. A special round-trip day tour between Raiatea and Tahaa is 5.000 CFP ($50) per person, including boat transportation and the land tour. Departure from the boat dock at Uturoa is at 8am, returning at 1:30pm. An air-conditioned 45-seat bus is available for large groups.

Sailing Charter Yachts

Archipels Polynesian Cruises, *Tel. 56.36.39,* has a nautical base at *Opunohu Bay in Moorea* and a yacht based permanently in Raiatea. Please see chapter on *Moorea* for details.

Danae Cruises, *B.P. 251, Uturoa, Raiatea, Tel. 689/66.12.50; Fax 689/ 66.39.37. This nautical base is located at Uturaerae Marina.* The Goche family have been operating the Danae Cruises in the Society Islands since 1972, and they proudly claim to be the oldest charter operation in Tahiti and Her Islands. *Danae III* is a 67-foot steel ketch with four double staterooms, fully crewed and offering complete services. The *Danae III* operates shared-boat cruises, with alternating weekly Monday departures from Raiatea and Bora Bora, ending on alternating Saturday afternoons at the same islands. These cruises are sold by the berth or cabin, and the sailing program is maintained even if there are only two people on board. The cost of this six-day cruise is 116.700 CFP ($1,167) per person, all on-board meals and activities included. Airfare is not included.

Danae IV is a fully air-conditioned 50-foot sailing trawler with two double staterooms, each with its own head and shower. This is an ideal yacht for a family or honeymooners or for private charters of three or more days. A couple can charter the *Danae IV* for a 3 day/2 night cruise for 90.000 CFP ($900) per person, including all meals, crew and services.

Dive Cruises to Tahaa and the atoll of Tupai are available for four to eight divers. If there are four divers, the per diver cost of 145.000 CFP ($1,450) includes a 6 day/5 night cruise, all meals and 10 dives, led by a qualified diving instructor. The cost is 160,000 CFP ($1,600) per diver for a minimum of two divers. Weekend dive cruises are also available.

The Moorings, *B.P. 165, Uturoa, Raiatea, Tel. 689/66.35.93/66.26.26; Fax 689/66.20.94. The nautical base is located at Apooiti Marina, 2 kilometers (1.2 miles) from the Raiatea airport and 4 kilometers (2.5 miles) from the boat dock in Uturoa.* The Moorings fleet has been operating in Raiatea since 1985 and has a fleet of monohull sailboats from 35 to 51 feet and catamarans 42 feet long. Yachts can be chartered bareboat or with skipper and hostess/cook, and provisioning is available on request. The Exclusive Line incorporates the newest yachts, up to two years old, with all the extras, such as satellite navigation systems or autopilot, downwind cruising sails, roller furling mainsails and compact disk players with cockpit speakers. The Club Line offers yachts ranging in age from brand new to four years. These are also fully equipped except for the autopilot and downwind cruising sail.

Bruno Cadoret heads a team of 17 employees who takes care of the American, French and German sailors who charter their yachts each year to cruise the Leeward Islands. Daily charter rates start at 31.000 CFP ($310) for a six-passenger Moorings 353. A 10-passenger Moorings 510 costs 62.000 CFP ($620) a day, and an eight-passenger 42-foot catamaran charters for 67.000 CFP ($670) per day. Weekly rentals and 10-day cruises are also available.

Stardust Marine, *B.P. 331, Uturoa, Raiatea, Tel. 689/66.23.18; Fax 689/66.23.19. The nautical base and marina are located at PK 12.5 in Faaroa Bay 8 miles from Uturoa,* with a fleet of 17 monohull sailboats ranging from 37 to 52 feet, and 3 catamarans 43 to 47 feet long. Stardust Marine has an office in Newport Beach, California, but their biggest market is French. The Europeans have also discovered the pleasures of cruising through the Leeward Islands, and up to eight yachts at a time are chartered by groups of Germans and Austrians.

The sailing range includes the neighboring Leeward Islands of Tahaa, Bora Bora and Huahine, and with special permission, Maupiti. Cruises are also available in the Marquesas Islands and Tuamotu atolls. One-way conveyance is possible. The sailing program includes a welcome with floral leis at the Uturoa airport and round-trip transportation between the airport and the Stardust Marine nautical base. The yachts are ready to sail away, complete with fuel, water, dinghy and outboard engine, bed linen and towels, barbecue grill and charcoal, snorkeling equipment and with complete provisions on request. Optional services include skippers and hostess-cooks. For security, each yacht is equipped with a radio-telephone and nautical charts of the islands to be visited.

Star Voyage, *B.P. 119, Uturoa, Raiatea, Tel. 689/66. 40.00; Fax 689/66.11.83. The base is at the Uturoa marina.* This French-owned company is the newest addition to the yacht charterers in Raiatea. The fleet includes Sun Odyssey monohulls from 32 to 42 feet long, Oceanis 381 and 461 yachts, and Privilege 37 and 42 catamarans. An 11 day/10 night itinerary takes you on a cruise from Raiatea through the Leeward Islands of Huahine, Tahaa, Bora Bora and back to Raiatea. Weekly charter rates start at 180.000 CFP ($1,800) for a Sun Odyssey 32.1 during the low season of November through March. The high season rate, from June 27 through August 28, 1998, for the same yacht is 238,000 CFP ($2,300).

   Tahiti Yacht Charter, *B.P. 608, Papeete, Tahiti, Tel. 689/45.04.00; Fax 689/42.76.00; e-mail: tyc@mail.pf is located on the yacht quay of Papeete and at the Apooiti Marina in Raiatea.* The fleet includes six monohulls from 32 to 50 feet and six catamarans from 35 to 46 feet, which can be chartered bareboat or provisioned with skipper and hostess/cook. Charter rates range from $350 a day to $5,740 a week, depending on season and yacht. Please see information in *Tahiti* chapter.

Scuba Diving

   A short boat ride takes you to the **natural aquarium** at Teavapiti, and 50 different exciting dive spots are found in the four most beautiful passes of the Raiatea-Tahaa lagoon. These include exploring a sunken three-masted yacht, the hull of a Catalina seaplane, feeding gray sharks, barracuda, moray eels and the Napoleon fish that inhabit an underwater wall. The Octopus Grotto is a cave 120 meters (394 feet) long at a depth of 50 meters (55 feet), a dive for experienced divers only. There are also rainbow-hued Jack trevally fish, caves of orange corals, black coral forests and dancing coral gardens of blues, violets and yellow. An exploratory or fun dive is 5.000 CFP ($50); a first dive or lesson costs 5.500 CFP ($55), and PADI open water diver certification costs 50.000 CFP ($500), including all the equipment.

   Hémisphère Sub Plongée, *Tel. 66.12.49/66.14.19, is based at the Marina Apooiti.* A team of qualified instructors led by dive master Hubert Clot offers French CMAS-certification courses and PADI lessons. Daily diving excursions leave the marina at 8:30am and 2:30pm to discover the lagoon, passes and open ocean depths around Raiatea and Tahaa. An exploratory dive is 5.000 CFP ($50). Introductory dives are made at 10:30am, and night dives are available on request. A day tour with a picnic lunch on a *motu* and diving cruises can also be arranged.

   Raiatea Plongée, *Tel. 66.37.10, VHF Channel 16-Raiatea Scuba,* is operated by Patrice Philip *at Chez Marie-France in Tepua Bay.* Patrice Philip is a highly qualified international diving monitor, who can teach beginners to dive in a specially built swimming pool, or give PADI certifications for resort divers, open water divers, advanced open water divers, master scuba divers and specialties. He can also give French exams for CMAS and FFESSM certificates. Dives are made two to three times daily, taking you to one or more of the special dive sites Patrice has discovered both inside and outside the coral reef since he opened his dive center in 1981. American standard equipment is provided and photo and video service is available. Guests staying at Marie-France pension get reduced diving rates. Raiatea Plongée will soon open a Scubapro dive center at the **Hotel Le Maitai Tenape** in Miri Miri Bay.

SHOPPING

The **Anuanua Art Gallery**, *Tel. 66.12.66, is close to the post office on the main street of Uturoa center.* A unique selection of paintings, sculptures, etchings, pottery, tapa, sandalwood and seashell jewelry is on display. **Galerie Art-Expo**, *Tel. 66.11.83, is located at the Marina Apooiti*, exhibiting lithographs by Moorea resident artists François Ravello and Michèle Dallet, and locally made *pareos*, shirts, tee-shirts, *tifaifai* bed covers, tapa bark paintings and black pearls.

Te Fare, *Tel. 66.17.17, is on the lagoon side close to the Lycée,* with a colorful selection of Polynesian art deco linens, pottery, basketware and jewelry. **Arii Boutique** sells hand painted *pareos* and tee-shirts, and you can also find locally made souvenir items at the **Handcrafts Center** *beside the tourist office at the Uturoa ferry dock.* The **Hawaiki Nui Association** *at the airport* sells *pareos* and tee-shirts, wood sculptures, and traditional woven hats and bags, plus seashell jewelry. **La Palme d'Or** in Uturoa sells black pearl jewelry.

PRACTICAL INFORMATION

Banks

Raiatea has four banks, which are all located *in the main town of Uturoa.* **Banque de Polynésie**, *Tel. 66.34.42,* is open Monday through Friday from 7:45am to 12pm and from 1 to 3:45pm; **Banque Socredo**, *66.30.64,* is open Monday through Friday from 7:30 am to 3pm; **Banque de Tahiti**, *Tel. 66.35.68,* is open Monday through Friday from 7:45 to 11:45am, and from 1:30 to 4:30pm; and **Banque Westpac**, *Tel. 66.32.48,* is open Monday, Wednesday and Thursday from 7:45am to 3:30pm, and on Tuesday and Friday from 7:15am to 3pm.

Bookstores

Librarie d'Uturoa, *Tel. 66.30.80,* is in the center of town, on the mountain side of the main street. **Polycentre**, *Tel. 66.31.13,* next door, has coffee table books about Tahiti and Her Islands.

Drugstore

The Pharmacie de Raiatea, *Tel. 66.15.56,* is adjacent to the Banque de Polynésie on the main street of Uturoa center. It is open Monday through

Friday from 7:30 to 11:30am and 2 to 5:30pm; on Saturday from 7:30 to 11:30am and on holidays from 9:30 to 10:30am.

Hospital

There is a government hospital close to the boat dock in Uturoa, *Tel. 66.35.03*, that serves all the Leeward Society Islands, and several private doctors and dentists have practices in Raiatea.

Police

The French *gendarmerie* is close to the post office *in Uturoa center, Tel. 66.31.07*.

Post Office and Telecommunications Office

The **Post Office** is in a modern building north of Uturoa on the main road, *Tel. 66.35.50*. All telecommunications and postal services are available here. Hours are Monday to Thursday from 7am to 3pm, Friday from 7am to 2pm, and on Saturday from 8 to 10am.

Tourist Bureau

A tourist information bureau is located on the quay in Uturoa and at the airport, *Tel. 66.23.33*.

19. TAHAA

You don't hear much about the quiet little island of **Tahaa**, which lives in the shadow of its big sister island of Raiatea and within sight of the glamorous island of Bora Bora. Without making much hoopla about it, Tahaa is stretching in many directions. Its reputation as Polynesia's vanilla island has now expanded to include one of the best hotels in French Polynesia and three dozen black pearl farms in the clear lagoon waters near the white sand beaches of the *motu* islets.

The Maohi pioneers who settled on this small circular island called it Uporu, a name that is also found in Western Samoa. Polynesian folklore declares that this island was the natal home of Hiro, the famous god of thieves in Polynesian mythology, whose favorite hangout was in the islands we now call the Leeward Society Islands. Huge black volcanic boulders on Tahaa's east coast are considered parts of Hiro's body or objects that belonged to him.

During the 17th century the kings of Raiatea and Tahaa fought for possession of Tahaa. Bora Bora's feared warriors were more powerful, and both Tahaa and Raiatea were subjugated to the rule of Bora Bora's King Tapoa, descendant of Puni the Conqueror.

Although the Leeward Islands became a possession of France in 1888, the French flag was raised in Tahaa only in 1897, following years of rebellion.

Several Frenchmen with yachts have chosen the now peaceful island of Tahaa as retirement retreats. There are good marina facilities and all yachts are welcomed.

Tahaa's inhabitants lead quiet, industrious lives, earning their living in agriculture, fishing and breeding livestock. Plantations of sumptuous fruits and vegetables add their lushness to the palette of vibrant colors

See page 351 for the map of Tahaa, which is joined to Raiatea.

you'll see all around the island. The produce from Tahaa is sold at the public market in Raiatea and the watermelons are shipped to the market in Papeete.

Tahaa is often called the **Vanilla Island** because of the numerous plantations of this aromatic "black gold" that flourish in the fertile valleys. After the vanilla beans are harvested and laid out to dry, the whole village is filled with the rich perfume of vanilla. You can visit a vanilla plantation and some of the black pearl farms that are built in the warm, clear lagoon near the *motu* islets.

Tahaa has no airport, but there are good port facilities, with inter-island ferry and cargo ship service several times a week, and water-taxi or shuttle boat service from Uturoa. Tahaa has a *gendarmerie*, infirmary and dispensary, post office, banks and small general stores. Accommodations are available on a small scale, either in traditional Polynesian style hotels, beach and overwater bungalows on a *motu*, a berth aboard a sailboat or a room in a village home. Wherever there is a room there is usually an excellent meal available.

You can paddle an outrigger canoe or hire a boat and guide to visit the *motu*, where you can picnic on the white sand beaches. The protected lagoon is also ideal for sailing, windsurfing, snorkeling and fishing. You can hike into the valleys or rent a car or bike to explore the island.

Tahaa is slowly awakening to the world of tourism, yet it remains virtually undiscovered by the general tourist market. Peace, tranquillity and natural beauty combine with a friendly, unhurried pace, offering you a relaxed and happy vacation with a taste of Polynesia of yesteryear.

ARRIVALS & DEPARTURES
Arriving By Air
There is no airport on the island of Tahaa. You can fly to Raiatea and take a boat to Tahaa. If you have made reservations at a hotel or pension on Tahaa, your host will send a boat to meet you at the airport. You can also go to the boat dock in Uturoa and get a regular shuttle boat to Tahaa or take a private taxi boat.

Arriving By Boat
Ono-Ono, *Tel. 45.35.35; Fax 43.83.45; e-mail: onoono@mail.pf* departs from the *Papeete boat dock, adjacent to the Moorea boats*, each Monday and Wednesday at 9am, arriving in Tahaa at 2:45pm. *The ticket office is located on the boat dock in Papeete.* One-way fare from Papeete to Tahaa is 6.055 CFP ($60.55). Be at the dock one hour prior to departure. A special weekend inter-island circuit arrives in Tahaa from Bora Bora each Saturday 9am, and from Huahine and Raiatea at 4:45pm the same day.

Taporo VI, *Tel. 42.63.93/43.79.72; Fax 42.06.17*, departs from *the Fare-Ute quay on the far side of the Papeete harbor*, each Monday, Wednesday and Friday, at 4pm, stopping in Huahine and Raiatea, arriving in Tahaa the following morning at 6:30am. One-way fare to Tahaa is 1,692 CFP ($16.92) on the bridge and 20.000 CFP ($200) for a cabin with four berths.

Vaeanu, *Tel. 41.25.35; Fax 41.24.34*, departs from the *Fare-Ute quay in Papeete* at 5pm on Monday, stopping in Huahine, Raiatea and Bora Bora, arriving in Tahaa the following day at 12:30pm. Each Friday the *Vaeanu* leaves Papeete at 5pm, stopping in Huahine and Raiatea, and arrives in Tahaa on Saturday at 7:30am. After spending the night in Bora Bora the ship arrives back in Tahaa on Sunday at 12pm. One-way fare for bridge passengers is 1.709 CFP ($17.09) and cabins cost 4.000 to 5.500 CFP ($40 to $55) per person. All the inter-island transport boats dock at the quay in Tapuamu.

Scheduled boat service between Raiatea and Tahaa is provided by several boats that depart from the public quay in Uturoa center, stopping at various villages around the island of Tahaa.

Maupiti Express, *Tel. 67.66.69*, arrives in Tahaa from Bora Bora each Wednesday and Friday at 8am, stopping at the Marina Iti pier. The boat goes on to Raiatea for the day and returns from Uturoa to Tahaa at 4:45pm. The one-way fare is 3.000 CFP ($30). Passengers under 15 years and over 60 years have a 20 percent reduction. *Reservations office in Tahiti, Tel. 48.05.81*. A Day Tour of Tahaa is available for 10.000 CFP ($100) a person, which includes a guided visit to the highlights of Tahaa, including a vanilla plantation, a black pearl farm and handcrafts centers. *Reservations can be made at Agence Blue Lagon, Tel. 66.17.28/65.67.10*.

Tahaa Transport Services, *Tel. 65.67.10*, operated by Yves Guilbert, has two launches for 57 people. The regularly scheduled shuttle boat *Uporu* departs from Uturoa for the west coast of Tahaa (Apu, Poutoru, Tiva and Tapuamu Bays) several times daily between 8:30am and 5:45pm Monday through Friday, and at 10:45am on Saturday. Boat service between Uturoa and Tahaa's east coast bays of Haamene and Faaaha is provided by the *Iripau*, starting at 6:40am and the last boat leaves Raiatea at 4:50pm. Each Monday, Wednesday and Friday a free shuttle bus service aboard an air-conditioned Mercedes 45-place bus connects with the *Iripau*, which leaves Uturoa at 11am and arrives in Faaaha at 12:10pm. The bus will take you from the Amaru Quay in Faaaha, at 12:10pm, to the village of Patio, arriving at 12:50pm, with stops at the *mairie* (town hall) of Faaaha, the Raai marina and the Hipu *mairie*, arriving at the *mairie* in Patio at 12:50pm.

Taxi Boats

Tahaa Transport Services, *Tel. 65.67.10*, provides daily taxi boat service between Uturoa and Tahaa on request.

Departing By Air

You can take a boat from Tahaa directly to the airport on Raiatea or go to Uturoa town by taxi boat and take a land taxi to the airport. Air Tahiti's number in Raiatea is *Tel. 66.32.50/66.30.51.*

Departing By Boat

You can continue on to Bora Bora by boat from Tahaa, or you can return to Papeete with stops in Raiatea and Huahine.

Ono Ono, *Tel. 66.24.25*, (Raiatea) leaves Tahaa for Bora Bora each Monday and Wednesday at 3pm. The Tahaa-Raiatea-Huahine-Papeete passages leave the boat dock in Tapuamu each Tuesday and Thursday at 8:15am, arriving in Tahiti at 2:15pm. A special inter-island circuit operates each weekend, leaving Tahaa for Raiatea and Huahine at 9:15am each Saturday, and departing for Bora Bora at 5pm Saturday afternoon. On Sundays the departure time from Tahaa to Raiatea, Huahine and Tahiti is at 1:15pm, arriving in Papeete at 7:15pm.

Taporo VI, *Tel. 66.32.29*, *(Raiatea)* leaves Tahaa at 5:30am each Tuesday, Thursday and Saturday at 7am for Bora Bora and from there goes to Raiatea and Huahine before arriving in Papeete at 4am the following morning. Buy your tickets on board.

Vaeanu, *Tel. 41.25.35*, leaves Tahaa at 1pm each Tuesday for Raiatea, Huahine and Tahiti, arriving in Papeete at 3am on Wednesday. On Saturday the *Vaeanu* leaves Tahaa at 8am for Bora Bora, and returns to Tahiti each Sunday, leaving Tahaa at 12pm, stopping in Raiatea and Huahine, and arriving in Papeete each Monday at 2am. Buy your ticket on board the ship.

Maupiti Express, *Tel. 67.66.69*, departs from the Marina Iti pier each Wednesday and Friday at 5pm, for Bora Bora. The one-way fare is 3.000 CFP ($30). Passengers under 15 years and over 60 years have a 20 percent reduction. *Reservations office in Tahiti, Tel. 48.05.81.*

Tahaa Transport Services, *Tel. 65.67.10*, has a shuttle boat service provided by the *Uporu* that departs from the Tapuamu port at 6:15am on Monday through Friday, Stops are made in Tiva, Patii, Poutoru and Apu Marina Iti, arriving at the Uturoa boat dock in Raiatea at 7:10am. The afternoon departure leaves Tapuamu at 1pm, arriving in Uturoa at 1:55pm. A Saturday departure leaves Tapuamu at 7am. A special run is made from the Apu Marina Iti at 9:30am, arriving in Uturoa at 9:50am. The *Iripau* leaves Haamene village Monday through Friday at 7:30am, stopping in Faaha, and arriving in Uturoa at 8:10am. The boat also leaves

Haamene at 12 and 4:40pm for Uturoa, arriving at 12:50 and 5:30pm. There is no scheduled service from the east coast on weekends, but you can charter a private taxi boat.

ORIENTATION

Tahaa lies three kilometers (2 miles) northwest of Uturoa, sharing the same coral foundation and reef protected lagoon that surrounds the island of Raiatea. The shape of the island, with its scalloped shoreline, resembles a hibiscus flower. The deeply indented bays of Apu, Haamene and Hurepiti on the south of the island are separated by a narrow isthmus. Some 60 *motu* islets lie inside the coral reef in the north and this protective barrier is unbroken except by the two navigable passes of Toahotu on the southeast side and Tiamahana on the southwest coast. Yachts and even ships can completely circumnavigate the island inside the lagoon, often accompanied by porpoises.

Tahaa has a land surface of 88 square kilometers (34 square miles), and **Mount Ohiri**, at 598 meters (1,961 feet), is the highest peak of the volcanic mountain range. The mountains are not high enough to attract enough rain to meet the needs of the 4,470 residents, who live in the small villages of Patio, Pahure, Hipu, Faaaha, Haamene, Motutiairi, Vaitoare, Poutoru, Patii, Tiva, Tapuamu and Murifenua. **Tiva** is considered the prettiest village, **Tapuamu** has the main port facilities, **Patio** is the administrative center, and **Haamene Bay** is six kilometers (3.7 miles) long, providing good anchorage and a haven for sailors.

A road winds 67 kilometers (42 miles) through the coastal villages and up mountain roads, where you have panoramic views of the bays, offshore islets and the ever-changing colors of the sea beyond the white foam on the barrier reef.

GETTING AROUND

Car & Scooter Rentals

Avis, *Tel. 65.66.77*. The main sales office is located *at the Haamene quay*. A 2-place Mega Ranch rents for 5.400 CFP ($54) for 4 hours and 6.800 CFP ($68) for 8 hours. A 4-door Ford Fiesta rents for 6.300 CFP ($63) for 4 hours, 7.100 CFP ($71) for 8 hours, and 7.900 CFP ($79) for 24 hours. These rates include 100 kilometers and insurance.

Europcar, *Tel. 65.67.00*. The main sales office is located *at the service station on the ferry dock of Tapuamu*. A Fiat Panda rents for 5.000 CFP ($50) for 4 hours, 6.000 CFP ($60) for 8 hours, 7.000 CFP ($70) for 24 hours, and 13.000 CFP ($130) for a weekend. A Fun Car is a cross between a car and a scooter and rents for 4.500 CFP ($45) for 4 hours and 5.000 CFP ($50) for 8 hours. Scooter rates start at 4.000 CFP ($40) for 4 hours. These rates include unlimited mileage and third party insurance. Gas is extra.

Tahaa Transport Services, *Tel. 65.67.10, at Hotel Marina Iti*, also rents cars and bicycles.

Pacificar Tahaa, (**Monique Location**) *Tel. 65.62.48*, is located *in Patio.*

Bicycles

Europcar, *Tel. 65.67.00*, rents bicycles and beach bikes for 1.200 CFP ($12) for 4 hours and 1.500 CFP ($15) for 8 hours. Longer rentals possible.

WHERE TO STAY

Expensive

HOTEL VAHINE ISLAND NOA NOA, *B.P. 510, Uturoa, Raiatea. Tel. 689/65.67.38; Fax 689/65.67.70. Reservations: South Pacific Marketing, B.P. 718, Papeete, Tahiti. Tel. 689/43.90.04; Fax 689/41.39.23. Located on Motu Tuvahine, a private islet in the Tahaa lagoon, facing Bora Bora, 15 kilometers (9.3 miles) from the Raiatea airport and 12 kilometers (7.4 miles) from the ferry dock in Raiatea. Round-trip boat transfers from Raiatea are 5.000 CFP ($50) per person. EP Rates: beach bungalow 30.000 CFP ($300) single/double; overwater bungalow 45.000 CFP ($450) single/double. Add 4.000 CFP ($40) for third person. Meal plan with breakfast and dinner is 5.900 CFP ($59) per person; meal plan with breakfast, lunch and dinner is 8.900 CFP ($89) per person. Add 7% hotel tax to room rates and 1% value added tax to room rates and meal plan. All major credit cards.*

This elegant hotel is located on an eight-acre *motu* off the village of Hipu on Tahaa's northeastern shore. Here you will find long stretches of white sand beaches, good snorkeling in the coral gardens of the lagoon, a lounge filled with a good selection of books, music and video films, and the perfect setting for relaxing. The eight beach bungalows are small, with room for a bed and closet on the ground floor, and a sleeping loft for a child. The three Polynesian style overwater bungalows are larger, with a bedroom and salon, and a hammock on the covered deck. The bamboo furniture and *pareo* cloth bedspreads, curtains and cushion covers provide a traditional Polynesian motif. A glass coffee table in the sitting area is a window to the marvelous marine world beneath the bungalow, where you can spy on the comings and goings of the multihued fish. All the bungalows have overhead fans, a mini-bar and private bathrooms with hot water showers.

Serge Gatinal, from Toulouse, France, is the enthusiastic and friendly young manager. His plans include adding Jacuzzis, traditional massages, sunset cruises and a list of other activities. A hotel activities desk can suggest several ways to enjoy the beautiful lagoon between Tahaa and

Raiatea and land tours on the main island. The restaurant and bar are open to the public, but reservations must be made for meals if you are not staying in the hotel. A helipad on the premises allows you to fly over from Bora Bora or Raiatea and land on Tuvahine Island, and you can also visit by boat.

Moderate
HOTEL MAREVA VILLAGE, *B.P. 214, Haamene, Tahaa. Tel./Fax 689/65.61.61. Beside the lagoon in Poutoru on the south coast of Tahaa, facing Raiatea. Round-trip boat transfers from Raiatea are 5.000 CFP ($50) for one to four people. MAP Rates: beach bungalow with breakfast and dinner, 7.000 CFP ($70) single/double. Third person add 1.000 CFP. Meal plan with breakfast and dinner is 13.000 CFP ($130) for two people. Add 7% hotel tax to room rates and 1% value added tax to room rates and meal plan. Mastercard, Visa.*

Six bungalows beside the lagoon offer first rate accommodations in attractive wooden bungalows on stilts. Each bungalow contains a living room with a couch that converts to a bed, a ceiling fan, television, kitchen with refrigerator and stove, and a bathroom with a hot water shower. A dining veranda overlooks the lagoon toward Raiatea. The restaurant and bar are across the road on a promontory, and activities can be arranged at the activities desk.

MARINA ITI, *B.P. 888, Uturoa, Raiatea. Tel. 689/65.61.01; Fax 689/65.63.87. Beside the lagoon in Vaitoare, 10 minutes by boat from Apooiti Marina in Raiatea. Round-trip boat transfers 3.000 CFP ($30) per person. EP Rates: garden double bungalow 6.000 CFP ($60) single/double; lagoon double bungalow 8.000 CFP ($80) single/double. Additional bed 2.000 CFP ($20). Meal plan with breakfast and dinner is 5.000 CFP ($50) per person; meal plan with breakfast, lunch and dinner is 8.000 CFP ($80) per person. Add 1% value added tax to room rates and meal plan. Mastercard, Visa.*

The main building of this small hotel could be used as a setting for a South Seas movie, with its open-air lounge, shell lamps and bamboo sofas, and the golden patina of aged woven bamboo and a thatched palm roof. The view of the sunsets here are truly remarkable, looking past the masts of the sailboats that are moored at the hotel pier.

The four bungalows include three double units, each containing a double bed and a single bed, a living room, terrace and private bathroom. The fourth bungalow is also double, with a bedroom, terrace and private bathroom with hot water. House linens are provided. Snorkeling equipment and paddle canoes are provided, and all other activities can be arranged at the activities desk.

This is a popular gathering place for residents of Raiatea, which is just 10 minutes by boat from the Apooiti Marina. The hotel has a private boat that can pick up guests at the airport, the marina or at the public pier in

Uturoa. People who live on Tahiti also come over for the weekend, and almost anyone with a boat at their disposal heads for the Marina Iti on weekends and holidays. The atmosphere is very European and the excellent cuisine served in the restaurant is definitely French.

CHEZ PERRETTE, *PK 10, Faaopore, Tahaa. Tel. 689/65.65.78. Beside the lagoon in Faaaha, 30 minutes by boat from airport and one kilometer (.62 miles) from the Tahaa ferry dock at Faaaha Bay. Round-trip transfers provided. Rates: bungalow with breakfast and dinner 8.500 CFP ($85) single/double; bungalow with breakfast, lunch and dinner 15.000 CFP ($150) single/double; mattress in dormitory 2.500 CFP ($25) per person. Add 1% value added tax to room rates and meal plan. No credit cards.*

There is one bungalow with a bedroom, living room, kitchen and private bathroom with cold water; and a colonial style house has two bedrooms and a dormitory on the mezzanine, with 8 mattresses. You share a communal bathroom with cold water. House linens are furnished. This place is clean and colorful, but it is remote and the setting is not very scenic. It's also rather pricey for what it offers.

PENSION HIBISCUS, *B.P. 184, Haamene, Tahaa. Tel. 689/65.61.06; Fax 689/65.65.65. At the end of Haamene Bay, 20 minutes by boat from the Raiatea ferry dock. Round-trip boat transfers are 2.500 CFP ($25) per person. EP Rates: bungalow with private bathroom 7.850 CFP ($78.50) for one to five people per day. A bungalow with outside communal bathroom is 5.750 CFP ($57.50) single/double/triple. Meal plan with breakfast and dinner is 3.500 CFP ($35) per person; meal plan with breakfast, lunch and dinner is 5.500 CFP ($55) per person. Reduced rates for longer stays. Add 1% value added tax to room rates and meal plan. American Express, Mastercard, Visa.*

This is primarily a nautical base that has three bungalows for rent. Each of the small bungalows contains a double bed and a single bed, a private bedroom with hot water and a small terrace. Two family bungalows each contain one room with a double bed and a single bed, kitchen and communal bathroom with hot water. House linens are provided and all the beds are covered by a mosquito net. Snorkeling equipment is provided and a wide range of activities is available, with Lolita frequently acting as your guide.

The main action is in the restaurant and bar, which also serves as a yacht club, decorated with flags and nautical pennants. The ambiance can become quite lively when a group of yachties tie up at the moorings provided at the big pier and adjourn to the "watering hole". If you're looking for a rollicking good time, with lots of sea tales, this is your place. If you seek a tranquil, private environment, give it a miss.

PENSION HERENUI, *B.P. 148, Haamene, Tahaa. Tel./Fax 689/ 65.62.60. On mountainside in Poutoru, next to the shuttle boat dock, 25 minutes by boat from the ferry dock in Raiatea. Round-trip boat transfers are 1.000 CFP*

($10) per person. EP Rates: bungalow 7.000 CFP ($70) single/double. Third person 1.000 CFP ($10). Meal plan with breakfast and dinner is 3.500 CFP ($35) per person; meal plan with breakfast, lunch and dinner is 5.000 CFP ($50) per person. Children under three years are free and children under 12 years pay 2.500 CFP ($25) a day for three meals and 1.750 CFP ($17.50) for breakfast and dinner. Add 1% value added tax to room rates and meal plan. No credit cards.

This is an attractive location even though it is not beside the lagoon. Three wooden bungalows contain two single beds that can be converted into a double bed, a private bathroom with hot water and a terrace. House linens are furnished. A "Club House" beside a fresh water swimming pool contains a communal kitchen and dining room. Owners Esther and Gilbert Delort prepare Polynesian style meals on request.

CHEZ PATRICIA & DANIEL, *BP 104, Haamene, Tahaa, Tel./Fax 689/65.60.83. On mountainside in Haamene, 20 minutes by boat from the Uturoa boat dock. Round-trip transfers 4.000 CFP ($40) for one to eight passengers. EP rates: bungalow 6.000 CFP ($60) single/double. Additional person 1.000 CFP ($10). Meal plan with breakfast and dinner add 2.500 CFP ($25) per person; meal plan with all meals add 3.500 CFP ($35) per person. Reduced rates for longer stays. Add 1% value added tax to room rates and meal plan. No credit cards.*

This small pension opened in July, 1997, with three thatched roof bungalows that were formerly used for the children of the family. They are situated on an immense grassy land facing the lagoon and the family's black pearl farm in Haamene. The thatched roof bungalows each contain a bedroom with two double beds and a private bathroom with hot water, plus closets and a small desk or dressing table, all with a Polynesian touch. A big open club house contains a kitchen, dining area and video room, and an arts and crafts shop also contains black pearls from the Amaru's own farm. The program of activities includes lagoon excursions aboard their private outrigger speed canoe.

Inexpensive

CHEZ PASCAL, *Tapuamu, Tahaa. Tel. 689/65.60.42. On mountainside in Tapuamu, one kilometer (.62 miles) from the Tahaa ferry dock and 40 minutes by boat from Raiatea airport. Round-trip transfers and all activities are included. EP rates: "fare" or room with breakfast 3.000 CFP ($30) per person. Room with breakfast and dinner 4.500 CFP ($45) per person. Room with all meals 6.000 CFP ($60). Add 1% value added tax to room rates and meal plan. No credit cards.*

If you're looking for total immersion into a Polynesian experience at the lowest rates available, this is the place to stay. There are three *fares*, which are large and simply furnished. One *fare* has a double bed and a single bed, a terrace and an outside private bathroom with cold water; one *fare* has a double bed and communal bathroom with cold water; a four-bedroom house has a double bed and a single bed in each room, with communal living room, kitchen and bathroom with cold water. House linens are furnished and the electricity is solar powered. Meals are served family style, with Pascal and his family joining guests at the table. This is the true Polynesian spirit.

WHERE TO EAT

HOTEL VAHINE ISLAND, *Tel. 689/65.67.38. Breakfast, lunch and dinner are served. All major credit cards. Reservations are required for guests not staying in the hotel.*

French cuisine and local dishes.

MARINA ITI, *Tel. 65.61.01. Breakfast, lunch and dinner are served. Diners, Mastercard and Visa. Reservations are required for guests not staying in the hotel.*

French cuisine is the specialty here.

HOTEL MAREVA VILLAGE, *Tel. 65.67.38. Breakfast, lunch and dinner. No credit cards. Reservations are required for guests not staying in the hotel.*

French and local cuisine.

PENSION HIBISCUS, *Tel. 65.61.06. Breakfast, lunch and dinner are served. American Express, Mastercard and Visa. Reservations are required for guests not staying in the hotel.*

The emphasis is on local specialties and the fish catch of the day. Frequent Tahitian *tamaara'a* feasts are held.

SNACK PAT MANOU, *close to the ferry dock in Tapuamu.*

Serves local cuisine in a lively Polynesian ambiance.

SNACK TISSAN, *Tel. 65.64.15, is at the boat dock in Patio. Open Friday, Saturday and Sunday for lunch and dinner. No credit cards.*

Take-away meals of local and Chinese cuisine are available.

SEEING THE SIGHTS

Vanilla Tours, *Tel. 65.62.46.* Christina and Alain Plantier have a 4 1/2 hour excursion that takes you on a mountain safari by 4-wheel drive vehicle through Tahaa's luxuriant vegetation, across the island, through the mountains and from bay to bay, to view the scenery from these vantage points. You will visit a tropical fruit garden and vanilla plantation, where you will learn about this fragrant "brown gold" and how it is "married" by hand. Fresh fruits and juice will be served. The tour costs 3.500 CFP ($35) per person if departing from the Plantier home in Hurepiti, and 4.000 CFP ($40) for hotel pick-up.

Hainanui Tours, *Tel. 65.61.90*, operated by Philippe Paoaafaite, has mini-bus tours daily, leaving the *Marina Iti hotel* at 9am and returning at 4:45pm. A complete sightseeing tour takes you across the island, to visit a vanilla farm, a cultured pearl farm and a turtle park.

Lolita Tours, *Tel. 65.61.06, is located at Hotel Hibiscus in Haamene.* Lolita is also known as Tearere Ariitu-Morou, and she leads daily walks, which start at the *quay in Haamene.* You will visit a vanilla plantation, copra drying platform, a black pearl farm and explore the fauna and flora of Tahaa, including a stop at the Hibiscus Foundation's turtle reserve. Lolita also operates 4WD excursions to discover the summits of Tahaa's lookout points.

Tahaa Transport Services, *Tel. 65.67.10*, owned by Yves Guilbert, has a 9-place *Navette des Iles* mini-truck for guided excursions of Tahaa, visiting the vanilla farms, fruit farms and pearl farms. A special round-trip day tour between Raiatea and Tahaa is 5.000 CFP ($50) per person, including boat transportation and the land tour. Departure from the boat dock at Uturoa is at 8am, returning at 1:30pm. An air-conditioned 45-seat bus is available for large groups.

SPORTS & RECREATION

Deep Sea Fishing

See the section on Deep Sea Fishing charters in the *Raiatea* chapter.

Lagoon Excursions

Fare Rama Excursions, *Tel. 65.62.06*, owned by Verdon Tefaatau, has two outrigger speed canoes for lagoon excursions and visits to black pearl farms and vanilla plantations.

Fun Club Marina Iti, *Tel. 65.61.01*, at *Hotel Marina Iti*, can arrange a lagoon fishing expedition with a local fisherman, outrigger canoe excursions, visits to black pearl farms and vanilla plantations, as well as sunset cruises.

Hibiscus Activities, *Tel. 65.61.06*, are available at the *Hotel Hibiscus in Haamene*. Boat transfers will take you to a *motu* for a half- or full-day outing. An island excursion by outrigger canoe takes you to a vanilla plantation, a *marae* stone temple and to arts and crafts workshops. Snorkeling and shelling expeditions also include a boat trip to visit fish enclosures and a black pearl farm. You can also go fishing by day or night inside the lagoon and walking on the reef. Leo Morou will take you to visit his nature reserve for turtles.

Poerangi Farm, owned by Rooveta Ebbs, *Tel. 65.60.25, is in Haamene Bay*. A one-hour excursion takes you to the pearl farm, where you will learn about how the oysters are grafted and the beautiful black pearls are produced. You can also buy Tahitian products here.

HIBISCUS FOUNDATION SAVES THE SEA TURTLES

Leo and Lolita Morou, who own the Hotel Hibiscus in Tahaa, started the **Hibiscus Foundation** *in 1992. Their goals are to fight against underwater spear-fishing and turtle poachers, and to rescue the turtles that have been injured or accidentally trapped in fish parks inside the lagoon near the passes. When they find these turtles Leo and his volunteer helpers shelter them in a special enclosure for a few days, then tag them for future identification before releasing the turtles into the open ocean. The Hibiscus Foundation has already saved hundreds of Chelonia mydas, the green sea turtle, which is the most common and the tastiest. The hawksbill turtle, Eretmochelys imbricata, the large-headed turtle, Caretta caretta gigas, and the lute turtle, Dermochelys coriacea, have also been rescued by Leo and Lolita, and their network of yachting friends.*

In the olden days when the arii, the Polynesian chiefs, ruled the people, the honu (turtles) were considered sacred and their meat was reserved only for the kings, priests and keepers of the marae, where the Maohi people worshipped their god Oro. The marae that were dedicated to Oro were distinguished by stones that were shaped in the form of turtle heads, and turtle petroglyphs were carved in the basaltic rocks. The turtles are just as tapu (taboo, sacred or forbidden) today as they were then, because they have been declared an endangered species by the local government.

Motu Pearl Farm Tour, *Tel. 65.69.18/65.66.67*, takes you aboard a 35-foot glass bottom boat on a half-day excursion to visit the black pearl farm of Linda and Hugh Laughlin in Faaaha Bay. You will receive a complete explanation of how the pearl is cultivated inside the mother-of-pearl oyster, and you'll surely want to see their collection of pearls for sale. Optional visits can also be made to visit a vanilla plantation and see the panoramic sights of Tahaa.

Tahaa Pearl Tour, *Tel. 65.67.80*, is operated by Bruno Fabre, who can take from two to 10 people in his covered outrigger speed canoe for half- or full-day excursions, departing from the pier at Hotel Marina Iti. On the all-day tour, from 9am to 4pm, you will visit a vanilla plantation, eat lunch with a local family and visit the pearl farm, where you will be given a demonstration of how the black lip oyster is cultivated to produce black pearls. Stops are also made at the fish enclosures inside the lagoon. This tour costs 6.000 CFP ($60) for adults and 4.500 CFP ($45) for children, lunch included.

Chez Aiho, *Tel. 65.60.75*, has a pearl farm you can visit close to Tiva village.

Chez Patricia and Daniel Amaru, *Tel. 65.60.83, in Haamene*, is a family pension, and they will take you in an outrigger canoe to visit their family pearl farm.

Charter Yachts
Archipels Polynesian Cruises, *Tel. 56.36.39*, has a nautical base at *Opunohu Bay in Moorea* and a yacht based permanently in Raiatea.

Danae Cruises, *Tel. 66.12.50*, has a nautical base at *Uturaerae Marina in Raiatea*.

The Moorings, *Tel. 66.35.93/66.26.26*, has a nautical base *at the Apooiti Marina*.

Stardust Marine, *Tel. 66.23.18*, has a nautical base and marina *at PK 12.5 in Faaroa Bay*.

Star Voyage, *Tel. 66. 40.00*, has a nautical base *at Apooiti Marina*.

Tahiti Yacht Charter, *Tel. 66.28.86*, has a nautical base *at Apooiti Marina* and the main office *is on the yacht quay in Papeete*.

VPM Dufour Tahiti, *Tel. 56.40.50*, is based *at the Vaiare Marina in Moorea*, and has a yacht based in Raiatea.

Additional information on the yacht charter companies is given in *Tahiti, Moorea* and *Raiatea* chapters.

Day Sailing
Fai Manu, *Tel. 65, 62.52*, is a 50-foot catamaran owned by Louis Corneglio that is based in *Apu Bay in Tahaa*. A maximum of six passengers can sail around the island, with a picnic on request. Weekly cruises are available, starting at 60.000 CFP ($600) per day. Add 5.000 CFP ($50) per person per day for all meals and 10.000 CFP ($100) for a hostess-cook.

Bisou Fute Charter, *Tel. 65.64.97*, is a 51-foot monohull owned by Jean-Yvon Nechaby that is based *in Apu Bay, Tahaa*. This yacht can transport eight passengers for full-day sailing cruises inside the Raiatea-Tahaa lagoon. The cost is 30.000 CFP ($300) per day for the boat, and lunch is an additional 3.000 CFP ($30) per person. Private cruises depart from Raiatea on Monday and arrive in Bora Bora on Saturday. The cost of 100.000 CFP ($1,000) includes all meals on-board, transfers, fuel, and linens. A hostess-cook is 10.000 CFP ($100) extra per day. Cruises are organized upon request to other Society Islands for 50.000 CFP ($500) per day for the yacht.

Scuba Diving
See the section on Scuba Diving centers in the *Raiatea* chapter.

SHOPPING

Motu Pearl Boutique, *Tel. 65.69.18, in Faaaha*, sells black pearls, keishis, mabes and black pearl jewelry. They also sell locally made clothing, *pareos*, curios, and traditional arts and crafts combining mother-of-pearl with local woods and woven coconut fibers. **Areiti Boutique**, *Tel. 65.62.60, in Poutoru*, has arts and crafts and hand painted *pareos*. **Chez Belloune**, *Tel. 65.62.52, in Poutoru*, sells hand painted *pareos* and clothing.

Chez Sophie, *Tel. 65.62.56, in Hurepiti Bay*, sells hand painted *pareos*. **Xavier Barff**, *Tel. 65.68.50, in Apu Bay*, sells mother-of-pearl shells. **Kaheilany**, *Tel. 65.63.77, in Haamene*, and **Mama Naumi**, *Tel. 65.63.42, in Tapuamu*, also sell locally made products.

PRACTICAL INFORMATION

Banks

Banque Socredo, *Tel. 65.66.55*, is located in Tapuamu. A **Banque de Tahiti** representative calls on their main clients around the island each Tuesday.

Doctors

There is a government operated infirmary in Patio, *Tel. 65.63.31*, and a dispensary in Haamene, *Tel. 65.61.03*. Doctor Marc Chabanne, *Tel. 65.60.60*, has a private practice in Haamene.

Police

A brigade of the French *gendarmerie* is posted in Tahaa, *Tel. 65.64.07*.

Post Office and Telecommunications Office

There is a **Post Office** in Haamene, *Tel. 65.60.11*, and another in Patio, *Tel. 65.64.70*. All telecommunications and postal services are available.

Tourist Bureau

A tourist information bureau is located in Haamene, *Tel. 65.69.00*.

Yacht Services

Hibiscus Yacht Club, *Tel. 65.61.06, VHF 68*, is located at the Hotel Hibiscus at the entrance to Haamene Bay. Free yacht moorings, fresh water, free showers, garbage disposal, message service and fresh bread are delivered to your yacht daily except Sunday.

Latitude 16 Sud, *Tel. 65.61.01, VHF 68*, is located at the Hotel Marina Iti in Apu Bay. Moorings are available for 12 boats at the quay.

20. BORA BORA

When you tell your friends: "I'm going to **Bora Bora**," you can be sure that this simple phrase will bring envy and longing to their romantic hearts and stir a feeling of wanderlust in their vagabonding souls.

Bora Bora has become the center of tourism in Tahiti and Her Islands. Some of the world's famous stars of stage, cinema and television vacation here, flying directly from the international airport in Tahiti to Bora Bora, without a thought of seeing the other islands of French Polynesia. European royalty, sheiks, maharajas and international jet-setters find the serenity and privacy they seek on this magnificent little island. Cinematographers discover the ideal tropical setting for movies, often starring the islanders themselves.

Bora Bora, perhaps more than any other island in the South Seas, teases the imagination of travel writers, who search for adequate phrases of 'purple prose' to describe the spectacular beauty of its craggy, sculpted mountains, the palm-crowned islets that seem to float just inside the coral reef, surrounded by a confection of white sandy beaches that dip down into a lagoon of opalescent blues and greens.

Bora Bora lies 260 kilometers (161 miles) northwest of Tahiti in the Leeward Society Islands. Your first glimpse of Bora Bora may be from the window of an Air Tahiti plane, at the end of a 45-minute direct flight from Tahiti. Be sure to sit on the left side of the aircraft so that you'll have the best view as the ATR-72 banks for landing on Motu Mute. Bora Bora from aloft appears as a precious emerald in a setting of turquoise, encircled by a protective necklace of sparkling pearls.

If you arrive in Bora Bora by cruise ship, inter-island ferry boat or by sailboat, you will also be impressed by the kaleidoscope of shimmering iridescence that greets your eye at every turn. Aquamarine. Lapis lazuli. Turquoise. Cobalt. Periwinkle. Sapphire. Emerald. Jade. Ultramarine. Indigo. You'll love counting the shades of color in the sparkling waters of Bora Bora's world-famous lagoon.

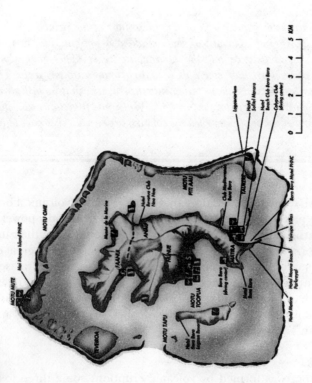

PAUL-EMILE VICTOR – THE COLORS OF BORA BORA

*Paul-Emile Victor, a French polar explorer, artist and writer, retired to Bora Bora with his wife **Colette**, and lived on Motu Tane in Bora Bora until his death in 1995. His impression of seeing Bora Bora from the cockpit of an airplane in 1958, after a 25-year absence from the island, was published in the 1970s in Distance, the in-flight magazine of the former UTA-French airline:*

"...Never before had I seen waters the colour of the rainbow or like fireworks, springing right out of some maddened imagination, or from Gauguin's own palette. Waters the colour of bronze, of copper, gold, silver, mother-of-pearl, pearl, jade, emeralds, moonlight or the aurora borealis. The stars themselves seemed to have fallen into the sea, scintillating brilliantly on the lagoon's surface, in bright sunlight... Who could find the words, what poet the images, what painter even the colours, to describe this scene? I give up.

Mythology

Polynesian mythology claims that Ofai Honu, a volcanic boulder carved with petroglyphs of turtles, was possessed with godly power and mated with the Pahia mountain, then called Hohorai. From their union a son was born, whose name was Firiamata O Vavau. This first great chief gave his name to the island and for many years this fabled paradise was known as **Vavau**, which means first born. Legend says that Vavau was the first island that sprang up after the mythical creation of the sacred island of Havai'i (Raiatea). The beautiful little islet beside the pass of Vavau was named Motu Tapu, the sacred islet.

Geology

Bora Bora was formed by volcanic eruptions some three to four million years ago. It is one of the oldest in the chain of the Leeward Islands. Through eons and centuries it has been eroding and sinking. One to two miles inside the fringing reef rise the sharp cliffs of basaltic rock that form the central mountain chain running through the principal island of Bora Bora. Mount Otemanu, at 727 meters (2,384 feet), Mount Pahia, at 661 meters (2,168 feet), and Mount Hue at 619 meters (2,030 feet), are the most spectacular chimney peaks of the crater that once spewed molten lava. The center of this sunken volcano lies far beneath the electric blue of Povai Bay, and the smaller islands of Toopua and Toopua-Iti are the opposite walls of the crater, formed when the earth erupted beneath the ocean. The Teavanui Pass is the only navigable break in the coral wall that has formed on top of the caldeira of the sunken volcano.

LEGEND OF HIRO

*One of the most famous characters in Polynesian oral history was **Hiro**, god of thieves. Hiro hid out on **Toopua Island**, across Povai Bay from the main island. Using the dragonfly to distract attention, Hiro and his band of thieves robbed their victims at night, between sunset and the first cockcrow. Hiro's constant companion was a white cock, the moa uo. This rooster became excited when Hiro was trying to steal Toopua Island and began to crow, breaking the magic power and so enraging Hiro that he hurled the bird against the face of Pahia mountain, where the imprint still remains. Although Hiro abandoned his plan to steal the island, he detached a large chunk of it that is called Toopua-Iti, the islet that is separated by only a few feet from Toopua.*

*The view of Bora Bora's famous mountains of **Otemanu** (sea of birds) and the twin peaks of **Pahia** and **Hue** are best photographed through this opening, where just underneath the clear surface of the lagoon lie rocks known as **Hiro's Canoe**. Ashore on Toopua Island are giant stones said to have been left by Hiro and his son Marama, tossed about in a game played by the two giants. Deep inside the coconut forest is a gigantic rock, **Hiro's Bell**, that reverberates when struck.*

The Exploitation of Bora Bora

I had not heard of Bora Bora until I read the *Sports Illustrated* magazine mentioned in the sidebar on the next page that showed Erwin Christian water-skiing in front of the Hotel Bora Bora. That was in January 1968. I was so impressed by the beauty of the purple-colored mountains of Bora Bora that I just had to see this scene in person. The article that accompanied the photos stated that the Hotel Bora Bora was the most expensive hotel in the South Pacific, and had the best restaurant. The rates were $35 for a single room and $48 for a double bungalow per day, American plan. The only other hotel on the island was Club Med's Noa Noa, with a few simple bungalows beside the lagoon in Vaitape village.

Today Bora Bora is an island devoted to tourism, with more luxurious hotels than on any other island of French Polynesia. And more hotels will open in Bora Bora by the time you read this book. In addition to the eight major hotels on the main island, there are three international class hotels on the offshore *motu* islets, plus a dozen pensions, hostels and lodging in family homes. There are currently some 800 rooms available on Bora Bora, with other hotel projects and expansion programs on the drawing board.

This development creates jobs for the local residents and most management level positions are filled by European personnel. What it

ERWIN CHRISTIAN

The January 15, 1968 edition of Sports Illustrated magazine included an article on the island of Bora Bora, with a photo of **Erwin Christian** *water-skiing in front of the Hotel Bora Bora. The story said that Christian (no relation to* **Fletcher Christian***, the Bounty mutineer) had jumped ship in Tahiti in 1963, where he scratched out a living for seven weeks while he explored the mountains and undersea world surrounding the island. His send-off party at the airport was so much fun that Christian changed his mind at the last moment and decided not to board his jet plane.*

Instead of going to Bermuda to accept a well-paying and challenging job in the hotel business there, the 27-year old native of Silesia eventually took a job as assistant manager of the Hotel Bora Bora, which at that time was an American-owned hotel with 18 small bungalows that had opened June 1, 1961. Christian soon fell in love with a beautiful and charming local girl named Ate (pronounced Ah-tay), and became a father. He created Moana Adventure Tours and served as director of the vast watery playground that is formed by the world's most beautiful lagoon.

After many years of taking tourists to visit the Bora Bora lagoon aboard his glass bottom boat, to walk on the reef, scuba dive, spearfish, to troll for fish or water-ski behind his runabout, Christian began to concentrate on his photography. He has taken thousands of pictures for post cards, calendars, posters and several coffee table books about Bora Bora and all the other island groups of French Polynesia. The bookstores, newsstands, gift shops and hotel boutiques carry Erwin Christian's photos, and you can see the whole collection when you visit his Moana Arts Boutique, adjacent to the Hotel Bora Bora.

does to the esthetics and ecology of the island should also be considered. More and more cruise ships, shuttle boats, outrigger speed canoes and jet-skis zoom about from the airport to the hotels and village, and around the island to the *motu*. According to Evan Temarii, a native of Bora Bora, who has operated lagoon excursions here for 20 years, there is less wildlife now, especially among the family of graceful manta rays. The coral reefs have suffered a lot of damage from cyclones, but also from humans who walk on the reef and collect coral souvenirs to take home.

Although **James Michener** wrote that "Bora Bora is the most beautiful island in the world," the truth is that the island itself has a lot of swamp area, and you'll see old wooden shacks with sheet metal roofing, sitting in the mire, with hundreds of *tupa* (land crab) holes all around their yards. Along with the old *marae* temples of coral stone, you'll see relics of World War II and the vestiges of an abandoned hotel project that was supposed to have been a Hyatt Hotel. More deserted bungalows in Vaitape village were once used as a Club Med, but after they were damaged by several cyclones, Club Med built another village on a more protected site. Outrigger Hotels is currently considering taking over the old Club Med bungalows. Matira Beach is billed as the most beautiful white sand beach in French Polynesia, yet I've been there when this natural site was totally littered with bottles, cans and disposable diapers. I collected a huge bag of trash from the beach and dropped it into an empty garbage can on the premises.

The next day the beach was in the same condition as before. A garbage dump at the end of Fitiiu Point, right next to the beautiful lagoon, is also visible from the circle island road. The new visitor's tax that went into effect in January, 1998, is supposed to be used to clean up the island and lagoon and keep them presentable. But everyone knows that it is not the tourists doing the littering.

In 1997 I visited Bora Bora twice, after an absence of about five years. I realized that many changes had taken place since my prior visits, and I expected to see more hotels, more restaurants, more boutiques, more black pearl shops and more tourist activities centers. But I was not prepared for the shock I received when I went to Point Matira. This used to be a tranquil setting, where you could snooze in the sun or splash around in the shallow tepid water. Naps are definitely out of the question now, because of all the jet-skis and scuba diving boats buzzing about.

The biggest change, however, is in the area between Point Matira and the Hotel Sofitel Marara. French Polynesia was always able to boast that there was no such thing as a "hotel row" in these islands. The rapid expansion on Bora Bora has changed that concept, and now there is hardly an empty space left on either side of the road in the Matira area. The sad thing is that some of these additions are not esthetically up to par with the privileged reputation of the island, and the prices that go with it.

ARRIVALS & DEPARTURES
Arriving By Air
Air Tahiti has two to four direct flights daily between Tahiti and Bora Bora. The 45-minute non-stop flight is 13.020 CFP ($132.20) one-way for adults, tax included. There are from one to five flights daily with stops in Moorea, Huahine or Raiatea. You can also fly to Bora Bora from Maupiti or Rangiroa. **Air Tahiti reservations**: *Tahiti, Tel. 86.42.42/86.41.84; Moorea, Tel. 56.10.34; Huahine, Tel. 68.82.65; Raiatea Tel. 66.32.50; Bora Bora, Tel. 67.70.35/67.70.85.*

The **Bora Bora airport** is located on Motu Mute, a 30-minute boat ride to the main village of Vaitape or by luxury launch direct to your deluxe hotel.

As soon as you step off the plane you can pick up brochures and get information inside the modern terminal building, which also has a snack bar, boutique and toilets. The boats leave for Vaitape village about 20 minutes after your flight arrives. The voyage across the emerald silk lagoon of Bora Bora will help to set the pace for a vacation on a small island, and you can take some fabulous photographs of the island during this crossing. If your hotel doesn't have a private launch to the airport, then you will be met at the boat dock in Vaitape village and driven to your hotel. Land transportation from the Vaitape quay to the small hotels, pensions and campgrounds is also provided by *le truck*, mini-vans or taxi. The Air Tahiti office is located on the quay of Vaitape, and there are public phone booths just outside.

Arriving By Boat

Ono-Ono, *Tel. 45.35.35; Fax 43.83.45; e-mail: onoono@mail.pf* has a ticket office on the Papeete boat dock. The *Ono-Ono* departs from *the Papeete boat dock, adjacent to the Moorea boats*, each Monday and Wednesday at 9am, with stops in Huahine, Raiatea and Tahaa, arriving in Bora Bora at 4pm. Each Friday it leaves Papeete at 4:30 p.m., stopping in Huahine and Raiatea, and arriving in Bora Bora at 11:20pm. A special weekend circuit from Huahine-Raiatea-Tahaa arrives in Bora Bora each Saturday at 6pm. The one-way fare from Papeete to Bora Bora is 6.610 CFP ($66.10). Be at the dock one hour prior to departure. There's a good snack bar on board and you can also buy food at the docks along the way.

Taporo VI, *Tel. 42.63.93/43.79.72; Fax 42.06.17* departs from the Fare-Ute quay, on the far side of the Papeete harbor, each Monday, Wednesday and Friday, at 4 p.m., with stops in Huahine, Raiatea and Tahaa, arriving in Bora Bora the following day at 1:30 a.m. One-way fare to Bora Bora is 1,692 CFP ($16.92) on the bridge and 20.000 CFP ($200) for a cabin with four berths.

Vaeanu, *Tel. 41.25.35, departs from the Fare-Ute quay in Papeete* at 5 pm on Monday, Wednesday and Friday, stopping in Huahine and Raiatea and arriving in Bora Bora the following morning between 9:30 and 10am. One-way fare to Bora Bora is 1.709 CFP ($17.09) on the bridge, and cabins cost between 4.000 and 5.500 CFP ($40 and $55) per person.

All the inter-island transport boats dock at the Fare Piti quay in Faanui, 3 kilometers (1.9 miles) from Vaitape village. It would be advisable to arrange with your hotel or pension to have someone meet you when you arrive. You can rent a car, scooter or mountain bike across the street. A *le truck* also provides service from the boat dock to the hotels in Matira.

Maupiti Express, *Tel. 67.66.69*, arrives at the Vaitape quay in Bora Bora at 6pm each Tuesday, Thursday, Saturday and Sunday, after a day spent in Maupiti. Each Wednesday and Friday the *Maupiti Express* arrives at Vaitape quay at 6pm, from Raiatea and Tahaa, following a round-trip rotation to those islands. The one-way fare is 3.000 CFP ($30). Passengers under 15 years and over 60 years have a 20 percent reduction. *Reservations office in Tahiti, Tel. 48.05.81.*

Departing By Air

The main office of **Air Tahiti**, *Tel. 67.70.35/67.70.85*, is at *the boat dock in Vaitape village.* Most of the hotels take care of reconfirming your departure flight, or you can do it yourself by telephone. Check-in time at the Air Tahiti office in Vaitape is 1 1/2 hours before each scheduled departure. That's to give you time to get across the lagoon to Motu Mute.

Departing By Boat

You have to be a hardy sailor to weather the trip from Bora Bora back to Tahiti. Complaints about seasickness aboard the *Ono Ono* are most frequent because it travels so rapidly through the rough seas. You may want to consider flying back to Tahiti.

Ono Ono, *Tel./Fax 67.78.00, has a ticket office on the Vaitape quay,* open 8 to 11am on Monday and Thursday, and another sales office at the Fare Piti quay, which is open for the arrivals and departures of the boat. *Ono Ono* leaves Bora Bora for Tahaa, Raiatea, Huahine and Tahiti each Tuesday and Thursday at 7am, arriving in Papeete at 2:15pm. An inter-island round-trip tour leaves Bora Bora each Saturday at 8am, with 15-minute stops in Tahaa and Raiatea, arriving in Huahine at 11am and departing at 3pm, returning to Raiatea and Tahaa and on to Bora Bora, arriving at 6pm. On Sunday the *Ono Ono* leaves Bora Bora at 12pm, stopping in Tahaa, Raiatea and Huahine, arriving in Papeete at 7:15pm.

Taporo VI, *Tel. 42.63.93*, leaves Bora Bora at 11:30am each Tuesday, Thursday and Saturday, with stops in Raiatea and Huahine, arriving in Papeete at 4 a.m. the following morning. Buy your tickets on board.

Vaeanu, *Tel. 41.25.35*, leaves Bora Bora at 10:30am each Tuesday, stops in Tahaa, Raiatea and Huahine, and arrives in Papeete at 3 a.m. on Wednesday. Thursday departures leave Bora Bora at 12pm, stopping in Raiatea and Huahine, arriving in Papeete at 4 a.m. on Friday. The Sunday departures leave Bora Bora at 9am, stopping in Tahaa, Raiatea and Huahine, and arriving in Papeete each Monday at 2 a.m. Buy your ticket on board the ship.

Maupiti Express, *Tel. 67.66.69*, departs from the Vaitape quay each Tuesday, Thursday, Saturday and Sunday at 8:30am for Maupiti, and departs from Bora Bora for Tahaa and Raiatea at 7am each Wednesday and Friday. The one-way fare is 3.000 CFP ($30). Passengers under 15 years and over 60 years have a 20 percent reduction. *Reservations office in Tahiti, Tel. 48.05.81.* A Day Tour of Tahaa is available for 10.000 CFP

($100) a person, which includes a guided visit to the highlights of Tahaa, including a vanilla plantation, a black pearl farm and handcrafts centers. *Reservations can be made at Agence Blue Lagon, Tel. 66.17.28/65.67.10.*

ORIENTATION

Close to the boat dock in **Vaitape village** you will find the *mairie* (town hall), *gendarmerie*, post office, banks, schools, churches, dispensary, pharmacy, Air Tahiti office, Bora Bora Visitors Center (also called the Tourism Committee), arts and crafts center, food stores, small restaurants and snack stands, shops, boutiques and rental agencies for cars, scooters and bicycles, plus service stations and public telephones.

Bora Bora's main island is only 10 kilometers (5.2 miles) long and 4 kilometers (2.5 miles) wide. A partially paved road circles the coastline, winding 29 kilometers (18 miles) through the colorful villages of Vaitape, Faanui and Anau. You'll see little settlements of modest *fares*, the homes of Bora Bora's 5,767 inhabitants, which are often surrounded by flower gardens.

GETTING AROUND

Car, Scooter & Bicycle Rentals

Avis-Pacificar, *Tel. 67.70.31*, has its office on the Vaitape Quay. Manager Alfredo Doom rents a 5-door Ford Fiesta for 4.200 CFP ($42) for 2 hours, 6.800 CFP ($68) for 8 hours and 8.400 CFP ($84) for 24 hours. Scooter rentals start at 3.000 CFP ($30) for 2 hours and 5.500 CFP ($55) for 8 hours. These rates include unlimited mileage and insurance. Gas is extra.

Europcar, *Tel. 67.70.15/67.70.03*, has its main sales office in Vaitape facing the quay, with sales desks at all the hotels. A Fiat Panda rents for 4.500 CFP ($45) for 2 hours, 5.000 CFP ($50) for 4 hours, 6.000 CFP ($60) for 8 hours and 7.000 CFP ($70) for 24 hours. A Fun Car is a cross between a car and a scooter and rents for 4.000 CFP ($40) for 2 hours and 4.500 CFP ($45) for 4 hours. Scooter rates start at 3.500 CFP ($35) for 2 hours. These rates include unlimited mileage and third party insurance. Gas is extra.

Fare Piti Rent A Car, *Tel. 67.65.28/67.71.58*, is at the boat dock in Faanui, where the inter-island ships arrive from Tahiti. The lowest car rental price for a Peugeot is 3.500 CFP ($35) for.2 hours and 5.500 CFP ($55) for 8 hours. Scooter rentals are 2.500 CFP ($25) for 2 hours and 5.400 CFP ($54) for 8 hours. These rates include unlimited mileage and insurance. Gas is extra.

Bicycles

Avis-Pacificar, *Tel. 67.70.31,* rents mountain bikes for 1.500 CFP ($15) for 4 hours and 2.000 CFP ($20) for 8 hours. Their bicycles are 1.000 CFP ($10) for 4 hours and 1.500 CFP ($15) for 8 hours. Longer rentals possible.

Europcar, *Tel. 67.70.15/67.70.03,* rents mountain bikes for 1.000 CFP ($10) for 3 hours and 1.600 CFP ($16) for 8 hours. Bicycles can be rented for 1.000 CFP ($10) for 2 hours and 1.500 CFP ($15) for 8 hours.

Fare Piti Rent A Car, *Tel. 67.65.28,* rents mountain bikes for 500 CFP ($5) for 2 hours and 1.000 CFP ($10) for 8 hours.

Hibiscus Rent A Bike, *Tel. 67.72.43,* is opposite the Club Med. Bicycles rent for 400 CFP ($4) for 2 hours, 600 CFP ($6) for 4 hours and 800 CFP ($8) for 8 hours.

Mautara Location, *Tel. 67.73.16,* in Tiipoto, also has bikes for rent.

Taxis

Taxi service is provided by Jacques Isnard, *Tel. 67.72.25,* **Bora Bora Tours**, *Tel. 67.70.31,* **Otemanu Tours**, *Tel. 67.70.49,* and Jeannine Buchin, *Tel. 67.74.14.*

Le Truck

Each hotel and pension has its own *le truck* or mini-van service between the hotel and the boat dock in Vaitape or Faanui. coordinating their runs with the arrivals and departures of Air Tahiti and the inter-island ferries. Some of them may stop for you if you flag them down, but there is no official public transportation service on Bora Bora.

BORA BORA TOURIST TAX

*All visitors staying on Bora Bora began paying a **tourist tax** on January 1, 1998, regardless of what type of accommodation you buy. The tax amounts to 150 CFP ($1.50) per person, per day, for all stays in classified hotels, pensions, hostels or campgrounds, and includes passengers aboard all cruise ships. All children ages 2-12 accompanied by a parent are exempt from the new tax. The rates quoted here do not include the value added tax (VAT) nor the special tourist tax.*

WHERE TO STAY
ON THE MAIN ISLAND
Expensive

HOTEL BORA BORA, *B.P. 1, 98730 Vaitape, Bora Bora. Tel. 689/ 60.44.60; Fax 689/60.44.66; Reservations Tel. 689/60.44.11; Fax 689/ 60.44.22. North America Reservations: Tel. 800/447-7462, New York Tel. 212/ 223-2848. Beside the lagoon at Raititi Point, 14 kilometers (8.7 miles) from the airport and 5.8 kilometers (3.6 miles) from the village of Vaitape. Round-trip transfers provided from airport to hotel by private launch. 55 bungalows. EP Rates: bungalow 39.500 CFP ($395) single/double; superior bungalow 49.500 CFP ($495) single/double; "fare" 60.000 CFP ($600) single/double; deluxe bungalow 65.000 CFP ($650) single/double; overwater bungalow 65.000 CFP ($650) single/double; "fare" with swimming pool 65.000 CFP ($650) single/ double; deluxe overwater bungalow 70.000 CFP ($700) single/double; deluxe overwater "fare" 70.000 CFP ($700) single/double. Add 7.500 CFP ($75) for additional person. Meals may be prearranged. Add 7% hotel tax to room rates and 1% value added tax to room rates and meals. All major credit cards.*

The Hotel Bora Bora was the first international class hotel built on Bora Bora, and naturally, the owners chose the best spot on the island. It is located on Point Raititi, a private peninsula that faces the southwest, with sunset views of the neighboring island of Maupiti. The famous Matira Beach is just an extension of one of the hotel's three private white-sand beaches.

This exclusive resort offers 55 individual Polynesian style guest bungalows and *fares* (villas), which are situated in tropical gardens with ocean views, on one of the beaches, or resting on columns over the water. All accommodations are spaciously designed and elegantly, but simply, appointed to maximize guest comfort. Each bungalow has a ceiling fan, bathtub and separate shower, hairdryer, private bar, coffee and tea facilities, radio/cassette player and personal safe. Telephone jacks are installed in each bungalow, should you wish to keep in touch with the outside world.

The Hotel Bora Bora was the first hotel to introduce overwater accommodations to French Polynesia over 30 years ago, and now they are the first to introduce the *fare* concept of a Tahitian home with a private swimming pool.

The hotel's facilities include the Matira Terrace restaurant overlooking Bora Bora's spectacular lagoon, the adjacent bar offering a light menu and tropical beverages, and the Pofai Beach Bar serving light meals and refreshments throughout the day. Afternoon Tea is served on the beach. A Wednesday night Beach Barbecue is followed by a Polynesian dance show and fire dancing on the beach. A Friday night Gastronomic Evening features "flaming" dishes and begins with an arts and crafts demonstration and entertainment by the "mamas" of Bora Bora.

The hotel's activities range from a full selection of nautical activities, including snorkeling, shark feeding, sunset cruises, deep-sea fishing, paddle canoes, and scuba diving, to tennis, volleyball, basketball, helicopter tours, horseback riding, jeep excursions, car, scooter and bicycle rentals. Other services include a boutique and general store, laundry, baby-sitting and foreign exchange.

See more information in the *Best Places to Stay* chapter.

HOTEL MOANA BEACH PARKROYAL, *B.P. 156, Vaitape, Bora Bora. Tel. 689/60.49.00. Reservations: 689/60.49.01/60.49.02; Fax 689/60.49.99; in US 800/835-7742. e-mail prkroyal@mail.pf Beside the lagoon on Point Matira. 51 bungalows. EP Rates single/double: beach bungalow 49.800 CFP ($498); overwater bungalow 63.800 CFP ($638); additional person 6.000 CFP ($60). Meal plan with breakfast and dinner 6.800 CFP ($68) per person; meal plan with breakfast, lunch and dinner 9.800 CFP ($98) per person. Round-trip boat transfers provided. Add 7% hotel tax to room rates and 1% value added tax to room rates and meal plan. All major credit cards.*

This beautiful hotel has 41 overwater bungalows and 10 beach bungalows that are built in the traditional Polynesian style of pointed pandanus thatch roofs, woven bamboo walls, rattan and bamboo furniture and tasteful decor in a Polynesian motif. All the bungalows are mini-suites, with a large terrace and sun deck, a living room, bedroom, dressing area and an attractive bathroom, with vanilla vines growing overhead the bathtub and shower, and a hair dryer tucked inside the lighted dressing table. Each bedroom is furnished with a king size bed that can be converted into twin beds, an overhead fan, an international direct dial telephone and personal safe. In the living room is a sofa that can sleep a third person, a color television with video, radio and music, writing desk, mini-bar, and coffee and tea facilities. A glass table in the overwater bungalows allows you to look at the fish swimming around the coral gardens in the crystalline lagoon. Maid service is provided twice a day and room service is available from 7am to 9pm.

The restaurant and bar and dining terrace overlook a beautiful white sand beach, where an interesting selection of water activities are available. An activities desk and car rental desk can help you to visit the island by land tours and excursions, and you will find a very chic boutique and black pearl shop on the premises. The personnel are dressed in white Polynesian style costumes and are very friendly yet professional and efficient. Special theme evenings include a Tuesday night barbecue buffet with a Tahitian dance show, a Polynesian evening on Thursdays, with a show presented by the "Mamas" of Bora Bora, and *La Soirée Merveilleuse* on Saturday nights, which is a seafood buffet followed by a Polynesian dance show on the beach.

See more information in the *Best Places to Stay* chapter.

HOTEL SOFITEL MARARA, *B.P. 6, Vaitape, Bora Bora. Tel. 689/ 67.70.56; Fax 689/67.74.03. Reservations: 689/41.05.05; Fax 689/41.04.04; in US Tel. 800/763-4835 or 914/472-0370; Fax 914/472-0451; Internet: http://www.sofitel.com Beside the lagoon at the end of Taahana Bay, north of Point Matira on the east side. 64 bungalows. EP Rates single/double: garden bungalow 30.000 CFP ($300); beach bungalow 39.000 CFP ($390); overwater bungalow 50.000 CFP ($500). Add 1.500 CFP ($15) per day for all rates during high season of January 1-15, July 15-August 31, and December 20-31. Third person add 4.500 CFP ($45). Meal plan with breakfast and dinner 5.600 CFP ($56) per person; meal plan with breakfast, lunch and dinner 8.100 CFP ($81) per person. Round-trip transfers provided. Private speedboat transfer to airport 6.500 CFP ($65) for two people with luggage. Add 7% hotel tax to room rates and 1% value added tax to room rates and meal plan. All major credit cards.*

This is the last hotel in the area generally known as Matira, at the end of a long white sand beach. The thatched roof hotel has 32 garden bungalows, 11 beach bungalows and 21 overwater bungalows. Each room has a ceiling fan, direct dial telephone, individual safe, tea and coffee facilities, mini-bar, bathroom with shower and separate toilet, hair dryer and Sofitel brand coconut soaps, *monoi* oils and other amenities. The overwater bungalows are some of the least expensive on the island, but ask for an overwater bungalow far away from the kitchen noises. The large bungalows are attractively decorated with bamboo furniture and contain king size beds, with a sliding window between the bathroom and bedroom so that you can see the lagoon from the dressing area. There is also piped in music if you want it, and black out curtains. Room service is available to the overwater bungalows. From the big semi-circular sun decks you can see Tahaa and Raiatea on the horizon, as well as the hotel's private *motu*, where barbecue picnics are held every Wednesday and Friday.

La Perouse Restaurant, Le Corail bar and the fresh water swimming pool all have views of the lagoon and *motu* islets. The restaurant serves French and international cuisine. A barbecue buffet is served every Tuesday evening, followed by the "Mamas" Polynesian show at 8:30pm; a seafood buffet is served on Thursday evening, followed by a coconut show; and a Saturday evening Tahitian buffet features *maa Tahiti* cooked in an underground oven, followed by the Marama Nui Polynesian dance show. Daily activities are posted in the reception area, and the activities desk can book any tour you want, plus rent you a car, scooter or bicycle. There is nightly entertainment at the bar, and a Happy Hour is held every night from 9 to 10pm. Wedding ceremonies are performed on the beach every Monday or Thursday at 5:30pm. Françoise is the wedding coordinator who will take care of all the details, for 40.000 CFP ($400) per couple, which does not include the room rate.

The ambiance at the Marara is a miniature version of Club Med, with several people gathered in one small area looking for some kind of entertainment. Some of Tahitian staff truly make wonderful vacation memories for the guests, while other employees lack professionalism or a sense of public relations. The lagoon under the overwater bungalows looks dirty because of the slimy green algae.

HOTEL LE MAITAI POLYNESIA, *B.P. 195, Vaitape, Bora Bora. Tel. 689/67.62.66; Fax 689/67.62.79. Reservations: Hotel Management & Services, Tel. 689/43.08.83/Fax 689/43.08.93. At Taahana Beach in the Matira area, 15 kilometers (9 miles) from the ferry dock and 12 kilometers (6 miles) from Vaitape. 75 units. EP Rates: air-conditioned room 20.000 CFP ($200) single/ double; villa suite 27.000 CFP ($270) single/double; beach bungalow 29.000 CFP ($290) single/double; overwater bungalow 36.000 CFP ($360) single/ double. Third person 5.500 CFP ($55). Add 7% hotel tax to room rates and 1% value added tax to room rates and meals.*

This three-star hotel is due to open in June, 1998, with 65 new units added to the existing 10 villa-suites with kitchens that owner Pauline Youssef is presently operating under the name Vairupe Villas. In addition to these mountainside villa-suites, Le Maitai Polynesia will consist of 20 garden bungalows, 6 beach bungalows, 11 overwater bungalows, and 28 air-conditioned rooms in three 2-level buildings with a lagoon view. As the name implies, Le Maitai Polynesia (good Polynesia) is a deluxe Polynesian style hotel, with pandanus roofs and bamboo wall coverings and furniture. Public areas will include 2 restaurants, 2 bars, a beach bar, swimming pool, conference room, 2 activities desks, a conference room, lobby and reception area.

Moderate

HOTEL BEACH CLUB BORA BORA, *B.P. 251, Vaitape, Bora Bora. Tel. 689/67.71.16; Fax 689/67.71.30. Reservations: Tahiti Resort Hotels, B.P. 13019, Papeete, Tahiti, Tel. 689/43.08.29; Fax 689/41.09.28; Telex 702/ 428FP. Located between the Bora Bora Motel and Sofitel Marara in the Matira area. 36 rooms. EP Rates single/double/triple: garden room 18.000 CFP ($180); beach room 20.000 CFP ($200); air-conditioned garden room 20.500 CFP ($205); air-conditioned beach room 22.500 CFP ($225). Meal plan with breakfast and dinner 4.000 CFP ($40) per person; meal plan with breakfast, lunch and dinner 5.600 CFP ($56) per person. Round-trip transfers 1.750 CFP ($17.50) per person. Add 7% hotel tax to room rates and 1% value added tax to room rates and meal plan. All major credit cards.*

A construction project will soon be underway to add 54 more rooms, with 48 garden rooms to be finished by June, 1998, and the remaining six rooms next to the lagoon scheduled to open in December, 1998. The entire hotel will be reconstructed in two stages without closing the hotel, and the end results will be a total of 90 rooms. This may be a noisy choice with all the construction work going on, but the location is good. The shingle-roof buildings contain small motel-style rooms, and each has air-conditioning or overhead fans. Some of the rooms are situated in a coconut grove on the mountain side of the road and some of the blocks are on the beach side, where you'll find lots of water sports, a pier and the white sand beach. There is a restaurant and bar, reception, activities desk and a boutique on the mountain side.

HOTEL MATIRA, *B. P. 31, Vaitape, Bora Bora. Tel. 689/67.70.51; Fax 689/67.77.02. On Matira Beach between Hotel Bora Bora and Moana Beach Parkroyal. 29 bungalows. EP Rates single/double: garden bungalow 12.000 CFP ($120); mountain side bungalow with kitchen 12.000 CFP ($120); beach bungalow with kitchen 17.000 CFP ($170); deluxe garden bungalow 19.000 CFP ($190); deluxe ocean view bungalow 24.000 CFP ($240); deluxe beach bungalow 29.000 CFP ($290); third person 4.000 CFP ($40). Meal plan with breakfast and dinner add 3.500 CFP ($35) per person. Round-trip transfers 1.000 CFP ($10) per person. Add 7% hotel tax to room rates and 1% value added tax to room rates and meal plan. American Express, Mastercard, Visa.*

The reception desk is in the Matira Restaurant and Bar beside the lagoon between the Hotel Bora Bora and Point Matira. A few of the bungalows are located across the road on the mountain side, and the majority of the bungalows are built right on the famous white sand beach at Point Matira, facing the Hotel Bora Bora and the sunset sea. You will see their sign just before the turnoff to the Moana Beach Parkroyal. 16 of the thatched roof bungalows on the beach have just been built, or will be completed by June, 1998. These bungalows have two double beds in the bedroom, a living room, toilet with hot water shower, unscreened louvered windows, an overhead fan, refrigerator and a terrace facing the lagoon. Some of the mountain side bungalows near the restaurant have kitchens.

CLUB MED BORA BORA, *B.P. 34, Vaitape, Bora Bora; Tel. 689/ 60.46.04; Fax 60.46.10. Reservations: 689/42.96.99; Fax 689/42.16.83; in US 800/528-3100. Beside the lagoon on Faaopore Bay, between the villages of Anau and Faanui, on the east coast. 150 twin-share units. AP Rates: garden room and all meals 19.000 CFP ($190) single, 38.000 CFP ($380) double; beach bungalows and all meals 22.800 CFP ($228) single, 45.600 CFP ($456) double. Add 7% hotel tax to room rates and 1% value added tax to room rates and meal plan. All major credit cards.*

The Club Med Coral Garden has 72 garden rooms and 78 beach rooms in two story motel-style buildings, duplex bungalows and stand-alone bungalows, all painted in pastel shades of yellow, chartreuse and mauve, to resemble a coral garden. The tastefully furnished bungalows are well spaced throughout the village, each with a view of the lagoon, and honeymooners enjoy the privacy of the beachfront bungalows, which are more elaborate. Each bungalow has an overhead fan, a luxurious bathroom and tiled floors. A thatched-roof beachside pavilion is the central gathering place, with the reception, boutiques, dining room, bar and night club located here. A full range of Club Med activities is presented, including a show nightly except Sunday. See *Where to Eat* in this chapter.

BORA BORA MOTEL, *B.P. 180, Vaitape, Bora Bora. Tel. 689/ 67.78.21; Fax 689/67.77.57. Beside the Taahana lagoon and white sand beach in Matira area, 15 kilometers (9 miles) from the ferry dock and 12 kilometers (6 miles) from Vaitape. EP Rates: studio 13.000 CFP ($130) single/double; apartment 17.000 CFP ($170) single/double. Third person 3.000 CFP ($30). Breakfast, lunch and dinner on request. Add 1% value added tax to room rates. Mastercard, Visa.*

The thatched roof Polynesian style units include four studios, each with a queen size bed with sitting area, bathroom with hot water shower and fully equipped kitchens with a large refrigerator; three apartments can sleep four adults, featuring a separate bedroom with a queen size bed, a living/dining area with a single sofa bed, kitchen and private bathroom with hot water. A separate bungalow on the beach can sleep up to three adults, and has a kitchen and the same amenities as the units. House linens are furnished. All units are equipped with overhead fans and have private terraces. A food market is across the road and there are several restaurants and snack bars very close by, as well as big hotels with a wide range of activities.

BORA BORA CONDOS, *B.P. 98, Vaitape, Bora Bora. Tel. 689/ 67.71.33. On the mountain side in Faanui 10 kilometers (6 miles) from Vaitape. Round-trip transfers are extra. EP Rates: mountain side bungalow 12.000 CFP ($120) for one to five people per day and 150.000 CFP ($1,500) per month; overwater bungalow 15.000 CFP ($150) for one to five people per day and 185.000 CFP ($1,850) per month. Add 1% value added tax to room rates. No credit cards.*

If you want to spend longer than a week on Bora Bora these 14 bungalows each have two bedrooms with a double bed in each room, a living room, kitchen, dining room, private bathroom with hot water, and terrace. House linens are provided. Use of the communal laundry room is extra. You have access to a private pontoon where you can leave your rental boat. Otherwise you will need a car, as there are no stores on this side of the island. The hillside condos are not recommended for anyone who cannot easily climb steps. The overwater bungalows are more easily accessible.

HOTEL REVATUA CLUB NOA NOA, *B.P. 159, Vaitape, Bora Bora. Tel. 689/67.71.67; Fax 689/67.76.59. Reservations: South Pacific Marketing, B. P. 718, Papeete, Tahiti, Tel. 689/42.68.55; Fax 689/41.39.23. Located between Anau and Faanui villages, 7 kilometers (4.3 miles) from Club Med, 11 kilometers (6.8 miles) from Point Matira and 14 kilometers (8.7 miles) from the boat dock in Vaitape village. 17 units. EP Rates: standard room 9.790 CFP ($97.90) single, 11.440 CFP ($114.40) double, 12.870 CFP ($128.70) triple; villa 16.600 CFP ($166) per day and 215.000 CFP ($2,150) per month. Continental breakfast 1.000 CFP ($10); American breakfast 1.500 CFP ($15); breakfast and dinner 3.800-4.900 CFP ($38-$49) per person; 3 meals daily 5.600-6.600 CFP ($56-$66) per person. Round-trip transfers 1.000 CFP ($10) per person. Add 7% hotel tax to room rates and 1% value added tax to room rates and meals. All major credit cards.*

This hotel is on the opposite side of the island from Vaitape village, and the management usually picks up its clients directly from the airport, which is facing the Revatua Club across the turquoise lagoon. The 16 fan-cooled rooms are located in neo-colonial one-story concrete buildings across the road from the reception, restaurant, bar and boutique. They each have pinewood furniture, a bathroom with hot water shower and a private terrace. A family-sized villa on the lagoon side has a separate lounge and kitchen area and an overwater terrace.

The restaurant has one of the best reputations in Bora Bora, and the complimentary activities offered here include a salt water swimming pool, a white sand mini-beach, bicycles, library, *pétanque* (bocci ball), snorkeling equipment and swings and slides. Paid activities include a lagoon tour of the island in a covered boat, shark feeding excursions, a visit to the coral gardens, transfers to a private *motu*, motor boat rental and water skiing. Rental cars are available.

Inexpensive

VILLAGE PAULINE, *B.P. 215, Vaitape, Bora Bora. Tel. 689/67.72.16; Fax 689/67.78.14. On the mountainside in Pofai Bay, between Bloody Mary's Restaurant and Honeymoon Boutique. EP rates: room 6.000 CFP ($60) single/ double; private bungalow 9.000 CFP ($90) single/double; dormitory 2.500 CFP ($25) per bed; camping 1.500 CFP ($15) per camper. Add 1% value added tax to room rates. Mastercard, Visa.*

For many years Chez Pauline, Pauline Camping and Village Pauline have been a password for budget travelers who visit Bora Bora. Campers could pitch their tents right on the white sand beach of Matira, and for just a few francs, have all the advantages of the Bora Bora lagoon that other tourists pay hundreds of dollars a day to enjoy while staying in the luxury hotels. That's all changed now, because Pauline Youssef has moved her village and camping facilities to make way for the Hotel Maitai Polynesia, which is programmed to open in June, 1998.

The new Village Pauline is now 1 1/2 kilometers (.9 mile) from Matira Beach, which is a five-minute bike ride or a 20-minute walk. Guests are given free bicycles to go to the beach or to the nearby food store. The new village has Polynesian style thatched roof and wooden structures providing rooms, a private bungalow with its own kitchen and bathroom facilities, a dormitory and a communal kitchen and bathrooms for those renting a room, dorm bed or camping space. All the activities that are available on Bora Bora can be booked at the reception and the excursion pick ups stop by Village Pauline. This is the only place on the island where you can rent a kayak, which costs 1.000 CFP ($10) and 4.000 CFP ($40) for an all-day rental from 9am to 6pm. A really big plus for this pension is Nir Shalev, the manager, who is extremely friendly, knowledgeable, helpful and cheerful.

Pauline has rented a 3-bedroom house across the road from Matira Beach, which is unofficially available for those people who demand a beach with their Bora Bora experience. The bathroom and kitchen facilities are shared with other guests, and free bikes are provided. Call Village Pauline and ask about the rooms in Matira.

TEMANUATA, *Vaitape, Bora Bora. Tel. 689/67.75.61. On the beach side at Point Matira, just past the turnoff to Moana Beach Parkroyal. Round trip transfers extra. EP Rates: garden bungalow, 7.000 CFP ($70) single/double; beach bungalow single/double 8.000 CFP ($80); extra person 1.500 CFP ($15). Special rates for 10 days or more. Continental breakfast 500 CFP ($5). Add 1% value added tax to room rates. Mastercard and Visa.*

Five small thatched roof bungalows sit in a spacious grassy area between the white sand beach and the Restaurant/Snack Temanuata. Four are garden bungalows and one is on the beach. They were opened in 1996 and are attractively decorated in an island style of bright *pareo* fabrics. Each bungalow has a double bed, a closet and fan, and private bathrooms with cold water. Marama will put in a television and refrigerator on request. His plans are to add five more bungalows in the garden during 1998. All the Matira Beach activities are very close to this pension.

CHEZ TEIPO, *B.P. 270, Vaitape, Bora Bora. Tel. 689/67.78.17; Fax 689/67.73.24. Beside the lagoon in Anau, 200 meters (656 feet) from Club Med. EP Rates: fare 6.000 CFP ($60) single; 7.000 CFP ($70) double. Third person 1.000 CFP ($10). Add 1% value added tax to room rates. No credit cards.*

Three small thatched roof bungalows, each containing a double bed, kitchen and private bathroom with cold water. House linens are furnished. Line fishing and reef fishing are available.

CHEZ MAEVA MASSON, *B.P. 33, Vaitape, Bora Bora. Tel. 689/ 67.72.04. Beside the beach at Point Matira, 13 kilometers (8 miles) from the ferry dock and 6.8 kilometers (4.2 miles) from Vaitape village. EP Rates: room on ground level 6.000 CFP ($60) single/double; add 1.000 CFP ($10) for one-night stay; upstairs room 5.500 CFP ($55) single/double; add 1.000 CFP ($10) for one-night stay; bed in dormitory 2.500 CFP ($25); add 500 CFP ($5) for one night stay. Additional bed 2.500 CFP; add 500 CFP for one night stay. Add 1% value added tax to room rates. Mastercard, Visa.*

This was the former home of artist Rosine Temauri-Masson and her late husband, the painter Jean Masson. Their daughter Maeva runs the pension, which still has the warmth of a home. The two-story wooden house has two bedrooms on the ground floor, each containing a double bed and fridge; two rooms upstairs each have a double bed; plus there is a 4-bed dormitory; with three sofa beds in the living room. The kitchen and bathroom with cold shower are communal. House linens are provided.

CHEZ NONO, *B.P. 282, Vaitape, Bora Bora. Tel. 689/67.71.38; Fax 689/67.74.27. On the white sand beach of Point Matira, facing the Hotel Bora Bora and the distant island of Maupiti, 13 kilometers (8 miles) from the ferry dock and 6.8 kilometers (4.2 miles) from Vaitape village. EP Rates: room in house 5.000 CFP ($50) single; 6.000 CFP ($60) double; 8.000 CFP ($80) triple; small bungalow 8.000 CFP ($80) single/double; family bungalow 10.000 CFP ($100) single/double. Third person 2.000 CFP ($20). Breakfast on request. Add 1% value added tax to room rates and meal plan. Mastercard, Visa.*

This is probably the best choice for a budget accommodation on Bora Bora, because of its excellent location right on the white sand beach of Matira, facing Maupiti and the sunset sea. Most of the guests stay in a six-bedroom house, which has two bedrooms on the ground level and two rooms upstairs. The communal kitchen and bathroom have hot water. There are also two small bungalows, each with a double bed and private bathroom with hot water; and two family bungalows, each with a double and single bed and private bathroom with hot water. House linens are provided. The family bungalows are especially recommended because they are your ideal Polynesian style *fare*, with a big thatched roof and half-walls of woven bamboo, overlooking the incredibly beautiful lagoon. The biggest drawback here is lack of privacy, as Matira Beach is Bora Bora's only public beach. Nono has an outrigger canoe and operates Teremoana Tours.

CHEZ ROSINA, *B.P. 51, Vaitape, Bora Bora. Tel./Fax 689/67.70.91. On mountain side in Paparoa section of Pofai Bay, 8 kilometers (5 miles) from the ferry dock and 4.5 kilometers (2.8 miles) from Vaitape village. Free round-trip transfers. EP Rates: room with breakfast 5.000 CFP ($50) single; 7.000 CFP ($70) double. Meal plan with breakfast and dinner 2.500 CFP ($25) single;*

5.000 CFP ($50) double. Half-rate for meals for child under 12 years. Add 1% value added tax to room rates. No credit cards.

This is a 4-bedroom house on the mountainside behind the Honeymoon Boutique. The rooms are rented individually and each contains a double bed with a private bathroom and hot water shower. You also have use of the living room, dining room and kitchen. House linens are provided.

CHEZ HENRIETTE, *B.P. 267, Vaitape, Bora Bora. Tel. 689/67.71.32. Beside the lagoon in Anau over the hill from Club Med. Round-trip transfers provided. EP Rates: bed in dormitory 1.500 CFP ($15); room 4.000 CFP ($40) single/double; camping 1.000 CFP ($10) per camper per day. Add 1% value added tax to room rates. No credit cards.*

This is the low-end accommodation for backpackers and campers. There are two dormitories containing eight-ten beds in each structure, plus two bedrooms with a double bed. Communal bath facilities have cold water showers. There's also a camp ground for 30 tents, sharing the kitchen and cold-water bath facilities. There is no beach here, but there is a warm family atmosphere. Stellio provides circle island tours, safari tours and lagoon tours.

ON THE MOTUS
Expensive

HOTEL BORA BORA LAGOON RESORT, *B.P. 175, 98730 Vaitape, Bora Bora. Tel. 689/60.40.00; Fax 689/60.40.03. US Reservations: 800/237-1236; Internet http://www.orient-expresshotels.com/ 80 units. EP Rates single/ double: garden bungalow 52.000 CFP ($520); beach bungalow 55.000 CFP ($550); overwater bungalow 71.000 CFP ($710); beach suites 82.000 CFP ($820); extra person 8.500 CFP ($85). Meal plan with breakfast and dinner add 8.000 CFP ($80) per person; meal plan with breakfast, lunch and dinner add 11.000 CFP ($110) per person. Add 7% hotel tax to room rates and 1% value added tax to room rates and meals. All major credit cards.*

This hideaway hotel is located on the sunset point of Motu Toopua, a small, roadless coral island a mile across the bay from Bora Bora's main island. It is the only resort on the little island, which faces Motu Tapu and the Teavanui Pass and the Otemanu mountain. There are 50 overwater bungalows, 12 garden bungalows, 16 beach bungalows and 2 beach suites. They are built in the traditional Tahitian *fare* style, with thatched roofs, and are arranged in three villages: Sunrise Bungalows, Coral Bungalows and Sunset Bungalows; each with easy access to the village center. Features include yucca wood floors, private lanai terraces, king or twin beds, writing desks, electric ceiling fans, baths with separate showers, mini-bars, private safe boxes, hair dryers, tea and coffee facilities, international direct dial telephones, multi-channel television, sun deck and daily laundry service. The overwater bungalows have glass-bottom coffee tables and private steps to the lagoon, with fresh water showers on the landing.

The Otemanu Restaurant serves international cuisine and the Cafe "Fare" serves buffets, barbecues and light meals beside the swimming pool. The Hiro Lounge & Bistro offers spectacular views of Bora Bora's mountains and lagoon. The Pub Heiva is an underground discothèque with drum style counters and furniture and a large, hand-painted wall mural depicting Bora Bora's famous Heiva Festival, which is held each July. The Pavilion library/lounge can also be used for private dining, small meetings and video presentations, and the Putari Boutique carries gift items, film and clothing. The Fitness Center overlooks the swimming pool, and two tennis courts are inland at the back of the property. Tahitian outrigger paddle canoes, deep sea fishing, beach volleyball, scuba diving, wind surfing and sailing, glass bottom boat rides, pedal boats, lagoon excursions, jeep excursions, and special children's programs will keep you occupied if you want activity. Entertainment includes local Tahitian musicians and a folkloric dance group performs twice a week.

HOTEL LE MERIDIEN BORA BORA, *Pre-opening address and Reservations: B.P. 380595, Punaauia 98718, Tahiti. Tel. 689/47.07.07; Fax 689/ 47.07.08; in US 800/543-4300. 100 units. EP Rates single/double: beach bungalow 55.000 CFP ($550); overwater bungalow 68.000 CFP ($680); rollaway bed 8.000 CFP ($80). Meal plan with breakfast and dinner 7.000 CFP ($70); meal plan with breakfast, lunch and dinner 10.800 CFP ($108). American buffet breakfast 2.000 CFP ($20); Set lunch menu at beach restaurant 3.800 CFP ($38); buffet dinner 7.000 CFP ($70). Add 7% hotel tax to room rates and 1% value added tax to room rates and meal plan. All major credit cards.*

This hotel is scheduled to open on June 10, 1998, with 85 overwater bungalows and 15 beachside bungalows, located on 9.5 hectares (23.47 acres) of land on the southern end of Motu Roa, an islet across the lagoon from the village of Anau on Bora Bora's main island. The view of Bora Bora's Otemanu mountain is at its best from this *motu*. The hotel is a 20-minute boat ride from the airport and five minutes by boat from the main island.

The 100 deluxe bungalows are built in the Polynesian traditional style, using natural materials of pandanus thatched roofs, bamboo and precious woods. They are decorated in a Polynesian motif with the warm colors of Tahiti. Each bungalow contains a large bedroom with a living area, overhead fan, television with pay-for-view movies, a fully stocked mini-bar, international direct dial telephone, safe, coffee and tea facilities, a bathroom and outdoor terrace. The large glass surface in the floor of the overwater bungalows, which has become standard in the overwater bungalows in French Polynesia, will allow you to watch the fish in the lagoon.

The restaurant Le Tipanier can seat 180 people and will present international and local cuisine. Le Te Ava, the 120-seat beachside restaurant, and Le Miki Miki beach bar are built as a Tahitian village, where you can enjoy romantic dinners and Polynesian barbecues. An unusual addition to this hotel is the construction of a levy on the ocean side, which is 3.5 meters (11.5 feet) high and 20 meters (66 feet) wide. This serves as a protective barrier in the event of big ocean swells, and it is camouflaged with sand and planted with trees to enhance the visual aspect of the wall. The beautiful white sand beach and aquamarine waters of Bora Bora's famous lagoon will be the highlights of the activities offered, which include all the excursions and outings available on Bora Bora. The Lagoonarium is just a five-minute walk along the white sand beach, where you can swim with the wild creatures that live inside this enclosure.

BORA BORA PEARL BEACH RESORT, *Reservations: South Pacific Marketing, B.P. 718, 98713 Papeete, Tahiti, Tel. 689/43.90.04; Fax 689/ 43.17.86. 60 bungalows. EP Rates single/double: beach bungalow 42.000 CFP ($420), overwater bungalow 52.000 CFP ($520), third person 4.000 CFP ($40). Meal plan with breakfast and dinner 6.200 CFP ($62) per person; meal plan with breakfast, lunch and dinner 8.500 CFP ($85). Full American breakfast 1.950 CFP ($19.50); Continental breakfast 1.450 CFP ($14.50); Outrigger canoe breakfast 2.900 CFP ($29); Romantic breakfast on the beach 2.900 CFP ($29); private Honeymoon Champagne Dinner under the Stars 7.800 CFP ($78); Fruit basket 2.200 CFP ($22). Add 7% hotel tax to room rates and 1% value added tax to room rates and meal plan. All major credit cards.*

This five-star hotel is due to open in June, 1998, on Motu Tevairoa, facing Faanui Bay. The 50 overwater bungalows and 10 beach bungalows are built in the traditional Polynesian style, with pandanus thatched roofs, local woods, woven pandanus wall coverings and a decor that includes tapa wall hangings and sculptures by Polynesian artists. The beach bungalows will be air-conditioned and the overwater bungalows will be cooled by the sea breezes and overhead fans. Each bungalow has a mini-bar refrigerator, coffee and tea facilities, international direct dial telephone, safe, television and sundeck. The beach bungalows are equipped with a shower and a Jacuzzi, and the overwater bungalows have a shower and separate bathtub. The overwater bungalows also have a glass bottom table with a view to the eco-system of the lagoon below. Bungalows for the handicapped are available on the beach and over the water.

In addition to the restaurant and bar, the hotel will have a gift shop and pearl boutique, a game room, billiards room, dive center, swimming pool, snorkeling equipment, outrigger paddle canoes, glass-bottom boat excursions, water-skiing, windsurfing, Hobie Cat sailing, lagoon fishing, deep sea fishing, outrigger canoe tours, sunset cruises, and all the land tours in Bora Bora will be available. The hotel is built on 19 hectares (47 acres) of land between the ocean and lagoon, and eventual plans include adding a 9-hole golf course.

MAI MOANA ISLAND, *B.P. 164, Vaitape, Bora Bora. Tel. 689/ 67.62.45; Fax 689/67.62.39. On Motu Iti, a private islet five minutes by boat from airport and 10 minutes from ferry dock. Free round-trip boat transfers. Minimum stay two nights. EP Rates: Fare 32.000 CFP ($320) single/double, including breakfast; lunch or dinner on request for 3.200 CFP ($32) per person. For six people maximum with all meals included 120.000 CFP ($1,200). Add 1% value added tax to room rates and meal plan. Mastercard, Visa.*

Stan Wisnieswski speaks English, French, German, Russian, Polish and Italian and he's a ham radio operator. His private paradise gets a lot of good comments from people who have stayed on Mai Moana Island, which is dotted with coconut palms and surrounded by a white sand beach. There are three deluxe *fares*, each with a double bedroom with telephone, television and video, dressing room and private bathroom with hot water. House linens are furnished. There is a small restaurant and bar on the premises plus snorkeling equipment, a motorboat, sailing dinghy and windsurf board. The entire islet can be rented as well.

OASIS DU LAGON, *B.P. 35, Vaitape, Bora Bora. Tel. 689/67.74.03. On Motu Iti A'au, a private islet six minutes by boat from Hotel Sofitel Marara and 20 minutes from the airport. Free round-trip boat transfers between Sofitel Marara and motu if you're staying a week or more. EP Rates: fare for one to six people 17.000-30.000-100.000 CFP ($170-$300-$1,000) per day. Dinner provided on request. Add 1% value added tax to room rates and meal plan. No credit cards.*

This was the first of the luxury accommodations built on the *motu* between the sea and the lagoon in Bora Bora, opening in 1991 for people who are willing to pay the price for looking at Otemanu mountain from a quiet distance. There are 5 *fares* in this deluxe complex on a private section of the *motu*. In 4 of the *fares* are two rooms or a mezzanine with a double bed, living room, terrace, and private bathroom with hot water. Inside a villa *fare* are three rooms, each with a double bed, and a fourth room on the mezzanine. There is also a kitchen and private bathroom with hot water. A club *fare* is a meeting place for leisure activities. House linens are furnished.

Moderate

FARE CORAIL, *B.P. 77, Vaitape, Bora Bora. Tel. 689/67.74.50. On Motu Tane, a private islet five minutes by boat from the airport and five minutes from the ferry dock. Round-trip transfers are extra. Minimum stay of three nights. EP Rates: bungalow 10.000 CFP ($100) single; 20.000 CFP ($200) double; 22.500 CFP ($225) triple; 25.000 CFP ($250) quadruple. Reduced rates for longer stays. Add 1% value added tax to room rates. No credit cards.*

Motu Tane was the private islet of a famous French explorer, artist and writer named Paul-Emile Victor, who spent a lot of time in the South Pole and among the Eskimos in the North Pole. When he retired to live in Bora Bora he and his wife Colette and their son Teva built their home on this little *motu*, along with a guest cottage. Paul-Emile died in 1995 and Colette still manages the place. The bungalow is made of coral stone and has a big bed in a sleeping alcove, plus a living/dining room, kitchen, terrace and outside private bathroom with cold water. It is very attractively decorated and house linens are furnished. The *fare* is on the other side of the islet from Colette's house and has its own white sand beach. Snorkeling equipment and a paddle canoe are provided.

LE PARADIS, *B.P. 243, Vaitape, Bora Bora. Tel. 689/67.75.53; Fax 689/67.72.88. On Motu Paahi, a private islet five minutes by boat from the Motu Mute airport and 10 minutes from the ferry dock. Round-trip boat transfers extra. EP Rates: fare 8.000 CFP ($80) single; 10.000 CFP ($100) double; deluxe fare 15.000 CFP ($150) double/triple. Meal plan with breakfast and dinner is 2.800 CFP ($28) per person. Add 1% value added tax to room rates and meal plan. No credit cards.*

The Tahitian couple who own this little pension have a very good reputation for their local style cuisine, especially the *maa Tahiti* they prepare in the underground oven. The 5 small thatched roof bungalows have bamboo walls and are located on a pretty white sand beach. Each *fare* has a double bed and a single bed, and house linens are supplied. You have to share a communal toilet and bathroom with cold water, located in a separate building. The water is potable. The Grandadam family will take you around the island by outrigger canoe with a picnic on a *motu* for 3.000 CFP ($30) a person, drive you around the big island by car for 2.000 CFP ($20) a person, or rent you a bike for 1.000 CFP ($10) to do your own tour. The Tahitian feast can be prepared for a minimum of six people at a cost of 30.000 CFP ($300).

Sat Sun Mon

WHERE TO EAT
Expensive
MATIRA TERRACE RESTAURANT, *Hotel Bora Bora, Tel. 60.44.60. All major credit cards. Open daily 7 to 10am, 12 to 2pm, and 6:30 to 9:30pm. Breakfast is also served for early morning departures.*

A Continental breakfast costs 1.800 CFP ($18), an American breakfast is 2.200 CFP ($22), and à la carte breakfasts cost between 1.000 and 2.500 CFP ($10 to $25). For lunch you can expect to pay 1.500 to 3.500 CFP ($15 to $35), and for dinner the cost is 3.500 to 6.500 CFP ($35 to $65). The refined cuisine of French and Continental dishes with a Polynesian flavor includes smoked salmon lasagna with spinach, flambéed fricassee of slipper lobster and morel mushrooms with brandy, filet of mahi mahi in a pastry crust with tropical fruit, chicken breast with papaya and a vanilla butter sauce, roasted duck breast with pineapple, grilled filet mignon and giant shrimp with Béarnaise sauce, and rack of lamb with a mustard and herb crust. A gourmet dinner may include such tempting treats as Polynesian clams on homemade pasta with a parsley cream sauce, a choice of sautéed marlin with shitaki mushrooms or veal Cordon Bleu, with your choice of divine desserts or a selection of fine French cheeses, all for 5.000 CFP ($50). The wine cellar has the right wine for every dish.

A Tahitian Beach Barbecue is held on the beach each Wednesday night. You dine under the stars with your feet in the white sand and watch a Polynesian dance show, which includes fire dancing. This costs 5.500 CFP ($55). On Friday evenings, starting at 6:30pm, the arts and crafts "mamas" entertain with music and singing on the beach, and demonstrate how to weave palm leaves into hats and baskets, how to make a *tifaifai* bed cover, and ways to use the coconut. Your Gastronomic Evening begins with your choice of a special flaming dish, which may be beef filet flambé with green pepper, shrimp flambé with whisky, filet mignon of pork flambé with porto, or slipper lobster flambé with ginger alcohol. Even the crêpes you order for dessert are flambéed at your table. This feast costs 5.000 CFP ($50) and is followed by a Polynesian dance show. Children under 12 years of age are extended a 50 percent reduction off all buffet style meals and barbecues.

OTEMANU RESTAURANT, *Bora Bora Lagoon Resort, Tel. 60.40.00. All major credit cards. Open daily for breakfast and dinner.*

This hotel restaurant is on Motu Toopua, facing the main island of Bora Bora and its famous mountain peaks. Seafood is prominent on the menu of international cuisine. A Tahitian feast is held twice a week, followed by a folkloric dance show. Lunch is served in the Cafe Fare by the pool.

NOA NOA RESTAURANT, *Moana Beach Parkroyal, Tel. 67.49.00. All major credit cards. Open daily for breakfast, lunch and dinner.*

A Continental breakfast is 1.650 CFP ($16.50) and a full American breakfast is 1.950 CFP ($19.50). Dinners start at 2.500 CFP ($25), and a set dinner menu is 5.200 CFP ($52). A complimentary cake is offered to anyone dining in the restaurant who is celebrating a birthday or wedding anniversary. A lavish seafood buffet under the stars is served each Saturday evening, during the *Soirée Merveilleuse* (marvelous evening), followed by a Polynesian dance show on the beach. The cost is 5.990 CFP ($59.90). A barbecue and buffet dinner highlights each Tuesday evening, with a Tahitian dance show, for 4.950 CFP ($49.50). Each Thursday evening is Polynesian Night, with a Tahitian dinner and song and dance show performed by the Mamas of Bora Bora. This costs 4.950 CFP

($49.50). A Moonlight Dinner Cruise, complete with musicians, is held each Friday evening, for 7.200 CFP ($72), drinks not included. You should book early for this romantic occasion. On the second Sunday of every month a traditional feast of *maa Tahiti* is cooked in an underground *ahima'a* oven, which is opened at 11am. Lunch starts at 12pm in the Noa Noa Restaurant and outside on the Vini Vini Terrace. The cost is 4.900 CFP ($49) for adults and 2.450 CFP ($24.50) for children under 12 years.

LA PEROUSE RESTAURANT, *Sofitel Marara, Tel. 67.70.46. All major credit cards. Open daily from 5:30 to 10:30am for breakfast, 12 to 3:30pm for lunch, and 7 to 9:30pm for dinner.*

The restaurant and bar are built on stilts over the lagoon, facing Tahaa and Raiatea. I have stayed here many times over the years and have eaten some pretty good food in this restaurant, but during my last trip in April, 1997, I found the food rather uninspired. The chefs change every year or so, and maybe the next one will be a culinary master. A Barbecue buffet followed by a Polynesian show takes place each Tuesday, starting at 8:30pm; a Seafood buffet and Polynesian show is held each Thursday at 8:30pm; and a Tamaara'a buffet and Polynesian show are on the bill for Saturday evenings, starting at 6:30pm with the opening of the Tahitian oven.

CLUB MEDITERANNEE, *Tel. 60.46.04. All major credit cards. Open daily for breakfast, lunch and dinner.*

Even if you are not staying at Club Med you can go for breakfast, lunch or dinner. The breakfast costs 2.060 CFP ($20.60), lunch is 4.635 ($46.35), and dinner is 5.150 CFP ($51.50). Beer and wine are included with lunch and dinner. Each Thursday night is Polynesian night, featuring traditional Tahitian foods cooked in an underground oven and a Tahitian dance show. There is no show on Sunday, but during the rest of the week a nightly show is presented by the Club Med staff, except on Fridays, when the guests, the *gentils membres,* are put on stage. Saturday night is disco night. You can attend the shows and disco without eating when you buy a necklace of plastic bar beads for 1.800 CFP ($18).

L'ESPADON RESTAURANT, *Revatua Club, 16 kilometers (10 miles) from Vaitape and 9 kilometers (6 miles) from Point Matira. Tel. 67.71.67. Mastercard and Visa. Open daily for dinner. Free transportation provided from your hotel or boat.*

This overwater restaurant is noted for its excellent French cuisine and seafood specialties, with main courses priced at 1.800 to 2.400 CFP ($18 to $24) for fish, and 1.400 to 2.600 CFP ($14 to $26) for meat dishes. There is a good choice of French wines. Snack Le Totara is open at lunch time. Be sure to feed the fish from the dock.

YACHT CLUB OF BORA BORA, *in Faanui, 1.6 kilometers (1 mile) north of Vaitape. Tel. 67.70.69, Mastercard and Visa. Open daily for breakfast, lunch and dinner. Free transportation is provided for dinner if you reserve in advance.*

This overwater dining terrace has a distinct nautical atmosphere, where Bora Bora residents go for fine French cuisine. Main dishes are 2.100 to 3.100 CFP ($21 to $31), which include prawns in coconut milk curry, mahi mahi with basil and tuna steaks. The decor isn't fancy, but the view of the bay, with yachts and floating bungalows tied to their moorings, and the *motu* islets and the vast ocean beyond the reef provide romantic scenery.

Note: This restaurant and the rental bungalows were destroyed during Cyclone Osea in November, 1997. Hopefully, the restaurant will be rebuilt by the time you arrive in Bora Bora.

BLOODY MARY'S, *on the mountainside in Pofai Bay, 5 kilometers (3 miles) from Vaitape and 1 kilometer (.62 miles) from the Hotel Bora Bora. Tel. 67.72.86. American Express, Mastercard and Visa. Open for lunch and dinner. Closed Sunday. Free dinner transportation is provided from your hotel or boat.*

This is where all the stars of stage, cinema and television go to eat when they visit Bora Bora. A panel beside the road has a long list of names of "Famous People Who Have Eaten at Bloody Mary's." Going to Bloody Mary's is not just a dining experience; for some people it's a Happening. Your host may be Rick Guenette, originally from Canada, who is one of the owners, or manager Craig Goold, an American expatriate. Both young men have lived in Bora Bora for many years and are married to local beauties. Bloody Mary's is the kind of place where people get to know one another very easily. You can't be too reserved while you are sitting on a coconut stump under a huge thatched roof and wiggling your toes in the white sand floor. Folks have a tendency to hoot and holler here, or at least strike up a friendly conversation with the guy on the next stool at the big U-shaped bar.

The bar opens at 9:30am and lunch is served between 11am and 3pm, which consists of salads and homemade pizzas. The dinner service starts at 6:30pm, when a variety of fresh fish and lobsters are displayed on a bed of ice. Craig or Rick will take your order while the chef looks on, ready for instructions on how you want your fish, shrimp, crab, lobster, steak or chicken cooked. They will even prepare vegetarian dishes at your request. The main courses include salad, rice and vegetables, and start at 2.400 CFP ($24) for one fish choice, 3.800 CFP ($38) for a lobster/fish combination, and 4.500 CFP ($45) for lobster. A 20 percent discount is given for return clients.

BAMBOO HOUSE, *on the mountain side in Pofai Bay, 3.5 kilometers (2 miles) from Vaitape toward Matira. Tel. 67.76.24. American Express, Mastercard* *and Visa. Open daily for lunch and dinner. Free transportation provided from your hotel or boat.*

The decor here is what the name implies, a little house made of bamboo walls and a thatched roof. Dining is inside or out in the courtyard. This restaurant gets high ratings from the residents of Bora Bora, although the service can be slow. Luncheon choices include burgers and chips, salads and pastas. The dinner menu features French cuisine and fresh fish, crab and lobster specialties from the Bora Bora lagoon. Meat courses are 2.300 to 2.800 CFP ($23 to $28) and fish dishes are 2.300 to 2.600 CFP ($23 to $26). Pasta dishes are 1.350 to 1.900 CFP ($13.50 to $19), which include a delicious prawn fettucine. You can also visit Gauguin's Garden in the same complex, which has Gauguin-type statues set in poses that resemble some of his paintings.

Moderate

TOOPITI RESTAURANT, *Beach Club Bora Bora, Tel. 67.71.16. All major credit cards. Open daily for breakfast, lunch and dinner.*

Dinner choices include sirloin steak for 1.300 CFP ($13), roast duck for 2.050 CFP ($20.50), shrimp curry for 1.750 CFP ($17.50), and lobster medallion for 2.700 CFP ($27). You can also get a fish or lobster soup or a Japanese plate of sushi. If you're in the mood for Mexican food served at Le Coin on the beach of Bora Bora, then you may appreciate the *guacamole* for 750 CFP ($7.50), chili con carne for 1.000 CFP ($10), enchiladas for 1.150 CFP ($11.50), and tacos for 1.100 CFP ($11). I didn't try them, so I cannot recommend them. Once a week the restaurant prepares a barbecue or veal on a spit, followed by a Tahitian dance show. This all depends on the number of guests in the hotel.

TEMANUATA, *on the lagoon side at Point Matira, just past the turnoff at Point Matira. Tel. 67.75.61. Mastercard and Visa. Open for lunch and dinner. Closed Sunday.*

This attractive little restaurant is built of coconut trunk walls, with a huge chandelier of bamboo and mother-of-pearl shells hanging from the cross beams under a thatched roof. Although the sign out front says Restaurant-Snack, the food here is of gourmet quality. I ordered the shrimp, breaded in coconut and sautéed, for 1.600 CFP ($16). It was beautifully presented on a plate decorated with rice and green beans and slices of Chinese starfruit. It was melt-in-your-mouth delicious. So was the coconut pie I ate afterward. Since then I have recommended this restaurant to several friends, who all praised the food.

The menu includes some tempting salads, *poisson cru*, sashimi, tuna tartare and carpaccio for 900 to 1.300 CFP ($9 to $13); a number of fish dishes from 1.300 to 1.600 CFP; meat dishes for 1.400 CFP ($14); and a number of Chinese dishes and pastas for 900 to 1.300 CFP ($9 to $13). The crêpes, fruit salad, homemade pies and profiteroles were 450 to 550 CFP ($4 to $5). The most expensive food item was American style lobster, for 3.200 CFP ($32). An impressive wine list showed prices ranging from 1.500 to 4.000 CFP ($15 to $40) for white or red French wines, and 10.000 CFP ($100) for a bottle of Moet et Chandon champagne.

The owner of Temanuata Restaurant-Snack is Marama Dugan, whose grandfather was an American soldier stationed in Bora Bora in World War II. Marama's chief cook and *patissier* are two local lads who learned their culinary skills at school in France. Marama also has a 5-bungalow pension adjacent to his restaurant.

LE TIARE, *on mountainside in Matira, opposite Bora Bora Motel. Tel. 67.61.39. American Express, Mastercard and Visa. Open for lunch and dinner. Closed Sunday.*

This restaurant is very conveniently located in the biggest concentration of hotels on Bora Bora, and is adjacent to the Tiare Market, a small food store also owned by Anne and Pierre English. I had a so-so Club sandwich at Le Tiare and I was the only customer for lunch. The dinner menu included shrimp in a light cheese sauce with wild mushrooms for 1.800 CFP ($18), fresh scallops on a skewer with white butter for 2.150 CFP ($21.50), and fondue Bourguignonne for two, for 1.850 CFP ($18.50) per person, which is beef fondue that you cook in hot oil at the table.

BEN'S PLACE, *on mountainside in Matira, between Hotel Bora Bora and Point Matira. Tel. 67.74.54. American Express, Mastercard and Visa. Open Friday through Wednesday 11am to 8pm for lunch and an early dinner. Closed Thursday.*

Ben Teraitepo, from Bora Bora, and his American wife, Robin, gave up their busy life in Southern California to settle in Bora Bora. They started out serving American breakfasts, burgers and pizzas on the front terrace of their house, across the road from the white sandy beach. Now they have eliminated the breakfasts and have evolved their menu to include spaghetti for 1.250 CFP ($12.50), lasagna for 1.900 CFP ($19), Mexican *fajitas* for 1.400 CFP ($14), and fish or steak with salad and chips for 1.900 CFP ($19).

LA BOUNTY, *on lagoon side in Matira, close to Hotel Le Polynesia and Bora Bora Motel. Tel. 67.70.43. Mastercard and Visa. Open for lunch and dinner. Closed Monday.*

This is a popular restaurant with a good location, close to several hotels and pensions. Starter courses are 750 to 900 CFP, pizza costs 1.000 to 1.400 CFP ($10 to $14), and fish and meat dishes range from 1.100 to 1.500 CFP ($11 to $15).

MAHANA VIEW, *on the beach at Point Matira, just before the turnoff when you're coming from Vaitape. American Express, Mastercard and Visa. Open for lunch and dinner. Closed Wednesday.*

Continental cuisine and seafood specialties include chicken curry, grilled chicken breast, pepper steak and shrimp, from 900 to 1.500 CFP ($9 to $15). Pasta and Chinese dishes are also prepared and you can buy a glass of wine for 350 CFP ($3.50).

POFAI BEACH BAR, *Hotel Bora Bora, Tel. 60.44.60. All major credit cards. Open daily 10:30am to 5pm.*

This excellent snack bar is my favorite. It is located on the white sand beach below the Hotel Bora Bora's main restaurant. You can order sandwiches, salads, *poisson cru*, fruit salads, milkshakes and cold beer or cocktails, and enjoy your lunch while you take a break from sunbathing. My favorite choice is a mahi mahi sandwich, which is served with fries, a slice of pineapple and a pretty flower to wear behind my ear.

RESTAURANT MATIRA, *on the beach in the Hotel Matira between the Hotel Bora Bora and Point Matira. Tel. 67.70.51. American Express, Mastercard and Visa. Open Tuesday through Sunday for breakfast, lunch and dinner. Closed Monday.*

This is a great place to watch the action on the beach while enjoying an average lunch of Chinese dishes from Cantonese recipes. The courses vary from 900 to 1.500 CFP ($9 to $15). The sunsets from the terrace are often spectacular.

Inexpensive

SNACK AU COCOTIER, *on mountainside in Vaitape, between Chin Lee's market and the pharmacy. Tel. 67.74.18. No credit cards. Open Monday through Saturday 6am to 8pm. Closed Sunday.*

The *poisson cru* served here has a reputation for being the best on the island, and many tourists have already discovered this small restaurant. The food is basically good portions of local Chinese and Tahitian dishes priced between 800 and 1.000 CFP ($8 to $10), with very special dishes prepared for 1.700 CFP ($17).

CHEZ MICHEL, *on the northern end of Vaitape about 90 meters (100 yards) from the Commercial Center, Tel. 67.71.43. No credit cards. Open for breakfast and lunch, Monday to Friday, and for dinner on Sunday. Closed Saturday.*

This neat little indoor-outdoor snack serves some of the best local style dishes you'll find on Bora Bora and the price is right. Daily specials of chow mien, steak and fries, and *maa tinito*, (Chinese food), which is a delicious combination of red beans, pork, vegetables and macaroni. It's very filling. The specials cost 700 to 900 CFP ($7 to $9) and you can get a *casse-croûte* sandwich for 100 CFP ($1).

BORA BORA BURGERS, *next door to the post office in Vaitape. No phone, no credit cards. Open Monday through Saturday 7:30am to 5pm.*

You can sit on a coconut bar stool or at one of the tables on the sidewalk in front of this small fast food stand and eat your burgers and fries, which are very reasonably priced for Bora Bora.

L'APPETISSERIE, *in Pahia Center in Vaitape village. Tel. 67.75.43. No credit cards. Open daily.*

You'll find just the treat for your sweet tooth in this air-conditioned pastry shop. In addition to cakes, ice cream and sorbets, you will also find homemade croissants, quiches and pizza.

SEEING THE SIGHTS

To explore the island by car, scooter or bicycle start at the Vaitape boat dock, if you head south around the island. All along the water's edge of Pofai (or Povai) Bay you will see spectacular views of the **Otemanu Mountain**. You'll pass Alain and Linda's Art Gallery on the right, and on the left you'll see Tautu's pile of junk that was supposed to be a museum. With his bulldozer he collected American defense guns, anchors and other heavy military paraphernalia, and at one time he even had the wrecks of two inter-island ships anchored and sinking in Pofai Bay. He's now abandoned the museum project and the ships were thankfully hauled away. Go past the museum and you'll see a road opposite the soccer field and gymnasium, which leads over the island to the village of Anau. The interior roads can only be traversed by mountain bike or on foot.

If you stay on the **circle island road** you'll see the Bamboo House Restaurant, Gauguin Boutique, Honeymoon Boutique, Chez Pauline Camping, Bloody Mary's Restaurant, Moana Art, and the Hotel Bora Bora, at Raititi Point. When the American Armed Forces were stationed on Bora Bora during World War II they installed a battery of coastal defense guns on the hillside above the Hotel Matira. You can reach them in just a 10-minute hike up a walking trail east of the hotel property.

The road continues on past Bora Bora Diving Center, Ben's Snack, and the Hotel Matira's bungalows on the beach at **Point Matira**. A sign indicates the turnoff at Point Matira, where you can visit the Hotel Moana Beach Parkroyal, and have a swim at Matira Beach. Chez Nono has a pension right on the white sand beach. Back on the main road, you'll see Galerie Rosine Temauri-Masson, Pension Maeva Masson, and the excellent Temanuata Restaurant on the right (the coconut shrimp is delicious), and Matira Pearls on the left (the prices are good).

Heading into hotel row along the east coast, you'll see the new Hotel Le Maitai Polynesia, with overwater bungalows. The Bora Bora Motel, La Bounty Restaurant, Calypso Club, Poeiti Tours, Beach Club Bora Bora, Taahana Tourisme, Tiare Market and Restaurant, and Hotel Sofitel Marara are all located on either side of this short stretch of road.

A steep hill leads you behind the Club Med Coral Garden Village at **Faaopore Bay**, just before Paoaoa Point. You can visit a lookout point on a ridge above the bay by taking Club Med's private tunnel under the road or by walking up the steps just beyond the Boutique Hibiscus on the left side of the road. A trail to the right of the hill will take you down to Marae Aehautai, where you will have a good view of Otemanu mountain and the islands of Tahaa and Raiatea beyond the reef. Other *marae* are also located in this vicinity, as well as coastal guns from World War II.

The road continues on to **Anau village**, which has a general store, a couple of roadside stands where you can buy shells and *pareos*, a church, school and some very modest homes, which are often unpainted. Across the lagoon you'll see the overwater bungalows of the luxurious Hotel Le Méridien Bora Bora.

After passing a few houses on the road beyond Fitiiu Point, you'll come to the Revatua Club on Taimoo Bay. If you're hungry or thirsty this is a good place to stop. You can also look at the fish and turtles in a lagoon enclosure beside the hotel pier.

For the next few miles the only thing you will see are coconut plantations and *tupa* crabs, until you come to the *Musée de la Mer*, the Marine Museum, which has replicas of famous ships that have visited Tahiti and Bora Bora. Just before Point Taihi you'll see a steep and muddy track that leads up to a World War II radar station on top of Popoti Ridge. You can also continue by foot or mountain bikes on this path to a lookout above Faanui village.

From the road at Point Taihi you will see the derelict buildings that were constructed in the mid-1980s to be used as a Hyatt Hotel. The project was abandoned when the owner ran out of money, and the slums that remain are sometimes used as homes for squatters. Across the lagoon you can see the Bora Bora airport on Motu Mute. The Bora Bora Condos are just beyond the Hyatt slums, and consist of overwater bungalows and mountainside apartments on stilts. Actors Marlon Brando and Jack Nicholson owned some of the overwater bungalows, but a couple of them were washed away during the cyclones of 1982-83.

At Tereia Point in **Faanui Bay** is an old shipping wharf and seaplane ramp that were built by the American Seabees during the war. Another US coastal gun is located on the hill above the concrete water tank, and right after the former submarine base is the Marae Fare-Opu, between the road and the bay. The stones of the temple are engraved with turtle petroglyphs. A road beside the Protestant church at the head of the bay runs inland, narrowing into an unmarked muddy track that you can follow with a guide over the saddle of the ridgetop to Bora Bora's east coast of Vairau Bay, south of Fitiiu Point.

On the western end of Faanui Bay is the main shipping wharf, where inter-island ferries and cargo vessels from Tahiti dock. This wharf was also built during the war. Just 100 meters west of the quay is the Marae

Marotetini, a coastal *marae* that was restored by Dr. Yosihiko Sinoto in 1968. This was a royal temple and members of Bora Bora's chiefly families are buried nearby.

Around the bend from the Faanui boat dock is the Bora Bora Yacht Club, which is also a restaurant and bar with bungalows and houseboats for rent. On the hillside facing the island's only pass are two defense guns left over from the war. The Safari Tour excursions will take you to visit these guns.

The next turn in the road passes the abandoned bungalows that were formerly used by Club Med and you are back in Vaitape village. If you feel in need of refreshment you'll find a good little *patisserie* in the modern Centre Commercial Le Pahia, or you can shop at Magasin Chin Lee, which is truly an establishment of village life in Bora Bora. In addition to cold juices and drinks you can choose a *casse-croûte*, sandwich, Tahitian and Chinese pastries or a take-away container of good hot food, usually rice and fish, chicken or meat.

Circle Island Tours $20 - $90

To fully appreciate the history and beauty of Bora Bora, climb aboard an excursion bus or *le truck* and settle back to listen, learn and enjoy as the English-speaking guide tells all about this little island and its colorful past, exciting present and plans for tomorrow. While passing through the little villages on the 29-kilometer (18-mile) circuit, you will see modest homes surrounded by pretty flower gardens, small snack stands and little boutiques selling *pareos* and shells.

The *marae* temples, where Polynesians used to worship in pre-Christian days, are pointed out, along with the Quonset huts, naval base and heavy artillery guns, left behind by the 5,000 American soldiers, sailors and Seabees who made a "friendly invasion" of Bora Bora during World War II, who also left many blue-eyed children. A tour by *le truck* or minibus starts at 2.000 CFP ($20); you can also tour the island by private air-conditioned limousine for 9.000 CFP ($90). Circle island tours can be booked with the following companies:

Bora Bora Tours, *Tel. 67.70.31*, is the company of Alfredo Doom, Bora Bora's "Mr. Transportation". Alfredo gave me my first circle island tour of Bora Bora in 1968, and he has trained his children and other employees in the fine art of tour guiding. Alfredo's 2-hour excursion departs in the morning and afternoon from the Hotel Bora Bora and Club Med.

Otemanu Tours, *Tel. 67.70.49*, is owned by Paul Desmet, who provides a 2-hour circle island tour daily, using *le truck* to show you the island.

Maire Tours, *Tel. 67.71.32*, is operated by Stellio Vaiho and his wife Henriette, who have a backpacker's lodging and campground in the village of Anau, which is called **Chez Henriette**. This is a 2 1/2 hour excursion.

Mountain Safari 4x4 Excursions

Viewing Bora Bora's majestic beauty takes on new dimensions when you bounce up and down the rutted mountain trails in a Land Rover or Jeep on a photographic safari excursion. Your guide will tell you the story of the American military base that was established in Bora Bora during World War II and you'll visit the gun emplacements and radar station on Popoti Ridge. At the end of the trail you walk uphill through the bush, where you are rewarded with a 360 degree panoramic vista of an ancient volcano crater, the lagoon and coral reefs around Bora Bora and the neighboring islands of Tahaa, Raiatea, Huahine, Maupiti and the atoll of Tupai, which are all clearly visible from this height. These tours also circle the island, where your guide points out the *marae* stone temples used by the ancient Polynesians, and the war relics used by the Americans. These are very interesting and scenic tours, but are not for the faint-hearted, pregnant or lazily inclined tourist.

Tupuna Mountain Expeditions, *Tel. 67.75.06*, is owned by Dany Leverd, who has several guides, including a very popular young man named Patrick Tairua, whose warm and friendly personality so impresses the people he meets that they write "Mauruuru Award" letters to the *Tahiti Beach Press*, singing his praises. They also like the music he plays on his "Indiana Jones" type journey. Patrick also performs a fire dance at the Moana Beach Parkroyal and the Hotel Bora Bora. This half-day morning or afternoon tour costs 5.750 CFP ($57.50).

Bora Bora Safari Land, *Tel. 67.71.32*, also has 4-wheel drive excursions. This is owned by Stellio Vaiho, who also operates pension Chez Henriette and Maire Tours.

Helicopter Tours

Héli-Inter Polynésie, *Tel. 67.62.59*, is next door to the Air Tahiti office on the Vaitape quay. A 6-seat "Ecureuil" helicopter will transfer you from the Bora Bora airport to your hotel for 5.000 CFP ($50) a person. Daily flights start at 5.800 CFP ($58), and you can even take a spectacular sunset flight for 15.000 CFP ($150). These tours are available daily except Sunday. You can also visit the neighboring islands by helicopter.

Special Activities & Sightseeing Stops

Alain Gerbault's grave opposite the *gendarmerie* on Vaitape quay will be pointed out to you during all guided land tours. This is a Frenchman who had sailed the seven seas aboard his yacht *Firecrest* before dropping anchor in Bora Bora. He was most attracted to the young boys of Bora Bora, to whom he introduced the game of soccer. Due to the politics of war Gerbault left Bora Bora in 1941, and died on the island of Timor. His remains were brought back to his beloved Bora Bora in 1947, and a small tomb in the form of a *marae* was built in his honor.

Ancient temples of coral stone called *marae* are scattered around the island and on a few of the surrounding *motu* islets. The most easily accessible of these pre-historic sites of worship and human sacrifice are: **Marae Marotetini**, on a point by the lagoon between the Bora Bora Yacht Club and the Faanui boat dock; **Marae Taianapa**, on private property well off the mountain side of the road in Faanui, close to the Electra power plant; and **Marae Aehautai**, located on the beach at Fitiiu Point overlooking Anau Bay. **Fare Opu**, "House of the Stomach" is located between the lagoon and the road, close to the old navy docks in Faanui, immediately before the Faanui village. Petroglyphs of turtles are incised into two of the coral slabs. Turtles were sacred to the Maohi ancestors of today's Polynesians.

Matira Beach begins at the Hotel Bora Bora and continues past the Hotel Matira on around Point Matira and past the Moana Beach Parkroyal. It joins Taahana Beach at Hotel Le Polynesia and Bora Bora Motel, but most people still refer to the entire area as Matira Beach. This is where you will find a concentration of hotels, pensions, boutiques, black pearl shops and all kinds of nautical activities. The west side of Matira Beach, facing the Hotel Bora Bora, is Bora Bora's most popular beach. The soft, white powdery sand slopes gently into the aquamarine lagoon, where the water is very shallow until you see the deepening shades of blue. Point Matira was named in memory of a British ship named *Mathilda*, which was wrecked on Moruroa Atoll in the Tuamotus in 1792. Three of the survivors remained in Tahiti, forming the first European colony. One of the crew, James O'Connor, married King Pomare's cousin, and their granddaughter was named Mathilda. She married a chief of the Leeward Islands and they settled in Bora Bora, where part of their property included the beautiful point and sand beach now called Matira, the Tahitian pronunciation of Mathilda.

Musée de la Marine, *Tel. 67.75.24,* is on the back side of the island, between the villages of Faanui and Anau. French architect Bertrand Darasse displays his collection of ship models, which includes models of Captain Cook's *Endeavour*, **Captain Bligh's** famous *Bounty*, and **Alain Gerbault's** *Firecrest*, which he sailed to Bora Bora. Admission to the maritime museum is free, but many disappointed tourists have found it closed when they arrived.

TUPAPAU

"Many vestiges of ancient times still linger on Bora Bora. The belief in **tupapau** *(TWO-pow-pow), ghosts of the dead, is prevalent among the islanders. Walk alone on a dark Bora Bora night and you'll see why. It is still a common practice to keep a lamp lit at night to ward off these evil spirits.*

In 1973 my son Tom and I discovered a human arm and a portion of jawbone in front of the altar of Marae Marotetini. They had been pushed to the surface by land crabs digging their burrows. Despite warnings from the locals, we took the bones as souvenirs. Shortly after the discovery, my right arm became swollen to twice its normal size, followed by a swelling of the right side of my jaw. Upon taking the bones back to Los Angeles, Tom's leg was broken in several places during a freak motorcycle accident. This was followed by a period of family sickness and bad luck that didn't cease until we returned the bones to Marae Marotetini in 1976.

In 1981, several giant human footprints were discovered at the water's edge near Marae Taianapa. The discovery was important enough to bring government officials and newsmen from Papeete to examine the huge prints and wonder at their origin. The elders of Bora Bora didn't wonder. They knew. The prints were an omen from the distant past." – From cinematographer Milas Hinshaw's booklet **"Bora Bora E."**

NIGHTLIFE & ENTERTAINMENT

The **Hotel Bora Bora**, **Moana Beach Parkroyal**, **Sofitel Marara** and **Club Med** have entertainment several nights a week. Details are given under *Where to Eat* in this chapter. The bar at Bloody Mary's is a very friendly place, where you can be assured of meeting other English-speaking people.

LE RÉCIF, *Tel. 67.73.87, is north of Vaitape towards Faanui.*

This is Bora Bora's only disco and it is open on Friday and Saturday nights. The ambiance in this dark and crowded room is very Tahitian. If you are curious as to how the locals whoop it up on Saturday night, the entry fee is 1.000 CFP ($10). The drinking and dancing goes on until the wee hours of the morning. You'll probably enjoy it more if you go with some local residents. Some of the young people who work at the hotels may be happy to go with you.

HEIVA IN BORA BORA -
WHERE THE FÊTE GOES ON AND ON

During the month of July, the island of Bora Bora pulsates to the rhythm of the **Heiva**, which means festival in Tahitian. Some people still call this event the Fête or Tiurai, the Tahitian word for July. Whatever name you choose to call it, this is the most colorful time to visit Bora Bora.

Most of the islands have their own Heiva celebrations, but the Fête in Bora Bora is the best, because the villagers put so much enthusiasm and effort into building their baraques (barracks). These are carnival type stalls or booths that are made of thatched roofs and walls woven of palm fronds. They are decorated with multicolored tifaifai wall hangings, ferns, bright blossoms and ti leaves. These baraques are transformed into restaurants, pool halls, shooting galleries and carnival booths with a roulette-type wheel called taviri. If you place a bet you may win a bar of soap, sack of rice or sugar, bolt of pareo cloth, or even a live suckling pig.

Each village presents a singing group and a troupe of dancers in the Heiva competitions. Some of these performers are just as talented as the professional entertainers in Tahiti, as Bora Bora has long been recognized for producing excellent dancers, choreography and costumes. The competitions are a big social event, when old friends get together to catch up on the latest happenings and to swap a choice bit of gossip. Seats are provided for the officials and those who wish to pay to sit down. Everyone else sits on the grass or white sand at Place Vaitape. The bicycle races around the island are fun to watch on July 14, as the supporters stand beside the road and spray the riders with water. The fruit-carriers' race, javelin-throwing contest, soccer matches and outrigger sailing canoe races are just warm-up events for the outrigger paddle canoe races.

July 14 is a good combination of old style Polynesian celebrations and the French version of honoring Bastille Day in the tropics. This is the time to drink champagne at the mayors office, aboard a visiting French ship and at the glamorous resort hotels. A huge fireworks display ends the day's festivities, and an all-night ball gets underway a little later. Although there are only two or three weeks of planned events during the Heiva in Bora Bora, the Fête still goes on and on, well into the month of August. After all, building the baraques did require a lot of work. What's more, they provide a great meeting place.

SPORTS & RECREATION
Hiking & Trekking
Ato Randonnees, *Tel. 67.77.27*, is a full-day excursion led by Ato Tinorua. This excursion departs from Pofai Bay by outrigger canoe at 10am, crossing over to the islet of Toopua. Ato will tell you the legend of Hiro, the Polynesian god of thieves and show you Hiro's bell, a rock that reverberates when struck. Then you'll walk to the top of the hill and over to another slope. Ato will then teach you how to prepare *poisson cru*, the many uses of the coconut and other Polynesian customs. Your lunch consists of fresh fruits from his garden. Ato says that your day will be full of new discoveries and you'll return to Pofai Bay on the main island at 5pm. This all-day tour is 4.000 CFP ($40).

Bora Bora Trekking, *Tel. 67.72.81.* You can drink champagne on a mountain summit and admire the views of the neighboring islands of Tahaa, Raiatea, Maupiti and Huahine. You are transferred to Mount Hue by helicopter and Christian Faye leads a 2-hour bush walk through cleared paths to Mount Pahia (661 meters/2,168 feet) and Mount Otemanu (727 meters/2,385 feet). Non-hikers can also enjoy the view and sip champagne on the top of Mount Hue (619 meters/2,030 feet). This outing operates daily except Sunday and costs 12.000 CFP ($120) per person.

Mont Pahia Excursions, *Tel. 67.70.49,* is owned by Paul Demest, who also has Otemanu Tours. Your guide will meet you in Vaitape village and lead you on a 3-hour hike up Mount Pahia, which is a 9 kilometer (5 mile) hike.

Horseback Riding
Reva Reva Ranch, *Tel. 67.63.63,* is located on Motu Piti A'au across the lagoon from the village of Anau. Olivier Ringeard will take you riding along secluded white sand beaches on New Zealand horses, with a choice of English and Western saddles. There are four rides daily at 8am, 10:30am, 2pm and 4pm, with moonlight rides on request. A 1-hour ride is 4.000 CFP ($40) and a 1 1/2 hour ride is 5.500 CFP ($55).

Boat Rental
René and Maguy Locations, *Tel. 67.60.61,* is located on Matira Beach close to the Sofitel Marara and Bora Bora Beach Club. You can rent a pedal boat for 3.500 CFP ($35) for 2 hours. An aluminum boat for four people, with a 6 horsepower engine, is 4.500 CFP ($45) for 2 hours, 6.500 CFP ($65) for half a day, and 9.500 CFP ($95) for a full day. No permit required. A transfer from the beach to the *motu* is 1.500 CFP ($15) per person.

Moana Adventure Tours, *Tel. 67.61.41,* adjacent to the Hotel Bora Bora, provides boat transfers upon request from the airport and resort hotels or private lodgings. A 13-foot or 17-foot Boston Whaler can be rented with a pilot, who will take you to places in the lagoon that visitors normally never get to see. A 17-foot Boston Whaler rents for 16.000 CFP ($160) for 2 hours, 23.500 CFP ($235) for 3 hours, and 28.000 CFP ($280) for 4 hours.

A 4-person Shuttle Craft or Jet Boat can be rented for day or night cruises. *Tel 67.63.48.*

Camera Rental

Camera Shop, *Tel. 67.76.63*, in the same complex as the Bamboo House and Boutique Gauguin, rents Minolta cameras or multi-system video cameras for snorkeling and scuba diving excursions. Your film can be developed in 24 hours. A roll of Kodak Gold film for 24 color prints costs 1.700 CFP ($17). Photocopies are 100 CFP ($1).

Coastal Fishing

Moana Adventure Tours, *Tel. 67.61.41/67.75.97*, uses a 13-foot or 17-foot Boston Whaler for fishing close to the outside reef, where currents and high seas attract bonito, tuna, mahi mahi, jacks, barracudas and wahoo. Half-day offshore fishing excursions are 29.500 CFP ($295).

Deep Sea Fishing

Sports fishing around Bora Bora is a very popular activity and the local fishing clubs hold tournaments throughout the year. There is even a Vahine Sport Fishing Club for the ladies, and any visiting female angler is welcome to join the competitions and fun. The fishing grounds are only 20 minutes away outside the barrier reef, and the waters around Bora Bora are filled with marlin, yellowfin tuna, sailfish, wahoo, mahi mahi and bonito. The marlin are tagged and released at the anglers' request. The cost of a half-day charter is 45.000 to 48.000 CFP ($450-$480), and a full-day charter costs 60.000 to 80.000 CFP ($600-$800), with drinks and picnic lunch included. Inter-island cruises are provided on request. The sea captains listed below all speak very good English, and some of them are expatriate Americans who chose Bora Bora as their home many years ago.

Jessie L, owned by Alain Loussan, *Tel. 67.70.59*, is a Luhrs 35; **Lady C**, owned by Steve Ellacott, *Tel. 67.72.12*, is a 29-foot Phoenix 29; **Mokalei**, a 37-foot Striker owned by Kirk Pearson, *Tel. 60.44.60/67.74.93*, operates out of the Hotel Bora Bora; **Te Aratai II**, *Tel. 67.71.96*, is Keith "Taaroa" Olson's 25-foot Farallon Fisherman. **Taravana** is a 50-foot prototype sportfishing/sailing catamaran owned by Richard Postma, which is based at the Hotel Bora Bora, *Tel. 67.77.79/60.44.05*. Half-day deep-sea fishing cruises, full-day trips to the atoll of Tupai, and three day charters to other islands can be arranged. Famous Hollywood stars who want to get away from it all find the privacy and tranquillity they seek when they charter the *Taravana*.

Lagoon Excursions by Outrigger Speed Canoe

Bora Bora's lovely lagoon offers many surprises, pleasures and photographic treasures. **A Boat Trip Around the Island** normally includes time for snorkeling, exploring a small Motu islet, walking on the living Coral Reef, searching for the graceful Manta Rays, sharing a kiss with the Sting Rays, diving for the Giant Mussels buried in the white sand lagoon bottom (the mussels are not removed from their habitat) and donning mask and snorkel to view the fish and coral in the Natural Aquarium. **Feeding the Sharks** is included in most **Circle Island Tours**, and is Bora Bora's most popular and thrilling excursion. A half-day tour starts at 3.500 CFP ($35). A **Picnic on a Motu** combined with your boat tour can mean you eat freshly grilled fish and fruit and drink coconut water, or you may be served a gourmet lunch, complete with cold drinks and wine. All lagoon activities depend on the whim of the weather and sea. Each of the following tour operators offers something different:

Bora Bora Lagoonarium, *Tel. 67.71.34*. A half-day excursion operated by Teura and Claudine Teheiura departs at 9:15am and returns you to your hotel at 12:45pm. Your destination is to their Lagoonarium on the northern point of Motu Piti A'au. A fenced-in section of the lagoon contains fish, sea turtles, rays, and a huge moray eel that likes to play kissy face when you feed it some fish. The cost of this tour is 4.000 CFP ($40), or you can stay all day and enjoy a picnic on the white sand beach, returning to your hotel at 5pm.

Matira Tours Excursions, *Tel. 67.70.97*, departs at 9am *from the end of Point Matira* at the beach of owner Ioane Tinorua, and returns at 3pm. His 25-passenger outrigger speed canoe will tour the island inside the lagoon, with visits to the sharks and manta rays, the *motu* islets and coral reef, and at the Lagoonarium for snorkeling. Ioane will prepare you a picnic on Motu Taufarii.

Moana Adventure Tours, *Tel. 67.61.41*. Owner Franck Sachsse offers barrier reef excursions, shark feeding and snorkeling, barbecue picnics on request, ordinary picnics on a *motu*, and private lagoon excursions.

Poeiti Tours, *Tel. 67.64.04*, is owned by Mike Henry, who also operates Taahana Tourisme between the Bora Bora Motel and the Bora Bora Beach Club. Mike, who is from New Zealand, offers a 3-hour express excursion for 3.500 CFP ($35). His full day circle island tour with picnic on a private *motu* departs daily at 9am and returns at 4:30pm. Your lunch includes a rum punch, assorted salads, chicken barbecue and chilled

French wine. The total cost is 5.300 CFP ($53) per adult, and half price for children under 10 years old.

Raanui Tours, *Tel. 67.61.79*, is operated by Arieta Onee *in Anau village*. Half-day excursions, from 9am to 12:30pm, include shark feeding, snorkeling, walking on the reef and a visit to Hiro's Bell on Toopua Motu.

BORA BORA'S SHARK FEEDING SHOW

Feeding the sharks is one of the most popular excursions on Bora Bora. Each morning the tourists board outrigger canoes to speed across the lagoon toward the barrier reef. When you make your own shark feeding tour, you will put on a mask and snorkel, and step into the clear waters of the warm lagoon, just inside the fringing reef. With just a few steps in water about 1.2 meters (4 feet) deep you will reach a rope that has been tied around two huge coral heads. You hold onto the rope for stability and watch through your mask as your guide performs the daily shark feeding show.

Thousands of tropical fish of all colors rush over to have a nibble at the huge head of tuna or mahi mahi that the guide holds out to them. You will see rainbow colored butterfly fish, black and white striped manini, the blue and yellow empress angel fish, the variegated and very territorial Picasso fish, plus many other families of more than 300 species of fish that inhabit the Bora Bora submarine gardens.

Gasps and squeals from the audience announce the arrival of the sharks as they appear for their breakfast. Sometimes you can see as many as 30 to 50 sharks, about 1.5 meters (5 feet) long. These are the Carcharhinus Melanopterus, commonly known as the **blackfin** *or* **blacktip reef shark***.*

The shark feeding show is so fascinating that you may forget your fear. As you are upcurrent of the sharks and the Tahitian guides keep their attention diverted with the proffered fish breakfast, the sharks normally pay little attention to their observers. If you are bold enough, you can even help to feed these hungry beasts. And if your nerve fails you, then the outrigger canoe is just a few steps away.

Shark Boy of Bora Bora, *Tel. 67.78.59/60.49.70*, is owned by Evan Temarii, whose four outrigger canoes make half-day excursions around the island, for 4.500 CFP ($45). Full-day excursions leave the hotel at 9:30am and return at 4:30pm, with fresh fruit and coconut water served on the *motu*. Evan works with the Moana Beach Parkroyal, Bora Bora Lagoon Resort and cruise ships. He has starred in two movies filmed in Bora Bora: starting when he was 11 years old with *Heart*, made for the Wonderful World of Disney, followed by *Call It Courage* when he was 18.

Evan traps the sharks with his bare hands and holds them over his head out of the water for the photographers. He was the first one to tame the sting rays, and even taught them how to kiss.

Teremoana Tours, *Tel. 67.71.38*, is operated by Noel "Nono" Leverd, who also owns Chez Nono pension on Matira Beach. His very popular excursions depart from the beach in front of his pension at 9:30am and return at 4:30pm. A fresh fruit lunch is served on the *motu*.

Sailing Charter Yachts

There is no big yacht charterer based in Bora Bora. You can rent a sailboat from one of the charter companies based in Tahiti, Moorea or Raiatea and sail to Bora Bora, or you can arrange for a yacht to be delivered to Bora Bora in time for your arrival. See Chapter 6, *Planning Your Trip*, section on Cruises.

Day Sailing Excursions

Coup De Coeur is a 40-foot Jeannot Sun Fizz sloop usually moored between the Moana Beach Parkroyal and the Hotel Bora Bora, owned by Thierry and Luisa Jubin, *Tel. 689/Radio Mahina 3698*. A half-day sail in the lagoon or open ocean is 4.500 CFP($45) and a full-day cruise with an on-board picnic is 8.700 CFP ($87). Weekend sails to Tupai atoll or cruises to the other Leeward Islands are also available for a maximum of six passengers.

Taaroa III, *Tel. 67.61.55*, is based at the Bora Bora Beach Club. Jean-Claude Rambert can accommodate 22 people aboard his Formula 40 racing catamaran for lagoon excursions and 10 passengers in the deep ocean. Morning excursions inside the lagoon are made daily except Sunday, from 9am to 12pm, for 4.500 CFP ($45); and sunset cruises, from 5:30 to 7pm daily except Sunday, cost 3.000 CFP ($30).

Taravana is a 50-foot prototype sportfishing/sailing catamaran owned by Richard Postma, which is based at the Hotel Bora Bora, *Tel. 67.77.79/ 60.44.05*. A maximum of 38 people can join a full-day picnic excursion inside the lagoon, departing at 9:30am and returning at 3:30pm. The sunset cruises aboard the *Taravana* are made for lovers, departing from the Hotel Bora Bora boat dock at 4:30pm and returning at 6:30pm. Private excursions can also be arranged. Some movie stars have even gotten married aboard Richard's famous catamaran.

Vehia, *Tel. 67.70.69*, is a 46-foot racing catamaran that can accommodate 35 people inside the lagoon and 8 passengers in the open ocean. Captain James Barbbadjan will take you for a half-day sail with drinks, a full-day excursion in the lagoon with a picnic, or for a sunset cruise from 4:30 to 6:30pm.

pub Morea,

Scuba Diving

Bora Bora's scuba diving clubs have qualified diving instructors who will introduce you to a large variety of diving spots inside the lagoon and beyond the barrier reef. Visibility is usually 20 to 30 meters, with an abundance of marine life, including manta rays, sharks, barracuda, dolphins and turtles. Initiation dives, fun dives and night dives are available, with up to four outings a day. Each regular dive costs about 5.500 CFP ($55), and two dives in the same day cost 10.000 CFP ($100), with all equipment included.

Bora Bora Calypso Club, *Tel. 67.63.33*, is on the mountainside between the Bora Bora Beach Club and Sofitel Marara, and is managed by Ben Heriteau; **Bora Bora Plongee**, *Tel. 67.64.83*, is based at the Yacht Club of Bora Bora, **Aqua Safari**, *Tel. 67.74.83*, is managed by Anne Condesse, at the Beach Club Bora Bora. **Bora Diving Center**, *Tel. 67.71.84*, is managed by Michel Condesse, next to the Hotel Bora Bora on the Matira side; **Moana Adventure Tours**, *Tel. 67.61.41*, at Pofai Bay, close to the Hotel Bora Bora, is run by Franck Sachsse; **Topdive**, *Tel. 60.50.50*, and **Maeva Scuba**, *Tel. 67.64.83*, are located at Point Matira; both under the management of Teiva Buchin.

Glass Bottom Boat Excursions

Moana Adventure Tours, *Tel. 67.61.41*, has a covered glass bottom boat that operates tours on Monday, Wednesday and Saturday, between 10:30 and 11:45am., for 2.750 CFP ($27.50), and half-price for children under 12 years.

Jet-Ski or Wave-Runner Excursions

You can rent a jet-ski for 30 minutes or 3 hours, with guides to take you around the island inside the lagoon. You'll stop on the *motu* islets, snorkel in beautiful coral gardens, feed the fish, visit the lagoonarium and even dive with the sharks and stingrays. The rental costs start at 10.000 CFP ($100) for one hour.

Heremiti Jet Tours, *Tel. 67.77.70*, is located in Vaitape; **Matira Jet Tours**, *Tel. 67.62.73*, and **Miki-Miki's Jet Tours**, *Tel. 67.76.44*, are located on the beach at Point Matira.

Pacific Bike Surf, *Tel. 67.63.48*, rents surf bikes at all the hotels on Bora Bora.

Bora Bora Parasail, *Tel. 67.70.34*, is located between the Bora Bora Beach Club and Sofitel Marara. Soar above the Bora Bora lagoon for 10 to 12 minutes, with gentle take-off and landing without even getting wet. Cost is 5.000 CFP ($50).

Water-skiing, *Tel. 67.63.76*, costs 3.800 CFP ($38) for a 15-minute tour.

SHOPPING

Galerie Alain and Linda, *Tel. 67.70.32*, is the name of an art gallery and boutique on the beach side of Pofai Bay, between Vaitape village and the Hotel Bora Bora. Linda, who is German, paints tableaux, and Alain, her French husband, paints the *pareos* and tee-shirts. They also exhibit paintings, sculptures and pottery by other artists who live in French Polynesia. If you're into metaphysics, you'll enjoy meeting Linda, a self-proclaimed "White Witch."

The Musée Jean Masson and **Galerie Rosine Temauri-Masson**, *Tel. 67.72.04*, is an art gallery at Matira Point, on the right just after the turnoff sign to the Moana Beach Parkroyal. Rosine, a native of Bora Bora, was married to a famous French artist named **Jean Masson**, who taught her to paint before he died. She raised her four children by selling her tableaux. Their paintings are on display and Rosine also sells *pareos*.

Garrick Yrondi has a gallery in the center that also contains the Bamboo House Restaurant and Gauguin's Garden, between Vaitape and the Hotel Bora Bora. His paintings, sculptures and bronzes are on display. Yrondi created the pink marble statue of *vahine ei'a*, the fish woman, which you should look for at the edge of the Motu Mute lagoon by the airport. This is the protector of Bora Bora.

Moana Art, *Tel. 67.70.33*, is adjacent to the Hotel Bora Bora beside Pofai Bay. This is the realm of photographer Erwin Christian, who has produced several beautiful and informative coffee table books on Bora Bora and all the islands in French Polynesia. In his boutique you will find his books, post cards and posters and greeting cards, in addition to local fashions and other souvenir items.

Art du Pacifique is in the same complex with the Yrondi gallery, the Bamboo House and Gauguin's Garden. This collection of South Seas primitive art includes ceremonial masks, drums and war clubs from the tribes of Papua New Guinea and other Melanesian and Polynesian islands.

Matira Pearls & Fashions, *Tel. 67.79.14*, is on the mountainside at Point Matira, just past the turnoff sign for the Moana Beach Parkroyal. The two American owners are both named Steve. Steve Fearon's family used to own the Hotel Bora Bora and the Hotel Tahara'a in Tahiti, and Steve Donnatin also worked in the hotel and restaurant business in Bora Bora before getting into the black pearl business. Stop by and meet them and have a look at their big collection of quality black pearls. Some of the big name black pearl companies from Tahiti, such as **Sibani** and **O.P.E.C.**, also have outlets in Bora Bora, and you will find black pearls in almost every shop you wander into.

All around the island you will find darling little boutiques and thatched roof stands that sell hand-printed *pareos*, tee-shirts, swimwear and all kinds of creative souvenir items that were actually made on Bora

Bora. Don't be fooled into buying an authentic made-in-Bali carving that has the name Bora Bora stamped on it. Look for **Boutique Gauguin** and **Honeymoon Boutique** in Pofai Bay, **Martine Creations** in Matira, **Boutique Hibiscus** opposite Club Med and **Pakalola Boutique** in Vaitape.

The **Arts and Crafts Center** at the Vaitape quay has grass skirts and coconut bras, shell jewelry and woven hats and bags that are handmade by the people who sell them.

PRACTICAL INFORMATION

Banks

Bora Bora has four banks, which are all located in Vaitape village. **Banque de Tahiti**, *Tel. 67.70.37,* **Banque Socredo,** *Tel. 67.71.11,* **Banque de Polynésie,** *Tel. 67.70.71,* and **Banque Westpac,** *Tel. 67.70.72.*

Doctors

There are three private doctors at the Vaitape Medical Cabinet and a government operated dispensary in the center of the village, *Tel. 67.70.77.* A dentist is located in the Pahia Center, *Tel. 67.70.55.*

Drugstore

The **Vaitape Pharmacy,** *Tel. 67.70.30,* is open Monday to Friday from 8am to 12pm and 3:30 to 6pm; on Saturday from 8am to 12pm and 5 to 6pm; and on Sunday from 9 to 9:30am.

Police

The French *gendarmerie* is on the mountainside opposite the quay in Vaitape, *Tel. 67.70.58.*

Post Office and Telecommunications Office

The **Post Office,** *Tel. 67.70.74,* is in Vaitape village on the circle island road near the quay. Hours are 8am to 3pm on Monday, 7am to 3pm Tuesday through Friday, and 7 to 9am on Saturday. All telecommunications and postal services are available here.

Tourist Bureau

The **Bora Bora Tourism Committee** has an informational desk at the airport and the main office is on the quay in Vaitape, *Tel. 67.76.36/ 67.70.31.* Hours are 7:30am to 12pm and 1:30 to 4pm Monday through Friday, and 8 to 11:30am on Saturday. **Taahana Tourisme,** *Tel. 689/ 67.64.04, in US 818/842-0057,* is an Excursions and Services Bureau located between the Bora Bora Motel and Bora Bora Beach Club at Matira Beach. Manager Mike Henry and his staff can arrange land, sea and sky tours and excursions for some 20 activities, as well as handling car, scooter and bicycle rentals. Open daily 8am to 7pm.

21. MAUPITI

If you appreciate the beauty of Bora Bora but not the mass tourism, **Maupiti** offers similar scenery, peace and tranquillity, as well as an authentic Polynesian experience, with genuinely friendly people who are not burned out by seeing too many tourists.

Lying just 40 kilometers (25 miles) west of bustling Bora Bora, Maupiti is considered the hidden jewel in the necklace of emerald islands and atolls that make up the Society Islands. Some people say it's one of the prettiest islands in the South Seas.

Like Bora Bora, Maupiti has a central island with a high mountain range of volcanic origins, and is surrounded by a shallow, sparkling lagoon with five long offshore *motu* islets bordered by beautiful white sand beaches. **Onoiau** is the name of a narrow pass leading into the lagoon. This formerly dangerous pass is more easily navigable since channel markers were added. The clear turquoise lagoon has pretty coral gardens, a plentiful supply of edible fish, lobsters, tridacna clams, *vana*, an edible sea urchin, and even *varo*, a sea centipede that is sought by gourmets. The *motus* provide coral gardens for watermelon and cantaloupe plantations, as well as secluded white sand beaches for sunbathing and excellent snorkeling grounds a few feet into the lagoon.

Mount Teurafaatiu rises 380 meters (1,246 feet) above the central island, and is relatively easy to scale for panoramic views. **Point Tereia** on the main island is a lovely white sand beach in a natural environment, a favorite swimming site for the young people from the villages. Some of the older folks compare this beach to what Point Matira in Bora Bora was like 50 years ago. From here you can walk across the lagoon to the *motu*, in waste-deep water. Although you may encounter a few curious sharks, just hit the water hard with the palm of your hand and yell at them, and they will swim away. It works for the locals, and no tourists have been injured to date by the "friendly" sharks who grew up inside the lagoon.

Geologists say that Maupiti is the oldest of the high islands in the Society archipelago, and was formed some four million years ago.

Dr. Yosihiko H. Sinoto and Dr. Kenneth P. Emory of the Bernice P. Bishop Museum in Honolulu excavated a burial site in Maupiti in 1962 and 1963, unearthing 13 skeletons from the ninth century. Inside the tombs on Motu Paeao were adzes, fish-hooks, lures and sperm whale tooth pendants that date back to circa 850 AD. This is one of the oldest archaeological sites in the Society Islands, and one of the most important. Doctor Sinoto said that the whale tooth pendants were the first material cultural link between the Society Islands and the New Zealand Maoris.

Other archaeological sites include two more *marae* on the *motus* and two *maraes* on the high island. In the valley of Heranae are petroglyphs representing turtles, a sacred animal for the ancient Maohi people.

At one time there were nine districts and nine royal Maohi chiefs on Maurua Ite Ra, as Maupiti was then called. Chiefs came from other islands to meet at the royal Marae Vaiahu for gatherings that included investiture ceremonies. A huge boulder at the stone temple has been engraved with the names of these nine chiefs, who came from Rimatara, Raivavae, Rapa, Atiu in the Cook Islands, and Hawaii. One of these kings was said to have come from Malaysia.

Maupiti was discovered by the Dutch explorer Roggeveen in 1722, 45 years before Tahiti was discovered by Samuel Wallis. It was united with Bora Bora during the reign of the last royal family. The nine villages of ancient times have dwindled to the three contiguous villages of Vai'ea, Fararuru and Pauma, where most of the 1,127 inhabitants live.

ARRIVALS & DEPARTURES
Arriving By Air
Air Tahiti, *Tel. 86.42.42/86.41.84*, has four flights a week from Tahiti to Maupiti, with stops in Raiatea and/or Bora Bora. The Tuesday flight leaves Tahiti at 6:15am, stopping in Raiatea and arriving in Maupiti at 7:25am. On Friday morning a flight leaves Tahiti at 6am, stopping in Raiatea and Bora Bora, arriving in Maupiti at 7:30am. On Friday afternoon the flight leaves Tahiti at 2:55pm, stopping in Raiatea and arriving in Maupiti at 4:05pm. On Sunday afternoon Air Tahiti leaves Papeete at 3:30pm, stops in Raiatea and Bora Bora, and arrives in Maupiti at 5pm.

The Maupiti airstrip is located on a *motu* islet across the lagoon from the main village. If you have reservations for a place to stay then you will be met at the airport and taken by boat to the pension. Otherwise, you can catch a ride with one of the taxi boats that goes to the airport for each flight arrival. The one-way airfares are: 13.335 CFP ($133.35) between Tahiti and Maupiti; 5.880 CFP ($58.80) between Raiatea and Maupiti; and 5.565 CFP ($55.65) between Bora Bora and Maupiti.

MAUPITI

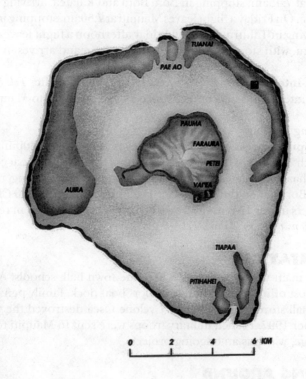

TUANAI

PAE AO

PAUMA

FARAURA

PETEI

VAI'EA

AURIA

TIAPAA

PITIHAHEI

0   2   4   6 KM

Arriving By Boat

Maupiti Express, *Tel. 67.66.69*, arrives in Maupiti from Bora Bora at 10am each Tuesday, Thursday, Saturday and Sunday, to spend the day. The one-way fare is 3.000 CFP ($30). Passengers under 15 years and over 60 years have a 20 percent reduction. *Reservations office in Tahiti, Tel. 48.05.81.*

Departing By Air

Air Tahiti, *Tel. 67.80.20/67.81.24*; *Tahiti Reservations Tel. 86.42.42/ 86.41.84.* Air Tahiti has four flights from Maupiti to Papeete each week, stopping at Bora Bora and/or Raiatea enroute. The Tuesday flight leaves Maupiti at 7:45am, stopping in Bora Bora and Raiatea, arriving in Tahiti at 9:15am. On Friday a flight leaves Maupiti at 7:50am, stopping in Raiatea and arriving in Tahiti at 9am. On Friday afternoon a flight leaves Maupiti at 4:25pm, with stops in Bora Bora and Raiatea, and arrives in Tahiti at 5:55pm.

Heli-Inter Polynesie, *Tel. 67.62.59*, and **Heli-Pacific**, *Tel. 85.68.00*, provide inter-island helicopter service from Bora Bora to Maupiti.

Departing By Boat

Maupiti Express, *Tel. 67.66.69*, leaves Maupiti at 4:30pm for Bora Bora each Tuesday, Thursday, Saturday and Sunday. The boat continues on to Tahaa and Raiatea each Wednesday and Friday morning, returning to Bora Bora late in the afternoon. The one-way fare is 3.000 CFP ($30). Passengers under 15 years and over 60 years have a 20 percent reduction. *Reservations office in Tahiti, Tel. 48.05.81.*

ORIENTATION

The main village is **Vai'ea**, where the town hall, schools, Air Tahiti office, post office, bank, church, airport boat dock, family pensions and a few small stores existed before Cyclone Osea destroyed the village in November 1997. French military troops were sent to Maupiti to rebuild the village, which is an ongoing project.

GETTING AROUND

Bicycles

Suzanne Tetuahiti has rental bicycles.

WHERE TO STAY & EAT

Note: The eye of Cyclone Osea passed over the island of Maupiti on November 25, 1997, and destroyed all the pensions and tourist lodgings, as well as 95% of the other structures on the island and *motu* islets. Some of the pensions are being rebuilt, while others wait for help from the government before rebuilding. The following listings tell you what pensions existed prior to the cyclone. Check with the Tahiti Tourist Bureau for an update on reconstruction.

Moderate
    KURIRI VILLAGE, *B.P. 23, Vai'ea, Maupiti. No telephone. Fax 689/ 67.82.00. Beside the ocean on Motu Tiapa'a, an islet 30 minutes by boat from the airport. Boat transfers are provided. Rates: bungalow with half-pension, including breakfast and dinner 8.000 CFP ($80) person; bungalow with full-pension, including breakfast, lunch and dinner 10.000 CFP ($100) person; bungalow with all meals and activities included 15.000 CFP ($150) person. Half-price for child under 12 years. Add 1% value added tax to room rates and meal plan. No credit cards.*

    Each of the four *fares* contains a double bedroom with mosquito net and private bathroom with cold water. House linens are furnished. Snorkeling equipment, outrigger canoe and kayak are available. Activities can be all-inclusive or selected at extra cost.

    FARE PA'EAO, *B.P. 33, Vai'ea, Maupiti. Tel/Fax 689/67.81.01. On Motu Pa'eao, 10 minutes by boat from the airport. Round-trip canoe transfers 1.000 CFP ($10) per person. EP Rates: bungalow 6.000 CFP ($60) single/ double; meal plan with breakfast, lunch and dinner, add 5.000 CFP ($50) per person. Extra mattress 1.500 CFP ($15). Half-price meals for child under 12 years. Add 1% value added tax to room rates and meal plan. No credit cards.*

    Three *fares* have a double bedroom and private bathroom with cold water. House linens are supplied and there is a restaurant on the premises.

    PENSION AUIRA, *B.P. 2, Vai'ea, Maupiti. Tel./Fax 689/67.80.26. On Motu Auira, 15 minutes by boat from the airport. Round-trip boat transfers 2.000 CFP ($20) per person. Rates: garden fare with breakfast and dinner 5.000 CFP ($50) person; garden fare with breakfast, lunch and dinner 7.000 CFP ($70) per person; beach fare with breakfast and dinner 6.000 CFP ($60) per person; beach fare with all meals 8.000 CFP ($80) per person; camping 1.000 CFP ($10) per camper per day. Child 3-12 years half-price. Add 1% value added tax to room rates and meal plan. Mastercard, Visa.*

    There are seven *fares*: 2 beach *fares* each contain a double bed and a single bed and a private bathroom with cold water; one family bungalow has a double and a single bed, plus a mezzanine with one double bed, a single bed on the terrace, and a private bathroom with cold water. Four garden *fares* each contain one double bed and a private bathroom with cold water. House linens are furnished. There is also a camp ground with a dining room *fare* and communal bath facilities with cold water. A restaurant-bar is on the premises. Paddle canoes are available for clients.

Inexpensive
PENSION PAPAHANI, *B.P. 1, Vai'ea, Maupiti. Tel. 689/67.81.58. On Motu Auira, 15 minutes by boat from the airport. Round-trip transfers 1.000 CFP ($10) per person. AP Rates: room with breakfast, lunch and dinner 6.500 CFP ($65) person per day; bungalow with all meals 7.500 CFP ($75) person per day. Add 1% value added tax to room rates and meal plan. No credit cards.*

There are three *fares* here. One *fare* has four rooms, each with one double bed. A dining room *fare* and communal bath facilities with cold water are outside. Two *fares* each have a bedroom and private bathroom with cold water. House linens are supplied.

CHEZ FLORIETTE, *B. P. 43, Vai'ea, Maupiti. Tel. 689/67.80.85. Beside lagoon in Vai'ea village, one kilometer (.62 miles) from the ferry dock and three kilometers (1.9 miles) from the airport. Round-trip boat transfers and all activities are included. Rates: Room with breakfast and dinner 5.000 CFP ($50) single; 7.800 CFP ($78) double; room with all meals 6.500 CFP ($65) single; 11.800 CFP ($118) double. Half-price for child under 12 years. Add 1% value added tax to room rates and meal plan. No credit cards.*

A four-bedroom house has two rooms with one double and one single bed in each room; two rooms have a double bed in each room. Guests share the living room with television, dining room, kitchen and communal bathroom with cold water. House linens are furnished.

PENSION ERI, *Vai'ea, Maupiti. Tel. 689/67.81.29. Beside the lagoon in Vai'ea village, 700 meters (763 yards) from the ferry dock and three kilometers from the airport. Round-trip boat transfers 1.000 CFP ($10) per person. Rates: Room with breakfast 2.500 CFP ($25) person; room with breakfast and dinner 4.800 CFP ($48) per person; room with all meals 5.500 CFP ($55) per person. Half-price for child under 12 years. Add 1% value added tax to room rates and meal plan. No credit cards.*

A four-bedroom house, with a double bed in each room. Guests share the kitchen, living room and bathroom with cold water. House linens are furnished.

PENSION TAMATI, *Vai'ea, Maupiti. Tel. 689/67.80.10. On the mountain side in the middle of Vai'ea village, 600 meters (1,968 feet) from the ferry dock and three kilometers (1.9 miles) from the airport. Round-trip boat transfers 800 CFP ($8) per person. Rates: room and breakfast 2.000 CFP ($20) per person; room with breakfast and dinner 3.300 CFP ($33) per person; room with all meals 4.600 CFP ($46) per person. Half-price for child under 12 years. Add 1% value added tax to room rates and meal plan. No credit cards.*

This is a two-story house with eight rooms: three rooms have a double and single bed; three rooms have a double bed and private bathroom with cold water; two rooms have one double and one single bed. All guests share a communal bathroom with cold water, the living room, dining room and kitchen. House linens are supplied.

PENSION MARAU, *Vai'ea, Maupiti. Tel. 689/67.81.19. On the mountain side in Vai'ea, 1.2 kilometers (.74 feet) from the boat dock and 3 kilometers (1.9 miles) from the airport. Round-trip boat transfers provided. Rates: room with breakfast and dinner 4.500 CFP ($45) per person; room with all meals 6.000 CFP ($60) per person. Add 1% value added tax to room rates and meal plan. No credit cards.*

This is a three bedroom house with guests sharing the living room, dining room, kitchen, terrace and communal bathroom with cold water. House linens are furnished.

CHEZ MARETA, *Vai'ea, Maupiti. Tel. 689/67.80.25. Beside the lagoon in Vai'ea village, 700 meters (763 yards) from the ferry dock and three kilometers (1.9 miles) from the airport. Round-trip boat transfers 800 CFP ($8) per person. Rates: room only 1.000 CFP ($10) per person; room with breakfast and dinner 3.000 CFP ($30) per person; room with all meals 4.000 CFP ($40) per person. Add 1% value added tax to room rates and meal plan. No credit cards.*

A two-bedroom house has a double bed in each room. Guests share the living room, dining room, kitchen, terrace and communal bathroom with cold water. House linens are supplied.

SEEING THE SIGHTS

You can walk around the main island of Maupiti in about two or three hours, depending on your pace, and how many times you stop to take pictures, shake down a ripe mango from a roadside tree or stop for a swim in the inviting lagoon. A road circles the island for 9.6 kilometers (5.9 miles). You can also bike around the island and visit the petroglyphs of turtles, the family and royal *marae* stone temples and other archeological sites. The *maraes* are located on some of the *motu* islets, as well as the central island.

SPORTS & RECREATION

Lagoon Excursions

Haranai Cruiser is a 28-foot covered boat for 20-30 people, owned by Richard Tefaatau, who takes groups on lagoon excursions, with a picnic on the *motu* if requested. Richard also makes trips to visit Mopelia, an atoll just west of Maupiti.

The hosts at each pension normally organize the activities for their guests, which include snorkeling and shelling, outrigger paddle canoes, fishing in the lagoon and pass for lobster and fish, and picnics on the *motu*.

22. TUAMOTU ISLANDS

The 77 atolls and one upraised island that form the **Tuamotu Archipelago** are mere specks of land out in the heart of the trade wind, lost in the vastness of the blue Pacific. Sprinkled across ten latitudes and covering a length of 1,500 kilometers (930 miles) and a width of 500 kilometers (310 miles), these are some of the most remote islands in the world.

This vast collection of coral islets conjures up castaway dreams on a tropical isle, the ultimate get-away for rejuvenation of the body and soul. Tiny green oases floating in the desert of the sea, with names as exotic as the trade winds and coconut trees. Wild windswept beaches, the sea and sunshine. And only the sound of the surf and the cries of the sea birds for company. Fragrant *miki miki* shrubs blend perfumes with aromas of salt spray and blossoms from the *tiare kahaia*, *geo geo* and *gapata* trees. The lagoons shimmer with a brilliance of light and color unsurpassed, and a submerged landscape of untouched magic and awesome beauty awaits beneath the sun-gilded waters tinged in turquoise.

Polynesian explorers, sailing from their homeland in the West, settled on the lonely shores of these atolls centuries ago. Pakamotu, they called their new home—a cloud of islands. Outcast chiefs from Tahiti and the Marquesas Islands named them Paumotu, the Submissive or Conquered Islands, the isles of Exiles. European ships from many nations rode the treacherous reef in this maritime maze, thus adding the names Low or Dangerous Archipelago and the Labyrinth. The **Paumotu people** now call their home the Tuamotu—many islands.

More than 400 varieties of fantastic, rainbow-hued fish glint like ornaments of gold in the iridescent waters of the sheltered lagoons, providing hours of enchantment for snorkelers and scuba divers. On many of the atolls you can visit black pearl farms and fish parks inside the lagoons, take boat tours to visit the various *motu* islets and picnic under the black-eyed gaze of the white fairy tern.

"MANY LAGOONS" BY RALPH VARADY

You have to see an atoll to get its feeling. It leaves a vastly different impression than a high island does. There is something about the atolls that is magnetic. They are lost and, for the greater part, deserted, full of flies and copra bugs. They are remote, a death trap in a hurricane, a danger to navigation and often inaccessible except by small boat. They offer the minimum of human comfort, their maximum asset being their copra; and yet there is something wonderful about them, and truly they belong to the list of nature's wonders.

Many of the islands are uninhabited and seldom visited. Nevertheless, the traveler who wanders into this maritime maze will be rewarded by what he sees. These Dangerous Islands are not sizable or comfortable, but they are rich in the realm of color. The debauch of color found in the Tuamotu lagoons is incomparable to that of any other island group.

Personally, I hope that these islands never have "facilities" so that they will be kept as they are now: unspoiled, beautiful and natural. It is good to know that some of these islands will remain out of reach of a fast-moving civilization."

You may also be invited to join in the volleyball and soccer games played by the villagers. You can go along on fishing expeditions, hunt for tiny shells to string into pretty necklaces, learn to weave hats, mats and baskets from palm fronds, and eat delicious seafood direct from its shell while you stand at the edge of a Technicolor reef. In the evening you can sit beside the Paumotu musicians under a starlit sky, watching the Southern Cross as you listen to melodic island tunes being played on guitars and ukuleles. Their songs tell of old gods and heroes, the spirits of sharks and fish, destructive hurricanes, people lost at sea, shipwrecks on the treacherous reef, *vahines* and *l'amour*.

At least two dozen of these atolls have airstrips and regular air service from Tahiti, and several inter-island trading schooners transport supplies and passengers. The lack of potable water remains a problem on many of these remote islands, while solar energy provides electricity and hot water for villages and remote pearl farms. This archipelago is rapidly being developed, with modern telecommunications services now reaching even the most distant of the settled islands.

Unfortunately, we are not able to give the details of each atoll in this book, but you can obtain a 1998 edition of *Le Guide*, which is published by the Tahiti Tourist Bureau, with information on each atoll, plus pictures, descriptions and the rates for each small hotel, pension, hostel, guest house and campground that exists in French Polynesia. The contact numbers are listed in the *Basic Information* chapter under *Where to Find More Information About Tahiti & French Polynesia.*

The atolls of Rangiroa, Manihi, Tikehau and Fakarava, which are described below, offer either international class hotels, small hotels, pensions, houses or a room in a family home, where guests can find simple accommodations. These are the destinations most frequently visited by tourists, but the number of visitors in the Tuamotus is so minute that these islands still offer a natural environment and miles of empty beaches.

RANGIROA

Rangiroa, also called **Rairoa**, means 'long sky' in the Paumotu dialect, the language of the Polynesian inhabitants. The coral ring encircling the pear-shaped atoll of Rangiroa contains more than 240 *motu* islets, separated by at least 100 very shallow *hoa* channels and three passes. The Tiputa Pass and Avatoru Pass on the north of the atoll are deep and wide enough for ships to enter the lagoon, and the Tivaru Pass on the west is narrow and shallow. A vast inland sea measures approximately 75 kilometers (47 miles) long by 25 kilometers (16 miles) wide, covering a distance of 1,020 square kilometers (393 square miles). This is the largest atoll in the Southern Hemisphere and the second largest in the world, after Kwajalein atoll in the Marshall Islands of Micronesia.

Cultivation pits and *marae* temples of coral stone are remains of settlements that existed on Rangiroa during the 14th and 15th centuries. To protect themselves from the aggressive 'Parata' warriors from the atoll of Anaa, the Rangiroa inhabitants took refuge on the southwest side of the atoll, close to Motu Taeo'o, known today as the Blue Lagoon. This village was destroyed by a natural disaster, probably a *tsunami*, in 1560, and the entire population disappeared.

Rangiroa and its surrounding atolls made up small independent kingdoms in the 17th and 18th centuries, and were known as the Mihiroa. Political relations were established with Tahiti, but the bloody battles with Anaa exterminated most of Rangiroa's population by 1800. The ancestors of Tahiti's King Pomare I were Anaa chiefs, and through his intervention the marauders ended their aggressions and cannibalism with their rival clans. The surviving Rangiroans went to the nearby atoll of Tikehau and to Tautira in Tahiti Iti, and returned to their atoll between 1823 and 1826.

The Dutch explorer Le Maire discovered Rangiroa in 1616, but the first European settlers did not arrive until 1851. The missionaries insisted that the population be grouped in Avatoru and Tiputa rather than dispersing in small villages around the atoll, where they could more likely continue their heathenistic practices. A cyclone in 1906 destroyed the village of Tivaru, and today the population of 1,913 inhabitants reside in the villages of Avatoru and Tiputa.

RANGIROA

TIVARO

Sables Roses

OTEPIPI

Hotel Kia Ora Sauvage

TIPUTA

Hotel Rangiroa Village

Relais Marama (diving center)

Hotel Kia Ora Village

Relais Mihiroa PNHC

Rangiroa Paradise (diving center)

Rangiroa Beach Club

Hotel Kiaroa Lagoon PNHC

The Six Passengers (diving center)

AVATORU

Blue Lagoon

FENUAROA

0 5 10 15 20 KM

Rangiroa is the administrative center of the northern Tuamotu atolls. Children from the small atolls are sent to junior high school and technical schools in Rangiroa, where they are lodged throughout the school year, some of the students returning to their homes only during the two month vacation in July and August.

Rangiroa's lagoon is world famous for unsurpassed scuba diving in the warmest and clearest water you can dream of. Favorite excursions include "shooting the pass," where hundreds of fish, moray eels and sharks swim beside and below you, swept along by the strong currents. You can view this exciting spectacle aboard a glass-bottom boat, or jump into the water with mask, snorkel, fins or even scuba diving bottles. Vacation memories are also made aboard a pedal boat, paddling an outrigger canoe, sailing inside the lagoon, line or drag fishing, on boat excursions to the pink sand beach of Vahituri, while admiring the fossilized coral formations on Reef Island, and during a full day picnic trip across the lagoon to Blue Lagoon and Motu Taeo'o.

Among this wealth of scenery is an attractive selection of international resort hotels, small hotels with thatched roof bungalows and simple family owned pensions with fresh lagoon fish on the menu. Across the lagoon from the villages are small hotels and camps that can be reached only by boat, where you can walk on beaches as remote as Robinson Crusoe's. On these beautiful little *motu* islets you can live a *sauvage* simplified life with lots of fresh food from the reef and lagoon.

ARRIVALS & DEPARTURES

Arriving By Air

Air Tahiti has one or two direct flights daily between Tahiti and Rangiroa and three or four direct flights on the weekends. The 55-minute non-stop flight is 14.210 CFP ($142.10) one-way for adults, tax included. You can also fly from Bora Bora to Rangiroa with 1 hour 20 minute direct flights on Wednesday, Friday and Sunday, for 21.735 CFP ($21.735). Flight service is also provided from Manihi, Tikehau, Fakarava, Arutua, Mataiva, Puka Puka, and the Marquesas Islands of Ua Pou and Atuona.

If you have reservations with a hotel, pension or yacht charter company, then you will be met at the airport and driven to your hotel. **Air Tahiti reservations**: *Tahiti, Tel. 86.42.42/86.41.84.*

Arriving By Boat

St. Xavier Maris Stella, *Tel. 42.23.58*, can transport 12 passengers with berths in cabins for 5.000 CFP ($50), or on the bridge for 2.000 CFP ($20). Three meals a day cost 2.000 CFP ($20) per person. Rangiroa is the first stop after a 20 hour crossing from Tahiti. The ship leaves Papeete every 15 days. Other inter-island ships that call at Rangiroa are: **Dory**, *Tel.*

42.30.55, **Manava II**, Tel. 43.83.84/42.25.53; and **Vai Aito**, *Tel. 43.99.96*. See more information in Chapter 6, *Planning Your Trip.*

Departing By Air

You can fly from Rangiroa direct to Tahiti, Bora Bora, Manihi, Tikehau, Fakarava, Kaukura, Apataki, Ahe, Puka Puka, and Napuka by **Air Tahiti**, *Tel. 96.05.03/96.03.41 in Rangiroa.* Tickets can be purchased at the airport. If you already have reservations and a ticket, reconfirmations should be made one day in advance, and most hotels will take care of this for you. Check-in time at the airport is one hour before scheduled departure.

Departing By Boat

St. Xavier Maris Stella, *Tel. 42.23.58*, leaves Rangiroa every 15 days for Ahe, Manihi, and all the western Tuamotu atolls, before returning to Papeete. Other inter-island ships that call at Rangiroa are: **Dory**, *Tel. 42.30.55*, which leaves Rangiroa once a week for Arutua, Kaukura and Papeete; **Manava II**, *Tel. 43.83.84/42.25.53*, which leaves Rangiroa every 15 days for Arutua, Apataki, Toau and Papeete; **Rairoa Nui**, *Tel. 42.91.69*, which leaves Rangiroa once a week for Papeete; and **Vai Aito**, *Tel. 43.99.96*, which leaves Rangiroa twice a month for Ahe, Manihi, Aratika, Kauehi, Raraka, Fakarava, Toau, Apataki, Kaukura and Papeete.

The *Aranui* calls at Rangiroa at the end of its 16-day round-trip voyage from Papeete to the Marquesas Islands, and continues on to Tahiti, arriving the following morning in Papeete. See more information in Chapter 6, *Planning Your Trip.*

ORIENTATION

The villages of **Avatoru** and **Tiputa** are located on the northern coast, where most of the population lives beside the deep passes. In these two villages you will find the churches, schools, small food stores and post offices. It is easy to walk around both villages, but you will probably find that the people in Tiputa village are more friendly to tourists. The airport and most of the hotels and pensions are located between the Tiputa Pass and Avatoru, a 45-minute boat ride apart.

You can explore Avatoru village to the Tiputa Pass by bicycle, minimoke or Fun Car, a two-passenger vehicle that is a cross between a scooter and a car. You have to take a boat across the Tiputa Pass to get to the village, which can be easily discovered in a short walk. Overlooking the Tiputa Pass is **Ohutu Point**, complete with covered picnic tables, benches and shade trees. This is a favorite destination in late afternoon, when dolphins can often be seen playing in the swift current that flows through the pass, between the open ocean and the interior lagoon.

GETTING AROUND

A flat paved road 10 kilometers (6.2 miles) long extends from the Avatoru Pass to the Tiputa Pass, with the ocean on one side and the lagoon on the other side. Most of the hotels and pensions are on the lagoon side of this road and the airport is about half-way between the two passes. The hosts at the hotels and pensions meet their guests at the airport and provide transportation to the lodging. To get to Tiputa from the Avatoru side you can usually catch a ride aboard one of the speedboats that travels between the boat dock adjacent to Pension Glorinne and Tiputa village.

Car, Scooter & Bicycle Rentals

Rangi-Location Europcar, *Tel 96.04.92,* has an office near Avatoru village and a desk at the Kia Ora Village. A Fiat Panda rents for 5.500 CFP ($55) for 4 hours, 6.500 CFP ($65) for 8 hours and 7.500 CFP ($75) for 24 hours. A Fun Car is a cross between a car and a scooter and rents for 2.000 CFP ($20) for 1 hour and 5.000 CFP ($50) for 4 hours. Scooter rates start at 4.000 CFP ($40) for 4 hours. These rates include unlimited mileage and insurance. Gas is extra. Bicycles can be rented for 800 CFP ($8) for four hours and 1.200 CFP ($12) for eight hours. Longer rentals are possible.

Arenahio Locations is operated by Pomare Temaehu *in Avatoru, Tel. 96.82.85,* with bicycle and scooter rentals. Bicycles can also be rented from several of the hotels and pensions.

Taxis

Rangi-Location, *Tel. 96.03.28,* provides taxi service in a 6-passenger mini-bus.

WHERE TO STAY

Expensive

HOTEL KIA ORA VILLAGE RANGIROA, *B.P. 1, Avatoru, Rangiroa; Tel. 689/96.03.84/96.02.22; Fax 689/96.04.93/96.02.20. Reservations: B.P. 4607, Papeete, Tahiti. Tel. 689/42.86.75; Fax 689/41.30.40. 45 units beside the lagoon in Avatoru commune, three kilometers (1.9 miles) east of the airport. EP Rates single/double: beach bungalow or family size garden suite 32.000 CFP ($320); overwater bungalow 49.000 CFP ($490). Additional person add 4.500 CFP ($45). Meal plan with breakfast and dinner is 5.500 CFP ($55) per person; meal plan with breakfast, lunch and dinner is 8.000 CFP ($80) per person. Round-trip transfers are provided. Add 7% hotel tax to room rates and 1% value added tax to room rates and meal plan. All major credit cards.*

Like a lovely jewel sparkling in the sunshine, the Kia Ora Village beams an invitation to you if you are sitting on the left side of the Air Tahiti flight when the plane approaches the airport in Rangiroa. Viewed from the air or from the roadside, the 40 acres of gardens and coconut trees and the white sand beach almost a mile long make a perfect setting for a Polynesian style hotel. And the coral studded lagoon that is the center of this precious gem glitters in agreement.

The Kia Ora Village was the first international class hotel on Rangiroa. It was opened in 1973 by three former Club Med employees with foresight. Laris Kindynis, Robin Angely and Serge Arnoux ran a successful operation for almost two decades, before selling the 30-bungalow hotel to the Tokyo Coca-Cola Bottling Company in 1990. The new management has continued to improve and expand the hotel, while maintaining a people-size establishment, where you can still feel you're "away from the madding crowd."

The Kia Ora Village now offers 30 beach bungalows situated along a very white sand beach and 5 garden suites. The highlights of these deluxe accommodations are the 10 overwater bungalows, which are so beautiful, comfortable and romantic you'll never want to leave. These spacious bungalows, made of thatched roofs, local woods and woven bamboo walls, are junior suites with a separate lounge and a glass bottom coffee table for fish watching. That can be a full-time occupation in Rangiroa's lagoon, with its wealth of marine flora and fauna. The decor is a subtle Polynesian design in cool colors to complement the blues and greens of the lagoon. Each overwater unit has a shiny, modern bathroom, telephone and safe, plus a big terrace and a private solarium, with steps leading into the inviting lagoon. All the bungalows at Kia Ora Village have private bathrooms with hot water showers, overhead fans, mini-refrigerators and hair-dryers.

Even if you're not staying in an overwater bungalow you can still fish watch through the floor of the spacious bar and lounge, or walk along the pier to see a variety of brightly colored tropical fish as they swim through the coral gardens in the translucent water. Or you can don mask and snorkel and jump in with them. The hotel provides free snorkeling equipment for its guests, as well as windsurf boards, fishing facilities, tennis, table tennis, French bowls, arts and crafts exhibits, frequent shows of Tahitian songs and dances, a boat ride to visit the little village of Tiputa, and a ride to the church on Sunday morning. Optional activities include pedal boat, bicycle and scooter rentals, glass bottom boat rides to snorkel and feed the sharks, lagoon tours to visit the dolphins and drift through the passes, picnic excursions to *motu* islets on the other side of the lagoon, deep-sea fishing, scuba diving, parasailing, visits to a black pearl farm, boat rentals, and excursions to visit the Kia Ora Sauvage.

The open-air dining room faces the white sand beach and shining lagoon, and the menu selections have been chosen to please the discerning clientele, who come from all parts of the world. Local fish and lobster are favorite choices, along with the fine French cuisine and the sumptuous buffet. The wine cellar contains just the right vintage to enhance your meal, and the service provided by the friendly staff is also commendable.

RANGIROA PEARL BEACH RESORT, *Reservations B.P. 718, 98713, Papeete, Tahiti; Tel. 689/43.90.04; Fax 689/41.39.23. 40 units. EP Rates single/double: beach suite 35.000 CFP ($350); deluxe overwater bungalow 46.000 CFP ($460); third person 4.000 CFP ($40). Meal plan with breakfast and dinner add 6.000 CFP ($60) per person; meal plan with breakfast, lunch and dinner add 8.500 CFP ($85) per person; full American breakfast 1.950 CFP ($19.50); outrigger canoe breakfast 2.950 CFP ($29.50); romantic breakfast on the beach 2.900 CFP ($29); private honeymoon champagne dinner under the stars 8.000 CFP ($80); fruit basket 2.000 CFP ($20); bottle of wine 2.400 CFP ($24); bottle of champagne 6.000 CFP ($60). One-way transfer from airport 600 CFP ($6) per person. Add 7% hotel tax to room rates and 1% value added tax to room rates and meal plan. All major credit cards.*

This five-star deluxe hotel is due to open in June, 1999, with 15 beach suites and 25 deluxe overwater bungalows. All the Polynesian style bungalows will have overhead fans, a mini-bar refrigerator, coffee/tea facilities, showers, international direct dial telephones, safes, hair-dryers and a terrace. The beach bungalows will also have a Jacuzzi and the overwater bungalows will have a glass bottom table for fish-watching. The hotel will have a restaurant and bar, boutique, black pearl shop, fresh water swimming pool, game room with billiards, and television/video room. Activities will include rental bicycles, outrigger canoes, kayaks, windsurf boards, snorkeling equipment, scuba diving, day sailing, reef walks, lagoon fishing, deep-sea fishing, boat excursions and sunset cruises.

HOTEL KIA ORA SAUVAGE RANGIROA, *Hotel Kia Ora Village, B.P. 1, Avatoru, Rangiroa; Tel. 689/96.03.84/96.02.22; Fax 689/96.04.93/96.02.20. Reservations: B.P. 4607, Papeete, Tahiti, Tel. 689/42.86.75; Fax 689/41.30.40. On a private motu islet, three kilometers (1.9 miles) east of the airport to Kia Ora Village, then one hour by boat across the lagoon to Motu Avea, 40 kilometers (25 miles) from main village. Round-trip car transfers included between airport and Kia Ora Village. Round-trip boat transfers to Kia Ora Sauvage are 7.500 CFP ($75) per person. EP Rates: beach bungalow single/double 24.000 CFP ($240); third person add 4.500 CFP ($45). Meal plan with breakfast, lunch and dinner included is 7.000 CFP ($70) per person. Add 7% hotel tax to room rates and 1% value added tax to room rates and meal plan. All major credit cards.*

Here is your ultimate Robinson Crusoe island. There are only five bungalows for a maximum of 12 guests. What you don't have here is of primary importance for your tranquillity and totally relaxed getaway. No electricity, no telephones, no jet-skis, no excursion boats or helicopters buzzing around and overhead the lagoon, no cars, motorcycles and other traffic noises, and no roosters to crow all night. Ugo and Celine are your host and hostess, and they will take care of your meals, which are served family style in the restaurant-bar or on the beach. Your bungalow is an attractive thatched roof *fare* built of local woods, and contains a king-size bed and a single bed, a private bathroom and a terrace overlooking the white sand beach. Two kerosene lamps are placed on your front steps each evening.

Activities include boat trips to nearby *motu* islets, fishing for dinner in the lagoon and trips to the reef for appetizers. You can also paddle an outrigger canoe, windsurf or feed the sharks. This little hotel is a favorite retreat for honeymooners and other travelers in the know. See more information in *Best Places to Stay* chapter.

Moderate

HOTEL RANGIROA BEACH CLUB, *B.P. 17, Avatoru, Rangiroa; Tel. 689/96.03.34; Fax 689/96.02.90. Reservations: Tahiti Resort Hotels, Tel. 689/43.08.29; Fax 689/41.09.28. In Avatoru, 150 meters (492 feet) from the airport and four kilometers (2.5 miles) from the boat dock. EP Rates single/ double/triple: garden bungalow 13.000 CFP ($130); beach-front bungalow 15.000 CFP ($150); two-room suite 20.000 CFP ($200). Meal plan with breakfast and dinner is 4.000 CFP ($40) per person; meal plan with all meals is 5.600 CFP ($56) per person. Round-trip transfers 600 CFP ($6) per person. Add 7% hotel tax to room rates and 1% value added tax to room rates and meal plan. All major credit cards.*

There are presently 6 garden bungalows and 5 beach bungalows, which will be replaced by 26 new bungalows by June, 1998. Four more bungalows will be added by December, 1998, and 5 more bungalows will be built by June, 1999, giving the hotel a total capacity of 35 bungalows. The hotel is built beside a white coral sand beach, which is not fine sand, and entry into the lagoon is made by walking across a slab of dead coral at the edge of the lagoon. The individual bungalows have a thatched roof and a covered terrace facing the lagoon. They are equipped with an overhead fan, rattan furniture, mini refrigerator, and a private bathroom with shower. The hotel's main building houses a restaurant and bar, reception, boutique and activities desk. There is a tennis court and volley ball net, and outrigger paddle canoes are provided for the guests. Excursions to the Blue Lagoon or Ile aux Récifs, reef island, cost 6.500 CFP ($65) per person, and you'll pay 9.500 CFP ($95) per person to visit the pink sand beach of Vahituri.

Pierre and Maryse Seybal, who manage the hotel, were looking pretty frazzled when I visited the hotel on a Sunday, following a big *fête* and all-night ball in Avatoru village the night before. None of the employees showed up, including the cook, and there was already a group of local people impatiently waiting to get a drink and be fed, while Pierre was cooking, driving clients to the airport, checking in new arrivals, and trying to get the bar and dining room cleaned up for lunch. Maryse was holding fort in the boutique, where she was so busy we couldn't even talk. All the bungalows were occupied so I didn't get to look inside, but they will all be replaced very soon.

HOTEL MIKI MIKI VILLAGE, *B.P. 5, Avatoru, Rangiroa. Tel./Fax 689/96.83.83. Beside the lagoon in Avatoru, five kilometers (3 miles) from the airport and one kilometer (.62 miles) from the Avatoru boat dock. MAP Rates: beach-front bungalow with breakfast and dinner included 9.000 CFP ($90) single; 16.000 CFP ($160) double; 20.000 CFP ($200) triple; and 24.000 CFP ($240) quadruple. Round-trip transfers provided. Add 7% hotel tax to room rates and 1% value added tax to room rates and meal plan. JCB, Mastercard, Visa.*

This little hotel was formerly the Rangiroa Village. The nine small bungalows face a white coral sand beach, and have been renovated, providing sleeping space for two to four people, an overhead fan, refrigerator, telephone, tea/coffee facilities, radio, television and private bathroom with hot water shower. There is a restaurant and bar, with an overwater dining terrace. Lagoon excursions and fishing trips can be arranged on request. A boat trip to the Blue Lagoon is 6.000 CFP ($60) per person, and 9.000 CFP ($90) to visit the Sables Roses or Ile aux Récifs. This is a convenient lodging if you want to be close to Avatoru village.

TURIROA VILLAGE, *B.P. 26, Avatoru, Rangiroa; Tel./Fax 689/ 96.04.27. Beside the lagoon in Avatoru, three kilometers (1.9 miles) from the boat dock and 500 meters (1,640 feet) west of the airport. Round-trip transfers provided. EP Rates: bungalow 8.000 CFP ($80) for one to five people; add 500 CFP ($5) per person for breakfast, 1.500 CFP ($15) for lunch and 1.500 CFP ($15) for dinner. Add 7% hotel tax to room rates and 1% value added tax to room rates and meal plan. No credit cards.*

This is the only pension on Rangiroa with a kitchen where you can cook your own meals. There are two garden and two beach bungalows, each containing a double bedroom and a mezzanine with two single or two double mattresses, plus kitchen, private bathroom with cold water, and terrace. House linens are furnished. The family style restaurant will serve your meals if you don't want to cook.

PENSION TUANAKE, *B. P. 21, Avatoru, Rangiroa; Tel. 689/96.04.45; Fax 689/96.03.29. Beside the lagoon in Avatoru, half-way between the airport and village. EP Rates: fare 5.000 CFP ($50) single; 8.000 CFP ($80) double/ triple; 10.000 CFP ($100) four-five people. Fare with breakfast: 5.800 CFP ($58) single; 9.600 CFP ($96) double; 10.400 CFP ($104) triple; 13.200 CFP ($132) for four people, and 14.000 CFP ($140) for five people. Fare with breakfast and dinner: 8.000 CFP ($80) single; 14.000 CFP ($140) double; 17.000 CFP ($170) triple; 22.000 CFP ($220) four people; and 25.000 CFP*

($250) for five people. Fare with all meals included: 10.000 CFP ($100) single; 18.000 CFP ($180) double; 23.000 CFP ($230) triple; 30.000 CFP ($300) for four people; and 35.000 CFP ($350) for five people. Round-trip transfers provided. Add 1% value added tax to room rates and meal plan. Mastercard, Visa.

There are four small *fares* on the white sand beach, two with two single beds and one berth, and a private bathroom in each with cold water; and two family *fares*, each with five-six beds; with a double and a single bed in the living room and three single beds on the mezzanine. Each *fare* is very clean and has a fan and private bathroom with cold water. A hot water shower is outside. House linens are furnished.

Roger Terorotua is the president of the Haere Mai Association, which represents the small hotels and pensions in French Polynesia. Therefore, he is very interested in tourism and presenting a good tourist product. A friendly, comfortable atmosphere reigns here, with beach chairs to read in the shade or sunbathe on the white coral beach. Roger's cuisine is also recommended, which he serves in an attractive dining room overlooking the beach and lagoon. The Gauguin's Pearl farm is next door.

RAIRA LAGON, *B.P. 87, Avatoru, Rangiroa; Tel. 689/96.04.23; Fax 689/96.05.86. Beside the lagoon in Avatoru commune, 4.5 kilometers (2.8 miles) east of the Avatoru boat dock and 1.5 kilometers (.93 miles) west of the airport. EP Rates: fare 4.000 CFP ($40) per person; fare with breakfast and dinner 8.000 CFP ($80) per person; fare with all meals 10.000 CFP ($100) per person. Half-price for children 3-12 years. Round-trip transfers provided. Add 1% value added tax to room rates and meal plan. Mastercard, Visa.*

There are nine comfortable and clean *fares* or individual little bungalows, with single or double beds and private bathrooms with hot or cold water. Each bungalow has a fan. The restaurant, which is on the beach, has one of the best culinary reputations on the island. This is where the local residents prefer to go when they want to choose from an *a la carte* menu and dine well at reasonable cost. There are beach chairs for guests under the shade trees or on the coral beach.

RELAIS MIHIROA, *B. P. 51, Tiputa, Rangiroa; Tel. 689/96.72.14; Fax 689/96.75.13. Beside the lagoon in Tiputa, four kilometers (2.5 miles) from the boat dock and the village, and a 15-minute boat ride from the airport. EP Rates: bungalow 7.200 CFP ($72) single/double/triple; bungalow with breakfast and dinner 6.000 CFP ($60) per person; bungalow with all meals 7.500 CFP ($75) per person. Half-price for children 3-12 years. Round-trip transfers 1.500 CFP ($15) per person for the boat ride and 400 CFP ($4) per car trip to the Tiputa boat landing. Add 1% value added tax to room rates and meal plan. Mastercard, Visa.*

This pension is east of Tiputa village, across the Tiputa Pass from the airport *motu*. You are transferred from the airport to the Tiputa boat dock by boat, then driven the four kilometers (2.5 miles) to the pension. The four small wooden bungalows with shingled roofs each contain a double bedroom where a mattress or berth can be added, a private bathroom with cold water, a fan and terrace. House linens, snorkeling equipment and beach chairs are provided. Local style meals and seafood specialties are served in the restaurant-bar *fare* facing the lagoon. The hosts will take you to the Blue Lagoon for 7.500 CFP ($75) per person and to the Sables Roses, the pink sand beach of Vahituri, for 8.500 CFP ($85) per person.

Inexpensive

PENSION GLORINNE, *Avatoru, Rangiroa; Tel./Fax 689/96.03.58. Beside the lagoon in Avatoru commune, 50 meters from the boat dock near Tiputa Pass and six kilometers (3.7 miles) east of the airport. Rates: bungalow with breakfast and dinner 5.500 CFP ($55) per person; bungalow with all meals provided 6.500 CFP ($65) per person; half-price for child under 12 years. Round-trip transfers 800 CFP ($8) per car. Add 1% value added tax to room rates and meal plan. No credit cards.*

This is the most popular pension on Rangiroa, and Glorinne is noted for her delicious food. See *Where to Eat* in this chapter. The biggest drawback here is the noise generated by the inter-island boats that bring fuel and other supplies to Rangiroa. They unload at the dock beside the pension, which may be disturbing to some guests. There is no beach here. Rangiroa Paradive is located adjacent to the pension.

There are three small thatched roof Polynesian style bungalows with single or double beds for two people, and three family bungalows, each with a private bathroom and cold water shower, and a veranda. House linens are furnished. A communal sitting room is furnished with information on activities and excursions available and paperback books to exchange. Beach chairs are scattered throughout the shaded and sunny lawn.

PENSION CECILE, *B. P. 98, Avatoru, Rangiroa; Tel. 689/96.05.06. In Avatoru, 2.5 kilometers (1.6 miles) from the boat dock and two kilometers (1.2 miles) from the airport. Round-trip transfers provided. Rates: bungalow 2.500 CFP ($25) per person; bungalow with breakfast and dinner 5.000 CFP ($50) person; bungalow with all meals 6.000 CFP ($60) per person; half-price for child under 12 years. Add 1% value added tax to room rates and meal plan. No credit cards.*

Here's another famous cook in Rangiroa. Cecile is very much appreciated by visitors because of her warm welcome and excellent meals, which she serves under a *fare pote'e* shelter facing the lagoon. There are six bungalows, each containing a double and single bed, with mosquito net, private bathroom and cold water. House linens, snorkeling equipment and bicycles are supplied. Your hosts will take you to visit a pearl farm, to go fishing in the lagoon and to learn about the culture of the Paumotu people. Access to the beach.

CHEZ LUCIEN, *B.P. 69, Tiputa, Rangiroa; Tel. 689/96.73.55. Near the pass in Tiputa village, 10 minutes by boat from the airport. Round-trip boat transfers 500 CFP ($5) per person. Rates: bungalow with breakfast and dinner 5.000 CFP ($50) per person; bungalow with all meals provided 6.000 CFP ($60) per person. Add 1% value added tax to room rates and meal plan. No credit cards.*

This well maintained pension is facing the lagoon at the edge of the Tiputa Pass. Two bungalows have room with two double beds, a mezzanine with one double bed and a private bathroom with cold water in each, and a two-bedroom house has sleeping space for several people, with a double bed in each room, plus a mezzanine with three double mattresses, a communal bathroom with cold water, and a terrace. House linens are furnished. The meals are generous and pleasant, served in a covered dining room beside the lagoon. Lucien treats his guests to a free picnic on a *motu* if they stay a minimum of three nights.

The other pensions in Rangiroa are: **CHEZ TEINA & MARIE**, *Tel. 96.03.94;* **CHEZ FELIX & JUDITH**, *Tel. 96.04.41;* **CHEZ HENRIETTE**, *Tel. 96.85.85;* **CHEZ MARTINE**, *Tel. 96.02.53;* **PENSION HERENUI**, *Tel. 96.84.71;* **PENSION HINANUI**, *Tel. 96.84.61;* **PENSION LOYNA**, *Tel. 96.82.09;* **RANGIROA LODGE**, *Tel. 96.82.13;* **PENSION ESTALL**, *Tel. 96.73.16;* **CHEZ PUNUA & MOANA**, *Tel. 96.84.73;* and **CHEZ NANUA**, *Tel. 96.83.88.*

WHERE TO EAT
Expensive
KIA ORA VILLAGE, *Tel. 96.03.84. All credit cards.*

This restaurant caters to international palates, served in an elegant setting by Polynesians who try to please everyone, which is sometimes difficult when the restaurant is full. The menu offers several choices, which usually include fresh fish from the lagoon or deep ocean, with a good selection of fine wines. A barbecue buffet is served twice a week, with grilled meat, chicken and fresh lagoon fish. The overwater bar can serve almost any drink you order.

Moderate
MIKI MIKI VILLAGE, *Tel. 96.83.63. Mastercard, Visa.*

The lunch menu for 2.200 CFP ($22) is very popular. You can dine on an overwater terrace.

RANGIROA BEACH CLUB, *Tel. 96.03.34. All major credit cards.*

You have your choice of meat, fish and poultry. The restaurant is on the beach.

RAIRA LAGOON, *Tel. 96.04.23. Mastercard, Visa.*

This beachfront restaurant is very popular with local residents because they can choose from an *a la carte* menu and the food is deliciously prepared and reasonably priced.

Inexpensive

CHEZ GLORINNE, *Tel. 96.03.58. Reservations. No credit cards.*

Glorinne's cooking has earned her a reputation for serving some of the best food on Rangiroa. She has combined recipes from her native island of Tubuai with the finest of *cordon bleu* cuisine from Paris. I still remember the excellent *poisson cru* and fried parrot fish croquettes she served me when I was on a yacht in Rangiroa in 1985, which was served beside the lagoon. Glorinne's guests still dine beside the lagoon under a *fare pote'e,* where they create their own sweet memories with her unforgettable meals.

CHEZ CECILE, *Tel. 96.05.06. No credit cards.*

Residents from Tahiti usually include Cecile's restaurant in their itinerary when visiting Rangiroa because her cooking is superb. You dine on local foods, including fresh fish and lobster, under a *fare pote'e* shelter facing the lagoon.

PENSION TUANAKE, *Avatoru, Tel. 96.04.45, open daily, reservations. Mastercard, Visa.*

Local cuisine and seafood specialties.

CHEZ TEINA & MARIE, *Ohutu Point, Tel. 96.03.94open daily, reservations. No credit cards.*

Beside the lagoon at the edge of the Tiputa Pass, serving local cuisine and seafood specialties.

ACAJOU, *Avatoru, Tel. 96.04.12. Closed Sunday.*

Chinese cuisine and take-away food.

OHUTU NUI is a *snack on the Ohutu quay, overlooking the Tiputa Pass. Open daily 9am to 6pm, No credit cards.*

Fruit juices, beer, *casse-croûtes*, shish kebabs and fish.

SPORTS & RECREATION

Motor Boat Rental

Heikura Iti has a 20-foot and a 25-foot fast Haura boat for hire with skipper. Contact Hiria Arnoux, *Tel. 96.02.88* at the Kia Ora Village. The cost per hour is 7.500 CFP ($75), with a two-hour minimum.

Deep Sea Fishing

Hiria Arnoux, *Tel. 96.02.88* at the Kia Ora Village, will take you deep sea fishing in a 20-foot or 25-foot fast Haura boat. The rates start at 20.000 CFP ($200) for a minimum of two hours.

Glass Bottom Boat Excursions

Matahi Excursions is a 20-passenger glass bottom boat named *Suzanne* that is operated by Matahi Tepa, *Tel. 96.84.48*, which is based at Ohutu Point in Avatoru. Departures for the 2-hour excursions are made according to the incoming current in Tiputa Pass. You'll view the amazing wealth of sea life from the dry comfort of the boat as you drift through the pass and stop at the fishermen's *motu* islet inside the pass, where you can watch the shark feeding. The cost is 1.800 CFP ($18) per person. Line fishing is available on request. Round-trip transfers are provided from your lodging to the boat.

Lagoon Excursions

The most popular destination of the lagoon excursions is the **Blue Lagoon**, which is an hour's boat ride from the hotels in Rangiroa, on the western edge of the atoll. This lagoon within a lagoon is formed by a natural pool of aquamarine water on the edge of the reef, known locally as Taeo'o. Several *motu* islets are separated by very shallow *hoa* channels, and you can walk from one white sand beach to another. Each hotel or pension has its own private *motu* used for barbecue picnics. The cost of an all-day picnic excursion to the Blue Lagoon ranges from 6.500 to 9.000 CFP ($65 to $90) per person, depending on your hotel or pension.

Reef Islet, also called **l'île aux Récifs**, and **Motu Ai Ai**, are on the south end of Rangiroa, an hour's boat ride across the lagoon. Here you can walk through razor sharp raised coral outcrops called *feo* that resemble miniature fairy castles formed during four million years of erosion. This excursion is sold for 6.500 to 9.000 CFP ($65 to $90).

The pink sand beaches of **Vahituri**, or **Les Sables Roses**, are 1 1/2 or 2 hours by boat from Avatoru to the southeastern edge of the lagoon. The pink reflections in the sand are caused by Foraminifera deposits and coral residues. You'll enjoy swimming and snorkeling in the lagoon in this lovely area. The cost of this excursion ranges from 8.500 CFP ($85) to 12.000 CFP ($120).

The following excursions will take you to discover the wonders of the Rangiroa lagoon.

Spirit of Ireland is a 60-foot Kevlar racing trimaran operated by Hiria Arnoux, *Tel. 96.02.88*, based at the Kia Ora Village. Day excursions for a maximum of 12 passengers are made to Ai Ai Motu inside the lagoon. Private charters are possible to visit the lagoons of Rangiroa and Tikehau.

Heikura Iti is operated by Hiria Arnoux, *Tel. 96.02.88*, with two fast Haura boats that will take a maximum of 10 passengers each on full-day excursions inside the Rangiroa Lagoon, departing the Kia Ora Village at 9am and returning at 4pm. Excursion choices include the Blue Lagoon of Motu Taeo'o, to the pink beaches of Vahituri and to the Reef Islet.

Snorkeling, shark feeding, walking on the reef and barbecue picnics on the *motu* are included. Boat rental with skipper for half-day and full-day excursions are made on request.

    Oviri Snorkeling is a new activity owned by Ugo Angely, manager of Hotel Kia Ora Sauvage, and his friend Christophe. They will take you on a snorkeling excursion aboard their new 25-foot motor boat *Tiputa/Avatoru*, which has an awning, two big ladders and a powerful Yamaha engine. The boat is based at the Avatoru marina and Christophe makes two excursions daily, at 9am and 2:30pm. Each outing lasts three hours and takes you to the Avatoru Pass, then to the fish enclosures inside the lagoon. While you pause for refreshments he will tell you about the marina flora and fauna around you. Then you'll head for the Tiputa pass, inside the lagoon, and snorkel around the little *motu* of Nuhi Nuhi, which is a natural aquarium. The grande finale for this excursion will be to watch the dolphins in Tiputa Pass. This excursion costs 4.000 CFP ($40) a person. *Tel. 96.05.87* or sign up at your hotel or pension.

    Rangiroa Activities, *Tel. 96.03.31*, is owned by Pascal and Cosetta, a young French and Italian couple, who use their 19-foot boat *Poevai* for 2-hour excursions to the pass and dolphin watching. When the current is incoming from the ocean to the lagoon Pascal will take you through the Tiputa Pass, where you can drift snorkel through the pass into the lagoon. When the current is outgoing you can watch the dolphins riding the current to the open ocean. You may see the big dolphins (*Tursiops truncatus*), a family of spinner dolphins (*Stenella longirostris*), or more rarely, the black and white dolphins (*Peponocephala electra*) that live around the coast of Rangiroa. The snorkeling excursion is 3.000 CFP ($30) and the dolphin watch is 4.000 CFP ($40).

    Te Tiare Excursions, Alphonse Tetua, *Tel. 96.85.85*, is based at the Avatoru Marina. A 26-foot aluminum boat for 4 to 16 passengers is used for daily excursions to the Blue Lagoon, with a picnic on Motu Taeo'o and visits to the surrounding islets, from 8:30 am to 3:30pm.

    Te Onoono, *Tel. 96.03.84/96.85.61*, based at the Kia Ora Village, is a locally-built 32 foot Glenn and can take 4–20 passengers on two daily excursions to Tiputa Pass and Avatoru Pass, with a swim stop at Motu Fara. You can swim through the Avatoru Pass with the fish and sharks. The morning excursion is from 9am to 12pm, and the afternoon outing is from 2 to 5pm. The half-day tour costs 4.000 CFP ($40) per person.

    Sharky Park is a 20-passenger outrigger speed canoe operated by Punua Tamaehu, *Tel. 96.84.73*. Half- or full-day excursions are made to visit the Blue Lagoon or the Reef Islet, departing at 8:30am and returning at 10:30am or 4pm, according to your choice. You can also explore the Avatoru Pass and visit the enclosures for the sharks, turtles, rays and tropical fish. Line fishing on request.

Parasailing

Rangiroa Parasail, *Tel. 96.04.96* at Kia Ora Village. Smooth and gentle take-off and landing on board the boat without getting wet. The cost is 5.000 CFP ($50). Parasailing flight can be coordinated with a boat excursion to the Blue Lagoon or to Reef Islet with a picnic included. Round-trip transfers provided between your lodging and the Kia Ora Village.

Pearl Farms

Gauguin's Pearl, operated by Philippe Cabrall, *Tel. 96.05.39*, is a visit to a black pearl farm, open Monday through Saturday 8:30am to 2pm. No admission fee.

Sailing Charter Yachts

Archipels Polynesian Cruises, *Tel. 56.36.39*, has a nautical base at Opunohu Bay in Moorea and a yacht based permanently in Rangiroa. A Tuesday to Friday 4 day/3 night Tuamotu cruise inside the atoll of Rangiroa is $1,030 per person. A Saturday to Monday 3 day/2 night cruise inside the lagoon is $790 per person. These cruises operate all year except in January and February. Dive Aboard Cruises "by the boat only" cost $2,450 a day in the Tuamotus. See information in *Moorea* chapter.

Scuba Diving

The lagoon of Rangiroa offers world-class diving. It is essentially a huge inland sea, with a maximum depth of about 27 meters (90 feet), which offers the finest and most abundant of nature's aquaculture. The two passes of **Tiputa** and **Avatoru** are submarine freeways for the passage of fish between the open ocean and the lagoon. The ocean normally has a moderate swell running and near the passes a five knot current enters or exits rhythmically with the rise and fall of the tide. Static dives in or near the passes can only be done twice a day when the water is still and clear, which is normally at 12 hour intervals. Drift dives are possible on nearly any day, and these "shooting the pass" dives are exhilarating, as you are surrounded by hordes of fish, jacks, tuna, barracuda, manta rays, eagle rays, turtles, dolphins and sharks.

Between December and March huge hammerhead sharks gather to mate outside Tiputa Pass, and the graceful manta rays are most plentiful during their mating season between July and October. There are 15 popular dive sites inside the lagoon, in the passes and on the outer coral reef of Rangiroa. The following diving clubs have qualified French instructors who speak English and schedule their dives between 8am and 2pm, depending on the tides, currents, swell and wind conditions. They all accept credit cards and charge 5.000 CFP ($50) a dive. Night dives and dive packages are also available. Equipment is included, but you may feel more secure if you bring your own buoyancy compensator, regulator and depth gauge. You'll also need to bring you certification papers and medical certificate.

Raie Manta Club, *Tel. 96.04.80*. Yves Lefevre, who is a PADI instructor and international CMAS two-star monitor, French State BEES, 1st level monitor and sea guide, was the first dive master to open a scuba diving center on Rangiroa in 1985. His main office *is* beside the lagoon near Avatoru village, between Pension Herenui and Rangiroa Lodge and he has an annex next to Chez Teina and Marie beside Tiputa Pass. The Raie Manta Club has an exclusive arrangement with the Kia Ora Village. Diving excursions can also be combined with a picnic on one of the *motu* islets across the lagoon. Yves is qualified to give all international examinations at any level. Video films of your dive are also available.

Rangiroa Paradive, *Tel. 96.05.55*, is next door to Pension Glorinne near the Tiputa Pass. Bernard Blanc is a PADI instructor, international CMAS two-star monitor, French State BEES second level monitor, sea guide and FFESSM instructor. He and his instructors also offer PADI and CMAS training and picnic dives.

The Six Passengers, *Tel. 96.03.05*, is headed by Frédéric Aragones, who opened his friendly dive shop close to the Kia Ora Village in 1995. He is an international CMAS three star monitor, BEES second level Federal instructor, PADI monitor and PADI dive master. As the name implies, his boats accommodate only six passengers for dives and diving picnics. All dives are photographed and shown at the center when you return.

SHOPPING

Ciao Rangiroa, *Tel. 96.02.60*, in Avatoru, rents waterproof video cameras to record your scuba diving memories.

Kia Ora Boutique sells local style clothing, curios, video film, post cards and jewelry.

Rangiroa Beach Club Boutique sells tee-shirts, pareos and local handcrafts.

Le Coquillage, *Tel. 96.05.08*, in Avatoru sells locally made clothing and curios.

Ocean Passion, near Avatoru village, sells beautiful original *pareos* and wall hangings of dolphins, rays, fish and the coral gardens of Rangiroa's lagoon.

PRACTICAL INFORMATION

Banks

Banque de Tahiti, *Tel. 96.85.52*, has an office in Avatoru village close to the Catholic church and the *mairie* (town hall). It is open Monday, Wednesday and Friday, from 8 to 11:30am and 1:30 to 4pm, and on Thursday from 1:30 to 4pm. In Tiputa village the Banque de Tahiti operates from the *mairie* on Tuesday from 1:30 to 4pm, and on Thursday from 8 to 11:30am.

Banque Socredo, *Tel. 96.85.63* is located in the *mairie* of Avatoru, and is open on Monday, Tuesday, Thursday and Friday from 8 to 10:30am, and on Wednesday from 8:30 to 10:30 am and 1:30 to 4pm. Banque Socredo, *Tel. 96.75.57*, also has an office at the *mairie* in Tiputa, which is open Monday and Thursday, 1:30 to 4pm.

You can exchange currency and withdraw cash with your credit card at either bank in Avatoru, but you can only exchange currency in Tiputa.

Hospitals

A government operated medical center is located in Avatoru village, *Tel. 96.03.75*, and there is an infirmary in Tiputa village, *Tel. 96.73.96*.

Police

The French *gendarmerie* is in Tiputa village, *Tel. 96.03.61*.

Post Office & Telecommunications Office

A Post Office is located in Avatoru village, *Tel. 96.83.81* and another is in Tiputa village, *Tel. 96.73.50*.

MANIHI

The first black pearl farm was started in **Manihi** in 1968, and with the development of the black pearl industry in the Tuamotu archipelago, the pretty little atoll of Manihi has become synonymous with the *po'e rava*. This is the Tahitian name for the rare and beautiful Tahitian black pearl. Manihi's famous lagoon, which is 5,6 kilometers (3 1/2 miles) wide by 30 kilometers (19 miles) long, is as lovely as the high quality rainbow-hued pearls that are produced in more than 60 black pearl farms that are built on stilts around the periphery of the transparent lagoon.

Seen from the air, the lagoon of Manihi presents a picturesque palette of glimmering greens and blues, with white and pink beaches in a framing of feathery green coconut palms. A close range view of this crystal clear lagoon is even better, as you can see the vividly painted tropical fish feeding in the coral gardens on the white sand bottom, several feet below the water's surface.

You can fly to Manihi from Tahiti in just one hour and fifteen minutes or hop aboard a cargo boat for an overnight cruise of 520 kilometers (322 miles). You'll be transferred by boat from the airport to your hotel or to the village of Turipaoa. This sun-baked little village, with colorful houses of limestone and clapboard lining the two streets, is shaded by breadfruit trees and bordered with frangipani, hibiscus and bougainvillea. This is home to some of Manihi's 769 inhabitants, while others remain on the pearl farms an hour's boat ride from the village. The favorite hangout in Turipaoa village is under the shade of a giant *tou* tree with orange flowers. The old folks sit on benches under the tree and watch the comings and goings of the boats from the pearl farms. This is more interesting to them than sitting at home watching television.

Almost everyone who lives in Manihi today is involved in the pearl business, even though they may have other jobs as well. Many of the Paumotu people, including grown men and women and even babies, wear necklaces, bracelets, earrings and rings of 18 karat gold and exquisite pearls of peacock blue, fly-wing green, aubergine or shiny black. Practically all the men own the latest models of fancy pickup trucks and the young people zoom about on motorcycles, although the road is not even a mile long!

The warm waters of Manihi are ideal for swimming, snorkeling, or diving at any time of the year. You can spear fish on the reef or drag fish in the lagoon. You can even watch the brilliantly colored parrot fish as they nibble their lunch in the live coral gardens. Manihi Blue Nui is a scuba diving center based at Manihi Pearl Beach Resort with a CMAS and PADI instructor, which offers diving in the lagoon, at the pass or outside the coral reef, plus night dives and underwater filming excursions.

ARRIVALS & DEPARTURES
Arriving by Air
Air Tahiti flies from Tahiti to Manihi seven days a week, with a one hour and 15 minute direct flight on Thursday. The other flights stop in Rangiroa, Takapoto or Takaroa, and there are two flights via Rangiroa on Saturdays. You can fly from Bora Bora to Manihi every Wednesday, Friday and Sunday, with an aircraft change in Rangiroa. The one-way fare from Tahiti to Manihi is 17.955 CFP ($179.55) and 24.570 CFP ($245.70) from Bora Bora to Manihi. **Air Tahiti reservations**: *Tahiti, Tel. 86.42.42/ 86.41.84.*

The airport is on a *motu* islet, and if you have reservations with a hotel, pension or yacht charter company, then you will be met at the airport and

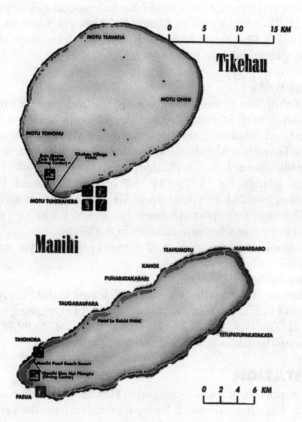

driven to your lodging or transferred by boat. Otherwise, you can catch a ride to the village with some of the residents who have come to meet arriving family members.

Arriving By Boat

St. Xavier Maris Stella, *Tel. 42.23.58*, can transport 12 passengers with berths in cabins for 5.000 CFP ($50), or on the bridge for 2.000 CFP ($20). Three meals a day cost 2.000 CFP ($20) per person. Manihi is the third stop after Rangiroa and Ahe, coming from Tahiti. The ship leaves Papeete every 15 days. Other inter-island ships that call at Manihi are: **Manava II**, *Tel. 43.83.84/42.25.53*; and **Vai Aito**, *Tel. 43.99.96*. See more information in Chapter 6, *Planning Your Trip*. All the ships stop at the Turipaoa quay beside the pass in Manihi.

Departing By Air

Air Tahiti flies from Manihi to Rangiroa and Papeete on Monday, Wednesday, Friday, Saturday and Sunday. A Manihi-Ahe-Papeete flight is scheduled each Thursday, and there is a direct Manihi-Papeete flight on Tuesday. There is a Manihi-Rangiroa-Bora Bora flight each Friday. A Saturday flight from Tahiti and Rangiroa will take you to Nuku Hiva in the Marquesas Islands, for 25.725 CFP ($257.25) from Manihi. Reconfirm your flight at least 24 hours in advance. **Air Tahiti** reservations in Manihi: *Tel. 96.43.34* and the airport number is *Tel. 96.42.71*. The Air Tahiti office is located in Jean Marie's supermarket in the village.

You should be at the airport 30 minutes prior to departure.

Departing By Boat

St. Xavier Maris Stella, *Tel. 42.23.58*, leaves Manihi every 15 days, stopping at 11 of the western Tuamotu atolls before returning to Papeete. **Manava II**, *Tel. 43.83.84/42.25.53*, and **Vai Aito**, *Tel. 43.99.96*, also visit the western Tuamotus before returning to Papeete.

ORIENTATION

The airport is at the southwest end of Manihi, on the same *motu* where the Manihi Pearl Beach Resort is located. Transfers from the airport to the hotel are made by boat or car. Either way, its only a two-minute ride. Manihi's only village, **Turipaoa**, is across the lagoon from the airport, also on the southwest end, the Tairapa Pass, which provides the only navigable entry into the lagoon. The village is about a 15-minute boat ride from the airport.

WHERE TO STAY
Expensive
MANIHI PEARL BEACH RESORT, *Tel. 689/96.42.73; Fax 689/96.42.72. Reservations: South Pacific Marketing, B.P. 2460, 98713 Papeete, Tahiti; Tel. 689/43.16.10; Fax 689/43.17.86; in US 607/273-5012; Fax 607/273-5302; E-mail: sales@tahiti-nui.com Internet: http://www.tahiti-nui.com 41 units. EP Rates single/double: beach bungalow 26.000 CFP ($260), deluxe overwater bungalow 46.000 CFP ($460); third person 4.000 CFP ($40); meal plan with breakfast and dinner 5.950 CFP ($59.50) per person; meal plan with breakfast, lunch and dinner 8.250 CFP ($82.50) per person; full American breakfast 1.800 CFP ($18); outrigger canoe breakfast 2.900 CFP ($29); romantic breakfast on the beach 2.800 CFP ($28); private honeymoon champagne dinner under the stars 7.500 CFP ($75) per person; fruit basket 1.850 CFP ($18.50); bottle of wine 2.250 CFP ($22.50); bottle of champagne 3.950 CFP ($39.50). One-way transfer 600 CFP ($6). Add 7% hotel tax to room rates and 1% value added tax to room rates and meal plan. All major credit cards.*

The hotel is located on the same *motu* with the airport, and is 4 kilometers (2.5 miles) across the lagoon from the main village. Each of the 22 beach bungalows and 19 deluxe overwater bungalows is built in the traditional Polynesian style of pointed pandanus thatched roof and local woods. Each of the very attractively decorated bungalows has an overhead fan, a mini-bar refrigerator, coffee/tea facilities, hot water shower, hair-dryer, international direct dial telephone, individual safe and sundeck. The overwater bungalows have a glass bottom table so that you can watch a family of parrot fish feeding in the clear lagoon below. There is even an overwater bungalow designed for handicapped clients.

The first-class restaurant serves French cuisine, seafood and local specialties. The bar, boutique, black pearl shop, television/video room and billiards room are all located in separate buildings. Beside the white sand beach and the lagoon is a large salt water swimming pool, and a scuba diving center is adjacent to the pier. Activities include lagoon excursions to black pearl farms, picnics on the *motu*, fishing trips and sunset cruises. Tahitian dance shows are presented each Thursday night during dinner.

See more information in *Best Places to Stay* chapter.

Moderate
CHEZ JEANNE, *98771 Motu Tangaraufara, Manihi; Tel. 689/96.42.90; Fax 689/96.42.91, is located on a private islet, 10 kilometers (6.2 miles) from the airport and 14 kilometers (8.7 miles) from the village. Round-trip boat transfers provided. EP Rates: beach bungalow 8.000 CFP ($80) single/double/triple; overwater bungalow 12.000 CFP ($120) single/double. Add 1% percent value added tax to room rates. Mastercard, Visa.*

Jeanne and Guy Huerta have two beach bungalows, each with a

double and single bed, kitchenette and private bathroom with cold water. They also have an overwater bungalow with a double bedroom, kitchenette and private bathroom with cold water. House linens are furnished, but you have to do the shopping and cooking yourself. The water is okay for showers but is not potable, so be sure to include a sufficient supply of bottled water for your needs. You can buy supplies from your hosts, including food and bottled mineral water. Beach chairs are provided to sit under the shade of the palm trees or on the white sand beach, and outrigger paddle canoes are available for exploring the lagoon. A visit to a pearl farm is included in your room charge.

Inexpensive
VAINUI PERLES, *98771 Motu Marakorako, Manihi; Tel. 689/96.42.89; Fax 689/96.42.00. On a private motu, 12 kilometers (7.5 miles) from the airport and main village. Round-trip boat transfers provided. AP Rates: fare or room with all meals included 7.000 CFP ($70) per person. Half-rate for child under 12 years. No credit cards.*

Accommodations are available in a separate *fare* with a double bedroom, and in a 3-bedroom house, with a communal bathroom and cold water shower. House linens are furnished, and there is a restaurant and bar. In addition to visiting a pearl farm you can line fish inside the lagoon.

WHERE TO EAT
POE RAVA RESTAURANT *at Manihi Pearl Beach Resort, Tel. 96.42.73.*
Open daily, serving breakfast from 7:30 to 9am, lunch from 12 to 2pm, and dinner from 7 to 9pm. The Miki Miki Bar serves *casse-croûtes* from 2 to 6:30pm.

SPORTS & RECREATION
Motor Boat Rental
You can rent a boat with pilot for 8.000 CFP ($80) an hour at the **Manihi Pearl Beach Resort**.

Deep Sea Fishing
The **Manihi Pearl Beach Resort** will rent you a boat and pilot for 10.000 CFP ($100) an hour to fish in the open ocean. An ice chest of drinks can also be included on request.

Lagoon Excursions
Each Monday, Friday and Sunday morning boat excursions from the **Manihi Pearl Beach Resort** will take you to visit a black pearl farm, for 2.000 CFP ($20) per person.

Every Tuesday, Thursday and Saturday a barbecue picnic is held on a private *motu* islet across the lagoon, reached by a 30-minute speed boat ride. Be sure to protect yourself from the sun during this crossing and while you're on the *motu*, as there is very little shade. You'll have plenty of time to snorkel inside the lagoon while the freshly speared lagoon fish is being cooked whole on a grill. This excursion costs 5.500 CFP ($55) per person.

Each Wednesday morning you can snorkel and dive in the pass, for 1.500 CFP ($15) a person. This outing is subject to change according to the currents in the pass.

Every Monday afternoon a boat will take you to the best fishing sites inside the lagoon, for 1.000 CFP ($10) a person.

A boat excursion each Wednesday and Friday afternoon will make a tour of the lagoon, where you will see pearl farms and uninhabited *motu* islets and swim in natural pools of crystal clear water. This excursion costs 4.500 CFP ($45) per person, for a minimum of four people.

A Sunday afternoon boat trip will take you to the reef, where you can search for seashells and observe the living ecosystem of a coral reef, for 1.000 CFP ($10) each.

Sunset cruises are held twice a week, each Monday and Saturday evening, departing aboard a speed boat that takes you outside the pass into the open ocean to watch the spectacular phenomenon of the enormous golden-orange sun dropping behind the horizon. If you are observant, you may even see the green flash. This excursion costs 1.200 CFP ($12) per person, and includes rum punch or juice and snacks.

You can also have a private excursion to a *motu* with pink sand, for 2.000 CFP ($20) per person, or 3.000 CFP ($30) per person with a picnic and drinks.

A PAUMOTU PICNIC

As beautiful as they are to look at, the parrot fish and some of the other fish species in Manihi are dangerous to eat because of **ciguatera**, *which I was told is caused by the iron fencing used for all the black pearl farms that now blanket the lagoon. When you take a lagoon excursion to the motu for a barbecue picnic, your guide will spear some fish for the grill. He knows which ones to choose, which will usually be grouper, a sweet tasting fish. If you don't like the idea of peeling away the charred skin with your fingers, and looking at the fish head and eyes, or fighting the flies for your meal, then choose a piece of chicken or steak instead. But if you want to have a Paumotu-style picnic on the motu, then you'll squeeze some lime juice on the fish and fan the flies away with a leaf and dig in for a delightful meal.*

Scuba Diving

Manihi Blue Nui Dive Center, *Tel. 96.42.73/96.42.17; Fax 96.42.72*, is located at the Manihi Pearl Beach Resort. This brand new dive shop has showers, lockers, hangers for wet suits, a Boston Whaler boat for six divers and a covered aluminum boat for 16 divers. Both boats have powerful twin engines. The diving gear is Sherwood brand, with 25 tanks and a complete range of equipment. Wetsuits and waterproof lights are available for rent for 500 CFP ($5) per dive. Manager Gilles Petre, who is a PADI, BEES and CMAS dive master, heads a team of qualified diving instructors, who speak good English. The rates are 5.500 CFP ($55) for one dive, 5.000 CFP ($50) per dive for five dives, and 4.500 CFP ($45) per dive for 10 dives. Night dives and initiation dives are 6.500 CFP ($65), including all the equipment. You can dive two or three times a day, in the morning, afternoon and at night.

Manihi offers excellent diving conditions in shallow, warm, clear water, with mild currents in the pass. The dive sites are only five minutes away from the dive center, reached by comfortable speed boats that are custom designed for diving. The pass is south to north with the main wind from the east, and for beginners, a protected site outside the reef is used that is protected from the main wind by the village of Turipaoa.

Tairapa Pass is one of the most popular dive sites, offering drift dives with the incoming or outgoing currents. You'll feel as though you are soaring through space with the tuna, sharks, schools of barracuda, jack fish, rays and turtles. **The Drop Off** is a wall dive on the ocean side of Manihi, which descends from 3 to 1,350 meters (10 to 4,500 feet) deep. This site abounds with gray sharks, Napoleon fish, giant jack fish, schools of snapper and sea pike barracuda, plus the deep sea fish like tuna and marlin. Each July thousands of groupers gather here to breed, offering one of the most fascinating underwater events in the world. **The Circus** is the name given to a location between the pass and the lagoon, which is a favorite hangout for eagle and manta rays. Underwater photographers can get close to the graceful manta rays as they glide up and down in an average underwater depth of 9 meters (30 feet). These curious and friendly creatures sometimes have a wing span up to four meters (13 feet) wide, and remain here all year long.

A scenic dive on the **West Point** of the ocean side reveals fire coral, antler coral and flower petal coral, among others, which are visible for up to 60 meters (200 feet) in the incredibly clear water. Shark feeding is best at **The Break**, a large cut in the outer reef, where a coral amphitheater provides the scenery for a multitude of reef sharks, including black tip, white tip, gray sharks and an occasional hammer head, who show up for the free handouts of tuna heads.

SHOPPING

The **Manihi Pearl Beach Resort** has a boutique and a black pearl shop. Pearls can also be purchased from the pearl farms directly, at less prices than you would pay in Papeete, but remember that the best quality pearls are usually shipped to Tahiti for sale in the various jewelry shops in the Society Islands.

PRACTICAL INFORMATION

Banks

There are no banks in Manihi.

Hospital

A government operated infirmary is located in Turipaoa village, *Tel. 96.43.67.*

Post Office

The **Post Office and Telecommunications Office**, *Tel. 96.42.22*, is located in Turipaoa village, upstairs in the white administration building. You'll find telephone booths on the ground floor of this building, at the airport and at the Manihi Pearl Beach Resort, which all accept phone cards.

TIKEHAU

Tikehau is a South Sea island dream come true, an escapist's haven of seclusion that is less than an hour's flight from Tahiti and just 20 minutes by plane from Rangiroa. Tikehau is one of the most popular atolls in the Tuamotu archipelago, because of its natural beauty and the friendliness of the 400 inhabitants.

In the Paumotu language Tikehau means "peaceful landing" and when the atoll was discovered by the Russian navigator Kotzbue in 1815, he named it Krusenstern Island. Most of the inhabitants live in Tuherahera on the southwest side of the atoll, which is a pretty little village, with lots of flowers and fruit trees. Here you'll find the *mairie* (town hall), post office and telecommunications center, school, infirmary, *magasin* stores, bakery, snacks, Protestant temple, Catholic church, Seventh-Day Adventist church, Sanito temple and most of the pensions and guest houses. There is no bank in Tikehau.

See map of Tikehau on page 461.

Tikehau's lagoon is rich with sea life, whose forms and hues defy even the most active imagination. There are brain coral and stag horn corals, in a myriad of shapes and colors. Soft corals and sponges, tubeworms with lively colored feathered tips. Mother-of-pearl oysters, reef clams, crown-of-thorn starfish, anemones, and a whole parade of brightly painted fish. When **Jacques Cousteau's** research group made a study of the Polynesian atolls in 1987, they declared the lagoon of Tikehau to contain the most fish of any of the lagoons in French Polynesia. Parrot fish, grouper and other choice lagoon fish are exported to Tahiti.

The air in Tikehau is laden with perfume from the pandanus, *tahinu, puatea* and *tiare kahaia* flowers that grow beside the long, clean beaches. When you finally leave the island, you'll have an odd sensation when you breathe plain air once more.

ARRIVALS & DEPARTURES

Arriving by Air

Air Tahiti flies direct from Tahiti to Tikehau each Wednesday, with 50-minute flights. Each Friday and Saturday the ATR flights from Tahiti to Tikehau stop in Rangiroa, and the Sunday's flight to Tikehau stops in Mataiva. **Air Tahiti reservations**: *Tahiti, Tel. 86.42.42/86.41.84.*

The one-way airfare from Tahiti to Tikehau is 14.280 CFP ($142.80), and the one-way fare from Rangiroa to Tikehau is 4.620 CFP ($46.20).

Arriving by Boat

The most direct way to get to Tikehau by sea is aboard the **Dory,** *Tel. 42.30.55,* which is a fishing boat with no cabin space and no meals. This boat leaves Tahiti each Monday and Tikehau is the first stop. The one-way fare is 2.500 CFP ($25). The **Manava II,** *Tel. 43.83.84/42.25.53,* has no cabins but does serve meals. This boat leaves Tahiti every 15 days, and one of its itineraries includes Tikehau as the second stop. The one-way fare is 2.700 CFP ($27), plus 1.800 CFP ($18) per day for three meals.

Departing by Air

Air Tahiti flies direct from Tikehau to Tahiti each Friday, Saturday and Sunday, and the flight from Tikehau stops in Rangiroa enroute to Tahiti on Wednesdays. **Air Tahiti reservations** in Tikehau, *Tel. 96.22.66.*

Departing by Boat

The **St. Xavier Maris Stella**, *Tel. 42.23.58,* calls at Tikehau at the end of its 15-day voyage through the western Tuamotus, so it would be convenient to take this ship directly back to Tahiti. There are cabins and meals on board. The one way deck fare is 2.000 CFP ($20) and a cabin is 5.000 CFP ($50); meals are 2.000 CFP ($20) per day. See more information under *Inter-Island Cruise Ships, Passenger Boats and Freighters* in Chapter 6, *Planning Your Trip.*

ORIENTATION

Most of the residents of Tikehau live in **Tuherahera village** on the southern end of the atoll, where small boats can enter the lagoon through a pass in the coral reef. The almost circular interior lagoon is 26 kilometers (16 miles) wide, bordered by white sand beaches. A 10-kilometer (6.2 mile) track circles the *motu* of Tuherahera, which you can explore on bicycle.

WHERE TO STAY & EAT

TIKEHAU VILLAGE, *98778 Tuherahera, Tikehau. Tel. 689/96.22.86, Fax 689/96.22.91. Beside the beach in Tematie village, 600 meters (654 yards) from the village and 400 meters (436 yards) from the airport. Rates: bungalow 2.500 CFP ($25) per person; fare with breakfast and dinner 5.500 CFP ($55) per person; fare with all meals 7.000 CFP ($70) per person; half-price for child under 12 years. Round-trip transfers are provided. Add 1% value added tax to room rates and meal plan. No credit cards.*

The eight thatched roof *fares* have fans and private or communal bathrooms with cold water showers. House linens are furnished. Restaurant and bar. Snorkeling equipment is provided and visits to the main village can be arranged. This is a popular place with residents of Tahiti, who stay here because the food is good. Tourists enjoy feeding the sharks and rays who come to the edge of the lagoon beside the white sand beach in search of handouts. Rental bicycles are available.

PANAU LAGON, *98778 Tuherahera, Tikehau. Tel. 689/96.22.99/ 96.22.34. Beside the white sand beach in Hotu Panau village, close to the airport. Rates: beach bungalow 2.500 CFP ($25) per person, family size beach bungalow 7.000 CFP ($70) single/double; breakfast and dinner add 3.000 CFP ($30) per person; breakfast, lunch and dinner add 3.500 CFP ($35) per person; half-price for child under 12 years. Round-trip transfers are provided. Add 1% value added tax to room rates and meal plan. No credit cards.*

There are six thatched roof *fares*, four with a double bed and single bed and private bathroom with cold water; one *fare* with two rooms and communal bathroom with cold water; and one overwater *fare* with two double beds and communal bathroom. House linens and mosquito nets are furnished. A restaurant is on the premises.

KAHAIA BEACH, *98778 Tuherahera, Tel./Fax 689/96.22.77. Beside the beach on the private Motu Kahaia, next to the airport. Rates: bungalow 2.500 CFP ($25) single, 4.000 CFP($40) double; for breakfast and dinner add 2.300 CFP ($23) per person; for breakfast, lunch and dinner add 4.000 CFP ($40) per* *person; half-rate meals for child under six years. Round-trip boat transfers included. Add 1% value added tax to room rates and meal plan. Mastercard, Visa.*

Two thatched roof beach bungalows and two overwater bungalows each have a double bed and living room. There are private and communal bathrooms with cold water. House linens are furnished. Local cuisine is served in the restaurant-bar.

CHEZ JUSTINE, *98778 Tuherahera, Tikehau. Tel. 689/96.22.37/ 96.22.88. Beside the white sand beach in Hotu Panau village, 200 meters (656 feet) from the airport. Rates: beach bungalow 2.500 CFP ($25) per person; bungalow with breakfast and dinner 5.000 CFP ($50) per person; bungalow with breakfast, lunch and dinner 6.500 CFP ($65) per person; half fare for child under 12 years. Round-trip transfers are provided. Add 1% value added tax to room rates and meal plan. No credit cards.*

Two thatched roof *fares* have two rooms with a double bed, private bathroom with cold water, and terrace. House linens are provided. The restaurant serves local-style meals. This pension offers peace and tranquillity in its isolated location.

CHEZ COLETTE, *98778 Tuherahera, Tikehau. Tel. 689/96.22.47. In the center of Tuherahera village, two kilometers (1.2 miles) from the airport. Rates: room only 2.000 CFP ($20) per person; room with breakfast and dinner 4.500 CFP ($45) per person; room with all meals 5.500 CFP ($55) per person; half-fare meals for child under 12 years. Round-trip transfers are provided. Add 1% value added tax to room rates and meal plan. No credit cards.*

This clean and well run pension has five guest rooms plus a living room, dining room, kitchen, private bathroom with cold water, and shaded terrace. House linens are provided. Car transfers to the beach on request and to visit the village. Chez Maui food shop is next door, if you want to cook your own meals. Colette will prepare local dishes for you, which will be sure to include some of the delicious lagoon fish and rock lobsters.

CHEZ ISIDORE & NINI, *98778 Tuherahera, Tikehau. Tel. 689/ 96.22.38. In the center of Tuherahera village, two kilometers (1.2 miles) from the airport. Rates: room only 2.000 CFP ($20) per person; room with breakfast and dinner 4.500 CFP ($45) per person; room with all meals 5.500 CFP ($55) per person; half-price for child 5-12 years. Round-trip transfers are provided. Add 1% value added tax to room rates and meal plan. No credit cards.*

A three-bedroom house is simply furnished with a double bed in each room, plus a living room, dining room, television, kitchen and communal bathroom with cold water. House linens are provided. The garden here is filled with fruit and flower trees and bushes.

SEEING THE SIGHTS

You can view the beauty of the fish and submarine gardens through a glass bottom boat, or scuba dive with qualified dive masters. Take a boat to **Motu Ohihi**, which is surrounded by shallow *hoa* channels and has a pink sand beach. Go to **Motu Puarua** and **Oeoe**, where snowy white fairy terns and noddy birds nest. Snorkeling is especially good in Tikehau's crystal clear lagoon.

Boat excursions will take you to visit the fish parks and pearl farms, and you have a choice of *motu* islets for a memorable picnic. Bike through the coconut groves to the rose-colored reef, and take a guided land tour to the village and surrounding area. You can fish by line or spear, or join the villagers in a tug-of-war with the rolling surf, as fishermen haul in a seine heavy with fish.

SPORTS & RECREATION

Sail & Dive Charters

Archipels Polynesian Cruises, *Tel. 56.36.39,* has a nautical base at *Opunohu Bay in Moorea* and a yacht based permanently in Rangiroa. Dive Aboard Cruises "by the boat only" cost $2,450 a day in the Tuamotus.

VPM Dufour Tahiti, *Tel. 689/56.40.50,* has a boat permanently based in Tikehau for cruising or dive cruises in the Tuamotu atolls. The main base for this yacht charter company is located at the Vaiare Marina in Moorea.

See more information on both charter companies in *Moorea* chapter.

Scuba Diving

Raie Manta Club Tikehau is based at the Tikehau Village, *Tel. 96.22.53.* Yannis Saint-Pe is a qualified diving instructor who charges 5.500 CFP ($55) for an exploration dive. Lagoon dives, open ocean dives and night dives are possible, and he can give you exams for CMAS certification. Diving in the Tuheiava Pass is an exciting experience, where you will be surrounded by sharks, tunas, barracudas, jackfish napoleon fish and other brilliantly colored schools of tropical fish. You may even see the graceful manta rays gliding by.

FAKARAVA

Fakarava is the second largest atoll in the Tuamotu archipelago, after Rangiroa, and its rectangular-shaped lagoon is 60 kilometers (37 miles) long by 25 kilometers (15 miles) wide. The atoll is 488 kilometers (303 miles) east-north-east of Tahiti and south-east of Rangiroa in the central Tuamotus.

A direct flight from Tahiti to Fakarava is just one hour and ten minutes, which is helping to turn this atoll into a dream location for scuba divers. The lagoon of Fakarava is a magnificent marine realm of sharks, graceful manta rays, giant sized fish and a whole parade of beautiful tropical fish. A Spiro dive center opened in February, 1996, in Fakarava's Rotoava village, offering a selection of exciting dives for experienced divers. This center was temporarily closed at publication time.

The Garuae pass on the northwest coast is one kilometer (.62 miles) wide, and the adjacent village of **Rotoava** is home to most of the atoll's 467 population, with only a small settlement in Tetamanu village.

Just a few decades ago Fakarava was the social, religious and cultural capital of the Tuamotu archipelago, known to the *Paumotu* people as Havaiki Nui. **Tetamanu village** was the principal settlement on Fakarava. It is located beside the Tumakohua pass on the southeast side of the atoll, and the lagoon here contains numerous fish parks and pearl farms. A variety of fresh vegetables and fruits are grown in soil imported from Tahiti.

Fakarava's lagoon provides a wealth of fresh fish, which the local fishermen catch by placing bottom lines attached to a buoy. When a fish strikes, the buoys jiggle up and down, and the ever watchful seabirds get into the act by squawking excitedly at the prospect of a fresh fish dinner. Your hosts will arrange boat trips for you to visit the pearl farms and some of the 80 *motu* islets inside the immense lagoon.

ARRIVALS & DEPARTURES

Arriving by Air

Air Tahiti flies direct from Tahiti to Fakarava each Monday and Wednesday, with 70-minute flights. Each Friday the ATR flight from Tahiti to Fakarava stops in Rangiroa. **Air Tahiti reservations**: *Tahiti, Tel. 86.42.42/86.41.84.*

The one-way airfare from Tahiti to Fakarava is 14.700 CFP ($147), and the one-way fare from Rangiroa to Fakarava is 4.400 CFP ($44). The airport is four kilometers (2.5 miles) from the village.

Air Oceania, *Tel. 82.10.47, Fax 689/85.52.12*, flies a nine-seater Cessna or a five-seater Aero Commander from Tahiti to Fakarava each Wednesday, for 14.000 CFP ($140) one way. Divers get a 1.000 CFP ($10) discount on the airfare.

Arriving by Boat

The **Au'ura Nui III**, *Tel. 43.92.40*, is a passenger-cargo ship owned by Sane Richmond, who also owns Tetamanu Village in Fakarava. During the voyages through the central Tuamotus, the ship stops first at Anaa, then at Tetamanu. The one-way fare for deck passage is 3.000 CFP ($30) per person, and 6.000 CFP ($60) in a cabin. Three daily meals cost 2.200 CFP ($22) per person.

Other ships serving Fakarava are: the **Manava II**, *Tel. 43.83.84/ 42.25.53*; **St.-Xavier Maris Stella**, *Tel. 42.23.58*; and the **Vai Ato**, *Tel. 43.99.96*.

Departing by Air

Air Tahiti flies direct from Fakarava to Tahiti each Wednesday and Friday, and the flight from Fakarava stops in Rangiroa enroute to Tahiti on Mondays. **Air Tahiti reservations** *in Fakarava, Tel. 98.42.30*.

Departing by Boat

If you take the *Au'ura Nui III* back to Papeete, you'll stop in Faaite, Katiu, Makemo, Taenga, Nihiru, Hikueru and Marokau before reaching the Papeete Pass. The *Manava II* will take you from Fakarava to Aratika, Raraka, Kauehi, Niau and Tahiti. The *St.-Xavier Maris Stella* will take you to Kauehi, Aratika, Toau, Arutua, Kaukura, Apataki, Mataiva, Tikehau and Papeete. And the *Vai Ato* will show you Toau, Apataki, and Kaukura on the way to Tahiti. There are no direct Fakarava-Tahiti passages.

WHERE TO STAY

TETAMANU VILLAGE, *B.P. 9364, Motu Uta, 98713 Papeete, Tahiti, Tel. 689/43.92.70/Fax 689/42.77.70. Beside the pass in Tetamanu village, 55 kilometers (34 miles) by boat from the airport and main village. AP Rates: bungalow with all meals 10.000 CFP ($100) per person per day; half-fare for child under 12 years. Minimum stay three nights. Round-trip boat transfers are provided. Add 1% value added tax to room rates and meal plan. No credit cards.*

There are six thatched roof beach bungalows, each with a double and single bed; outside communal bath facilities with cold water, a separate *fare* for dining and bar; solar freezer and electricity, house linens are provided. This pension is right at the edge of the pass, where a private pontoon is built over the water for line fishing and swimming. The activities are centered around the lagoon, and a trawler with three cabins is used for excursions on the lagoon and to the neighboring atolls.

FAKARAVA PARADIS, *B.P. 7, 98763 Rotoava, Fakarava, Tel. 689/ 98.42.89, Fax 689/98.42.00. On Motu Maiuru, a private islet 15 minutes by boat from the airport. Rates: fare with breakfast 5.000 CFP ($50) per person; fare with breakfast, lunch and dinner 6.500 CFP ($65) per person. Round-trip boat transfers 2.000 CFP ($20) per person. Add 1% value added tax to room rates and meal plan. No credit cards.*

Three little *fares* each have a double bed, and guests share the dining room and communal bathroom with cold water shower. House linens are furnished. Free activities include snorkeling equipment, net or line fishing, shark feeding and boat excursions to visit the *motu* islets inside the lagoon.

RELAIS MARAMA, *98763, Rotoava, Tel. 689/98.42.25. Beside the ocean in Rotoava Village, 6 kilometers (3.7 miles) from the airport. EP Rates: room 2.500 CFP($25) single, 4.000 CFP ($40) double; garden bungalow 5.000 CFP ($50) single/double; add 1.000 CFP ($10) per day for extra person; room or bungalow and all meals 6.000 CFP ($60) per person a day. Round-trip transfers provided. Add 1% value added tax to room rates and meal plan. No credit cards.*

A small house with a sheet metal roof has three bedrooms with single or double beds, a communal living room with television, kitchen, dining room, and bathroom with a cold water shower. A separate thatched roof garden bungalow has a double bed and fan, and shares the communal bath facilities. House linens are furnished.

SPORTS & RECREATION
Sail & Dive Charters
VPM Dufour Yachting, *Tel. 689/56.40.50,* offers 8 day/7 night Sail & Dive Cruises in the Tuamotu archipelago. On Monday you fly from Papeete to Fakarava by Air Tahiti and board the 82-foot catamaran *Nemo*. You will dive the passes of Fakarava, Kauehi and Toau during the week and fly back from Fakarava to Tahiti the following Monday. See further information in *Moorea* chapter.

Scuba Diving
Spiro Dive Center Rotoava, *B.P. 33002, Paea, Tahiti, Tel. 689/43.07.50, Fax 689/43.07.54,* was opened in 1996 by Marc-Antoine Baudart, an international CMAS two-star monitor and BEES 1 professional diver. This center is located next to Kiritia Village, a six-bungalow hostel with accommodations for the divers. Tetamanu Village is also used to house the scuba divers.

Using the latest and most sophisticated Spirotechnique equipment, Baudart and his assistant, Noël Pourcelot, a CMAS and PADI instructor, take divers to explore some of the best dive sites in the wide and deep passes, inside the lagoon and outside the coral reef. You can also visit several of the 80 *motu* islets, which are bordered by white sand beaches.

Note: At publication time the Spiro Dive Center was closed, pending a hearing on a diving accident that resulted in the death of a client. The Kiritia Village was also closed.

23. MARQUESAS ISLANDS

The South Seas Island image of tranquil lagoons protected by coral reefs are not part of the scenery in the **Marquesas Islands**. Rising like a mirage from the swells of the cobalt blue Pacific, the rugged volcanic cliffs soar like rock fortresses thousands of feet above the thundering sea. The wild ocean beats endlessly against the craggy, sculpted coasts, unbroken by any barriers for almost 6,400 km. (4,000 miles).

Beyond the tumbling breakers lie the fjord-like bays, the narrow shores and curving beaches of golden black sand. Sheltered coves reveal a turquoise tide with pink and white sand beaches. Behind the seaside cliffs the electric green grasslands wander gently upward. Brooding and black with frequent rains, the jagged peaks and spires become a fairy castle in the clouds of the setting sun.

Lying north-northwest by south-southeast along a 350 kilometer (217 mile) submarine chain, the Marquesas Islands are all of volcanic origin. Scientists believe that these islands rose from the oceanic depths and their foundations are submerged 4,000 meters (13,120 feet) below sea level. The island of Fatu Hiva is the youngest of the chain, with an age of only 1.35 million years, while the most ancient island in the Marquesas group is the uninhabited island of Ei'ao, which was formed 5.2 to 7.5 million years ago. This is the youngest group of islands in French Polynesia and the farthest removed from any continent.

The Marquesas Islands are 7.50 to 10.35 degrees south of the Equator, and 138.25 to 140.50 degrees west longitude. They form two geographical groups about 111 kilometers (69 miles) apart, with a combined land area of 1,279 square kilometers (492 square miles) for the 20 or so islands,

The southern group consists of the three inhabited islands of **Hiva Oa**, **Tahuata** and **Fatu Hiva**, plus a few smaller islets. The northern group comprises the three principal islands of **Ua Pou**, **Nuku Hiva** and **Ua Huka**, and several uninhabited islands, including **Eiao** and **Hatutu**, which lie about 80 kilometers(50 miles) northwest of the other islands in the northern group.

Nuku Hiva, the administrative center of the northern Marquesas, is about 1,500 kilometers (932 miles) northeast of Tahiti, and Hiva Oa, the main island in the southern group, lies approximately 1,400 kilometers (868 miles) northeast of Tahiti, a 3 1/2 hour flight by Air Tahiti's 46-passenger ATR 42 airplanes. Marquesan time is one-half hour ahead of the rest of the islands in French Polynesia. When it is 6am in Tahiti, it is 6:30am in the Marquesas.

The average temperature of the Marquesas is about 27 degrees Celsius (80 degrees Fahrenheit), with the hottest weather in March and the coolest temperatures in August. Although there is usually more than 80 percent humidity, the climate is healthy and fairly pleasant. The trade winds prevail between April and October, but at other times of the year there can be some hot, calm days. The annual rainfall varies greatly and is unevenly distributed. Fatu Hiva is the most lush island of all, therefore, it receives the greatest amount of rain.

Land of the Men

Maohi people, whom the Europeans called Polynesians, settled in the valleys of these islands some 2,000 to 2,500 years ago, sailing their double-hulled canoes from Samoa or Tonga. Their legends tell of the god **Tiki**, ancestor of man, who conjured up a dozen islands from the ocean depths. These proud and fierce warriors were divided into clans, living in isolated valleys, separated by steep, knife-edge ridges. They had abundance, but also seasons of draught, famine and tribal wars. They tattooed their bodies in intricate patterns learned from their god Tiki. As they evolved they made exquisite carvings in wood, stone, ivory and bone. They built their homes on *paepae* platforms, worshipped their gods in *me'ae* temples of stone, and were feared cannibals. In the northern islands they called their adopted home *Te Henua Te Enata*, and in the southern group it was *Te Henua Te Enana*, "Land of The Men."

In later years the descendants of The Men learned the origins of their islands from their legends, and had a story for the way their islands were named. Folklore tells that the islands were born of a marriage between the sea and sky. Their god Atua built a house: Nuku Hiva was its pointed roof; Ua Pou was its support posts or pillars; Ua Huka was the binding; Hiva Oa was the ridge pole; Fatu Hiva was the thatched roof; and Tahuata was the celebration of its completion.

European Conquerors

The history of the Marquesas with the arrival of the Europeans was varied and often tragic. In 1595 Spanish explorer Alvaro de Mendaña discovered the southern group, which he named Las Marquesas de Mendoza—in honor of the wife of his patron, Don Garcia Hurtado de

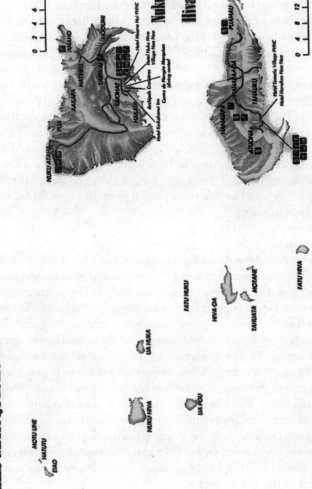

Mendoza, Marquis de Canete, Viceroy of Peru. When Mendaña sailed away 200 islanders lay dead on the beach of Tahuata.

Captain James Cook claimed the southern group for England in 1774, estimating the population at 100,000. Joseph Ingraham of Boston discovered the northern group in 1791, and explorers from France, Germany and Russia also planted their flags on these distant shores.

These islands became a regular port-of-call for the men sailing the Pacific—crews hungry for a touch of land, women and recreation. Australians seeking the valuable sandalwood that grew in abundance in the valleys of the Marquesas brought their sailors to these shores. Later the American whaling ships arrived, often leaving behind those deserters who had jumped ship. Over the years there were all kinds of blackbirders, profiteers, beachcombers and adventurers who sought refuge in the Marquesas. They brought guns, alcohol, opium, smallpox, syphilis and other deadly diseases, which almost decimated the entire population.

In 1842 the whole archipelago was annexed to France under the name *Iles Marquises*. Catholic missionaries were installed and a new rule began. Yet the decline of the population continued. When the French took control in 1842 there were 20,000 people living in the Marquesas Islands. Thirty years later that number dropped to 6,200. The all-time low of 2,225 people was recorded in 1926, and 131 of this number were non-natives. The population at the last census in 1996 was 8,064, still only a fraction of what it was a century and a half ago, but on the rise again. More than 50 percent of this number are under the age of 19 years. Most of the inhabitants are Catholics.

Modern Marquesas

The Marquesas Islands today are quite modern, with electricity, international communications services, a television station, airports on the islands of Nuku Hiva, Hiva Oa, Ua Pou and Ua Huka, and efficient boat docks in the larger villages for the supply ships that provide regular service from Tahiti.

Farming and fishing are carried out on a family scale. The villagers live mostly from the land and sea, earning money for purchased supplies by copra production. A recent addition to the cash economy is generated by the wild pickings of the *noni*, the *Morinda Citrifolia*, a potato-like fruit that grows on a tall bush. The juice from this fruit is sold as a tonic to cure anything from sore throats to syphilis, or as a panacea to heal a wide range of ailments from colds to cancers. While encouraging the exploitation of this business, the local government tries to discourage the islanders from abandoning their subsidized copra plantations in favor of planting *noni* to be shipped to the US market.

There are airstrips on four of the six main islands. The *Aranui* cruises to the Marquesas Islands 15 times a year, during its 16-day round-trip voyages from Tahiti. The ship calls at every principal valley and many smaller ones on each inhabited island. This is the most practical and enjoyable way to make a brief visit to the Marquesas, as the costs of land and sea transportation are very expensive for individual travelers. See information on the *Aranui* under *Inter-Island Cruises, Passenger Boats and Freighters* in the chapter on *Planning Your Trip.*

Accommodations are available in small hotels, pensions and family homes on each island, and two small hotels will open in 1999 on Nuku Hiva and Hiva Oa. The 6-bungalow Keikahanui Inn in Taiohae will be closed in early April, 1998, rebuilt and enlarged to 20 bungalows, opening in June 1999, as the **Keikahanui Noa Noa**. The 6-bungalow Hotel Hanakee in Atuona will be enlarged to 20 bungalows and renamed the **Hotel Hanakee Noa Noa**, also reopening in June, 1999.

Activities in the Marquesas Islands include 4-wheel drive excursions, helicopter flights, horseback riding, hiking over mountain trails and to inland cascades, picnics on the beach or in the mountains, deep-sea fishing, sailing, motorboat rides, scuba diving, visits to archaeological sites and stone tikis, and visits to the workshops of crafts people to buy wood carvings and tapa hangings.

A fragrant bouquet of flowers and herbs is worn in the hair or around the necks of the Marquesan women. This is called *kumu hei* in the northern group and *umu hei* in the southern islands. Their *monoi* is a delightful blend of coconut oil, sandalwood, spearmint, jasmine, ginger root, pineapple, sweet basil, gardenia, pandanus fruit, ylang-ylang and other mysterious herbs. This is used as perfume, for massages, to seduce a boyfriend or to ward off mosquitoes.

NUKU HIVA

In Marquesan mythology, **Nuku Hiva** was the first island to be raised from the ocean depths by the god Tiki. who created a wife from a pile of sand. Even today this beautiful emerald isle, located about 1,500 kilometers (932 miles) northeast of Tahiti, is the leader of the Marquesas archipelago.

Captain Joseph Ingraham from Boston discovered Nuku Hiva in 1791, followed the same year by French Etienne Marchand. When Russian Admiral Krusenstern landed in Taiohae Bay in 1804 they found an Englishman and a Frenchman, who had deserted their ships to settle in Nuku Hiva. Cabry, the Frenchman, was tattooed from head to foot, just like his hosts in Taiohae.

AN AMERICAN COLONY

In October 1813, Taiohae was invaded by the United States Navy and Marine Corps. They arrived aboard the Essex, a 32-gun, 14-year-old frigate commanded by **Captain David Porter**. *Under the steve of her bowsprit stood a grim carved figurehead, an Indian chieftain with a raised tomahawk held ready in his right hand and a scalping knife clasped in his left. The ship flew a long white pennant from her mainmast with the words of her motto: "Free Trade and Sailor's Rights." Porter was also in charge of the Essex Junior, a small sloop-of-war he had taken as a prize, along with 200 English captives.*

Although he came to Nuku Hiva in peace, Porter was convinced by the Te'i'i chief **Keatanui** *of Taiohae to help defend his people against the Hapa'a tribe. When they were subdued by the American guns the Hapa'a warriors joined forces with the Te'i'i to build a village for the Americans, which Porter named Madison City. A stout coconut log fort was called Fort Madison.*

On November 19, 1813, Porter took possession of Nuku Hiva, declaring it to be a United States possession, Madison's Island Colony, in honor of the United States President James Madison. The island had already been named by earlier European or American explorers Federal, Franklin, Ile Baux, Adams and Sir Henry Maryin's Island, before the Essex arrived.

Five weeks after his arrival in Nuku Hiva Porter launched an attack against the raiding Taipi tribes. His first attempt from the sea was a failure. Porter's 200 men then hauled the ship's guns up the mountain to Muake Pass and made an overland attack, which killed several of the Taipi.

Porter left one of his lieutenants in charge of the fort and sailed to Valparaiso for a year. No sooner had the sails of the Essex disappeared over the horizon when the remaining Americans and Englishmen were imprisoned and tortured. They eventually escaped and sailed to Hawaii aboard the Essex Junior. Thus ended the first American colony in the South Pacific. But for the next 30 years the war drums were to beat their rhythm of death. War conches were to awaken the anger of ancient, terrible gods, who called their vengeance upon any remnant of the once-feared white warriors, who had burned the temples and made the proud chiefs of Taipi kneel in submission. Because of Porter's exploit in Nuku Hiva, the lives of no white man were safe until France assumed control in 1842.

With a surface area of 330 square kilometers (127 square miles), Nuku Hiva is the largest island of the Marquesas group. The beauty of

Nuku Hiva is truly breathtaking, whether viewed from the sea or the mountain heights. On the crenelated north coast is Taiohae Bay, a spectacular giant amphitheater dominated by emerald peaks and waterfalls. This is a welcome haven for cruising yachts from all over the world, who drop anchor here after a month or more at sea. Taiohae is a pleasant village bordering the sea and serves as the administrative, economic, educational and health center of the Marquesas Islands. Here are the French and Territorial administrators, government buildings, *gendarmerie*, post office, general hospital, town hall, Air Tahiti office, banks and schools.

The 2,375 inhabitants live in the villages of Taiohae, Taipivai, Hatiheu, Aakapa, Pua, Houmi, Anaho and Hakaui, which are separated by serrated mountain ranges, and connected by rutted roads best suited for four-wheel drive vehicles and horses. These residents work for the government, the community, Catholic church or school system, or for themselves—chopping copra high in the mountains, fishing, raising cattle and other livestock, or sculpting bowls, platters, Marquesan ceremonial clubs, tikis and ukuleles.

The Notre-Dame Cathedral of the Marquesas Islands contains magnificently carved sculptures by craftsmen from each of the Marquesas Islands. You can visit the sculptors' workshops and arts and crafts centers in the villages of Taiohae, Hatiheu and Taipivai. You can rent a horse, a 4WD or pickup truck with chauffeur, or a speed boat with pilot. A scuba diving center is located in Taiohae and two yacht charter companies have catamarans based here year-round. You can hang glide from the peaks of Nuku Hiva or take a helicopter flight to Hakaui Valley, with its steep gorges and Ahuii waterfall, one of the world's highest cascades, at an altitude of 350 meters (1,148 feet). Near Hatiheu and Taipivai are ceremonial platforms, stone tikis and petroglyphs hidden deep in the valleys.

Accommodations are available in small hotels and pensions. Taiohae has a few restaurants and snack bars, a public market with fresh produce, and stores well stocked with food, clothing and household items. In Hatiheu you will find one of the best restaurants in the Marquesas Islands.

ARRIVALS & DEPARTURES

Arriving By Air

Air Tahiti, *Tel. 86.42.42/86.41.84*, flies ATR 42 turbo jet planes direct from Tahiti to Nuku Hiva each Wednesday, Thursday and Sunday in 3 1/2 hours. Each Tuesday's flight stops in Hiva Oa and each Saturday's flight stops in Rangiroa and Manihi. The one-way airfare from Tahiti to Nuku Hiva is 30.135 CFP ($30.135); from Rangiroa or Manihi to Nuku Hiva the one-way fare is 25.725 CFP ($257.25); and from Hiva Oa to Nuku Hiva the one-way fare is 9.240 CFP ($92.40). You can also fly to Nuku Hiva from Ua Pou or Ua Huka each Thursday for a one-way fare of 5.355 CFP ($53.55) from either island, aboard 19-passenger Dornier aircraft. These inter-Marquesas flights correspond to the schedule of the ATR 42 flights to Tahiti. See further information under *Hiva Oa*, *Ua Pou* and *Ua Huka* in this chapter.

The 32-kilometer (20 mile) road between the Nuku Ataha airport and Taiohae village takes about two hours in a four-wheel drive vehicle. The unpaved road winds across the Toovii Plateau and the road is rutted, often very muddy and always uncomfortable. Most people prefer to take the helicopter shuttle service.

Arriving By Boat

The *Aranui* includes stops at Taiohae, Hatiheu and Taipivai during its 16-day round-trip cruise program from Tahiti to the Marquesas. The *Taporo IV* includes Taiohae in its 10-day round-trip voyages from Tahiti. See details in section on *Inter-Island Cruise Ships and Cargo/Passenger Boats* in Chapter 6, *Planning Your Trip*.

Departing By Air

There is a direct ATR 42 flight between Nuku Hiva and Tahiti each Tuesday, Wednesday, Thursday and Friday. You can fly ATR 42 aircraft from Nuku Hiva to Hiva Oa each Wednesday and Sunday, and continue on to Tahiti from Atuona on Sunday. The Dornier 19-passenger flights will take you from Nuku Hiva to Ua Pou or Ua Huka on Thursdays. **Air Tahiti reservations** *in Taiohae, Tel. 92.03.41/92.05.02; Nuku Ataha airport, Tel. 92.01.45.*

Departing By Boat

The *Aranui* arrives in Taiohae Bay on the sixth day of its 16-day voyage from Tahiti to the Marquesas Islands. An alternative to taking the entire trip is to fly to Nuku Hiva and join the ship there, which will give you the opportunity of visiting all the inhabited islands in the Marquesas, with a stop in Rangiroa on the return trip to Tahiti. Or you can make the round of the Marquesas on board the ship and fly back to Tahiti. If you're just looking for a one-way passage from the Marquesas to Tahiti, the *Aranui* calls at Nuku Hiva on the 13th day of its schedule, and from there goes to Ua Pou, Rangiroa and Tahiti, which will give you only three nights aboard the ship. See details in section on *Inter-Island Cruise Ships and Cargo/Passenger Boats* in Chapter 6, *Planning Your Trip*.

ORIENTATION

Nuku Ataha airport is a 3 1/2 hour direct flight from Tahiti, and can be reached from Hiva Oa, Ua Pou and Ua Huka, with connections to Rangiroa and Manihi. The principal town of **Taiohae** is 32 kilometers (20 miles) from the airport at La Terre Deserte. A twisting dirt road from the airport winds through the mountains and the Toovii plateau, 800 meters (2,624 feet) above the valleys of ferns, giant mango trees and coconut palms.

The village of Taiohae follows the semicircular curve of **Taiohae Bay** for about 3.5 kilometers (2 miles), from the ship dock on the east to the **Keikahanui Inn Noa Noa** on the west. Flowering flamboyant trees shade the road that passes through the village between the bay and the administrative buildings, hospital, church, school, post office, bank, shops, boutiques and small hotels. Sundays and holidays are just as busy as any work day, when the villagers drive back and forth along the seafront road in their four-wheel drive vehicles, calling out to their friends and stopping to join the game of petanque being played beside the black sand beach. Nearby the women sit under a shelter and play bingo, while the children splash in the rollers that crash onto the beach.

GETTING AROUND

Helicopter Flights

Heli-Inter Marquises, *Tel. 92.00.54/92.02.17 Taiohae office; Tel 92.04.40 Nuku Ataha airport.* Two AS 355 helicopters can transport six passengers each for sightseeing tours over Nuku Hiva or for air transport between the Nuku Ataha Airport and Taiohae Village, or between the airport and the Nuku Hiva villages of Taipivai, Hatiheu and Aakapa. The round-trip transfer is 13.800 CFP ($138) per passenger. Inter-island flights between Taiohae and Ua Pou are made each Wednesday, Friday and Sunday for 12.000 CFP ($120) per person.

4-Wheel Drive Vehicle (4x4) Rentals

Teiki Transports in Taiohae village is operated by Joseph Teiki Puhetini, *Tel. 92.03.47.* He will drive you from Taiohae to Taipivai, Hatiheu or to Aakapa and back to Taiohae, or to the Nuku Ataha airport. Be prepared to pay a minimum of 10.000 CFP ($100) and often much more when you hire a car with chauffeur.

Charles Monbaerts at Hotel Moana Nui, *Tel. 92.03.30,* will rent you a self-drive vehicle.

WHERE TO STAY
Expensive
KEIKAHANUI INN NOA NOA, *B.P. 21, 98742 Taiohae, Nuku Hiva, Tel. 689/92.03.82; Fax 689/92.00.74. Reservations: South Pacific Marketing, B.P. 718, 98713 Papeete, Tahiti, Tel. 689/43.90.04; Fax 689/41.39.23. Overlooking Taiohae Bay, 2 kilometers (1.2 miles) from the Taiohae pier and 32 kilometers (20 miles) from the airport. EP Rates: Ocean view bungalow 20.000 CFP ($200) single/double; add 3.000 CFP ($30) for third person. Meal plan with breakfast and dinner add 5.300 CFP ($53) per person; meal plan with breakfast, lunch and dinner add 7.500 CFP ($75) per person; full American breakfast 1.600 CFP ($16); fruit basket 1.800 CFP ($18); bottle of champagne 5.500 CFP ($55). Add 7% hotel tax to room rates and 1% value added tax to room rates and meal plan. One-way transfer from airport to hotel by 4WD 4.000 CFP ($40) per person; one-way transfer from airport to Taiohae village by helicopter 7.000 CFP ($70); one-way transfer from Taiohae village to hotel by 4WD 900 CFP ($9) per person. All major credit cards.*

This 6-bungalow hotel is scheduled to close in April, 1998, and will reopen in June, 1999, with 20 ocean view bungalows. Each bungalow will have an overhead fan or air-conditioner, mini-bar refrigerator, tea and coffee making facilities, international direct dial telephone, safe, shower, hair dryer and terrace. The public facilities will include a restaurant and bar, reception, boutique and swimming pool. Room service will also be available. Activities will include bicycle and 4-wheel drive rentals, helicopter tours, deep sea fishing, horseback riding, boat excursions, scuba diving, Jeep safari tours, visits to handcrafts centers and wood sculptors workshops, historical tours and walks in the mountains.

Moderate
NUKU HIVA VILLAGE NOA NOA, *B.P. 82, 98742 Taiohae, Nuku Hiva. Tel. 689/92.01.94; Fax 689/92.05.97. Reservations: South Pacific Marketing, B.P. 718, 98713 Papeete, Tahiti, Tel. 689/43.90.04; Fax 689/ 41.39.23. On mountain side, 2 kilometers (1.2 miles) from the Taiohae pier and 32 kilometers (20 miles) from the airport. 15 bungalows. EP Rates: bungalow 6.500 CFP ($65) single; 7.500 CFP ($75) double. Meal plan with breakfast and dinner add 3.500 CFP ($35) per person; meal plan with breakfast, lunch and dinner add 4.700 CFP ($47) per person. Add 1% value added tax to room rates and meal plan. Round-trip transfers: 7.000 CFP ($70) per person by 4WD; 13.800 CFP ($138) per person by helicopter. American Express, Mastercard, Visa.*

The 15 thatched roof bungalows spread out on a big grassy lawn facing Taiohae Bay are typically Polynesian style, with woven bamboo walls and a private terrace. Each room contains a double bed and a single bed, a private bathroom with hot water and an overhead fan. The restaurant and bar are very popular with local residents, especially on weekends, when there may be music and singing and dancing.

MOANA NUI, *B.P. 93, 98742 Taiohae, Nuku Hiva. Tel. 689/92.03.30; Fax 689/92.00.02. On mountain side 600 meters (654 yards) from the boat dock and 32 kilometers (20 miles) from the airport. EP Rates: room with breakfast 4.000 CFP ($40) single; 4.500 CFP ($45) double; Meal plan with room, breakfast and dinner 6.500 CFP ($65) single, 9.500 CFP ($95) double; meal plan with room, breakfast, lunch and dinner 9.500 CFP ($95) single, 13.000 CFP ($130) double; house 10.000 CFP ($100) per day, 60.000 ($600) per week, 100.000 CFP ($1,000) for two weeks. Add 1% value added tax to room rates and meal plan. Round-trip transfers: 7.000 CFP ($70) per person by 4WD; 13.800 CFP ($138) per person by helicopter. Mastercard, Visa.*

This two-story building has seven rooms upstairs, with single or double beds and private bathrooms with hot water showers. House linens are furnished. The restaurant and bar downstairs serves three daily meals, which may be steak and fries or Marquesan seafood specialties. A one bedroom house separate from the hotel premises is practical for cooking your own meals. It has a kitchen, dining room with television, private bathroom with hot water shower, washing machine and house linens. There's nothing fancy about this hotel, but it's conveniently located if you want to be in Taiohae village.

Inexpensive

MOETAI VILLAGE, *98742, Nuku Ataha, Nuku Hiva. Tel. 689/ 92.04.91. On mountain side, 500 meters (545 yards) from the Nuku Ataha airport and 32 kilometers (20 miles) from Taiohae village. EP Rates: Room plus breakfast 2.500 CFP ($25) single, 3.500 CFP ($35) double, 4.500 CFP ($45) triple. Meal plan with room and all meals 6.000 CFP ($60) per person; add 1.000 CFP ($10) per day for additional person. Add 1% value added tax to room rates and meal plan. Round-trip transfers provided. No credit cards.*

If you need a place to stay next to the airport, this small hotel with five bungalows offers accommodations for three to four people in each unit. Private bathrooms with cold water and house linens are supplied, and there is a restaurant on the premises.

CHEZ FETU, *B.P. 22, 98728 Taiohae, Nuku Hiva. Tel. 689/92.03.66. On mountain side in Taiohae village, 1.5 kilometers (.9 miles) from the boat dock and 32 kilometers (20 miles) from the airport. EP Rates: Bungalow or room 2.000 CFP ($20) single, 4.000 CFP ($40) double, 6.000 CFP ($60) triple; 50.000 CFP ($500) single/double per month. Breakfast on request. Add 1% value added tax to room rates and meal plan. Round-trip transfers: 7.000 CFP ($70) per person by 4WD; 13.800 CFP ($138) per person by helicopter. No credit cards.*

You have a choice of a bungalow with a private bathroom and cold water or a 4-bedroom house with a communal bathroom with cold water, a kitchen and dining room. House linens are furnished. This is in the center of Taiohae village and you can easily walk to the stores, banks, cathedral and beach.

CHEZ YVONNE, *B.P. 199, 98742, Taiohae, Nuku Hiva. Tel. 689/ 92.02.97; Fax 689/92.01.28. On mountain side in Hatiheu village, 500 meters (545 yards) from the Hatiheu boat landing and 28 kilometers (17 miles) from Taiohae Bay. EP Rates: Bungalow plus breakfast 2.500 CFP ($25) single, 4.800 CFP ($48) double. Meal plan with breakfast and dinner add 3.000 to 3.800 CFP ($30-$38) per person. Add 1% value added tax to room rates and meal plan. Round-trip transfers: 7.000 CFP ($70) per person by 4WD; 13.800 CFP ($138) per person by helicopter. No credit cards.*

Yvonne Katupa is the energetic mayor of Hatiheu and she finds time to cook the best food you can find in the Marquesas Islands. The five little bungalows adjacent to the restaurant have a double bed or two single beds, with a private bathroom and cold water shower in each room. House linens are included. This pension is in the center of Hatiheu village and you can walk to the church, archaeological sites and artisan center. A black sand beach is in front of the bungalows.

TE PUA HINAKO, *B.P. 202, 98742, Taiohae, Nuku Hiva. Tel. 689/ 92.04.14. Beside the beach in Anaho Bay, 2 kilometers (1.2 miles) from Hatiheu village and 30 kilometers (19 miles) from Taiohae Bay. EP Rates: Room plus breakfast 2.000 CFP ($20) per person; meal plan with room, breakfast and dinner 3.500 CFP ($35) per person; meal plan with room, breakfast, lunch and dinner 5.000 CFP ($50) per person. Add 1% value added tax to room rates and meal plan. Round-trip transfers: 10.000 CFP ($100) for 6 passengers in boat, 13.800 CFP ($138) per person by helicopter. No credit cards.*

It's worth staying here just to swim in the beautiful Anaho Bay, bordered by a beach of soft pink sand. A two-bedroom house has both single and double beds, a communal bathroom with cold water, and house linens are furnished. A restaurant and bar are on the premises. Activities include line fishing, free diving, swimming and shelling. You can also find a horse to ride along the beach if you just ask Juliette.

KAOHA TIARE, *B.P. 290, 98742 Taiohae, Nuku Hiva. Tel. 689/ 92.00.08/92.02.66. Beside the beach in Anaho Bay, 2 kilometers (1.2 miles) from Hatiheu village and 30 kilometers (19 miles) from Taiohae Bay. EP Rates: bungalow 3.000 CFP ($30) single, 4.000 CFP ($40) double; meal plan with bungalow, breakfast, lunch and dinner 6.000 CFP ($60) per person. Add 1% value added tax to room rates and meal plan. Round-trip transfers: 7.000 CFP ($70) per person by 4WD; 13.800 CFP ($138) per person by helicopter. No credit cards.*

This five-bungalow pension is due to open in June, 1998, at Anaho Bay. Each bungalow will be furnished with a double bed and a private bathroom with cold water, a terrace and house linens. I'm not sure whether they will serve food or if you will have to make arrangements with Juliette at Te Pua Hinako for your meals.

CHEZ MARTINE, *B.P. 60, 98742 Taiohae, Nuku Hiva. Tel. 689/ 92.01.19; Fax 689/92.05.34. On mountain side in Taipivai Valley, 20 kilometers (12.4 miles) from the boat dock in Taiohae Bay. EP Rates: room and breakfast 2.000 CFP ($20) per person; meal plan with room, breakfast and dinner 4.000 CFP ($40) per person; meal plan with room, breakfast, lunch and dinner 6.000 CFP ($60) per person. Add 1% value added tax to room rates and meal plan. Round-trip transfers: 13.800 CFP ($138) per person by helicopter. No credit cards.*

If you have a desire to spend a few days in the valley that Herman Melville made famous in his book *Typee*, this four-bedroom house will provide simple but comfortable accommodations. The communal bathroom has hot water, the linens are furnished and Martine will serve you Marquesan style meals in her restaurant.

ANDY'S DREAM, *B.P. 111, 98742 Taiohae, Nuku Hiva. Tel. 689/ 92.00.80; Fax 689/92.04.05. On mountain side in Hoata Valley, 1 kilometer (.62 miles) from the boat dock in Taiohae Bay and 32 kilometers (20 miles) from the airport. EP Rates: Room or bungalow and breakfast 3.000 CFP ($30) per person; meal plan with room or bungalow, breakfast and dinner 5.000 CFP ($50) per person; meal plan with room or bungalow, breakfast, lunch and dinner 7.000 CFP ($70). Four night stay with all meals and activities included 100.000 CFP ($1,000) per person. Add 1% value added tax to room rates and meal plan. Round-trip transfers: 7.000 CFP ($70) per person by 4WD; 13.800 CFP ($138) per person by helicopter. No credit cards.*

These two little bungalows have corrugated metal roofs and concrete walls, which are a far cry from the escapist's dream of a South Seas thatched roof bungalow by the sea. However, the Marquesas Islands are not the Tuamotus or the Society Islands. It has a different energy, and Andy's Dream is brightly decorated, which may offset the brooding mountains that tower above the island. You have a choice of one or two bedrooms. Each bungalow has a kitchen, television, terrace and bathroom with cold water. House linens are furnished.

WHERE TO EAT
Moderate
NUKU HIVA VILLAGE, *Taiohae, Tel. 92.01.94. Reserve. All major credit cards.*

Open daily for breakfast, lunch and dinner. French and local cuisine is served, featuring tuna salad for 700 CFP ($7), hamburgers for 950 CFP ($9.50), grilled fish for 1.100 CFP ($11), steak for 1.350 to 1.500 CFP ($13.50 to $15), *magret de canard* for 1.800 CFP ($18); and grilled lobster for 2.500 CFP ($25). Desserts include a fresh fruit cup, banana split and *pêche melba.*

MOANA NUI, *Taiohae, Tel. 92.03.30. Reserve. All major credit cards.* Open daily except Sunday for breakfast, lunch and dinner. Local and French cuisine and buffet dinners are served.

LE KOVIVI, *Taiohae, Tel. 92.03.85. Reserve. No credit cards.* Open daily except Sunday for breakfast, lunch and dinner. The menu includes French and local cuisine, and you can get take-away meals.

MOETAI VILLAGE, *Nuku Ataha Airport, Tel. 92.04.91. Reserve. No credit cards.* Open daily for breakfast, lunch and dinner, serving local style dishes and French cuisine.

NUKU ATAHA AIRPORT, *Tel. 92.02.94. No credit cards.* Breakfast, lunch and dinner served when the airport is open for each arrival and departure of Air Tahiti flights. Local style cuisine and snacks are served.

CHEZ MARTINE HAITI, *Tel. 92.01.19, in Taipivai. Reserve. No credit cards.* Open daily, serves breakfast, lunch and dinner, specializing in local cuisine.

CHEZ YVONNE KATUPA, *Tel. 92.02.97 in Hatiheu village. Reservations are a must at this popular restaurant. No credit cards.* Open for breakfast, lunch and dinner. Yvonne's cuisine is famous throughout Polynesia. Her specialty is the fresh water shrimp that are caught in the river nearby, which she lightly batters and fries. She also cooks very tasty barbecued chicken legs, tuna fritters and grilled lobster.

SEEING THE SIGHTS

The **Notre-Dame Cathedral of the Marquesas Islands** is located in the Catholic mission on the west side of Taiohae village. The cathedral was built in 1977, using stones from all the inhabited islands in the archipelago. The magnificent carvings were made by several of the local sculptors.

The **Herman Melville memorial** is a wooden sculpture made by Kahee Taupotini in 1992, which is on the bayside between the cemetery and the nautical club at the west end of the village. Melville wrote two books, *Typee* and *Omoo*, based on his short visit to Nuku Hiva in 1842, when he jumped ship from an American whaler and lived among the Taipi cannibals in Taipivai Valley for three weeks.

Behind Taiohae village you can have a panoramic view of Taiohae Bay and the island of Ua Pou from the summit of **Muake mountain**, which rises 864 meters (2,834 feet). You can get there on foot, by horse or by 4WD.

Hakaui Valley is on the southern coast, about a 20-minute boat ride from Taiohae. You'll have to hike inland over stones for about two hours to reach the **Ahuii waterfall**. This is one of the world's highest cascades, with a single jet of water tumbling from the basaltic rock at an altitude of 350 meters (1,148 feet). You can also reach Hakaui from Taiohae on horseback, riding 12 kilometers (8 miles) along a bridleway that ranges from 400 to 500 meters (1,312 to 1,640 feet) in altitude. You'll appreciate the refreshing pool of water when you get to the waterfall. It's best to go with a guide, and take mosquito repellent, plastic shoes and your swimsuit with you.

Taipivai Valley is 16 kilometers (10 miles) northeast of Taiohae, which you can reach in 30 minutes by boat from Taiohae, or in two hours by 4WD over a rutted road that crosses the **Toovii Plateau**, which has an average altitude of 800 meters (2,624 feet). A navigable river connects Contrôleur Bay with the village boat dock and follows the single dirt road through the village into the valley. American writer Herman Melville made this village famous with his published account of the Taipi tribe who welcomed him into their village in 1842. A **'Cite Melville'** sign marks the place where Melville was supposed to have stayed during his three-week visit. It's on the left side of the Hatiheu road about 4.5 kilometers (2.8 miles) from the bridge in Taipivai village.

The **Paeke archaeological site** in Taipivai has two *me'ae* temples and 11 tikis of reddish colored stone. The trailhead, about four kilometers (2.5 miles) from where the valley begins, is not marked, so it is best to go with a guide. In 1957 American archaeologist **Robert Suggs** excavated **Te Ivi o Hou**, a *tohua* ceremonial site that is 274 meters (300 yards long). You'll need a guide to reach this hidden site, way back in the valley. **Pukiki** in Taipivai, *Tel. 91.01.26*, is familiar with both sites. Protect yourself against *nonos* in the valleys as well as on the beaches.

Hatiheu, on the northern coast, is 28 kilometers (17 miles) from Taiohae and 12 kilometers (7.5 miles) from Taipivai. Hatiheu was the favorite village of the Scottish writer, **Robert Louis Stevenson**, when he visited the Marquesas Islands in 1888 aboard his yacht *Casco*. This is also my first choice on Nuku Hiva, for the beauty and layout of the village, for the food at Chez Yvonne Katupa's restaurant and for the **Hikokua** *tohua* in the valley, beside the road to Taipivai. This archaeological site is about one kilometer (.62 miles) from Chez Yvonne, and it was restored for the Marquesas Festival of Arts. It is a large flat surface 120 meters (394 feet) long, used for dances and other public ceremonies. The *me'ae* are decorated with ancient stone tikis and modern sculptures also decorate the *paepaes*.

At the entrance to the site is a phallic-shaped fertility tiki. It is said that infertile women who touch the tiki will soon become pregnant. A 15-

minute walk up the road brings you to **Kamuihei**, a sacred place shaded by old banyan trees. Here there are boulders carved with petroglyphs of fish, turtles and humans. Just beyond the petroglyph site is a *tohua* complex of boulders and stone platforms in a mysterious dark jungle setting. In Hatiheu village a small **museum** inside the *mairie* (town hall) has a collection of traditional artifacts found in the valley. A white statue of the Virgin Mary was placed on one of the cathedral-shaped peaks overlooking Hatiheu in 1872, 300 meters (984 feet) above the sea. The wooden Catholic church in this village is ideally situated, facing the sea with a backdrop of rolling hills carpeted in shades of green.

Anaho is just a 10-minute boat ride from Hatiheu, and you can also get there by 4WD, horse or hiking the 2-kilometer (1.2-mile) trail, which takes about 90 minutes round trip. Anaho Bay is one of the loveliest spots in the Marquesas Islands, with good swimming in tranquil turquoise water and a crescent-shaped beach with golden-pink sand. Only a few families live in this valley, and the simple little chapel here is perhaps the smallest church in French Polynesia. The manta rays and leopard rays live in the depths of this bay, and the dreaded *nono* hangs out in the beach area. Bring your repellent.

Land Tours

Pua Excursions Nuku Hiva is operated by Georges Pua Taupotini, *Tel. 92.02.94/92.04.18*. He leads guided excursions by 4WD, horseback or hiking. A three-day excursion will take you to the Valley of the Kings, to visit Hakaui Valley and to climb above the Taipivai Valley. You can ride a horse from Taiohae to Anaho and return by motor boat.

An eight-day excursion will take you to the Valley of the Kings by motor boat, a visit to Hakaui Valley to the Ahuii waterfall, to the royal *marae* stone temple of Taiohae and the Cathedral. A mountain excursion by 4WD includes a picnic on Muake peak, and a hike up Taipivai Valley. From Hatiheu Valley you can hike or ride a horse to Aakapa, swim in the afternoon and ride a horse to Anaho to visit the Haatuatua Valley.

SPORTS & RECREATION

Horseback Riding

Sabine Teikiteetini, *Tel. 92.05.68/92.02.60, in Taiohae village*, has six Marquesan horses for rent for one hour, half-day or full-day rides. She will organize excursions for you to explore the valleys by horseback, with or without a guide.

The Ranch is operated by Patrice Temarii, *Tel. 92.06.35*, who has five horses for rent. He can arrange a full-day ride with a picnic and excursions to Hatiheu or Taipivai, with overnight lodging. The cost is 1.000 CFP ($10) per hour and 6.000 CFP ($60) for the day.

Parapente - Hang Gliding

Upe O Te Henua Enana Club is run by Arai Tuheiava and Valérie Tetuanui, *Tel. 92.01.61/92.05.23, Fax 92.03.62 in Taiohae.* Parapente platforms are located on Muake, Vaioa and Paahatea peaks, with five landing sites in football fields or near Taiohae Village, at Tevanui, Paahatea or the Mission. Discovery flights on Tekao mountain overhanging Toovii Plateau to Hatuatua Bay will give you a panoramic view of Taiohae Bay. You can join the parapente club on a three-month temporary basis, which will allow you to rent the parapente for 3.000 CFP ($30). One-week courses are available for 22.500 CFP ($225), and you'll also have to pay 11.400 CFP ($114) for insurance and a license.

Motor Boat Rental

Heetai is a locally built 36-foot tuna fishing boat based at the Taiohae Marina, owned by Laurent Teiki Falchetto, *Tel. 92.05.78.* He will take a maximum of eight passengers to Ua Pou or Ua Huka or to the airport on request.

Makuita is a 36-foot Fiberglas boat owned by Xavier Curvat, *Tel. 92.00.88.* He can take a maximum of 15 passengers on round-trip interisland excursions to Ua Pou and Ua Huka, or to the Nuku Ataha airport.

Sailing Charter Yachts

Archipels Croisières, *B.P. 1160, Moorea, Tel. 689/56.36.39, Fax 689/56.35.87.* This yacht charter company keeps an 8-passenger 57-foot deluxe catamaran based year-round in Taiohae Bay. The four guest cabins are air-conditioned and there are four private heads. One of the 8 day/7 night sailing programs is a Discovery of the Marquesas Cruise that begins in Nuku Hiva on a Sunday and ends in Hiva Oa the following Sunday. During the week you'll visit the islands of Nuku Hiva, Ua Huka, Hiva Oa, Tahuata, Fatu Hiva, back to Tahuata and on to Hiva Oa.

The cost of $2,050 per person is based on "by the cabin" double-occupancy accommodations, and includes all meals and hotel services aboard, transfers between the airport and yacht and all excursions and events specified in the program. The yacht may also be chartered by the day for $2,090.

Dive Cruises can be organized for a minimum of four divers for $2,450 per person. The boat is equipped with two Bauer electric compressors and the necessary number of dive tanks. Two 12-foot dinghies are used for up to five divers. The *Makuita*, a 10 meter (33 foot) deep sea boat owned by the Centre Plongée Marquises (CPM) dive club, is used for six or more divers. This cruise departs from the island of Nuku Hiva, with a minimum of three dives per day in the northern group of Nuku Hiva,

Eiao, Hatutu and Motu One. Scenic land and cultural excursions are also included.

VPM Dufour Tahiti, *Tel. 92.05.13*, has a yacht based in Taiohae Bay that will take you for daysails, leaving at 7:30am and returning around 5pm. A minimum of five passengers are required, and the per person cost is 9.000 CFP ($90), not including meals. The catamaran is 14.5 meters (48 feet) long and has four double cabins, one single cabin and four heads. You can charter this boat with or without a skipper. See *Moorea* chapter for more information.

Scuba Diving

Centre de Plongee Marquises (CPM) is based at the Taiohae Quay, *Tel./Fax 92.00.88.* Xavier Curvat is a French Federal Instructor who has lived in the Marquesas Islands for 15 years. He is a PADI OWSI, BEES 1 and CMAS two-star instructor, and he can give exams for diving certificates. His dive boat is the 33-foot *Makuita*, with complete equipment for 15 divers, plus a compressor and additional bottles. He can take you to more than 20 dive sites in the immediate proximity of Taiohae, or on day trips to Ua Pou, Ua Huka and the other islands in the northern Marquesas group.

You can see an abundance of marine life near the rocky points, where the water is oxygenated continuously by the surf. Among the profusion of color, species and movement, you may see red snappers, groupers, perch and other rock fish seeking shelter in the hollows of rock slides and caves sculpted in volcanic stones, hiding from their predators—tuna, surgeon fish, lionfish and four kinds of jacks or trevally. Curious manta rays, with their graceful ballet movements, will approach you for a closer look. And everywhere you will see sting, eagle and marble rays, lobsters, sponges and rare seashells. A little deeper you can observe barracudas and sharks,. These may include reef sharks, silvertip sharks, Galapagos and silky sharks, hammerhead sharks and melon-head whales.

SHOPPING

You can visit the sculptors' workshops to buy carved bowls, platters, saddles, tikis, ceremonial clubs and intricately carved tables. You can also visit the arts and crafts centers to buy wood carvings. Damien Haturau, *Tel. 92.05.56,* is the best known of the Marquesan sculptors. His works include the statues in the cathedral in Taiohae and the Virgin with Child at the Vaitahu church in Tahuata.

Other noted wood carvers include: Edgard Tamarii, *Tel. 92.01.67*; Tahiahui Haiti, Charles Deane, *Tel. 92.04.13*; Damien Huukena, Bernard Taupotini, *Tel. 92.01.07*; Pierrot Keuvahana, *Tel. 92.06.14*; and Tora Huukena.

PRACTICAL INFORMATION

Banks

Banque Socredo, *Tel. 92.03.63*, has a branch office in Taiohae. It is open Monday to Friday from 7:30 to 11am and 1:30 to 4pm. You can exchange currency and make credit card withdrawals here.

Hospitals

There is a government-operated hospital in Taiohae, *Tel. 92.03.75*, and a dental center. The villages of Hatiheu and Taipivai each have an infirmary.

Police

The French gendarmerie has an office in Taiohae, *Tel. 92.03.61 or 17*.

Post Office & Telecommunications Office

All telecommunications and postal services are available at the post office, which is close to the boat dock in Taiohae, *Tel. 92.03.50*. It is open Monday to Thursday from 8am to 3pm and on Friday from 7:30am to 4:30pm.

Tourist Bureau

Nuku Hiva Visitors Bureau is located on the mountain side between the marina and *mairie* (town hall) in Taiohae village and is open in the mornings only. Deborah Kimitete is the president, *Tel. 92.03.73/92.01.95*.

UA POU

When the Polynesians first settled on the island of **Ua Pou** they named it for the pillars of rock that resemble great cathedral spires. The mountain called Oave Needle, the tallest of the fantastic monoliths, thrusts 1,232 meters (4,040 feet) into the clouds, and Ua Pou's dramatic silhouette is visible from Nuku Hiva, 35 kilometers (22 miles) across the sea, and even from Ua Huka, some 56 kilometers (35 miles) distant.

From the time of the old Polynesian chiefs Ua Pou has always been different from the rest of the Marquesas Islands. Although they formed tribes in the isolated valleys they recognized the authority of a single chief. The people seemed to be more peaceful, more unified and friendly, and the girls of Ua Pou are still considered the prettiest in all of Polynesia.

Ua Pou is the third largest island in the Marquesas archipelago, with 114 square kilometers (44 square miles) of surface area. The 2,013 inhabitants live in the villages of Hakahau, Hakahetau, Haakuti, Hakamaii, Hakamoui, Hakatao, Hohoi and Anahoa. Air Tahiti has 20-minute flight connections to Nuku Hiva and 35 minute flights to Hiva Oa.

The first stone church built in the Marquesas was constructed in Hakahau in 1859, and in Haakuti and Hakahetau villages there are small Catholic churches built on top of old *paepae* platforms. The main village of **Hakahau** has a hospital, *gendarmerie*, bank, post office, food stores, boutiques, Air Tahiti office, port facilities, schools, small family pensions, plus a few simple restaurants and bars.

Ua Pou has experienced a cultural revival within the past several years. **Paepae Teavatuu** is a restored meeting platform in Hakahau, where traditional reenactments are held. **Rataro** is a talented young singer from Ua Pou, who has become very popular throughout the Polynesian triangle and beyond. Video tapes and musical cassettes featuring his all-male performers are fast selling items throughout the islands.

The **Kanahau Trio** is another popular singing group from Ua Pou. The sculptors sell their wood or stone carvings from their homes and in the handcrafts centers in the villages. Horseback or 4x4 vehicle excursions can be arranged to visit the **Valley of the Kings** at Hakamoui, archaeological sites in the interior valleys, to picnic on the white sand beach of Anahoa or to discover the flower stones (*phonolitis*) of Hoho'i, with their multicolored drawings. Boats with pilot can be chartered for off-shore fishing or to visit **Motu Ua**, a bird sanctuary on the south coast.

ARRIVALS & DEPARTURES

Arriving By Air

Air Tahiti, *Tel. 86.42.42/86.41.84*, has five ATR 42 flights per week from Tahiti to the Marquesas Islands of Nuku Hiva or Hiva Oa, and connecting to Ua Pou by a 19-passenger Dornier. There is a flight from Nuku Hiva to Ua Pou each Thursday, departing Nuku Hiva at 11:20am and arriving at the Aneou airport in Ua Pou at 11:40am. There is also a Thursday flight from Hiva Oa to Ua Pou, departing Atuona at 3:35pm and arriving in Ua Pou at 4:10pm. One-way airfare from Tahiti to Ua Pou is 31.500 CFP ($315). The one-way fare from Nuku Hiva to Ua Pou is 5.355 CFP ($53.55). If you have reservations with a pension then you will be met at the Ua Pou airport and driven to your lodging. You can also ride to the village in a taxi operated by Tina Klima, who is the Air Tahiti agent in Ua Pou. It's a 45-minute trip between the airport and Hakahau.

Heli-Inter Marquises, *Tel. 92.02.17*, flies from Nuku Hiva to Ua Pou every Wednesday, Friday and Sunday, departing Taiohae Bay at 4:30pm and arriving in Hakahau at 4:45pm. The one-way fare is 12.000 CFP ($129) per person.

Arriving By Boat

The *Aranui* includes stops at Hakahetau and Hakahau during its 16-day round-trip cruise program from Tahiti to the Marquesas. The *Taporo*

IV includes Ua Pou in its 10-day round-trip voyages from Tahiti. See details in section on *Inter-Island Cruise Ships and Cargo/Passenger Boats* in Chapter 6, *Planning Your Trip*.

Motor boats can be rented in Nuku Hiva for trips to Ua Pou. See details in *Nuku Hiva* section.

Departing By Air

The **Air Tahiti** *office in Ua Pou is in Hakahau at the Kanahau Boutique, 92.53.414/92.51.08*. The departure flight leaves from the Aneou airfield at 12pm each Thursday, arriving in Nuku Hiva at 12:20pm, to connect with a direct flight to Tahiti, which leaves Nuku Hiva at 2:10pm, arriving in Tahiti at 5:25pm. There is also a Thursday flight from Ua Pou to Hiva Oa, departing Ua Pou at 9am and arriving in Atuona at 9:35am. An alternate Friday flight from Ua Pou departs one week at 7:25am, arriving in Atuona at 8am, and the next week it leaves Ua Pou at 8:10am, arriving in Atuona at 8:45am. The Friday flights stop in Puka Puka and Rangiroa before arriving in Tahiti.

Heli-Inter Marquises, *Tel. 92.02.17*, flies from Ua Pou to Nuku Hiva each Wednesday, Friday and Sunday, departing Hakahau at 5pm and arriving in Taiohae at 5:15pm. The cost is 12.000 CFP ($120) per person.

Departing By Boat

See information on the *Aranui* and *Taporo IV* in Chapter 6, *Planning Your Trip* (section on Inter-Island Cruise Ships and Passenger Boats). It is also possible to make arrangements with the numerous speed boats and *bonitiers* that frequently make the crossing from Ua Pou to Nuku Hiva.

ORIENTATION

The **Aneou airport** is located between Hakahetau and Hakahau, half an hour's distance to the main village. **Hakahau** is spread along the Bay of Hakahau and continues inland for several blocks. Sailboats drop anchor in the bay, adjacent to a concrete dock for inter-island ships. The "pillars" rise above the seaside cliffs, and are often covered by clouds. A paved road leads from the boat dock throughout the village, and it is also an easy walk from the dock to the village center, where you'll find *magasins*, a few snack bars and the Catholic church in the south end of the village. A museum was built for the Marquesas Festival of Arts that was held in Hakahau in 1995, but when I visited in June 1997, it was empty.

A 22-kilometer (14-mile) dirt road from Hakahau to the airport and **Hakahetau** continues on to the tiny valley of **Haakuti** on the southwest side of the island, with a track from there to the village of **Hakamaii**, which is more accessible by boat. The dirt road from Hakahau to the south leads to the villages of **Hakamoui**, **Haakau** and **Hoho'i**. A track leads from this road to **Pa'aumea**, but all the villages along this southeast coast are better reached by boat. The white sand beach of **Anahoa** is a 25-minute walk east of Hakahau. This is also a nice ride on horseback, where you have panoramic views of the volcanic mountains and Hakahau Bay. Look for the Restaurant Pukuee sign, which also gives directions to Anahoa Beach.

GETTING AROUND

Car Rentals

Etienne Hokaupoko, *Tel. 92.51.03*, in Hakahetau, has a transfer service between the airport and the villages of Hakahetau, Haakuti and Hakahau for four passengers.

Valja Klima, *Tel. 92.53.37*, in Hakahau, can take six passengers on half-day round-trip guided excursions from Hakahau to Hohoi, from Hakahau to Hakahetau, or from Hakahau to the airport.

WHERE TO STAY

PENSION PUKUEE, *B.P. 31, 91745 Hakahau; Tel./Fax. 689/92.50.83. Overlookiing Hakahau Bay, 12 kilometers (7.5 miles) from the airport and 300 meters (984 feet) from the boat dock. Round-trip transfers 2.000 CFP ($20) per car. Rates: room and breakfast 3.000 CFP ($30) per person; room with breakfast and dinner 5.000 CFP ($50); room with all meals 6.000 CFP ($60). Child under 6 years is free. Add 1% value added tax to room rates and meal plan. No credit cards.*

A big 7-room house sits on a hill overlooking the boat harbor, with a good view of the sugar-loaf mountains of Ua Pou. Guests share the two bathrooms with cold water. A very spacious terrace is also used as a dining area for the restaurant. Hélène Kautai is from Ua Pou and spent several years in France with her French husband, before coming home to open her own pension. She serves French cuisine and local products with a French flavor and takes very good care of her guests.

CHEZ MARGUERITE DORDILLON, *B.P. 87, 91745 Hakahau; Tel. 689/92.51.36. In Hakahau village, 10 kilometers (6.2 miles) from the airport and 300 meters (984 feet) from the boat dock. Round-trip transfers 1.000 CFP ($10) per person. EP Rates: room 2.500 CFP ($25) per person for one night; 2.000 CFP ($20) per person for two or more nights. Add 1% value added tax to room rates and meal plan. No credit cards.*

This two-bungalow pension is located a couple of blocks inland from the beach, in the center of the village close to the post office and town hall. The manager does not live on the premises, so you are truly on your own. Each of the concrete bungalows contains two bedrooms, a living room, equipped kitchen and private bathroom with cold water. House linens are furnished.

WHERE TO EAT

PUKUE'E, *Tel. 92.50.83, overlooking Hakahau Bay. No credit cards. Reservations required.*

Open daily, serving French and local cuisine.

CHEZ ADRIENNE, *Tel. 92.52.16, in Hakahau. No credit cards. Reservations required.*

Open daily, serving local cuisine. .

CHEZ ROSALIE, *Tel. 92.51.77, in the center of Hakahau village. No credit cards. Reservations required.*

Open daily, serving local cuisine. This is where the passengers from the *Aranui* have a Marquesan feast when the ship arrives in port. This delicious buffet features lobster, *poisson cru*, roast pork, goat with coconut milk and vegetables, octopus, *uru*, *fei*, banana *po'e*, mangoes and papaya. A fantastic *kai kai*!

SEEING THE SIGHTS

Saint Etienne Catholic Church in Hakahau village is on the site where the first church in the Marquesas Islands was built in 1859. The carvings inside this stone and wood church include a pulpit of *tou* wood that represents the prow of a boat with a fishnet filled with fish. Adam and Eve and the serpent in the Garden of Eden and other Biblical designs are also presented. The statue of Christ rests his feet on the head of a tiki and the Virgin Mary and Christ child have Polynesian faces. These exquisite carvings were created by Alfred Hatuuku, who lives in Hakahau.

Excursions by horseback or four-wheel drive vehicle will take you to visit the white sand beach of **Anahoa** and the flower stones of **Hohoi**. These amber colored stones are pieces of volcanic phonolite that make a pinging noise when struck. Archaeological sites in the **Valley of the Kings** in Hakamoui and Hakaohoka valley include *paepae* platforms, *tohua* ceremonial plazas, *me'ae* temples and tikis.

Above the village of **Haakuti** a small Catholic church is built on a high *paepae* stone terrace. **Hakahetau** also has an interesting Catholic church with a red tower. Hakanai Bay, 11 kilometers (7 miles) from Hakahau, below the track leading to Hakahetau, is a good picnic spot. This cove is also called Shark Beach.

SPORTS & RECREATION

Horseback Riding

Francis Aka *in Hakahau* has horses for rent. Albert Kohumoetini, *Tel. 92.52.28, in Hakahau,* has a horse for hire. André Kohumoetini *in Hakahau,* has half-day guided rides on request to visit the valleys of Hakahau/Hakahetau and Hakahau/Haakuti.

Motor Boat Rental & Fishing Excursions

The following locally built speed boats are available for inter-island transfers between Ua Pou and Taiohae or the Nuku Ataha airport on Nuku Hiva, for excursions around the island, and for fishing trips.

Guy Hikutini, *Tel. 92.53.08,* in Hakahau, has a 22-foot fishing boat that can take a maximum of three passengers for half-day island tours while fishing.

Charles Tissot, *Tel. 92.51.92,* in Hakamaii, has a 24-foot fishing boat for round-trip inter-valley rotations between Hakamaii and Hakahau. He also has guided excursions to Haakuti and Hakahetau valleys.

Julien Tissot, *Tel. 92.50.22,* in Hakamaii, has a 39-foot fishing boat for 8 passengers, for round-trip inter-valley rotations to Hakatao and Hakahau.

Alain Alho, *Tel. 92.52.80,* in Hakatao, has a 26-foot fishing boat for 8 passengers, for round-trip inter-valley outings between Hakatao and Hakahau.

SHOPPING

Kanahau Boutique, *Tel. 92.53.37,* in Hakahau, sells curios, local clothing and perfumes. There is an arts and crafts center near the boat dock in Hakahau. Some two dozen wood or stone sculptors live on the island of Ua Pou, and you can visit their workshops beside their homes. One of the finest sculptors is Alfred Hatuuku, who carved the pulpit in the Catholic church. He lives between the seafront and Snack Vehine.

William Aka, *Tel. 92.53.90,* close to Snack Guéranger, makes and sells jewelry, small tikis, lizards and miniature saddles of semi-precious woods. Other artisans include Eugène and Tahia Hapipi, Aimé Kohumoetini, Pierre and Petero Ohotoua, Jean and Philippe Teikitohe, Lino Taera and Marcel Bruneau. In Hakahetau village you'll find sculptors Apataroma Hikutini and Tony Tereino; in Hakamaii, José Kaiha, *Tel. 92.50.07,* makes tikis and ceremonial clubs; and in Hohoi, Uri Ah Lo makes tikis, spears and dugout canoes. He lives in the blue house on the right toward the beach.

PRACTICAL INFORMATION
Bank

Banque Socredo, *Tel. 92.53.63,* is located in the same building as the Hakahau Mairie. The bank is open Monday to Thursday from 7:30 to 11:30am and 1:30 to 4:30pm, and on Friday from 7:30am to 2:30pm.

Hospital

A government operated medical center is located in Hakahau, *Tel. 92.53.75,* and every village has an infirmary.

Police
There is a French *gendarmerie* in Hakahau, *Tel. 92.53.61.*

Post Office & Telecommunications Office
The post office is in Hakahau, open Monday to Thursday from 7:30 to 11:30am and 1:30 to 4:30 pm, and on Friday from 7:30 to 11:30am and 12 to 2pm. All telecommunications and postal services are available here. Phonecard telephone booths are located beside the post office, on the quay and opposite the Air Tahiti office.

UA HUKA

Welcome to **Ua Huka**, Marquesan cowboy country by the sea. On the southern coast wild horses gallop freely in the wind on the tablelands. Herds of cows and goats graze in the ferns, wild cotton and scrub brush that grow in the desert-like topography on a vast plateau. Above this incredible and beautiful scene rises Mount Hitikau, the highest mountain at 855 meters (2,804 feet). Breathtaking panoramas of the rugged coast and the sparkling sea greet the eye at every turn on the narrow winding mountain road that connects Vaipae'e, Hane and Hokatu, the three valleys where the 571 inhabitants live.

Ua Huka lies 35 kilometers (22 miles) east of Nuku Hiva, and 56 kilometers (35 miles) northeast of Ua Pou. It is the smallest of the inhabited islands in the northern Marquesas group, with just 81 square kilometers (31 square miles) of land. This crescent-shaped island is 8 kilometers (5 miles) long and 14 kilometers (8.7 miles) wide.

Ua Huka is one of the most interesting of all the Polynesian islands. The fern-covered valleys conceal *tohua* ceremonial plazas, *me'ae* stone temples and *tokai* burial platforms for deceased pregnant or birthing women. Among the ruins from the seven tribes who formerly inhabited the island are petroglyphs that can be seen at the archeological site of Vaikiki valley. From Hane you can hike uphill for half an hour to a restored *me'ae*, a sacred place where three tikis are sculpted from red rock.

In 1964 and 1965, **Doctor Yosihiko H. Sinoto**, Senior Anthropologist at the Bishop Museum in Honolulu, excavated a coastal village in Hane that was buried under sand dunes two meters (6.6 feet) high. Among his findings were two fragments of pottery, dating from around 380 A.D., which Sinoto said is the oldest site yet discovered by anyone in Eastern Polynesia, and an important link between Western and Eastern Polynesia. Other scientists claim to have found evidence that the Marquesas were settled between 500-200 BC, but Sinoto remains confident in his theory.

Captain Joseph Ingraham, of the American trading ship *Hope*, sailed by Ua Huka in 1791. The northern Marquesas islands were visited in quick succession by Captain Marchand of the French ship *La Solide*; Lieutenant Hergest aboard the *Doedalus*, who surveyed the islands, and by Captain Josiah Roberts of the American ship *Jefferson* in 1793. Ua Huka was spared most of the carnage wreaked on the other Marquesas Islands by European discoverers, whalers and sandalwood seekers. During this period of discovery Ua Huka was named Ile Solide, Washington Island, Massachusetts, Ouahouka, Riou, Roahouga and Rooahooga.

Accommodations for tourists are available in the villages of Vaipae'e, Hane and Hokatu, and in the private valley of Haavei. These lodgings are located in separate houses and small bungalows, or in family homes or pensions. Prospective plans are to build a small five-star hotel for 40 guests before the year 2000. The site chosen is just two minutes from the airport at a place by the sea called Tetumu, the former habitat of wild goats.

With the addition of a new deluxe hotel the airplane service to Ua Huka, which is presently only once a week, will surely improve.

ARRIVALS & DEPARTURES
Arriving By Air
Air Tahiti, *Tel. 86.42.42/86.41.84*, has five ATR 42 flights per week from Tahiti to the Marquesas Islands of Nuku Hiva or Hiva Oa, and connects with a 19-passenger Dornier from Nuku Hiva to Ua Huka each Thursday. The flight leaves Nuku Hiva at 12:50pm and arrives at the Nukumoo airport in Ua Huka at 1:10pm. One-way airfare from Tahiti to Ua Huka is 31.500 CFP ($315) and the one-way fare from Nuku Hiva is 5.355 CFP ($53.55). If you have reservations with a pension then you will be met at the Ua Huka airport and driven to your lodging.

Helicopter Service is provided by **Heli-Inter Marquises** in Taiohae, Nuku Hiva, *Tel. 92.02.17.*

Arriving By Boat
The *Aranui* includes stops at Vaipae'e and Hane in its 16-day round-trip cruise program from Tahiti to the Marquesas. The *Taporo IV* includes Ua Huka in its 10-day round-trip voyages from Tahiti. See details in the section on Inter-Island Cruise Ships and Cargo/Passenger Boats in Chapter 6, *Planning Your Trip*. Motor boats can be rented in Nuku Hiva for trips to Ua Huka. See details in Nuku Hiva section.

Departing By Air
Air Tahiti reservations in Ua Huka is *Tel. 92.60.44/92.60.85*. The departure flight leaves Ua Huka at 1:30pm each Thursday, connecting in Nuku Hiva for a direct flight to Tahiti.

Departing By Boat

See information on the *Aranui* and *Taporo IV* in Chapter 6, *Planning Your Trip*, section on Inter-Island Cruise Ships and Passenger Boats.

Motor boats can be rented in Ua Huka to visit Nuku Hiva. Please see information in this chapter under Motor Boat Rentals.

ORIENTATION

Ua Huka's three villages of **Vaipae'e**, **Hane** and **Hokatu** are connected by an unpaved road that winds along the edge of the cliffs for 14 kilometers (8.7 miles). Four-wheel drive vehicles (4x4) and horses are the means of transportation. The surf crashes against the steeply rising rocks of the coastline, creating a continuous spray that splashes high into the sky, reflecting the sun in multiple shades of blue. After a rain the hills and plains glimmer in varying shades of green, but the plateaus become brown and desolate during the arid seasons.

If you arrive by ship you will probably disembark in **Vaipae'e Bay**, also called Invisible Bay, because a wall of basaltic rock protects the bay from the open sea. Landings are made by small boat onto a concrete pier. Vaipae'e is the largest village on Ua Huka, with the *Mairie*, post office and the Museum of Marquesan artifacts all in the same complex.

The airport is located between Vaipae'e and Hane villages, and the arboretum is close to the small airstrip. **Hane Bay** is distinguished by Motu Hane that sits just offshore facing the pretty little village. This is a dark violet and red rock 152 meters (508 feet) high, shaped like a sugar loaf. A structure of stones on top of this huge rock looks like a giant tiki has been carved there. In Hane there is a post office, an infirmary, schools and churches. Small *magasins* offer limited food supplies in Vaipae'e, Hane and Hokatu. Handcrafts centers and wood carvers' shops are found in each village.

The coast off Haavei is rich in sea life, filled with sharks, dolphins, manta ray, big turtles, lobster and a variety of fish. Boats with captains can be rented for deep-sea fishing and excursions to Anaa Atua grotto and the islets of Teuaua and Tiotio. On these bird islands thousands of white and sooty terns (*kaveka*), red-footed booby birds, blue noddy birds, frigates, tropic birds, petrels and shearwaters lay their eggs. They screech and squawk as they feed on the abundance of fish in this area, while their fluffy white fledglings sit on the hard ground of these upraised *motu* islets, waiting for dinner to be served.

GETTING AROUND

Four-wheel drive vehicles (4x4) can be rented with a driver from Marcel Fournier, *Tel. 92.60.20*; Maurice Rootuehine, *Tel. 92.60.55*; and Jean Fournier, *Tel. 92.60.68*, who all have pensions.

WHERE TO STAY

AUBERGE HITIKAU, *98744, Hane. Tel. 689/92.60.68. In Hane valley, 5 kilometers (3 miles) from the airport and 11 kilometers (7 miles) from the Vaipae'e boat landing. Round-trip transfers included. EP Rates: room 2.000 CFP ($20) single, 3.000 CFP ($30) double; room with breakfast and dinner 5.100 CFP ($51) per person; room with all meals 7.600 CFP ($76) per person. Add 1% value added tax to room rates and meal plan. No credit cards.*

This is a concrete building, constructed especially for use as a pension and restaurant. The four bedrooms are clean and spacious, each containing a double bed, closet and desk, with curtains over the entry to each room. Shared bath facilities have cold water showers. House linens are furnished. A big terrace in front is also shared by guests who come to eat in the Hitikau restaurant and bar, also operated by the Fournier family.

CHEZ ALEXIS, *98744 Vaipae'e. Tel. 689/ 92.61.16. In Vaipae'e valley, 5.5 kilometers (3.4 miles) from the airport and 2 kilometers (1.2 miles) from the Vaipae'e boat landing. Round-trip transfers included. EP Rates: room 1.500 CFP ($15) per person; room with breakfast and dinner 3.500 CFP ($35); room with all meals 4.500 CFP ($45). Add 1% value added tax to room rates and meal plan. No credit cards.*

This is a concrete house with four rooms for rent beside the main road in Vaipae'e village. Look for the sign on the right. Each room contains a double bed and a single bed. The living room with television, large kitchen, living room, terrace and two bathrooms with cold water are shared. House linens are furnished.

MANA TUPUNA VILLAGE, *98744, Vaipae'e. Tel./Fax. 689/92.60.08. In Vaipae'e valley, 5.5 kilometers (3.4 miles) from the airport and 2 kilometers (1.2 miles) from the Vaipae'e boat landing. Round-trip transfers included. MAP Rates: bungalow with breakfast and dinner 5.500 CFP ($55) single, 10.000 CFP ($100) double. Half-price for child under 12 years. Add 1% value added tax to room rates and meal plan. No credit cards.*

Three small wooden A-frame bungalows on stilts overlook Vaipae'e valley, where you can see goats and horses roaming freely and feeding on wild grass. Each of these *ha'e* contains a double bed and a single bed, a private bathroom with hot water, and a covered terrace. The furniture is made of bamboo and the posts on the terrace are sculpted coconut trunks from Ua Huka. House linens are provided and there is a restaurant and bar on the premises for breakfast and dinner.

CHEZ MAURICE & DELPHINE, *98744 Hokatu. Tel./Fax. 689/ 92.60.55. In Hokatu valley, 7 kilometers (4.4 miles) from the airport, 13 kilometers (8 miles) from the boat landing of Vaipae'e and 2 kilometers (1.2 miles) from Hane village. At the entry to Hokatu it's the first house on the left. Round-trip transfers included. Rates: room with breakfast 1.700 CFP ($17) per person; bungalow with breakfast 2.500 CFP ($25) per person; room and all meals 3.600*

CFP ($36); bungalow and all meals 4.400 CFP ($44). Add 1% value added tax to room rates and meal plan. No credit cards.

Two bungalows overlooking the sea and Mount Hitikau contain a double bed in the bedroom, a living room with a sofa, private bathroom with cold water, and a terrace. There are also three bedrooms in a concrete house, with a double bed in each room. Guests share the living room, equipped kitchen, terrace and two bathrooms with cold water. House linens are furnished.

CHEZ JOSEPH LICHTLE, *98744 Haavei. Tel. 689/92.60.72. Beside the beach in Haavei valley, 5 kilometers (3.1 miles) from Vaipae'e village and the boat landing. Round-trip transfers 1.000 CFP ($10) per person. Rates: room or bungalow with breakfast included 2.500 CFP ($25) per person; room or bungalow with all meals 5.500 CFP ($55) per person. Add 1% value added tax to room rates and meal plan. No credit cards.*

Haavei valley is reached by boat, 4-wheel drive vehicle or by horseback. There are no families living here, so it is rather isolated, but this is one of the most beautiful spots in the Marquesas Islands. There are two bungalows built beside a white sand beach, each containing a double bed and private bathroom with cold water, and a terrace overlooking the sea. There are also two houses for rent. One house has three bedrooms, with a double bed in each room, plus a living room with a double bed and six sofas. There is a bathroom with cold water, and a terrace. The other house has two bedrooms with a double bed in each room and a sofa in the living room. The bathroom with cold water, the outside kitchen and the terrace are shared with other guests, if there are any. Electricity is by solar power. House linens are furnished.

There is good swimming from the white sand beach, and the view of the sunset from here is spectacular. Joseph Lichtle has cattle, horses, pigs, chickens and ducks, plus a garden filled with vegetables and fruits. The ocean here is especially rich in all kinds of fish, rays and big sharks.

CHEZ CHRISTELLE, *98744 Vaipae'e. Tel. 689/92.60.34/92.60.85. In Vaipae'e valley, 7 kilometers (4.4 miles) from the airport and 2 kilometers (1.2 miles) from the boat landing. It's the seventh house on the left from the bridge, 5 meters (16 feet) after Chez Alexis. Round-trip transfers included. Rates: room with breakfast 2.000 CFP ($20) per person; room with breakfast and dinner 3.500 CFP ($35); room with all meals 5.000 CFP ($50). Child under 12 years 500 CFP ($5) for room, 2.500 CFP ($25) for room, breakfast and dinner, and 4.000 CFP ($40) for room and all meals. Add 1% value added tax to room rates and meal plan. No credit cards.*

This is a 4-bedroom concrete house, with a double bed in each room. Guests share the living room with television, equipped kitchen, dining room, two bathrooms with cold water shower, and terrace. House linens are furnished. There is also a large garden here.

WHERE TO EAT

In Vaipae'e village each morning around 9am, Rose sells *casse-croûtes* from her green pickup truck, for 100 or 200 CFP ($1 or $2). She also has fried chicken legs, fish, banana fritters and a selection of sandwiches.

When the *Aranui* arrives in Vaipae'e, the mamas of the village sell soft drinks and *casse-croûtes* at the boat landing around 10am.

For more extensive meals, try:

AUBERGE HITIKAU, *Hane village, Tel. 92.60.68. Advance reservations are needed for all meals.*

Breakfast costs 500 CFP ($5), and lunch and dinner are each 1.500 CFP ($15). Special feasts are prepared for groups, such as the *Aranui* passengers. These buffets may include kaveka (sooty tern) omelets, hard boiled kaveka eggs, goat cooked in coconut milk, *poisson cru*, roast pig, goat and fish cooked in an underground oven, plus rice, *fei, uru,* banana *po'e, sashimi,* cake and wine and coffee.

CHEZ ALEXIS, *Vaipae'e village, Tel. 92.61.16.*

If you reserve in advance, Alexis can prepare you some of his specialties, which include grilled lobster with *uru* fries, grilled fish, goat in coconut milk, sashimi, *poisson cru*, banana fritters or fruit salad. Breakfast is 500 CFP ($5), and lunch and dinner cost 1.500 CFP ($15) each.

CHEZ MAURICE & DELPHINE, *Hokatu village, Tel. 92.60.55.*

You can eat three meals a day for 3.000 CFP ($30) or arrange for an individual meal by calling in advance.

SEEING THE SIGHTS

The **Arboretum**, between Vaipae'e and Hane, is a botanical and plant nursery with more than 400 species of flora, including 120 varieties of citrus plants. This nursery was started in the early 1970s by Leon Lichtle, who is now the mayor of Ua Huka. The gardens comprise 14 hectares (35 acres) and contain every kind of plant and flower you can think of that grows in this climate. There are huge trees of *miro* (rosewood), *tou,* bamboo, banyan, *uru,* teak, *puatea, pakai, cerrettes, tutui,* all-spice, acacia, mangoes, mountain apples, custard apples, star apples, carambola and guava. You'll find several species of bananas and plantains, pomegranates, coffee, cacao, vanilla, hot peppers, hibiscus, auti and jasmine. Plus there are many bushes of Tiare Tahiti and Tiare Moorea. This is a refreshing stop in the shade of the lovely trees, as well as a very interesting and informative botanical lesson. The arboretum is open to the public from 6:30am to 2:30pm Monday through Friday. There is no admission charge.

The **Historic Museum of Vaipae'e**, *Tel. 92.60.13, is adjacent to the Mairie or town hall of Vaipae'e on the left of the main road from the boat landing.*

At the entry way is a small sandalwood tree, perhaps the only one you will see in the Marquesas Islands. The small museum is filled with old photographs and ancient Marquesan artifacts, including replicas of a chief's burial grotto and a Marquesan stove. The sculptures were carved by Joseph Vaatete, who also takes care of the museum. Open Monday to Friday from 7am to 3pm.

The **Musée de la Mer** *beside the sea in Hane village* contains an old anchor, fish nets, ancient fish hooks, reproductions of outrigger canoes, and drawings of the Polynesian triangle, retracing the route of the first Polynesian sailors who settled the South Pacific islands. An arts and crafts center shares the building with the Museum of the Sea.

Land Tours

Land tours include visiting the three villages, the archaeological sites, arboretum, museums and the arts and crafts shops. To arrange for an excursion by four-wheel drive vehicle (4x4) you can ask at the pension where you're staying, or you can hire the following people: in Vaipae'e valley contact Jean Tamarii, *Tel. 92.60.67*, or Benoît Teatiu, *Tel. 92. 61.22*; in Hane village contact Léon Fournier, *Tel. 92.60.61*, or Richard Teikihuavanaka, *Tel. 92.60.78*. The cost of visiting all three valleys is 10.000 CFP ($100) per car.

In Hokatu valley arrangements can be made at *magasin* Maurice, *Tel. 92.60.55*, for land tours, horseback riding and boat rentals.

SPORTS & RECREATION

Horseback Riding

Seeing Ua Huka on horseback is the way to go. The small Marquesan horses you see wandering around the desert-like plains are descendants from Chilean stock imported in 1856. You can ride bareback or astride wooden saddles softened by piling on copra sacks. The cost of horseback riding in Ua Huka is 5.000 CFP ($50) per day. The following men rent horses and will accompany you on your outing.

Joseph Lichtle, *Tel. 92.60.72*, rents riding horses *in Haavei valley* for half- and full-day excursions. Horses can also be rented from Alexis Fournier *in Vaipae'e, Tel. 92.60.05*, and Edmond Lichtle *in Vaipae'e, Tel. 92.60.87*. In Hane valley Pierre Brown, *Tel. 92.60.65*, and Emile Panau, *Tel. 92.60.56*, will take you horseback riding.

Motor Boat Rental

Offshore excursions can be made by speedboat to visit Ua Huka's unusual sites. A full day's outing will cost about 30.000 CFP ($300) for the boat. Half-day excursions and picnics are also possible. Boats with captains can be rented for deep-sea fishing and excursions to **Anaa Atua** grotto and the bird islands of **Teuaua** and **Tiotio**.

Bird Island or **Teuaua Motu** is a steep rock 6 meters (20 feet) high, 150 meters (492 feet) long and 100 meters (328 feet) wide, lying offshore Haavei valley. Attracted by the numerous fish in this area, millions of sooty terns lay their eggs on the open ground on top of this small island. You have to climb to the top by rope, which is very tricky and dangerous. The small eggs are white with black spots and the yolk is very orange. People gather these eggs by the bucket to boil or use in omelets.

The imprint of human footsteps can be seen in the sand at low tide in the **Anaa Atua** grotto and they disappear during high tide. Petroglyphs can be visited at the pretty beach of **Hatuana**. The **Pahonu beach** near the airport is a good place to swim and can be reached by boat.

Alexis Fournier, in Vaipae'e, *Tel. 92.60.05/92.60.72*, has a locally built 20-foot fishing boat for six passengers. Round-trip inter-island rotations are made from Ua Huka to Nuku Hiva, and excursions around Ua Huka include half-day outings to Bird Island and Anaa Atua grotto. Full-day excursions around the island of Ua Huka also include a picnic.

Maurice Rootuehine, in Hokatu, *Tel. 92.60.55*, has a locally built 25-foot fishing boat for 7 passengers, which is available for inter-island round-trips between Ua Huka and Nuku Hiva, and excursions around Ua Huka.

Jean Tamarii, *Tel. 92.60.07*, Paul Teatiu, *Tel. 92.60.88*, and Paul Teikiteputini, *Tel. 92.60.48*, also have locally built fishing boats available for hire.

SHOPPING

Arts and crafts centers are located in the villages of Vaipae'e, Hane and Hokatu. The prices here are less expensive than in the other islands. You can also visit the sculptors' workshops at their homes. Joseph Vaatete is one of the most noted sculptors in wood and stone, who makes pieces for the museums in Ua Huka. He lives in Hane village, a couple of blocks from the sea, on the left side of the road that goes up the valley. You can recognize his house by the tree trunks and pieces of wood and stone in his yard. Two of Joseph's statues are located at the International Airport of Tahiti-Faaa, and another carving is located at the *Mairie* of Papeete. Joseph also takes care of the historical museum adjacent to the *Mairie* of Vaipae'e.

PRACTICAL INFORMATION

Infirmary

A government-operated infirmary is located in the village of Hane, *Tel. 92.60.58*.

Post Office & Telecommunications Office

The Post Office is located in the main village of Vaipae'e, *Tel. 92.60.26*. All telecommunications and postal services are available here.

Magasin stores are located in each village and are also open on Sundays.

HIVA OA

According to some Marquesan legends, **Hiva Oa** was the first island in this archipelago settled by the Polynesians before they reached Nuku Hiva. Archaeological findings support this theory, based on a charcoal sample taken from a fireplace in a rock shelter at Anapua. This site was excavated in 1981 by Pierre Ottino of the ORSTOM research center in Tahiti, and the charcoal dates 150+-95 years B.C. This is the oldest date thus uncovered reflecting the presence of human occupancy in Eastern Polynesia.

Hiva Oa is located 1,400 kilometers (868 miles) northeast of Tahiti. It is one of the youngest islands in the Marquesas chain, and has been described as a seahorse whose head faces the setting sun. The island measures 40 kilometers (25 miles) long east to west and averages 10 kilometers (6.2 miles) north to south. Atuona sits in the center of three adjoining craters, and the ridge of mountains is crowned by Temetiu, whose peak reaches into the clouds 1,190 meters (3,900 feet) above the picturesque bays. The steep slopes of high altitude interior plateaus dominate this large fertile island of 330 square kilometers (127 square miles). The 1,837 inhabitants live in the villages of Atuona, Puamau, Hanaiapa, Hanapaaoa, Nahoe, Tahauku and Taaoa, which are separated into isolated valleys by the dorsal spine and ridges.

The French painter **Paul Gauguin** came to Hiva Oa in 1901 in search of a primitive culture and savage wildness, and here he died in 1903. He is buried in Calvary Cemetery on a hill behind Atuona village. Fragrant petals from a gnarled old frangipani tree shower down on the simple grave, and a statue of Oviri, "the savage" stands at the head of the tombstone.

A few graves distant is the final resting place of the famous Belgian singer **Jacques Brel**, who lived in Atuona from 1975 until his death in 1978. Many of Brel's European fans make a pilgrimage to his grave, which is always decorated with flowers.

In **Atuona** village you'll find a replica of Gauguin's *Maison de Jouir* "House of Pleasure" adjacent to the **Ségalen-Gauguin Museum**, which has an exhibit of 160 reproductions of Gauguin's paintings. Outside the museum is Jacques Brel's Beechcraft airplane named JoJo.

Gauguin's descendants still live in the Puamau valley, 48 kilometers (30 miles) from Atuona. The restored archaeological site of I'ipona is also located in this valley. In this religious sanctuary is a *me'ae* on two large terraces, with five huge stone tikis. The most famous stone tiki represents the god Takaii. Carved from porous red rock, this statue is 2.35 meters (7.7 feet) tall, and is the largest stone tiki in French Polynesia.

Other excursions reveal the bays of Nahoe and Hanamenu, the black sand beach of Taaoa and the lovely white sand beach of Hanatekua. Near the little village of Hanaiapa is a cascade that splashes down a 249-meter (800-foot) cliff into the surging sea, wetting the black rocks so they sparkle like vaults of mica. Petroglyphs carved on stone have been found in the valleys of Eiaone and Punaei, and many other archaeological sites exist all over the island of Hiva Oa.

Atuona is the administrative center for the southern Marquesas. Framed in a theater of mountains with the Tahauku Bay providing safe anchorage, Atuona is a favorite port of call for yachts and copra/cargo ships. Atuona village has a *gendarmerie*, infirmary, post office, bank, weather station, Air Tahiti office, restaurants and snack bars, stores and shops. There is a Catholic mission with a boarding school and a Protestant church.

You can rent a car with or without a driver or charter a boat for a trip to **Motane**, the sheep island. You can go deep-sea fishing, scuba diving, sailing, explore woodcarvers' shops, ride along a black sand beach on a Marquesan horse or visit nearby islands by speedboat. Accommodations on Hiva Oa are found in small hotels overlooking the cobalt blue Pacific and in family homes near the villages.

ARRIVALS & DEPARTURES

Arriving By Air

Air Tahiti, *Tel. 86.42.42/86.41.84*, flies ATR 42 turbo jet planes direct from Tahiti to Hiva Oa every Tuesday in 2 hours and 35 minutes. The Wednesday and Sunday flights stop in Nuku Hiva first. A Thursday ATR-42 flight from Tahiti to Nuku Hiva connects with a Dornier 19-passenger flight to Atuona, and Dornier service is provided from Ua Pou to Atuona each Thursday, corresponding with the schedule of the ATR-42 flights to Tahiti. There is also a Friday flight from Ua Pou to Atuona, with the schedule varying every other week. You can also fly from Tahiti to Rangiroa, Puka Puka or Napuka to Atuona alternately each Wednesday with the Dornier service. The one-way airfare from Tahiti to Hiva Oa is 31.500 CFP ($315); the one-way fare from Nuku Hiva to Atuona is 9.240 CFP ($92.40).

Note: The airstrip in Atuona is currently under repair, and the work is expected to continue at least through June 1998. Until the work is completed the ATR-42 aircraft will not land in Hiva Oa, but the Dornier service continues to operate.

Arriving By Boat

The *Aranui* includes stops at Atuona, Puamau, and Hanaiapa in Hiva Oa during its 16-day round-trip cruise program from Tahiti to the Marquesas. The *Taporo IV* includes Hiva Oa in its 10-day round-trip voyages from Tahiti. See details in section on *Inter-Island Cruise Ships and Cargo/Passenger Boats* in Chapter 6, *Planning Your Trip*.

The communal boats from Tahuata and Fatu Hiva connect their islands with Atuona once or twice a week. See further information for these two islands in this chapter.

Departing By Air

Air Tahiti reservations in Atuona, *Tel. 92.73.41/92.72.31*. You can fly from Atuona direct to Tahiti each Sunday, and the Wednesday flight from Atuona stops in Nuku Hiva first. You can fly from Atuona to Nuku Hiva aboard a Dornier-19 passenger plane each Thursday to connect with the ATR-42 flight to Tahiti. A Thursday afternoon flight connects Atuona with Ua Pou, and a Friday flight from Atuona takes you to Puka Puka, Rangiroa and Tahiti on board a Dornier plane.

Departing By Boat

Pua Ote Tai is a locally built 30-foot tuna fishing boat owned by Gabriel Heitaa of Atuona, *Tel./Fax 92.73.02*, which can transport 10 passengers. The round-trip inter-island rotations include: Atuona-Puamau (Hiva Oa), Atuona-Vaitahu and Hapatoni (Tahuata), and Atuona-Omoa (Fatu Hiva).

Denise II is a locally built 36-foot tuna fishing boat owned by Ozanne Rohi of Atuona, *Tel./Fax. 92.73.43*. He makes round-trip inter-island rotations to Tahuata and Fatu Hiva, and will arrange deep sea fishing and picnics on request.

The Tahuata communal boat *Te Pua O Mioi* makes twice-weekly rotations from Vaitahu to Atuona and back to Tahuata. The boat leaves Atuona each Tuesday and Thursday at 12pm. The one-way fare to Tahuata is 500 CFP ($5). *Reserve at Tel. 92.92.19; Fax 92.92.10*.

The communal boat of Fatu Hiva, *Auona II*, can transport 15 passengers during the weekly rotations between Fatu Hiva and Atuona. The 45-foot catamaran leaves Atuona at 2pm for Fatu Hiva. The one-way fare is 3.000 CFP ($30).

ORIENTATION

A road 17 kilometers long (10.5 feet) is built on the **Tepuna Plateau**, 440 meters (1,443 feet) above the sea, connecting the airport with **Atuona**

village. The town is at the north end of Taaoa Bay, 3 kilometers (1.9 miles) from **Tahauku Bay**, also known as Traitors' Bay, which provides a safe harbor for yachts and the inter-island cargo vessels that dock at the concrete pier.

Three paved roads pass through Atuona and it is easy to walk around the town center, where most of the businesses and administrative offices are concentrated, as well as the medical facilities, churches and Catholic schools.

GETTING AROUND

When you make reservations with a hotel or pension your hosts will meet you at the airport or boat dock on your arrival. The transfer costs vary according to your lodging, which are listed under *Where to Stay*. An excursion by 4WD from Atuona to Taaoa is a distance of 7 kilometers (4.4 miles). The 15-20 minute ride costs approximately 8.000 CFP ($80). The 2 1/2 hour ride to Puamau, a distance of 48 kilometers (30 miles), costs 20.000 CFP ($200) per car for six passengers maximum.

Car Rentals

David Kaimuko at **David Locations**, *Tel. 92.72.87*, in Atuona, has two 4WD vehicles that you can drive yourself or with a chauffeur if you prefer.

Ozanne Rohi, *Tel 92.73.43*, at **Pension J. Ozanne**, has a 4WD vehicle his clients can rent.

Taxis

Ida Clark, *Tel. 92.71.33*, in Atuona, provides 4WD transfers between the airport and Atuona village, and tours to visit the archaeological sites and villages of Taaoa, Hanaiapa and Puamau.

WHERE TO STAY

Expensive

HOTEL HANAKEE NOA NOA, *B.P. 57, Atuona, Hiva Oa, Tel. 689/ 92.71.62/92.73.25, Fax 689/92.72.51. Reservations: South Pacific Marketing, Tel. 689/ 43.90.04; Fax 689/41.39.23. 20 bungalows. EP Rates: ocean view bungalow 20.000 CFP ($200) single/double; add 3.000 CFP ($30) for third person; add 5.300 CFP ($53) per person for breakfast and dinner; add 7.500 CFP ($75) per person for all meals; full American breakfast 1.600 CFP ($16); fruit basket 1.800 CFP ($18); bottle of champagne 5.500 CFP ($55); one-way transfer 2.100 CFP ($21) per person. Add 7% hotel tax to room rates and 1% value added tax to room rates and meal plan. All major credit cards.*

This hotel has closed its six bungalows to add 14 more units, and will reopen in June, 1999. The bungalows are built on the hillside overlooking Tahauku Bay, above the port for the inter-island ships. The new hotel will offer rooms with air-conditioning and fans, a mini-bar refrigerator, tea and coffee making facilities, international direct dial telephones, showers with hot water, hair dryers, terraces and room service. The main building will house the reception and boutique, and a desk for excursions and car rentals. There will also be a restaurant and bar, and a swimming pool.

Inexpensive

TEMETIU VILLAGE, *B.P. 52, 98741 Atuona, Hiva Oa, Tel./Fax 689/ 92.73.02. MAP Rates: room with breakfast and dinner 5.500 CFP ($55) single/ 10.000 CFP ($100) double. Lunch on request. Half-fare for child under 12 years. Round-trip transfers 3.600 CFP ($36) per person. Add 1% value added tax to room rates and meal plan. Mastercard, Visa.*

Three neat and clean bungalows sit on the hillside above Tahauku Bay with a beautiful view of the bay and ocean. One bungalow has two bedrooms, each with three single beds, and two bungalows each have a double bed. Each bungalow has a private bathroom with hot water, and house linens are furnished. There is also a living room with television, and a lending library. Meals are served on the dining terrace overlooking the bay. Snorkeling equipment is provided.

This is a favorite lodging because of its location, but mainly because of the owners, who are warm and welcoming. "Gaby" owns the *Pua Ote Tai* boat that provides transportation service to other villages and islands. His wife speaks English and will guide you on a complimentary tour of Atuona village and the other main points of interest.

PENSION GAUGUIN, *B.P. 34, 98741 Atuona, Hiva Oa, Tel./Fax 689/ 92.73.51. Rates: room 3.000 CFP ($30) per person; room with breakfast and dinner 5.500 CFP ($55) per person; room with all meals 7.500 CFP ($75) per person; half-fare for child under 12 years. Round-trip transfers 3.600 CFP ($36) per person. Add 1% value added tax to room rates and meal plan. No credit cards.*

This popular small hotel overlooks the road that leads to Tahauku port at the eastern end of Atuona Bay, 7 kilometers (4.4 miles) from the airport and 2.5 kilometers (1.6 miles) from the boat dock. The 2-story building has four rooms, each with a double bed, with a communal living room with television, dining room, kitchen, laundry and bathroom with hot water. The house linens are furnished. A big terrace has a panoramic view of the bay. The atmosphere is very homey and clean and the meals are good. The Make Make Snack is also close by, should you want a change. André will organize interesting excursions for you to visit the sites in Hiva Oa and to spend the day on Tahuata.

PENSION J. OZANNE, *B.P. 43, 98741 Atuona, Hiva Oa, Tel/Fax 689/ 92.73.43. Rates: room only 1.500 CFP ($15) single/2.500 CFP ($25) double; room with breakfast and dinner 3.500 CFP ($35) per person; room with all meals 5.000 CFP ($50) per person; bungalow 2.000 CFP ($20) single/3.500 CFP*

($35) double; bungalow with breakfast and dinner 4.000 CFP ($40) per person; bungalow with all meals 5.500 CFP ($55) per person. Round-trip transfers 3.000 CFP ($30) per car. Add 1% value added tax to room rates and meal plan. No credit cards.

This pension is on the hillside on the eastern edge of Atuona, providing accommodations in a 2-bedroom house and a bungalow. There is a double bed and fan in each bedroom. The house contains a living room with television, a terrace and a communal bathroom with hot water, and the bungalow has a kitchen and private bathroom. The house linens are furnished. The Marquesan style meals are eaten with the family under a *fare pote'e* shelter overlooking the black sand beach and ocean. Ozanne will rent you a 4WD vehicle and you may want to join him aboard his *Denise II* boat for deep sea fishing, picnics and visits to Tahuata and Fatu Hiva.

CHEZ MARIE-ANTOINETTE, *98741 Puamau, Hiva Oa, Tel. 689/ 92.72.27. Rates: room only 1.000 CFP ($10) per person; room with breakfast and dinner 3.000 CFP ($30) per person; room with all meals 4.500 CFP ($45) per person. Round-trip transfers between airport and pension 20.000 CFP ($200) per car. Add 1% value added tax to room rates and meal plan. No credit cards.*

This pension is in the valley of Puamau, on the northeast coast of Hiva Oa, 40 kilometers (25 miles) from the airport, beside the road leading to the I'ipona or Oipona archaeological site with the five big tikis. Two simply furnished rooms in the mayor's home, Bernard "Vohi" Heitaa, each contain a double and a single bed. The bathroom with hot water is shared, and there is a living room with television, a dining room and laundry. The house linens are furnished.

WHERE TO EAT
Moderate
TE HOA NUI, *Tel. 92.73.63, in Atuona village. No credit cards. Reservations required.*

Open daily for lunch, serving local cuisine and seafood specialties. Marquesan feasts of lobster, goat, fresh water shrimp, smoked chicken, *fafa poulet*, banana *po'e* and other delicious treats are served to groups such as the *Aranui* passengers.

TEMETIU VILLAGE, *Tel. 92.73.02. Reservations are necessary. Mastercard, Visa.*

Serves lunch and dinner on their terrace overlooking Tahauku and Taaoa bays. Local seafood specialties and Marquesan foods, such as goat in coconut milk are served.

Inexpensive

SNACK MAKE MAKE, *Tel. 92.74.26, on the mountain side in the center of Atuona village.*

Fresh fish, Chinese dishes, *poisson cru* and sandwiches are very reasonably priced. Open from 7am to 6pm.

SEEING THE SIGHTS

In the center of Atuona you can visit the **Ségalen-Gauguin Museum**, *Tel. 92.73.77*, which has exhibits of drawings, photographs, letters and souvenirs of **Paul Gauguin** and his friend **Victor Ségalen**, a writer-physician who landed in Atuona in 1903. The museum was built in 1992 and is managed by Ernest Teapuaoteani, who said that a new museum should be finished by June 7, 1998, in time to commemorate the 150th anniversary of Gauguin's birth. The new buildings will reflect the three periods of Gauguin's life in Brittany, Tahiti and the Marquesas.

In Atuona you can also visit a replica of Gauguin's house and *atelier*, which he named **La Maison du Jouir**. This is an arts and crafts center today, and is adjacent to the **Pepeu** *tohua* meeting ground, which was the site of the Marquesas Festival of Arts in 1991. In **Calvary Cemetery** behind the village you can visit the graves of **Paul Gauguin** and **Jacques Brel**. A memorial to the Belgian singer was erected by the tourist office on a piece of open ground overlooking the Hotel Hanakée.

Sightseeing highlights away from Atuona include: a visit to **Puamau Valley** to visit the giant tikis at the **I'ipona** (or Oipona) archaeological site; the tiki and *paepae* platforms of **Taaoa Valley**; the petroglyphs on the **Tehueto** site in the **Faakua Valley**; the **Moe One tiki** in **Hanapaaoa Valley**; and the *paepae* and pretty little village of **Hanaiapa Valley**.

Ida Clark, *Tel. 92.71.33*, will drive you to visit the archaeological sites and villages of Taaoa, Hanaiapa and Puamau.

David Locations, *Tel. 92.72.87*, has 4WD vehicles with or without chauffeur available to explore the highlights of Hiva Oa.

André Teissier at Pension Gauguin, *Tel. 92.73.51*, leads excursions to the historical sites in Hiva Oa.

SPORTS & RECREATION

Horseback Riding

Etienne Heitaa in Puamau, *Tel. 92.75.28*, has Marquesan horses for rent, with a guide if requested. Check with your hotel or pension for other possibilities of renting a horse.

Motor Boat Rental

Gisele and Georges Gramont at **Temetieu Boat Rentals** in Atuona, *Tel. 92.73.69*, have boats available for picnic outings.

Deep Sea Fishing
Ozanne Rohi, *Tel 92.73.43,* at **Pension J. Ozanne**, will take you fishing aboard the *Denise II*, a 36-foot tuna fishing boat.

Sailing Charter Yachts
OMATI Marquises, *B.P. 106, Atuona, Hiva Oa, Tel./Fax 689/92.75.20,* offers customized sailing charters in the southern or northern groups of the Marquesas Islands. *Omati* is a comfortable and strong catamaran that is 13.50 meters (44 feet) long, with three cabins, which is based at Tahauku Bay in Atuona. All meals are included in the rates, which vary according to how many passengers are aboard.

Archipels Croisières, *Tel. 689/56.36.39,* whose main office is in Moorea, has a 57-foot deluxe catamaran based year-round in the Marquesas Islands. One of the itineraries in the Discovery of the Marquesas Cruise program begins in Hiva Oa and ends in Nuku Hiva. During the 8-day/7 night cruise you'll visit Hiva Oa, Tahuata, Fatu Hiva, Ua Huka and Nuku Hiva, with guided tours to the archaeological sites and highlights of each island. The cost of $2,050 per person is based on "by the cabin" double-occupancy accommodations, and includes all meals and hotel services aboard, transfers between the airport and yacht and all excursions and events specified in the program. The yacht may also be chartered by the day for $2,090. Dive Aboard Cruises for groups cost $2,450 per person. See additional information in the *Moorea* chapter.

SHOPPING

One of several arts and crafts centers in Atuona is adjacent to the Gauguin Museum, and a very good handcrafts shop and boutique is across the road. You can buy tee-shirts with Marquesan designs, hand-painted pareos, *monoi* oil made with sandalwood and a thousand flowers, and *mille fleurs* honey. Artisan shops are also located in Puamau and Taaoa.

If you want to buy wood carvings you can visit the sculptors at their home workshops. These artisans include: Jean-Marie Otomimi, *Tel. 92.74.35*; Gilbert "Tuarai" Peterano, Antoine and Mathias Tohetiaatua, Noël Scallamera in Tahauku, *Tel. 92.71.19*; Noël Kaimuko; and Axel Kimitete, *Tel. 92.73.81.*

PRACTICAL INFORMATION
Banks
Banque Socredo, *Tel. 92.73.54,* has a branch on the main street in Atuona. Business hours are: Monday, Tuesday, Thursday and Friday 7:30 to 11:30am, and 1:30 to 4pm; Wednesday 7:30 to 11:30am.

Hospitals

There's a government-operated infirmary in Atuona, *Tel. 92.73.75*, a dental center, *Tel. 92.73.58*, an infirmary in Puamau, *Tel. 92.74.96*, and first aid stations in Nahoe and Hanapaoa.

Police

The French *gendarmerie* has a brigade in the center of Atuona, *Tel. 92.73.61*.

Post Office & Telecommunications Office

The post office is located adjacent to the town hall (*mairie*) in the center of Atuona village, *Tel. 92.73.50*. It is open Monday-Thursday from 7:30 to 11:30am and from 1:30 to 4:30pm, and on Friday until 3:30pm; on Saturday it is open from 7:30-8:30am.

Tourist Bureau

The **Hiva Oa Tourist Bureau** is located at the Museum of Atuona, and is open from 7:30 to 11:30am and from 1:30 to 3:30pm. *Tel. 92.75.10*.

TAHUATA

Tahuata has the only coral gardens in the Marquesas and the prettiest white sand beaches. There is no airport and no helicopter service, but you can easily reach Tahuata by boat from Hiva Oa, which is just an hour's ride across the Bordelais Channel. This is a popular port-of-call for cruising yachts, who drop anchor in coves with beautiful secluded beaches that are accessible only by boat. The *Aranui* passengers enjoy visiting the friendly little village of Hapatoni and playing on the beach at Hanemoenoe.

Tahuata is the smallest populated island in the Marquesas archipelago, with only 50 square kilometers (19 square miles) of land. A central mountain range crowns the crescent shaped island, reaching 1,040 meters (3,465 feet) into the ocean sky.

It was in Tahuata's Vaitahu Bay that Alvaro de Mendaña's expedition of four caravelles anchored in 1595. He named the island group *Las Marquesas de Garcia de Mendoza de Canete*, in honor of the wife of Peru's viceroy. The Spanish explorer came ashore at Vaitahu Bay, which he named *Madre de Dios*, Mother of God. It was here that the first crosses were raised and Mass was said. When the Spanish-Peruvian ships set sail, 200 inhabitants lay massacred on the beach.

Following Captain James Cook's visit in 1774, Vaitahu's harbor was named Resolution Bay. When the first Protestant missionaries came in 1797, the generous local chief left his wife with missionary John Harris, with instructions that he should treat her as his own wife. Harris fled when the wife and five of her women friends visited his room.

The French took possession of the Marquesas in Vaitahu, establishing a garrison at Fort Halley in 1842. Monuments, ruins and graves of the French soldiers killed during the skirmishes can be seen in Vaitahu, but no indication is given to the Marquesans who lost their lives. The Catholic missionaries chose Tahuata as the site of their first Marquesan church. The Catholic church that stands today in Vaitahu was built in 1988 with funds from the Vatican. It has a stained-glass window depicting a Marquesan Madonna, plus carvings from the wood sculptors.

Although Tahuata's past has been violent and grim, the 637 inhabitants live a quiet life today, working peacefully in their verdant valleys, raising livestock and making copra. The rich waters surrounding the island attract an amazing variety of fish, sharks and even whales.

Boat day in Tahuata's small villages is a main event, when the copra ship arrives with food and supplies. The 60 residents of Hapatoni are especially welcoming, and the seafront road is shaded by the sacred *tamanu* trees, which are made almost entirely of ancient paved stones.

ARRIVALS & DEPARTURES
Arriving By Boat
The *Aranui* includes stops at Vaitahu, Hapatoni and Hanemoenoe during its 16-day round-trip cruise program from Tahiti to the Marquesas. The *Taporo IV* includes Tahuata in its 10-day round-trip voyages from Tahiti. See details in section on *Inter-Island Cruise Ships and Cargo/ Passenger Boats* in Chapter 6, *Planning Your Trip*.

Te Pua O Mioi is the name of a locally built 42-foot Fiberglas fishing boat that is used by the Commune of Tahuata to transport passengers between Atuona on Hiva Oa to Vaitahu and Hapatoni on Tahuata. The boat leaves the quay of Atuona at 12pm each Tuesday for Vaitahu, and each Thursday the boat leaves Atuona at 12pm for Vaitahu and Hapatoni. The one-way fare is 500 CFP($5). Advance reservations are essential as the boat can transport a maximum of 15 passengers. Reserve at the Mairie of Tahuata, *Tel. 689/92.92.19; Fax 689/92.92.10.*

Departing By Boat
Te Pua O Mioi departs Vaitahu each Tuesday and Thursday at 6:30am for Atuona. The boat stops at Hapatoni village each Thursday enroute to Hiva Oa. Reservations are a must. See information above under *Arriving by Boat*.

ORIENTATION

You can walk from the boat landing to the small village of **Vaitahu**. **Hapatoni** is just a 10-minute boat ride from Vaitahu, or you can take the bridleway. The **Valley of Hanatehau** is a 30-minute horse ride from Hapatoni. A track joins Vaitahu and **Motopu** in the northeast, a distance of about 17 kilometers, which is ideal for riders.

WHERE TO STAY

There are no organized tourist lodgings in Tahuata, but you can rent a room in a family home. Jeanne and Louis Timau, *Tel. 689/92.92.71*, have a house in Vaitahu where you can rent one or two rooms when their children are away at school in Hiva Oa. You can arrange your meals with Jeanne.

PENSION BARSINAS, *Vaitahu, Tahuata, Tel. 689/ 92.92.26.*

There are three very simply furnished rooms upstairs in a split-level house, with a kitchen and communal bathroom with cold water. You can buy supplies at the *magasin* next door and cook your own meals, or arrange with Marie to prepare your meals. You'll pay about 1.500 CFP ($15) a night for the room.

SEEING THE SIGHTS

Vaitahu is the main village, and the small museum **Haina Kakiu** is located in the *mairie* (town hall), which contains exhibits, photos and illustrations of an archaeological site excavated in Hanamiai. **Monuments** in Vaitahu commemorate: the 400th anniversary of the Spanish discovery of the Marquesas Islands; the 150th anniversary of **Iotete**, the first Marquesan chief; French Admiral Dupetit-Thouars; and the French-Marquesan battle of 1842. There are also the remains of a French fort and the graves of French sailors.

The big **Meipe Eia** in Hapatoni is being renovated by the youths from the village. **Petroglyphs** can be found in the Hanatu'una valley, which can be reached by boat or horseback from Hapatoni. There are also stone **petroglyphs** in Hanatehau and **archaeological sites** in Vaitahu valley.

In front of the **Notre Dame de l'Enfant Jesus Catholic Church** in Vaitahu is a wooden statue of the *Virgin with Child* that is nearly four meters (13 feet) tall. This beautiful work of art was carved by **Damien Haturau** of Nuku Hiva, whose Christ child is holding an *uru* (breadfruit) as an offering.

To rent a boat or horse, see the Mayor in Vaitahu.

SHOPPING

A specialty of Tahuata is the fragrant *monoi* oil made from coconuts, herbs and flowers, sandalwood, pineapple and other aromatic plants. You will also enjoy the smoke flavored dried bananas wrapped in leaves. Wood carvers have their workshops in the valleys of Vaitahu, Hapatoni, Hanatetena and Motopu.

The most noted sculptors in Vaitahu are: Teiki Barsinas, *Tel. 92.92.67*; Edwin and Felix Fii, *Tel. 92.93.04*; and Ronald Teiefitu. In Hapatoni contact Frédéric Timau, *Tel. 92.92.55*, Jules Timau, and Sébastien "Kehu" Barsinas.

FATU HIVA

The beautiful island of **Fatu Hiva** will show you the mysterious Marquesas you have dreamed of discovering. Deep within **Hanavave Bay** you may feel that you are inside a gigantic cathedral, a green mansion of moss and fern covered mountains, often encased in misty rain. White patches of goats and sheep look down from their green mansions above the quiet harbor. Nature's chiseled image of the Polynesian god Tiki is visible in the mountain formations, which may give inspiration to the talented sculptors of wood and stone. This is the famous Bay of Virgins, so named by Catholic missionaries, who said that the phallic shaped stone outcrops were formed as veiled virgins.

When the Spanish explorer Alvaro de Mendaña sighted the island of Fatu Hiva in 1595, he believed he had discovered Solomon's kingdom, complete with gold mines. He named the island La Magdalena and killed his first Polynesian on the shore of Omoa village.

The wild, spectacularly beautiful island of Fatu Hiva is the most remote, the furthest south and the wettest and greenest of the Marquesas Islands. Stretching 15 kilometers (9.3 miles) long, a rugged mountain range is topped by Mt. Tauaouoho, at 960 meters (3,149 feet), overlooking 80 square kilometers (31 square miles) of land.

Fatu Hiva is about 70 kilometers (43 miles) south of Hiva Oa, and can be reached by helicopter, communal catamaran, private bonito boats or inter-island ships. As there is no airport the only approach is by sea, and this view alone is worth a trip to the Marquesas Islands.

The jungle greenery begins at the edge of the sea, which is like blue glass after a rain. Narrow ravines, deep gorges and luxuriant valleys briefly open to view as your boat glides past, close to the sheer cliffs that plunge straight into the splashing surf.

Due to the abundant rain and rich, fertile soil, sweet and juicy citrus fruits fill the gardens. Large, tasty shrimp live in the rivers that rush through each valley and rock lobsters are plentiful in the submerged reefs offshore Omoa.

Fatu Hiva is a center of Marquesan crafts. In the villages you will see the women producing tapa cloth from the inner bark of mulberry, banyan or breadfruit trees. They hammer the bark on a log until the fibers adhere, and when it is dry they paint it with the old Marquesan designs like their ancestors wore as tattoos. Sculptors carve the semi-precious woods of *miro* (rosewood), *tou* and sandalwood, as well as coconuts, basaltic stones and bones. They produce bowls, platters, small canoes, turtles, tiki statues and war clubs. You are welcome to visit their workshops at their homes.

A rare collection of ancient Marquesan woodcarvings can be viewed at a private museum in Omoa. You can rent a horse for a bareback ride into the valley, charter a motorized outrigger canoe to explore the coastline and line fish, swim in the rivers or open ocean, go shrimping or lobstering with the locals, and if you're really adventurous, you can join a Marquesan wild pig hunt.

Smoke flavored dried bananas are a specialty of the industrious people of **Omoa village**. Fatu Hiva's special bouquet is the *umu hei*—a delightful blend of sandalwood powder, spearmint, jasmine, ginger root, pineapple, vanilla, sweet basil, gardenia, pandanus fruit, ylang-ylang and other mysterious herbs. This seductive concoction is all tied together and worn around your neck or in your hair.

ARRIVALS & DEPARTURES
Arriving By Boat
The *Aranui* includes stops at Hanavave Bay and Omoa during its 16-day round-trip cruise program from Tahiti to the Marquesas. See details in Chapter 6, *Planning Your Trip*, section on Inter-Island Cruise Ships and Cargo/Passenger Boats.

Departing By Boat
Auona II is a locally built 45-foot catamaran owned by the Commune of Omoa, *Tel. 92.80.23*, that can transport 15 passengers. A weekly round-trip voyage leaves Fatu Hiva at 6am for Atuona, Hiva Oa, and departs Atuona at 2pm to return to Fatu Hiva. The per person cost is 3.000 CFP ($30) from Fatu Hiva to Tahuata, Atuona or Puamau (on the island of Hiva Oa). You can also charter the boat for 60.000 CFP ($600).

ORIENTATION
The 631 inhabitants of Fatu Hiva live in the villages of **Omoa** and **Hanavave**, which are separated by five kilometers (3 miles) of sea. Omoa, in the south of the island, is a wide open valley with a black sand beach lined with several outrigger canoes painted blue. Just behind the beach is a soccer field and the one road that leads through the village past the little

Catholic church, which has a lovely background of mountainous peaks and spires. Almost every house is surrounded by beautiful flower gardens, *pamplemousse* (grapefruit) trees, citrons and oranges, bananas and other tropical fruit trees. This village is clean and the people are open and friendly.

Hanavave village is narrow and closed in between the fantastic rock formations. The beach is dirty and the most of the houses are old and shabby. The people seem to reflect their environment and suffer from an apathy that I have noticed in other enclosed valleys in the Marquesas Islands.

Getting ashore at either village can be an adventure in itself, as small boat landings consist of slippery concrete piers. When the ocean is wild, as it often is, the whale boat bobs up and down beside the pier and you have to time your jump with the crest of the waves. If you arrive with the *Aranui*, the ship's crew will help you to get ashore and back into the whale boat.

A serpentine path winds over the mountains between the two villages, offering a 17 kilometer (10.5 mile) challenging hike and panoramic views through the curtains of rock. Majestic waterfalls are visible from the path deep inside **Vaie'enui Valley**. Facilities include food stores, a post office, a town hall and primary schools in each village.

GETTING AROUND
Car Rentals
Didier Gilmore at Chez Cecile in Omoa village, *Tel. 92.80.54*, will drive you to Hanavave in his 4WD vehicle for 10.000 CFP ($100) one-way.

WHERE TO STAY
Inexpensive
PENSION HEIMATA, *98740 Omoa, Fatu Hiva, Tel. 689/92.80.58. Rates: room with breakfast 2.500 CFP ($25) per person; room with breakfast and dinner 4.000 CFP ($40) per person; room with all meals 5.500 CFP ($55) per person; half-fare for children 6 to 11 years; no charge for children under 6 years. Round-trip transfers from boat landing to pension are included. Add 1% value added tax to room rates and meal plan. No credit cards.*

This two bedroom house is beside the road in the village, and is very clean, homey and brightly decorated. There's a double bed in each room, a living room, dining room, terrace and bathroom with hot water. House linens are furnished and Albertine's husband Teva will arrange excursions for you on request. Albertine serves good Marquesan food, which includes lots of fresh fish, fruits and vegetables.

CHEZ NORMA ROPATI, *98740 Omoa, Fatu Hiva, Tel. 689/92.80.13. Rates: room with breakfast 2.000 CFP ($20) per person; room with all meals 5.500 CFP ($55) per person. Round-trip transfers from boat landing to pension are included. Add 1% value added tax to room rates and meal plan. No credit cards.*

Norma's guest house is in the middle of the village, across the road from Chez Cecile. It is totally surrounded by beautiful flowers and colorful bushes and shrubs. The 4-bedroom house has a double bed in each room, and the living room with television, dining room, kitchen, and communal bathroom with hot water are all shared. The house linens are furnished. Norma's Marquesan style meals are generous and very tasty.

PENSION CHEZ JOSEPH, *98740 Omoa, Fatu Hiva, Tel./Fax 689/92.80.09. EP Rates: room 2.000 CFP ($20) single; 3.500 CFP ($35) double. Meals are prepared on request. Round-trip transfers from boat landing to pension are included. Add 1% value added tax to room rates and meal plan. No credit cards.*

This pension opened in 1997 above the new concrete *magasin* store in the center of the village. Each of the two bedrooms contains a king size bed and there's a small balcony overlooking the flower garden and the mountains. The kitchen and bathroom facilities are shared and house linens are supplied.

CHEZ CECILE GILMORE, *98740 Omoa, Fatu Hiva, Tel. 689/92.80.54. EP Rates: room 3.500 CFP ($35) per person; room with all meals 5.000 CFP ($50) per person. Round-trip transfers from boat landing to pension are included. Add 1% value added tax to room rates and meal plan. No credit cards.*

This simple pension is beside the road in the center of the village. Each of the two bedrooms contains a double bed, and you share the living room, dining room, kitchen and bathroom with cold water. House linens are supplied.

CHEZ MARIE-CLAIRE, *98740 Omoa, Fatu Hiva, Tel. 689/92.80.75. EP Rates: room 3.000 CFP ($30) per person per day; half-fare for children 6 to 11 years; no charge for children under 6 years; house 50.000 CFP ($500) per month. Round-trip transfers from boat landing to pension are included. Add 1% value added tax to room rates. No credit cards.*

This little two-bedroom house is beside the road in the center of the village, just a five minute walk from the beach. There's a double bed in each room, plus a living room, dining room, kitchen and bathroom with hot water. House linens are supplied and Marie-Claire will wash them free of charge for long-term guests. This is a good choice if you want to stay in Omoa for a few days or weeks. You can do your own cooking or make arrangements with one of the other pensions for your meals.

WHERE TO EAT

Inexpensive

You'll eat very well for inexpensive costs at either of the pensions listed below. There are two *magasin* stores in Omoa village that sell food supplies and cold beer. There are no snacks or restaurants.

PENSION HEIMATA, *Tel. 92.80.58. Please reserve.*

Breakfast is 500 CFP ($5) and lunch or dinner is 1.500 CFP ($15), featuring Marquesan specialties.

CHEZ NORMA ROPATI, *Tel. 92.80.13. Reservations are required.*

Marquesan specialties.

SEEING THE SIGHTS

The most beautiful sight in Fatu Hiva is the **Bay of Virgins** in Hanavave, which is best seen from the sea. In Omoa a giant **petroglyph** featuring a huge fish and stick figures is engraved in a boulder at the edge of the village, and there are stone *paepae* house terraces in the valleys. A private collection of ancient Marquesan woodcarvings that belonged to former chief **Willie Grellet** are on display in a house owned by his grandchildren in Omoa. The **Catholic church** in Omoa, with its red roof, white walls and rock fence, is one of the most picturesque scenes in any Marquesan village.

A 17-kilometer (10.5-mile) **hiking trail** will lead you across the rugged mountains between Omoa and Hanavave village. You'll see towering cliffs and majestic waterfalls and a secluded jungle pool awaits you at the end of the hike, where you can swim in an ideal setting for a South Pacific movie. Walking alone in the mountains of Fatu Hiva is not recommended, even if you are an experienced hiker.

SPORTS & RECREATION

Horseback Riding

In Omoa village you can rent a Marquesan horse with a wooden saddle for daily excursions to Hanavave Bay or to ride around Omoa Valley. Contact Roberto Maraetaata, *Tel. 92.80.23*, or Isidore Mose, *Tel. 92.80.28*.

Boat Rental

You can rent an outrigger canoe with an engine and guide to get from Omoa to Hanavave Bay or vice-versa. Skimming across the incredibly blue water close to the untamed shore and gazing up at the rock formations and the wild cattle and goats staring down at you are moments to remember forever.

In Omoa contact: Xavier Gilmore, Napoléon Gilmore or Edwin Tametona at *Tel. 92.80.54*; or Stellio Tehevini, *Tel. 92.80.79*.

Deep Sea Fishing

The Marquesan men are experienced fishermen and you can arrange with your pension to accompany one of them. Most of the boats used for fishing are the outrigger speed canoes.

SHOPPING

Most of the women in Fatu Hiva make tapa bark paintings, which they sell from their homes or take to Papeete for arts and crafts exhibits. They also make *monoi* oils, *umu hei* and dried bananas. Appoline Teaiho in Omoa village is one of the most noted tapa makers, who demonstrates to groups how the bark cloth is made. Marie-Noëlle Ehueinana, who also lives in Omoa, has won prizes for her tapa paintings.

Some of the men are sculptors of wood, stone and even coconuts, which they carve into lovely designs taken from the ancient Marquesan tattoos. There are at least 10 sculptors in Omoa village and two or three in Hanavave.

PRACTICAL INFORMATION

Doctors

There is a government-operated **infirmary** in Omoa village, *Tel. 92.80.36*, and a **First Aid Station** (*Poste de Secours*) in Hanavave village, *Tel. 92.80.61*.

Post Office and Telecommunications Office

There is a **post office** in Omoa Village, *Tel. 92.83.74*.

24. THE AUSTRAL ISLANDS

In the Polynesian language, the **Austral Islands** of French Polynesia are collectively known as *Tuhaa Pae*, referring to the five parts or islands that make up the archipelago. Folklore tells of Maui, the South Seas Superman, who fished up this chain of islands from the sea, using a magical fishhook that now forms the tail of Scorpio in the sky. This same hero is said to have cut away the great octopus that held the earth and the sky together, and he pushed up the sky so that people could walk upright. The arms of this octopus fell to the earth to form the Austral Islands, with Tubuai as its head.

Tane was a powerful god who used his many colored seashells to help separate the earth and sky, decorated the Austral heavens with twinkling stars, a golden sun and silvery moon, cool winds and billowing clouds. R'o, God of Agriculture and the Harvest, can be seen as a gilded rainbow and heard as the voice of thunder. Ruahatu-Tinirau, a Polynesian Neptune known as God of the Ocean and Lord of the Abyss, is said to have a man's body joined to a swordfish tail. Everyone knows that this powerful god lives in the reefs of Raivavae. And Tuivao, a fishing hero from Rurutu, sailed on the back of a whale to an enchanted island ruled by the goddess Tareparepa. Fleeing her spell Tuivao rode his whale to the island of Raivavae, where the mammal landed so hard on the beach that its imprint is still seen there today.

Past and present blend in harmony in the Austral Islands today. Islands of quiet beauty, peace and pride, these are Polynesia's Temperate Isles.

The Austral Islands include the high islands of **Rurutu**, **Tubuai**, **Rimatara**, **Raivavae** and **Rapa**, plus the low, uninhabited islands of **Maria** (or Hull) and the **Marotiri** (or Bass) **Rocks**. These islands lie on both sides of the Tropic of Capricorn, extending in a northwest-southeasterly direction across 1,280 kilometers (794 miles) of ocean. They are part of a vast mountain range, an extension of the same submerged chain that comprises the Cook Islands 960 kilometers (595 miles) further to the northwest.

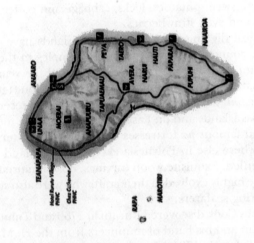

ILES AUSTRALES

ILES MARIA

RIMATARA   RURUTU

TUBUAI   RAIVAVAE

RAPA   MAROTIRI

0   100   200   300   400   500 KM

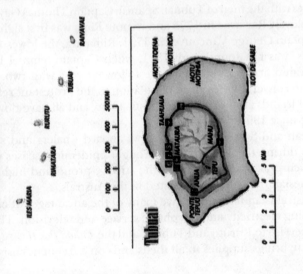

Tubuai

0   1   2   3   4   5 KM

MOTU TOENA   MOTU ROA

MOTU MOTHAA

TAAHUAIA

MAHU

MATAURA

ANUA   TEPU

POINTE ANUA

ROT DE SABLE

The 141 square kilometers (54 square miles) of land surface in the Austral Islands is home to some 6,500 Polynesians, who live peaceful lives in their attractive villages, where their houses and churches are usually built of coral limestone. Due to the rich soil and the cooler climate of the Australs, good quality vegetables can be produced, including taro, manioc, potatoes, sweet potatoes, leeks, cabbage and coffee, as well as apples, peaches and even strawberries.

Archaeological diggings in these isolated islands have uncovered habitation sites, council platforms and *marae* temples in the village of Vitaria on Rurutu, showing man's presence around the year 900 A.D. Tubuai and Rimatara also have ruins of open-air *marae* stone temples, and giant sized stone *tikis* have been found on Raivavae that resemble those in the Marquesas Islands and on Easter Island. On Rapa there are the remains of seven famous *pa* fortresses on superimposed terraces, that were found nowhere else in Polynesia except New Zealand where the Maori people settled. Exquisite wood carvings, now in museums, tell of an artistic people highly evolved in their craft, who were also superb boat builders and daring seafarers.

Captain James Cook discovered Rurutu in 1769 and Tubuai in 1777. Fletcher Christian and his band of mutineers from the H. M. S. *Bounty* tried to settle in Tubuai in 1789, but were forced to flee the island because of skirmishes with the men of Tubuai. Spanish Captain Thomas Gayangos discovered lovely Raivavae in 1775 and remote Rapa was first sighted by English Captain George Vancouver in 1791. Rimatara, the lowest of the high islands, was not found until 1821, when Captain Samuel Pinder Henry of Tahiti arrived, returning the following year with two native teachers who converted the entire population to the Protestant religion. The Austral Islands are mostly Evangelistic today and all have flown the French flag since 1901.

European and South American crews aboard whalers and sandal-wood ships during the 19th century brought epidemic diseases to the islands, which practically decimated the strong, proud and highly cultured Polynesian race that once existed in the Australs.

The Austral Islanders today have many of the advantages of civilization, including electricity and telephone service and television. There is regular air service to Rurutu and Tubuai, and the *Tuhaa Pae II* cargo ship from Papeete brings supplies to all the islands on a frequent basis.

RURUTU

Rurutu is the most northerly of the Austral Islands, 572 kilometers (355 miles) southwest of Tahiti. A very pretty island with a circumference of 30 kilometers (19 miles), Rurutu is an upthrust limestone island with steep cliffs rising dramatically from the sea. The crannies in these bluffs were formerly used as shelters and burial chambers. There are also caves and grottoes decorated with stalactites and stalagmites. Rurutu's highest mountain, **Manureva**, reaches an elevation of 385 meters (1,263 feet), and the coral reefs that surrounded the island eons ago are now raised bluffs some 90 meters (300 feet) high above the sea. Rurutu does not have the wide lagoons found in the Society Islands or in Tubuai and Raivavae. Swimming and snorkeling are still possible in certain areas, however, and there are a few white sand beaches.

The original name of this island was *Eteroa*, which means a long measuring string. The current name of *Rurutu tu noa* is an old Polynesian saying that means a mast standing straight. *Manureva* (soaring bird), was formerly the name of one of Rurutu's famous sailing boats that carried produce between the islands. The men are still noted sailors, and several of them work aboard the inter-island cargo ships that serve as a life line between Tahiti and the remote islands of French Polynesia.

The people of Rurutu were also highly skilled wood carvers, but no longer practice this craft. Most of the ancient tiki statues were destroyed by the missionaries, and one of them, the statue of the Rurutu ancestor god A'a, was taken to London by John Williams, one of the pioneering missionaries. This original tiki, which is 45 inches tall and weighs 282 pounds, is in the Museum of Mankind in London, but five plaster of Paris molds were made of this statue by the British Museum, and one of them has been willed to the people of Rurutu by an American man who recently died. Christi's has evaluated each of the A'a tiki statues to be worth $50,000. The tiki is currently on display at the Museum of Tahiti and Her Islands, and will be sent to Rurutu in the near future.

In the old village of **Vitaria** is the **Marae Taaroa** or **Arii**, which dates from the year 900. This is the oldest known site of man's habitation in the Austral Islands. Nearby is a council platform and 70 house sites of a former village and warriors' house. In ancient times the warriors of Rurutu were feared for their strength. Today they are admired for their industriousness, seamanship, dancing skills and physical beauty.

The 2,015 handsome, intelligent and industrious Polynesians who live in the three villages of Moerai, Avera and Hauti, have colorful houses of coral limestone, bordered by flower gardens and low fences of limestone, painted white.

In the main village of **Moerai** there is a gendarmerie, a post office and infirmary with a doctor and dentist, a bank, primary and junior high schools, a few small stores and a couple of snack bars. Each village is dominated by a Protestant temple, with smaller churches for the Catholic, Mormon, Adventist and Jehovah's Witness faiths.

The men harvest their taro, tapioca, sweet potatoes, cabbages, leeks and carrots. The women form artisan groups to weave specially grown fibers of *paeore* pandanus into attractive hats, bags and mats, which are sold both locally and in Tahiti. The people of Rurutu enjoy a pleasant communal spirit, working together, singing *himenes* in their Evangelical churches, and pitching in to prepare a big feast.

A New Year's custom on Rurutu is to visit each house in the village, where you are sprinkled with talcum powder before entering to partake of the refreshments. Also during the month of January the youth groups of the Protestant churches participate in a ritual called the *Tere*. A long caravan of flower-decorated pickup trucks, 4-wheel drive vehicles and motorcycles makes a tour of the island, stopping at each historical site, where one of the orators recites the legends of each significant stone or cave. One of the stops is on top of a mountain, where you have a lovely view of the village of Avera. Here is the Ofai Maramaiterai (intelligence that lightens the sky), which folklore claims is the center and origin of the island.

During the *Tere* circle island tour and also during the July Festival the young men and women of each village prove themselves in a show of strength. Following a custom called *amoraa ofai*, unique to Rurutu, they attempt to lift huge volcanic stones to their shoulders. The village champions hoist one sacred stone that weighs 150 kilograms (330 pounds). This accomplishment is followed by exuberant feasting and dancing.

Activities on Rurutu include horseback riding and hiking to waterfalls, where refreshing showers cascade into fern bordered pools. The limestone grottoes form a natural stage for cultural reenactment ceremonies and cinematographers from all parts of the world come here to film these natural formations. Circle island tours by four-wheel drive vehicle wind over rutted roads into cool valleys where fields of wild miri (sweet basil) scent the breeze. Picnic lunches can be packed for these trips or to play in the sun on deserted white sand beaches. Humpback whales can be seen offshore Rurutu during the austral winter months of July-October.

The aroma of pineapple mingles pleasantly with *ylang ylang*, Tiare Tahiti, wild *miri* basil and *avaro*, some of the fragrant flowers, fruits and spices that are used to make the welcoming leis you will smell as soon as you arrive on this island of fragrant perfumes.

ARRIVALS & DEPARTURES
Arriving By Air
Air Tahiti flies has a 1 1/2 hour direct flight from Tahiti to Rurutu each Monday and Wednesday, and a flight each Friday and Sunday via Tubuai. The one way airfare from Tahiti to Rurutu is 18.585 CFP

($185.85) and the fare from Tubuai to Rurutu is 8.715 ($87.15). **Air Tahiti reservations**: *Tahiti Tel. 86.42.42/86.41.84.*

Arriving By Boat

Tuhaa Pae II, *Tel. 42.93.67,* makes a voyage from Tahiti to the Austral Islands every 15 days, calling at Tubuai, Rimatara, Raivavae and Rurutu, then returning to Papeete. This itinerary may change according to the freight requirements of each voyage. The one-way fare to Rurutu is 3.761 CFP ($37.61) on the deck, 5.265 CFP ($52.65) in a berth on deck, and 65.83 ($65.83) in a cabin. Meals are 2.300 CFP ($23) per day. See further information in Chapter 6, *Planning Your Trip.*

Departing By Air

You can fly from Rurutu to Tubuai and on to Tahiti each Monday and Wednesday. The Friday and Sunday departures from Rurutu are direct flights to Tahiti. **Air Tahiti reservations** in Rurutu, *Tel. 94.03.57.*

Departing By Boat

The *Tuhaa Pae II* calls at Moerai village in Rurutu on its way back to Papeete or enroute to the other Austral Islands, according to the needs of the islanders. You can purchase your ticket on board the ship.

ORIENTATION

The oblong-shaped island of Rurutu is 10 kilometers (6.2 miles) long and 5.5 kilometers (3.4 miles) wide, or 36 square kilometers (14 square miles) in circumference. The main village of **Moerai** on the east coast is about four kilometers (2.5 miles) from the airport, connected by a paved road, which also extends to the village of **Hauti**, also on the east coast. Another sealed road links Moerai with **Avera**, on the western coast, which has a small harbor for fishing boats, within the island's only real bay. The road does not circle the coastline, but climbs up and down, from sea-level to almost 200 meters (656 feet). There are also several off-track dirt roads that can be explored by 4WD, horseback or on foot.

GETTING AROUND

If you reserve a room at the Rurutu Village or Chez Catherine they will provide free round-trip transportation between the airport and the lodging. You can rent a car at Chez Catherine for 3.500 CFP ($35) for a half day, or 6.000 CFP ($60) for a full day. The Rurutu Village has bicycles for the use of their guests. You can arrange an island tour with either lodging for 4.500 CFP ($45) per person.

WHERE TO STAY

RURUTU VILLAGE, *B.P. 22, 98753 Moerai, Rurutu, Tel. 689/94.03.92, Fax 689/94.05.01. Beside the lagoon 1 kilometer (.62 miles) from the airport. 8 bungalows. EP Rates: room 3.500 CFP ($35) single; 4.500 CFP ($45) double; add 500 CFP ($5) per day for additional person; add 3.500 CFP ($35) per person for breakfast and dinner; add 5.300 CFP ($53) per person for breakfast, lunch and dinner. Round-trip transfers included. Add 1% value added tax to room rates and meal plan. Mastercard, Visa.*

Eight bungalows of coral and limestone face the white sand beach on the northwest coast. These units are furnished with two single beds, a bathroom with a tub and hot water, and a terrace. House linens are furnished.

The main building houses the reception, lounge area, bar and a big dining room serving generous helpings of food. A fresh water swimming pool is just outside, which is actually preferable to swimming in the lagoon here, because it is difficult to get into the lagoon due to the fringing reef. This was once a first class little hotel, but it was badly damaged by a cyclone in 1995, and the tennis courts have been converted into a pig pen. The rooms were all rebuilt and are once again in operation.

Paid activities include a full-day excursion around the island, with a picnic on the beach, visits to the Vitaria and Peva grottoes and arts and crafts centers. Deep sea fishing can be arranged on request.

CHEZ CATHERINE, *B.P. 11, 98753 Moerai, Rurutu, Tel. 689/94.02.43, Fax 689/94.06.99. In Moerai village facing the port. 10 rooms. EP Rates: room 3.000 CFP ($30) single, 4.000 CFP ($40) double; add 2.500 CFP ($25) per person for breakfast and dinner; add 4.000 CFP ($40) for breakfast, lunch and dinner. Monthly rentals are 40.000 CFP ($400) single and $50.000 ($500) double. Round-trip transfers included. Add 1% value added tax to room rates and meal plan. Mastercard, Visa.*

Five rooms contain a double bed and a berth for a child, and five rooms contain two single beds and a small berth. Each room has a private bathroom with a hot water shower. House linens are furnished. The main building contains a living room with television and a lending library, plus a restaurant/bar featuring French and local cuisine.

You can sit on the front terrace and watch the ocean while listening to the *himene* singing coming from the Protestant church in the center of Moerai village. From here it's very convenient to walk around the village or along the road beside the sea, up to the limestone caves overlooking the ocean. There's nothing fancy about this place, but it is well managed.

You can rent a car or take a guided tour around the island with a picnic included, stopping at the artisan's centers and at the cultural sites of Vitaria and Peva grottoes. You can also go line fishing in the open ocean or shrimping in the rivers in the valley. Picnics can be prepared for hikes into the interior of the island.

WHERE TO EAT

Rurutu Village serves breakfast for 500 CFP ($5) and lunch or dinner for 2.500 CFP ($25). **Chez Catherine** serves breakfast for 500 CFP ($5) and lunch or dinner for 2.000 CFP ($20). Some of the main courses cost between 1.000-1.800 CFP ($10-$18). Each restaurant features fresh fish, lobster, steaks and local dishes, which may include some of Rurutu's delicious taro. **Snack-Restaurant Chez Titine** is in Avera Village, *Tel. 94.05.14.*

SEEING THE SIGHTS

Some of the interesting sites you will want to visit in Rurutu are the grottoes and *marae* temples of Vitaria, the Tetuanui Plateau and dam, the beautiful view of Matotea between Vitaria and Avera, the Lookout Point at Taura'ma, where you can see the villages of Avera and Hauti, the beautiful white sand beaches of Naairoa, Narui and Peva, the Vairuauri Grotto at Paparai, and the Underwater Grotto of Te Ana Maro at Teava Nui.

You may also be interested in visiting the final resting place of **Eric de Bisschop**, a French explorer who was noted for his ocean voyages in unseaworthy rafts. He died at Rakahanga in the Cook Islands in 1972, and is buried in the second cemetery of Moerai, off the main road, south of the village.

SPORTS & RECREATION
Diving

Te Ava Ma'o Dive Club in Moerai is operated by Bertrand Devaux and Louis Teinaore, Jr., *Tel. 94.02.29.*

The host at your pension can arrange activities for you. See information under *Where to Stay* above.

SHOPPING

The "mamas" of Rurutu are noted for their finely made hats, baskets, tote bags, mats and other woven products. You can visit the arts and crafts shops and you will also see the women sitting together on the grass or on their front terraces, creating an outlandish hat for them to wear to church or a beautiful traditional hat for you to buy.

PRACTICAL INFORMATION

Banks

Banque Socredo, *Tel. 94.04.75*, has an agency in Moerai village.

Doctors

There is a small medical center in Moerai, *Tel. 94.03.12*, and an infirmary in Avera village, *Tel. 94.03.21*.

Police

The French gendarmerie of Rurutu, *Tel. 94.03.61*, is located in Moerai.

Post Office

There is a Post Office and Telecommunications Center in Moerai, *Tel. 94.03.50*.

Tourist Bureau

Rurutu Visitors Bureau, *Tel. 94.02.43*, is in Moerai. Yves Gentilhomme, from Chez Catherine, is president.

TUBUAI

Tubuai is 568 kilometers (352 miles) due south of Tahiti, located just above the Tropic of Capricorn in the center of the Austral Island group, offering a pleasant combination of the tropics and temperate zone

This is the largest of the Austral Islands, with a land area of 45 square kilometers (17 square miles) and a population of 2,049 inhabitants. An immense turquoise lagoon is bordered by brilliant white sand beaches and dotted by seven palm shaded *motu* islets, surrounded by superb snorkeling grounds. These warm and shallow lagoon waters provide an ideal nursery for colorful and delicious tropical fish, clams, sea urchins and lobsters. There are three main passes and several smaller passes through the coral reef into the calm lagoon, and the cargo ships can offload supplies at a concrete pier near Mataura village. This sheltered harbor is located close to the former site where Fort George was established by Fletcher Christian and his mutineers from the *H.M.S. Bounty* when they tried to settle on Tubuai in 1789. This was one of the most important events in the history of Tubuai, when the mutineers tried twice to settle on the island, but were fought off by the unfriendly warriors of the island.

Captain James Cook landed in Tubuai in 1777 during his third voyage to Tahiti. The London Missionary Society sent native teachers to the island to convert souls to Christianity in 1822. The Protestant faith is still predominant in Tubuai, and the Mormon religion is also an important part of today's lifestyle.

Tubuai is the administrative center for the archipelago, and the main village of **Mataura** has the administrative offices, town hall, gendarmerie, small hospital, post office, schools and churches. Chinese families operate the island's grocery stores and bake bread. Electricity and hot water are usually included in the small family pensions and prepared meals can sometimes be arranged with the landlady. Fresh fish, fruits and vegetables can be obtained with the family's assistance. You can rent a bicycle, horse or car, and boat trips to explore the *motu* islets can be arranged with your hosts.

Tubuai is a pretty island but it does not have the dramatic coastlines of Rurutu, Raivavae and Rapa, and the people here seem to lack the zestful spirit, the *joie de vivre* that you'll find on Rurutu.

ARRIVALS & DEPARTURES
Arriving By Air
Air Tahiti has a 1 hour and 40 minute direct flight from Tahiti to Tubuai each Friday and Sunday, and a flight each Monday and Wednesday via Rurutu. The one way airfare from Tahiti to Tubuai is 20.790 CFP ($20.790) and the fare from Rurutu to Tubuai is 8.715 ($87.15). **Air Tahiti reservations**: *Tahiti Tel. 86.42.42/86.41.84.*

Arriving By Boat
Tuhaa Pae II, *Tel. 42.93.67*, makes a voyage from Tahiti to the Austral Islands every 15 days, calling at Tubuai, Rimatara, Raivavae and Rurutu, then returning to Papeete. This itinerary may change according to the freight requirements of each voyage. The one-way fare to Tubuai is 3.761 CFP ($37.61) on the deck, 5.265 CFP ($52.65) in a berth on deck, and 65.83 ($65.83) in a cabin. Meals are 2.300 CFP ($23) per day. See further information in Chapter 6, *Planning Your Trip*.

Departing By Air
You can fly direct from Tubuai to Tahiti each Monday and Wednesday. The Friday and Sunday departures from Tubuai make a brief stop in Rurutu before returning to Tahiti. **Air Tahiti reservations** *in Tubuai, Tel. 95.04.76.*

Departing By Boat
The *Tuhaa Pae II* calls at Tubuai enroute to the other Austral Islands or on its way back to Papeete. You can purchase your ticket on board the ship.

ORIENTATION

Tubuai is an oval shaped island with no indented bays. Two mountain ranges rise from the heart of the island, with **Mount Taita** the highest peak at 422 meters (1,393 feet) in altitude. A 24-kilometer (15 mile) paved road circles the island, connecting the quiet villages of **Mataura**, **Taahuaia** and **Mahu**. An interior road winds through fertile plains and marshlands, where taro, potatoes, sweet potatoes and peaches grow, alongside coffee, corn and oranges. The airport is about four kilometers (2.5 miles) from Mataura village.

GETTING AROUND

You will be met at the airport or boat dock by someone from the pension where you've reserved accommodations. There is no public transportation system on Tubuai and no taxi service outside the pensions. Check with your host for the possibility of renting a car, 4WD, scooter or bicycle.

WHERE TO STAY

CHEZ DOUDOU, *B.P. 64, 98754 Mataura, Tubuai, Tel. 689/95.06.71. On mountain side in Mataura, 3 kilometers (1.9 miles) from the airport and two kilometers (1.2 miles) from the boat dock. EP Rates: Room 3.000 CFP ($30) single, 4.500 CFP ($45) double; add 1.000 CFP ($10) for additional person; add 500 CFP ($5) for child under 12 years; add 500 CFP ($5) for one night's stay only; add 2.300 CFP ($23) per person for breakfast and dinner; add 4.100 CFP ($41) per person for all meals; half-price for child under 12 years. Round-trip transfers 1.000 CFP ($10). Add 1% value added tax to room rates and meal plan. Major credit cards accepted.*

This small hotel has 20 rooms in a new two-story motel-like building. Each room contains a fan and private bathroom with hot water, and a private balcony or terrace. The restaurant and bar serves local style cuisine and Tahitian food. House linens are furnished. A laundry is available for guest use and activities can be arranged.

PENSION VAITEA NUI, *B.P. 141, 98754 Mataura, Tubuai, Tel/Fax 689/95.04.19. On mountain side in Mataura, 5 kilometers (3.1 miles) from the airport. EP Rates: room 2.500 CFP ($25) single, 4.000 CFP ($40) double; room with breakfast 3.000 CFP ($30) single, 5.000 CFP ($50) double; room with breakfast and dinner 5.000 CFP ($50) single, 7.000 CFP ($70) double; room with all meals 6.000 CFP ($60) single, 10.000 CFP ($100) double. Half-price for child under 10 years. Round-trip transfers included. Add 1% value added tax to room rates and meal plan. No credit cards.*

This is a 5-room one-story motel-like structure. Each room has a double bed and private bathroom with hot water, and a chair on the long front terrace. Local style and French cuisine is served in the big family style dining room. House linens are furnished. This pension is conveniently located near the post office, food stores and town hall. Access to the beach. Camping is possible in the big garden. Car and bike rentals are available.

CHEZ SAM ET YOLANDE, *B.P. 77, 98754 Mataura, Tubuai, Tel./Fax 689/95.05.52. On the beach in Mataura, 2 kilometers (1.2 miles) from the airport and 3 kilometers (1.9 miles) from the boat dock. EP Rates: room 2.500 CFP ($25) single, 4.000 CFP ($40) double; room with breakfast 3.000 CFP ($30) single, 5.000 CFP ($50) double; room with breakfast and dinner 5.000 CFP ($50) single, 7.000 CFP ($70) double; room with all meals 6.000 CFP ($60) single, 10.000 CFP ($100) double. Half-price for child under 10 years. Round-trip transfers included. Add 1% value added tax to room rates and meal plan. No credit cards.*

This modern and attractive 4-room house has a double bed and fan in each room. The kitchen, living room with television, dining room, laundry room and bathroom with hot water are shared. House linens are furnished.

MANU PATIA, *B.P. 7, 98754 Mataura, Tubuai, Tel. 689/95.03.27. Beside lagoon in Taahuaia, 9 kilometers (6 miles) from the airport and 3.5 kilometers (2.2 miles) from the boat dock. EP Rates: room 2.500 CFP ($25) per person; room with all meals 5.000 CFP ($50) per person; apartment 55.000 CFP ($550) per month. Round-trip transfers included. Add 1% value added tax to room rates and meal plan. No credit cards.*

This is a simple little concrete house with a sheet metal roof and two apartments. One apartment has two bedrooms, a living room with television and a private bathroom with hot water. The other apartment has one bedroom, a kitchen, living room with television and a private bathroom with hot water. Each apartment has a fan. House linens are furnished. The prepared meals are Tahitian style cuisine.

LE BOUNTY, *B.P. 74, 98754 Mataura, Tubuai, Tel. 689/95.03.32, Fax 689/95.05.58. In Taahuaia, 12 kilometers (7.5 miles) from the airport and 2.5 kilometers (1.6 miles) from the boat dock. EP Rates: house 3.000 CFP ($30) single; 5.000 CFP ($50) up to four people. Round-trip transfers included. Add 1% value added tax to room rates and meal plan. No credit cards.*

This is a two-bedroom house with a double bed and two single beds in each room. The living room with television, dining room, kitchen, terrace and bathroom with hot water are communal. House linens are furnished. A washing machine and bicycles are also available for guests' use. A food store is close by.

WHERE TO EAT

LE MOTU *in Taahuaia village, Tel. 95.05.27. Please reserve. No credit cards.*

Serves lunch and dinner, featuring French and local cuisine. Closed on Sunday.

VAITEA NUI *in Taahuaia village, Tel. 95.04.19. Please reserve. No credit cards.*

Serves lunch and dinner, featuring local style cooking and seafood specialties. Closed on Sunday.

SEEING THE SIGHTS

The hosts at your pension will help you to rent a boat with chauffeur to visit the lagoon and the offshore *motu* islets, or to go line fishing inside the emerald-tinted lagoon. Some of the pensions will pack you a picnic lunch to take along. **Mount Taita** is an attraction for hikers, who will enjoy the view from the summit, which is 422 meters (1,384 feet) high. A drive around the island is quickly done, but is not very inspiring.

SPORTS & RECREATION

Hang Gliding

Matai Reva Nui is a hang gliding club operated by Jean-Yves Ly Tham, *Tel. 95.03.65/95.03.33*, who will take you to the island's highest peaks to soar over Tubuai like a bird. He can also arrange boat trips to visit the lagoon and *motu* islets.

Horseback Riding

Lucien Viriamu, *Tel. 95.03.97*, in Mataura village, rents horses by the hour, half-day or full-day. You can also hike to Taitaa peak, which is a three-hour excursion, visit Haramea village during a four-hour outing, and visit the interior of the island. Excursions are arranged on request.

SHOPPING

Each village has an arts and crafts center, where you can buy locally made hats, mats, bags, clothing, *pareos* and *tifaifai* bed covers. There is also an artisan center at the *mairie* (town hall) in Mataura. The best place to see the handcrafts is at the airport, where the "mamas" display their hand made products before the departure of each Air Tahiti flight.

PRACTICAL INFORMATION

Banks

Banque Socredo, *Tel. 95.04.86/95.06.88*, has an agency in Mataura village.

Banque de Tahiti, *Tel. 95.03.63*, in Mataura village, serves all the Austral Islands.

Doctors
There is a hospital in Mataura, which serves all the Austral Islanders, *Tel. 95.03.79*. There is also a dental center in this complex.

Police
French *gendarmerie*: *Tel. 95.03.33*.

Post Office
There is a Post Office and Telecommunications Center in Mataura, *Tel. 95.03.50*.

Tourist Bureau
The **Tubuai Visitors Bureau**, *Tel. 95.04.19,* is in Mataura, presided by Melinda Bodin.

RIMATARA

When the *Tuhaa Pae II* ship anchors offshore **Rimatara** every few weeks to bring supplies, the passengers come ashore by whaleboat, surfing over the reef in turbulent waves that beat against the island's limestone cliffs. Upon landing on the beautiful white sand beach of Amaru the visitors are required to follow an old custom of the island and walk through a cloud of smoke to purify them before being welcomed ashore.

Far removed from the beaten path of tourists and even cruising yachts, Rimatara has no airport, no sheltered boat harbor or dock, and no hotel. For the island's 929 inhabitants (1996 census), who live in blissful isolation from the world's problems and turmoil, Rimatara is a joyful and tranquil refuge and the people here even have their own dialect. Located 538 kilometers (334 miles) southwest of Tahiti and 150 kilometers (93 miles) westsouthwest of Rurutu, the circular island of Rimatara is the smallest and lowest of the inhabited Austral Islands. The land surface is only 8 square kilometers (3 square miles) and Mount Vahu is the highest peak at 83 meters (274 feet). A narrow fringing reef hugs the uneven shore of the island and there is no lagoon.

Amaru is the principal village, with the town hall, *gendarmerie*, post office and infirmary, plus a school and a couple of stores. **Anapoto** and **Mutuaura** villages are reached by rutted dirt roads. There is a severe water shortage during dry seasons. The hosts at your pension will provide car transportation from the boat landing, and can perhaps find a horse for you to ride to explore the island. There are no rental bicycles, cars or boats available, no restaurants or bars, and alcohol is not sold on Rimatara. Bring your own supplies.

WHERE TO STAY

UMARERE, *B.P. 20595, 98713, Papeete, Tahiti, Tel. 689/83.25.84. EP Rates: room 2.000 CFP ($20) per person per day, 60.000 CFP ($600) per month. Round-trip transfers are provided from the boat landing. No credit card. Add 1% value added tax to room rates and meal plan.*

This brightly painted salmon colored concrete house has two bedrooms for rent in Mutuaura village, five kilometers (3.1 miles) from the boat dock. The living room, dining room, kitchen, laundry facilities, terrace and bathroom with cold water are shared. House linens are furnished. Tahitian style meals are available on request.

RAIVAVAE

Raivavae is one of the most exquisite islands in the South Pacific, still aloof from the world of tourism and modern influences. Located 632 kilometers (392 miles) southeast of Tahiti, this island of 16 square kilometers (6 square miles) can be reached only by boat. Fern covered mountains reach 437 meters (1,442 feet) into the mist of clouds. Sea birds soar around a dozen picturesque islets that seem to float on the emerald lagoon protected by a distant coral reef. Tranquillity reigns on Raivavae, even in the five pretty villages of **Rairua**, **Mahanatoa**, **Anatonu**, **Vaiuru** and **Matotea**. These neat and clean villages, with their pastel colored limestone houses, are home to the island's 1,049 inhabitants. The women of Raivavae compete with one another to see who can make the most original hat to wear to the Evangelical church services. Some of the decorations consist of plastic fruit, golf balls and even blinking lights.

The *Tuhaa Pae II* ship docks every few weeks at the quay in Rairua. Nearby is the town hall, *gendarmerie*, school and a Chinese store. There is also a post office and small dispensary on the island and a road connects the villages.

Car transfers are provided for pension guests, and you can visit the archaeological sites, which include three tiki statues of stone. Boat trips can be arranged for fishing in the lagoon and to visit the *motu* islets with a picnic lunch. Visitors who plan to sojourn on this beautiful island should bring their own bicycles or other transportation, meats and other food products, including bread, and whatever alcoholic beverages you want. There is a plentiful variety of seafood—fish, lobster, sea urchins and tridacna clams from the lagoon. Taro is a staple vegetable, and Raivavae also grows good cabbages, carrots, potatoes, coffee and oranges.

WHERE TO STAY

CHEZ VAITE, *B.P. 55, 98750, Mahanatoa, Raivavae, Tel. 689/95.42.85, Fax 689/95.42.00. Beside the sea in Mahanatoa village, five kilometers (3.1 miles) from the boat dock. MAP Rates: room with breakfast and dinner 4.000 CFP($40) single, 7.000 CFP ($70) double. Reduced rates for longer stays. Round-trip transfers from boat dock provided. Add 1% value added tax to room rates and meal plan. No credit cards.*

This modern concrete house has three bedrooms, each containing a double bed. The living room with television, dining room, kitchen, terrace and bathroom with cold water are shared. House linens are furnished. Bike rentals are available.

PENSION MOANA, *98750 Mahanatoa, Tel. 689/95.42.47. Beside the sea in Mahanatoa village, two kilometers (1.2 miles) from the boat dock. MAP Rates: room with breakfast and dinner 4.000 CFP($40) single, 7.000 CFP($70) double. Reduced rates for longer stays. Round-trip transfers from boat dock provided. Add 1% value added tax to room rates and meal plan. No credit cards.*

This is a concrete house with three bedrooms, a living room with television, dining room, kitchen, terrace and communal bathroom with cold water. House linens are furnished. Bike rentals are available.

CHEZ ANNIE FLORES, *98750, Rairua, Raivavae, Tel./Fax 689/ 95.43.28. Beside the boat dock in Rairua village. EP Rates: room 2.000 CFP ($20) per person per day, 35.000 CFP ($350) per month. Round-trip transfers provided. Add 1% value added tax to room rates and meal plan. No credit cards.*

This is an older house with a sheet metal roof and two bedrooms, a kitchen and bathroom with cold water shower. House linens are furnished. The owner sells food at the boat dock when the *Tuhaa Pae II* arrives, and you can probably arrange a few local style meals with her.

RAPA

Remote **Rapa** stands proudly alone 1,074 kilometers (666 miles) southeast of Tahiti, below the tropical zone. Rapa-Iti, as the island is also called, has a strong cultural connection to Rapa-Nui, the Polynesian name for Easter Island. Archaeological ruins include strong *pa* fortresses built among volcanic pinnacles. **Mount Perehau**, the tallest of six peaks, reaches 650 meters (2,145 feet) above the island, whose fjord-like coastline has 12 deeply indented bays. Several sugar loaf-shaped islets lie just offshore and there is no fringing reef in these cold waters. White puffs of sheep and wild goats perch on precipitous cliffs over the sea and bay, and herds of cattle roam the velvety green mountain ranges.

Rapa's 521 inhabitants live in **Haurei Village**, where there are 70 houses, and in the smaller village of Area, with about 30 houses, which is reached only by boat, one kilometer distant across Haurei Bay. The land is owned by the entire community and the simple houses are grouped together, reminiscent of a small Mexican village, with a goat tied outside each house. There is a town hall, post office, infirmary, weather station and school. A cooperative store provides the villagers with basic supplies and many of the homes have television and telephone service.

The temperature in this southerly clime can drop to a low 5 degrees Celsius (41 degrees Fahrenheit) during the austral winter in July and August. Because it is below the tropical zone, the coconut trees on Rapa do not produce many nuts. A very tasty variety of taro is grown, which the Rapans make into popoi or a paté called *takae*. Other root vegetables include *tarua* and *aki*, part of a fern. A sweet-tasting rose colored flower called *mangu* is like candy for the children, and oranges from Rapa are especially succulent. There are peaches, passion fruit and figs, plus three varieties of apples grown here. An excellent grade of coffee is grown on Rapa and shipped to Papeete, while the islanders drink instant Nescafé. The daily fare for a Rapan family includes fresh salmon, mussels, oysters, raw crabs and *bêche de mer*, shrimp, sea urchin, cold water lobster and tender goat meat. The South Seas staple of canned corned beef is scorned in favor of fresh food. This sometimes includes a portion of fresh beef from the cooperative store.

There is no airport in Rapa and the *Tuhaa Pae II* supply ship docks in Haurei Bay every 6-8 weeks, the island's only regular connection to the outside world. Research ships call infrequently, and private yachts are allowed to stay only a few days, for refueling. Small specialized passenger ships visit briefly once or twice a year.

There are no tourist activities and excursions in Rapa, but you can join the locals when they go fishing and lobstering, or when they organize a hunt for wild beef in the mountains.

Even though Rapa is difficult to reach, there are still those adventurous souls who heed the call to those exotic places far from the world of tourism.

WHERE TO STAY

CHEZ CERDAN FARAIRE, *98751 Ahurei, Rapa, Tel. 689/95.72.84, Fax 689/95.72.00. A 2-bedroom house in the main village has a double bed in each room, a living room, dining room and private bathroom with hot water. House linens are furnished. Free round-trip transportation from the boat dock is included. AP Rates: room with all meals 4.500 CFP ($45) per person. No credit cards. Add 1% value added tax to room rates and meal plan.*

CHEZ PUNUA MAKE, *98751 Ahurei, Rapa, Tel./Fax 95.72.00.*

25. GAMBIER ISLANDS

MANGAREVA

If you have a quest for remote islands in temperate climes, **Mangareva** may qualify as your Garden of Eden. This island, which is 1,650 kilometers (1,023 miles) southeast of Tahiti, is the largest of the **Gambier Archipelago**, just above the Tropic of Capricorn. The climate in these southern latitudes is very pleasant, with cooler temperatures than in Tahiti.

Mangareva and the other high islands of Aukena, Akamaru and Taravai are partially enclosed by a barrier reef that stretches for 80 kilometers (50 miles). Also sharing this protected lagoon are six smaller islands and 25 *motu* islets surrounded by white coral sand beaches. Three passes lead into the sun-gilded waters of the turquoise lagoon, which are a haven for the *Pinctada Margaritefera*, the black-lipped oyster that produces some of the world's finest black pearls in the farms of Mangareva and its neighboring islands.

In addition to raising cows and pigs, coffee, oranges and watermelons, many of the 1,087 inhabitants of the Gambier Islands are employed in the black pearl business.

History

Polynesian oral tradition claims that expeditions of Polynesians from the eastern and western Pacific used to stop at Mangareva, and that it was settled by people from the Marquesas Islands during three migratory waves. Archaeologists have found similarities between the Marquesas Islands stone temples and the *marae* found on the islet of Timoe, 50 kilometers (31 miles) southeast of Mangareva, outside the protective coral reef. Carbon-14 dating confirms human occupations on Mangareva around the year 1200.

English Captain Wilson of the London Missionary Society's (LMS) chartered ship, *H.M.S. Duff*, sailed past Mangareva in May, 1797, and named it after **Captain Gambier**, a descendant of the French Huguenots who had supported the LMS expedition. F. W. Beechey, another Englishman, landed on the island in 1826, and the island became a popular port-of-call for ships who traded for the mother-of-pearl shell from the lagoon.

Mangareva's history is strongly connected with Catholic missionaries from the Sacred Heart of Picpus, who arrived in the Gambiers in 1834. Under the staff of Father Honoré Laval, these docile, gentle people were converted to Catholicism and taught to spin, weave, print, construct boats, and above all, to build churches.

Laval organized a native police force, commanded the girls to become nuns and the men to become monks, and forced the islanders to work night and day to construct a neo-gothic city of coral and stone. Great blocks of coral were used to build a cathedral large enough for 2,000 people, and a church replaced every *marae* altar that existed on the island.

Also constructed were chapels, a convent, a monastery, a school, triumphal arches of great size, and a large number of palatial and unhealthy stone houses for King Maputeoa and the aristocrats of the island. Laval also had a number of houses built for his own use.

The people began to die under the enforced labor, and in 1864, the new Governor of Tahiti, Comte Emile de la Roncière, visited Mangareva to investigate the stories he had heard of Laval's behavior, which included trafficking in pearls and shell. When the governor ordered the prisons opened, he found two boys in a dungeon. Their offense had been to laugh during Mass.

Laval's rule ended in 1871 when he departed for Tahiti, where he died in 1880. Some 116 coral and stone buildings of the neo-gothic design still stand today. These include the 2,000 seat cathedral, another silent witness to Father Laval's driving need to build.

It was thanks to Father Laval and his assistant François Caret that Tahiti was brought to the attention of the French government. Soon after they arrived in the Gambier Islands the two priests went to Tahiti to establish a Catholic mission in the staunch English Protestant territory. They were literally removed from the island, which began a mighty dispute between the English Protestants and French Catholics, and resulted in France establishing a protectorate over the islands in 1842. The Gambier Islands remained relatively independent until their official annexation in 1881.

In 1982 the Frères of the Sacred Heart of Québec opened a **Center for Education and Development** in Mangareva, to train the youths in mechanics and carpentry. A visit to the sculptors' workshop in the village is one of the activities provided for visitors.

Lodging is available in the main village of **Rikitea**, where comfortable and clean cottages or modern style houses welcome the traveler, with a choice of European or local-style cuisine.

MANGAREVA

0 1 2 3 4 5 6 7 8 KM

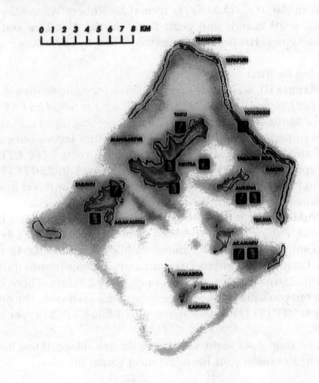

ARRIVALS & DEPARTURES

Arriving By Air

Air Tahiti flies from Tahiti to the Gambier Islands each Tuesday, using ATR turbo jets for the 3 hour and 40 minute flights. The flight leaves Tahiti at 10:50am and arrives in the Gambiers at 3:30pm, which is an hour ahead of Tahiti time. The cost of a one-way fare from Tahiti is 30.000 CFP ($300) if you purchase your ticket in Tahiti, and 5 percent more if you buy it overseas. **Air Tahiti reservations**: *Tahiti, Tel. 86.42.42/86.41.84.* The airport of Totegegie is built on one of the flat *motu* islets across the lagoon from Rikitea, the principal village of Mangareva. Your pension will send a boat to transport you across the lagoon, which is a 15-minute ride. Air Tahiti also has charter flights that can take you to the Gambier Islands.

Wan Air, *Tel. 85.55.54*, is owned by Robert Wan, who also owns several pearl islands and pearl farms in the Gambier and Tuamotu archipelagoes. His fleet of planes frequently fly to Mangareva.

Arriving By Boat

Manava III, *Société Compagnie de Développement Maritime des Tuamotu, B. P. 1291, Papeete, Tahiti; Tel. 689/43.32.65; Fax 689/41.31.65.* The office is at the Motu-Uta goëlette pier. This big steel boat offers cabins and meals and is owned by Béné Richmond, who provides service once a month to the Gambier Islands. The 18-day round-trip costs 7.500 CFP ($75) for deck space and 15.000 CFP ($150) for a cabin. Add 2.500 CFP ($25) per person for three meals daily. The itinerary is usually direct from Papeete to Rikitea.

Nuku Hau, *Sociéte Compagnie de Développement Maritime Intersulaire, B.P. 635, Papeete, Tahiti, Tel. 689/45.23.24, Fax 689/45.24.44.* This is a cargo ship managed by Raymond Paquier that can take 12 passengers from Tahiti to the eastern Tuamotu and Gambier Islands during the 18-day round-trip voyages it makes once every 25 days. There is no cabin space but you will be served three meals a day on board. The one-way fare is 7.400 CFP ($74) for deck space, plus 1.800 CFP ($18) per day for the meals.

The ships dock at the wharf near Rikitea village. If you have reservations in a pension your hosts will meet you at the pier.

Departing By Air

Air Tahiti's weekly departure from the Gambiers is at 9am local time each Wednesday morning. The plane stops at Hao in the Tuamotus and arrives in Papeete at 12:55pm Tahiti time. Be sure to set your watch back an hour. **Air Tahiti reservations** in Rikitea, *Tel. 97.82.65.*

Departing By Boat

Manava III stops at the Tuamotu atoll of Marutea Sud (South) on the return trip to Papeete; *Nuku Hau* calls at Tematangi and Hereheretue on the return trip to Tahiti, and may stop on request at other atolls.

ORIENTATION

Mangareva is 8 kilometers (5 miles) long and 1.5 kilometers (.9 miles) wide. A road encircles the island for 28 kilometers (17.3 miles), offering picturesque views of the luminescent bays and inlets and other islands. **Mount Duff**, at 441 meters (1,455 ft.) high, is the highest point on Mangareva. The hillsides of the island turn yellowish-brown during the dry seasons. **Rikitea**, the main village, is a quiet little oasis of verdure.

WHERE TO STAY

CHEZ BIANCA & BENOIT, *B.P. 19, 98755 Rikitea, Mangareva, Tel. 689/97.83.76. EP Rates: room 2.000 CFP ($20) single, 3.000 CFP ($30) double, 3.500 CFP ($35) triple. Room with breakfast and dinner 4.000 CFP ($40) single, 7.000 CFP ($70) double, 10.000 CFP ($100) triple. Room with breakfast, lunch and dinner 6.000 CFP ($60) single, 11.000 CFP ($110) double, 16.000 CFP ($160) triple. Round-trip transfers 1.000 CFP ($10) per adult and 500 CFP ($5) per child. Add 1% value added tax to room rates and meals. No credit cards.*

This large modern house is on an elevated position in Rikitea village, at the foot of Mount Duff, with a magnificent panoramic view of Rikitea Bay. The top floor is reserved for visitors and contains three bedrooms, a lounge with television and telephone, a kitchen and a bathroom with hot water. House linens are furnished. The dining terrace overlooks the bay. The food is European and local cuisine.

Your hosts will take you on guided tours to visit the churches, and the island, with trips to other islands and a picnic on the *motu*. This is the primary choice of the lodgings in Mangareva.

CHEZ HELENE & TERII, *98755 Rikitea, Mangareva, Tel. 689/97.82.80. In the center of the village, 200 meters (56 feet) from the boat dock. EP Rates: room 2.000 CFP ($20) single, 3.000 CFP ($30) double, 3.500 CFP ($35) triple. Room with breakfast and dinner 4.000 CFP ($40) single, 7.000 CFP ($70) double, 10.000 CFP ($100) triple. Room with breakfast, lunch and dinner 6.000 CFP ($60) single, 11.000 CFP ($110) double, 16.000 CFP ($160) triple. Additional bed 1.000 CFP ($10). Round-trip transfers 1.000 CFP ($10) per adult and 500 CFP ($5) per child. Add 1% value added tax to room rates and meals. No credit cards.*

This small 2-bedroom house is in the heart of the village, with a shared living room with television, kitchen and bathroom with cold water. House linens are furnished.

CHEZ MARIETTE & PIERRE, *B.P. 298, 98755 Rikitea, Mangareva, Tel. 689/97.82.87. In the center of the village, 200 meters (56 feet) from the boat dock. EP Rates: room 2.000 CFP ($20) single, 3.000 CFP ($30) double, 3.500 CFP ($35) triple. Room with breakfast, lunch and dinner 4.000 CFP ($40) single, 7.000 CFP ($70) double, 10.000 CFP ($100) triple. Room with breakfast, lunch and dinner 6.000 CFP ($60) single, 11.000 CFP ($110) double, 16.000 CFP ($160) triple. Round-trip transfers 1.000 CFP ($10) per adult and 500 CFP ($5) per child. Add 1% value added tax to room rates and meals. No credit cards.*

This 3-bedroom house is on the mountain side with a shared living room with television, dining room, kitchen, terrace and bathroom with hot water. House linens are furnished.

CHEZ JOJO, *B.P. 1, Rikitea, Mangareva, Tel./Fax 689/97.82.61. Beside the sea away from the village. EP Rates: room 2.000 CFP ($20) single, 3.500 CFP ($35) double. Room with breakfast and dinner 4.000 CFP ($40) single, 7.000 CFP ($70) double. Room with breakfast, lunch and dinner 6.000 CFP ($60) single, 11.000 CFP ($110) double. Camping 1.000 CFP ($10). Round-trip transfers 1.000 CFP ($10) per adult and 500 CFP ($5) per child. Add 1% value added tax to room rates and meals. No credit cards.*

This two-story house beside the sea has a big lawn for campers. The house has two bedrooms, shared living room with television, dining room, kitchen and bathroom with hot water, and terrace. House linens are furnished.

SEEING THE SIGHTS

Activities include lagoon excursions by outrigger speed canoe, boat trips to visit the various *motu* islets around the island, fishing, visits to the family-owned pearl farms, land tours of the island, with stops at the religious and historic sites. You can also hike up the mountains and visit the sculptors' workshop for mother-of-pearl carvings.

PRACTICAL INFORMATION

Doctor

There is a government-operated infirmary in Rikitea, *Tel. 97.82.16.*

Police

The French *gendarmerie* is located in Rikitea, *Tel. 97.82.68.*

Post Office & Telecommunications Office

The post office is located in Rikitea, *Tel. 97.82.22.*

GLOSSARY

The **Tahitian alphabet** contains 13 letters. A is pronounced ah, as in father, E is pronounced e, as in fate, F is pronounced fa as in farm, H is pronounced he as in heaven, I is pronounced i as me, M is pronounced mo as in mote, N is pronounced nu as in noon, O is pronounced o as in go, P is pronounced p as in pat, R is pronounced ro as in rode, T is pronounced t as in time, U is pronounced u as in rule, V is pronounced v as in veer.

The Tahitian dialect abounds in vowels, such as Faaa, the name of Tahiti's largest commune, where the international airport is located. This is pronounced Fah-ah-ah, but most people lazily forget the last syllable. Tahitian words have no "s" for the plural. There are no hard consonants in the Tahitian alphabet, such as the letter "B"; however, the name Bora Bora is accepted as the legal name for the island that was formerly called Pora Pora.

a'ahi - tuna, *thon* on French menus
ahima'a - underground oven used for cooking traditional Polynesian food; also *hima'a*
ahu - the most sacred place on a marae, an altar that took many forms, including pyramid shaped
aita - Tahitian for "no"
aita e peapea - no problem; also used as "you're welcome"
aita maitai - no good
aito - ironwood tree, also a strong warrior
aparima - a Polynesian story-telling group dance
api - new, young
arii - Polynesian high chief, a sacred being or princely caste
arioi - a religious sect or fraternity in the Society Islands in pre-Christian days
atoll - a low coral island, usually no more than six feet above sea level
atua - Polynesian gods
baguette - long loaf of crusty French bread

barrier reef - coral reef between the shoreline and the ocean, separated from the land by a lagoon

belvédère - panoramic lookout

bonitier - bonito boat

BP - *bôite postale*, post office box

breadfruit - a football-size starchy green fruit that grows on a breadfruit tree, eaten as a staple with fish, pork or canned corned beef and coconut milk

bringue - a party or fête, usually with lots of music, singing, dancing and Hinano beer

cascade - French for waterfall

casse-croûte - sandwich made with *baguette* bread

CEP - *Centre d'expérimentation du Pacifique*; the French nuclear-testing program that was carried out in French Polynesia from 1966-1996

CFP - *cours de franc Pacifique*; the French Pacific franc is the local currency

chevrette - French for sea shrimp, as opposed to fresh water *crevettes*

CMAS - *Conféderation Mondiale des Activités Subaquatiques*; the World Underwater Federation, France's scuba diving equivalent to PADI

copra - dried coconut meat used to make oil and monoi

coral - a white calcareous skeletal structure inhabited by Madreporaria, organisms that comprise the living polyps inside the skeletal pores, giving color to the coral

croque madame - also called *croque vahine*, is a toasted ham and cheese sandwich with a fried egg on top

croque monsieur - toasted ham and cheese sandwich

cyclone - tropical storm rotating around a low-pressure 'eye'; the equivalent to a typhoon in the western Pacific and a hurricane in the Caribbean

demi-pension - half board (bed, breakfast and dinner), see also *pension complète*

demis - half caste Tahitian-European

e - Tahitian for "yes"

espadon - French for sword fish

faa'amu - to feed; an informal child adoption system in Polynesia

faa'apu - farm

fafa - the green tops of the taro plant, similar to spinach

fafaru - stinky fish dish

fare - traditional Polynesian house, home, hut

fare iti - little house, outdoor toilet

fare manihini - visitor's bureau

fare moni - bank

fare ohipa - office

fare pape - bathroom

fare pote'e - chief's house or community meeting place, oval shaped
fare pure - church
fare purera'a rahi - cathedral
fare rata - post office
fare taoto -sleeping house
fare toa - store
fare tutu - kitchen
fei - plantain, Tahitian cooking banana
fête - festival, party, celebration
fiu - bored, fed up
fringing reef - a coral reef along the shoreline
FFESSM - *Fèderation Française des Activités Subaquatiques,* or French
   Underwater Federation of Scuba Divers
gendarmerie - French national police station
goëlette - French for schooner; inter-island cargo or freighter ships
haere mai - come here
haere maru - take it easy
haura - swordfish or marlin
heiva - festival, an assembly for dancing
heiva vaevae - big festival parade
here here - romance
high island - an island created by volcanic action or geological upheaval
himenes - Tahitian for songs or hymns
hinano - flower of the pandanus tree, girl's name, Tahiti's favorite beer
Hiro - Polynesian god of thieves; Raiatea's first king was named Hiro
hoa - shallow channel across the outer reef of an atoll that carries water
   into or out of the central lagoon at high tide or with big ocean swells
hoe - ceremonial canoe paddle
honu - turtle
ia ora na - hello, good morning, good afternoon, good evening, pronounced similar to "your honor" (yore-ronah)
ia'ota - marinated fish salad, *poisson cru*
ipo - a dumpling made with breadfruit and coconut water
iti - small, little
kaina - a slang term similar to hick or hillbilly, usually applied to out-
   islanders; country music
kava - mildly intoxicating drink made from the root of piper methysticum,
   the pepper plant; a fruit tree
kaveu - coconut crab
keshi - a pearl without a nucleus
lagoon - a body of normally calm water inside a coral reef
leeward - on the downwind side, sheltered from the prevailing winds
le truck - Tahiti's public transportation system

LMS - London Missionary Society, the first Protestants to bring the Gospel to Tahiti in 1797

ohipa - work

opani - out of order, broken, closed

maa - food, also spelled **ma'a**

maa tahiti - traditional Tahitian food

maa tinito - Chinese food

maa tinito haricots rouge - a popular dish with red beans, macaroni, pork or chicken

mabe - blister pearl that is grown inside the mother-of-pearl shell

maeva; manava - greetings, welcome

magasin - small food store

mahi mahi - dolphinfish, *dorade Coryphène*

mahu - Tahitian for transvestite or female impersonator

maitai - good; also a potent rum drink

maiore - another name for uru or breadfruit

mana - spiritual power

manahune - the common people or peasant class in pre-European Polynesia; servants, tillers of the soil, fishermen, prisoners of war and slaves

manuia - cheers, a toast to your health

mako, mao - shark

maniota - manioc root

manu - bird

maoa - sea snails

Maohi - Tahitian Polynesians; the ancestors of today's Tahitians, some of whom sailed to New Zealand and are called Maori

mape - Tahitian chestnut

maraamu - southeast trade winds that can often blow for days, bringing rain, rough seas and cooler weather

marae - traditional Polynesian temple of coral or basaltic stone, usually built with an ahu altar at one end

marara - flying fish

mauruuru - thank you

mauruuru roa - thank you very much

me'ae - Marquesan word for marae

mei'a - banana

meka - a melt-in-your-mouth swordfish from the ocean depths. French menus sometimes list it as *espadon de nuit*

miti ha'ari - fresh coconut milk poured over traditional Tahitian foods

miti hue - a fermented coconut milk used as a dipping sauce for breadfruit, taro, fei, bananas, fish, pork and canned corned beef

mona mona - sweet, candy

monoi - oil made from coconut oil, flavored with Tiare Tahiti, ylang ylang, pitate and other flowers, also with sandalwood powder or vanilla. It is used as an emollient, perfume, hair dressing, suntan oil and mosquito repellent

mo'o - lizard

mo'o rea - yellow lizard, name of the island of Moorea

more - Tahitian grass skirts made from the purau tree

mou'a - mountain

motu - a coral islet inside the lagoon, between the outer reef and a high island

mutoi - Tahitian municipal police

nacre - mother-of-pearl shell

naissain - larva of an oyster

nao nao -mosquito

navette - shuttle boat

nehenehe - pretty; handsome

neo neo - stinky smell

noa noa - fragrant, sweet smelling

nohu - stone fish

noni - Marquesan for *Morinda citrifolia*, a plant whose juice is used as a tonic

nono - sand flea; also Tahitian word for *Morinda citrifolia*

nucleus - a small sphere of calcium carbonate that is grafted into the gonads of the pearl oyster to produce a pearl. The fresh water mussel from the Mississippi River provides the best nucleus and helps to produce the finest black pearls

nui - big, new

oa oa - happy, joyful, merry

ono ono - barracuda

Oro - Polynesian god of war who demanded human sacrifices at the *marae* in pre-Christian days

otea - legendary group dance performed in grass skirts

PADI - Professional Association of Diving Instructors, the American system of scuba diving

pae pae - stone paved floor of pre-European houses or meeting platforms

pahua - clam; *bénitier* on French menus

painapo - pineapple, *anana*

pandanus - palm tree with aerial roots whose leaves are used for weaving roofs, hats, mats and bags

pape - water

pareo, pareu - a sarong-like garment that is hand-painted or tie-dyed

pass - channel through the outer reef of an atoll or the barrier reef around a high island that allows water to flow into and out of the lagoon

Paumotu - inhabitants of the Tuamotu atolls
peapea - problems, worries
pension - boarding house, hostel
pension complète - full-board (bed and all meals)
penu - pestle
pétanque - also known as *boules* or bocci-ball; a French game of bowls, where metal balls are thrown to land as near as possible to a target ball. A very competitive sport in Tahiti
peue - mats woven of coconut or pandanus fronds
pia - beer
pirogue - French word for outrigger canoe
PK - *poste kilometre*, the number of kilometers from the *mairie* or post office
plat du jour - daily special, plate of the day
po'e - a sticky pudding made with papaya, bananas or pumpkin, corn starch and coconut milk
poe rava - black pearl that comes from the *Pinctada Margaritifera*, the black-lip oyster
poisson cru - fish marinated in lime juice and served cold with tomatoes, onions, carrots, cucumbers and coconut milk. In Tahitian it's *i'a ota*
popaa - foreigner, Europeans, westerners, white people
popoi - fermented breadfruit eaten as a bread substitute or sweetened with sugar and coconut cream as a dessert
poulet - French for chicken
poulet fafa - chicken cooked with taro leaves and coconut milk
pu - conch shell blown to announce the arrival of a delegation, dancers, or the fish truck
puaa - pig, the basic food for all Tahitian *tamaara'a* feasts
pua'a'toro - beef; canned corned beef, the staple of the South Seas
purau - wild hibiscus tree, whose inner bark is used to make grass skirts
rae rae - a slang term for *mahu*, usually implying homosexuality
raatira - the intermediary caste of the ancient Polynesian society, between the *arii* and the *manahune*
rori - sea slug, sea cucumber
roulotte - mobile dining van
sennit - woven fiber from coconut husks
siki - dark skinned people
Taaroa - Polynesian creator god
tahua - priests of ancient Polynesian religion
taioro - fermented grated coconut sauce that may contain *pahua* clams or *maoa* sea snails
tamaara'a - Tahitian feast
tama'a maitai - enjoy your meal, *bon appetit*
tamure - Tahiti's national hip swiveling, rubber-legging dance

tane - man, husband, boyfriend, Mr.

tapa - bark-cloth, traditional clothing of the pre-European Polynesians; wall hangings

tapu - tabu, taboo, sacred, forbidden

taramea - crown-of-thorns starfish that eats the coral animals and destroys the reefs

taro - root vegetable that is one of the staple foods in Polynesia

tarua - a tuber usually cooked in the *ahima'a* oven

tatau - Tahitian word for tattoo

tiane'e - slipper lobster; *cigalle de mer* on French menus

tiare - flower

Tiare Tahiti - fragrant white petalled *gardenia taitensis*, Tahiti's national flower

tifaifai - colorful bed and cushion covers or wall hangings sewn in patchwork or appliquéd designs

tii - Tahitian name for human-like wooden or stone statues that had a religious significance in pre-European Polynesia

tiki - a Marquesan word for the Tahitian *tii*; some of these statues are still found on the *me'ae* in the Marquesas Islands

Tinito - Tahitian name for Chinese

tiurai - Tahitian for July, the major festival of July

TPE - *traitement paiement electronique*, an automatic teller machine equivalent to the ATM. Nobody calls this a TPE, however, but a *distributeur*

toe toe - cold

toere - wooden slit drum played for Tahitian dance shows

tohua - a place for meetings or festivals in pre-European Polynesia

tupa - land crab

tupapau - spirit ghosts of the Polynesian religion, still feared by some people

ufi - a huge root vegetable similar to yams, cooked in underground *ahima'a* oven

umara - sweet potato

umete - wooden dish or bowl used for serving foods or holding fruits and flowers

upa upa - music

uru - breadfruit

vaa - Tahitian word for outrigger canoe

vahine - Tahitian word for woman, wife, Ms.

vehine- Marquesan word for woman, wife, Ms.

vana- black sea urchin whose meat is good to eat

vanira - vanilla

varo - sea centipede, a gourmet's delicacy

V.A.T. - value added tax; called T.V.A. in French Polynesia

vea vea - hot
vivo - nose flute
VTT or vélo or tout terrain - mountain bike
windward - facing the wind; the opposite of leeward
4x4 or 4WD - a 4-wheel drive vehicle, such as a Landrover, Jeep or pick-up truck

THINGS CHANGE!

Phone numbers, prices, addresses, quality of food, etc, all change. If you come across any new information, we'd appreciate hearing from you. No item is too small! Drop us an e-mail note at: Jopenroad@aol.com, or write us at:

Tahiti & French Polynesia Guide
Open Road Publishing, P.O. Box 284
Cold Spring Harbor, NY 11724

TRAVEL NOTES

TRAVEL NOTES

TRAVEL NOTES

TRAVEL NOTES

TRAVEL NOTES

TRAVEL NOTES

TRAVEL NOTES